FREE MONEY™ FROM THE FEDERAL GOVERNMENT FOR SMALL BUSINESSES AND ENTREPRENEURS

Other Books by Laurie Blum

Childcare/Education

Free Money for Day Care
Free Money for Private Schools
Free Money for Foreign Study
Free Money for Graduate School (revised)
Free Money for College
Free Money from Colleges and Universities
Free Money for College from the Government
Free Money for Athletic Scholarships
Free Money for Children's Medical Expenses
Free Money for Childhood Behavioral and Genetic Disorders

Healthcare

Free Money for Heart Disease and Cancer Care
Free Money for Diseases of Aging
Free Money for Infertility Treatments
Free Money for Mental/Emotional Disorders

The Arts

Free Money for People in the Arts

Business

Free Money for Small Business and Entrepreneurs
How to Invest in Real Estate Using Free Money
Free Money When You're Unemployed

Other

Free Dollars from the Federal Government
The Complete Guide to Getting a Grant

FREE MONEY™ FROM THE FEDERAL GOVERNMENT FOR SMALL BUSINESSES AND ENTREPRENEURS

Laurie Blum

John Wiley & Sons, Inc.

New York • Chichester • Brisbane • Toronto • Singapore

Library of Congress Cataloging-in-Publication Data:

Blum, Laurie.
    Free money from the federal government for small businesses and
entrepreneurs / Laurie Blum.
       p. cm.
    Includes bibliographical references and index.
    ISBN 0-471-59942-5 (cloth). — ISBN 0-471-59943-3 (paper)
     1. Small business—United States—Finance—Directories.
    2. Commercial loans—United States—Directories.   3. Federal aid to
community development—United States—Directories. I. Title.
HG4027.7.B6   1993
658.15'224—dc20   93-11505

Printed in the United States of America

10 9 8 7 6 5 4 3 2 1

I would like to briefly but sincerely thank Cybèle Fisher, Walter Goldenberg, Shira Levin, Ken Rose, Sylvia Szeker, my wonderful editor PJ Dempsey, Chris Jackson, and Ron Stone.

Contents

Introduction

This is a book that many of my readers have asked me to write. It is the federal version of my very popular book, *Free Money for Small Businesses and Entrepreneurs*.

According to the *Catalog of Federal Domestic Assistance*, over $735 million and nearly 1,200 federal assistance programs (administered by 52 federal agencies) were available in 1990. Approximately 71 percent of these monies and programs offer eligibility through direct payments (including entitlements such as veterans benefits, social security, etc.), direct loans, project grants, and "other." Although these figures do not directly reflect the exact number of grant dollars and programs available specifically to individuals, they are an indication of the millions of dollars provided through the thousands of funding programs existing at the federal level.

HOW TO USE THIS BOOK

Substantial funding is available from agencies at the various levels of government: federal, state, county, and city.

Because the nature of many government publications and other reference guides makes accessing this information nearly impossible, I have written this book as an easy-to-use directory listing grant programs in seven general areas. Available grants are organized by field of interest: community development, real estate, minorities, and so on. Underneath the grant or government program (where appropriate) are individual state or regional offices through which an individual from a given state should apply.

Check these seven general grant "subject" areas to see which grants apply to you. Remember, regardless of what type of business or enterprise you have or want to undertake, there should be a government funding source that's right for you.

Introduction

I've also included an important section on how to write a proposal. Unlike private funders, government agencies almost always use a printed application form. Detailed instructions are usually provided, with little room for free-form creative writing. From my own experience in writing many successful proposals for government grants, however, I have found a number of rules that must be adhered to in order to produce a successful proposal.

I am also including a bibliography that lists government source books, private foundation source books, and some books on how to go about seeking government grants (including my recently published *The Complete Guide to Getting a Grant*) which I thought the reader would find helpful.

HOW TO WRITE A PROPOSAL

Once you have identified which government programs are likely prospects for support, your next step is to contact them directly. Request any information that they make available to prospective applicants, including the application form and instruction booklet. (You may apply for more than one grant. Because federal grants are much more complicated and labor-intensive than private foundation or corporate grants, however, I would not recommend applying for more than two or three grants.) In addition, try to identify the contact person at the funding program you are applying for. After you receive information about the program and determine that you are eligible for funding, try to speak with the contact person; if that is not possible, write to the contact person. Ask what the government official's agency is looking for in proposals or applications. Are there particular types of projects it wants? Don't hesitate to ask questions about completing the application. The government does not expect you to be totally knowledgeable in government grantsmanship.

Most government funding boards make available application forms or formats for proposals. The proposal or the application is a very important document, for it is your opportunity to demonstrate who you are, what you hope to accomplish, and how you are especially qualified to work toward the objectives that you have set forth. Again, if you have any questions that arise while you are preparing your written materials, speak or write to the government official you have previously contacted.

Begin your proposal with a title page. Include:

- The amount requested
- The name of the funding agency
- The purpose of the grant
- A short descriptive title

- The time frame of the project
- Your full name and affiliation, if any
- Your address and phone number
- The date of submission

The title page should be followed by a clear and precise statement of purpose. Your statement of purpose should answer these three questions:

1. What do you hope to accomplish?
2. How do you plan to obtain your goals? (What activities, programs, or services will you undertake to accomplish your goals? Would you characterize these efforts as service-related, advocacy-focused, or public education-related?)
3. For whose benefit will your project function? (How specifically can you define your prime constituents: by age, sex, geography, minority-group status, or income?)

The proposal should always include an evaluation section briefly outlining how you intend to show that the proposed results were achieved.

The budget reflects the cost of the project in detail. It should be justified in relation to the tasks. Job descriptions of all staff should be presented, with an outline of the overall organizational structure.

The budget section is followed by a section called the capability of the contractor, documenting the reasons why you are in a strong position to conduct this project. Your resume, resources, and letters of support should be included.

Frequently government grant proposals are lengthier than foundation and corporate proposals, because of the detail required. Detail does not mean verbosity; rather, clarity and succinct prose are in order.

Be sure to observe grant deadlines. Like deadlines for tax returns, they require close adherence.

THE YES

Congratulations! You have been awarded a grant. As you will be receiving public tax dollars, make sure you understand all the financial reporting requirements that accompany your award. You may also want to clarify when you will receive your funds. Given the red tape inherent in any bureaucracy, you may have to wait a number of months before you actually receive the monies, so plan accordingly.

THE NO

Don't despair! Inquire why your proposal was rejected. If possible, ask the contact person for a specific reason. Find out the strengths and weaknesses of your proposal. Ask how you can submit an application the next time around that addresses the issues that have been raised during your discussion with the government official. You can always apply again. Persistence will be your best ally as long as any subsequent application demonstrates that you have dealt with the concerns that prompted the rejection.

Be sure that you are on the mailing list of the targeted agency to receive future requests for proposals and any other information that they periodically make available to prospective applicants. Thank the official with whom you have been in touch for his or her time and help.

Remember, do not apply for government grants unless you are willing to play the game by the funders' rules. You must have a certain tolerance for frustration and a willingness to confront red tape. Patience is an absolute necessity to government grant seekers.

One last note. By the time this book is published, some of the information contained here will have changed. Names, addresses, dollar amounts, telephone numbers, and other data are always in flux; however, most of the information will not have changed.

FREE MONEY™ FROM THE FEDERAL GOVERNMENT FOR SMALL BUSINESSES AND ENTREPRENEURS

Agriculture

Assistance is widely available from the federal government for owners, landlords, or sharecroppers on a farm or ranch for the following:

1. Assistance for agricultural conservation programs, such as cotton production stabilization; emergency livestock assistance; feed grain, rice, and wheat production; or forestry incentive programs
2. Various loan programs (i.e., loans for commodity purchases and payments; emergency loans for natural disasters; or soil and water loans)
3. Assistance for agricultural research grants

You will need to consult the list of addresses in this chapter for your nearest local or regional Agricultural and Conservation Service office or Farmers Home Administration (FmHA) office.

AGRICULTURE CONSERVATION PROGRAM

Department of Agriculture
Agricultural Stabilization and Conservation Service (ASCS)
P.O. Box 2415
Washington, DC 20013
(202) 720-6221

Description: Direct payments for specified use to any owner, landlord, tenant, or sharecropper on a farm or ranch, (including associated groups), who bears part of the cost of an approved conservation practice.
$ Given: Payment range: $3–$3,500; average: $990. Pooling agreement range: $3–$10,000; average: $1,600.
Application Information: Form ACP-245 for annual cost-sharing or Form ACP-310 for long-term agreements to be filed at your local ASCS office in the county in which the land is located.
Deadline: Application for payment must be filed with county ASCS committee after the practice is completed.
Contact: Your local, state, and/or regional ASCS office

Alabama
Albert C. McDonald
P.O. Box 891
474 South Court Street, Room 749
Montgomery, AL 36104-4184
(205) 832-7230

Alaska
Teresa Weiland
Alaska State ASCS Office
800 West Evergreen, Suite 216
Palmer, AK 99645-6389
(907) 745-7982

Arizona
Arden J. Palmer
Arizona State ASCS Office
201 East Indianola, Suite 325
Phoenix, AZ 85012-2054
(602) 640-5200

Arkansas
Dotson Collins·
P.O. Box 2781
New Federal Building, Room 5102
700 West Capitol Street
Little Rock, AR 72201-3225
(501) 378-5220

California
John Smythe
California State ASCS Office
1303 J. Street, Suite 300
Sacramento, CA 95814-2916
(916) 551-1801

Colorado
Lloyd C. Sommerville
Colorado State ASCS Office
655 Parfet Street
Room E 305, Third Floor
Lakewood, CO 80215
(303) 236-2866

Connecticut
David T. Schreiber
88 Day Hill Road
Windsor, CT 06095
(203) 285-8483

Delaware
Earle Isaacs, Jr.
179 West Chestnut Hill Road, Suite 7
Newark, DE 19713-2295
(302) 573-6536

Florida
Eugene C. Badger
P.O. Box 141030
4440 Northwest 25th Place, Suite 1
Gainesville, FL 32614-1030
(904) 372-8549

Georgia
James E. Harrison
P.O. Box 1907
Federal Building, Room 102
344 East Hancock Avenue
Athens, GA 30601-2775
(404) 546-2266

Hawaii
Ralph K. Ajifu
Hawaii State ASCS Office
300 Ala Moana Boulevard,
Room 4202
P.O. Box 50008
Honolulu, HI 96850-0002
(808) 551-2644

Idaho
Trent Clark
Idaho State ASCS Office
3220 Elder Street
Boise, ID 83705-5820
(208) 334-1486

Illinois
William G. Beeler
P.O. Box 19273
3500 Wabash Avenue
Springfield, IL 62707
(217) 492-4180

Indiana
Don Villwoch
Indiana State ASCS Office
5981 Lakeside Boulevard
Indianapolis, IN 46278-1996
(317) 290-3030

Iowa
Robert Furleigh
10500 Buena Vista Court
Urbandale, IA 50322
(515) 254-1540

Kansas
Frank A. Mosier
Kansas State ASCS Office
2601 Anderson Avenue
Manhattan, KS 66502-2898
(913) 539-3531

Kentucky
Kenneth Ashby
Kentucky State ASCS Office
771 Corporate Drive,
Suite 100
Lexington, KY 40503-5477
(606) 233-2726

Louisiana
Willie F. Cooper
3737 Government Street
Alexandria, LA 71302-3395
(318) 473-7721

Maine
David P. Staples
44 Stillwater Avenue
P.O. Box 406
Bangor, ME 04401-3521
(207) 942-0342

Maryland
James Richardson
Rivers Center
10270 B Columbia Road
Columbia, MD 21046-9998
(301) 381-4550

Massachusetts
Raymond E. Duda
451 West Street
Amherst, MA 01002-2953
(413) 256-0232

Michigan
David Conklin
1405 South Harrison Road,
Room 116
East Lansing, MI 48823-5202
(517) 337-6659

Minnesota
Donald L. Friedrich
Minnesota State ASCS Office
400 Farm Credit Service
Building
375 Jackson Street
St. Paul, MN 55101-1852
(612) 290-3651

Mississippi
Charles R. Hull
Mississippi State ASCS
Office
6310 I-55 North
Jackson, MS 39236
(601) 965-4300

Missouri
Morris G. Westfall
601 Parkdale Plaza Business
Loop
70 West, Suite 225
Columbia, MO 65203
(314) 875-5201

Montana
Donald Anderson
P.O. Box 670
Bozeman, MT 59771-0670
(406) 587-6872

Nebraska
John Neuberger
Nebraska State ASCS Office
P.O. Box 57975
Lincoln, NE 68505-7975
(402) 437-5581

Nevada
C. Richard Capurro
Nevada State ASCS Office
1755 East Plumb Lane,
Suite 202
Reno, NV 89502-3207

Agriculture

New Hampshire
Peter M. Thomson
USDA - New Hampshire
State ASCS Office
22 Bridge Street,
Fourth Floor
Concord, NH 03301-5605
(603) 224-7941

New Jersey
Peter de Wilde
Mastoris Professional Plaza
163 Route 130
Building 1, Suite E
Bordentown, NJ 08505
(609) 298-3446

New Mexico
David Turner
New Mexico State ASCS
Office
P.O. Box 1458
Federal Building, Room 4408
517 Gold Avenue, SW
Albuquerque, NM
87102-3156
(505) 766-2472

New York
John Steele
811 James H. Hanley Federal
Building
100 South Clinton Street
Syracuse, NY 13260-0066
(315) 423-5176

North Carolina
John J. Cooper
P.O. Box 27327
Federal Building, Suite 175
4407 Bland Road
Raleigh, NC 27611
(919) 790-2957

North Dakota
Robert J. Christiman
North Dakota State ASCS
Office
P.O. Box 3046
Fargo, ND 58108-3046
(701) 239-5224

Ohio
Dorothy Leslie
Federal Building, Room 540
200 North High Street
Columbus, OH 43215-2495
(614) 469-6735

Oklahoma
Bart Brorsen
USDA Agriculture Center
Building
Farm Road and McFarland
Street
Stillwater, OK 74074-2531
(405) 624-4110

Oregon
Glen E. Stonebrink
Oregon State ASCS Office
P.O. Box 1300
Tualatin, OR 97062-1300
(503) 692-6830

Pennsylvania
Donald Unangst
One Credit Union Place,
Suite 320
228 Walnut Street
Harrisburg, PA 17101-1701
(717) 782-4547

Rhode Island
Alfred R. Bettencourt, Jr.
Aldeic Complex
60 Quaker Lane
West Warwick, RI 02893-2120
(401) 828-8232

South Carolina
Thomas H. Herlong
Strom Thurmond Mall
Columbia, SC 29207
(803) 765-5186

South Dakota
Dean W. Anderson
Federal Building, Room 208
200 Fourth Street, SW
Huron, SD 57350-2478
(605) 353-1092

Tennessee
Charles Ben Thompson
U.S. Courthouse, Room 579
801 Broadway
Nashville, TN 37203-3816
(615) 736-5555

Texas
Donnie Bownan Aeting
Texas State ASCS Office
P.O. Box 2900
College Station, TX
77841-0001
(409) 260-9207

Utah
Royal K. Norman
Utah State ASCS Office
P.O. Box 11547
Salt Lake City, UT
84147-2547
(801) 524-5013

Vermont
David Newton
Executive Square Office
Building
346 Shelburne Street
Burlington, VT 05401-4495
(802) 658-2803

4

Virginia
Mahlon K. Rudy
Federal Building, Room 7105
400 North 8th Street
Richmond, VA 23240-9990
(804) 771-2581

Washington
Robert Deife
Washington State ASCS
Office
Rock Pointe Tower, Suite 568
316 West Boone Avenue
Spokane, WA 99201-2350
(509) 353-1092

West Virginia
Donald W. Brown
P.O. Box 1049
New Federal Building,
Room 239
75 High Street
Morgantown, WV 26505-7558
(304) 291-4351

Wisconsin
Peter C. Senn
Wisconsin State ASCS Office
6515 Watts Road, Room 100
Madison, WI 53719-2797
(608) 264-5301

Wyoming
Harold Hellbaum
P.O. Box 920
100 East B. Street,
Room 3001
Casper, WY 82602-0920
(307) 261-5231

Caribbean Area
Herberto J. Martinez
Caribbean Area ASCS Office
Cobran's Plaza, Suite 309
1609 Ponce DeLeon Avenue
Santurce, Puerto Rico
00909-0001
(809) 729-6872

BUSINESS AND INDUSTRIAL LOANS

Department of Agriculture
Farmers Home
Administration (FmHA)
Washington, DC
20250-0700
(202) 690-1553

Description: Guaranteed and insured loans for individuals, cooperatives, corporations, partnerships, trusts, Indian tribes, or subdivisions of states located in rural areas. Applicants must be in rural areas other than cities with populations of 50,000 or more and adjacent to urban areas with a population density of more than 100 persons per square mile.
$ Given: Business and Industrial loan range: $30,000–$7.5 million. Development loan range: $35,000–$500,000.
Application Information: File Form FmHA 449-1 for guaranteed loans at your FmHA state office.
Deadline: Contact your local or state FmHA office.
Contact: Consult your local telephone directory under U.S. Government, Department of Agriculture, for FmHA county office number or contact your FmHA state office.

Alabama
Aronov Building, Room 717
474 South Court Street
Montgomery, AL 36104
(205) 223-7077

Alaska
634 South Bailey, Suite 103
Palmer, AK 99645
(907) 745-2176

Arizona
201 East Indianola, Suite 275
Phoenix, AZ 85012
(602) 640-5086

Agriculture

Arkansas
700 West Capitol
P.O. Box 2778
Little Rock, AR 72203
(501) 324-6281

California
194 West Main Street,
Suite F
Woodland, CA 95695-2915
(916) 666-3382

Colorado
655 Parfet Street,
Room E-100
Lakewood, CO 80215
(303) 236-2801

Connecticut
451 West Street
Amherst, MA 01002
(413) 253-4300

Delaware
4611 South Dupont Highway
P.O. Box 400
Camden, DE 19934-9998
(302) 697-4300

District of Columbia
4611 South Dupont Highway
P.O. Box 400
Camden, DE 19934-9998
(302) 697-4300

Florida
Federal Building
4440 NW 25th Place
P.O. Box 147010
Gainesville, FL 32614-7010
(904) 338-3400

Georgia
Stephens Federal Building
355 East Hancock Avenue
Athens, GA 30610
(404) 546-2162

Hawaii
Federal Building, Room 311
154 Waianuenue Avenue
Hilo, HI 967720
(808) 933-3000

Idaho
3232 Elder Street
Boise, ID 83720
(808) 933-3000

Illinois
Illini Plaza
1817 South Neil Street
Champaign, IL 61820
(217) 398-5235

Indiana
5975 Lakeside Boulevard
Indianapolis, IN 46278
(317) 290-3100

Iowa
Federal Building, Room 873
210 Walnut Street
Des Moines, IA 50309
(515) 284-4663

Kansas
1201 SW Summit Executive
Court
P.O. Box 4653
Topeka, KS 66604
(913) 271-2700

Kentucky
333771 Corporate Plaza,
Suite 200
Lexington, KY 40503
(606) 224-7300

Louisiana
3727 Government Street
Alexandria, LA 71302
(318) 473-7920

Maine
444 Stillwater Avenue,
Suite 2
P.O. Box 405
Bangor, ME 04402-0405
(207) 990-9106

Maryland
4611 South Dupont Highway
P.O. Box 400
Camden, DE 19934-9998
(302) 697-4300

Massachusetts
451 West Street
Amherst, MA 01002
(413) 253-4300

Michigan
Manly Miles Building,
Room 209
1405 South Harrison Road
East Lansing, MI 48823
(517) 337-6631

Minnesota
410 Farm Credit Building
375 Jackson Street
St. Paul, MN 55101
(612) 290-3842

Mississippi
Federal Building, Suite 831
100 West Capitol
Jackson, MS 39269
(601) 965-4316

Missouri
601 Business Loop, 70 West
Parkade Center, Suite 235
Columbia, MO 65203
(314) 876-0976

Montana
900 Technology Boulevard,
Suite B
P.O. Box 850
Bozeman, MT 59771
(406) 585-2500

Nebraska
Federal Building, Room 308
100 Centennial Mall North
Lincoln, NE 68508
(402) 437-5551

Nevada
194 West Main Street,
Suite F
Woodland, CA 95695-2915
(916) 666-3382

New Hampshire
City Center, Third Floor
89 Main Street
Montpelier, VT 05602
(802) 223-2371

New Jersey
Tarnsfield and Woodlane
Roads
Tarnsfield Plaza, Suite 22
Mt. Holly, NJ 08060
(609) 265-3600

New Mexico
Federal Building, Room 3414
517 Gold Avenue, SW
Albuquerque, NM 87102
(505) 766-2462

New York
Federal Building, Room 871
100 South Clinton Street
Syracuse, NY 13261-7318
(315) 423-5290

North Carolina
4405 South Bland Road,
Suite 260
Raleigh, NC 27609
(919) 790-2731

North Dakota
Federal Building, Room 208
Third and Rosser
P.O. Box 1737
Bismarck, ND 58502
(701) 250-4781

Ohio
Federal Building, Room 507
200 North High Street
Columbus, OH 43215
(614) 469-5606

Oklahoma
USDA Agricultural Center
Office Building
Stillwater, OK 74074
(405) 624-4250

Oregon
Federal Building, Room 1590
1220 SW 3rd Avenue
Portland, OR 97204
(503) 326-2731

Pennsylvania
One Credit Union Place,
Suite 330
Harrisburg, PA 17110-2996
(717) 782-4476

Puerto Rico
New San Juan Center
Building, Room 501
159 Carlos E. Chardon Street
G.P.O. Box 6106G
Hato Rey, PR 00918-5481
(809) 766-5095

Rhode Island
451 West Street
Amherst, MA 01002
(413) 253-4300

South Carolina
Strom Thurmond Federal
Building, Room 1007
1835 Assembly Street
Columbia, SC 29201
(803) 765-5163

South Dakota
Huron Federal Building,
Room 308
200 Fourth Street, SW
Huron, SD 57350
(605) 353-1430

Tennessee
3322 West End Avenue,
Suite 300
Nashville, TN 37203-1071
(615) 736-7341

Texas
Federal Building, Suite 102
101 South Main
Temple, TX 76501
(817) 774-1301

Utah
Federal Building, Room 5438
125 South State Street
Salt Lake City, UT 84138
(801) 524-4063

Vermont
City Center, Third Floor
89 Main Street
Montpelier, VT 05602
(802) 223-2371

Virgin Islands
City Center, Third Floor
89 Main Street
Montpelier, VT 05602
(802) 223-2371

Virginia
Federal Building, Room 8213
400 North 8th Street
Richmond, VA 23240
(804) 771-2451

Washington
Federal Building, Room 319
P.O. Box 2427
Wenatchee, WA 98807
(509) 662-4352

West Virginia
75 High Street
P.O. Box 678
Morgantown, WV 26505
(304) 291-4791

Wisconsin
4949 Kirschling Court
Stevens Point, WI 54481
(715) 345-7600

Wyoming
Federal Building, Room 1005
100 East B Street
P.O. Box 820
Casper, WY 82602
(307) 261-5271

COLORADO RIVER BASIN SALINITY CONTROL PROGRAM

Department of Agriculture
Agricultural Stabilization
and Conservation Service
Conservation and
Environmental Protection
Division
P.O. Box 2415
Washington, DC 20013
(202) 720-6221

Description: Direct payments for specified use to individuals, Indian tribes, partnerships, firms, associations, corporations, joint stock companies, and state or local public or nonpublic entities not included in the above, to treat salinity problems caused by agricultural irrigation activities.
$ Given: Not identified or established.
Application Information: Complete Form CRSC-1 at your county ASCS office.
Deadline: None
Contact: Your local, state, and/or regional ASCS office

Alabama
Albert C. McDonald
P.O. Box 891
474 South Court Street,
Room 749
Montgomery, AL 36104-4184
(205) 832-7230

Alaska
Teresa Weiland
Alaska State ASCS Office
800 West Evergreen,
Suite 216
Palmer, AK 99645-6389
(907) 745-7982

Arizona
Arden J. Palmer
Arizona State ASCS Office
201 East Indianola, Suite 325
Phoenix, AZ 85012-2054
(602) 640-5200

Arkansas
Dotson Collins
P.O. Box 2781
New Federal Building,
Room 5102
700 West Capitol Street
Little Rock, AR 72201-3225
(501) 378-5220

California
John Smythe
California State ASCS Office
1303 J. Street, Suite 300
Sacramento, CA 95814-2916
(916) 551-1801

Colorado
Lloyd C. Sommerville
Colorado State ASCS Office
655 Parfet Street
Room E 305, Third Floor
Lakewood, CO 80215
(303) 236-2866

Connecticut
David T. Schreiber
88 Day Hill Road
Windsor, CT 06095
(203) 285-8483

Delaware
Earle Isaacs, Jr.
179 West Chestnut Hill Road,
Suite 7
Newark, DE 19713-2295
(302) 573-6536

Florida
Eugene C. Badger
P.O. Box 141030
4440 Northwest 25th Place,
Suite 1
Gainesville, FL 32614-1030
(904) 372-8549

Georgia
James E. Harrison
P.O. Box 1907
Federal Building, Room 102
344 East Hancock Avenue
Athens, GA 30601-2775
(404) 546-2266

Hawaii
Ralph K. Ajifu
Hawaii State ASCS Office
300 Ala Moana Boulevard,
Room 4202
P.O. Box 50008
Honolulu, HI 96850-0002
(808) 551-2644

Idaho
Trent Clark
Idaho State ASCS Office
3220 Elder Street
Boise, ID 83705-5820
(208) 334-1486

Illinois
William G. Beeler
P.O. Box 19273
3500 Wabash Avenue
Springfield, IL 62707
(217) 492-4180

Indiana
Don Villwoch
Indiana State ASCS Office
5981 Lakeside Boulevard
Indianapolis, IN 46278-1996
(317) 290-3030

Iowa
Robert Furleigh
10500 Buena Vista Court
Urbandale, IA 50322
(515) 254-1540

Kansas
Frank A. Mosier
Kansas State ASCS Office
2601 Anderson Avenue
Manhattan, KS 66502-2898
(913) 539-3531

Kentucky
Kenneth Ashby
Kentucky State ASCS Office
771 Corporate Drive,
Suite 100
Lexington, KY 40503-5477
(606) 233-2726

Louisiana
Willie F. Cooper
3737 Government Street
Alexandria, LA 71302-3395
(318) 473-7721

Maine
David P. Staples
44 Stillwater Avenue
P.O. Box 406
Bangor, ME 04401-3521
(207) 942-0342

Maryland
James Richardson
Rivers Center
10270 B Columbia Road
Columbia, MD 21046-9998
(301) 381-4550

Massachusetts
Raymond E. Duda
451 West Street
Amherst, MA 01002-2953
(413) 256-0232

Michigan
David Conklin
1405 South Harrison Road,
Room 116
East Lansing, MI 48823-5202
(517) 337-6659

Minnesota
Donald L. Friedrich
Minnesota State ASCS Office
400 Farm Credit Service
Building
375 Jackson Street
St. Paul, MN 55101-1852
(612) 290-3651

Mississippi
Charles R. Hull
Mississippi State ASCS
Office
6310 I-55 North
Jackson, MS 39236
(601) 965-4300

Missouri
Morris G. Westfall
601 Parkdale Plaza Business
Loop
70 West, Suite 225
Columbia, MO 65203
(314) 875-5201

Montana
Donald Anderson
P.O. Box 670
Bozeman, MT 59771-0670
(406) 587-6872

Nebraska
John Neuberger
Nebraska State ASCS Office
P.O. Box 57975
Lincoln, NE 68505-7975
(402) 437-5581

Nevada
C. Richard Capurro
Nevada State ASCS Office
1755 East Plumb Lane,
Suite 202
Reno, NV 89502-3207

New Hampshire
Peter M. Thomson
USDA - New Hampshire
State ASCS Office
22 Bridge Street,
Fourth Floor
Concord, NH 03301-5605
(603) 224-7941

New Jersey
Peter de Wilde
Mastoris Professional Plaza
163 Route 130
Building 1, Suite E
Bordentown, NJ 08505
(609) 298-3446

New Mexico
David Turner
New Mexico State ASCS
Office
P.O. Box 1458
Federal Building, Room 4408
517 Gold Avenue, SW
Albuquerque, NM
87102-3156
(505) 766-2472

New York
John Steele
811 James H. Hanley Federal
Building
100 South Clinton Street
Syracuse, NY 13260-0066
(315) 423-5176

North Carolina
John J. Cooper
P.O. Box 27327
Federal Building, Suite 175
4407 Bland Road
Raleigh, NC 27611
(919) 790-2957

North Dakota
Robert J. Christiman
North Dakota State ASCS
Office
P.O. Box 3046
Fargo, ND 58108-3046
(701) 239-5224

Ohio
Dorothy Leslie
Federal Building, Room 540
200 North High Street
Columbus, OH 43215-2495
(614) 469-6735

Oklahoma
Bart Brorsen
USDA Agriculture Center
Building
Farm Road and McFarland
Street
Stillwater, OK 74074-2531
(405) 624-4110

Oregon
Glen E. Stonebrink
Oregon State ASCS Office
P.O. Box 1300
Tualatin, OR 97062-1300
(503) 692-6830

Pennsylvania
Donald Unangst
One Credit Union Place,
Suite 320
228 Walnut Street
Harrisburg, PA 17101-1701
(717) 782-4547

Rhode Island
Alfred R. Bettencourt, Jr.
Aldeic Complex
60 Quaker Lane
West Warwick, RI 02893-2120
(401) 828-8232

South Carolina
Thomas H. Herlong
Strom Thurmond Mall
Columbia, SC 29207
(803) 765-5186

South Dakota
Dean W. Anderson
Federal Building, Room 208
200 Fourth Street, SW
Huron, SD 57350-2478
(605) 353-1092

Tennessee
Charles Ben Thompson
U.S. Courthouse, Room 579
801 Broadway
Nashville, TN 37203-3816
(615) 736-5555

Texas
Donnie Bowman Aeting
Texas State ASCS Office
P.O. Box 2900
College Station, TX
77841-0001
(409) 260-9207

Utah
Royal K. Norman
Utah State ASCS Office
P.O. Box 11547
Salt Lake City, UT
84147-2547
(801) 524-5013

Vermont
David Newton
Executive Square Office
Building
346 Shelburne Street
Burlington, VT 05401-4495
(802) 658-2803

Virginia
Mahlon K. Rudy
Federal Building, Room 7105
400 North 8th Street
Richmond, VA 23240-9990
(804) 771-2581

Washington
Robert Deife
Washington State ASCS
Office
Rock Pointe Tower, Suite 568
316 West Boone Avenue
Spokane, WA 99201-2350
(509) 353-1092

West Virginia
Donald W. Brown
P.O. Box 1049
New Federal Building,
Room 239
75 High Street
Morgantown, WV 26505-7558
(304) 291-4351

Wisconsin
Peter C. Senn
Wisconsin State ASCS Office
6515 Watts Road, Room 100
Madison, WI 53719-2797
(608) 264-5301

Wyoming
Harold Hellbaum
P.O. Box 920
100 East B. Street,
Room 3001
Casper, WY 82602-0920
(307) 261-5231

Caribbean Area
Herberto J. Martinez
Caribbean Area ASCS Office
Cobran's Plaza, Suite 309
1609 Ponce DeLeon Avenue
Santurce, Puerto Rico
00909-0001
(809) 729-6872

COMMODITY LOANS AND PURCHASES

Department of Agriculture
Agricultural Stabilization
and Conservation Service
Cotton, Grain, and Rice
Support Division
P.O. Box 2415
Washington, DC 20013
(202) 720-7617

Description: Direct loans and payments with unrestricted use to owners, landlords, tenants, or sharecroppers on a farm with a history of producing eligible commodities. Record of farming operation must be on file in the ASCS county office.
$ Given: Loan range: $50–$76 million.
Application Information: Write for guidelines.
Deadline: Based on type of crop
Contact: Your state ASCS office

Agriculture

Alabama
Albert C. McDonald
P.O. Box 891
474 South Court Street,
Room 749
Montgomery, AL 36104-4184
(205) 832-7230

Alaska
Teresa Weiland
Alaska State ASCS Office
800 West Evergreen,
Suite 216
Palmer, AK 99645-6389
(907) 745-7982

Arizona
Arden J. Palmer
Arizona State ASCS Office
201 East Indianola, Suite 325
Phoenix, AZ 85012-2054
(602) 640-5200

Arkansas
Dotson Collins
P.O. Box 2781
New Federal Building,
Room 5102
700 West Capitol Street
Little Rock, AR 72201-3225
(501) 378-5220

California
John Smythe
California State ASCS Office
1303 J. Street, Suite 300
Sacramento, CA 95814-2916
(916) 551-1801

Colorado
Lloyd C. Sommerville
Colorado State ASCS Office
655 Parfet Street
Room E 305, Third Floor
Lakewood, CO 80215
(303) 236-2866

Connecticut
David T. Schreiber
88 Day Hill Road
Windsor, CT 06095
(203) 285-8483

Delaware
Earle Isaacs, Jr.
179 West Chestnut Hill Road,
Suite 7
Newark, DE 19713-2295
(302) 573-6536

Florida
Eugene C. Badger
P.O. Box 141030
4440 Northwest 25th Place,
Suite 1
Gainesville, FL 32614-1030
(904) 372-8549

Georgia
James E. Harrison
P.O. Box 1907
Federal Building, Room 102
344 East Hancock Avenue
Athens, GA 30601-2775
(404) 546-2266

Hawaii
Ralph K. Ajifu
Hawaii State ASCS Office
300 Ala Moana Boulevard,
Room 4202
P.O. Box 50008
Honolulu, HI 96850-0002
(808) 551-2644

Idaho
Trent Clark
Idaho State ASCS Office
3220 Elder Street
Boise, ID 83705-5820
(208) 334-1486

Illinois
William G. Beeler
P.O. Box 19273
3500 Wabash Avenue
Springfield, IL 62707
(217) 492-4180

Indiana
Don Villwoch
Indiana State ASCS Office
5981 Lakeside Boulevard
Indianapolis, IN 46278-1996
(317) 290-3030

Iowa
Robert Furleigh
10500 Buena Vista Court
Urbandale, IA 50322
(515) 254-1540

Kansas
Frank A. Mosier
Kansas State ASCS Office
2601 Anderson Avenue
Manhattan, KS 66502-2898
(913) 539-3531

Kentucky
Kenneth Ashby
Kentucky State ASCS Office
771 Corporate Drive,
Suite 100
Lexington, KY 40503-5477
(606) 233-2726

Louisiana
Willie F. Cooper
3737 Government Street
Alexandria, LA 71302-3395
(318) 473-7721

Maine
David P. Staples
44 Stillwater Avenue
P.O. Box 406
Bangor, ME 04401-3521
(207) 942-0342

Maryland
James Richardson
Rivers Center
10270 B Columbia Road
Columbia, MD 21046-9998
(301) 381-4550

Massachusetts
Raymond E. Duda
451 West Street
Amherst, MA 01002-2953
(413) 256-0232

Michigan
David Conklin
1405 South Harrison Road,
Room 116
East Lansing, MI 48823-5202
(517) 337-6659

Minnesota
Donald L. Friedrich
Minnesota State ASCS Office
400 Farm Credit Service
Building
375 Jackson Street
St. Paul, MN 55101-1852
(612) 290-3651

Mississippi
Charles R. Hull
Mississippi State ASCS
Office
6310 I-55 North
Jackson, MS 39236
(601) 965-4300

Missouri
Morris G. Westfall
601 Parkdale Plaza Business
Loop
70 West, Suite 225
Columbia, MO 65203
(314) 875-5201

Montana
Donald Anderson
P.O. Box 670
Bozeman, MT 59771-0670
(406) 587-6872

Nebrasksa
John Neuberger
Nebraska State ASCS Office
P.O. Box 57975
Lincoln, NE 68505-7975
(402) 437-5581

Nevada
C. Richard Capurro
Nevada State ASCS Office
1755 East Plumb Lane,
Suite 202
Reno, NV 89502-3207

New Hampshire
Peter M. Thomson
USDA - New Hampshire
State ASCS Office
22 Bridge Street,
Fourth Floor
Concord, NH 03301-5605
(603) 224-7941

New Jersey
Peter de Wilde
Mastoris Professional Plaza
163 Route 130
Building 1, Suite E
Bordentown, NJ 08505
(609) 298-3446

New Mexico
David Turner
New Mexico State ASCS
Office
P.O. Box 1458
Federal Building, Room 4408
517 Gold Avenue, SW
Albuquerque, NM
87102-3156
(505) 766-2472

New York
John Steele
811 James H. Hanley Federal
Building
100 South Clinton Street
Syracuse, NY 13260-0066
(315) 423-5176

North Carolina
John J. Cooper
P.O. Box 27327
Federal Building, Suite 175
4407 Bland Road
Raleigh, NC 27611
(919) 790-2957

North Dakota
Robert J. Christiman
North Dakota State ASCS
Office
P.O. Box 3046
Fargo, ND 58108-3046
(701) 239-5224

Ohio
Dorothy Leslie
Federal Building, Room 540
200 North High Street
Columbus, OH 43215-2495
(614) 469-6735

Oklahoma
Bart Brorsen
USDA Agriculture Center
Building
Farm Road and McFarland
Street
Stillwater, OK 74074-2531
(405) 624-4110

Oregon
Glen E. Stonebrink
Oregon State ASCS Office
P.O. Box 1300
Tualatin, OR 97062-1300
(503) 692-6830

Agriculture

Pennsylvania
Donald Unangst
One Credit Union Place,
Suite 320
228 Walnut Street
Harrisburg, PA 17101-1701
(717) 782-4547

Rhode Island
Alfred R. Bettencourt, Jr.
Aldeic Complex
60 Quaker Lane
West Warwick, RI 02893-2120
(401) 828-8232

South Carolina
Thomas H. Herlong
Strom Thurmond Mall
Columbia, SC 29207
(803) 765-5186

South Dakota
Dean W. Anderson
Federal Building, Room 208
200 Fourth Street, SW
Huron, SD 57350-2478
(605) 353-1092

Tennessee
Charles Ben Thompson
U.S. Courthouse, Room 579
801 Broadway
Nashville, TN 37203-3816
(615) 736-5555

Texas
Donnie Bownan Aeting
Texas State ASCS Office
P.O. Box 2900
College Station, TX
77841-0001
(409) 260-9207

Utah
Royal K. Norman
Utah State ASCS Office
P.O. Box 11547
Salt Lake City, UT
84147-2547
(801) 524-5013

Vermont
David Newton
Executive Square Office
Building
346 Shelburne Street
Burlington, VT 05401-4495
(802) 658-2803

Virginia
Mahon K. Rudy
Federal Building, Room 7105
400 North 8th Street
Richmond, VA 23240-9990
(804) 771-2581

Washington
Robert Deife
Washington State ASCS
Office
Rock Pointe Tower, Suite 568
316 West Boone Avenue
Spokane, WA 99201-2350
(509) 353-1092

West Virginia
Donald W. Brown
P.O. Box 1049
New Federal Building,
Room 239
75 High Street
Morgantown, WV 26505-7558
(304) 291-4351

Wisconsin
Peter C. Senn
Wisconsin State ASCS Office
6515 Watts Road, Room 100
Madison, WI 53719-2797
(608) 264-5301

Wyoming
Harold Hellbaum
P.O. Box 920
100 East B. Street,
Room 3001
Casper, WY 82602-0920
(307) 261-5231

Caribbean Area
Herberto J. Martinez
Caribbean Area ASCS Office
Cobran's Plaza, Suite 309
1609 Ponce DeLeon Avenue
Santurce, Puerto Rico
00909-0001
(809) 729-6872

CONSERVATION RESERVE PROGRAM

**Department of
Agriculture**
Agricultural Stabilization
and Conservation Service
Conservation and
Environmental Protection
Division
P.O. Box 2415
Washington, DC 20013
(202) 720-6221

Description: Direct payments for specified use to individuals, partnerships, associations, corporations, estates, trusts, and other legal entities. Cropland must be owned or operated for at least three years prior to close of annual sign-up period, unless acquired by will or succession, or if the department determines that ownership was not acquired to place land in conservation reserve.
$ Given: Payment range: $50–$50,000; average: $5,324.
Application Information: Submit rental rate per acre bid to local ASCS office.
Deadline: N/A
Contact: Your local, state, and/or regional ASCS office

Alabama
Albert C. McDonald
P.O. Box 891
474 South Court Street,
Room 749
Montgomery, AL 36104-4184
(205) 832-7230

Alaska
Teresa Weiland
Alaska State ASCS Office
800 West Evergreen,
Suite 216
Palmer, AK 99645-6389
(907) 745-7982

Arizona
Arden J. Palmer
Arizona State ASCS Office
201 East Indianola, Suite 325
Phoenix, AZ 85012-2054
(602) 640-5200

Arkansas
Dotson Collins
P.O. Box 2781
New Federal Building,
Room 5102
700 West Capitol Street
Little Rock, AR 72201-3225
(501) 378-5220

California
John Smythe
California State ASCS Office
1303 J. Street, Suite 300
Sacramento, CA 95814-2916
(916) 551-1801

Colorado
Lloyd C. Sommerville
Colorado State ASCS Office
655 Parfet Street
Room E 305, Third Floor
Lakewood, CO 80215
(303) 236-2866

Connecticut
David T. Schreiber
88 Day Hill Road
Windsor, CT 06095
(203) 285-8483

Delaware
Earle Isaacs, Jr.
179 West Chestnut Hill Road,
Suite 7
Newark, DE 19713-2295
(302) 573-6536

Florida
Eugene C. Badger
P.O. Box 141030
4440 Northwest 25th Place,
Suite 1
Gainesville, FL 32614-1030
(904) 372-8549

Georgia
James E. Harrison
P.O. Box 1907
Federal Building, Room 102
344 East Hancock Avenue
Athens, GA 30601-2775
(404) 546-2266

Agriculture

Hawaii
Ralph K. Ajifu
Hawaii State ASCS Office
300 Ala Moana Boulevard,
Room 4202
P.O. Box 50008
Honolulu, HI 96850-0002
(808) 551-2644

Idaho
Trent Clark
Idaho State ASCS Office
3220 Elder Street
Boise, ID 83705-5280
(208) 334-1486

Illinois
William G. Beeler
P.O. Box 19273
3500 Wabash Avenue
Springfield, IL 62707
(217) 492-4180

Indiana
Don Villwoch
Indiana State ASCS Office
5981 Lakeside Boulevard
Indianapolis, IN 46278-1996
(317) 290-3030

Iowa
Robert Furleigh
10500 Buena Vista Court
Urbandale, IA 50322
(515) 254-1540

Kansas
Frank A. Mosier
Kansas State ASCS Office
2601 Anderson Avenue
Manhattan, KS 66502-2898
(913) 539-3531

Kentucky
Kenneth Ashby
Kentucky State ASCS Office
771 Corporate Drive, Suite
100
Lexington, KY 40503-5477
(606) 233-2726

Louisiana
Willie F. Cooper
3737 Government Street
Alexandria, LA 71302-3395
(318) 473-7721

Maine
David P. Staples
44 Stillwater Avenue
P.O. Box 406
Bangor, ME 04401-3521
(207) 942-0342

Maryland
James Richardson
Rivers Center
10270 B Columbia Road
Columbia, MD 21046-9998
(301) 381-4550

Massachusetts
Raymond E. Duda
451 West Street
Amherst, MA 01002-2953
(413) 256-0232

Michigan
David Conklin
1405 South Harrison Road,
Room 116
East Lansing, MI 48823-5202
(517) 337-6659

Minnesota
Donald L. Friedrich
Minnesota State ASCS Office
400 Farm Credit Service
Building
375 Jackson Street
St. Paul, MN 55101-1852
(612) 290-3651

Mississippi
Charles R. Hull
Mississippi State ASCS
Office
6310 I-55 North
Jackson, MS 39236
(601) 965-4300

Missouri
Morris G. Westfall
601 Parkdale Plaza Business
Loop
70 West, Suite 225
Columbia, MO 65203
(314) 875-5201

Montana
Donald Anderson
P.O. Box 670
Bozeman, MT 59771-0670
(406) 587-6872

Nebraska
John Neuberger
Nebraska State ASCS Office
P.O. Box 57975
Lincoln, NE 68505-7975
(402) 437-5581

Nevada
C. Richard Capurro
Nevada State ASCS Office
1755 East Plumb Lane,
Suite 202
Reno, NV 89502-3207

New Hampshire
Peter M. Thomson
USDA - New Hampshire
State ASCS Office
22 Bridge Street,
Fourth Floor
Concord, NH 03301-5605
(603) 224-7941

New Jersey
Peter de Wilde
Mastoris Professional Plaza
163 Route 130
Building 1, Suite E
Bordentown, NJ 08505
(609) 298-3446

New Mexico
David Turner
New Mexico State ASCS
Office
P.O. Box 1458
Federal Building, Room 4408
517 Gold Avenue, SW
Albuquerque, NM
87102-3156
(505) 766-2472

New York
John Steele
811 James H. Hanley Federal
Building
100 South Clinton Street
Syracuse, NY 13260-0066
(315) 423-5176

North Carolina
John J. Cooper
P.O. Box 27327
Federal Building, Suite 175
4407 Bland Road
Raleigh, NC 27611
(919) 790-2957

North Dakota
Robert J. Christiman
North Dakota State ASCS
Office
P.O. Box 3046
Fargo, ND 58108-3046
(701) 239-5224

Ohio
Dorothy Leslie
Federal Building, Room 540
200 North High Street
Columbus, OH 43215-2495
(614) 469-6735

Oklahoma
Bart Brorsen
USDA Agriculture Center
Building
Farm Road and McFarland
Street
Stillwater, OK 74074-2531
(405) 624-4110

Oregon
Glen E. Stonebrink
Oregon State ASCS Office
P.O. Box 1300
Tualatin, OR 97062-1300
(503) 692-6830

Pennsylvania
Donald Unangst
One Credit Union Place,
Suite 320
228 Walnut Street
Harrisburg, PA 17101-1701
(717) 782-4547

Rhode Island
Alfred R. Bettencourt, Jr.
Aldeic Complex
60 Quaker Lane
West Warwick, RI 02893-2120
(401) 828-8232

South Carolina
Thomas H. Herlong
Strom Thurmond Mall
Columbia, SC 29207
(803) 765-5186

South Dakota
Dean W. Anderson
Federal Building, Room 208
200 Fourth Street, SW
Huron, SD 57350-2478
(605) 353-1092

Tennessee
Charles Ben Thompson
U.S. Courthouse, Room 579
801 Broadway
Nashville, TN 37203-3816
(615) 736-5555

Texas
Donnie Bownan Aeting
Texas State ASCS Office
P.O. Box 2900
College Station, TX
77841-0001
(409) 260-9207

Utah
Royal K. Norman
Utah State ASCS Office
P.O. Box 11547
Salt Lake City, UT
84147-2547
(801) 524-5013

Vermont
David Newton
Executive Square Office
Building
346 Shelburne Street
Burlington, VT 05401-4495
(802) 658-2803

Virginia
Mahlon K. Rudy
Federal Building, Room 7105
400 North 8th Street
Richmond, VA 23240-9990
(804) 771-2581

Washington
Robert Deife
Washington State ASCS
Office
Rock Pointe Tower, Suite 568
316 West Boone Avenue
Spokane, WA 99201-2350
(509) 353-1092

West Virginia
Donald W. Brown
P.O. Box 1049
New Federal Building,
Room 239
75 High Street
Morgantown, WV 26505-7558
(304) 291-4351

Wisconsin
Peter C. Senn
Wisconsin State ASCS Office
6515 Watts Road, Room 100
Madison, WI 53719-2797
(608) 264-5301

Wyoming
Harold Hellbaum
P.O. Box 920
100 East B. Street,
Room 3001
Casper, WY 82602-0920
(307) 261-5231

Caribbean Area
Herberto J. Martinez
Caribbean Area ASCS Office
Cobran's Plaza, Suite 309
1609 Ponce DeLeon Avenue
Santurce, Puerto Rico
00909-0001
(809) 729-6872

COTTON PRODUCTION STABILIZATION

Department of Agriculture
Agricultural Stabilization
and Conservation Service
P.O. Box 2415
Washington, DC 20013
(202) 447-6734

Description: Direct payments with unrestricted use are made to owners, landlords, tenants, or sharecroppers on a farm who meet the requirements announced by the Secretary. Record of farming operation must be on file in the ASCS county office.
$ Given: Up to $250,000 per person.
Application Information: Write for guidelines.
Deadline: N/A
Contact: Your local ASCS office. If unlisted, contact your state or regional ASCS office.

Alabama
Albert C. McDonald
P.O. Box 891
474 South Court Street,
Room 749
Montgomery, AL 36104-4184
(205) 832-7230

Alaska
Teresa Weiland
Alaska State ASCS Office
800 West Evergreen,
Suite 216
Palmer, AK 99645-6389
(907) 745-7982

Arizona
Arden J. Palmer
Arizona State ASCS Office
201 East Indianola, Suite 325
Phoenix, AZ 85012-2054
(602) 640-5200

Arkansas
Dotson Collins
P.O. Box 2781
New Federal Building,
Room 5102
700 West Capitol Street
Little Rock, AR 72201-3225
(501) 378-5220

California
John Smythe
California State ASCS Office
1303 J. Street, Suite 300
Sacramento, CA 95814-2916
(916) 551-1801

Colorado
Lloyd C. Sommerville
Colorado State ASCS Office
655 Parfet Street
Room E 305, Third Floor
Lakewood, CO 80215
(303) 236-2866

Connecticut
David T. Schreiber
88 Day Hill Road
Windsor, CT 06095
(203) 285-8483

Delaware
Earle Isaacs, Jr.
179 West Chestnut Hill Road,
Suite 7
Newark, DE 19713-2295
(302) 573-6536

Florida
Eugene C. Badger
P.O. Box 141030
4440 Northwest 25th Place,
Suite 1
Gainesville, FL 32614-1030
(904) 372-8549

Georgia
James E. Harrison
P.O. Box 1907
Federal Building, Room 102
344 East Hancock Avenue
Athens, GA 30601-2775
(404) 546-2266

Hawaii
Ralph K. Ajifu
Hawaii State ASCS Office
300 Ala Moana Boulevard,
Room 4202
P.O. Box 50008
Honolulu, HI 96850-0002
(808) 551-2644

Idaho
Trent Clark
Idaho State ASCS Office
3220 Elder Street
Boise, ID 83705-5820
(208) 334-1486

Illinois
William G. Beeler
P.O. Box 19273
3500 Wabash Avenue
Springfield, IL 62707
(217) 492-4180

Indiana
Don Villwoch
Indiana State ASCS Office
5981 Lakeside Boulevard
Indianapolis, IN 46278-1996
(317) 290-3030

Iowa
Robert Furleigh
10500 Buena Vista Court
Urbandale, IA 50322
(515) 254-1540

Kansas
Frank A. Mosier
Kansas State ASCS Office
2601 Anderson Avenue
Manhattan, KS 66502-2898
(913) 539-3531

Kentucky
Kenneth Ashby
Kentucky State ASCS Office
771 Corporate Drive,
Suite 100
Lexington, KY 40503-5477
(606) 233-2726

Louisiana
Willie F. Cooper
3737 Government Street
Alexandria, LA 71302-3395
(318) 473-7721

Maine
David P. Staples
44 Stillwater Avenue
P.O. Box 406
Bangor, ME 04401-3521
(207) 942-0342

Maryland
James Richardson
Rivers Center
10270 B Columbia Road
Columbia, MD 21046-9998
(301) 381-4550

Massachusetts
Raymond E. Duda
451 West Street
Amherst, MA 01002-2953
(413) 256-0232

Michigan
David Conklin
1405 South Harrison Road,
Room 116
East Lansing, MI 48823-5202
(517) 337-6659

Minnesota
Donald L. Friedrich
Minnesota State ASCS Office
400 Farm Credit Service
Building
375 Jackson Street
St. Paul, MN 55101-1852
(612) 290-3651

Mississippi
Charles R. Hull
Mississippi State ASCS
Office
6310 I-55 North
Jackson, MS 39236
(601) 965-4300

Missouri
Morris G. Westfall
601 Parkdale Plaza Business
Loop
70 West, Suite 225
Columbia, MO 65203
(314) 875-5201

Montana
Donald Anderson
P.O. Box 670
Bozeman, MT 59771-0670
(406) 587-6872

Nebraska
John Neuberger
Nebraska State ASCS Office
P.O. Box 57975
Lincoln, NE 68505-7975
(402) 437-5581

Nevada
C. Richard Capurro
Nevada State ASCS Office
1755 East Plumb Lane,
Suite 202
Reno, NV 89502-3207

New Hampshire
Peter M. Thomson
USDA - New Hampshire
State ASCS Office
22 Bridge Street,
Fourth Floor
Concord, NH 03301-5605
(603) 224-7941

New Jersey
Peter de Wilde
Mastoris Professional Plaza
163 Route 130
Building 1, Suite E
Bordentown, NJ 08505
(609) 298-3446

New Mexico
David Turner
New Mexico State ASCS
Office
P.O. Box 1458
Federal Building, Room 4408
517 Gold Avenue, SW
Albuquerque, NM
87102-3156
(505) 766-2472

New York
John Steele
811 James H. Hanley Federal
Building
100 South Clinton Street
Syracuse, NY 13260-0066
(315) 423-5176

North Carolina
John J. Cooper
P.O. Box 27327
Federal Building, Suite 175
4407 Bland Road
Raleigh, NC 27611
(919) 790-2957

North Dakota
Robert J. Christman
North Dakota State ASCS
Office
P.O. Box 3046
Fargo, ND 58108-3046
(701) 239-5224

Ohio
Dorothy Leslie
Federal Building, Room 540
200 North High Street
Columbus, OH 43215-2495
(614) 469-6735

Oklahoma
Bart Brorsen
USDA Agriculture Center
Building
Farm Road and McFarland
Street
Stillwater, OK 74074-2531
(405) 624-4110

Oregon
Glen E. Stonebrink
Oregon State ASCS Office
P.O. Box 1300
Tualatin, OR 97062-1300
(503) 692-6830

Pennsylvania
Donald Unangst
One Credit Union Place,
Suite 320
228 Walnut Street
Harrisburg, PA 17101-1701
(717) 782-4547

Rhode Island
Alfred R. Bettencourt, Jr.
Aldeic Complex
60 Quaker Lane
West Warwick, RI 02893-2120
(401) 828-8232

South Carolina
Thomas H. Herlong
Strom Thurmond Mall
Columbia, SC 29207
(803) 765-5186

South Dakota
Dean W. Anderson
Federal Building, Room 208
200 Fourth Street, SW
Huron, SD 57350-2478
(605) 353-1092

Tennessee
Charles Ben Thompson
U.S. Courthouse, Room 579
801 Broadway
Nashville, TN 37203-3816
(615) 736-5555

Texas
Donnie Bownan Aeting
Texas State ASCS Office
P.O. Box 2900
College Station, TX
77841-0001
(409) 260-9207

Utah
Royal K. Norman
Utah State ASCS Office
P.O. Box 11547
Salt Lake City, UT
84147-2547
(801) 524-5013

Vermont
David Newton
Executive Square Office
Building
346 Shelburne Street
Burlington, VT 05401-4495
(802) 658-2803

Virginia
Mahlon K. Rudy
Federal Building, Room 7105
400 North 8th Street
Richmond, VA 23240-9990
(804) 771-2581

Washington
Robert Deife
Washington State ASCS
Office
Rock Pointe Tower, Suite 568
316 West Boone Avenue
Spokane, WA 99201-2350
(509) 353-1092

West Virginia
Donald W. Brown
P.O. Box 1049
New Federal Building,
Room 239
75 High Street
Morgantown, WV 26505-7558
(304) 291-4351

Wisconsin
Peter C. Senn
Wisconsin State ASCS Office
6515 Watts Road, Room 100
Madison, WI 53719-2797
(608) 264-5301

Wyoming
Harold Hellbaum
P.O. Box 920
100 East B. Street,
Room 3001
Casper, WY 82602-0920
(307) 261-5231

Caribbean Area
Herberto J. Martinez
Caribbean Area ASCS Office
Cobran's Plaza, Suite 309
1609 Ponce DeLeon Avenue
Santurce, Puerto Rico
00909-0001
(809) 729-6872

DAIRY INDEMNITY PROGRAM

Department of Agriculture
Agricultural Stabilization
and Conservation Service
Emergency Operations
and Livestock Program
Division
P.O. Box 2415
Washington, DC 20013
(202) 720-7673

Description: Direct payments with unrestricted use to dairy farmers whose milk has been removed from the market by a public agency because of residue of any violating substance in milk and to manufacturers of dairy products whose product has been removed from the market by a public agency because of pesticide residue.
$ Given: Payment range: $88–$95,000
Application Information: Producers should file application for payment on Form ASCS-373 with local county ASCS office. Manufacturers must file information on cause and amount of loss with local county ASCS office.
Deadline: Claims must be filed by December 31, following the fiscal year in which the loss is incurred.
Contact: Your local ASCS office or, if not listed, the appropriate state and/or regional office.

Alabama
Albert C. McDonald
P.O. Box 891
474 South Court Street,
Room 749
Montgomery, AL 36104-4184
(205) 832-7230

Alaska
Teresa Weiland
Alaska State ASCS Office
800 West Evergreen,
Suite 216
Palmer, AK 99645-6389
(907) 745-7982

Arizona
Arden J. Palmer
Arizona State ASCS Office
201 East Indianola, Suite 325
Phoenix, AZ 85012-2054
(602) 640-5200

Arkansas
Dotson Collins
P.O. Box 2781
New Federal Building,
Room 5102
700 West Capitol Street
Little Rock, AR 72201-3225
(501) 378-5220

California
John Smythe
California State ASCS Office
1303 J. Street, Suite 300
Sacramento, CA 95814-2916
(916) 551-1801

Colorado
Lloyd C. Sommerville
Colorado State ASCS Office
655 Parfet Street
Room E 305, Third Floor
Lakewood, CO 80215
(303) 236-2866

Connecticut
David T. Schreiber
88 Day Hill Road
Windsor, CT 06095
(203) 285-8483

Delaware
Earle Isaacs, Jr.
179 West Chestnut Hill Road,
Suite 7
Newark, DE 19713-2295
(302) 573-6536

Florida
Eugene C. Badger
P.O. Box 141030
4440 Northwest 25th Place,
Suite 1
Gainesville, FL 32614-1030
(904) 372-8549

Georgia
James E. Harrison
P.O. Box 1907
Federal Building, Room 102
344 East Hancock Avenue
Athens, GA 30601-2775
(404) 546-2266

Hawaii
Ralph K. Ajifu
Hawaii State ASCS Office
300 Ala Moana Boulevard,
Room 4202
P.O. Box 50008
Honolulu, HI 96850-0002
(808) 551-2644

Idaho
Trent Clark
Idaho State ASCS Office
3220 Elder Street
Boise, ID 83705-5820
(208) 334-1486

Illinois
William G. Beeler
P.O. Box 19273
3500 Wabash Avenue
Springfield, IL 62707
(217) 492-4180

Indiana
Don Villwoch
Indiana State ASCS Office
5981 Lakeside Boulevard
Indianapolis, IN 46278-1996
(317) 290-3030

Iowa
Robert Furleigh
10500 Buena Vista Court
Urbandale, IA 50322
(515) 254-1540

Kansas
Frank A. Mosier
Kansas State ASCS Office
2601 Anderson Avenue
Manhattan, KS 66502-2898
(913) 539-3531

Kentucky
Kenneth Ashby
Kentucky State ASCS Office
771 Corporate Drive,
Suite 100
Lexington, KY 40503-5477
(606) 233-2726

Louisiana
Willie F. Cooper
3737 Government Street
Alexandria, LA 71302-3395
(318) 473-7721

Maine
David P. Staples
44 Stillwater Avenue
P.O. Box 406
Bangor, ME 04401-3521
(207) 942-0342

Maryland
James Richardson
Rivers Center
10270 B Columbia Road
Columbia, MD 21046-9998
(301) 381-4550

Massachusetts
Raymond E. Duda
451 West Street
Amherst, MA 01002-2953
(413) 256-0232

Michigan
David Conklin
1405 South Harrison Road,
Room 116
East Lansing, MI 48823-5202
(517) 337-6659

Minnesota
Donald L. Friedrich
Minnesota State ASCS Office
400 Farm Credit Service
Building
375 Jackson Street
St. Paul, MN 55101-1852
(612) 290-3651

Mississippi
Charles R. Hull
Mississippi State ASCS
Office
6310 I-55 North
Jackson, MS 39236
(601) 965-4300

Missouri
Morris G. Westfall
601 Parkdale Plaza Business
Loop
70 West, Suite 225
Columbia, MO 65203
(314) 875-5201

Montana
Donald Anderson
P.O. Box 670
Bozeman, MT 59771-0670
(406) 587-6872

Nebraska
John Neuberger
Nebraska State ASCS Office
P.O. Box 57975
Lincoln, NE 68505-7975
(402) 437-5581

Nevada
C. Richard Capurro
Nevada State ASCS Office
1755 East Plumb Lane,
Suite 202
Reno, NV 89502-3207

New Hampshire
Peter M. Thomson
USDA - New Hampshire
State ASCS Office
22 Bridge Street, Fourth
Floor
Concord, NH 03301-5605
(603) 224-7941

New Jersey
Peter de Wilde
Mastoris Professional Plaza
163 Route 130
Building 1, Suite E
Bordentown, NJ 08505
(609) 298-3446

New Mexico
David Turner
New Mexico State ASCS
Office
P.O. Box 1458
Federal Building, Room 4408
517 Gold Avenue, SW
Albuquerque, NM
87102-3156
(505) 766-2472

New York
John Steele
811 James H. Hanley Federal
Building
100 South Clinton Street
Syracuse, NY 13260-0066
(315) 423-5176

North Carolina
John J. Cooper
P.O. Box 27327
Federal Building, Suite 175
4407 Bland Road
Raleigh, NC 27611
(919) 790-2957

North Dakota
Robert J. Christiman
North Dakota State ASCS
Office
P.O. Box 3046
Fargo, ND 58108-3046
(701) 239-5224

Ohio
Dorothy Leslie
Federal Building, Room 540
200 North High Street
Columbus, OH 43215-2495
(614) 469-6735

Oklahoma
Bart Brorsen
USDA Agriculture Center
Building
Farm Road and McFarland
Street
Stillwater, OK 74074-2531
(405) 624-4110

Oregon
Glen E. Stonebrink
Oregon State ASCS Office
P.O. Box 1300
Tualatin, OR 97062-1300
(503) 692-6830

Agriculture

Pennsylvania
Donald Unangst
One Credit Union Place,
Suite 320
228 Walnut Street
Harrisburg, PA 17101-1701
(717) 782-4547

Rhode Island
Alfred R. Bettencourt, Jr.
Aldeic Complex
60 Quaker Lane
West Warwick, RI 02893-2120
(401) 828-8232

South Carolina
Thomas H. Herlong
Strom Thurmond Mall
Columbia, SC 29207
(803) 765-5186

South Dakota
Dean W. Anderson
Federal Building, Room 208
200 Fourth Street, SW
Huron, SD 57350-2478
(605) 353-1092

Tennessee
Charles Ben Thompson
U.S. Courthouse, Room 579
801 Broadway
Nashville, TN 37203-3816
(615) 736-5555

Texas
Donnie Bownan Aeting
Texas State ASCS Office
P.O. Box 2900
College Station, TX
77841-0001
(409) 260-9207

Utah
Royal K. Norman
Utah State ASCS Office
P.O. Box 11547
Salt Lake City, UT
84147-2547
(801) 524-5013

Vermont
David Newton
Executive Square Office
Building
346 Shelburne Street
Burlington, VT 05401-4495
(802) 658-2803

Virginia
Mahlon K. Rudy
Federal Building, Room 7105
400 North 8th Street
Richmond, VA 23240-9990
(804) 771-2581

Washington
Robert Deife
Washington State ASCS
Office
Rock Pointe Tower, Suite 568
316 West Boone Avenue
Spokane, WA 99201-2350
(509) 353-1092

West Virginia
Donald W. Brown
P.O. Box 1049
New Federal Building,
Room 239
75 High Street
Morgantown, WV 26505-7558
(304) 291-4351

Wisconsin
Peter C. Senn
Wisconsin State ASCS Office
6515 Watts Road, Room 100
Madison, WI 53719-2797
(608) 264-5301

Wyoming
Harold Hellbaum
P.O. Box 920
100 East B. Street,
Room 3001
Casper, WY 82602-0920
(307) 261-5231

Caribbean Area
Herberto J. Martinez
Caribbean Area ASCS Office
Cobran's Plaza, Suite 309
1609 Ponce DeLeon Avenue
Santurce, Puerto Rico
00909-0001
(809) 729-6872

ECONOMIC INJURY DISASTER LOANS

Small Business Administration (SBA)
Office of Disaster Assistance
409 3rd Street, SW
Washington, DC 20416
(202) 205-6734

Description: Direct, guaranteed, and insured loans for small businesses or agricultural cooperatives that are victims of drought, to pay liabilities from disaster or to provide working capital to continue operations until conditions return to normal.
$ Given: Direct loans to $500,000; average: $70,667.
Application Information: Write for guidelines.
Deadline: N/A
Contact: Your state and/or regional office

Alabama
1375 Peachtree Street, NE, Fifth Floor
Atlanta, GA 30367-8102
(404) 347-2797

Alaska
2615 4th Avenue, Room 440
Seattle, WA 98121
(206) 553-5676

Arizona
71 Stevenson Street, Twentieth Floor
San Francisco, CA 94105-2939
(415) 744-6402

Arkansas
8625 King George Drive, Building C
Dallas, TX 75235-3391
(214) 767-7633

California
71 Stevenson Street, Twentieth Floor
San Francisco, CA 94105-2939
(415) 744-6402

Colorado
999 18th Street, Suite 701
Denver, CO 80202
(303) 294-7186

Connecticut
155 Federal Street, Ninth Floor
Boston, MA 02110
(617) 451-2023

Delaware
475 Allendale Road, Suite 201
King of Prussia, PA 19406
(215) 962-3700

District of Columbia
475 Allendale Road, Suite 201
King of Prussia, PA 19406
(215) 962-3700

Florida
1375 Peachtree Street, NE, Fifth Floor
Atlanta, GA 30367-8102
(404) 347-2797

Georgia
1375 Peachtree Street, NE, Fifth Floor
Atlanta, GA 30367-8102
(404) 347-2797

Hawaii
71 Stevenson Street, Twentieth Floor
San Francisco, CA 94105-2939
(415) 744-6402

Idaho
2615 4th Avenue, Room 440
Seattle, WA 98121
(206) 553-5676

Illinois
Federal Building
300 South Riverside Plaza, 1975 South
Chicago, IL 60606-6617
(312) 353-5000

Iowa
911 Walnut Street, Thirteenth Floor
Kansas City, MO 64106
(816) 426-3608

Agriculture

Indiana
Federal Building
300 South Riverside Plaza,
1975 South
Chicago, IL 60606-6617
(312) 353-5000

Kansas
911 Walnut Street, Thirteenth
Floor
Kansas City, MO 64106
(816) 426-3608

Kentucky
1375 Peachtree Street, NE,
Fifth Floor
Atlanta, GA 30367-8102
(404) 347-2797

Louisiana
8624 King George Drive,
Building C
Dallas, TX 75235-3391
(214) 767-7633

Maine
155 Federal Street,
Ninth Floor
Boston, MA 02110
(617) 451-2023

Maryland
475 Allendale Road,
Suite 201
King of Prussia, PA 19406
(215) 962-3700

Massachusetts
155 Federal Street,
Ninth Floor
Boston, MA 02110
(617) 451-2023

Michigan
Federal Building
300 South Riverside Plaza,
1975 South
Chicago, IL 60606-6617
(312) 353-5000

Minnesota
Federal Building
300 South Riverside Plaza,
1975 South
Chicago, IL 60606-6617
(312) 353-5000

Mississippi
1375 Peachtree Street, NE,
Fifth Floor
Atlanta, GA 30367-8102
(404) 347-2797

Missouri
911 Walnut Street,
Thirteenth Floor
Kansas City, MO 64106
(816) 426-3608

Montana
999 18th Street, Suite 701
Denver, CO 80202
(303) 294-7186

Nebraska
911 Walnut Street,
Thirteenth Floor
Kansas City, MO 64106
(816) 426-3608

Nevada
71 Stevenson Street,
Twentieth Floor
San Francisco, CA
94105-2939
(415) 744-6402

New Hampshire
155 Federal Street,
Ninth Floor
Boston, MA 02110
(617) 451-2023

New Jersey
26 Federal Plaza,
Room 31-08
New York, NY 10278
(212) 264-7772

New Mexico
8625 King George Drive,
Building C
Dallas, TX 75235-3391
(214) 767-7633

New York
26 Federal Plaza,
Room 31-08
New York, NY 10278
(212) 264-7772

North Carolina
1375 Peachtree Street, NE,
Fifth Floor
Atlanta, GA 30367-8102
(404) 347-2797

North Dakota
999 18th Street, Suite 701
Denver, CO 80202
(303) 294-7186

Ohio
Federal Building
300 South Riverside Plaza,
1975 South
Chicago, IL 60606-6617
(312) 353-5000

Oklahoma
8625 King George Drive,
Building C
Dallas, TX 75235-3391
(214) 767-7633

Oregon
2615 4th Avenue, Room 440
Seattle, WA 98121
(206) 553-5676

Pacific Islands
71 Stevenson Street,
Twentieth Floor
San Francisco, CA
94105-2939
(415) 744-6402

Pennsylvania
475 Allendale Road,
Suite 201
King of Prussia, PA 19406
(215) 962-3700

Puerto Rico
26 Federal Plaza,
Room 31-08
New York, NY 10278
(212) 264-7772

Rhode Island
155 Federal Street,
Ninth Floor
Boston, MA 02110
(617) 451-2023

South Carolina
1375 Peachtree Street, NE,
Fifth Floor
Atlanta, GA 30367-8102
(404) 347-2797

South Dakota
999 18th Street, Suite 701
Denver, CO 80202
(303) 294-7186

Tennessee
1375 Peachtree Street, NE,
Fifth Floor
Atlanta, GA 30367-8102
(404) 347-2797

Texas
8625 King George Drive,
Building C
Dallas, TX 75235-3391
(214) 767-7633

Utah
999 18th Street, Suite 701
Denver, CO 80202
(303) 294-7186

Vermont
155 Federal Street,
Ninth Floor
Boston, MA 02110
(617) 451-2023

Virgin Islands
26 Federal Plaza,
Room 31-08
New York, NY 10278
(212) 264-7772

Virginia
475 Allendale Road,
Suite 201
King of Prussia, PA 19406
(215) 962-3700

Washington
2615 4th Avenue, Room 440
Seattle, WA 98121
(206) 553-5676

West Virginia
475 Allendale Road,
Suite 201
King of Prussia, PA 19406
(215) 962-3700

Wisconsin
Federal Building
300 South Riverside Plaza,
1975 South
Chicago, IL 60606-6617
(312) 353-5000

Wyoming
999 18th Street, Suite 701
Denver, CO 80202
(303) 294-7186

EMERGENCY CONSERVATION PROGRAM

Department of Agriculture
Agricultural Stabilization and Conservation Service
P.O. Box 2415
Washington, DC 20013
(202) 720-6221

Description: Direct payments for specified use to owners, landlords, tenants, or sharecroppers on farms or ranches, including associated groups, who bear part of the cost of an approved conservation practice in a disaster area. Proof of contribution to cost of performing conservation practice must be demonstrated.
$ Given: Payment range: $3–$64,000; average: $1,780.
Application Information: File Form ACP-245, for cost-sharing, at county ASCS office for county in which the land is located.
Deadline: N/A
Contact: Your local ASCS office or, if not listed, the appropriate state and/or regional office.

Alabama
Albert C. McDonald
P.O. Box 891
474 South Court Street,
Room 749
Montgomery, AL 36104-4184
(205) 832-7230

Alaska
Teresa Weiland
Alaska State ASCS Office
800 West Evergreen,
Suite 216
Palmer, AK 99645-6389
(907) 745-7982

Arizona
Arden J. Palmer
Arizona State ASCS Office
201 East Indianola, Suite 325
Phoenix, AZ 85012-2054
(602) 640-5200

Arkansas
Dotson Collins
P.O. Box 2781
New Federal Building,
Room 5102
700 West Capitol Street
Little Rock, AR 72201-3225
(501) 378-5220

California
John Smythe
California State ASCS Office
1303 J. Street, Suite 300
Sacramento, CA 95814-2916
(916) 551-1801

Colorado
Lloyd C. Sommerville
Colorado State ASCS Office
655 Parfet Street
Room E 305, Third Floor
Lakewood, CO 80215
(303) 236-2866

Connecticut
David T. Schreiber
88 Day Hill Road
Windsor, CT 06095
(203) 285-8483

Delaware
Earle Isaacs, Jr.
179 West Chestnut Hill Road,
Suite 7
Newark, DE 19713-2295
(302) 573-6536

Florida
Eugene C. Badger
P.O. Box 141030
4440 Northwest 25th Place,
Suite 1
Gainesville, FL 32614-1030
(904) 372-8549

Georgia
James E. Harrison
P.O. Box 1907
Federal Building, Room 102
344 East Hancock Avenue
Athens, GA 30601-2775
(404) 546-2266

Hawaii
Ralph K. Ajifu
Hawaii State ASCS Office
300 Ala Moana Boulevard,
Room 4202
P.O. Box 50008
Honolulu, HI 96850-0002
(808) 551-2644

Idaho
Trent Clark
Idaho State ASCS Office
3220 Elder Street
Boise, ID 83705-5820
(208) 334-1486

Illinois
William G. Beeler
P.O. Box 19273
3500 Wabash Avenue
Springfield, IL 62707
(217) 492-4180

Indiana
Don Villwoch
Indiana State ASCS Office
5981 Lakeside Boulevard
Indianapolis, IN 46278-1996
(317) 290-3030

Iowa
Robert Furleigh
10500 Buena Vista Court
Urbandale, IA 50322
(515) 254-1540

Kansas
Frank A. Mosier
Kansas State ASCS Office
2601 Anderson Avenue
Manhattan, KS 66502-2898
(913) 539-3531

Kentucky
Kenneth Ashby
Kentucky State ASCS Office
771 Corporate Drive,
Suite 100
Lexington, KY 40503-5477
(606) 233-2726

Louisiana
Willie F. Cooper
3737 Government Street
Alexandria, LA 71302-3395
(318) 473-7721

Maine
David P. Staples
44 Stillwater Avenue
P.O. Box 406
Bangor, ME 04401-3521
(207) 942-0342

Maryland
James Richardson
Rivers Center
10270 B Columbia Road
Columbia, MD 21046-9998
(301) 381-4550

Massachusetts
Raymond E. Duda
451 West Street
Amherst, MA 01002-2953
(413) 256-0232

Michigan
David Conklin
1405 South Harrison Road,
Room 116
East Lansing, MI 48823-5202
(517) 337-6659

Minnesota
Donald L. Friedrich
Minnesota State ASCS Office
400 Farm Credit Service
Building
375 Jackson Street
St. Paul, MN 55101-1852
(612) 290-3651

Mississippi
Charles R. Hull
Mississippi State ASCS
Office
6310 I-55 North
Jackson, MS 39236
(601) 965-4300

Missouri
Morris G. Westfall
601 Parkdale Plaza Business
Loop
70 West, Suite 225
Columbia, MO 65203
(314) 875-5201

Montana
Donald Anderson
P.O. Box 670
Bozeman, MT 59771-0670
(406) 587-6872

Nebraska
John Neuberger
Nebraska State ASCS Office
P.O. Box 57975
Lincoln, NE 68505-7975
(402) 437-5581

Nevada
C. Richard Capurro
Nevada State ASCS Office
1755 East Plumb Lane,
Suite 202
Reno, NV 89502-3207

New Hampshire
Peter M. Thomson
USDA - New Hampshire
State ASCS Office
22 Bridge Street,
Fourth Floor
Concord, NH 03301-5605
(603) 224-7941

New Jersey
Peter de Wilde
Mastoris Professional Plaza
163 Route 130
Building 1, Suite E
Bordentown, NJ 08505
(609) 298-3446

New Mexico
David Turner
New Mexico State ASCS
Office
P.O. Box 1458
Federal Building, Room 4408
517 Gold Avenue, SW
Albuquerque, NM
87102-3156
(505) 766-2472

New York
John Steele
811 James H. Hanley Federal
Building
100 South Clinton Street
Syracuse, NY 13260-0066
(315) 423-5176

North Carolina
John J. Cooper
P.O. Box 27327
Federal Building, Suite 175
4407 Bland Road
Raleigh, NC 27611
(919) 790-2957

North Dakota
Robert J. Christman
North Dakota State ASCS
Office
P.O. Box 3046
Fargo, ND 58108-3046
(701) 239-5224

Ohio
Dorothy Leslie
Federal Building, Room 540
200 North High Street
Columbus, OH 43215-2495
(614) 469-6735

Oklahoma
Bart Brorsen
USDA Agriculture Center
Building
Farm Road and McFarland
Street
Stillwater, OK 74074-2531
(405) 624-4110

Oregon
Glen E. Stonebrink
Oregon State ASCS Office
P.O. Box 1300
Tualatin, OR 97062-1300
(503) 692-6830

Pennsylvania
Donald Unangst
One Credit Union Place,
Suite 320
228 Walnut Street
Harrisburg, PA 17101-1701
(717) 782-4547

Rhode Island
Alfred R. Bettencourt, Jr.
Aldeic Complex
60 Quaker Lane
West Warwick, RI 02893-2120
(401) 828-8232

South Carolina
Thomas H. Herlong
Strom Thurmond Mall
Columbia, SC 29207
(803) 765-5186

South Dakota
Dean W. Anderson
Federal Building, Room 208
200 Fourth Street, SW
Huron, SD 57350-2478
(605) 353-1092

Tennessee
Charles Ben Thompson
U.S. Courthouse, Room 579
801 Broadway
Nashville, TN 37203-3816
(615) 736-5555

Texas
Donnie Bownan Aeting
Texas State ASCS Office
P.O. Box 2900
College Station, TX
77841-0001
(409) 260-9207

Utah
Royal K. Norman
Utah State ASCS Office
P.O. Box 11547
Salt Lake City, UT
84147-2547
(801) 524-5013

Vermont
David Newton
Executive Square Office
Building
346 Shelburne Street
Burlington, VT 05401-4495
(802) 658-2803

Virginia
Mahlon K. Rudy
Federal Building, Room 7105
400 North 8th Street
Richmond, VA 23240-9990
(804) 771-2581

Washington
Robert Deife
Washington State ASCS
Office
Rock Pointe Tower, Suite 568
316 West Boone Avenue
Spokane, WA 99201-2350
(509) 353-1092

West Virginia
Donald W. Brown
P.O. Box 1049
New Federal Building,
Room 239
75 High Street
Morgantown, WV 26505-7558
(304) 291-4351

Wisconsin
Peter C. Senn
Wisconsin State ASCS Office
6515 Watts Road, Room 100
Madison, WI 53719-2797
(608) 264-5301

Wyoming
Harold Hellbaum
P.O. Box 920
100 East B. Street,
Room 3001
Casper, WY 82602-0920
(307) 261-5231

Caribbean Area
Herberto J. Martinez
Caribbean Area ASCS Office
Cobran's Plaza, Suite 309
1609 Ponce DeLeon Avenue
Santurce, Puerto Rico
00909-0001
(809) 729-6872

EMERGENCY LIVESTOCK ASSISTANCE

**Department of
Agriculture**
Agricultural Stabilization
and Conservation Service
Emergency Operation and
Livestock Program
Division
P.O. Box 2415
Washington, DC 20013
(202) 720-5621

Description: Direct payments with unrestricted use to
individuals, farm cooperatives, private domestic
corporations, partnerships or joint ventures, Indian
tribes, or Indian organizations. Must have annual gross
revenue of less than $2.5 million.
$ Given: Payment range: $10–$50,000; average: $3,411.
Application Information: Write for guidelines.
Deadline: N/A
Contact: Your local, state, and/or regional ASCS office

Alabama
Albert C. McDonald
P.O. Box 891
474 South Court Street,
Room 749
Montgomery, AL 36104-4184
(205) 832-7230

Alaska
Teresa Weiland
Alaska State ASCS Office
800 West Evergreen,
Suite 216
Palmer, AK 99645-6389
(907) 745-7982

Arizona
Arden J. Palmer
Arizona State ASCS Office
201 East Indianola, Suite 325
Phoenix, AZ 85012-2054
(602) 640-5200

Arkansas
Dotson Collins
P.O. Box 2781
New Federal Building,
Room 5102
700 West Capitol Street
Little Rock, AR 72201-3225
(501) 378-5220

California
John Smythe
California State ASCS Office
1303 J. Street, Suite 300
Sacramento, CA 95814-2916
(916) 551-1801

Colorado
Lloyd C. Sommerville
Colorado State ASCS Office
655 Parfet Street
Room E 305, Third Floor
Lakewood, CO 80215
(303) 236-2866

Agriculture

Connecticut
David T. Schreiber
88 Day Hill Road
Windsor, CT 06095
(203) 285-8483

Delaware
Earle Isaacs, Jr.
179 West Chestnut Hill Road,
Suite 7
Newark, DE 19713-2295
(302) 573-6536

Florida
Eugene C. Badger
P.O. Box 141030
4440 Northwest 25th Place,
Suite 1
Gainesville, FL 32614-1030
(904) 372-8549

Georgia
James E. Harrison
P.O. Box 1907
Federal Building, Room 102
344 East Hancock Avenue
Athens, GA 30601-2775
(404) 546-2266

Hawaii
Ralph K. Ajifu
Hawaii State ASCS Office
300 Ala Moana Boulevard,
Room 4202
P.O. Box 50008
Honolulu, HI 96850-0002
(808) 551-2644

Idaho
Trent Clark
Idaho State ASCS Office
3220 Elder Street
Boise, ID 83705-5820
(208) 334-1486

Illinois
William G. Beeler
P.O. Box 19273
3500 Wabash Avenue
Springfield, IL 62707
(217) 492-4180

Indiana
Don Villwoch
Indiana State ASCS Office
5981 Lakeside Boulevard
Indianapolis, IN 46278-1996
(317) 290-3030

Iowa
Robert Furleigh
10500 Buena Vista Court
Urbandale, IA 50322
(515) 254-1540

Kansas
Frank A. Mosier
Kansas State ASCS Office
2601 Anderson Avenue
Manhattan, KS 66502-2898
(913) 539-3531

Kentucky
Kenneth Ashby
Kentucky State ASCS Office
771 Corporate Drive,
Suite 100
Lexington, KY 40503-5477
(606) 233-2726

Louisiana
Willie F. Cooper
3737 Government Street
Alexandria, LA 71302-3395
(318) 473-7721

Maine
David P. Staples
44 Stillwater Avenue
P.O. Box 406
Bangor, ME 04401-3521
(207) 942-0342

Maryland
James Richardson
Rivers Center
10270 B Columbia Road
Columbia, MD 21046-9998
(301) 381-4550

Massachusetts
Raymond E. Duda
451 West Street
Amherst, MA 01002-2953
(413) 256-0232

Michigan
David Conklin
1405 South Harrison Road,
Room 116
East Lansing, MI 48823-5202
(517) 337-6659

Minnesota
Donald L. Friedrich
Minnesota State ASCS Office
400 Farm Credit Service
Building
375 Jackson Street
St. Paul, MN 55101-1852
(612) 290-3651

Mississippi
Charles R. Hull
Mississippi State ASCS
Office
6310 I-55 North
Jackson, MS 39236
(601) 965-4300

Missouri
Morris G. Westfall
601 Parkdale Plaza Business
Loop
70 West, Suite 225
Columbia, MO 65203
(314) 875-5201

Montana
Donald Anderson
P.O. Box 670
Bozeman, MT 59771-0670
(406) 587-6872

Nebraska
John Neuberger
Nebraska State ASCS Office
P.O. Box 57975
Lincoln, NE 68505-7975
(402) 437-5581

Nevada
C. Richard Capurro
Nevada State ASCS Office
1755 East Plumb Lane,
Suite 202
Reno, NV 89502-3207

New Hampshire
Peter M. Thomson
USDA - New Hampshire
State ASCS Office
22 Bridge Street,
Fourth Floor
Concord, NH 03301-5605
(603) 224-7941

New Jersey
Peter de Wilde
Mastoris Professional Plaza
163 Route 130
Building 1, Suite E
Bordentown, NJ 08505
(609) 298-3446

New Mexico
David Turner
New Mexico State ASCS
Office
P.O. Box 1458
Federal Building, Room 4408
517 Gold Avenue, SW
Albuquerque, NM
87102-3156
(505) 766-2472

New York
John Steele
811 James H. Hanley Federal
Building
100 South Clinton Street
Syracuse, NY 13260-0066
(315) 423-5176

North Carolina
John J. Cooper
P.O. Box 27327
Federal Building
4407 Bland Road, Suite 175
Raleigh, NC 27611
(919) 790-2957

North Dakota
Robert J. Christman
North Dakota State ASCS
Office
P.O. Box 3046
Fargo, ND 58108-3046
(701) 239-5224

Ohio
Dorothy Leslie
Federal Building, Room 540
200 North High Street
Columbus, OH 43215-2495
(614) 469-6735

Oklahoma
Bart Brorsen
USDA Agriculture Center
Building
Farm Road and McFarland
Street
Stillwater, OK 74074-2531
(405) 624-4110

Oregon
Glen E. Stonebrink
Oregon State ASCS Office
P.O. Box 1300
Tualatin, OR 97062-1300
(503) 692-6830

Pennsylvania
Donald Unangst
One Credit Union Place,
Suite 320
228 Walnut Street
Harrisburg, PA 17101-1701
(717) 782-4547

Rhode Island
Alfred R. Bettencourt, Jr.
Aldeic Complex
60 Quaker Lane
West Warwick, RI 02893-2120
(401) 828-8232

South Carolina
Thomas H. Herlong
Strom Thurmond Mall
Columbia, SC 29207
(803) 765-5186

South Dakota
Dean W. Anderson
Federal Building, Room 208
200 Fourth Street, SW
Huron, SD 57350-2478
(605) 353-1092

Tennessee
Charles Ben Thompson
U.S. Courthouse, Room 579
801 Broadway
Nashville, TN 37203-3816
(615) 736-5555

Texas
Donnie Bownan Aeting
Texas State ASCS Office
P.O. Box 2900
College Station, TX
77841-0001
(409) 260-9207

Agriculture

Utah
Royal K. Norman
Utah State ASCS Office
P.O. Box 11547
Salt Lake City, UT
84147-2547
(801) 524-5013

Vermont
David Newton
Executive Square Office
Building
346 Shelburne Street
Burlington, VT 05401-4495
(802) 658-2803

Virginia
Mahlon K. Rudy
Federal Building, Room 7105
400 North 8th Street
Richmond, VA 23240-9990
(804) 771-2581

Washington
Robert Deife
Washington State ASCS
Office
Rock Pointe Tower, Suite 568
316 West Boone Avenue
Spokane, WA 99201-2350
(509) 353-1092

West Virginia
Donald W. Brown
P.O. Box 1049
New Federal Building,
Room 239
75 High Street
Morgantown, WV 26505-7558
(304) 291-4351

Wisconsin
Peter C. Senn
Wisconsin State ASCS Office
6515 Watts Road, Room 100
Madison, WI 53719-2797
(608) 264-5301

Wyoming
Harold Hellbaum
P.O. Box 920
100 East B. Street,
Room 3001
Casper, WY 82602-0920
(307) 261-5231

Caribbean Area
Herberto J. Martinez
Caribbean Area ASCS Office
Cobran's Plaza, Suite 309
1609 Ponce DeLeon Avenue
Santurce, Puerto Rico
00909-0001
(809) 729-6872

EMERGENCY LOANS

**Department of
Agriculture**
Farmers Home
Administration
Washington, DC 20250
(202) 690-1533

Description: Direct loans to family farmers, ranchers, or aquaculture operators. Must be a U.S. citizen or legal resident alien who was conducting a farming operation at the time of a designated natural disaster and suffered substantial crop loss or physical property damages.
$ Given: Loan range: $500–$500,000.
Application Information: Application Form FmHA 410-1 provided by the Farmers Home Administration must be presented with supporting information to your FmHA county office. FmHA personnel will assist applicants in completing forms.
Deadline: Eight months from date of declaration for losses. Consult your local FmHA office.
Contact: Consult your local telephone directory under U.S. Government, Department of Agriculture, for your FmHA county office number or contact your FmHA state office.

Alabama
Aronov Building, Room 717
474 South Court Street
Montgomery, AL 36104
(205) 223-7077

Alaska
634 South Bailey, Suite 103
Palmer, AK 99645
(907) 745-2176

Arizona·
201 East Indianola, Suite 275
Phoenix, AZ 85012
(602) 640-5086

Arkansas
700 West Capitol
P.O. Box 2778
Little Rock, AR 72203
(501) 324-6281

California
194 West Main Street,
Suite F
Woodland, CA 95695-2915
(916) 666-3382

Colorado
655 Parfet Street,
Room E-100
Lakewood, CO 80215
(303) 236-2801

Connecticut
451 West Street
Amherst, MA 01002
(413) 253-4300

Delaware
4611 South Dupont Highway
P.O. Box 400
Camden, DE 19934-9998
(302) 697-4300

District of Columbia
4611 South Dupont Highway
P.O. Box 400
Camden, DE 19934-9998
(302) 697-4300

Florida
Federal Building
4440 NW 25th Place
P.O. Box 147010
Gainesville, FL 32614-7010
(904) 338-3400

Georgia
Stephens Federal Building
355 East Hancock Avenue
Athens, GA 30610
(404) 546-2162

Hawaii
Federal Building, Room 311
154 Waianuenue Avenue
Hilo, HI 967720
(808) 933-3000

Idaho
3232 Elder Street
Boise, ID 83720
(808) 933-3000

Illinois
Illini Plaza
1817 South Neil Street
Champaign, IL 61820
(217) 398-5235

Indiana
5975 Lakeside Boulevard
Indianapolis, IN 46278
(317) 290-3100

Iowa
Federal Building, Room 873
210 Walnut Street
Des Moines, IA 50309
(515) 284-4663

Kansas
1201 SW Summit Executive
Court
P.O. Box 4653
Topeka, KS 66604
(913) 271-2700

Kentucky
333771 Corporate Plaza,
Suite 200
Lexington, KY 40503
(606) 224-7300

Louisiana
3727 Government Street
Alexandria, LA 71302
(318) 473-7920

Maine
444 Stillwater Avenue,
Suite 2
P.O. Box 405
Bangor, ME 04402-0405
(207) 990-9106

Maryland
4611 South Dupont Highway
P.O. Box 400
Camden, DE 19934-9998
(302) 697-4300

Massachusetts
451 West Street
Amherst, MA 01002
(413) 253-4300

Michigan
Manly Miles Building,
Room 209
1405 South Harrison Road
East Lansing, MI 48823
(517) 337-6631

Minnesota
410 Farm Credit Building
375 Jackson Street
St. Paul, MN 55101
(612) 290-3842

Mississippi
Federal Building, Suite 831
100 West Capitol
Jackson, MS 39269
(601) 965-4316

Missouri
601 Business Loop, 70 West
Parkade Center, Suite 235
Columbia, MO 65203
(314) 876-0976

Montana
900 Technology Boulevard,
Suite B
P.O. Box 850
Bozeman, MT 59771
(406) 585-2500

Nebraska
Federal Building, Room 308
100 Centennial Mall North
Lincoln, NE 68508
(402) 437-5551

Nevada
194 West Main Street,
Suite F
Woodland, CA 95695-2915
(916) 666-3382

New Hampshire
City Center, Third Floor
89 Main Street
Montpelier, VT 05602
(802) 223-2371

New Jersey
Tarnsfield and Woodlane
Roads
Tarnsfield Plaza, Suite 22
Mt. Holly, NJ 08060
(609) 265-3600

New Mexico
Federal Building, Room 3414
517 Gold Avenue, SW
Albuquerque, NM 87102
(505) 766-2462

New York
Federal Building, Room 871
100 South Clinton Street
Syracuse, NY 13261-7318
(315) 423-5290

North Carolina
4405 South Bland Road,
Suite 260
Raleigh, NC 27609
(919) 790-2731

North Dakota
Federal Building, Room 208
Third and Rosser
P.O. Box 1737
Bismarck, ND 58502
(701) 250-4781

Ohio
Federal Building, Room 507
200 North High Street
Columbus, OH 43215
(614) 469-5606

Oklahoma
USDA Agricultural Center
Office Building
Stillwater, OK 74074
(405) 624-4250

Oregon
Federal Building, Room 1590
1220 SW 3rd Avenue
Portland, OR 97204
(503) 326-2731

Pennsylvania
One Credit Union Place,
Suite 330
Harrisburg, PA 17110-2996
(717) 782-4476

Puerto Rico
New San Juan Center
Building, Room 501
159 Carlos E. Chardon Street
G.P.O. Box 6106G
Hato Rey, PR 00918-5481
(809) 766-5095

Rhode Island
451 West Street
Amherst, MA 01002
(413) 253-4300

South Carolina
Strom Thurmond Federal
Building, Room 1007
1835 Assembly Street
Columbia, SC 29201
(803) 765-5163

South Dakota
Huron Federal Building,
Room 308
200 Fourth Street, SW
Huron, SD 57350
(605) 353-1430

Tennessee
3322 West End Avenue,
Suite 300
Nashville, TN 37203-1071
(615) 736-7341

Texas
Federal Building, Suite 102
101 South Main
Temple, TX 76501
(817) 774-1301

Utah
Federal Building, Room 5438
125 South State Street
Salt Lake City, UT 84138
(801) 524-4063

Vermont
City Center, Third Floor
89 Main Street
Montpelier, VT 05602
(802) 223-2371

Virgin Islands
City Center, Third Floor
89 Main Street
Montpelier, VT 05602
(802) 223-2371

Virginia
Federal Building, Room 8213
400 North 8th Street
Richmond, VA 23240
(804) 771-2451

Washington
Federal Building, Room 319
P.O. Box 2427
Wenatchee, WA 98807
(509) 662-4352

West Virginia
75 High Street
P.O. Box 678
Morgantown, WV 26505
(304) 291-4791

Wisconsin
4949 Kirschling Court
Stevens Point, WI 54481
(715) 345-7600

Wyoming
Federal Building, Room 1005
100 East B Street
P.O. Box 820
Casper, WY 82602
(307) 261-5271

FARM LABOR HOUSING LOANS AND GRANTS

Department of Agriculture
Farmers Home
Administration
Multifamily Housing
Processing Division
Washington, DC 20250
(202) 720-1604

Description: Project grants and guaranteed and insured loans for farmers. Grants only given when there is a pressing need and when it is doubtful that facilities could be provided unless grant assistance is available.
$ Given: Initial grant range: $135,000–$2 million. Initial individual loan range: $20,000–$200,000. Initial organizational loan range: $165,000–$670,000.
Application Information: Write for guidelines.
Deadline: None
Contact: Consult your local telephone directory under U.S. Government, Department of Agriculture, for FmHA county office number or contact your FmHA state office.

Alabama
Aronov Building, Room 717
474 South Court Street
Montgomery, AL 36104
(205) 223-7077

Alaska
634 South Bailey, Suite 103
Palmer, AK 99645
(907) 745-2176

Arizona
201 East Indianola, Suite 275
Phoenix, AZ 85012
(602) 640-5086

Agriculture

Arkansas
700 West Capitol
P.O. Box 2778
Little Rock, AR 72203
(501) 324-6281

California
194 West Main Street,
Suite F
Woodland, CA 95695-2915
(916) 666-3382

Colorado
655 Parfet Street,
Room E-100
Lakewood, CO 80215
(303) 236-2801

Connecticut
451 West Street
Amherst, MA 01002
(413) 253-4300

Delaware
4611 South Dupont Highway
P.O. Box 400
Camden, DE 19934-9998
(302) 697-4300

District of Columbia
4611 South Dupont Highway
P.O. Box 400
Camden, DE 19934-9998
(302) 697-4300

Florida
Federal Building
4440 NW 25th Place
P.O. Box 147010
Gainesville, FL 32614-7010
(904) 338-3400

Georgia
Stephens Federal Building
355 East Hancock Avenue
Athens, GA 30610
(404) 546-2162

Hawaii
Federal Building, Room 311
154 Waianuenue Avenue
Hilo, HI 967720
(808) 933-3000

Idaho
3232 Elder Street
Boise, ID 83720
(808) 933-3000

Illinois
Illini Plaza
1817 South Neil Street
Champaign, IL 61820
(217) 398-5235

Indiana
5975 Lakeside Boulevard
Indianapolis, IN 46278
(317) 290-3100

Iowa
Federal Building, Room 873
210 Walnut Street
Des Moines, IA 50309
(515) 284-4663

Kansas
1201 SW Summit Executive
Court
P.O. Box 4653
Topeka, KS 66604
(913) 271-2700

Kentucky
333771 Corporate Plaza,
Suite 200
Lexington, KY 40503
(606) 224-7300

Louisiana
3727 Government Street
Alexandria, LA 71302
(318) 473-7920

Maine
444 Stillwater Avenue,
Suite 2
P.O. Box 405
Bangor, ME 04402-0405
(207) 990-9106

Maryland
4611 South Dupont Highway
P.O. Box 400
Camden, DE 19934-9998
(302) 697-4300

Massachusetts
451 West Street
Amherst, MA 01002
(413) 253-4300

Michigan
Manly Miles Building,
Room 209
1405 South Harrison Road
East Lansing, MI 48823
(517) 337-6631

Minnesota
410 Farm Credit Building
375 Jackson Street
St. Paul, MN 55101
(612) 290-3842

Mississippi
Federal Building, Suite 831
100 West Capitol
Jackson, MS 39269
(601) 965-4316

Missouri
601 Business Loop, 70 West
Parkade Center, Suite 235
Columbia, MO 65203
(314) 876-0976

Montana
900 Technology Boulevard,
Suite B
P.O. Box 850
Bozeman, MT 59771
(406) 585-2500

Nebraska
Federal Building, Room 308
100 Centennial Mall North
Lincoln, NE 68508
(402) 437-5551

Nevada
194 West Main Street,
Suite F
Woodland, CA 95695-2915
(916) 666-3382

New Hampshire
City Center, Third Floor
89 Main Street
Montpelier, VT 05602
(802) 223-2371

New Jersey
Tarnsfield and Woodlane
Roads
Tarnsfield Plaza, Suite 22
Mt. Holly, NJ 08060
(609) 265-3600

New Mexico
Federal Building, Room 3414
517 Gold Avenue, SW
Albuquerque, NM 87102
(505) 766-2462

New York
Federal Building, Room 871
100 South Clinton Street
Syracuse, NY 13261-7318
(315) 423-5290

North Carolina
4405 South Bland Road,
Suite 260
Raleigh, NC 27609
(919) 790-2731

North Dakota
Federal Building, Room 208
Third and Rosser
P.O. Box 1737
Bismarck, ND 58502
(701) 250-4781

Ohio
Federal Building, Room 507
200 North High Street
Columbus, OH 43215
(614) 469-5606

Oklahoma
USDA Agricultural Center
Office Building
Stillwater, OK 74074
(405) 624-4250

Oregon
Federal Building, Room 1590
1220 SW 3rd Avenue
Portland, OR 97204
(503) 326-2731

Pennsylvania
One Credit Union Place,
Suite 330
Harrisburg, PA 17110-2996
(717) 782-4476

Puerto Rico
New San Juan Center
Building, Room 501
159 Carlos E. Chardon Street
G.P.O. Box 6106G
Hato Rey, PR 00918-5481
(809) 766-5095

Rhode Island
451 West Street
Amherst, MA 01002
(413) 253-4300

South Carolina
Strom Thurmond Federal
Building, Room 1007
1835 Assembly Street
Columbia, SC 29201
(803) 765-5163

South Dakota
Huron Federal Building,
Room 308
200 Fourth Street, SW
Huron, SD 57350
(605) 353-1430

Tennessee
3322 West End Avenue,
Suite 300
Nashville, TN 37203-1071
(615) 736-7341

Texas
Federal Building, Suite 102
101 South Main
Temple, TX 76501
(817) 774-1301

Utah
Federal Building, Room 5438
125 South State Street
Salt Lake City, UT 84138
(801) 524-4063

Vermont
City Center, Third Floor
89 Main Street
Montpelier, VT 05602
(802) 223-2371

Virgin Islands
City Center, Third Floor
89 Main Street
Montpelier, VT 05602
(802) 223-2371

Virginia
Federal Building, Room 8213
400 North 8th Street
Richmond, VA 23240
(804) 771-2451

Washington
Federal Building, Room 319
P.O. Box 2427
Wenatchee, WA 98807
(509) 662-4352

West Virginia
75 High Street
P.O. Box 678
Morgantown, WV 26505
(304) 291-4791

Wisconsin
4949 Kirschling Court
Stevens Point, WI 54481
(715) 345-7600

Wyoming
Federal Building, Room 1005
100 East B Street
P.O. Box 820
Casper, WY 82602
(307) 261-5271

FARM OPERATING LOANS

Department of Agriculture
Farmers Home Administration
Farmer Programs Loan Making Division
Washington, DC 20250
(202) 720-1632

Description: Direct, guaranteed, and insured loans to individuals, as well as to certain corporations, cooperatives, partnerships, and joint operations operating family-sized farms. Applicant must have farm experience or training, have a good credit history, be a U.S. citizen, and comply with the highly erodible land and wetland conservation provisions.
$ Given: Guaranteed loans to $400,000; insured loans to $200,000.
Application Information: An informal conference with the local county staff is recommended. File Form FmHA 1910-1 with supporting information. Form FmHA 449-6 for guaranteed loans should be filed with the prospective lender.
Deadline: None
Contact: Consult your local telephone directory under U.S. Government, Department of Agriculture, for FmHA county office number or contact your FmHA state office.

Alabama
Aronov Building, Room 717
474 South Court Street
Montgomery, AL 36104
(205) 223-7077

Alaska
634 South Bailey, Suite 103
Palmer, AK 99645
(907) 745-2176

Arizona
201 East Indianola, Suite 275
Phoenix, AZ 85012
(602) 640-5086

Arkansas
700 West Capitol
P.O. Box 2778
Little Rock, AR 72203
(501) 324-6281

California
194 West Main Street,
Suite F
Woodland, CA 95695-2915
(916) 666-3382

Colorado
655 Parfet Street,
Room E-100
Lakewood, CO 80215
(303) 236-2801

Connecticut
451 West Street
Amherst, MA 01002
(413) 253-4300

Delaware
4611 South Dupont Highway
P.O. Box 400
Camden, DE 19934-9998
(302) 697-4300

District of Columbia
4611 South Dupont Highway
P.O. Box 400
Camden, DE 19934-9998
(302) 697-4300

Florida
Federal Building
4440 NW 25th Place
P.O. Box 147010
Gainesville, FL 32614-7010
(904) 338-3400

Georgia
Stephens Federal Building
355 East Hancock Avenue
Athens, GA 30610
(404) 546-2162

Hawaii
Federal Building, Room 311
154 Waianuenue Avenue
Hilo, HI 967720
(808) 933-3000

Idaho
3232 Elder Street
Boise, ID 83720
(808) 933-3000

Illinois
Illini Plaza
1817 South Neil Street
Champaign, IL 61820
(217) 398-5235

Indiana
5975 Lakeside Boulevard
Indianapolis, IN 46278
(317) 290-3100

Iowa
Federal Building, Room 873
210 Walnut Street
Des Moines, IA 50309
(515) 284-4663

Kansas
1201 SW Summit Executive
Court
P.O. Box 4653
Topeka, KS 66604
(913) 271-2700

Kentucky
333771 Corporate Plaza,
Suite 200
Lexington, KY 40503
(606) 224-7300

Louisiana
3727 Government Street
Alexandria, LA 71302
(318) 473-7920

Maine
444 Stillwater Avenue,
Suite 2
P.O. Box 405
Bangor, ME 04402-0405
(207) 990-9106

Maryland
4611 South Dupont Highway
P.O. Box 400
Camden, DE 19934-9998
(302) 697-4300

Massachusetts
451 West Street
Amherst, MA 01002
(413) 253-4300

Michigan
Manly Miles Building,
Room 209
1405 South Harrison Road
East Lansing, MI 48823
(517) 337-6631

Minnesota
410 Farm Credit Building
375 Jackson Street
St. Paul, MN 55101
(612) 290-3842

Mississippi
Federal Building, Suite 831
100 West Capitol
Jackson, MS 39269
(601) 965-4316

Missouri
601 Business Loop, 70 West
Parkade Center, Suite 235
Columbia, MO 65203
(314) 876-0976

Agriculture

Montana
900 Technology Boulevard,
Suite B
P.O. Box 850
Bozeman, MT 59771
(406) 585-2500

Nebraska
Federal Building, Room 308
100 Centennial Mall North
Lincoln, NE 68508
(402) 437-5551

Nevada
194 West Main Street,
Suite F
Woodland, CA 95695-2915
(916) 666-3382

New Hampshire
City Center, Third Floor
89 Main Street
Montpelier, VT 05602
(802) 223-2371

New Jersey
Tarnsfield and Woodlane
Roads
Tarnsfield Plaza, Suite 22
Mt. Holly, NJ 08060
(609) 265-3600

New Mexico
Federal Building, Room 3414
517 Gold Avenue, SW
Albuquerque, NM 87102
(505) 766-2462

New York
Federal Building, Room 871
100 South Clinton Street
Syracuse, NY 13261-7318
(315) 423-5290

North Carolina
4405 South Bland Road,
Suite 260
Raleigh, NC 27609
(919) 790-2731

North Dakota
Federal Building, Room 208
Third and Rosser
P.O. Box 1737
Bismarck, ND 58502
(701) 250-4781

Ohio
Federal Building, Room 507
200 North High Street
Columbus, OH 43215
(614) 469-5606

Oklahoma
USDA Agricultural Center
Office Building
Stillwater, OK 74074
(405) 624-4250

Oregon
Federal Building, Room 1590
1220 SW 3rd Avenue
Portland, OR 97204
(503) 326-2731

Pennsylvania
One Credit Union Place,
Suite 330
Harrisburg, PA 17110-2996
(717) 782-4476

Puerto Rico
New San Juan Center
Building, Room 501
159 Carlos E. Chardon Street
G.P.O. Box 6106G
Hato Rey, PR 00918-5481
(809) 766-5095

Rhode Island
451 West Street
Amherst, MA 01002
(413) 253-4300

South Carolina
Strom Thurmond Federal
Building, Room 1007
1835 Assembly Street
Columbia, SC 29201
(803) 765-5163

South Dakota
Huron Federal Building,
Room 308
200 Fourth Street, SW
Huron, SD 57350
(605) 353-1430

Tennessee
3322 West End Avenue,
Suite 300
Nashville, TN 37203-1071
(615) 736-7341

Texas
Federal Building, Suite 102
101 South Main
Temple, TX 76501
(817) 774-1301

Utah
Federal Building, Room 5438
125 South State Street
Salt Lake City, UT 84138
(801) 524-4063

Vermont
City Center, Third Floor
89 Main Street
Montpelier, VT 05602
(802) 223-2371

Virgin Islands
City Center, Third Floor
89 Main Street
Montpelier, VT 05602
(802) 223-2371

Washington
Federal Building, Room 319
P.O. Box 2427
Wenatchee, WA 98807
(509) 662-4352

Wisconsin
4949 Kirschling Court
Stevens Point, WI 54481
(715) 345-7600

Virginia
Federal Building, Room 8213
400 North 8th Street
Richmond, VA 23240
(804) 771-2451

West Virginia
75 High Street
P.O. Box 678
Morgantown, WV 26505
(304) 291-4791

Wyoming
Federal Building, Room 1005
100 East B Street
P.O. Box 820
Casper, WY 82602
(307) 261-5271

FARM OWNERSHIP LOANS

Department of Agriculture
Farmers Home Administration
Washington, DC 20250
(202) 720-1632

Description: Direct, guaranteed, and insured loans to individuals of family-sized farms engaged primarily and directly in farming in the United States, or cooperatives, corporations, joint operations, or partnerships controlled by U.S. farmers or ranchers. Individual applicants must not have a combined farm ownership, soil and water, and recreation loan indebtedness to FmHA of more than $200,000 for insured loans and $300,000 for guaranteed loans.
$ Given: Maximum insured loans to $200,000; maximum guaranteed loans to $300,000.
Application Information: File Form FmHA 1910-1, application for FmHA services, with supporting information, at your local county office of the Farmers Home Administration. File Form FmHA 449-6, application for guaranteed loans, with prospective lender.
Deadline: None.
Contact: Consult your local telephone directory under U.S. Government, Department of Agriculture, for FmHA county office number or contact your FmHA state office.

Alabama
Aronov Building, Room 717
474 South Court Street
Montgomery, AL 36104
(205) 223-7077

Alaska
634 South Bailey, Suite 103
Palmer, AK 99645
(907) 745-2176

Arizona
201 East Indianola, Suite 275
Phoenix, AZ 85012
(602) 640-5086

Agriculture

Arkansas
700 West Capitol
P.O. Box 2778
Little Rock, AR 72203
(501) 324-6281

California
194 West Main Street,
Suite F
Woodland, CA 95695-2915
(916) 666-3382

Colorado
655 Parfet Street,
Room E-100
Lakewood, CO 80215
(303) 236-2801

Connecticut
451 West Street
Amherst, MA 01002
(413) 253-4300

Delaware
4611 South Dupont Highway
P.O. Box 400
Camden, DE 19934-9998
(302) 697-4300

District of Columbia
4611 South Dupont Highway
P.O. Box 400
Camden, DE 19934-9998
(302) 697-4300

Florida
Federal Building
4440 NW 25th Place
P.O. Box 147010
Gainesville, FL 32614-7010
(904) 338-3400

Georgia
Stephens Federal Building
355 East Hancock Avenue
Athens, GA 30610
(404) 546-2162

Hawaii
Federal Building, Room 311
154 Waianuenue Avenue
Hilo, HI 967720
(808) 933-3000

Idaho
3232 Elder Street
Boise, ID 83720
(808) 933-3000

Illinois
Illini Plaza
1817 South Neil Street
Champaign, IL 61820
(217) 398-5235

Indiana
5975 Lakeside Boulevard
Indianapolis, IN 46278
(317) 290-3100

Iowa
Federal Building, Room 873
210 Walnut Street
Des Moines, IA 50309
(515) 284-4663

Kansas
1201 SW Summit Executive
Court
P.O. Box 4653
Topeka, KS 66604
(913) 271-2700

Kentucky
333771 Corporate Plaza,
Suite 200
Lexington, KY 40503
(606) 224-7300

Louisiana
3727 Government Street
Alexandria, LA 71302
(318) 473-7920

Maine
444 Stillwater Avenue,
Suite 2
P.O. Box 405
Bangor, ME 04402-0405
(207) 990-9106

Maryland
4611 South Dupont Highway
P.O. Box 400
Camden, DE 19934-9998
(302) 697-4300

Massachusetts
451 West Street
Amherst, MA 01002
(413) 253-4300

Michigan
Manly Miles Building,
Room 209
1405 South Harrison Road
East Lansing, MI 48823
(517) 337-6631

Minnesota
410 Farm Credit Building
375 Jackson Street
St. Paul, MN 55101
(612) 290-3842

Mississippi
Federal Building, Suite 831
100 West Capitol
Jackson, MS 39269
(601) 965-4316

Missouri
601 Business Loop, 70 West
Parkade Center, Suite 235
Columbia, MO 65203
(314) 876-0976

Montana
900 Technology Boulevard,
Suite B
P.O. Box 850
Bozeman, MT 59771
(406) 585-2500

Nebraska
Federal Building, Room 308
100 Centennial Mall North
Lincoln, NE 68508
(402) 437-5551

Nevada
194 West Main Street,
Suite F
Woodland, CA 95695-2915
(916) 666-3382

New Hampshire
City Center, Third Floor
89 Main Street
Montpelier, VT 05602
(802) 223-2371

New Jersey
Tarnsfield and Woodlane
Roads
Tarnsfield Plaza, Suite 22
Mt. Holly, NJ 08060
(609) 265-3600

New Mexico
Federal Building, Room 3414
517 Gold Avenue, SW
Albuquerque, NM 87102
(505) 766-2462

New York
Federal Building, Room 871
100 South Clinton Street
Syracuse, NY 13261-7318
(315) 423-5290

North Carolina
4405 South Bland Road,
Suite 260
Raleigh, NC 27609
(919) 790-2731

North Dakota
Federal Building, Room 208
Third and Rosser
P.O. Box 1737
Bismarck, ND 58502
(701) 250-4781

Ohio
Federal Building, Room 507
200 North High Street
Columbus, OH 43215
(614) 469-5606

Oklahoma
USDA Agricultural Center
Office Building
Stillwater, OK 74074
(405) 624-4250

Oregon
Federal Building, Room 1590
1220 SW 3rd Avenue
Portland, OR 97204
(503) 326-2731

Pennsylvania
One Credit Union Place,
Suite 330
Harrisburg, PA 17110-2996
(717) 782-4476

Puerto Rico
New San Juan Center
Building, Room 501
159 Carlos E. Chardon Street
G.P.O. Box 6106G
Hato Rey, PR 00918-5481
(809) 766-5095

Rhode Island
451 West Street
Amherst, MA 01002
(413) 253-4300

South Carolina
Strom Thurmond Federal
Building, Room 1007
1835 Assembly Street
Columbia, SC 29201
(803) 765-5163

South Dakota
Huron Federal Building,
Room 308
200 Fourth Street, SW
Huron, SD 57350
(605) 353-1430

Tennessee
3322 West End Avenue,
Suite 300
Nashville, TN 37203-1071
(615) 736-7341

Texas
Federal Building, Suite 102
101 South Main
Temple, TX 76501
(817) 774-1301

Utah
Federal Building, Room 5438
125 South State Street
Salt Lake City, UT 84138
(801) 524-4063

Vermont
City Center, Third Floor
89 Main Street
Montpelier, VT 05602
(802) 223-2371

Virgin Islands
City Center, Third Floor
89 Main Street
Montpelier, VT 05602
(802) 223-2371

Virginia
Federal Building, Room 8213
400 North 8th Street
Richmond, VA 23240
(804) 771-2451

Washington
Federal Building, Room 319
P.O. Box 2427
Wenatchee, WA 98807
(509) 662-4352

West Virginia
75 High Street
P.O. Box 678
Morgantown, WV 26505
(304) 291-4791

Wisconsin
4949 Kirschling Court
Stevens Point, WI 54481
(715) 345-7600

Wyoming
Federal Building, Room 1005
100 East B Street
P.O. Box 820
Casper, WY 82602
(307) 261-5271

FEED GRAIN PRODUCTION STABILIZATION

Department of Agriculture
Agricultural Stabilization
and Conservation Service
P.O. Box 2415
Washington, DC 20013
(202) 720-4418

Description: Direct payments with unrestricted use to owners, landlords, tenants, or sharecroppers on farms. Commodity planted must meet program requirements as announced by the secretary.
$ Given: Up to $250,000 per person
Application Information: Write for guidelines.
Deadline: N/A
Contact: Your local, state, and/or regional ASCS office

Alabama
Albert C. McDonald
P.O. Box 891
474 South Court Street,
Room 749
Montgomery, AL 36104-4184
(205) 832-7230

Alaska
Teresa Weiland
Alaska State ASCS Office
800 West Evergreen,
Suite 216
Palmer, AK 99645-6389
(907) 745-7982

Arizona
Arden J. Palmer
Arizona State ASCS Office
201 East Indianola, Suite 325
Phoenix, AZ 85012-2054
(602) 640-5200

Arkansas
Dotson Collins
P.O. Box 2781
New Federal Building,
Room 5102
700 West Capitol Street
Little Rock, AR 72201-3225
(501) 378-5220

California
John Smythe
California State ASCS Office
1303 J. Street, Suite 300
Sacramento, CA 95814-2916
(916) 551-1801

Colorado
Lloyd C. Sommerville
Colorado State ASCS Office
655 Parfet Street
Room E 305, Third Floor
Lakewood, CO 80215
(303) 236-2866

Connecticut
David T. Schreiber
88 Day Hill Road
Windsor, CT 06095
(203) 285-8483

Delaware
Earle Isaacs, Jr.
179 West Chestnut Hill Road,
Suite 7
Newark, DE 19713-2295
(302) 573-6536

Florida
Eugene C. Badger
P.O. Box 141030
4440 Northwest 25th Place,
Suite 1
Gainesville, FL 32614-1030
(904) 372-8549

Georgia
James E. Harrison
P.O. Box 1907
Federal Building, Room 102
344 East Hancock Avenue
Athens, GA 30601-2775
(404) 546-2266

Hawaii
Ralph K. Ajifu
Hawaii State ASCS Office
300 Ala Moana Boulevard,
Room 4202
P.O. Box 50008
Honolulu, HI 96850-0002
(808) 551-2644

Idaho
Trent Clark
Idaho State
ASCS Office
3220 Elder Street
Boise, ID 83705-5820
(208) 334-1486

Illinois
William G. Beeler
P.O. Box 19273
3500 Wabash Avenue
Springfield, IL 62707
(217) 492-4180

Indiana
Don Villwoch
Indiana State ASCS Office
5981 Lakeside Boulevard
Indianapolis, IN 46278-1996
(317) 290-3030

Iowa
Robert Furleigh
10500 Buena Vista Court
Urbandale, IA 50322
(515) 254-1540

Kansas
Frank A. Mosier
Kansas State ASCS Office
2601 Anderson Avenue
Manhattan, KS 66502-2898
(913) 539-3531

Kentucky
Kenneth Ashby
Kentucky State ASCS Office
771 Corporate Drive,
Suite 100
Lexington, KY 40503-5477
(606) 233-2726

Louisiana
Willie F. Cooper
3737 Government Street
Alexandria, LA 71302-3395
(318) 473-7721

Maine
David P. Staples
44 Stillwater Avenue
P.O. Box 406
Bangor, ME 04401-3521
(207) 942-0342

Maryland
James Richardson
Rivers Center
10270 B Columbia Road
Columbia, MD 21046-9998
(301) 381-4550

Massachusetts
Raymond E. Duda
451 West Street
Amherst, MA 01002-2953
(413) 256-0232

Michigan
David Conklin
1405 South Harrison Road,
Room 116
East Lansing, MI 48823-5202
(517) 337-6659

Minnesota
Donald L. Friedrich
Minnesota State ASCS Office
400 Farm Credit Service
Building
375 Jackson Street
St. Paul, MN 55101-1852
(612) 290-3651

Mississippi
Charles R. Hull
Mississippi State ASCS
Office
6310 I-55 North
Jackson, MS 39236
(601) 965-4300

Missouri
Morris G. Westfall
601 Parkdale Plaza Business
Loop
70 West, Suite 225
Columbia, MO 65203
(314) 875-5201

Montana
Donald Anderson
P.O. Box 670
Bozeman, MT 59771-0670
(406) 587-6872

Nebraska
John Neuberger
Nebraska State ASCS Office
P.O. Box 57975
Lincoln, NE 68505-7975
(402) 437-5581

Nevada
C. Richard Capurro
Nevada State ASCS Office
1755 East Plumb Lane,
Suite 202
Reno, NV 89502-3207

New Hampshire
Peter M. Thomson
USDA - New Hampshire
State ASCS Office
22 Bridge Street, Fourth
Floor
Concord, NH 03301-5605
(603) 224-7941

New Jersey
Peter de Wilde
Mastoris Professional Plaza
163 Route 130
Building 1, Suite E
Bordentown, NJ 08505
(609) 298-3446

New Mexico
David Turner
New Mexico State ASCS
Office
P.O. Box 1458
Federal Building, Room 4408
517 Gold Avenue, SW
Albuquerque, NM
87102-3156
(505) 766-2472

New York
John Steele
811 James H. Hanley Federal
Building
100 South Clinton Street
Syracuse, NY 13260-0066
(315) 423-5176

North Carolina
John J. Cooper
P.O. Box 27327
Federal Building, Suite 175
4407 Bland Road
Raleigh, NC 27611
(919) 790-2957

North Dakota
Robert J. Christiman
North Dakota State ASCS
Office
P.O. Box 3046
Fargo, ND 58108-3046
(701) 239-5224

Ohio
Dorothy Leslie
Federal Building, Room 540
200 North High Street
Columbus, OH 43215-2495
(614) 469-6735

Oklahoma
Bart Brorsen
USDA Agriculture Center
Building
Farm Road and McFarland
Street
Stillwater, OK 74074-2531
(405) 624-4110

Oregon
Glen E. Stonebrink
Oregon State ASCS Office
P.O. Box 1300
Tualatin, OR 97062-1300
(503) 692-6830

Pennsylvania
Donald Unangst
One Credit Union Place,
Suite 320
228 Walnut Street
Harrisburg, PA 17101-1701
(717) 782-4547

Rhode Island
Alfred R. Bettencourt, Jr.
Aldeic Complex
60 Quaker Lane
West Warwick, RI 02893-2120
(401) 828-8232

South Carolina
Thomas H. Herlong
Strom Thurmond Mall
Columbia, SC 29207
(803) 765-5186

South Dakota
Dean W. Anderson
Federal Building, Room 208
200 Fourth Street, SW
Huron, SD 57350-2478
(605) 353-1092

Tennessee
Charles Ben Thompson
U.S. Courthouse, Room 579
801 Broadway
Nashville, TN 37203-3816
(615) 736-5555

Texas
Donnie Bownan Aeting
Texas State ASCS Office
P.O. Box 2900
College Station, TX
77841-0001
(409) 260-9207

Utah
Royal K. Norman
Utah State ASCS Office
P.O. Box 11547
Salt Lake City, UT
84147-2547
(801) 524-5013

Vermont
David Newton
Executive Square Office
Building
346 Shelburne Street
Burlington, VT 05401-4495
(802) 658-2803

Virginia
Mahlon K. Rudy
Federal Building, Room 7105
400 North 8th Street
Richmond, VA 23240-9990
(804) 771-2581

Washington
Robert Deife
Washington State ASCS
Office
Rock Pointe Tower, Suite 568
316 West Boone Avenue
Spokane, WA 99201-2350
(509) 353-1092

West Virginia
Donald W. Brown
P.O. Box 1049
New Federal Building,
Room 239
75 High Street
Morgantown, WV 26505-7558
(304) 291-4351

Wisconsin
Peter C. Senn
Wisconsin State ASCS Office
6515 Watts Road, Room 100
Madison, WI 53719-2797
(608) 264-5301

Wyoming
Harold Hellbaum
P.O. Box 920
100 East B. Street,
Room 3001
Casper, WY 82602-0920
(307) 261-5231

Caribbean Area
Herberto J. Martinez
Caribbean Area ASCS Office
Cobran's Plaza, Suite 309
1609 Ponce DeLeon Avenue
Santurce, Puerto Rico
00909-0001
(809) 729-6872

FORESTRY INCENTIVE PROGRAM

**Department of
Agriculture**
Agricultural Stabilization
and Conservation Service
P.O. Box 2415
Washington, DC 20013
(202) 720-6221

Description: Direct payment for specified use to individuals, groups, associations, Indian tribes or other native groups, corporations whose stocks are not publicly traded, or other legal entities that own nonindustrial, private forestlands producing industrial wood crops. Limited to ownership of not more than 1,000 acres of nonindustrial private forestland that can produce at least 50 cubic feet of wood per acre per year, except by special approval. Program is available to eligible landowners in the United States or any U.S. territory.
$ Given: Payment range: $3–$10,000 per year; average: $1,600.
Application Information: Form ACP-245 or FIP-11 filed at any time of year with your county ASCS office in which the land is located.
Deadline: As announced by the ASC committee.
Contact: Your local, state, and/or regional ASCS office

Agriculture

Alabama
Albert C. McDonald
P.O. Box 891
474 South Court Street,
Room 749
Montgomery, AL 36104-4184
(205) 832-7230

Alaska
Teresa Weiland
Alaska State ASCS Office
800 West Evergreen,
Suite 216
Palmer, AK 99645-6389
(907) 745-7982

Arizona
Arden J. Palmer
Arizona State ASCS Office
201 East Indianola, Suite 325
Phoenix, AZ 85012-2054
(602) 640-5200

Arkansas
Dotson Collins
P.O. Box 2781
New Federal Building,
Room 5102
700 West Capitol Street
Little Rock, AR 72201-3225
(501) 378-5220

California
John Smythe
California State ASCS Office
1303 J. Street, Suite 300
Sacramento, CA 95814-2916
(916) 551-1801

Colorado
Lloyd C. Sommerville
Colorado State ASCS Office
655 Parfet Street
Room E 305, Third Floor
Lakewood, CO 80215
(303) 236-2866

Connecticut
David T. Schreiber
88 Day Hill Road
Windsor, CT 06095
(203) 285-8483

Delaware
Earle Isaacs, Jr.
179 West Chestnut Hill Road,
Suite 7
Newark, DE 19713-2295
(302) 573-6536

Florida
Eugene C. Badger
P.O. Box 141030
4440 Northwest 25th Place,
Suite 1
Gainesville, FL 32614-1030
(904) 372-8549

Georgia
James E. Harrison
P.O. Box 1907
Federal Building, Room 102
344 East Hancock Avenue
Athens, GA 30601-2775
(404) 546-2266

Hawaii
Ralph K. Ajifu
Hawaii State ASCS Office
300 Ala Moana Boulevard,
Room 4202
P.O. Box 50008
Honolulu, HI 96850-0002
(808) 551-2644

Idaho
Trent Clark
Idaho State ASCS Office
3220 Elder Street
Boise, ID 83705-5820
(208) 334-1486

Illinois
William G. Beeler
P.O. Box 19273
3500 Wabash Avenue
Springfield, IL 62707
(217) 492-4180

Indiana
Don Villwoch
Indiana State ASCS Office
5981 Lakeside Boulevard
Indianapolis, IN 46278-1996
(317) 290-3030

Iowa
Robert Furleigh
10500 Buena Vista Court
Urbandale, IA 50322
(515) 254-1540

Kansas
Frank A. Mosier
Kansas State ASCS Office
2601 Anderson Avenue
Manhattan, KS 66502-2898
(913) 539-3531

Kentucky
Kenneth Ashby
Kentucky State ASCS Office
771 Corporate Drive,
Suite 100
Lexington, KY 40503-5477
(606) 233-2726

Louisiana
Willie F. Cooper
3737 Government Street
Alexandria, LA 71302-3395
(318) 473-7721

Maine
David P. Staples
44 Stillwater Avenue
P.O. Box 406
Bangor, ME 04401-3521
(207) 942-0342

Maryland
James Richardson
Rivers Center
10270 B Columbia Road
Columbia, MD 21046-9998
(301) 381-4550

Massachusetts
Raymond E. Duda
451 West Street
Amherst, MA 01002-2953
(413) 256-0232

Michigan
David Conklin
1405 South Harrison Road,
Room 116
East Lansing, MI 48823-5202
(517) 337-6659

Minnesota
Donald L. Friedrich
Minnesota State ASCS Office
400 Farm Credit Service
Building
375 Jackson Street
St. Paul, MN 55101-1852
(612) 290-3651

Mississippi
Charles R. Hull
Mississippi State ASCS
Office
6310 I-55 North
Jackson, MS 39236
(601) 965-4300

Missouri
Morris G. Westfall
601 Parkdale Plaza Business
Loop
70 West, Suite 225
Columbia, MO 65203
(314) 875-5201

Montana
Donald Anderson
P.O. Box 670
Bozeman, MT 59771-0670
(406) 587-6872

Nebraska
John Neuberger
Nebraska State ASCS Office
P.O. Box 57975
Lincoln, NE 68505-7975
(402) 437-5581

Nevada
C. Richard Capurro
Nevada State ASCS Office
1755 East Plumb Lane,
Suite 202
Reno, NV 89502-3207

New Hampshire
Peter M. Thomson
USDA - New Hampshire
State ASCS Office
22 Bridge Street,
Fourth Floor
Concord, NH 03301-5605
(603) 224-7941

New Jersey
Peter de Wilde
Mastoris Professional Plaza
163 Route 130
Building 1, Suite E
Bordentown, NJ 08505
(609) 298-3446

New Mexico
David Turner
New Mexico State ASCS
Office
P.O. Box 1458
Federal Building, Room 4408
517 Gold Avenue, SW
Albuquerque, NM
87102-3156
(505) 766-2472

New York
John Steele
811 James H. Hanley Federal
Building
100 South Clinton Street
Syracuse, NY 13260-0066
(315) 423-5176

North Carolina
John J. Cooper
P.O. Box 27327
Federal Building, Suite 175
4407 Bland Road
Raleigh, NC 27611
(919) 790-2957

North Dakota
Robert J. Christman
North Dakota State ASCS
Office
P.O. Box 3046
Fargo, ND 58108-3046
(701) 239-5224

Ohio
Dorothy Leslie
Federal Building, Room 540
200 North High Street
Columbus, OH 43215-2495
(614) 469-6735

Oklahoma
Bart Brorsen
USDA Agriculture Center
Building
Farm Road and McFarland
Street
Stillwater, OK 74074-2531
(405) 624-4110

Oregon
Glen E. Stonebrink
Oregon State ASCS Office
P.O. Box 1300
Tualatin, OR 97062-1300
(503) 692-6830

Agriculture

Pennsylvania
Donald Unangst
One Credit Union Place,
Suite 320
228 Walnut Street
Harrisburg, PA 17101-1701
(717) 782-4547

Rhode Island
Alfred R. Bettencourt, Jr.
Aldeic Complex
60 Quaker Lane
West Warwick, RI 02893-2120
(401) 828-8232

South Carolina
Thomas H. Herlong
Strom Thurmond Mall
Columbia, SC 29207
(803) 765-5186

South Dakota
Dean W. Anderson
Federal Building, Room 208
200 Fourth Street, SW
Huron, SD 57350-2478
(605) 353-1092

Tennessee
Charles Ben Thompson
U.S. Courthouse, Room 579
801 Broadway
Nashville, TN 37203-3816
(615) 736-5555

Texas
Donnie Bownan Aeting
Texas State ASCS Office
P.O. Box 2900
College Station, TX
77841-0001
(409) 260-9207

Utah
Royal K. Norman
Utah State ASCS Office
P.O. Box 11547
Salt Lake City, UT
84147-2547
(801) 524-5013

Vermont
David Newton
Executive Square Office
Building
346 Shelburne Street
Burlington, VT 05401-4495
(802) 658-2803

Virginia
Mahlon K. Rudy
Federal Building, Room 7105
400 North 8th Street
Richmond, VA 23240-9990
(804) 771-2581

Washington
Robert Deife
Washington State ASCS
Office
Rock Pointe Tower, Suite 568
316 West Boone Avenue
Spokane, WA 99201-2350
(509) 353-1092

West Virginia
Donald W. Brown
P.O. Box 1049
New Federal Building,
Room 239
75 High Street
Morgantown, WV 26505-7558
(304) 291-4351

Wisconsin
Peter C. Senn
Wisconsin State ASCS Office
6515 Watts Road, Room 100
Madison, WI 53719-2797
(608) 264-5301

Wyoming
Harold Hellbaum
P.O. Box 920
100 East B. Street,
Room 3001
Casper, WY 82602-0920
(307) 261-5231

Caribbean Area
Herberto J. Martinez
Caribbean Area ASCS Office
Cobran's Plaza, Suite 309
1609 Ponce DeLeon Avenue
Santurce, Puerto Rico
00909-0001
(809) 729-6872

GRAIN RESERVE PROGRAM

Department of Agriculture
Agricultural Stabilization and Conservation Service
Cotton, Grain, and Rice Price Support Division
P.O. Box 2415
Washington, DC 20013
(202) 720-9886

Description: Direct payments with unrestricted use to individual producers or approved cooperatives having a conservation loan on wheat, corn, barley, oats, or sorghum.
$ Given: Payment range: $1–$122,863; average: $2,661.
Application Information: Visit, call, or write your county ASCS office during announced availability period.
Deadline: Announced time of availability.
Contact: Your local, state, and/or regional office

Alabama
Albert C. McDonald
P.O. Box 891
474 South Court Street, Room 749
Montgomery, AL 36104-4184
(205) 832-7230

Alaska
Teresa Weiland
Alaska State ASCS Office
800 West Evergreen, Suite 216
Palmer, AK 99645-6389
(907) 745-7982

Arizona
Arden J. Palmer
Arizona State ASCS Office
201 East Indianola, Suite 325
Phoenix, AZ 85012-2054
(602) 640-5200

Arkansas
Dotson Collins
P.O. Box 2781
New Federal Building, Room 5102
700 West Capitol Street
Little Rock, AR 72201-3225
(501) 378-5220

California
John Smythe
California State ASCS Office
1303 J. Street, Suite 300
Sacramento, CA 95814-2916
(916) 551-1801

Colorado
Lloyd C. Sommerville
Colorado State ASCS Office
655 Parfet Street
Room E 305, Third Floor
Lakewood, CO 80215
(303) 236-2866

Connecticut
David T. Schreiber
88 Day Hill Road
Windsor, CT 06095
(203) 285-8483

Delaware
Earle Isaacs, Jr.
179 West Chestnut Hill Road, Suite 7
Newark, DE 19713-2295
(302) 573-6536

Florida
Eugene C. Badger
P.O. Box 141030
4440 Northwest 25th Place, Suite 1
Gainesville, FL 32614-1030
(904) 372-8549

Georgia
James E. Harrison
P.O. Box 1907
Federal Building, Room 102
344 East Hancock Avenue
Athens, GA 30601-2775
(404) 546-2266

Hawaii
Ralph K. Ajifu
Hawaii State ASCS Office
300 Ala Moana Boulevard, Room 4202
P.O. Box 50008
Honolulu, HI 96850-0002
(808) 551-2644

Idaho
Trent Clark
Idaho State ASCS Office
3220 Elder Street
Boise, ID 83705-5820
(208) 334-1486

Illinois
William G. Beeler
P.O. Box 19273
3500 Wabash Avenue
Springfield, IL 62707
(217) 492-4180

Indiana
Don Villwoch
Indiana State ASCS Office
5981 Lakeside Boulevard
Indianapolis, IN 46278-1996
(317) 290-3030

Iowa
Robert Furleigh
10500 Buena Vista Court
Urbandale, IA 50322
(515) 254-1540

Kansas
Frank A. Mosier
Kansas State ASCS Office
2601 Anderson Avenue
Manhattan, KS 66502-2898
(913) 539-3531

Kentucky
Kenneth Ashby
Kentucky State ASCS Office
771 Corporate Drive,
Suite 100
Lexington, KY 40503-5477
(606) 233-2726

Louisiana
Willie F. Cooper
3737 Government Street
Alexandria, LA 71302-3395
(318) 473-7721

Maine
David P. Staples
44 Stillwater Avenue
P.O. Box 406
Bangor, ME 04401-3521
(207) 942-0342

Maryland
James Richardson
Rivers Center
10270 B Columbia Road
Columbia, MD 21046-9998
(301) 381-4550

Massachusetts
Raymond E. Duda
451 West Street
Amherst, MA 01002-2953
(413) 256-0232

Michigan
David Conklin
1405 South Harrison Road,
Room 116
East Lansing, MI 48823-5202
(517) 337-6659

Minnesota
Donald L. Friedrich
Minnesota State ASCS Office
400 Farm Credit Service
Building
375 Jackson Street
St. Paul, MN 55101-1852
(612) 290-3651

Mississippi
Charles R. Hull
Mississippi State ASCS
Office
6310 I-55 North
Jackson, MS 39236
(601) 965-4300

Missouri
Morris G. Westfall
601 Parkdale Plaza Business
Loop
70 West, Suite 225
Columbia, MO 65203
(314) 875-5201

Montana
Donald Anderson
P.O. Box 670
Bozeman, MT 59771-0670
(406) 587-6872

Nebraska
John Neuberger
Nebraska State ASCS Office
P.O. Box 57975
Lincoln, NE 68505-7975
(402) 437-5581

Nevada
C. Richard Capurro
Nevada State ASCS Office
1755 East Plumb Lane,
Suite 202
Reno, NV 89502-3207

New Hampshire
Peter M. Thomson
USDA - New Hampshire
State ASCS Office
22 Bridge Street,
Fourth Floor
Concord, NH 03301-5605
(603) 224-7941

New Jersey
Peter de Wilde
Mastoris Professional Plaza
163 Route 130
Building 1, Suite E
Bordentown, NJ 08505
(609) 298-3446

New Mexico
David Turner
New Mexico State ASCS
Office
P.O. Box 1458
Federal Building, Room 4408
517 Gold Avenue, SW
Albuquerque, NM
87102-3156
(505) 766-2472

New York
John Steele
811 James H. Hanley Federal Building
100 South Clinton Street
Syracuse, NY 13260-0066
(315) 423-5176

North Carolina
John J. Cooper
P.O. Box 27327
Federal Building, Suite 175
4407 Bland Road
Raleigh, NC 27611
(919) 790-2957

North Dakota
Robert J. Christiman
North Dakota State ASCS Office
P.O. Box 3046
Fargo, ND 58108-3046
(701) 239-5224

Ohio
Dorothy Leslie
Federal Building, Room 540
200 North High Street
Columbus, OH 43215-2495
(614) 469-6735

Oklahoma
Bart Brorsen
USDA Agriculture Center Building
Farm Road and McFarland Street
Stillwater, OK 74074-2531
(405) 624-4110

Oregon
Glen E. Stonebrink
Oregon State ASCS Office
P.O. Box 1300
Tualatin, OR 97062-1300
(503) 692-6830

Pennsylvania
Donald Unangst
One Credit Union Place, Suite 320
228 Walnut Street
Harrisburg, PA 17101-1701
(717) 782-4547

Rhode Island
Alfred R. Bettencourt, Jr.
Aldeic Complex
60 Quaker Lane
West Warwick, RI 02893-2120
(401) 828-8232

South Carolina
Thomas H. Herlong
Strom Thurmond Mall
Columbia, SC 29207
(803) 765-5186

South Dakota
Dean W. Anderson
Federal Building, Room 208
200 Fourth Street, SW
Huron, SD 57350-2478
(605) 353-1092

Tennessee
Charles Ben Thompson
U.S. Courthouse, Room 579
801 Broadway
Nashville, TN 37203-3816
(615) 736-5555

Texas
Donnie Bownan Aeting
Texas State ASCS Office
P.O. Box 2900
College Station, TX 77841-0001
(409) 260-9207

Utah
Royal K. Norman
Utah State ASCS Office
P.O. Box 11547
Salt Lake City, UT 84147-2547
(801) 524-5013

Vermont
David Newton
Executive Square Office Building
346 Shelburne Street
Burlington, VT 05401-4495
(802) 658-2803

Virginia
Mahlon K. Rudy
Federal Building, Room 7105
400 North 8th Street
Richmond, VA 23240-9990
(804) 771-2581

Washington
Robert Deife
Washington State ASCS Office
Rock Pointe Tower, Suite 568
316 West Boone Avenue
Spokane, WA 99201-2350
(509) 353-1092

West Virginia
Donald W. Brown
P.O. Box 1049
New Federal Building, Room 239
75 High Street
Morgantown, WV 26505-7558
(304) 291-4351

Wisconsin
Peter C. Senn
Wisconsin State ASCS Office
6515 Watts Road, Room 100
Madison, WI 53719-2797
(608) 264-5301

Wyoming
Harold Hellbaum
P.O. Box 920
100 East B. Street,
Room 3001
Casper, WY 82602-0920
(307) 261-5231

Caribbean Area
Herberto J. Martinez
Caribbean Area ASCS Office
Cobran's Plaza, Suite 309
1609 Ponce DeLeon Avenue
Santurce, Puerto Rico
00909-0001
(809) 729-6872

INTEREST AND ASSISTANCE PROGRAM

Department of Agriculture
Farmers Home Administration
Washington, DC 20250
(202) 720-1604

Description: Guaranteed and insured loans for individuals, partnerships, joint operators, legal resident aliens, corporations, or cooperatives that conduct family-size farming or ranching operations.
$ Given: Loan range: $1–$400,000.
Application Information: Write for guidelines.
Deadline: Program expires September 30, 1995. No other deadlines are applicable.
Contact: Consult your local telephone directory under U.S. Government, Department of Agriculture, for FmHA county office number or contact your FmHA state offices.

Alabama
Aronov Building, Room 717
474 South Court Street
Montgomery, AL 36104
(205) 223-7077

Alaska
634 South Bailey, Suite 103
Palmer, AK 99645
(907) 745-2176

Arizona
201 East Indianola, Suite 275
Phoenix, AZ 85012
(602) 640-5086

Arkansas
700 West Capitol
P.O. Box 2778
Little Rock, AR 72203
(501) 324-6281

California
194 West Main Street,
Suite F
Woodland, CA 95695-2915
(916) 666-3382

Colorado
655 Parfet Street,
Room E-100
Lakewood, CO 80215
(303) 236-2801

Connecticut
451 West Street
Amherst, MA 01002
(413) 253-4300

Delaware
4611 South Dupont Highway
P.O. Box 400
Camden, DE 19934-9998
(302) 697-4300

District of Columbia
4611 South Dupont Highway
P.O. Box 400
Camden, DE 19934-9998
(302) 697-4300

Florida
Federal Building
4440 NW 25th Place
P.O. Box 147010
Gainesville, FL 32614-7010
(904) 338-3400

Georgia
Stephens Federal Building
355 East Hancock Avenue
Athens, GA 30610
(404) 546-2162

Hawaii
Federal Building, Room 311
154 Waianuenue Avenue
Hilo, HI 967720
(808) 933-3000

Idaho
3232 Elder Street
Boise, ID 83720
(808) 933-3000

Illinois
Illini Plaza
1817 South Neil Street
Champaign, IL 61820
(217) 398-5235

Indiana
5975 Lakeside Boulevard
Indianapolis, IN 46278
(317) 290-3100

Iowa
Federal Building, Room 873
210 Walnut Street
Des Moines, IA 50309
(515) 284-4663

Kansas
1201 SW Summit Executive
Court
P.O. Box 4653
Topeka, KS 66604
(913) 271-2700

Kentucky
333771 Corporate Plaza,
Suite 200
Lexington, KY 40503
(606) 224-7300

Louisiana
3727 Government Street
Alexandria, LA 71302
(318) 473-7920

Maine
444 Stillwater Avenue,
Suite 2
P.O. Box 405
Bangor, ME 04402-0405
(207) 990-9106

Maryland
4611 South Dupont Highway
P.O. Box 400
Camden, DE 19934-9998
(302) 697-4300

Massachusetts
451 West Street
Amherst, MA 01002
(413) 253-4300

Michigan
Manly Miles Building,
Room 209
1405 South Harrison Road
East Lansing, MI 48823
(517) 337-6631

Minnesota
410 Farm Credit Building
375 Jackson Street
St. Paul, MN 55101
(612) 290-3842

Mississippi
Federal Building, Suite 831
100 West Capitol
Jackson, MS 39269
(601) 965-4316

Missouri
601 Business Loop, 70 West
Parkade Center, Suite 235
Columbia, MO 65203
(314) 876-0976

Montana
900 Technology Boulevard,
Suite B
P.O. Box 850
Bozeman, MT 59771
(406) 585-2500

Nebraska
Federal Building, Room 308
100 Centennial Mall North
Lincoln, NE 68508
(402) 437-5551

Nevada
194 West Main Street,
Suite F
Woodland, CA 95695-2915
(916) 666-3382

New Hampshire
City Center, Third Floor
89 Main Street
Montpelier, VT 05602
(802) 223-2371

New Jersey
Tarnsfield and Woodlane
Roads
Tarnsfield Plaza, Suite 22
Mt. Holly, NJ 08060
(609) 265-3600

New Mexico
Federal Building, Room 3414
517 Gold Avenue, SW
Albuquerque, NM 87102
(505) 766-2462

Agriculture

New York
Federal Building, Room 871
100 South Clinton Street
Syracuse, NY 13261-7318
(315) 423-5290

North Carolina
4405 South Bland Road,
Suite 260
Raleigh, NC 27609
(919) 790-2731

North Dakota
Federal Building, Room 208
Third and Rosser
P.O. Box 1737
Bismarck, ND 58502
(701) 250-4781

Ohio
Federal Building, Room 507
200 North High Street
Columbus, OH 43215
(614) 469-5606

Oklahoma
USDA Agricultural Center
Office Building
Stillwater, OK 74074
(405) 624-4250

Oregon
Federal Building, Room 1590
1220 SW 3rd Avenue
Portland, OR 97204
(503) 326-2731

Pennsylvania
One Credit Union Place,
Suite 330
Harrisburg, PA 17110-2996
(717) 782-4476

Puerto Rico
New San Juan Center
Building, Room 501
159 Carlos E. Chardon Street
G.P.O. Box 6106G
Hato Rey, PR 00918-5481
(809) 766-5095

Rhode Island
451 West Street
Amherst, MA 01002
(413) 253-4300

South Carolina
Strom Thurmond Federal
Building, Room 1007
1835 Assembly Street
Columbia, SC 29201
(803) 765-5163

South Dakota
Huron Federal Building,
Room 308
200 Fourth Street, SW
Huron, SD 57350
(605) 353-1430

Tennessee
3322 West End Avenue, Suite
300
Nashville, TN 37203-1071
(615) 736-7341

Texas
Federal Building, Suite 102
101 South Main
Temple, TX 76501
(817) 774-1301

Utah
Federal Building, Room 5438
125 South State Street
Salt Lake City, UT 84138
(801) 524-4063

Vermont
City Center, Third Floor
89 Main Street
Montpelier, VT 05602
(802) 223-2371

Virgin Islands
City Center, Third Floor
89 Main Street
Montpelier, VT 05602
(802) 223-2371

Virginia
Federal Building, Room 8213
400 North 8th Street
Richmond, VA 23240
(804) 771-2451

Washington
Federal Building, Room 319
P.O. Box 2427
Wenatchee, WA 98807
(509) 662-4352

West Virginia
75 High Street
P.O. Box 678
Morgantown, WV 26505
(304) 291-4791

Wisconsin
4949 Kirschling Court
Stevens Point, WI 54481
(715) 345-7600

Wyoming
Federal Building, Room 1005
100 East B Street
P.O. Box 820
Casper, WY 82602
(307) 261-5271

NATIONAL WOOL ACT PAYMENTS

Department of Agriculture
Agricultural Stabilization and Conservation Service
P.O. Box 2415
Washington, DC 20013
(202) 720-6734

Description: Direct payments with unrestricted use to anyone owning sheep, lambs, or angora goats for 30 days or more and who sell wool or unshorn lambs or mohair produced during marketing year. Applicant must meet regulatory definition of the term "person."
$ Given: Wool: Up to $649,100. Mohair: Up to $548,920.
Application Information: Contact your local ASCS county office.
Deadline: Dates vary from state to state.
Contact: Your local, state, and/or regional ASCS office

Alabama
Albert C. McDonald
P.O. Box 891
474 South Court Street,
Room 749
Montgomery, AL 36104-4184
(205) 832-7230

Alaska
Teresa Weiland
Alaska State ASCS Office
800 West Evergreen,
Suite 216
Palmer, AK 99645-6389
(907) 745-7982

Arizona
Arden J. Palmer
Arizona State ASCS Office
201 East Indianola, Suite 325
Phoenix, AZ 85012-2054
(602) 640-5200

Arkansas
Dotson Collins
P.O. Box 2781
New Federal Building,
Room 5102
700 West Capitol Street
Little Rock, AR 72201-3225
(501) 378-5220

California
John Smythe
California State ASCS Office
1303 J. Street, Suite 300
Sacramento, CA 95814-2916
(916) 551-1801

Colorado
Lloyd C. Sommerville
Colorado State ASCS Office
655 Parfet Street
Room E 305, Third Floor
Lakewood, CO 80215
(303) 236-2866

Connecticut
David T. Schreiber
88 Day Hill Road
Windsor, CT 06095
(203) 285-8483

Delaware
Earle Isaacs, Jr.
179 West Chestnut Hill Road,
Suite 7
Newark, DE 19713-2295
(302) 573-6536

Florida
Eugene C. Badger
P.O. Box 141030
4440 Northwest 25th Place,
Suite 1
Gainesville, FL 32614-1030
(904) 372-8549

Georgia
James E. Harrison
P.O. Box 1907
Federal Building, Room 102
344 East Hancock Avenue
Athens, GA 30601-2775
(404) 546-2266

Hawaii
Ralph K. Ajifu
Hawaii State ASCS Office
300 Ala Moana Boulevard,
Room 4202
P.O. Box 50008
Honolulu, HI 96850-0002
(808) 551-2644

Idaho
Trent Clark
Idaho State ASCS Office
3220 Elder Street
Boise, ID 83705-5820
(208) 334-1486

Agriculture

Illinois
William G. Beeler
P.O. Box 19273
3500 Wabash Avenue
Springfield, IL 62707
(217) 492-4180

Indiana
Don Villwoch
Indiana State ASCS Office
5981 Lakeside Boulevard
Indianapolis, IN 46278-1996
(317) 290-3030

Iowa
Robert Furleigh
10500 Buena Vista Court
Urbandale, IA 50322
(515) 254-1540

Kansas
Frank A. Mosier
Kansas State ASCS Office
2601 Anderson Avenue
Manhattan, KS 66502-2898
(913) 539-3531

Kentucky
Kenneth Ashby
Kentucky State ASCS Office
771 Corporate Drive,
Suite 100
Lexington, KY 40503-5477
(606) 233-2726

Louisiana
Willie F. Cooper
3737 Government Street
Alexandria, LA 71302-3395
(318) 473-7721

Maine
David P. Staples
44 Stillwater Avenue
P.O. Box 406
Bangor, ME 04401-3521
(207) 942-0342

Maryland
James Richardson
Rivers Center
10270 B Columbia Road
Columbia, MD 21046-9998
(301) 381-4550

Massachusetts
Raymond E. Duda
451 West Street
Amherst, MA 01002-2953
(413) 256-0232

Michigan
David Conklin
1405 South Harrison Road,
Room 116
East Lansing, MI 48823-5202
(517) 337-6659

Minnesota
Donald L. Friedrich
Minnesota State ASCS Office
400 Farm Credit Service
Building
375 Jackson Street
St. Paul, MN 55101-1852
(612) 290-3651

Mississippi
Charles R. Hull
Mississippi State ASCS
Office
6310 I-55 North
Jackson, MS 39236
(601) 965-4300

Missouri
Morris G. Westfall
601 Parkdale Plaza Business
Loop
70 West, Suite 225
Columbia, MO 65203
(314) 875-5201

Montana
Donald Anderson
P.O. Box 670
Bozeman, MT 59771-0670
(406) 587-6872

Nebraska
John Neuberger
Nebraska State ASCS Office
P.O. Box 57975
Lincoln, NE 68505-7975
(402) 437-5581

Nevada
C. Richard Capurro
Nevada State ASCS Office
1755 East Plumb Lane,
Suite 202
Reno, NV 89502-3207

New Hampshire
Peter M. Thomson
USDA - New Hampshire
State ASCS Office
22 Bridge Street,
Fourth Floor
Concord, NH 03301-5605
(603) 224-7941

New Jersey
Peter de Wilde
Mastoris Professional Plaza
163 Route 130
Building 1, Suite E
Bordentown, NJ 08505
(609) 298-3446

New Mexico
David Turner
New Mexico State ASCS
Office
P.O. Box 1458
Federal Building, Room 4408
517 Gold Avenue, SW
Albuquerque, NM
87102-3156
(505) 766-2472

New York
John Steele
811 James H. Hanley Federal Building
100 South Clinton Street
Syracuse, NY 13260-0066
(315) 423-5176

North Carolina
John J. Cooper
P.O. Box 27327
Federal Building, Suite 175
4407 Bland Road
Raleigh, NC 27611
(919) 790-2957

North Dakota
Robert J. Christiman
North Dakota State ASCS Office
P.O. Box 3046
Fargo, ND 58108-3046
(701) 239-5224

Ohio
Dorothy Leslie
Federal Building, Room 540
200 North High Street
Columbus, OH 43215-2495
(614) 469-6735

Oklahoma
Bart Brorsen
USDA Agriculture Center Building
Farm Road and McFarland Street
Stillwater, OK 74074-2531
(405) 624-4110

Oregon
Glen E. Stonebrink
Oregon State ASCS Office
P.O. Box 1300
Tualatin, OR 97062-1300
(503) 692-6830

Pennsylvania
Donald Unangst
One Credit Union Place, Suite 320
228 Walnut Street
Harrisburg, PA 17101-1701
(717) 782-4547

Rhode Island
Alfred R. Bettencourt, Jr.
Aldeic Complex
60 Quaker Lane
West Warwick, RI 02893-2120
(401) 828-8232

South Carolina
Thomas H. Herlong
Strom Thurmond Mall
Columbia, SC 29207
(803) 765-5186

South Dakota
Dean W. Anderson
Federal Building, Room 208
200 Fourth Street, SW
Huron, SD 57350-2478
(605) 353-1092

Tennessee
Charles Ben Thompson
U.S. Courthouse, Room 579
801 Broadway
Nashville, TN 37203-3816
(615) 736-5555

Texas
Donnie Bownan Aeting
Texas State ASCS Office
P.O. Box 2900
College Station, TX 77841-0001
(409) 260-9207

Utah
Royal K. Norman
Utah State ASCS Office
P.O. Box 11547
Salt Lake City, UT 84147-2547
(801) 524-5013

Vermont
David Newton
Executive Square Office Building
346 Shelburne Street
Burlington, VT 05401-4495
(802) 658-2803

Virginia
Mahlon K. Rudy
Federal Building, Room 7105
400 North 8th Street
Richmond, VA 23240-9990
(804) 771-2581

Washington
Robert Deife
Washington State ASCS Office
Rock Pointe Tower, Suite 568
316 West Boone Avenue
Spokane, WA 99201-2350
(509) 353-1092

West Virginia
Donald W. Brown
P.O. Box 1049
New Federal Building, Room 239
75 High Street
Morgantown, WV 26505-7558
(304) 291-4351

Wisconsin
Peter C. Senn
Wisconsin State ASCS Office
6515 Watts Road, Room 100
Madison, WI 53719-2797
(608) 264-5301

Wyoming
Harold Hellbaum
P.O. Box 920
100 East B. Street,
Room 3001
Casper, WY 82602-0920
(307) 261-5231

Caribbean Area
Herberto J. Martinez
Caribbean Area ASCS Office
Cobran's Plaza, Suite 309
1609 Ponce DeLeon Avenue
Santurce, Puerto Rico
00909-0001
(809) 729-6872

RICE PRODUCTION STABILIZATION

Department of Agriculture
Agricultural Stabilization
and Conservation Service
P.O. Box 2415
Washington, DC 20013
(202) 720-7923

Description: Direct payments with unrestricted use to owners, landlords, tenants, or sharecroppers on farms. Commodity planted must meet program requirements as announced by the secretary.
$ Given: Up to $250,000 per person.
Application Information: Visit your ASCS office prior to prescribed final date to sign application. File Forms ASCS-477 and ASCS-578.
Deadline: N/A
Contact: Your local, state, and/or regional ASCS office

Alabama
Albert C. McDonald
P.O. Box 891
474 South Court Street,
Room 749
Montgomery, AL 36104-4184
(205) 832-7230

Alaska
Teresa Weiland
Alaska State ASCS Office
800 West Evergreen,
Suite 216
Palmer, AK 99645-6389
(907) 745-7982

Arizona
Arden J. Palmer
Arizona State ASCS Office
201 East Indianola, Suite 325
Phoenix, AZ 85012-2054
(602) 640-5200

Arkansas
Dotson Collins
P.O. Box 2781
New Federal Building,
Room 5102
700 West Capitol Street
Little Rock, AR 72201-3225
(501) 378-5220

California
John Smythe
California State ASCS Office
1303 J. Street, Suite 300
Sacramento, CA 95814-2916
(916) 551-1801

Colorado
Lloyd C. Sommerville
Colorado State ASCS Office
655 Parfet Street
Room E 305, Third Floor
Lakewood, CO 80215
(303) 236-2866

Connecticut
David T. Schreiber
88 Day Hill Road
Windsor, CT 06095
(203) 285-8483

Delaware
Earle Isaacs, Jr.
179 West Chestnut Hill Road,
Suite 7
Newark, DE 19713-2295
(302) 573-6536

Florida
Eugene C. Badger
P.O. Box 141030
4440 Northwest 25th Place,
Suite 1
Gainesville, FL 32614-1030
(904) 372-8549

Georgia
James E. Harrison
P.O. Box 1907
Federal Building, Room 102
344 East Hancock Avenue
Athens, GA 30601-2775
(404) 546-2266

Hawaii
Ralph K. Ajifu
Hawaii State ASCS Office
300 Ala Moana Boulevard,
Room 4202
P.O. Box 50008
Honolulu, HI 96850-0002
(808) 551-2644

Idaho
Trent Clark
Idaho State ASCS Office
3220 Elder Street
Boise, ID 83705-5820
(208) 334-1486

Illinois
William G. Beeler
P.O. Box 19273
3500 Wabash Avenue
Springfield, IL 62707
(217) 492-4180

Indiana
Don Villwoch
Indiana State ASCS Office
5981 Lakeside Boulevard
Indianapolis, IN 46278-1996
(317) 290-3030

Iowa
Robert Furleigh
10500 Buena Vista Court
Urbandale, IA 50322
(515) 254-1540

Kansas
Frank A. Mosier
Kansas State ASCS Office
2601 Anderson Avenue
Manhattan, KS 66502-2898
(913) 539-3531

Kentucky
Kenneth Ashby
Kentucky State ASCS Office
771 Corporate Drive,
Suite 100
Lexington, KY 40503-5477
(606) 233-2726

Louisiana
Willie F. Cooper
3737 Government Street
Alexandria, LA 71302-3395
(318) 473-7721

Maine
David P. Staples
44 Stillwater Avenue
P.O. Box 406
Bangor, ME 04401-3521
(207) 942-0342

Maryland
James Richardson
Rivers Center
10270 B Columbia Road
Columbia, MD 21046-9998
(301) 381-4550

Massachusetts
Raymond E. Duda
451 West Street
Amherst, MA 01002-2953
(413) 256-0232

Michigan
David Conklin
1405 South Harrison Road,
Room 116
East Lansing, MI 48823-5202
(517) 337-6659

Minnesota
Donald L. Friedrich
Minnesota State ASCS Office
400 Farm Credit Service
Building
375 Jackson Street
St. Paul, MN 55101-1852
(612) 290-3651

Mississippi
Charles R. Hull
Mississippi State ASCS
Office
6310 I-55 North
Jackson, MS 39236
(601) 965-4300

Missouri
Morris G. Westfall
601 Parkdale Plaza Business
Loop
70 West, Suite 225
Columbia, MO 65203
(314) 875-5201

Montana
Donald Anderson
P.O. Box 670
Bozeman, MT 59771-0670
(406) 587-6872

Nebraska
John Neuberger
Nebraska State ASCS Office
P.O. Box 57975
Lincoln, NE 68505-7975
(402) 437-5581

Nevada
C. Richard Capurro
Nevada State ASCS Office
1755 East Plumb Lane,
Suite 202
Reno, NV 89502-3207

Agriculture

New Hampshire
Peter M. Thomson
USDA - New Hampshire
State ASCS Office
22 Bridge Street,
Fourth Floor
Concord, NH 03301-5605
(603) 224-7941

New Jersey
Peter de Wilde
Mastoris Professional Plaza
163 Route 130
Building 1, Suite E
Bordentown, NJ 08505
(609) 298-3446

New Mexico
David Turner
New Mexico State ASCS
Office
P.O. Box 1458
Federal Building, Room 4408
517 Gold Avenue, SW
Albuquerque, NM
87102-3156
(505) 766-2472

New York
John Steele
811 James H. Hanley Federal
Building
100 South Clinton Street
Syracuse, NY 13260-0066
(315) 423-5176

North Carolina
John J. Cooper
P.O. Box 27327
Federal Building, Suite 175
4407 Bland Road
Raleigh, NC 27611
(919) 790-2957

North Dakota
Robert J. Christiman
North Dakota State ASCS
Office
P.O. Box 3046
Fargo, ND 58108-3046
(701) 239-5224

Ohio
Dorothy Leslie
Federal Building, Room 540
200 North High Street
Columbus, OH 43215-2495
(614) 469-6735

Oklahoma
Bart Brorsen
USDA Agriculture Center
Building
Farm Road and McFarland
Street
Stillwater, OK 74074-2531
(405) 624-4110

Oregon
Glen E. Stonebrink
Oregon State ASCS Office
P.O. Box 1300
Tualatin, OR 97062-1300
(503) 692-6830

Pennsylvania
Donald Unangst
One Credit Union Place,
Suite 320
228 Walnut Street
Harrisburg, PA 17101-1701
(717) 782-4547

Rhode Island
Alfred R. Bettencourt, Jr.
Aldeic Complex
60 Quaker Lane
West Warwick, RI 02893-2120
(401) 828-8232

South Carolina
Thomas H. Herlong
Strom Thurmond Mall
Columbia, SC 29207
(803) 765-5186

South Dakota
Dean W. Anderson
Federal Building, Room 208
200 Fourth Street, SW
Huron, SD 57350-2478
(605) 353-1092

Tennessee
Charles Ben Thompson
U.S. Courthouse, Room 579
801 Broadway
Nashville, TN 37203-3816
(615) 736-5555

Texas
Donnie Bownan Aeting
Texas State ASCS Office
P.O. Box 2900
College Station, TX
77841-0001
(409) 260-9207

Utah
Royal K. Norman
Utah State ASCS Office
P.O. Box 11547
Salt Lake City, UT
84147-2547
(801) 524-5013

Vermont
David Newton
Executive Square Office
Building
346 Shelburne Street
Burlington, VT 05401-4495
(802) 658-2803

Virginia
Mahlon K. Rudy
Federal Building, Room 7105
400 North 8th Street
Richmond, VA 23240-9990
(804) 771-2581

Washington
Robert Deife
Washington State ASCS
Office
Rock Pointe Tower, Suite 568
316 West Boone Avenue
Spokane, WA 99201-2350
(509) 353-1092

West Virginia
Donald W. Brown
P.O. Box 1049
New Federal Building,
Room 239
75 High Street
Morgantown, WV 26505-7558
(304) 291-4351

Wisconsin
Peter C. Senn
Wisconsin State ASCS Office
6515 Watts Road, Room 100
Madison, WI 53719-2797
(608) 264-5301

Wyoming
Harold Hellbaum
P.O. Box 920
100 East B. Street,
Room 3001
Casper, WY 82602-0920
(307) 261-5231

Caribbean Area
Herberto J. Martinez
Caribbean Area ASCS Office
Cobran's Plaza, Suite 309
1609 Ponce DeLeon Avenue
Santurce, Puerto Rico
00909-0001
(809) 729-6872

RURAL CLEAN WATER PROGRAM

Department of Agriculture
Agricultural Stabilization
and Conservation Service
Conservation and
Environmental Protection
Division
P.O. Box 2415
Washington, DC 20013
(202) 720-6221

Description: Direct payments for specified use to private landowners and operators, partnerships, cooperatives, and Indian tribes, as well as for technical assistance.
$ Given: Maximum payment is $50,000 per individual for the life of the contract.
Application Information: Write to your local ASCS office for Form RCWP-1.
Deadline: N/A
Contact: Your local, state, and/or regional ASCS office

Alabama
Albert C. McDonald
P.O. Box 891
474 South Court Street,
Room 749
Montgomery, AL 36104-4184
(205) 832-7230

Alaska
Teresa Weiland
Alaska State ASCS Office
800 West Evergreen,
Suite 216
Palmer, AK 99645-6389
(907) 745-7982

Arizona
Arden J. Palmer
Arizona State ASCS Office
201 East Indianola, Suite 325
Phoenix, AZ 85012-2054
(602) 640-5200

Arkansas
Dotson Collins
P.O. Box 2781
New Federal Building,
Room 5102
700 West Capitol Street
Little Rock, AR 72201-3225
(501) 378-5220

California
John Smythe
California State ASCS Office
1303 J. Street, Suite 300
Sacramento, CA 95814-2916
(916) 551-1801

Colorado
Lloyd C. Sommerville
Colorado State ASCS Office
655 Parfet Street
Room E 305, Third Floor
Lakewood, CO 80215
(303) 236-2866

Agriculture

Connecticut
David T. Schreiber
88 Day Hill Road
Windsor, CT 06095
(203) 285-8483

Delaware
Earle Isaacs, Jr.
179 West Chestnut Hill Road,
Suite 7
Newark, DE 19713-2295
(302) 573-6536

Florida
Eugene C. Badger
P.O. Box 141030
4440 Northwest 25th Place,
Suite 1
Gainesville, FL 32614-1030
(904) 372-8549

Georgia
James E. Harrison
P.O. Box 1907
Federal Building, Room 102
344 East Hancock Avenue
Athens, GA 30601-2775
(404) 546-2266

Hawaii
Ralph K. Ajifu
Hawaii State ASCS Office
300 Ala Moana Boulevard,
Room 4202
P.O. Box 50008
Honolulu, HI 96850-0002
(808) 551-2644

Idaho
Trent Clark
Idaho State ASCS Office
3220 Elder Street
Boise, ID 83705-5820
(208) 334-1486

Illinois
William G. Beeler
P.O. Box 19273
3500 Wabash Avenue
Springfield, IL 62707
(217) 492-4180

Indiana
Don Villwoch
Indiana State ASCS Office
5981 Lakeside Boulevard
Indianapolis, IN 46278-1996
(317) 290-3030

Iowa
Robert Furleigh
10500 Buena Vista Court
Urbandale, IA 50322
(515) 254-1540

Kansas
Frank A. Mosier
Kansas State ASCS Office
2601 Anderson Avenue
Manhattan, KS 66502-2898
(913) 539-3531

Kentucky
Kenneth Ashby
Kentucky State ASCS Office
771 Corporate Drive,
Suite 100
Lexington, KY 40503-5477
(606) 233-2726

Louisiana
Willie F. Cooper
3737 Government Street
Alexandria, LA 71302-3395
(318) 473-7721

Maine
David P. Staples
44 Stillwater Avenue
P.O. Box 406
Bangor, ME 04401-3521
(207) 942-0342

Maryland
James Richardson
Rivers Center
10270 B Columbia Road
Columbia, MD 21046-9998
(301) 381-4550

Massachusetts
Raymond E. Duda
451 West Street
Amherst, MA 01002-2953
(413) 256-0232

Michigan
David Conklin
1405 South Harrison Road,
Room 116
East Lansing, MI 48823-5202
(517) 337-6659

Minnesota
Donald L. Friedrich
Minnesota State ASCS Office
400 Farm Credit Service
Building
375 Jackson Street
St. Paul, MN 55101-1852
(612) 290-3651

Mississippi
Charles R. Hull
Mississippi State ASCS
Office
6310 I-55 North
Jackson, MS 39236
(601) 965-4300

Missouri
Morris G. Westfall
601 Parkdale Plaza Business
Loop
70 West, Suite 225
Columbia, MO 65203
(314) 875-5201

Montana
Donald Anderson
P.O. Box 670
Bozeman, MT 59771-0670
(406) 587-6872

Nebraska
John Neuberger
Nebraska State ASCS Office
P.O. Box 57975
Lincoln, NE 68505-7975
(402) 437-5581

Nevada
C. Richard Capurro
Nevada State ASCS Office
1755 East Plumb Lane,
Suite 202
Reno, NV 89502-3207

New Hampshire
Peter M. Thomson
USDA - New Hampshire
State ASCS Office
22 Bridge Street,
Fourth Floor
Concord, NH 03301-5605
(603) 224-7941

New Jersey
Peter de Wilde
Mastoris Professional Plaza
163 Route 130
Building 1, Suite E
Bordentown, NJ 08505
(609) 298-3446

New Mexico
David Turner
New Mexico State ASCS
Office
P.O. Box 1458
Federal Building, Room 4408
517 Gold Avenue, SW
Albuquerque, NM
87102-3156
(505) 766-2472

New York
John Steele
811 James H. Hanley Federal
Building
100 South Clinton Street
Syracuse, NY 13260-0066
(315) 423-5176

North Carolina
John J. Cooper
P.O. Box 27327
Federal Building, Suite 175
4407 Bland Road
Raleigh, NC 27611
(919) 790-2957

North Dakota
Robert J. Christman
North Dakota State ASCS
Office
P.O. Box 3046
Fargo, ND 58108-3046
(701) 239-5224

Ohio
Dorothy Leslie
Federal Building, Room 540
200 North High Street
Columbus, OH 43215-2495
(614) 469-6735

Oklahoma
Bart Brorsen
USDA Agriculture Center
Building
Farm Road and McFarland
Street
Stillwater, OK 74074-2531
(405) 624-4110

Oregon
Glen E. Stonebrink
Oregon State ASCS Office
P.O. Box 1300
Tualatin, OR 97062-1300
(503) 692-6830

Pennsylvania
Donald Unangst
One Credit Union Place,
Suite 320
228 Walnut Street
Harrisburg, PA 17101-1701
(717) 782-4547

Rhode Island
Alfred R. Bettencourt, Jr.
Aldeic Complex
60 Quaker Lane
West Warwick, RI 02893-2120
(401) 828-8232

South Carolina
Thomas H. Herlong
Strom Thurmond Mall
Columbia, SC 29207
(803) 765-5186

South Dakota
Dean W. Anderson
Federal Building, Room 208
200 Fourth Street, SW
Huron, SD 57350-2478
(605) 353-1092

Tennessee
Charles Ben Thompson
U.S. Courthouse, Room 579
801 Broadway
Nashville, TN 37203-3816
(615) 736-5555

Texas
Donnie Bownan Aeting
Texas State ASCS Office
P.O. Box 2900
College Station, TX
77841-0001
(409) 260-9207

Agriculture

Utah
Royal K. Norman
Utah State ASCS Office
P.O. Box 11547
Salt Lake City, UT
84147-2547
(801) 524-5013

Vermont
David Newton
Executive Square Office
Building
346 Shelburne Street
Burlington, VT 05401-4495
(802) 658-2803

Virginia
Mahlon K. Rudy
Federal Building, Room 7105
400 North 8th Street
Richmond, VA 23240-9990
(804) 771-2581

Washington
Robert Deife
Washington State ASCS
Office
Rock Pointe Tower, Suite 568
316 West Boone Avenue
Spokane, WA 99201-2350
(509) 353-1092

West Virginia
Donald W. Brown
P.O. Box 1049
New Federal Building,
Room 239
75 High Street
Morgantown, WV 26505-7558
(304) 291-4351

Wisconsin
Peter C. Senn
Wisconsin State ASCS Office
6515 Watts Road, Room 100
Madison, WI 53719-2797
(608) 264-5301

Wyoming
Harold Hellbaum
P.O. Box 920
100 East B. Street,
Room 3001
Casper, WY 82602-0920
(307) 261-5231

Caribbean Area
Herberto J. Martinez
Caribbean Area ASCS Office
Cobran's Plaza, Suite 309
1609 Ponce DeLeon Avenue
Santurce, Puerto Rico
00909-0001
(809) 729-6872

SOIL AND WATER LOANS

**Department of
Agriculture**
Farmers Home
Administration
Washington, DC 20250
(202) 720-1632

Description: Direct, guaranteed, and insured loans for farming partnerships, joint operators, cooperatives, or corporations, as well as individual farm owners or tenants. Borrower must have or obtain training in financial and farm management concepts associated with commercial farming.
$ Given: Range: $4,000–$101,000.
Application Information: File Form FmHA 1910-1, application for FmHa services, with supporting information, at your local county office of the Farmers Home Administration. File Form FmHA 449-6, application for guaranteed loans, with prospective lender.
Deadline: None
Contact: Consult your local telephone directory under U.S. Government, Department of Agriculture, for FmHa county office number or contact your FmHA state offices.

Alabama
Aronov Building, Room 717
474 South Court Street
Montgomery, AL 36104
(205) 223-7077

Alaska
634 South Bailey, Suite 103
Palmer, AK 99645
(907) 745-2176

Arizona
201 East Indianola, Suite 275
Phoenix, AZ 85012
(602) 640-5086

Arkansas
700 West Capitol
P.O. Box 2778
Little Rock, AR 72203
(501) 324-6281

California
194 West Main Street,
Suite F
Woodland, CA 95695-2915
(916) 666-3382

Colorado
655 Parfet Street,
Room E-100
Lakewood, CO 80215
(303) 236-2801

Connecticut
451 West Street
Amherst, MA 01002
(413) 253-4300

Delaware
4611 South Dupont Highway
P.O. Box 400
Camden, DE 19934-9998
(302) 697-4300

District of Columbia
4611 South Dupont Highway
P.O. Box 400
Camden, DE 19934-9998
(302) 697-4300

Florida
Federal Building
4440 NW 25th Place
P.O. Box 147010
Gainesville, FL 32614-7010
(904) 338-3400

Georgia
Stephens Federal Building
355 East Hancock Avenue
Athens, GA 30610
(404) 546-2162

Hawaii
Federal Building, Room 311
154 Waianuenue Avenue
Hilo, HI 967720
(808) 933-3000

Idaho
3232 Elder Street
Boise, ID 83720
(808) 933-3000

Illinois
Illini Plaza
1817 South Neil Street
Champaign, IL 61820
(217) 398-5235

Indiana
5975 Lakeside Boulevard
Indianapolis, IN 46278
(317) 290-3100

Iowa
Federal Building, Room 873
210 Walnut Street
Des Moines, IA 50309
(515) 284-4663

Kansas
1201 SW Summit Executive
Court
P.O. Box 4653
Topeka, KS 66604
(913) 271-2700

Kentucky
333771 Corporate Plaza,
Suite 200
Lexington, KY 40503
(606) 224-7300

Louisiana
3727 Government Street
Alexandria, LA 71302
(318) 473-7920

Maine
444 Stillwater Avenue,
Suite 2
P.O. Box 405
Bangor, ME 04402-0405
(207) 990-9106

Maryland
4611 South Dupont Highway
P.O. Box 400
Camden, DE 19934-9998
(302) 697-4300

Massachusetts
451 West Street
Amherst, MA 01002
(413) 253-4300

Michigan
Manly Miles Building,
Room 209
1405 South Harrison Road
East Lansing, MI 48823
(517) 337-6631

Minnesota
410 Farm Credit Building
375 Jackson Street
St. Paul, MN 55101
(612) 290-3842

Mississippi
Federal Building, Suite 831
100 West Capitol
Jackson, MS 39269
(601) 965-4316

Missouri
601 Business Loop, 70 West
Parkade Center, Suite 235
Columbia, MO 65203
(314) 876-0976

Montana
900 Technology Boulevard,
Suite B
P.O. Box 850
Bozeman, MT 59771
(406) 585-2500

Nebraska
Federal Building, Room 308
100 Centennial Mall North
Lincoln, NE 68508
(402) 437-5551

Nevada
194 West Main Street,
Suite F
Woodland, CA 95695-2915
(916) 666-3382

New Hampshire
City Center, Third Floor
89 Main Street
Montpelier, VT 05602
(802) 223-2371

New Jersey
Tarnsfield and Woodlane
Roads
Tarnsfield Plaza, Suite 22
Mt. Holly, NJ 08060
(609) 265-3600

New Mexico
Federal Building, Room 3414
517 Gold Avenue, SW
Albuquerque, NM 87102
(505) 766-2462

New York
Federal Building, Room 871
100 South Clinton Street
Syracuse, NY 13261-7318
(315) 423-5290

North Carolina
4405 South Bland Road,
Suite 260
Raleigh, NC 27609
(919) 790-2731

North Dakota
Federal Building, Room 208
Third and Rosser
P.O. Box 1737
Bismarck, ND 58502
(701) 250-4781

Ohio
Federal Building, Room 507
200 North High Street
Columbus, OH 43215
(614) 469-5606

Oklahoma
USDA Agricultural Center
Office Building
Stillwater, OK 74074
(405) 624-4250

Oregon
Federal Building, Room 1590
1220 SW 3rd Avenue
Portland, OR 97204
(503) 326-2731

Pennsylvania
One Credit Union Place,
Suite 330
Harrisburg, PA 17110-2996
(717) 782-4476

Puerto Rico
New San Juan Center
Building, Room 501
159 Carlos E. Chardon Street
G.P.O. Box 6106G
Hato Rey, PR 00918-5481
(809) 766-5095

Rhode Island
451 West Street
Amherst, MA 01002
(413) 253-4300

South Carolina
Strom Thurmond Federal
Building, Room 1007
1835 Assembly Street
Columbia, SC 29201
(803) 765-5163

South Dakota
Huron Federal Building,
Room 308
200 Fourth Street, SW
Huron, SD 57350
(605) 353-1430

Tennessee
3322 West End Avenue,
Suite 300
Nashville, TN 37203-1071
(615) 736-7341

Texas
Federal Building, Suite 102
101 South Main
Temple, TX 76501
(817) 774-1301

Utah
Federal Building, Room 5438
125 South State Street
Salt Lake City, UT 84138
(801) 524-4063

Vermont
City Center, Third Floor
89 Main Street
Montpelier, VT 05602
(802) 223-2371

Virgin Islands
City Center, Third Floor
89 Main Street
Montpelier, VT 05602
(802) 223-2371

Virginia
Federal Building, Room 8213
400 North 8th Street
Richmond, VA 23240
(804) 771-2451

Washington
Federal Building, Room 319
P.O. Box 2427
Wenatchee, WA 98807
(509) 662-4352

West Virginia
75 High Street
P.O. Box 678
Morgantown, WV 26505
(304) 291-4791

Wisconsin
4949 Kirschling Court
Stevens Point, WI 54481
(715) 345-7600

Wyoming
Federal Building, Room 1005
100 East B Street
P.O. Box 820
Casper, WY 82602
(307) 261-5271

VERY LOW-INCOME HOUSING REPAIR LOANS AND GRANTS

Department of Agriculture
Farmers Home Administration
Washington, DC 20250
(202) 720-1474

Description: Direct loans and project grants for very low-income owners-occupants in rural areas to repair or improve dwellings. Grant recipient must be 62 or older and unable to repay a loan. Applicant's income should range from $8,000 to $19,000 for a single-person household, depending on area's median income.
$ Given: Loan range: $200–$15,000; grant range: $200–$5,000.
Application Information: File Form FmHA 410-4 at your FmHA county office.
Deadline: None
Contact: Consult your local telephone directory under U.S. Government, Department of Agriculture, for FmHA county office number or contact your FmHA state offices.

Alabama
Aronov Building, Room 717
474 South Court Street
Montgomery, AL 36104
(205) 223-7077

Alaska
634 South Bailey, Suite 103
Palmer, AK 99645
(907) 745-2176

Arizona
201 East Indianola, Suite 275
Phoenix, AZ 85012
(602) 640-5086

Agriculture

Arkansas
700 West Capitol
P.O. Box 2778
Little Rock, AR 72203
(501) 324-6281

California
194 West Main Street,
Suite F
Woodland, CA 95695-2915
(916) 666-3382

Colorado
655 Parfet Street,
Room E-100
Lakewood, CO 80215
(303) 236-2801

Connecticut
451 West Street
Amherst, MA 01002
(413) 253-4300

Delaware
4611 South Dupont Highway
P.O. Box 400
Camden, DE 19934-9998
(302) 697-4300

District of Columbia
4611 South Dupont Highway
P.O. Box 400
Camden, DE 19934-9998
(302) 697-4300

Florida
Federal Building
4440 NW 25th Place
P.O. Box 147010
Gainesville, FL 32614-7010
(904) 338-3400

Georgia
Stephens Federal Building
355 East Hancock Avenue
Athens, GA 30610
(404) 546-2162

Hawaii
Federal Building, Room 311
154 Waianuenue Avenue
Hilo, HI 967720
(808) 933-3000

Idaho
3232 Elder Street
Boise, ID 83720
(808) 933-3000

Illinois
Illini Plaza
1817 South Neil Street
Champaign, IL 61820
(217) 398-5235

Indiana
5975 Lakeside Boulevard
Indianapolis, IN 46278
(317) 290-3100

Iowa
Federal Building, Room 873
210 Walnut Street
Des Moines, IA 50309
(515) 284-4663

Kansas
1201 SW Summit Executive
Court
P.O. Box 4653
Topeka, KS 66604
(913) 271-2700

Kentucky
333771 Corporate Plaza,
Suite 200
Lexington, KY 40503
(606) 224-7300

Louisiana
3727 Government Street
Alexandria, LA 71302
(318) 473-7920

Maine
444 Stillwater Avenue,
Suite 2
P.O. Box 405
Bangor, ME 04402-0405
(207) 990-9106

Maryland
4611 South Dupont Highway
P.O. Box 400
Camden, DE 19934-9998
(302) 697-4300

Massachusetts
451 West Street
Amherst, MA 01002
(413) 253-4300

Michigan
Manly Miles Building,
Room 209
1405 South Harrison Road
East Lansing, MI 48823
(517) 337-6631

Minnesota
410 Farm Credit Building
375 Jackson Street
St. Paul, MN 55101
(612) 290-3842

Mississippi
Federal Building, Suite 831
100 West Capitol
Jackson, MS 39269
(601) 965-4316

Missouri
601 Business Loop, 70 West
Parkade Center, Suite 235
Columbia, MO 65203
(314) 876-0976

Montana
900 Technology Boulevard,
Suite B
P.O. Box 850
Bozeman, MT 59771
(406) 585-2500

Nebraska
Federal Building, Room 308
100 Centennial Mall North
Lincoln, NE 68508
(402) 437-5551

Nevada
194 West Main Street,
Suite F
Woodland, CA 95695-2915
(916) 666-3382

New Hampshire
City Center, Third Floor
89 Main Street
Montpelier, VT 05602
(802) 223-2371

New Jersey
Tarnsfield and Woodlane
Roads
Tarnsfield Plaza, Suite 22
Mt. Holly, NJ 08060
(609) 265-3600

New Mexico
Federal Building, Room 3414
517 Gold Avenue, SW
Albuquerque, NM 87102
(505) 766-2462

New York
Federal Building, Room 871
100 South Clinton Street
Syracuse, NY 13261-7318
(315) 423-5290

North Carolina
4405 South Bland Road,
Suite 260
Raleigh, NC 27609
(919) 790-2731

North Dakota
Federal Building, Room 208
Third and Rosser
P.O. Box 1737
Bismarck, ND 58502
(701) 250-4781

Ohio
Federal Building, Room 507
200 North High Street
Columbus, OH 43215
(614) 469-5606

Oklahoma
USDA Agricultural Center
Office Building
Stillwater, OK 74074
(405) 624-4250

Oregon
Federal Building, Room 1590
1220 SW 3rd Avenue
Portland, OR 97204
(503) 326-2731

Pennsylvania
One Credit Union Place,
Suite 330
Harrisburg, PA 17110-2996
(717) 782-4476

Puerto Rico
New San Juan Center
Building, Room 501
159 Carlos E. Chardon Street
G.P.O. Box 6106G
Hato Rey, PR 00918-5481
(809) 766-5095

Rhode Island
451 West Street
Amherst, MA 01002
(413) 253-4300

South Carolina
Strom Thurmond Federal
Building, Room 1007
1835 Assembly Street
Columbia, SC 29201
(803) 765-5163

South Dakota
Huron Federal Building,
Room 308
200 Fourth Street, SW
Huron, SD 57350
(605) 353-1430

Tennessee
3322 West End Avenue,
Suite 300
Nashville, TN 37203-1071
(615) 736-7341

Texas
Federal Building, Suite 102
101 South Main
Temple, TX 76501
(817) 774-1301

Utah
Federal Building, Room 5438
125 South State Street
Salt Lake City, UT 84138
(801) 524-4063

Vermont
City Center, Third Floor
89 Main Street
Montpelier, VT 05602
(802) 223-2371

Virgin Islands
City Center, Third Floor
89 Main Street
Montpelier, VT 05602
(802) 223-2371

VERY LOW- TO MODERATE-INCOME HOUSING LOANS

**Department of
Agriculture**
Farmers Home
Administration
Washington, DC 20250
(202) 447-7967

Description: Direct, guaranteed, and insured loans for construction repair or housing purchase, adequate sewage disposal facilities, and/or sewage water supply for household; weatherization; essential equipment; purchase site for dwelling; and under certain conditions, to finance a manufactured home and its site. Housing debts may be refinanced under certain circumstances. Dwelling financed must be modest in size, design, and cost and located in a rural area with a population of less than 10,000 (25,000 in extreme cases).
$ Given: Loan range: $10,000–$105,000.
Application Information: For direct loans, file with your FmHA county office. For guaranteed loans, contact a local lender.
Deadline: None
Contact: Consult your local telephone directory under U.S. Government, Department of Agriculture, for FmHA county office number or contact your FmHA state offices.

Arkansas
700 West Capitol
P.O. Box 2778
Little Rock, AR 72203
(501) 324-6281

California
194 West Main Street,
Suite F
Woodland, CA 95695-2915
(916) 666-3382

Colorado
655 Parfet Street,
Room E-100
Lakewood, CO 80215
(303) 236-2801

Connecticut
451 West Street
Amherst, MA 01002
(413) 253-4300

Delaware
4611 South Dupont Highway
P.O. Box 400
Camden, DE 19934-9998
(302) 697-4300

District of Columbia
4611 South Dupont Highway
P.O. Box 400
Camden, DE 19934-9998
(302) 697-4300

Florida
Federal Building
4440 NW 25th Place
P.O. Box 147010
Gainesville, FL 32614-7010
(904) 338-3400

Georgia
Stephens Federal Building
355 East Hancock Avenue
Athens, GA 30610
(404) 546-2162

Hawaii
Federal Building, Room 311
154 Waianuenue Avenue
Hilo, HI 967720
(808) 933-3000

Idaho
3232 Elder Street
Boise, ID 83720
(808) 933-3000

Illinois
Illini Plaza
1817 South Neil Street
Champaign, IL 61820
(217) 398-5235

Indiana
5975 Lakeside Boulevard
Indianapolis, IN 46278
(317) 290-3100

Iowa
Federal Building, Room 873
210 Walnut Street
Des Moines, IA 50309
(515) 284-4663

Kansas
1201 SW Summit Executive
Court
P.O. Box 4653
Topeka, KS 66604
(913) 271-2700

Kentucky
333771 Corporate Plaza,
Suite 200
Lexington, KY 40503
(606) 224-7300

Louisiana
3727 Government Street
Alexandria, LA 71302
(318) 473-7920

Maine
444 Stillwater Avenue,
Suite 2
P.O. Box 405
Bangor, ME 04402-0405
(207) 990-9106

Maryland
4611 South Dupont Highway
P.O. Box 400
Camden, DE 19934-9998
(302) 697-4300

Massachusetts
451 West Street
Amherst, MA 01002
(413) 253-4300

Michigan
Manly Miles Building,
Room 209
1405 South Harrison Road
East Lansing, MI 48823
(517) 337-6631

Minnesota
410 Farm Credit Building
375 Jackson Street
St. Paul, MN 55101
(612) 290-3842

Mississippi
Federal Building, Suite 831
100 West Capitol
Jackson, MS 39269
(601) 965-4316

Missouri
601 Business Loop, 70 West
Parkade Center, Suite 235
Columbia, MO 65203
(314) 876-0976

Agriculture

Montana
900 Technology Boulevard,
Suite B
P.O. Box 850
Bozeman, MT 59771
(406) 585-2500

Nebraska
Federal Building, Room 308
100 Centennial Mall North
Lincoln, NE 68508
(402) 437-5551

Nevada
194 West Main Street,
Suite F
Woodland, CA 95695-2915
(916) 666-3382

New Hampshire
City Center, Third Floor
89 Main Street
Montpelier, VT 05602
(802) 223-2371

New Jersey
Tarnsfield and Woodlane
Roads
Tarnsfield Plaza, Suite 22
Mt. Holly, NJ 08060
(609) 265-3600

New Mexico
Federal Building, Room 3414
517 Gold Avenue, SW
Albuquerque, NM 87102
(505) 766-2462

New York
Federal Building, Room 871
100 South Clinton Street
Syracuse, NY 13261-7318
(315) 423-5290

North Carolina
4405 South Bland Road,
Suite 260
Raleigh, NC 27609
(919) 790-2731

North Dakota
Federal Building, Room 208
Third and Rosser
P.O. Box 1737
Bismarck, ND 58502
(701) 250-4781

Ohio
Federal Building, Room 507
200 North High Street
Columbus, OH 43215
(614) 469-5606

Oklahoma
USDA Agricultural Center
Office Building
Stillwater, OK 74074
(405) 624-4250

Oregon
Federal Building, Room 1590
1220 SW 3rd Avenue
Portland, OR 97204
(503) 326-2731

Pennsylvania
One Credit Union Place,
Suite 330
Harrisburg, PA 17110-2996
(717) 782-4476

Puerto Rico
New San Juan Center
Building, Room 501
159 Carlos E. Chardon Street
G.P.O. Box 6106G
Hato Rey, PR 00918-5481
(809) 766-5095

Rhode Island
451 West Street
Amherst, MA 01002
(413) 253-4300

South Carolina
Strom Thurmond Federal
Building, Room 1007
1835 Assembly Street
Columbia, SC 29201
(803) 765-5163

South Dakota
Huron Federal Building,
Room 308
200 Fourth Street, SW
Huron, SD 57350
(605) 353-1430

Tennessee
3322 West End Avenue,
Suite 300
Nashville, TN 37203-1071
(615) 736-7341

Texas
Federal Building, Suite 102
101 South Main
Temple, TX 76501
(817) 774-1301

Utah
Federal Building, Room 5438
125 South State Street
Salt Lake City, UT 84138
(801) 524-4063

Vermont
City Center, Third Floor
89 Main Street
Montpelier, VT 05602
(802) 223-2371

Virgin Islands
City Center, Third Floor
89 Main Street
Montpelier, VT 05602
(802) 223-2371

Virginia
Federal Building, Room 8213
400 North 8th Street
Richmond, VA 23240
(804) 771-2451

Washington
Federal Building, Room 319
P.O. Box 2427
Wenatchee, WA 98807
(509) 662-4352

West Virginia
75 High Street
P.O. Box 678
Morgantown, WV 26505
(304) 291-4791

Wisconsin
4949 Kirschling Court
Stevens Point, WI 54481
(715) 345-7600

Wyoming
Federal Building, Room 1005
100 East B Street
P.O. Box 820
Casper, WY 82602
(307) 261-5271

WATER BANK PROGRAM

Department of Agriculture
Agricultural Stabilization and Conservation Service
P.O. Box 2415
Washington, DC 20013
(202) 720-6221

Description: Direct payments for specified use to landowners and operators of specified types of wetlands in designated migratory waterfowl, nesting, breeding, and feeding areas.
$ Given: $7 to $66 per acre; average: $15 per acre.
Application Information: Apply at your county ASCS office for the county in which the land is located.
Deadline: None
Contact: Your local, state, and/or regional ASCS office

Alabama
Albert C. McDonald
P.O. Box 891
474 South Court Street,
Room 749
Montgomery, AL 36104-4184
(205) 832-7230

Alaska
Teresa Weiland
Alaska State ASCS Office
800 West Evergreen,
Suite 216
Palmer, AK 99645-6389
(907) 745-7982

Arizona
Arden J. Palmer
Arizona State ASCS Office
201 East Indianola, Suite 325
Phoenix, AZ 85012-2054
(602) 640-5200

Arkansas
Dotson Collins
P.O. Box 2781
New Federal Building,
Room 5102
700 West Capitol Street
Little Rock, AR 72201-3225
(501) 378-5220

California
John Smythe
California State ASCS Office
1303 J. Street, Suite 300
Sacramento, CA 95814-2916
(916) 551-1801

Colorado
Lloyd C. Sommerville
Colorado State ASCS Office
655 Parfet Street
Room E 305, Third Floor
Lakewood, CO 80215
(303) 236-2866

Agriculture

Connecticut
David T. Schreiber
88 Day Hill Road
Windsor, CT 06095
(203) 285-8483

Delaware
Earle Isaacs, Jr.
179 West Chestnut Hill Road,
Suite 7
Newark, DE 19713-2295
(302) 573-6536

Florida
Eugene C. Badger
P.O. Box 141030
4440 Northwest 25th Place,
Suite 1
Gainesville, FL 32614-1030
(904) 372-8549

Georgia
James E. Harrison
P.O. Box 1907
Federal Building, Room 102
344 East Hancock Avenue
Athens, GA 30601-2775
(404) 546-2266

Hawaii
Ralph K. Ajifu
Hawaii State ASCS Office
300 Ala Moana Boulevard,
Room 4202
P.O. Box 50008
Honolulu, HI 96850-0002
(808) 551-2644

Idaho
Trent Clark
Idaho State ASCS Office
3220 Elder Street
Boise, ID 83705-5820
(208) 334-1486

Illinois
William G. Beeler
P.O. Box 19273
3500 Wabash Avenue
Springfield, IL 62707
(217) 492-4180

Indiana
Don Villwoch
Indiana State ASCS Office
5981 Lakeside Boulevard
Indianapolis, IN 46278-1996
(317) 290-3030

Iowa
Robert Furleigh
10500 Buena Vista Court
Urbandale, IA 50322
(515) 254-1540

Kansas
Frank A. Mosier
Kansas State ASCS Office
2601 Anderson Avenue
Manhattan, KS 66502-2898
(913) 539-3531

Kentucky
Kenneth Ashby
Kentucky State ASCS Office
771 Corporate Drive,
Suite 100
Lexington, KY 40503-5477
(606) 233-2726

Louisiana
Willie F. Cooper
3737 Government Street
Alexandria, LA 71302-3395
(318) 473-7721

Maine
David P. Staples
44 Stillwater Avenue
P.O. Box 406
Bangor, ME 04401-3521
(207) 942-0342

Maryland
James Richardson
Rivers Center
10270 B Columbia Road
Columbia, MD 21046-9998
(301) 381-4550

Massachusetts
Raymond E. Duda
451 West Street
Amherst, MA 01002-2953
(413) 256-0232

Michigan
David Conklin
1405 South Harrison Road,
Room 116
East Lansing, MI 48823-5202
(517) 337-6659

Minnesota
Donald L. Friedrich
Minnesota State ASCS Office
400 Farm Credit Service
Building
375 Jackson Street
St. Paul, MN 55101-1852
(612) 290-3651

Mississippi
Charles R. Hull
Mississippi State ASCS
Office
6310 I-55 North
Jackson, MS 39236
(601) 965-4300

Missouri
Morris G. Westfall
601 Parkdale Plaza Business
Loop
70 West, Suite 225
Columbia, MO 65203
(314) 875-5201

Montana
Donald Anderson
P.O. Box 670
Bozeman, MT 59771-0670
(406) 587-6872

Nebraska
John Neuberger
Nebraska State ASCS Office
P.O. Box 57975
Lincoln, NE 68505-7975
(402) 437-5581

Nevada
C. Richard Capurro
Nevada State ASCS Office
1755 East Plumb Lane,
Suite 202
Reno, NV 89502-3207

New Hampshire
Peter M. Thomson
USDA - New Hampshire
State ASCS Office
22 Bridge Street,
Fourth Floor
Concord, NH 03301-5605
(603) 224-7941

New Jersey
Peter de Wilde
Mastoris Professional Plaza
163 Route 130
Building 1, Suite E
Bordentown, NJ 08505
(609) 298-3446

New Mexico
David Turner
New Mexico State ASCS
Office
P.O. Box 1458
Federal Building, Room 4408
517 Gold Avenue, SW
Albuquerque, NM
87102-3156
(505) 766-2472

New York
John Steele
811 James H. Hanley Federal
Building
100 South Clinton Street
Syracuse, NY 13260-0066
(315) 423-5176

North Carolina
John J. Cooper
P.O. Box 27327
Federal Building, Suite 175
4407 Bland Road
Raleigh, NC 27611
(919) 790-2957

North Dakota
Robert J. Christiman
North Dakota State ASCS
Office
P.O. Box 3046
Fargo, ND 58108-3046
(701) 239-5224

Ohio
Dorothy Leslie
Federal Building, Room 540
200 North High Street
Columbus, OH 43215-2495
(614) 469-6735

Oklahoma
Bart Brorsen
USDA Agriculture Center
Building
Farm Road and McFarland
Street
Stillwater, OK 74074-2531
(405) 624-4110

Oregon
Glen E. Stonebrink
Oregon State ASCS Office
P.O. Box 1300
Tualatin, OR 97062-1300
(503) 692-6830

Pennsylvania
Donald Unangst
One Credit Union Place,
Suite 320
228 Walnut Street
Harrisburg, PA 17101-1701
(717) 782-4547

Rhode Island
Alfred R. Bettencourt, Jr.
Aldeic Complex
60 Quaker Lane
West Warwick, RI 02893-2120
(401) 828-8232

South Carolina
Thomas H. Herlong
Strom Thurmond Mall
Columbia, SC 29207
(803) 765-5186

South Dakota
Dean W. Anderson
Federal Building, Room 208
200 Fourth Street, SW
Huron, SD 57350-2478
(605) 353-1092

Tennessee
Charles Ben Thompson
U.S. Courthouse, Room 579
801 Broadway
Nashville, TN 37203-3816
(615) 736-5555

Texas
Donnie Bownan Aeting
Texas State ASCS Office
P.O. Box 2900
College Station, TX
77841-0001
(409) 260-9207

Utah
Royal K. Norman
Utah State ASCS Office
P.O. Box 11547
Salt Lake City, UT
84147-2547
(801) 524-5013

Vermont
David Newton
Executive Square Office
Building
346 Shelburne Street
Burlington, VT 05401-4495
(802) 658-2803

Virginia
Mahlon K. Rudy
Federal Building, Room 7105
400 North 8th Street
Richmond, VA 23240-9990
(804) 771-2581

Washington
Robert Deife
Washington State ASCS
Office
Rock Pointe Tower, Suite 568
316 West Boone Avenue
Spokane, WA 99201-2350
(509) 353-1092

West Virginia
Donald W. Brown
P.O. Box 1049
New Federal Building,
Room 239
75 High Street
Morgantown, WV 26505-7558
(304) 291-4351

Wisconsin
Peter C. Senn
Wisconsin State ASCS Office
6515 Watts Road, Room 100
Madison, WI 53719-2797
(608) 264-5301

Wyoming
Harold Hellbaum
P.O. Box 920
100 East B. Street,
Room 3001
Casper, WY 82602-0920
(307) 261-5231

Caribbean Area
Herberto J. Martinez
Caribbean Area ASCS Office
Cobran's Plaza, Suite 309
1609 Ponce DeLeon Avenue
Santurce, Puerto Rico
00909-0001
(809) 729-6872

WHEAT PRODUCTION STABILIZATION

Department of Agriculture
Agricultural Stabilization
and Conservation Service
P.O. Box 2415
Washington, DC 20013
(202) 720-4417

Description: Direct payments with unrestricted use to owners, landlords, tenants, or sharecroppers on farms. Commodity planted must meet program requirements as announced by the secretary.
$ Given: Up to $250,000 per person.
Deadline: Dates vary from state to state.
Contact: Your local, state, and/or regional ASCS office

Alabama
Albert C. McDonald
P.O. Box 891
474 South Court Street,
Room 749
Montgomery, AL 36104-4184
(205) 832-7230

Alaska
Teresa Weiland
Alaska State ASCS Office
800 West Evergreen,
Suite 216
Palmer, AK 99645-6389
(907) 745-7982

Arizona
Arden J. Palmer
Arizona State ASCS Office
201 East Indianola, Suite 325
Phoenix, AZ 85012-2054
(602) 640-5200

Arkansas
Dotson Collins
P.O. Box 2781
New Federal Building,
Room 5102
700 West Capitol Street
Little Rock, AR 72201-3225
(501) 378-5220

California
John Smythe
California State ASCS Office
1303 J. Street, Suite 300
Sacramento, CA 95814-2916
(916) 551-1801

Colorado
Lloyd C. Sommerville
Colorado State ASCS Office
655 Parfet Street
Room E 305, Third Floor
Lakewood, CO 80215
(303) 236-2866

Connecticut
David T. Schreiber
88 Day Hill Road
Windsor, CT 06095
(203) 285-8483

Delaware
Earle Isaacs, Jr.
179 West Chestnut Hill Road,
Suite 7
Newark, DE 19713-2295
(302) 573-6536

Florida
Eugene C. Badger
P.O. Box 141030
4440 Northwest 25th Place,
Suite 1
Gainesville, FL 32614-1030
(904) 372-8549

Georgia
James E. Harrison
P.O. Box 1907
Federal Building, Room 102
344 East Hancock Avenue
Athens, GA 30601-2775
(404) 546-2266

Hawaii
Ralph K. Ajifu
Hawaii State ASCS Office
300 Ala Moana Boulevard,
Room 4202
P.O. Box 50008
Honolulu, HI 96850-0002
(808) 551-2644

Idaho
Trent Clark
Idaho State ASCS Office
3220 Elder Street
Boise, ID 83705-5820
(208) 334-1486

Illinois
William G. Beeler
P.O. Box 19273
3500 Wabash Avenue
Springfield, IL 62707
(217) 492-4180

Indiana
Don Villwoch
Indiana State ASCS Office
5981 Lakeside Boulevard
Indianapolis, IN 46278-1996
(317) 290-3030

Iowa
Robert Furleigh
10500 Buena Vista Court
Urbandale, IA 50322
(515) 254-1540

Kansas
Frank A. Mosier
Kansas State ASCS Office
2601 Anderson Avenue
Manhattan, KS 66502-2898
(913) 539-3531

Kentucky
Kenneth Ashby
Kentucky State ASCS Office
771 Corporate Drive,
Suite 100
Lexington, KY 40503-5477
(606) 233-2726

Louisiana
Willie F. Cooper
3737 Government Street
Alexandria, LA 71302-3395
(318) 473-7721

Maine
David P. Staples
44 Stillwater Avenue
P.O. Box 406
Bangor, ME 04401-3521
(207) 942-0342

Maryland
James Richardson
Rivers Center
10270 B Columbia Road
Columbia, MD 21046-9998
(301) 381-4550

Massachusetts
Raymond E. Duda
451 West Street
Amherst, MA 01002-2953
(413) 256-0232

Michigan
David Conklin
1405 South Harrison Road,
Room 116
East Lansing, MI 48823-5202
(517) 337-6659

Agriculture

Minnesota
Donald L. Friedrich
Minnesota State ASCS Office
400 Farm Credit Service
Building
375 Jackson Street
St. Paul, MN 55101-1852
(612) 290-3651

Mississippi
Charles R. Hull
Mississippi State ASCS
Office
6310 I-55 North
Jackson, MS 39236
(601) 965-4300

Missouri
Morris G. Westfall
601 Parkdale Plaza Business
Loop
70 West, Suite 225
Columbia, MO 65203
(314) 875-5201

Montana
Donald Anderson
P.O. Box 670
Bozeman, MT 59771-0670
(406) 587-6872

Nebraska
John Neuberger
Nebraska State ASCS Office
P.O. Box 57975
Lincoln, NE 68505-7975
(402) 437-5581

Nevada
C. Richard Capurro
Nevada State ASCS Office
1755 East Plumb Lane,
Suite 202
Reno, NV 89502-3207

New Hampshire
Peter M. Thomson
USDA - New Hampshire
State ASCS Office
22 Bridge Street, Fourth
Floor
Concord, NH 03301-5605
(603) 224-7941

New Jersey
Peter de Wilde
Mastoris Professional Plaza
163 Route 130
Building 1, Suite E
Bordentown, NJ 08505
(609) 298-3446

New Mexico
David Turner
New Mexico State ASCS
Office
P.O. Box 1458
Federal Building, Room 4408
517 Gold Avenue, SW
Albuquerque, NM
87102-3156
(505) 766-2472

New York
John Steele
811 James H. Hanley Federal
Building
100 South Clinton Street
Syracuse, NY 13260-0066
(315) 423-5176

North Carolina
John J. Cooper
P.O. Box 27327
Federal Building, Suite 175
4407 Bland Road
Raleigh, NC 27611
(919) 790-2957

North Dakota
Robert J. Christiman
North Dakota State ASCS
Office
P.O. Box 3046
Fargo, ND 58108-3046
(701) 239-5224

Ohio
Dorothy Leslie
Federal Building, Room 540
200 North High Street
Columbus, OH 43215-2495
(614) 469-6735

Oklahoma
Bart Brorsen
USDA Agriculture Center
Building
Farm Road and McFarland
Street
Stillwater, OK 74074-2531
(405) 624-4110

Oregon
Glen E. Stonebrink
Oregon State ASCS Office
P.O. Box 1300
Tualatin, OR 97062-1300
(503) 692-6830

Pennsylvania
Donald Unangst
One Credit Union Place,
Suite 320
228 Walnut Street
Harrisburg, PA 17101-1701
(717) 782-4547

Rhode Island
Alfred R. Bettencourt, Jr.
Aldeic Complex
60 Quaker Lane
West Warwick, RI 02893-2120
(401) 828-8232

South Carolina
Thomas H. Herlong
Strom Thurmond Mall
Columbia, SC 29207
(803) 765-5186

South Dakota
Dean W. Anderson
Federal Building, Room 208
200 Fourth Street, SW
Huron, SD 57350-2478
(605) 353-1092

Tennessee
Charles Ben Thompson
U.S. Courthouse, Room 579
801 Broadway
Nashville, TN 37203-3816
(615) 736-5555

Texas
Donnie Bownan Aeting
Texas State ASCS Office
P.O. Box 2900
College Station, TX
77841-0001
(409) 260-9207

Utah
Royal K. Norman
Utah State ASCS Office
P.O. Box 11547
Salt Lake City, UT
84147-2547
(801) 524-5013

Vermont
David Newton
Executive Square Office
Building
346 Shelburne Street
Burlington, VT 05401-4495
(802) 658-2803

Virginia
Mahlon K. Rudy
Federal Building, Room 7105
400 North 8th Street
Richmond, VA 23240-9990
(804) 771-2581

Washington
Robert Deife
Washington State ASCS
Office
Rock Pointe Tower, Suite 568
316 West Boone Avenue
Spokane, WA 99201-2350
(509) 353-1092

West Virginia
Donald W. Brown
P.O. Box 1049
New Federal Building,
Room 239
75 High Street
Morgantown, WV 26505-7558
(304) 291-4351

Wisconsin
Peter C. Senn
Wisconsin State ASCS Office
6515 Watts Road, Room 100
Madison, WI 53719-2797
(608) 264-5301

Wyoming
Harold Hellbaum
P.O. Box 920
100 East B. Street,
Room 3001
Casper, WY 82602-0920
(307) 261-5231

Caribbean Area
Herberto J. Martinez
Caribbean Area ASCS Office
Cobran's Plaza, Suite 309
1609 Ponce DeLeon Avenue
Santurce, Puerto Rico
00909-0001
(809) 729-6872

Community Development

Assistance is widely available from the federal government for community development for the following:

1. Assistance for projects that promote long-term economic development and employment, as well as research projects that determine causes of unemployment in the United States.
2. Loans to businesses for local development, construction, or modernization of buildings; for projects serving low-income areas with high unemployment or that have experienced natural disasters; or for projects serving disadvantaged individuals

You will need to consult the list of addresses in this chapter for your nearest local or regional Small Business Administration office or Economic Development office.

BUSINESS LOANS FOR SBA PROGRAM PARTICIPANTS

**Small Business
Administration
Loan Policy and
Procedures Branch**
409 3rd Street, SW
Washington, DC 20416
(202) 205-6570

Description: Direct, guaranteed, and insured loans to small business concerns owned by socially and economically disadvantaged persons to construct, expand, or convert facilities; or to acquire equipment, building materials, or supplies. Loans for working capital limited to manufacturers.
$ Given: Direct loans to $150,000; guaranteed loans to $750,000; average: $113,636.
Application Information: Write for guidelines.
Deadline: None
Contact: Your state and/or regional office

Alabama
1375 Peachtree Street, NE,
Fifth Floor
Atlanta, GA 30367-8102
(404) 347-2797

Alaska
2615 4th Avenue, Room 440
Seattle, WA 98121
(206) 553-5676

Arizona
71 Stevenson Street,
Twentieth Floor
San Francisco, CA
94105-2989
(415) 744-6402

Arkansas
8625 King George Drive,
Building C
Dallas, TX 75235-3391
(214) 767-7633

California
71 Stevenson Street,
Twentieth Floor
San Francisco, CA
94105-2939
(415) 744-6402

Colorado
999 18th Street, Suite 701
Denver, CO 80202
(303) 294-7186

Connecticut
155 Federal Street,
Ninth Floor
Boston, MA 02110
(617) 451-2023

Delaware
475 Allendale Road,
Suite 201
King of Prussia, PA 19406
(215) 962-3700

District of Columbia
475 Allendale Road,
Suite 201
King of Prussia, PA 19406
(215) 962-3700

Florida
1375 Peachtree Street, NE,
Fifth Floor
Atlanta, GA 30367-8102
(404) 347-2797

Georgia
1375 Peachtree Street, NE,
Fifth Floor
Atlanta, GA 30367-8102
(404) 347-2797

Hawaii
71 Stevenson Street,
Twentieth Floor
San Francisco, CA
94105-2939
(415) 744-6402

Idaho
2615 4th Avenue, Room 440
Seattle, WA 98121
(206) 553-5676

Illinois
Federal Building
300 South Riverside Plaza,
1975 South
Chicago, IL 60606-6617
(312) 353-5000

Indiana
Federal Building
300 South Riverside Plaza,
1975 South
Chicago, IL 60606-6617
(312) 353-5000

Community Development

Iowa
911 Walnut Street,
Thirteenth Floor
Kansas City, MO 64106
(816) 426-3608

Kansas
911 Walnut Street,
Thirteenth Floor
Kansas City, MO 64106
(816) 426-3608

Kentucky
1375 Peachtree Street, NE,
Fifth Floor
Atlanta, GA 30367-8102
(404) 347-2797

Louisiana
8625 King George Drive,
Building C
Dallas, TX 75235-3391
(214) 767-7633

Maine
155 Federal Street,
Ninth Floor
Boston, MA 02110
(617) 451-2023

Maryland
475 Allendale Road,
Suite 201
King of Prussia, PA 19406
(215) 962-3700

Massachusetts
155 Federal Street,
Ninth Floor
Boston, MA 02110
(617) 451-2023

Michigan
Federal Building
300 South Riverside Plaza,
1975 South
Chicago, IL 60606-6617
(312) 353-5000

Minnesota
Federal Building
300 South Riverside Plaza,
1975 South
Chicago, IL 60606-6617
(312) 353-5000

Mississippi
1375 Peachtree Street, NE,
Fifth Floor
Atlanta, GA 30367-8102
(404) 347-2797

Missouri
911 Walnut Street,
Thirteenth Floor
Kansas City, MO 64106
(816) 426-3608

Montana
999 18th Street, Suite 701
Denver, CO 80202
(303) 294-7186

Nebraska
911 Walnut Street,
Thirteenth Floor
Kansas City, MO 64106
(816) 426-3608

Nevada
71 Stevenson Street,
Twentieth Floor
San Francisco CA 94105-2939
(415) 744-6402

New Hampshire
155 Federal Street,
Ninth Floor
Boston, MA 02110
(617) 451-2023

New Jersey
26 Federal Plaza,
Room 31-08
New York, NY 10278
(212) 264-7772

New Mexico
8625 King George Drive,
Building C
Dallas, TX 75235-3391
(214) 767-7633

New York
26 Federal Plaza,
Room 31-08
New York, NY 10278
(212) 264-7772

North Carolina
1375 Peachtree Street, NE,
Fifth Floor
Atlanta, GA 30367-8102
(404) 347-2797

North Dakota
999 18th Street, Suite 701
Denver, CO 80202
(303) 294-7186

Ohio
Federal Building
300 South Riverside Plaza,
1975 South
Chicago, IL 60606-6617
(312) 353-5000

Oklahoma
8625 King George Drive,
Building C
Dallas, TX 75235-3391
(214) 767-7633

Oregon
2615 4th Avenue, Room 440
Seattle, WA 98121
(206) 553-5676

Pacific Islands
71 Stevenson Street,
Twentieth Floor
San Francisco, CA
94105-2939
(415) 744-6402

Pennsylvania
475 Allendale Road,
Suite 201
King of Prussia, PA 19406
(215) 962-3700

Puerto Rico
26 Federal Plaza,
Room 31-08
New York, NY 10278
(212) 264-7772

Rhode Island
155 Federal Street,
Ninth Floor
Boston, MA 02110
(617) 451-2023

South Carolina
1375 Peachtree Street, NE,
Fifth Floor
Atlanta, GA 30367-8102
(404) 347-2797

South Dakota
999 18th Street, Suite 701
Denver, CO 80202
(303) 294-7186

Tennessee
1375 Peachtree Suite, NE,
Fifth Floor
Atlanta, GA 30367-8102
(404) 347-2797

Texas
8625 King George Drive,
Building C
Dallas, TX 75235-3391
(214) 767-7633

Utah
999 18th Street, Suite 701
Denver, CO 80202
(303) 294-7186

Vermont
155 Federal Street, Ninth
Floor
Boston, MA 02110
(617) 451-2023

Virgin Islands
26 Federal Plaza,
Room 31-08
New York, NY 10278
(212) 264-7772

Virginia
475 Allendale Road,
Suite 201
King of Prussia, PA 19406
(215) 962-3700

Washington
2615 4th Avenue, Room 440
Seattle, WA 98121
(206) 553-5676

West Virginia
475 Allendale Road,
Suite 201
King of Prussia, PA 19406
(215) 962-3700

Wisconsin
Federal Building
300 South Riverside Plaza,
1975 South
Chicago, IL 60606-6617
(312) 353-5000

Wyoming
999 18th Street, Suite 701
Denver, CO 80202
(303) 294-7186

ECONOMIC DEVELOPMENT—BUSINESS DEVELOPMENT ASSISTANCE

Department of Commerce
Herbert C. Hoover
Building, Room H7830B
Washington, DC 20230
(202) 377-4731

Description: Loan guarantees and grants to businesses for projects when financial assistance is not available from other sources. Business must create or retain permanent jobs; must establish or expand plants in redevelopment areas; must not relocate with a resultant loss of employment; must not produce a product for which there is no market demand; and must not use funds for research and development or marketing.

$ Given: Grant range: $500,000–$111 million; average: $2 million.

Application Information: Preliminary proposal followed by detailed proposal.

Deadline: June 30

Contact: John McNamee, Director, Credit and Debt Management Division, Economic Development Administration, above address

ECONOMIC DEVELOPMENT—PUBLIC WORKS IMPACT PROGRAM

Economic Development Administration
Public Works Division
Herbert C. Hoover
Building, Room H7326
Washington, DC 20230
(202) 377-5265

Description: Project grants to redevelop an area and promote long-term economic development and employment. Renovation or construction of public works and development facilities must provide immediate jobs in project area.

$ Given: Priority given to projects of $600,000 or less.

Application Information: Contact your economic development representative at the appropriate regional office listed below, or contact David L. McIlwain, Director, at the above address.

Deadline: 30 days after formal application has been invited.

Contact: Your appropriate regional and/or state office

Community Development

Alabama
Charles E. Oxley
Regional Director
401 West Peachtree Street,
NW, Suite 1820
Atlanta, GA 30308-3510
(404) 730-3002

Alaska
John D. Woodward
Regional Director
915 Second Avenue
Jackson Federal Building,
Suite 1856
Seattle, WA 98174
(206) 553-0596

American Samoa
John D. Woodward
Regional Director
915 Second Avenue
Jackson Federal Building,
Suite 1856
Seattle, WA 98174
(206) 553-0596

Arizona
John D. Woodward
Regional Director
915 Second Avenue
Jackson Federal Building,
Suite 1856
Seattle, WA 98174
(206) 553-0596

Arkansas
Henry N. Troell
Regional Director
Grant Building, Suite 201
611 East Sixth Street
Austin, TX 78701
(512) 482-5461

California
John D. Woodward
Regional Director
915 Second Avenue
Jackson Federal Building,
Suite 1856
Seattle, WA 98174
(206) 553-0596

Colorado
Steven R. Brennen
Regional Director
1244 Speer Boulevard,
Room 670
Denver, CO 80204
(303) 844-4714

Connecticut
John E. Corrigan
Regional Director
Curtis Center, Independence
Square West
6th and Walnut Street
Philadelphia, PA 19106
(215) 597-4603

Delaware
John E. Corrigan
Regional Director
Curtis Center, Independence
Square West
6th and Walnut Street
Philadelphia, PA 19106
(215) 597-4603

District of Columbia
John E. Corrigan
Regional Director
Curtis Center, Independence
Square West
6th and Walnut Street
Philadelphia, PA 19106
(215) 597-4603

Florida
Charles E. Oxley
Regional Director
401 West Peachtree Street,
NW, Suite 1820
Atlanta, GA 30308-3510
(404) 730-3002

Georgia
Charles E. Oxley
Regional Director
401 West Peachtree Street,
NW, Suite 1820
Atlanta, GA 30308-3510
(404) 730-3002

Guam
John D. Woodward
Regional Director
915 Second Avenue
Jackson Federal Building,
Suite 1856
Seattle, WA 98174
(206) 553-0596

Hawaii
John D. Woodward
Regional Director
915 Second Avenue
Jackson Federal Building,
Suite 1856
Seattle, WA 98174
(206) 553-0596

Idaho
John D. Woodward
Regional Director
915 Second Avenue
Jackson Federal Building,
Suite 1856
Seattle, WA 98174
(206) 553-0596

Illinois
Edward G. Jeep
Regional Director
111 North Canal, Suite 855
Chicago IL 60606-7204
(312) 353-7706

Community Development

Indiana
Edward G. Jeep
Regional Director
111 North Canal, Suite 855
Chicago, IL 60606-7204
(312) 353-7706

Iowa
Steven R. Brennen
Regional Director
1244 Speer Boulevard,
Room 670
Denver, CO 80204
(303) 844-4714

Kansas
Steven R. Brennen
Regional Director
1244 Speer Boulevard,
Room 670
Denver, CO 80204
(303) 844-4714

Kentucky
Charles E. Oxley
Regional Director
401 West Peachtree Street,
NW, Suite 1820
Atlanta, GA 30308-3510
(404) 730-3002

Louisiana
Henry N. Troell
Regional Director
Grant Building, Suite 201
611 East Sixth Street
Austin, TX 78701
(512) 482-5461

Maine
John E. Corrigan
Regional Director
Curtis Center, Independence
Square West
6th and Walnut Street
Philadelphia, PA 19106
(215) 597-4603

Marshall Islands
John D. Woodward
Regional Director
915 Second Avenue
Jackson Federal Building,
Suite 1856
Seattle, WA 98174
(206) 553-0596

Maryland
John E. Corrigan
Regional Director
Curtis Center, Independence
Square West
6th and Walnut Street
Philadelphia, PA 19106
(215) 597-4603

Massachusetts
John E. Corrigan
Regional Director
Curtis Center, Independence
Square West
6th and Walnut Street
Philadelphia, PA 19106
(215) 597-4603

Michigan
Edward C. Jeep
Regional Director
111 North Canal, Suite 855
Chicago, IL 60606-7204
(312) 353-7706

Minnesota
Edward G. Jeep
Regional Director
111 North Canal, Suite 855
Chicago, IL 60606-7204
(312) 353-7706

Mississippi
Charles E. Oxley
Regional Director
401 West Peachtree Street,
NW, Suite 1820
Atlanta, GA 30308-3510
(404) 730-3002

Missouri
Steven R. Brennen
Regional Director
1244 Speer Boulevard,
Room 670
Denver, CO 80204
(303) 844-4714

Montana
Steven R. Brennen
Regional Director
1244 Speer Boulevard,
Room 670
Denver, CO 80204
(303) 844-4714

Nebraska
Steven R. Brennen
Regional Director
1244 Speer Boulevard,
Room 670
Denver, CO 80204
(303) 844-4714

Nevada
John D. Woodward
Regional Director
915 Second Avenue
Jackson Federal Building,
Suite 1856
Seattle, WA 98174
(206) 553-0596

New Hampshire
John E. Corrigan
Regional Director
Curtis Center, Independence
Square West
6th and Walnut Street
Philadelphia, PA 19106
(215) 597-4603

New Jersey
John E. Corrigan
Regional Director
Curtis Center, Independence
Square West
6th and Walnut Street
Philadelphia, PA 19106
(215) 597-4603

New Mexico
Henry N. Troell
Regional Director
Grant Building, Suite 201
611 East Sixth Street
Austin, TX 78701
(512) 482-5461

New York
John E. Corrigan
Regional Director
Curtis Center, Independence
Square West
6th and Walnut Street
Philadelphia, PA 19106
(215) 597-4603

North Carolina
Charles E. Oxley
Regional Director
401 West Peachtree Street,
NW, Suite 1820
Atlanta, GA 30308-3510
(404) 730-3002

North Dakota
Steven R. Brennen
Regional Director
1244 Speer Boulevard,
Room 670
Denver, CO 80204
(303) 844-4714

Northern Mariana Islands
John D. Woodward
Regional Director
915 Second Avenue
Jackson Federal Building,
Suite 1856
Seattle, WA 98174
(206) 553-0596

Ohio
Edward G. Jeep
Regional Director
111 North Canal, Suite 855
Chicago, IL 60606-7204
(312) 353-7706

Oklahoma
Henry N. Troell
Regional Director
Grant Building, Suite 201
611 East Sixth Street
Austin, TX 78701
(512) 482-5461

Oregon
John D. Woodward
Regional Director
915 Second Avenue
Jackson Federal Building,
Suite 1856
Seattle, WA 98174
(206) 553-0596

Pennsylvania
John E. Corrigan
Regional Director
Curtis Center, Independence
Square West
6th and Walnut Street
Philadelphia, PA 19106
(215) 597-4603

Puerto Rico
John E. Corrigan
Regional Director
Curtis Center, Independence
Square West
6th and Walnut Street
Philadelphia, PA 19106
(215) 597-4603

Rhode Island
John E. Corrigan
Regional Director
Curtis Center, Independence
Square West
6th and Walnut Street
Philadelphia, PA 19106
(215) 597-4603

South Carolina
Charles E. Oxley
Regional Director
401 West Peachtree Street,
NW, Suite 1820
Atlanta, GA 30308-3510
(404) 730-3002

South Dakota
Steven R. Brennen
Regional Director
1244 Speer Boulevard,
Room 670
Denver, CO 80204
(303) 844-4714

Tennessee
Charles E. Oxley
Regional Director
401 West Peachtree, NW,
Suite 1820
Atlanta, GA 30308-3510
(404) 730-3002

Texas
Henry N. Troell
Regional Director
Grant Building, Suite 201
611 East Sixth Street
Austin, TX 78701
(512) 482-5461

Utah
Steven R. Brennen
Regional Director
1244 Speer Boulevard,
Room 670
Denver, CO 80204
(303) 844-4714

Vermont
John E. Corrigan
Regional Director
Curtis Center, Independence
Square West
6th and Walnut Street
Philadelphia, PA 19106
(215) 597-4603

Virgin Islands
John E. Corrigan
Regional Director
Curtis Center, Independence
Square West
6th and Walnut Street
Philadelphia, PA 19106
(215) 597-4603

Virginia
John E. Corrigan
Regional Director
Curtis Center, Independence
Square West
6th and Walnut Street
Philadelphia, PA 19106
(215) 597-4603

Washington
John D. Woodward
Regional Director
915 Second Avenue
Jackson Federal Building,
Suite 1856
Seattle, WA 98174
(206) 553-0596

West Virginia
John E. Corrigan
Regional Director
Curtis Center, Independence
Square West
6th and Walnut Street
Philadelphia, PA 19106
(215) 597-4603

Wisconsin
Edward G. Jeep
Regional Director
111 North Canal, Suite 855
Chicago, IL 60606-7204
(312) 353-7706

Wyoming
Steven R. Brennen
Regional Director
1244 Speer Boulevard,
Room 670
Denver, CO 80204
(303) 844-4714

ECONOMIC INJURY DISASTER LOANS

**Small Business
Administration**
Office of Disaster
Assistance
409 3rd Street, SW
Washington, DC 20416
(202) 205-6734

Description: Direct, guaranteed, and insured loans for small businesses or agricultural cooperatives that are victims of drought, to pay liabilities from disaster or to provide working capital to continue operations until conditions return to normal.
$ Given: Direct loans to $500,000; average: $70,667.
Application Information: Write for guidelines.
Deadline: N/A
Contact: Your state and/or regional office

Alabama
1375 Peachtree Street, NE,
Fifth Floor
Atlanta, GA 30367-8102
(404) 347-2797

Alaska
2615 4th Avenue, Room 440
Seattle, WA 98121
(206) 553-5676

Arizona
71 Stevenson Street,
Twentieth Floor
San Francisco, CA
94105-2939
(415) 744-6402

Arkansas
8625 King George Drive,
Building C
Dallas, TX 75235-3391
(214) 767-7633

California
71 Stevenson Street,
Twentieth Floor
San Francisco, CA
94105-2939
(415) 744-6402

Colorado
999 18th Street, Suite 701
Denver, CO 80202
(303) 294-7186

Connecticut
155 Federal Street,
Ninth Floor
Boston, MA 02110
(617) 451-2023

Delaware
475 Allendale Road,
Suite 201
King of Prussia, PA 19406
(215) 962-3700

District of Columbia
475 Allendale Road,
Suite 201
King of Prussia, PA 19406
(215) 962-3700

Florida
1375 Peachtree Street, NE,
Fifth Floor
Atlanta, GA 30367-8102
(404) 347-2797

Georgia
1375 Peachtree Street, NE,
Fifth Floor
Atlanta, GA 30367-8102
(404) 347-2797

Hawaii
71 Stevenson Street,
Twentieth Floor
San Francisco, CA
94105-2939
(415) 744-6402

Idaho
2615 4th Avenue, Room 440
Seattle, WA 98121
(206) 553-5676

Illinois
Federal Building
300 South Riverside Plaza,
1975 South
Chicago, IL 60606-6617
(312) 353-5000

Iowa
911 Walnut Street,
Thirteenth Floor
Kansas City, MO 64106
(816) 426-3608

Indiana
Federal Building
300 South Riverside Plaza,
1975 South
Chicago, IL 60606-6617
(312) 353-5000

Kansas
911 Walnut Street,
Thirteenth Floor
Kansas City, MO 64106
(816) 426-3608

Kentucky
1375 Peachtree Street, NE,
Fifth Floor
Atlanta, GA 30367-8102
(404) 347-2797

Louisiana
8625 King George Drive,
Building C
Dallas, TX 75235-3391
(214) 767-7633

Maine
155 Federal Street,
Ninth Floor
Boston, MA 02110
(617) 451-2023

Maryland
475 Allendale Road,
Suite 201
King of Prussia, PA 19406
(215) 962-3700

Massachusetts
155 Federal Street,
Ninth Floor
Boston, MA 02110
(617) 451-2023

Michigan
Federal Building
300 South Riverside Plaza,
1975 South
Chicago, IL 60606-6617
(312) 353-5000

Minnesota
Federal Building
300 South Riverside Plaza,
1975 South
Chicago, IL 60606-6617
(312) 353-5000

Mississippi
1375 Peachtree Street, NE,
Fifth Floor
Atlanta, GA 30367-8102
(404) 347-2797

Community Development

Missouri
911 Walnut Street,
Thirteenth Floor
Kansas City, MO 64106
(816) 426-3608

Montana
999 18th Street, Suite 701
Denver, CO 80202
(303) 294-7186

Nebraska
911 Walnut Street,
Thirteenth Floor
Kansas City, MO 64106
(816) 426-3608

Nevada
71 Stevenson Street,
Twentieth Floor
San Francisco, CA
94105-2939
(415) 744-6402

New Hampshire
155 Federal Street,
Ninth Floor
Boston, MA 02110
(617) 451-2023

New Jersey
26 Federal Plaza,
Room 31-08
New York, NY 10278
(212) 264-7772

New Mexico
8625 King George Drive,
Building C
Dallas, TX 75235-3391
(214) 767-7633

New York
26 Federal Plaza,
Room 31-08
New York, NY 10278
(212) 264-7772

North Carolina
1375 Peachtree Street, NE,
Fifth Floor
Atlanta, GA 30367-8102
(404) 347-2797

North Dakota
999 18th Street, Suite 701
Denver, CO 80202
(303) 294-7186

Ohio
Federal Building
300 South Riverside Plaza,
1975 South
Chicago, IL 60606-6617
(312) 353-5000

Oklahoma
8625 King George Drive,
Building C
Dallas, TX 75235-3391
(214) 767-7633

Oregon
2615 4th Avenue, Room 440
Seattle, WA 98121
(206) 553-5676

Pacific Islands
71 Stevenson Street,
Twentieth Floor
San Francisco, CA
94105-2939
(415) 744-6402

Pennsylvania
475 Allendale Road,
Suite 201
King of Prussia, PA 19406
(215) 962-3700

Puerto Rico
26 Federal Plaza,
Room 31-08
New York, NY 10278
(212) 264-7772

Rhode Island
155 Federal Street,
Ninth Floor
Boston, MA 02110
(617) 451-2023

South Carolina
1375 Peachtree Street, NE,
Fifth Floor
Atlanta, GA 30367-8102
(404) 347-2797

South Dakota
999 18th Street, Suite 701
Denver, CO 80202
(303) 294-7186

Tennessee
1375 Peachtree Street, NE,
Fifth Floor
Atlanta, GA 30367-8102
(404) 347-2797

Texas
8625 King George Drive,
Building C
Dallas, TX 75235-3391
(214) 767-7633

Utah
999 18th Street, Suite 701
Denver, CO 80202
(303) 294-7186

Vermont
155 Federal Street,
Ninth Floor
Boston, MA 02110
(617) 451-2023

Virgin Islands
26 Federal Plaza,
Room 31-08
New York, NY 10278
(212) 264-7772

Virginia
475 Allendale Road,
Suite 201
King of Prussia, PA 19406
(215) 962-3700

West Virginia
475 Allendale Road,
Suite 201
King of Prussia, PA 19406
(215) 962-3700

Wyoming
999 18th Street, Suite 701
Denver, CO 80202
(303) 294-7186

Washington
2615 4th Avenue, Room 440
Seattle, WA 98121
(206) 553-5676

Wisconsin
Federal Building
300 South Riverside Plaza,
1975 South
Chicago, IL 60606-6617
(312) 353-5000

LOANS FOR SMALL BUSINESSES

**Small Business
Administration**
Loan Policy and
Procedures Branch
409 Third Street, SW
Washington, DC 20416
(202) 205-6570

Description: Provides direct loans to small businesses owned by low-income persons or located in areas with high percentage of unemployment. Business must meet SBA standards and be independently owned and operated and not dominant in its field. Excludes publishing media, radio and TV, nonprofit, lending, investment, or gambling enterprises, speculation in property, and financing real property held for investment.
$ Given: Loans up to $150,000; average: $67,694.
Application Information: Application filed in field office in area in which the business is located.
Deadline: None
Contact: Director

Alabama
Regional Office
1375 Peachtree Street, NE,
Fifth Floor
Atlanta, GA 30367-8102
(404) 347-2797

District Office
Birmingham District Office
2121 8th Avenue North,
Suite 200
Birmingham, AL 35203-2398
(205) 731-1344

Alaska
Regional Office
2615 4th Avenue, Room 440
Seattle, WA 98121
(206) 442-5676

District Office
Anchorage District Office
222 West 8th Avenue,
Room A36
Anchorage, AK 99513
(907) 271-4022

Arizona
Regional Office
71 Stevenson Street,
Twentieth Floor
San Francisco, CA
94105-2939
(415) 744-6402

District Office
Phoenix District Office
2828 North Central Avenue,
Suite 800
Phoenix, AZ 85004-1025
(602) 379-3732

Community Development

Arkansas

Regional Office
8625 King George Drive,
Building C
Dallas, TX 75235-3391
(214) 767-7643

District Office
Little Rock District Office
Post Office and Court House
Building, Room 601
320 West Capitol Avenue
Little Rock, AR 72201
(501) 378-5871

California

Regional Office
71 Stevenson Street,
Twentieth Floor
San Francisco, CA
94105-2939
(415) 744-6402

District Offices
Santa Ana District Office
901 West Civic Center Drive,
Suite 160
Santa Ana, CA 92703-2352
(714) 836-2494

San Diego District Office
880 Front Street,
Room 4-S-29
San Diego, CA 92188-0270
(619) 557-5440

San Francisco District Office
211 Main Street,
Fourth Floor
San Francisco, CA
94105-1988
(415) 744-6804

Fresno District Office
2719 North Air Fresno Drive
Fresno, CA 93727-1547
(209) 487-5189

Los Angeles District Office
330 North Grand Boulevard,
Suite 1200
Glendale, CA 91203-2304
(213) 894-2956

Colorado

Regional Office
999 18th Street, Suite 701
Denver, CO 80202
(303) 294-7001

District Office
Denver District Office
721 19th Street, Room 407
Denver, CO 80201-0660
(303) 844-3984

Connecticut

Regional Office
155 Federal Street,
Ninth Floor
Boston, MA 02110
(617) 451-2023

District Office
Hartford District Office
Federal Building,
Second Floor
330 Main Street
Hartford, CT 06106
(203) 240-4700

Delaware

Regional Office
475 Allendale Road,
Suite 201
King of Prussia, PA 19406
(215) 962-3700

Florida

Regional Office
1375 Peachtree Street, NE,
Fifth Floor
Atlanta, GA 30367-8102
(404) 347-2797

District Offices
Jacksonville District Office
7825 Baymeadows Way,
Suite 100-B
Jacksonville, FL 32256-7504
(904) 443-1900

Miami District Office
1320 South Dixie Highway,
Suite 501
Coral Gables, FL 33146
(305) 536-5521

Georgia

Regional Office
1375 Peachtree Street, NE,
Fifth Floor
Atlanta, GA 30367-8102
(404) 347-2797

District Office
Atlanta District Office
1720 Peachtree Road, NW,
Sixth Floor
Atlanta, GA 30309
(404) 347-4749

Hawaii

Regional Office
71 Stevenson Street,
Twentieth Floor
San Francisco, CA
94105-2939
(415) 744-6402

District Office
Honolulu District Office
300 Ala Moana Boulevard,
Room 2213
Honolulu, HI 96850-4981
(808) 541-2990

Idaho

Regional Office
2615 4th Avenue, Room 440
Seattle, WA 98121
(206) 442-5676

District Office
Boise District Office
1020 Main Street, Suite 290
Boise, ID 83702
(208) 334-9635

Illinois

Regional Office
Federal Building, Room 1975
300 South Riverside Plaza
Chicago IL 60606-6611
(312) 353-0359

District Office
Chicago District Office
500 West Madison Street,
Room 1250
Chicago, IL 60661
(312) 353-4528

Indiana

Regional Office
Federal Building
300 South Riverside Plaza,
Room 1975
Chicago, IL 60606-6611
(312) 353-0359

District Office
Indianapolis District Office
429 North Pennsylvania
Street, Suite 100
Indianapolis, IN 46204-1873
(317) 226-7272

Iowa

Regional Office
911 Walnut Street,
Thirteenth Floor
Kansas City, MO 64106
(816) 426-3608

District Offices
Des Moines District Office
New Federal Building,
Room 749
210 Walnut Street
Des Moines, IA 50309
(515) 284-4762

Cedar Rapids District Office
373 Collins Road, NE,
Room 100
Cedar Rapids, IA 52402-3147
(319) 393-8630

Kansas

Regional Office
911 Walnut Street,
Thirteenth Floor
Kansas City, MO 64106
(816) 426-3608

District Office
Wichita District Office
110 East Waterman Street,
First Floor
Wichita, KS 67202
(316) 269-6273

Kentucky

Regional Office
1375 Peachtree Street, NE,
Fifth Floor
Atlanta, GA 30367-8102
(404) 347-2797

District Office
Louisville District Office
Federal Building, Room 188
600 Martin Luther King Jr.
Place
Louisville, KY 40202
(502) 582-5976

Louisiana

Regional Office
8625 King George Drive,
Building C
Dallas, TX 75235-3391
(214) 767-7643

District Office
New Orleans District Office
1661 Canal Street,
Suite 2000
New Orleans, LA 70112
(504) 589-6685

Maine

Regional Office
155 Federal Street,
Ninth Floor
Boston, MA 02110
(617) 451-2023

District Office
Augusta District Office
Federal Building, Room 512
40 Western Avenue
August, ME 04330
(207) 622-8378

Massachusetts

Regional Office
155 Federal Street,
Ninth Floor
Boston, MA 02110
(617) 451-2023

District Office
Boston District Office
10 Causeway Street,
Room 265
Boston, MA 02222-1093
(617) 565-5590

Michigan

Regional Office
Federal Building, Room 1975
300 South Riverside Plaza
Chicago, IL 60606-6611
(312) 353-0359

District Office
Detroit District Office
477 Michigan Avenue,
Room 515
Detroit, MI 48226
(313) 226-6075

Minnesota

Regional Office
Federal Building, Room 1975
300 South Riverside Plaza
Chicago, IL 60606-6611
(312) 353-0359

District Office
Minneapolis District Office
100 North 6th Street,
Suite 610
Minneapolis, MN 55403-1563
(612) 370-2324

Community Development

Mississippi
Regional Office
1375 Peachtree Street, NE,
Fifth Floor
Atlanta, GA 30367-8102
(404) 347-2797

District Office
Jackson District Office
100 West Capitol Street,
Suite 400
Jackson, MS 39201
(601) 965-5325

Missouri
Regional Office
911 Walnut Street,
Thirteenth Floor
Kansas City, MO 64106
(816) 426-3608

District Offices
St. Louis District Office
815 Olive Street, Room 242
St. Louis, MO 63101
(314) 539-6600

Kansas City District Office
323 West 8th Street,
Suite 501
Kansas City, MO 64105
(816) 374-6762

Montana
Regional Office
999 18th Street, Suite 701
Denver, CO 80202
(303) 294-7001

District Office
Helena District Office
301 South Park Avenue,
Room 528
Helena, MT 59626
(406) 449-5381

Nebraska
Regional Office
911 Walnut Street,
Thirteenth Floor
Kansas City, MO 64106
(816) 426-3608

District Office
Omaha District Office
11145 Mill Valley Road
Omaha, NB 64154
(402) 221-3604

Nevada
Regional Office
71 Stevenson Street,
Twentieth Floor
San Francisco, CA
94105-2939
(415) 744-6402

District Office
Las Vegas District Office
301 East Steward Street,
Room 301
Las Vegas, NV 89125-2527
(702) 388-6611

New Hampshire
Regional Office
155 Federal Street,
Ninth Floor
Boston, MA 02110
(617) 451-2023

District Office
Concord District Office
143 North Main Street,
Suite 202
Concord, NH 03302-1257
(603) 225-1400

New Jersey
Regional Office
26 Federal Plaza,
Room 31-08
New York, NY 10278
(212) 264-7772

District Office
Newark District Office
Military Park Building,
Fourth Floor
60 Park Place
Newark, NJ 07102
(201) 341-2434

New Mexico
Regional Office
8625 King George Drive,
Building C
Dallas, TX 75235-3391
(214) 767-7643

District Office
Albuquerque District Office
625 Silver Avenue, SW,
Suite 320
Albuquerque, NM 87102
(505) 766-1870

New York
Regional Office
26 Federal Plaza,
Room 31-08
New York, NY 10278
(212) 264-7772

District Offices
Buffalo District Office
Federal Building 1311
111 West Huron Street
Buffalo, NY 14202
(716) 846-4301

Syracuse District Office
100 South Clinton Street,
Room 1071
Syracuse, NY 13260
(315) 423-5383

North Carolina
Regional Office
1375 Peachtree Street, NE,
Fifth Floor
Atlanta, GA 30367-8102
(404) 347-2797

District Office
Charlotte District Office
200 North College Street
Charlotte, NC 28202
(704) 344-6563

North Dakota
Regional Office
999 18th Street, Suite 701
Denver, CO 80202
(303) 294-7001

District Office
Federal Building, Room 218
657 2nd Avenue, North
Fargo, ND 58108-3086
(701) 239-5131

Ohio
Regional Office
Federal Building, Room 1975
300 South Riverside Plaza
Chicago, IL 60606-6611
(312) 353-0359

District Office
Columbus District Office
85 Marconi Boulevard,
Room 512
Columbus, OH 43215
(614) 469-6860

Oklahoma
Regional Office
8625 King George Drive,
Building C
Dallas, TX 75235-3391
(214) 767-7643

District Office
Oklahoma City District Office
200 NW 5th Street, Suite 670
Oklahoma City, OK 73102
(405) 231-4301

Oregon
Regional Office
2615 4th Avenue, Room 440
Seattle, WA 98121
(206) 442-5676

District Office
Portland District Office
222 SW Columbia Street,
Suite 500
Portland, OR 97201-6605
(503) 326-2682

Pacific Islands
Regional Office
71 Stevenson Street,
Twentieth Floor
San Francisco, CA
94105-2939
(415) 744-6402

District Office
Agana Branch Office
Pacific Daily News Building,
Room 508
238 Archbishop F.C.
Flores Street
Agana, GM 96910
(671) 472-7277

Pennsylvania
Regional Office
475 Allendale Road,
Suite 201
King of Prussia, PA 19406
(215) 962-3700

District Office
Pittsburgh District Office
960 Penn Avenue, Fifth Floor
Pittsburgh, PA 15222
(412) 644-2780

Puerto Rico
Regional Office
26 Federal Plaza,
Room 31-08
New York, NY 10278
(212) 264-7772

District Office
Federico Degetau Federal
Building, Room 691
Carlos Chardon Avenue
Hato Rey, PR 00918
(809) 766-5002

Rhode Island
Regional Office
155 Federal Street,
Ninth Floor
Boston, MA 02110
(617) 451-2023

District Office
Providence District Office
380 Westminster Mall,
Fifth Floor
Providence, RI 02903
(401) 528-4561

South Carolina
Regional Office
1375 Peachtree Street, NE,
Fifth Floor
Atlanta, GA 30367-8102
(404) 347-2797

District Office
Columbia District Office
1835 Assembly Street,
Room 358
Columbia, SC 29202
(803) 765-5376

South Dakota
Regional Office
999 18th Street, Suite 701
Denver, CO 80202
(303) 294-7001

District Office
Sioux Falls District Office
101 South Main Avenue,
Suite 101
Sioux Falls, SD 57102-0527
(605) 336-4231

Tennessee
Regional Office
1375 Peachtree Street, NE,
Fifth Floor
Atlanta, GA 30367-8102
(404) 347-2797

District Office
Nashville District Office
50 Vantage Way, Suite 201
Nashville, TN 37338-1500
(615) 736-7176

Community Development

Texas
Regional Office
8625 King George Drive,
Building C
Dallas, TX 75235-3391
(214) 767-7643

District Offices
San Antonio District Office
7400 Blanco Road, Suite 200
San Antonio, TX 78216
(512) 229-4535

Dallas District Office
1100 Commerce Street,
Room 3C36
Dallas, TX 75242
(214) 767-0608

El Paso District Office
10737 Gateway West,
Suite 320
El Paso, TX 79935
(915) 541-5586

Utah
Regional Office
999 18th Street, Suite 701
Denver, CO 80202
(303) 294-7001

District Office
Salt Lake City District Office
Federal Building, Room 2237
125 South State Street
Salt Lake City, UT
84138-1195
(801) 524-5800

Vermont
Regional Office
155 Federal Street,
Ninth Floor
Boston, MA 02110
(617) 451-2023

District Office
Montpelier District Office
Federal Building, Room 205
87 State Street
Montpelier, VT 05602
(802) 828-4474

Virgin Islands
Regional Office
26 Federal Plaza,
Room 31-08
New York, NY 10278
(212) 264-7772

District Offices
Federico Degetau Federal
Building, Room 691
Carlos Chardon Avenue
Hato Rey, PR 00918
(809) 766-5002

St. Croix Post-of-Duty
United Shopping Plaza
4C & 4D Este Sion Farm,
Room 7
Christiansted, St. Croix, VI
00820
(809) 778-5380

St. Thomas Post-of-Duty
Federal Office Building,
Room 283
Veterans Drive
St. Thomas, VI 00801
(809) 774-8530

Virginia
Regional Office
475 Allendale Road,
Suite 201
King of Prussia, PA 19406
(215) 962-3700

District Office
Richmond District Office
Federal Building, Room 3015
400 North 8th Street
Richmond, VA 23240
(804) 771-2400

Washington
Regional Office
2615 4th Avenue, Room 440
Seattle, WA 98121
(206) 442-5676

District Offices
Spokane District Office
West 601 First Avenue,
Tenth Floor East
Spokane, WA 99204
(509) 353-2807

Seattle District Office
915 Second Avenue,
Room 1792
Seattle, WA 98174-1088
(206) 553-1420

Washington, DC
District Office
475 Allendale Road,
Suite 201
King of Prussia, PA 19406
(215) 962-3700

District Office
Washington District Office
1111 18th Street, NW,
Sixth Floor
Washington, DC 20036
(202) 634-1500

West Virginia
Regional Office
475 Allendale Road,
Suite 201
King of Prussia, PA 19406
(215) 962-3700

District Office
Clarksburg District Office
168 West Main Street,
Fifth Floor
Clarksburg, WV 26301
(304) 623-5631

Wisconsin
Regional Office
Federal Building, Room 1975
300 South Riverside Plaza
Chicago, IL 60606-6611
(312) 353-0359

District Office
Madison District Office
212 East Washington Avenue,
Room 213
Madison, WI 53703
(608) 264-5261

Wyoming
Regional Office
999 18th Street, Suite 701
Denver, CO 80202
(303) 294-7001

District Office
Casper District Office
Federal Building, Room 4001
100 East B Street
Casper, WY 82602-2839
(307) 261-5761

LOCAL DEVELOPMENT COMPANY LOANS

**Small Business
Administration**
Office of Rural Affairs and
Economic Development
409 3rd Street, SW
Washington, DC 20416
(202) 205-6485

Description: Guaranteed and insured loans to local development companies that are incorporated. Loans are for the purchase of land, buildings, machinery, and equipment for constructing, expanding, or modernizing buildings. Loans are not available to provide working capital for refinancing purposes. Loans may not exceed 25 years.
$ Given: Range: $62,000–$1 million; average: $358,646.
Application Information: Applications must be made on SBA Form 1244 for local development company loans and the requirements set forth thereon must be complied with.
Deadline: None
Contact: Your state and/or regional SBA office

Alabama
1375 Peachtree Street, NE,
Fifth Floor
Atlanta, GA 30367-8102
(404) 347-2797

Alaska
2615 4th Avenue, Room 440
Seattle, WA 98121
(206) 553-5676

Arizona
71 Stevenson Street,
Twentieth Floor
San Francisco, CA
94105-2939
(415) 744-6402

Arkansas
8625 King George Drive,
Building C
Dallas, TX 75235-3391
(214) 767-7633

California
71 Stevenson Street,
Twentieth Floor
San Francisco, CA
94105-2939
(415) 744-6402

Colorado
999 18th Street, Suite 701
Denver, CO 80202
(303) 294-7186

Connecticut
155 Federal Street,
Ninth Floor
Boston, MA 02110
(617) 451-2023

Delaware
475 Allendale Road,
Suite 201
King of Prussia, PA 19406
(215) 962-3700

District of Columbia
475 Allendale Road,
Suite 201
King of Prussia, PA 19406
(215) 962-3700

Community Development

Florida
1375 Peachtree Street, NE,
Fifth Floor
Atlanta, GA 30367-8102
(404) 347-2797

Georgia
1375 Peachtree Street, NE,
Fifth Floor
Atlanta, GA 30367-8102
(404) 347-2797

Hawaii
71 Stevenson Street,
Twentieth Floor
San Francisco, CA
94105-2939
(415) 744-6402

Idaho
2614 4th Avenue, Room 440
Seattle, WA 98121
(206) 553-5676

Illinois
Federal Building
300 South Riverside Plaza,
1975 South
Chicago, IL 60606-6617
(312) 353-5000

Indiana
Federal Building
300 South Riverside Plaza,
1975 South
Chicago, IL 60606-6617
(312) 353-5000

Iowa
911 Walnut Street,
Thirteenth Floor
Kansas City, MO 64106
(816) 426-3608

Kansas
911 Walnut Street,
Thirteenth Floor
Kansas City, MO 64106
(816) 426-3608

Kentucky
1375 Peachtree Street, NE,
Fifth Floor
Atlanta, GA 30367-8102
(404) 347-2797

Louisiana
8625 King George Drive,
Building C
Dallas, TX 75235-3391
(214) 767-7633

Maine
155 Federal Street,
Ninth Floor
Boston, MA 02110
(617) 451-2023

Maryland
475 Allendale Road,
Suite 201
King of Prussia, PA 19406
(215) 962-3700

Massachusetts
155 Federal Street,
Ninth Floor
Boston, MA 02110
(617) 451-2023

Michigan
Federal Building
300 South Riverside Plaza,
1975 South
Chicago, IL 60606-6617
(312) 353-5000

Minnesota
Federal Building
300 South Riverside Plaza,
1975 South
Chicago, IL 60606-6617
(312) 353-5000

Mississippi
1375 Peachtree Street, NE,
Fifth Floor
Atlanta, GA 30367-8102
(404) 347-2797

Missouri
911 Walnut Street,
Thirteenth Floor
Kansas City, MO 64106
(816) 426-3608

Montana
999 18th Street, Suite 701
Denver, CO 80202
(303) 294-7186

Nebraska
911 Walnut Street,
Thirteenth Floor
Kansas City, MO 64106
(816) 426-3608

Nevada
71 Stevenson Street,
Twentieth Floor
San Francisco, CA
94105-2939
(415) 744-6402

New Hampshire
155 Federal Street,
Ninth Floor
Boston, MA 02110
(617) 451-2023

New Jersey
26 Federal Plaza,
Room 31-08
New York, NY 10278
(212) 264-7772

New Mexico
8625 King George Drive,
Building C
Dallas, TX 75235-3391
(214) 767-7633

New York
26 Federal Plaza,
Room 31-08
New York, NY 10278
(212) 264-7772

North Carolina
1375 Peachtree Street, NE,
Fifth Floor
Atlanta, GA 30367-8102
(404) 347-2797

North Dakota
999 18th Street, Suite 701
Denver, CO 80202
(303) 294-7186

Ohio
Federal Building
300 South Riverside Plaza,
1975 South
Chicago, IL 60606-6617
(312) 353-5000

Oklahoma
8625 King George Drive,
Building C
Dallas, TX 75235-3391
(214) 767-7633

Oregon
2615 4th Avenue, Room 440
Seattle, WA 98121
(206) 553-5676

Pacific Islands
71 Stevenson Street,
Twentieth Floor
San Francisco, CA
94105-2939
(415) 744-6402

Pennsylvania
475 Allendale Road,
Suite 201
King of Prussia, PA 19406
(215) 962-3700

Puerto Rico
26 Federal Plaza,
Room 31-08
New York, NY 10278
(212) 264-7772

Rhode Island
155 Federal Street,
Ninth Floor
Boston, MA 02110
(617) 451-2023

South Carolina
1375 Peachtree Street, NE,
Fifth Floor
Atlanta, GA 30367-8102
(404) 347-2797

South Dakota
999 18th Street, Suite 701
Denver, CO 80202
(303) 294-7186

Tennessee
1375 Peachtree Street, NE,
Fifth Floor
Atlanta, GA 30367-8102
(404) 347-2797

Texas
8625 King George Drive,
Building C
Dallas, TX 75235-3391
(214) 767-7633

Utah
999 18th Street, Suite 701
Denver, CO 80202
(303) 294-7186

Vermont
155 Federal Street,
Ninth Floor
Boston, MA 02110
(617) 451-2023

Virgin Islands
26 Federal Plaza,
Room 31-08
New York, NY 10278
(212) 264-7772

Virginia
475 Allendale Road,
Suite 201
King of Prussia, PA 19406
(215) 962-3700

Washington
2615 4th Avenue, Room 440
Seattle, WA 98121
(206) 553-5676

West Virginia
475 Allendale Road,
Suite 201
King of Prussia, PA 19406
(215) 962-3700

Wisconsin
Federal Building
300 South Riverside Plaza,
1975 South
Chicago, IL 60606-6617
(312) 353-5000

Wyoming
999 18th Street, Suite 701
Denver, CO 80202
(303) 294-7186

MANAGEMENT TECHNICAL ASSISTANCE FOR SOCIALLY AND ECONOMICALLY DISADVANTAGED BUSINESSES

Small Business Administration
409 Third Street, SW
Washington, DC 20416
(202) 205-6423

Description: Grants to provide management and technical assistance to existing or potential businesses that are economically and socially disadvantaged and/or operated in areas of high unemployment or low income.
$ Given: $1,800–$388,000; average: $78,620.
Application Information: Application or proposal forwarded to Assistant Regional Administrator for Minority Small Businesses and Capital Ownership Development—SBA regional office for appropriate area.
Deadline: As announced within individual "Request for Application Proposals."
Contact: Appropriate regional office

Alabama

Regional Office
1375 Peachtree Street, NE,
Fifth Floor
Atlanta, GA 30367-8102
(404) 347-2797

District Office
Birmingham District Office
2121 8th Avenue North,
Suite 200
Birmingham, AL 35203-2398
(205) 731-1344

Alaska

Regional Office
2615 4th Avenue, Room 440
Seattle, WA 98121
(206) 442-5676

District Office
Anchorage District Office
222 West 8th Avenue,
Room A36
Anchorage, AK 99513
(907) 271-4022

Arizona

Regional Office
71 Stevenson Street,
Twentieth Floor
San Francisco, CA
94105-2939
(415) 744-6402

District Office
Phoenix District Office
2828 North Central Avenue,
Suite 800
Phoenix, AZ 85004-1025
(602) 379-3732

Arkansas

Regional Office
8625 King George Drive,
Building C
Dallas, TX 75235-3391
(214) 767-7643

District Office
Little Rock District Office
Post Office and Court House
Building, Room 601
320 West Capitol Avenue
Little Rock, AR 72201
(501) 378-5871

California

Regional Office
71 Stevenson Street,
Twentieth Floor
San Francisco, CA
94105-2939
(415) 744-6402

District Offices
Santa Ana District Office
901 West Civic Center Drive,
Suite 160
Santa Ana, CA 92703-2352
(714) 836-2494

San Diego District Office
880 Front Street,
Room 4-S-29
San Diego, CA 92188-0270
(619) 557-5440

San Francisco District Office
211 Main Street,
Fourth Floor
San Francisco, CA
94105-1988
(415) 744-6804

Fresno District Office
2719 North Air Fresno Drive
Fresno, CA 93727-1547
(209) 487-5189

Los Angeles District Office
330 North Grand Boulevard,
Suite 1200
Glendale, CA 91203-2304
(213) 894-2956

Colorado
Regional Office
999 18th Street, Suite 701
Denver, CO 80202
(303) 294-7001

District Office
Denver District Office
721 19th Street, Room 407
Denver, CO 80201-0660
(303) 844-3984

Connecticut
Regional Office
155 Federal Street,
Ninth Floor
Boston, MA 02110
(617) 451-2023

District Office
Hartford District Office
Federal Building,
Second Floor
330 Main Street
Hartford, CT 06106
(203) 240-4700

Delaware
Regional Office
475 Allendale Road,
Suite 201
King of Prussia, PA 19406
(215) 962-3700

Florida
Regional Office
1375 Peachtree Street, NE,
Fifth Floor
Atlanta, GA 30367-8102
(404) 347-2797

District Offices
Jacksonville District Office
7825 Baymeadows Way,
Suite 100-B
Jacksonville, FL 32256-7504
(904) 443-1900

Miami District Office
1320 South Dixie Highway,
Suite 501
Coral Gables, FL 33146
(305) 536-5521

Georgia
Regional Office
1375 Peachtree Street, NE,
Fifth Floor
Atlanta, GA 30367-8102
(404) 347-2797

District Office
Atlanta District Office
1720 Peachtree Road, NW,
Sixth Floor
Atlanta, GA 30309
(404) 347-4749

Hawaii
Regional Office
71 Stevenson Street,
Twentieth Floor
San Francisco, CA
94105-2939
(415) 744-6402

District Office
Honolulu District Office
300 Ala Moana Boulevard,
Room 2213
Honolulu, HI 96850-4981
(808) 541-2990

Idaho
Regional Office
2615 4th Avenue, Room 440
Seattle, WA 98121
(206) 442-5676

District Office
Boise District Office
1020 Main Street, Suite 290
Boise, ID 83702
(208) 334-9635

Illinois
Regional Office
Federal Building, Room 1975
300 South Riverside Plaza
Chicago, IL 60606-6611
(312) 353-0359

District Office
Chicago District Office
500 West Madison Street,
Room 1250
Chicago, IL 60661
(312) 353-4528

Indiana
Regional Office
Federal Building
300 South Riverside Plaza,
Room 1975
Chicago, IL 60606-6611
(312) 353-0359

District Office
Indianapolis District Office
429 North Pennsylvania
Street, Suite 100
Indianapolis, IN 46204-1873
(317) 226-7272

Iowa
Regional Office
911 Walnut Street,
Thirteenth Floor
Kansas City, MO 64106
(816) 426-3608

District Offices
Des Moines District Office
New Federal Building,
Room 749
210 Walnut Street
Des Moines, IA 50309
(515) 284-4762

Community Development

Cedar Rapids District Office
373 Collins Road, NE,
Room 100
Cedar Rapids, IA 52402-3147
(319) 393-8630

Kansas
Regional Office
911 Walnut Street,
Thirteenth Floor
Kansas City, MO 64106
(816) 426-3608
District Office
Wichita District Office
110 East Waterman Street,
First Floor
Wichita, KS 67202
(316) 269-6273

Kentucky
Regional Office
1375 Peachtree Street, NE,
Fifth Floor
Atlanta, GA 30367-8102
(404) 347-2797
District Office
Louisville District Office
Federal Building, Room 188
600 Martin Luther
King Jr. Place
Louisville, KY 40202
(502) 582-5976

Louisiana
Regional Office
8625 King George Drive,
Building C
Dallas, TX 75235-3391
(214) 767-7643
District Office
New Orleans District Office
1661 Canal Street,
Suite 2000
New Orleans, LA 70112
(504) 589-6685

Maine
Regional Office
155 Federal Street,
Ninth Floor
Boston, MA 02110
(617) 451-2023
District Office
Augusta District Office
Federal Building, Room 512
40 Western Avenue
Augusta, ME 04330
(207) 622-8378

Massachusetts
Regional Office
155 Federal Street,
Ninth Floor
Boston, MA 02110
(617) 451-2023
District Office
Boston District Office
10 Causeway Street,
Room 265
Boston, MA 02222-1093
(617) 565-5590

Michigan
Regional Office
Federal Building, Room 1975
300 South Riverside Plaza
Chicago, IL 60606-6611
(312) 353-0359
District Office
Detroit District Office
477 Michigan Avenue,
Room 515
Detroit, MI 48226
(313) 226-6075

Minnesota
Regional Office
Federal Building, Room 1975
300 South Riverside Plaza
Chicago, IL 60606-6611
(312) 353-0359

District Office
Minneapolis District Office
100 North 6th Street,
Suite 610
Minneapolis, MN 55403-1563
(612) 370-2324

Mississippi
Regional Office
1375 Peachtree Street, NE,
Fifth Floor
Atlanta, GA 30367-8102
(404) 347-2797
District Office
Jackson District Office
100 West Capitol Street,
Suite 400
Jackson, MS 39201
(601) 965-5325

Missouri
Regional Office
911 Walnut Street,
Thirteenth Floor
Kansas City, MO 64106
(816) 426-3608
District Offices
St. Louis District Office
815 Olive Street, Room 242
St. Louis, MO 63101
(314) 539-6600

Kansas City District Office
323 West 8th Street,
Suite 501
Kansas City, MO 64105
(816) 374-6762

Montana
Regional Office
999 18th Street, Suite 701
Denver, CO 80202
(303) 294-7001

District Office
Helena District Office
301 South Park Avenue,
Room 528
Helena, MT 59626
(406) 449-5381

Nebraska
Regional Office
911 Walnut Street,
Thirteenth Floor
Kansas City, MO 64106
(816) 426-3608

District Office
Omaha District Office
11145 Mill Valley Road
Omaha, NB 64154
(402) 221-3604

Nevada
Regional Office
71 Stevenson Street,
Twentieth Floor
San Francisco, CA
94105-2939
(415) 744-6402

District Office
Las Vegas District Office
301 East Steward Street,
Room 301
Las Vegas, NV 89125-2527
(702) 388-6611

New Hampshire
Regional Office
155 Federal Street,
Ninth Floor
Boston, MA 02110
(617) 451-2023

District Office
Concord District Office
143 North Main Street,
Suite 202
Concord, NH 03302-1257
(603) 225-1400

New Jersey
Regional Office
26 Federal Plaza,
Room 31-08
New York, NY 10278
(212) 264-7772

District Office
Newark District Office
Military Park Building,
Fourth Floor
60 Park Place
Newark, NJ 07102
(201) 341-2434

New Mexico
Regional Office
8625 King George Drive,
Building C
Dallas, TX 75235-3391
(214) 767-7643

District Office
Albuquerque District Office
625 Silver Avenue, SW,
Suite 320
Albuquerque, NM 87102
(505) 766-1870

New York
Regional Office
26 Federal Plaza,
Room 31-08
New York, NY 10278
(212) 264-7772

District Offices
Buffalo District Office
Federal Building 1311
111 West Huron Street
Buffalo, NY 14202
(716) 846-4301

Syracuse District Office
100 South Clinton Street,
Room 1071
Syracuse, NY 13260
(315) 423-5383

North Carolina
Regional Office
1375 Peachtree Street, NE,
Fifth Floor
Atlanta, GA 30367-8102
(404) 347-2797

District Office
Charlotte District Office
200 North College Street
Charlotte, NC 28202
(704) 344-6563

North Dakota
Regional Office
999 18th Street, Suite 701
Denver, CO 80202
(303) 294-7001

District Office
Federal Building, Room 218
657 2nd Avenue, North
Fargo, ND 58108-3086
(701) 239-5131

Ohio
Regional Office
Federal Building, Room 1975
300 South Riverside Plaza
Chicago, IL 60606-6611
(312) 353-0359

District Office
Columbus District Office
85 Marconi Boulevard,
Room 512
Columbus, OH 43215
(614) 469-6860

Oklahoma
Regional Office
8625 King George Drive,
Building C
Dallas, TX 75235-3391
(214) 767-7643

District Office
Oklahoma City District Office
200 NW 5th Street, Suite 670
Oklahoma City, OK 73102
(405) 231-4301

Community Development

Oregon
Regional Office
2615 4th Avenue, Room 440
Seattle, WA 98121
(206) 442-5676

District Office
Portland District Office
222 SW Columbia Street,
Suite 500
Portland, OR 97201-6605
(503) 326-2682

Pacific Islands
Regional Office
71 Stevenson Street,
Twentieth Floor
San Francisco, CA
94105-2939
(415) 744-6402

District Office
Agana Branch Office
Pacific Daily News Building,
Room 508
238 Archbishop F.C.
Flores Street
Agana, GM 96910
(671) 472-7277

Pennsylvania
Regional Office
475 Allendale Road,
Suite 201
King of Prussia, PA 19406
(215) 962-3700

District Office
Pittsburgh District Office
960 Penn Avenue, Fifth Floor
Pittsburgh, PA 15222
(412) 644-2780

Puerto Rico
Regional Office
26 Federal Plaza,
Room 31-08
New York, NY 10278
(212) 264-7772

District Office
Federico Degetau Federal
Building, Room 691
Carlos Chardon Avenue
Hato Rey, PR 00918
(809) 766-5002

Rhode Island
Regional Office
155 Federal Street,
Ninth Floor
Boston, MA 02110
(617) 451-2023

District Office
Providence District Office
380 Westminster Mall,
Fifth Floor
Providence, RI 02903
(401) 528-4561

South Carolina
Regional Office
1375 Peachtree Street, NE,
Fifth Floor
Atlanta, GA 30367-8102
(404) 347-2797

District Office
Columbia District Office
1835 Assembly Street,
Room 358
Columbia, SC 29202
(803) 765-5376

South Dakota
Regional Office
999 18th Street, Suite 701
Denver, CO 80202
(303) 294-7001

District Office
Sioux Falls District Office
101 South Main Avenue,
Suite 101
Sioux Falls, SD 57102-0527
(605) 336-4231

Tennessee
Regional Office
1375 Peachtree Street, NE,
Fifth Floor
Atlanta, GA 30367-8102
(404) 347-2797

District Office
Nashville District Office
50 Vantage Way, Suite 201
Nashville, TN 37338-1500
(615) 736-7176

Texas
Regional Office
8625 King George Drive,
Building C
Dallas, TX 75235-3391
(214) 767-7643

District Offices
San Antonio District Office
7400 Blanco Road, Suite 200
San Antonio, TX 78216
(512) 229-4535

Dallas District Office
1100 Commerce Street,
Room 3C36
Dallas, TX 75242
(214) 767-0608

El Paso District Office
10737 Gateway West,
Suite 320
El Paso, TX 79935
(915) 541-5586

Utah
Regional Office
999 18th Street, Suite 701
Denver, CO 80202
(303) 294-7001

District Office
Salt Lake City District Office
Federal Building, Room 2237
125 South State Street
Salt Lake City, UT
84138-1195
(801) 524-5800

Vermont
Regional Office
155 Federal Street,
Ninth Floor
Boston, MA 02110
(617) 451-2023

District Office
Montpelier District Office
Federal Building, Room 205
87 State Street
Montpelier, VT 05602
(802) 828-4474

Virgin Islands
Regional Office
26 Federal Plaza,
Room 31-08
New York, NY 10278
(212) 264-7772

District Offices
Federico Degetau Federal
Building, Room 691
Carlos Chardon Avenue
Hato Rey, PR 00918
(809) 766-5002

St. Croix Post-of-Duty
United Shopping Plaza
4C & 4D Este Sion Farm,
Room 7
Christiansted, St. Croix, VI
00820
(809) 778-5380

St. Thomas Post-of-Duty
Federal Office Building,
Room 283
Veterans Drive
St. Thomas, VI 00801
(809) 774-8530

Virginia
Regional Office
475 Allendale Road,
Suite 201
King of Prussia, PA 19406
(215) 962-3700

District Office
Richmond District Office
Federal Building, Room 3015
400 North 8th Street
Richmond, VA 23240
(804) 771-2400

Washington
Regional Office
2615 4th Avenue, Room 440
Seattle, WA 98121
(206) 442-5676

District Offices
Spokane District Office
West 601 First Avenue,
Tenth Floor East
Spokane, WA 99204
(509) 353-2807

Seattle District Office
915 Second Avenue,
Room 1792
Seattle, WA 98174-1088
(206) 553-1420

Washington, DC
Regional Office
475 Allendale Road,
Suite 201
King of Prussia, PA 19406
(215) 962-3700

District Office
Washington District Office
1111 18th Street, NW,
Sixth Floor
Washington, DC 20036
(202) 634-1500

West Virginia
Regional Office
475 Allendale Road,
Suite 201
King of Prussia, PA 19406
(215) 962-3700

District Office
Clarksburg District Office
168 West Main Street,
Fifth Floor
Clarksburg, WV 26301
(304) 623-5631

Wisconsin
Regional Office
Federal Building, Room 1975
300 South Riverside Plaza
Chicago, IL 60606-6611
(312) 353-0359

District Office
Madison District Office
212 East Washington Avenue,
Room 213
Madison, WI 53703
(608) 264-5261

Wyoming
Regional Office
999 18th Street, Suite 701
Denver, CO 80202
(303) 294-7001

District Office
Casper District Office
Federal Building, Room 4001
100 East B Street
Casper, WY 82602-2839
(307) 261-5761

PHYSICAL DISASTER LOANS

Small Business Administration
Office of Disaster Assistance
409 3rd Street, SW
Washington, DC 20416
(202) 205-6734

Description: Direct, guaranteed, and insured loans to individuals, businesses, charitable, and nonprofit organizations to repair and/or replace damaged and/or destroyed real and/or personal property to predisaster conditions.

$ Given: Direct loans to $120,000 plus $100,000 additional in special cases. Direct business loans to $150,000 with additional amounts available for major sources of employment.

Application Information: Write for application. When feasible, interviews are held with disaster victims and the program is explained.

Deadline: 60 days from date of disaster declaration.

Contact: Your state and/or regional office

Alabama
1375 Peachtree Street, NE,
Fifth Floor
Atlanta, GA 30367-8102
(404) 347-2797

Alaska
2615 4th Avenue, Room 440
Seattle, WA 98121
(206) 553-5676

Arizona
71 Stevenson Street,
Twentieth Floor
San Francisco, CA
94105-2939
(415) 744-6402

Arkansas
8625 King George Drive,
Building C
Dallas, TX 75235-3391
(214) 767-7633

California
71 Stevenson Street,
Twentieth Floor
San Francisco, CA
94105-2939
(415) 744-6402

Colorado
999 18th Street, Suite 701
Denver, CO 80202
(303) 294-7186

Connecticut
155 Federal Street,
Ninth Floor
Boston, MA 02110
(617) 451-2023

Delaware
475 Allendale Road,
Suite 201
King of Prussia, PA 19406
(215) 962-3700

District of Columbia
475 Allendale Road,
Suite 201
King of Prussia, PA 19406
(215) 962-3700

Florida
1375 Peachtree Street, NE,
Fifth Floor
Atlanta, GA 30367-8102
(404) 347-2797

Georgia
1375 Peachtree Street, NE,
Fifth Floor
Atlanta, GA 30367-8102
(404) 347-2797

Hawaii
71 Stevenson Street,
Twentieth Floor
San Francisco, CA
94105-2939
(415) 744-6402

Idaho
2615 4th Avenue, Room 440
Seattle, WA 98121
(206) 553-5676

Illinois
Federal Building
300 South Riverside Plaza,
1975 South
Chicago, IL 60606-6617
(312) 353-5000

Indiana
Federal Building
300 South Riverside Plaza,
1975 South
Chicago, IL 60606-6617
(312) 353-5000

Iowa
911 Walnut Street,
Thirteenth Floor
Kansas City, MO 64106
(816) 426-3608

Kansas
911 Walnut Street,
Thirteenth Floor
Kansas City, MO 64106
(816) 426-3608

Kentucky
1375 Peachtree Street, NE,
Fifth Floor
Atlanta, GA 30367-8102
(404) 347-2797

Louisiana
8625 King George Drive,
Building C
Dallas, TX 75235-3391
(214) 767-7633

Maine
155 Federal Street,
Ninth Floor
Boston, MA 02110
(617) 451-2023

Maryland
475 Allendale Road,
Suite 201
King of Prussia, PA 19406
(215) 962-3700

Massachusetts
155 Federal Street,
Ninth Floor
Boston, MA 02110
(617) 451-2023

Michigan
Federal Building
300 South Riverside Plaza,
1975 South
Chicago, IL 60606-6617
(312) 353-5000

Minnesota
Federal Building
300 South Riverside Plaza,
1975 South
Chicago, IL 60606-6617
(312) 353-5000

Mississippi
1375 Peachtree Street, NE,
Fifth Floor
Atlanta, GA 30367-8102
(404) 347-2797

Missouri
911 Walnut Street,
Thirteenth Floor
Kansas City, MO 64106
(816) 426-3608

Montana
999 18th Street, Suite 701
Denver, CO 80202
(303) 294-7186

Nebraska
911 Walnut Street,
Thirteenth Floor
Kansas City, MO 64106
(816) 426-3608

Nevada
71 Stevenson Street,
Twentieth Floor
San Francisco, CA
94105-2939
(415) 744-6402

New Hampshire
155 Federal Street,
Ninth Floor
Boston, MA 02110
(617) 451-2023

New Jersey
26 Federal Plaza,
Room 31-08
New York, NY 10278
(212) 264-7772

New Mexico
8625 King George Drive,
Building C
Dallas, TX 75235-3391
(214) 767-7633

New York
26 Federal Plaza,
Room 31-08
New York, NY 10278
(212) 264-7772

North Carolina
1375 Peachtree Street, NE,
Fifth Floor
Atlanta, GA 30367-8102
(404) 347-2797

North Dakota
999 18th Street, Suite 701
Denver, CO 80202
(303) 294-7186

Ohio
Federal Building
300 South Riverside Plaza,
1975 South
Chicago, IL 60606-6617
(312) 353-5000

Oklahoma
8625 King George Drive,
Building C
Dallas, TX 75235-3391
(214) 767-7633

Oregon
2615 4th Avenue, Room 440
Seattle, WA 98121
(206) 553-5676

Pacific Islands
71 Stevenson Street,
Twentieth Floor
San Francisco, CA
94105-2939
(415) 744-6402

Pennsylvania
475 Allendale Road,
Suite 201
King of Prussia, PA 19406
(215) 962-3700

Puerto Rico
26 Federal Plaza,
Room 31-08
New York, NY 10278
(212) 264-7772

Rhode Island
155 Federal Street,
Ninth Floor
Boston, MA 02110
(617) 451-2023

South Carolina
1375 Peachtree Street, NE,
Fifth Floor
Atlanta, GA 30367-8102
(404) 347-2797

South Dakota
999 18th Street, Suite 701
Denver, CO 80202
(303) 294-7186

Tennessee
1375 Peachtree Street, NE,
Fifth Floor
Atlanta, GA 30367-8102
(404) 347-2797

Texas
8625 King George Drive,
Building C
Dallas, TX 75235-3391
(214) 767-7633

Utah
999 18th Street, Suite 701
Denver, CO 80202
(303) 294-7186

Vermont
155 Federal Street,
Ninth Floor
Boston, MA 02110
(617) 451-2023

Virgin Islands
26 Federal Plaza,
Room 31-08
New York, NY 10278
(212) 264-7772

Virginia
475 Allendale Road,
Suite 201
King of Prussia, PA 19406
(215) 962-3700

Washington
2615 4th Avenue, Room 440
Seattle, WA 98121
(206) 553-5676

West Virginia
475 Allendale Road,
Suite 201
King of Prussia, PA 19406
(215) 962-3700

Wisconsin
Federal Building
300 South Riverside Plaza,
1975 South
Chicago, IL 60606-6617
(312) 353-5000

Wyoming
999 18th Street, Suite 701
Denver, CO 80202
(303) 294-7186

RESEARCH AND EVALUATION PROGRAM

**Department of
Commerce**
Economic Development
Administration
Washington, DC 20230
(202) 377-4085

Description: Project grants to individuals,
partnerships, corporations, colleges, universities, and
for-profit or nonprofit organizations to determine
causes of unemployment in various areas of the
United States.
$ Given: Range: $7,500–$350,000.
Application Information: Write for guidelines.
Deadline: See Federal Register.
Contact: David Geddes, Director, Technical Assistance
and Research Division, EDA Room H-7319, above
address

Environment/Conservation

Many funds are available from the federal government for the environment/conservation for the following:

1. Assistance for projects or for research on pathogenic agents and biological or environmental hazards as well as the health risks associated with these hazards, the toxicology of chemicals, environmental protection, pesticides control, and climate and air quality research

2. Assistance for projects that assess ocean resource conservation, marine environmental effects, or water pollution controls

3. Support for the Superfund Program, which aids environmental technologies

You will need to consult the list of addresses in this chapter for your nearest local or regional Environmental Protection Agency office.

AIR POLLUTION CONTROL RESEARCH

Environmental Protection Agency
Grants Administration
Division, Room 216
Washington, DC 20460
(202) 260-7473

Description: Project grants to states, universities and colleges, hospitals, laboratories, state and local health departments, public or private nonprofit institutes, and individuals who have demonstrated unusually high scientific ability.
$ Given: Range: $1,000–$1.8 million; average: $145,198.
Application Information: Request application from above address.
Deadline: None
Contact: Your state and/or regional EPA office

Alabama
William McBride
Grants and Contracts
Administration Section
Management Division
345 Courtland Street, NE
Atlanta, GA 30365
(404) 347-2200

Alaska
Oddvar Aurdal, Chief
Grants Administration
Section, MS 321
1200 6th Avenue
Seattle, WA 98101
(206) 442-2930

American Samoa
Mike Schulz, Chief
1235 Missouri Street
Grants and Policy Branch
San Francisco, CA 94105
(415) 744-1623

Arizona
Mike Schulz, Chief
1235 Missouri Street
Grants and Policy Branch
San Francisco, CA 94105
(415) 744-1623

Arkansas
Julie Jensen, Chief
First International Building
1445 Ross Avenue
Grants Audit Section
(6M-PG)
Management Division
Dallas, TX 75270
(214) 655-6530

California
Mike Schulz, Chief
1235 Missouri Street
Grants and Policy Branch
San Francisco, CA 94105
(415) 744-1623

Connecticut
Robert Goetzl
John F. Kennedy Federal
Building, Tenth Floor
(PAS-205)
Grants Information and
Management Section
Boston, MA 02203
(617) 565-3395

Colorado
Martha Nicodemus, Chief
Grants Administration
Branch, 8PM-GFM
999 18th Street, Suite 1300
Denver, CO 80202-2413
(303) 293-1672

Delaware
Fred Warren
Grants Management Section
Office of the Comptroller,
3PM32
841 Chestnut Building
Philadelphia, PA 19107
(215) 597-6166

District of Columbia
Fred Warren
Grants Management Section
Office of the Comptroller,
3PM32
841 Chestnut Building
Philadelphia, PA 19107
(215) 597-6166

Florida
William McBride
Grants and Contracts
Administration Section
Management Division
345 Courtland Street, NE
Atlanta, GA 30365
(404) 347-2200

Georgia
William McBride
Grants and Contracts
Administration Section
Management Division
345 Courtland Street, NE
Atlanta, GA 30365
(404) 347-2200

Hawaii
Mike Schulz, Chief
1235 Missouri Street
Grants and Policy Branch
San Francisco, CA 94105
(415) 744-1623

Idaho
Oddvar Aurdal, Chief
Grants Administration
Section, MS 321
1200 6th Avenue
Seattle, WA 98101
(206) 442-2930

Illinois
Ivavs Anteus, Contracts
and Grants Branch
230 South Dearborn Street
Chicago, IL 60604
(312) 886-9841

Indiana
Ivavs Anteus, Contracts
and Grants Branch
230 South Dearborn Street
Chicago, IL 60604
(312) 886-9841

Iowa
Carol Rompage
726 Minnesota Avenue
Grants Administration
Branch
Kansas City, KS 66101
(913) 551-7346

Kansas
Carol Rompage
726 Minnesota Avenue
Grants Administration
Branch
Kansas City, KS 66101
(913) 551-7346

Kentucky
William McBride
Grants and Contracts
Administration Section
Management Division
345 Courtland Street, NE
Atlanta, GA 30365
(404) 347-2200

Louisiana
Julie Jensen, Chief
First International Building
1445 Ross Avenue
Grants Audit Section
(6M-PG)
Management Division
Dallas, TX 75270
(214) 655-6530

Maine
Robert Goetzl
John F. Kennedy Federal
Building, Tenth Floor
(PAS-205)
Grants Information and
Management Section
Boston, MA 02203
(617) 565-3395

Maryland
Fred Warren
Grants Management Section
Office of the Comptroller,
3PM32
841 Chestnut Building
Philadelphia, PA 19107
(215) 597-6166

Massachusetts
Robert Goetzl
John F. Kennedy Federal
Building, Tenth Floor
(PAS-205)
Grants Information and
Management Section
Boston, MA 02203
(617) 565-3395

Michigan
Ivavs Anteus, Contracts
and Grants Branch
230 South Dearborn Street
Chicago, IL 60604
(312) 886-9841

Minnesota
Ivavs Anteus, Contracts
and Grants Branch
230 South Dearborn Street
Chicago, IL 60604
(312) 886-9841

Mississippi
William McBride
Grants and Contracts
Administration Section
Management Division
345 Courtland Street, NE
Atlanta, GA 30365
(404) 347-2200

Missouri
Carol Rompage
726 Minnesota Avenue
Grants Administration
Branch
Kansas City, KS 66101
(913) 551-7346

Montana
Martha Nicodemus, Chief
Grants Administration
Branch, 8PM-GFM
999 18th Street, Suite 1300
Denver, CO 80202-2413
(303) 293-1672

Nebraska
Carol Rompage
726 Minnesota Avenue
Grants Administration
Branch
Kansas City, KS 66101
(913) 551-7346

Nevada
Mike Schulz, Chief
1235 Missouri Street
Grants and Policy Branch
San Francisco, CA 94105
(415) 744-1623

New Hampshire
Robert Goetzl
John F. Kennedy Federal
Building, Tenth Floor
(PAS-205)
Grants Information and
Management Section
Boston, MA 02203
(617) 565-3395

New Jersey
Helen Beggun, Chief
Grants Administration
Branch, 2MGT
26 Federal Plaza, Room 937A
New York, NY 10278
(212) 264-9860

New Mexico
Julie Jensen, Chief
First International Building
1445 Ross Avenue
Grants Audit Section
(6M-PG)
Management Division
Dallas, TX 75270
(214) 655-6530

New York
Helen Beggun, Chief
Grants Administration
Branch, 2MGT
26 Federal Plaza, Room 937A
New York, NY 10278
(212) 264-9860

North Carolina
William McBride
Grants and Contracts
Administration Section
Management Division
345 Courtland Street, NE
Atlanta, GA 30365
(404) 347-2200

North Dakota
Martha Nicodemus, Chief
Grants Administration
Branch, 8PM-GFM
999 18th Street, Suite 1300
Denver, CO 80202-2413
(303) 293-1672

Ohio
Ivavs Anteus, Contracts
and Grants Branch
230 South Dearborn Street
Chicago, IL 60604
(312) 886-9841

Oklahoma
Julie Jensen, Chief
First International Building
1445 Ross Avenue
Grants Audit Section
(6M-PG)
Management Division
Dallas, TX 75270
(214) 655-6530

Oregon
Oddvar Aurdal, Chief
Grants Administration
Section, MS 321
1200 6th Avenue
Seattle, WA 98101
(206) 442-2930

Pennsylvania
Fred Warren
Grants Management Section
Office of the Comptroller,
3PM32
841 Chestnut Building
Philadelphia, PA 19107
(215) 597-6166

Puerto Rico
Helen Beggun, Chief
Grants Administration
Branch, 2MGT
26 Federal Plaza, Room 937A
New York, NY 10278
(212) 264-9860

Rhode Island
Robert Goetzl
John F. Kennedy Federal
Building, Tenth Floor
(PAS-205)
Grants Information and
Management Section
Boston, MA 02203
(617) 565-3395

South Carolina
William McBride
Grants and Contracts
Administration Section
Management Division
345 Courtland Street, NE
Atlanta, GA 30365
(404) 347-2200

South Dakota
Martha Nicodemus, Chief
Grants Administration
Branch, 8PM-GFM
999 18th Street, Suite 1300
Denver, CO 80202-2413
(303) 293-1672

Tennessee
William McBride
Grants and Contracts
Administration Section
Management Division
345 Courtland Street, NE
Atlanta, GA 30365
(404) 347-2200

Texas
Julie Jensen, Chief
First International Building
1445 Ross Avenue
Grants Audit Section
(6M-PG)
Management Division
Dallas, TX 75270
(214) 655-6530

Utah
Martha Nicodemus, Chief
Grants Administration
Branch, 8PM-GFM
999 18th Street, Suite 1300
Denver, CO 80202-2413
(303) 293-1672

Vermont
Robert Goetzl
John F. Kennedy Federal
Building, Tenth Floor
(PAS-205)
Grants Information and
Management Section
Boston, MA 02203
(617) 565-3395

Virgin Islands
Helen Beggun, Chief
Grants Administration
Branch, 2MGT
26 Federal Plaza, Room 937A
New York, NY 10278
(212) 264-9860

Virginia
Fred Warren
Grants Management Section
Office of the Comptroller,
3PM32
841 Chestnut Building
Philadelphia, PA 19107
(215) 597-6166

Washington
Oddvar Aurdal, Chief
Grants Administration
Section, MS 321
1200 6th Avenue
Seattle, WA 98101
(206) 442-2930

West Virginia
Fred Warren
Grants Management Section
Office of the Comptroller,
3PM32
841 Chestnut Building
Philadelphia, PA 19107
(215) 597-6166

Wisconsin
Ivavs Anteus, Contracts
and Grants Branch
230 South Dearborn Street
Chicago, IL 60604
(312) 886-9841

Wyoming
Martha Nicodemus, Chief
Grants Administration
Branch, 8PM-GFM
999 18th Street, Suite 1300
Denver, CO 80202-2413
(303) 293-1672

ANADROMOUS FISH CONSERVATION

Department of the Interior
Division of Fish and Wildlife Management Assistance
Fish and Wildlife Service
Washington, DC 20240
(703) 358-1718

Description: Project grants to individual entities with professional fishery capabilities to conserve anadromous fish resources (fish that ascend streams to spawn), particularly in the Great Lakes and Lake Champlain regions, and to determine the cause of the drastic decline in the Atlantic coastal migratory striped bass population. Nineteen inland states are ineligible.
$ Given: Nationwide FY 92 est. $100,000 (exclusive of striped bass study, for which $298,000 was given).
Application Information: Submit standard project application form to regional office.
Deadline: None
Contact: Regional Fish and Wildlife Service field office

Alabama
James W. Pulliam, Jr.
75 Spring Street, SW
Atlanta, GA 30303
(404) 331-3588

Alaska
Walter O. Stieglitz
1011 East Tudor Road
Anchorage, AK 99503
(907) 869-3542

Arizona
Michael J. Spear
P.O. Box 1306
500 Gold Avenue, SW,
Room 3018
Albuquerque, NM 87102
(505) 766-2321

Arkansas
James W. Pulliam, Jr.
75 Spring Street, SW
Atlanta, GA 30303
(404) 331-3588

California
Marvin L. Plenert
911 NE 11th Avenue
Portland, OR 97232-4181
(503) 231-6118

Colorado
Galen L. Buterbaugh
P.O. Box 25486
Denver Federal Center
Denver, CO 80025
(303) 236-7920

Connecticut
Ronald E. Lambertson
One Gateway Center,
Suite 700
Newton Corner, MA 02158
(617) 965-5100

Delaware
Ronald E. Lambertson
One Gateway Center,
Suite 700
Newton Corner, MA 02158
(617) 965-5100

District of Columbia
Ronald E. Lambertson
One Gateway Center,
Suite 700
Newton Corner, MA 02158
(617) 965-5100

Florida
James W. Pulliam, Jr.
75 Spring Street, SW
Atlanta, GA 30303
(404) 331-3588

Georgia
James W. Pulliam, Jr.
75 Spring Street, SW
Atlanta, GA 30303
(404) 331-3588

Hawaii
Marvin L. Plenert
911 NE 11th Avenue
Portland, OR 97232-4181
(503) 231-6118

Idaho
Marvin L. Plenert
911 NE 11th Avenue
Portland, OR 97232-4181
(503) 231-6118

Illinois
James C. Gritman
Federal Building,
Fort Snelling
Twin Cities, MN 55111
(612) 725-3563

Indiana
James C. Gritman
Federal Building,
Fort Snelling
Twin Cities, MN 55111
(612) 725-3563

Iowa
James C. Gritman
Federal Building,
Fort Snelling
Twin Cities, MN 55111
(612) 725-3563

Kansas
Galen L. Buterbaugh
P.O. Box 25486
Denver Federal Center
Denver, CO 80025
(303) 236-7920

Kentucky
James W. Pulliam, Jr.
75 Spring Street, SW
Atlanta, GA 30303
(404) 331-3588

Louisiana
James W. Pulliam, Jr.
75 Spring Street, SW
Atlanta, GA 30303
(404) 331-3588

Maine
Ronald E. Lambertson
One Gateway Center,
Suite 700
Newton Corner, MA 02158
(617) 965-5100

Maryland
Ronald E. Lambertson
One Gateway Center,
Suite 700
Newton Corner, MA 02158
(617) 965-5100

Massachusetts
Ronald E. Lambertson
One Gateway Center,
Suite 700
Newton Corner, MA 02158
(617) 965-5100

Michigan
James C. Gritman
Federal Building,
Fort Snelling
Twin Cities, MN 55111
(612) 725-3563

Minnesota
James C. Gritman
Federal Building,
Fort Snelling
Twin Cities, MN 55111
(612) 725-3563

Mississippi
James W. Pulliam, Jr.
75 Spring Street, SW
Atlanta, GA 30303
(404) 331-3588

Missouri
James C. Gritman
Federal Building,
Fort Snelling
Twin Cities, MN 55111
(612) 725-3563

Montana
Galen L. Buterbaugh
P.O. Box 25486
Denver Federal Center
Denver, CO 80025
(303) 236-7920

Nebraska
Galen L. Buterbaugh
P.O. Box 25486
Denver Federal Center
Denver, CO 80025
(303) 236-7920

Nevada
Marvin L. Plenert
911 NE 11th Avenue
Portland, OR 97232-4181
(503) 231-6118

New Hampshire
Ronald E. Lambertson
One Gateway Center,
Suite 700
Newton Corner, MA 02158
(617) 965-5100

New Jersey
Ronald E. Lambertson
One Gateway Center,
Suite 700
Newton Corner, MA 02158
(617) 965-5100

New Mexico
Michael J. Spear
P.O. Box 1306
500 Gold Avenue, SW,
Room 3018
Albuquerque, NM 87102
(505) 766-2321

New York
Ronald E. Lambertson
One Gateway Center,
Suite 700
Newton Corner, MA 02158
(617) 965-5100

North Carolina
James W. Pulliam, Jr.
75 Spring Street, SW
Atlanta, GA 30303
(404) 331-3588

North Dakota
Galen L. Buterbaugh
P.O. Box 25486
Denver Federal Center
Denver, CO 80025
(303) 236-7920

Ohio
James C. Gritman
Federal Building,
Fort Snelling
Twin Cities, MN 55111
(612) 725-3563

Oklahoma
Michael J. Spear
P.O. Box 1306
500 Gold Avenue, SW,
Room 3018
Albuquerque, NM 87102
(505) 766-2321

Oregon
Marvin L. Plenert
911 NE 11th Avenue
Portland, OR 97232-4181
(503) 231-6118

Pennsylvania
Ronald E. Lambertson
One Gateway Center,
Suite 700
Newton Corner, MA 02158
(617) 965-5100

Puerto Rico
James W. Pulliam, Jr.
75 Spring Street, SW
Atlanta, GA 30303
(404) 331-3588

Rhode Island
Ronald E. Lambertson
One Gateway Center,
Suite 700
Newton Corner, MA 02158
(617) 965-5100

South Carolina
James W. Pulliam, Jr.
75 Spring Street, SW
Atlanta, GA 30303
(404) 331-3588

South Dakota
Galen L. Buterbaugh
P.O. Box 25486
Denver Federal Center
Denver, CO 80025
(303) 236-7920

Tennessee
James W. Pulliam, Jr.
75 Spring Street, SW
Atlanta, GA 30303
(404) 331-3588

Texas
Michael J. Spear
P.O. Box 1306
500 Gold Avenue, SW,
Room 3018
Albuquerque, NM 87102
(505) 766-2321

Utah
Galen L. Buterbaugh
P.O. Box 25486
Denver Federal Center
Denver, CO 80025
(303) 236-7920

Vermont
Ronald E. Lambertson
One Gateway Center,
Suite 700
Newton Corner, MA 02158
(617) 965-5100

Virgin Islands
James W. Pulliam, Jr.
75 Spring Street, SW
Atlanta, GA 30303
(404) 331-3588

Virginia
Ronald E. Lambertson
One Gateway Center,
Suite 700
Newton Corner, MA 02158
(617) 965-5100

Washington
Marvin L. Plenert
911 NE 11th Avenue
Portland, OR 97232-4181
(503) 231-6118

West Virginia
Ronald E. Lambertson
One Gateway Center,
Suite 700
Newton Corner, MA 02158
(617) 965-5100

Wisconsin
James C. Gritman
Federal Building,
Fort Snelling
Twin Cities, MN 55111
(612) 725-3563

Wyoming
Galen L. Buterbaugh
P.O. Box 25486
Denver Federal Center
Denver, CO 80025
(303) 236-7920

APPLIED TOXICOLOGICAL RESEARCH AND TESTING (BIOASSAY OF CHEMICALS AND TEST DEVELOPMENT)

Department of Health and Human Services
Scientific Programs Branch
Division of Extramural Research and Training
National Institute of Environmental Health Sciences
National Institutes of Health
Public Health Service
P.O. Box 12233
Research Triangle Park, NC 27709
(919) 541-7634

Description: Project grants to for-profit organizations (includes Small Business Innovation Research grants [SBIRs]) to conduct research in toxicology of hazardous chemicals.
$ Given: Nationwide FY 93 est. $6.8 million in total grants. Range: $67,920–$436,776; average: $129,000.
Application Information: Submit standard applications.
Deadline: Research grants: February 1, June 1, October 1; SBIRs: April 15, August 15, December 15.
Contact: Dr. Christopher Schonwalder, Chief, above address

BIOLOGICAL RESPONSE TO ENVIRONMENTAL HEALTH HAZARDS

Department of Health and Human Services
Scientific Programs Branch
Division of Extramural Research and Training
National Institute of Environmental Health Sciences
National Institutes of Health
Public Health Service
P.O. Box 12233
Research Triangle Park, NC 27709
(919) 541-7634

Description: Project grants, including SBIRs, to private for-profit organizations to foster research on pathogenic agents and other biological hazards. Special grants to purchase low-cost research equipment. SBIRs in two phases, I and II (feasibility and continuation). Maximum funds: $50,000 for Phase I, $500,000 for Phase II. Various other restrictions apply. Funds to be used in manner consistent with research grants.
$ Given: Nationwide FY 93 est. $76 million in total grants. Range (excluding SBIRs): $25,022–$1.6 million; average: $179,664.
Application Information: Submit standard application.
Deadline: Research grants: February 1, June 1, October 1; SBIRs: April 15, August 15, December 15.
Contact: Dr. Christopher Schonwalder, Chief, above address

BIOMETRY AND RISK ESTIMATION—HEALTH RISKS FROM ENVIRONMENTAL EXPOSURES

Department of Health and Human Services
Scientific Programs Branch
Division of Extramural Research and Training
National Institute of Environmental Health Sciences
National Institutes of Health
Public Health Service
P.O. Box 12233
Research Triangle Park, NC 27709
(919) 541-7634

Description: Project grants to for-profit organizations (includes SBIRs) to conduct research in estimating probable health risks from various environmental hazards.
$ Given: Nationwide FY 93 est. $6.4 million in total grants. Range: $52,272–$864,117; average: $257,044.
Application Information: Submit standard applications.
Deadline: Research grants: February 1, June 1, October 1; SBIRs: April 15, August 15, December 15.
Contact: Dr. Christopher Schonwalder, Chief, above address

CLIMATE AND AIR QUALITY RESEARCH

Department of Commerce
National Oceanic and Atmospheric Administration
1335 East West Highway
Silver Spring, MD 20910
(301) 713-2458

Description: Project grants to individuals, technical schools, and laboratories to develop knowledge required to predict short-term and long-term fluctuations and trends in climate and air quality. Funds to be used for research and development, advisory services, and operational systems.
$ Given: Nationwide FY 93 est. $50,000. Range: $2,000–$10,000.
Application Information: Submit standard application with statement of work to be performed and proposed amount.
Deadline: None
Contact: Alan Thomas or Director, Office of Climate and Environmental Research Laboratories, Office of Oceanic and Atmospheric Research, above address

CLIMATE AND RESEARCH

Department of Commerce
National Oceanic and Atmospheric Administration
1335 East West Highway
Silver Spring, MD 20910
(301) 427-2089

Description: Project grants to any individual, technical school, or laboratory to develop ability to predict short-range and long-range climatic fluctuations and trends. Funds must be used for research and development, advisory services, or operational systems.
$ Given: Nationwide FY 93 est. $17.9 million. Range: $10,000–$220,000; average: $85,000.
Application Information: Submit standard application with statement of work to be performed and proposed amount.
Deadline: None
Contact: Director, Office of Global Programs, above address

ENVIRONMENTAL PROTECTION—CONSOLIDATED RESEARCH

Environmental Protection Agency
Grants Administration Division, Room 216
Washington, DC 20460
(202) 260-7473

Description: Project grants to states, universities and colleges, hospitals, laboratories, public or private nonprofit institutes, and individuals who have demonstrated unusually high scientific ability.
$ Given: Range: $2,000–$2.5 million; average: $140,000.
Application Information: Request application from above address.
Deadline: None
Contact: Your state and/or regional EPA office

Alabama
William McBride
Grants and Contracts
Administration Section
Management Division
345 Courtland Street, NE
Atlanta, GA 30365
(404) 347-2200

Alaska
Oddvar Aurdal, Chief
Grants Administration
Section, MS 321
1200 6th Avenue
Seattle, WA 98101
(206) 442-2930

American Samoa
Mike Schulz, Chief
1235 Missouri Street
Grants and Policy Branch
San Francisco, CA 94105
(415) 744-1623

Arizona
Mike Schulz, Chief
1235 Missouri Street
Grants and Policy Branch
San Francisco, CA 94105
(415) 744-1623

Arkansas
Julie Jensen, Chief
First International Building
1445 Ross Avenue
Grants Audit Section
(6M-PG)
Management Division
Dallas, TX 75270
(214) 655-6530

California
Mike Schulz, Chief
1235 Missouri Street
Grants and Policy Branch
San Francisco, CA 94105
(415) 744-1623

Connecticut
Robert Goetzl
John F. Kennedy Federal
Building, Tenth Floor
(PAS-205)
Grants Information and
Management Section
Boston, MA 02203
(617) 565-3395

Colorado
Martha Nicodemus, Chief
Grants Administration
Branch, 8PM-GFM
999 18th Street, Suite 1300
Denver, CO 80202-2413
(303) 293-1672

Delaware
Fred Warren
Grants Management Section
Office of the Comptroller,
3PM32
841 Chestnut Building
Philadelphia, PA 19107
(215) 597-6166

District of Columbia
Fred Warren
Grants Management Section
Office of the Comptroller,
3PM32
841 Chestnut Building
Philadelphia, PA 19107
(215) 597-6166

Florida
William McBride
Grants and Contracts
Administration Section
Management Division
345 Courtland Street, NE
Atlanta, GA 30365
(404) 347-2200

Georgia
William McBride
Grants and Contracts
Administration Section
Management Division
345 Courtland Street, NE
Atlanta, GA 30365
(404) 347-2200

Hawaii
Mike Schulz, Chief
1235 Missouri Street
Grants and Policy Branch
San Francisco, CA 94105
(415) 744-1623

Idaho
Oddvar Aurdal, Chief
Grants Administration
Section, MS 321
1200 6th Avenue
Seattle, WA 98101
(206) 442-2930

Illinois
Ivavs Anteus, Contracts
and Grants Branch
230 South Dearborn Street
Chicago, IL 60604
(312) 886-9841

Indiana
Ivavs Anteus, Contracts
and Grants Branch
230 South Dearborn Street
Chicago, IL 60604
(312) 886-9841

Iowa
Carol Rompage
726 Minnesota Avenue
Grants Administration
Branch
Kansas City, KS 66101
(913) 551-7346

Kansas
Carol Rompage
726 Minnesota Avenue
Grants Administration
Branch
Kansas City, KS 66101
(913) 551-7346

Kentucky
William McBride
Grants and Contracts
Administration Section
Management Division
345 Courtland Street, NE
Atlanta, GA 30365
(404) 347-2200

Louisiana
Julie Jensen, Chief
First International Building
1445 Ross Avenue
Grants Audit Section
(6M-PG)
Management Division
Dallas, TX 75270
(214) 655-6530

Maine
Robert Goetzl
John F. Kennedy Federal
Building, Tenth Floor
(PAS-205)
Grants Information and
Management Section
Boston, MA 02203
(617) 565-3395

Maryland
Fred Warren
Grants Management Section
Office of the Comptroller,
3PM32
841 Chestnut Building
Philadelphia, PA 19107
(215) 597-6166

Massachusetts
Robert Goetzl
John F. Kennedy Federal
Building, Tenth Floor
(PAS-205)
Grants Information and
Management Section
Boston, MA 02203
(617) 565-3395

Michigan
Ivavs Anteus, Contracts
and Grants Branch
230 South Dearborn Street
Chicago, IL 60604
(312) 886-9841

Minnesota
Ivavs Anteus, Contracts
and Grants Branch
230 South Dearborn Street
Chicago, IL 60604
(312) 886-9841

Mississippi
William McBride
Grants and Contracts
Administration Section
Management Division
345 Courtland Street, NE
Atlanta, GA 30365
(404) 347-2200

Missouri
Carol Rompage
726 Minnesota Avenue
Grants Administration
Branch
Kansas City, KS 66101
(913) 551-7346

Montana
Martha Nicodemus, Chief
Grants Administration
Branch, 8PM-GFM
999 18th Street, Suite 1300
Denver, CO 80202-2413
(303) 293-1672

Nebraska
Carol Rompage
726 Minnesota Avenue
Grants Administration
Branch
Kansas City, KS 66101
(913) 551-7346

Nevada
Mike Schulz, Chief
1235 Missouri Street
Grants and Policy Branch
San Francisco, CA 94105
(415) 744-1623

New Hampshire
Robert Goetzl
John F. Kennedy Federal
Building, Tenth Floor
(PAS-205)
Grants Information and
Management Section
Boston, MA 02203
(617) 565-3395

New Jersey
Helen Beggun, Chief
Grants Administration
Branch, 2MGT
26 Federal Plaza, Room 937A
New York, NY 10278
(212) 264-9860

New Mexico
Julie Jensen, Chief
First International Building
1445 Ross Avenue
Grants Audit Section
(6M-PG)
Management Division
Dallas, TX 75270
(214) 655-6530

New York
Helen Beggun, Chief
Grants Administration
Branch, 2MGT
26 Federal Plaza, Room 937A
New York, NY 10278
(212) 264-9860

North Carolina
William McBride
Grants and Contracts
Administration Section
Management Division
345 Courtland Street, NE
Atlanta, GA 30365
(404) 347-2200

North Dakota
Martha Nicodemus, Chief
Grants Administration
Branch, 8PM-GFM
999 18th Street, Suite 1300
Denver, CO 80202-2413
(303) 293-1672

Ohio
Ivavs Anteus, Contracts
and Grants Branch
230 South Dearborn Street
Chicago, IL 60604
(312) 886-9841

Oklahoma
Julie Jensen, Chief
First International Building
1445 Ross Avenue
Grants Audit Section
(6M-PG)
Management Division
Dallas, TX 75270
(214) 655-6530

Oregon
Oddvar Aurdal, Chief
Grants Administration
Section, MS 321
1200 6th Avenue
Seattle, WA 98101
(206) 442-2930

Pennsylvania
Fred Warren
Grants Management Section
Office of the Comptroller,
3PM32
841 Chestnut Building
Philadelphia, PA 19107
(215) 597-6166

Puerto Rico
Helen Beggun, Chief
Grants Administration
Branch, 2MGT
26 Federal Plaza, Room 937A
New York, NY 10278
(212) 264-9860

Rhode Island
Robert Goetzl
John F. Kennedy Federal
Building, Tenth Floor
(PAS-205)
Grants Information and
Management Section
Boston, MA 02203
(617) 565-3395

South Carolina
William McBride
Grants and Contracts
Administration Section
Management Division
345 Courtland Street, NE
Atlanta, GA 30365
(404) 347-2200

South Dakota
Martha Nicodemus, Chief
Grants Administration
Branch, 8PM-GFM
999 18th Street, Suite 1300
Denver, CO 80202-2413
(303) 293-1672

Tennessee
William McBride
Grants and Contracts
Administration Section
Management Division
345 Courtland Street, NE
Atlanta, GA 30365
(404) 347-2200

Texas
Julie Jensen, Chief
First International Building
1445 Ross Avenue
Grants Audit Section
(6M-PG)
Management Division
Dallas, TX 75270
(214) 655-6530

Utah
Martha Nicodemus, Chief
Grants Administration
Branch, 8PM-GFM
999 18th Street, Suite 1300
Denver, CO 80202-2413
(303) 293-1672

Vermont
Robert Goetzl
John F. Kennedy Federal
Building, Tenth Floor
(PAS-205)
Grants Information and
Management Section
Boston, MA 02203
(617) 565-3395

Virgin Islands
Helen Beggun, Chief
Grants Administration
Branch, 2MGT
26 Federal Plaza, Room 937A
New York, NY 10278
(212) 264-9860

Virginia
Fred Warren
Grants Management Section
Office of the Comptroller,
3PM32
841 Chestnut Building
Philadelphia, PA 19107
(215) 597-6166

Washington
Oddvar Aurdal, Chief
Grants Administration
Section, MS 321
1200 6th Avenue
Seattle, WA 98101
(206) 442-2930

West Virginia
Fred Warren
Grants Management Section
Office of the Comptroller,
3PM32
841 Chestnut Building
Philadelphia, PA 19107
(215) 597-6166

Wisconsin
Ivavs Anteus, Contracts
and Grants Branch
230 South Dearborn Street
Chicago, IL 60604
(312) 886-9841

Wyoming
Martha Nicodemus, Chief
Grants Administration
Branch, 8PM-GFM
999 18th Street, Suite 1300
Denver, CO 80202-2413
(303) 293-1672

FINANCIAL ASSISTANCE FOR OCEAN RESOURCES CONSERVATION AND ASSESSMENT PROGRAM

Department of Commerce
National Ocean Service
6001 Executive Avenue,
Room 212
Rockville, MD 20852

Description: Project grants (cooperative agreements) to individuals and corporations to assess long-term impact of human activities on coastal and marine environment and to define and assess techniques to minimize adverse effects. Recipient must demonstrate expertise in priority objectives and win approval for proposed methods.
$ Given: Nationwide FY 93 est. $850,000. Range: $20,000–$200,000; average: $80,000.
Application Information: Standard application forms required.
Deadline: None. Proposals reviewed several times a year.
Contact: Office of Ocean Resources Conservation and Marine Assessment, (N/ORCA), above address

PESTICIDES CONTROL RESEARCH

**Environmental
Protection Agency**
Grants Administration
Division, Room 216
Washington, DC 20460
(202) 260-7473

Description: Project grants to states, universities and colleges, hospitals, laboratories, state and local governments, and individuals.
$ Given: Range: $10,000–$450,000; average: $110,000.
Application Information: Request application from above address.
Deadline: None
Contact: Your state and/or regional EPA office

Alabama
William McBride
Grants and Contracts
Administration Section
Management Division
345 Courtland Street, NE
Atlanta, GA 30365
(404) 347-2200

Alaska
Oddvar Aurdal, Chief
Grants Administration
Section, MS 321
1200 6th Avenue
Seattle, WA 98101
(206) 442-2930

American Samoa
Mike Schulz, Chief
1235 Missouri Street
Grants and Policy Branch
San Francisco, CA 94105
(415) 744-1623

Arizona
Mike Schulz, Chief
1235 Missouri Street
Grants and Policy Branch
San Francisco, CA 94105
(415) 744-1623

Arkansas
Julie Jensen, Chief
First International Building
1445 Ross Avenue
Grants Audit Section
(6M-PG)
Management Division
Dallas, TX 75270
(214) 655-6530

California
Mike Schulz, Chief
1235 Missouri Street
Grants and Policy Branch
San Francisco, CA 94105
(415) 744-1623

Connecticut
Robert Goetzl
John F. Kennedy Federal
Building, Tenth Floor
(PAS-205)
Grants Information and
Management Section
Boston, MA 02203
(617) 565-3395

Colorado
Martha Nicodemus, Chief
Grants Administration
Branch, 8PM-GFM
999 18th Street, Suite 1300
Denver, CO 80202-2413
(303) 293-1672

Delaware
Fred Warren
Grants Management Section
Office of the Comptroller,
3PM32
841 Chestnut Building
Philadelphia, PA 19107
(215) 597-6166

District of Columbia
Fred Warren
Grants Management Section
Office of the Comptroller,
3PM32
841 Chestnut Building
Philadelphia, PA 19107
(215) 597-6166

Florida
William McBride
Grants and Contracts
Administration Section
Management Division
345 Courtland Street, NE
Atlanta, GA 30365
(404) 347-2200

Georgia
William McBride
Grants and Contracts
Administration Section
Management Division
345 Courtland Street, NE
Atlanta, GA 30365
(404) 347-2200

Hawaii
Mike Schulz, Chief
1235 Missouri Street
Grants and Policy Branch
San Francisco, CA 94105
(415) 744-1623

Idaho
Oddvar Aurdal, Chief
Grants Administration
Section, MS 321
1200 6th Avenue
Seattle, WA 98101
(206) 442-2930

Illinois
Ivavs Anteus, Contracts
and Grants Branch
230 South Dearborn Street
Chicago, IL 60604
(312) 886-9841

Indiana
Ivavs Anteus, Contracts
and Grants Branch
230 South Dearborn Street
Chicago, IL 60604
(312) 886-9841

Iowa
Carol Rompage
726 Minnesota Avenue
Grants Administration
Branch
Kansas City, KS 66101
(913) 551-7346

Kansas
Carol Rompage
726 Minnesota Avenue
Grants Administration
Branch
Kansas City, KS 66101
(913) 551-7346

Kentucky
William McBride
Grants and Contracts
Administration Section
Management Division
345 Courtland Street, NE
Atlanta, GA 30365
(404) 347-2200

Louisiana
Julie Jensen, Chief
First International Building
1445 Ross Avenue
Grants Audit Section
(6M-PG)
Management Division
Dallas, TX 75270
(214) 655-6530

Maine
Robert Goetzl
John F. Kennedy Federal
Building, Tenth Floor
(PAS-205)
Grants Information and
Management Section
Boston, MA 02203
(617) 565-3395

Maryland
Fred Warren
Grants Management Section
Office of the Comptroller,
3PM32
841 Chestnut Building
Philadelphia, PA 19107
(215) 597-6166

Massachusetts
Robert Goetzl
John F. Kennedy Federal
Building, Tenth Floor
(PAS-205)
Grants Information
and Management Section
Boston, MA 02203
(617) 565-3395

Michigan
Ivavs Anteus, Contracts
and Grants Branch
230 South Dearborn Street
Chicago, IL 60604
(312) 886-9841

Minnesota
Ivavs Anteus, Contracts
and Grants Branch
230 South Dearborn Street
Chicago, IL 60604
(312) 886-9841

Mississippi
William McBride
Grants and Contracts
Administration Section
Management Division
345 Courtland Street, NE
Atlanta, GA 30365
(404) 347-2200

Missouri
Carol Rompage
726 Minnesota Avenue
Grants Administration
Branch
Kansas City, KS 66101
(913) 551-7346

Montana
Martha Nicodemus, Chief
Grants Administration
Branch, 8PM-GFM
999 18th Street, Suite 1300
Denver, CO 80202-2413
(303) 293-1672

Nebraska
Carol Rompage
726 Minnesota Avenue
Grants Administration
Branch
Kansas City, KS 66101
(913) 551-7346

Nevada
Mike Schulz, Chief
1235 Missouri Street
Grants and Policy Branch
San Francisco, CA 94105
(415) 744-1623

New Hampshire
Robert Goetzl
John F. Kennedy Federal
Building, Tenth Floor
(PAS-205)
Grants Information and
Management Section
Boston, MA 02203
(617) 565-3395

New Jersey
Helen Beggun, Chief
Grants Administration
Branch, 2MGT
26 Federal Plaza, Room 937A
New York, NY 10278
(212) 264-9860

New Mexico
Julie Jensen, Chief
First International Building
1445 Ross Avenue
Grants Audit Section
(6M-PG)
Management Division
Dallas, TX 75270
(214) 655-6530

New York
Helen Beggun, Chief
Grants Administration
Branch, 2MGT
26 Federal Plaza, Room 937A
New York, NY 10278
(212) 264-9860

North Carolina
William McBride
Grants and Contracts
Administration Section
Management Division
345 Courtland Street, NE
Atlanta, GA 30365
(404) 347-2200

North Dakota
Martha Nicodemus, Chief
Grants Administration
Branch, 8PM-GFM
999 18th Street, Suite 1300
Denver, CO 80202-2413
(303) 293-1672

Ohio
Ivavs Anteus, Contracts
and Grants Branch
230 South Dearborn Street
Chicago, IL 60604
(312) 886-9841

Oklahoma
Julie Jensen, Chief
First International Building
1445 Ross Avenue
Grants Audit Section
(6M-PG)
Management Division
Dallas, TX 75270
(214) 655-6530

Oregon
Oddvar Aurdal, Chief
Grants Administration
Section, MS 321
1200 6th Avenue
Seattle, WA 98101
(206) 442-2930

Pennsylvania
Fred Warren
Grants Management Section
Office of the Comptroller,
3PM32
841 Chestnut Building
Philadelphia, PA 19107
(215) 597-6166

Puerto Rico
Helen Beggun, Chief
Grants Administration
Branch, 2MGT
26 Federal Plaza, Room 937A
New York, NY 10278
(212) 264-9860

Rhode Island
Robert Goetzl
John F. Kennedy Federal
Building, Tenth Floor
(PAS-205)
Grants Information and
Management Section
Boston, MA 02203
(617) 565-3395

South Carolina
William McBride
Grants and Contracts
Administration Section
Management Division
345 Courtland Street, NE
Atlanta, GA 30365
(404) 347-2200

South Dakota
Martha Nicodemus, Chief
Grants Administration
Branch, 8PM-GFM
999 18th Street, Suite 1300
Denver, CO 80202-2413
(303) 293-1672

Tennessee
William McBride
Grants and Contracts
Administration Section
Management Division
345 Courtland Street, NE
Atlanta, GA 30365
(404) 347-2200

Texas
Julie Jensen, Chief
First International Building
1445 Ross Avenue
Grants Audit Section
(6M-PG)
Management Division
Dallas, TX 75270
(214) 655-6530

Utah
Martha Nicodemus, Chief
Grants Administration
Branch, 8PM-GFM
999 18th Street, Suite 1300
Denver, CO 80202-2413
(303) 293-1672

Vermont
Robert Goetzl
John F. Kennedy Federal
Building, Tenth Floor
(PAS-205)
Grants Information and
Management Section
Boston, MA 02203
(617) 565-3395

Virgin Islands
Helen Beggun, Chief
Grants Administration
Branch, 2MGT
26 Federal Plaza, Room 937A
New York, NY 10278
(212) 264-9860

Virginia
Fred Warren
Grants Management Section
Office of the Comptroller,
3PM32
841 Chestnut Building
Philadelphia, PA 19107
(215) 597-6166

Washington
Oddvar Aurdal, Chief
Grants Administration
Section, MS 321
1200 6th Avenue
Seattle, WA 98101
(206) 442-2930

West Virginia
Fred Warren
Grants Management Section
Office of the Comptroller,
3PM32
841 Chestnut Building
Philadelphia, PA 19107
(215) 597-6166

Wisconsin
Ivavs Anteus, Contracts
and Grants Branch
230 South Dearborn Street
Chicago, IL 60604
(312) 886-9841

Wyoming
Martha Nicodemus, Chief
Grants Administration
Branch, 8PM-GFM
999 18th Street, Suite 1300
Denver, CO 80202-2413
(303) 293-1672

POLLUTION PREVENTION GRANTS PROGRAM

**Environmental
Protection Agency
Pollution Prevention
Division
Office of Pollution
Prevention and Toxics,**
PM-222B
401 M Street, SW
Washington, DC 20460
(202) 260-4167 or
260-2237

Description: Provides direct technical assistance to businesses in need of information and training in source reduction techniques. These programs are administered by the states. Applicants should contact the office designated as the single point of contact for his or her state, or to the regional EPA office.
$ Given: FY 93 est. $6 million. Range: $50,000–$200,000; average: $160,000.
Application Information: See contact listed below.
Deadline: N/A
Contact: Regional EPA office or state single point of contact

Environment/Conservation

Alabama
William McBride
Grants and Contracts
Administration Section
Management Division
345 Courtland Street, NE
Atlanta, GA 30365
(404) 347-2200

Alaska
Oddvur Aurdal, Chief
Grants Administration
Section, MS 321
1200 6th Avenue
Seattle, WA 98101
(206) 442-2930

Arizona
Janice Dunn
Arizona State Clearinghouse
3800 North Central Avenue,
Fourteenth Floor
Phoenix, AZ 85012
(602) 280-1315

Arkansas
Joseph Gillespie, Manager
State Clearinghouse
Office of Intergovernmental
Service
Department of Finance and
Administration
P.O. Box 3278
Little Rock, AK 72203
(501) 371-1074

California
Glenn Stober
Grants Coordinator
Office of Planning
and Research
1400 Tenth Street
Sacramento, CA 95814
(916) 323-7480

Colorado
State Single Point of Contact
State Clearinghouse
Division of Local
Government
1313 Sherman Street,
Room 520
Denver, CO 80203
(303) 866-2156

Connecticut
William T. Quiqq
Intergovernmental Review
Coordinator
State Single Point of Contact
Office of Policy and
Management
Intergovernmental Policy
Division
80 Washington Street
Hartford, CT 06106-4459
(203) 566-3410

Delaware
Francine Booth
State Single Point of Contact
Executive Department
Thomas Collins Building
Dover, DE 19903
(302) 736-3326

District of Columbia
Lovetta Davis
State Single Point of Contact
Executive Office
of the Mayor
Office of Intergovernmental
Relations
District Building, Room 416
1350 Pennsylvania
Avenue, NW
Washington, DC 20004
(202) 727-9111

Florida
Janice L. Alcott, Director
Florida State Clearinghouse
Executive Office
of the Governor
Office of Planning
and Budgeting
The Capitol
Tallahassee, FL 32399-0001
(904) 488-8114

Georgia
Charles H. Badger,
Administrator
Georgia State Clearinghouse
270 Washington Street, SW
Atlanta, GA 30334
(404) 656-3855

Hawaii
Mary Lou Kobayashi
Planning Program Manager
Office of State Planning
Office of the Governor
P.O. Box 3540
Honolulu, HI 96811
(808) 587-2802

Idaho
Grants Administration
Section, MS 321
1200 6th Avenue
Seattle, WA 98101
(206) 442-2930

Illinois
Tom Berkshire
State Single Point of Contact
Office of the Governor
State of Illinois
Springfield, IL 62706
(217) 782-8639

Indiana
Frank Sullivan
Budget Director
State Budget Agency
212 State House
Indianapolis, IN 46204
(317) 232-5610

Iowa
Steven R. McCann
Division for Community
Progress
Iowa Department of
Economic Development
200 East Grand Avenue
Des Moines, IA 50309

Kansas
Carol Rompage
726 Minnesota Avenue
Grants Administration
Branch
Kansas City, KS 66101
(913) 551-7346

Kentucky
Ronald W. Cook
Office of the Governor
Department of Local
Government
1024 Capitol Center Drive
Frankfort, KY 40601
(502) 564-2382

Louisiana
Julie Jensen, Chief
First International Building
1445 Ross Avenue
Grants Audit Section
(6M-PG)
Management Division
Dallas, TX 75270
(214) 655-6530

Maine
Joyce Benson
State Planning Office
State House Station No. 38
Augusta, ME 04333
(207) 289-3261

Maryland
Mary Abrams, Chief
Maryland State
Clearinghouse
Department of State
Planning
301 West Preston Street
Baltimore, MD 21201
(301) 225-4490

Massachusetts
State Clearinghouse
Executive Office of
Communities and
Development
100 Cambridge Street,
Room 1803
Boston, MA 02202
(617) 727-7001

Michigan
Manager, Federal Project
Review
Michigan Department of
Commerce
Michigan Neighborhood
Builders Alliance
P.O. Box 30242
Lansing, MI 48909
(517) 373-6223

Minnesota
Environmental Protection
Agency, Region V
77 West Jackson Boulevard
Chicago, IL 60604
(312) 353-2000

Mississippi
Cathy Mallette
Clearinghouse Officer
Office of Policy Development
Department of Finance
and Administration
455 North Lamar Street,
Suite 120
Jackson, MS 39202
(601) 359-6765

Missouri
Lois Pohl
Federal Assistance
Clearinghouse
Office of Administration
P.O. Box 809
Truman Building, Room 430
Jefferson City, MO 65102
(314) 751-4834

Montana
Martha Nicodemus, Chief
Grants Administration
Branch, 8PM-GFM
999 18th Street, Suite 1300
Denver, CO 80202-2413
(303) 293-1672

Nebraska
Carol Rompage
726 Minnesota Avenue
Grants Administration
Branch
Kansas City, KS 66101
(913) 551-7346

Nevada
Department of
Administration
State Clearinghouse
Capitol Complex
Carson City, NV 89710
Attn: Dana G. Strum
Clearinghouse Coordinator
(702) 687-4065

New Hampshire
Jeffery H. Taylor, Director
New Hampshire Office of
State Planning
Attn: Intergovernmental
Review Process, James E.
Bieber
2½ Beacon Street
Concord, NH 03301
(603) 271-2155

New Jersey
Andrew J. Jaskolka
State Review Process
Division of Community
Resources
CN 814, Room 609
Trenton, NJ 08625-0814
(609) 292-9025

New Mexico
George Elliott
Deputy Director
State Budget Division
Bataan Memorial Building,
Room 190
Santa Fe, NM 87503
(505) 827-3640

New York
New York State
Clearinghouse
Division of the Budget
State Capitol
Albany, NY 12224
(518) 474-1605

North Carolina
Chrys Baggett, Director
Intergovernmental Relations
North Carolina Department
of Administration
116 West Jones Street
Raleigh, NC 27611
(919) 733-0499

North Dakota
State Single Point of Contact
Office of Intergovernmental
Assistance
Office of Management
and Budget
600 East Boulevard Avenue
Bismarck, ND 58505-0170
(701) 224-2094

Ohio
Larry Weaver
State Single Point of Contact
State/Federal Funds
Coordinator
State Clearinghouse
Office of Budget and
Management
30 East Broad Street,
Thirty-fourth Floor
Columbus, OH 43266-0411
(614) 466-0698

Oklahoma
Julie Jensen, Chief
First International Building
1445 Ross Avenue
Grants Audit Section
(6M-PG)
Management Division
Dallas, TX 75270
(214) 655-6530

Oregon
Oddvar Aurdal, Chief
Grants Administration
Section, MS 321
1200 6th Avenue
Seattle, WA 98101
(206) 442-2930

Pennsylvania
Fred Warren
Grants Management Section
Office of the Comptroller,
3PM32
841 Chestnut Building
Philadelphia, PA 19107
(215) 597-6166

Puerto Rico
Partia CustodioIsrael
Soto Marrero
Chairman/Director
Puerto Rico Planning Board
Manillas Government Center
P.O. Box 41119
San Juan, PR 00940-9985
(809) 727-4444

Rhode Island
Review Coordinator
Office of Strategic Planning
265 Melrose Street
Providence, RI 02907
(401) 277-2656

South Carolina
State Single Point of Contact
Grant Services
Office of the Governor
1205 Pendleton Street,
Room 477
Columbia, SC 29201
(803) 734-0493

South Dakota
Susan Comer
State Clearinghouse
Coordinator
Office of the Government
500 East Capitol
Pierre, SD 57501

Tennessee
Charles Brown
State Single Point of Contact
State Planning Office
500 Charlotte Avenue
309 John Sevier Building
Nashville, TN 37219
(615) 741-1676

Texas
Tom Adams
Governor's Office of Budget
and Planning
P.O. Box 12428
Austin, TX 78711
(512) 463-1778

Utah
Utah State Clearinghouse
Office of Planning
and Budget
Attn: Carolyn Wright
State Capitol, Room 116
Salt Lake City, UT 84114
(801) 538-1535

Vermont
Bernard D. Johnson,
Assistant Director
Office of Policy Research
and Coordination
Pavilion Office Building
109 State Street
Montpelier, VT 05602
(802) 828-3326

Virgin Islands
Helen Beggun, Chief
Grants Administration
Branch, 2MGT
26 Federal Plaza, Room 937A
New York, NY 10278
(212) 264-9860

Virginia
Fred Warren
Grants Management Section
Office of the Comptroller,
3PM32
841 Chestnut Building
Philadelphia, PA 19107
(215) 597-6166

Washington
Oddval Aurdal, Chief
Grants Administration
Section, MS 321
1200 6th Avenue
Seattle, WA 98101
(206) 442-2930

West Virginia
Fred Cutlip, Director
Community Development
Division
Governor's Office of
Community Industrial
Development
Building No. 6, Room 553
Charleston, WV 25305
(304) 348-4010

Wisconsin
William C. Carey,
Section Chief
Federal/State
Relations Office
Wisconsin Department
of Administration
101 South Webster Street
Milwaukee, WI 53707
(608) 266-0267

Wyoming
Ann Redman
State Single Point of Contact
Wyoming State
Clearinghouse
State Planning Coordinator's
Office
Capitol Building
Cheyenne, WY 82002
(307) 777-7574

SUPERFUND INNOVATIVE TECHNOLOGY EVALUATION PROGRAM (SITE)

Environmental Protection Agency Office of Environmental Engineering Technology Demonstration
401 M Street, SW
(RD-681)
Washington, DC 20460
(202) 260-2583

Description: Aid to environmental technologies that are still in the bench/laboratory stage to bring them up to pilot scale. Provides assistance to developers of new technologies through field demonstrations at hazardous waste sites. This program is available to any private individual or business that has a new or innovative technology for recycling, separation, detoxification, destruction, stabilization, and handling of hazardous materials.

$ Given: FY 93 est. $17.6 million. The Emerging Technologies Program provides two-year funding at up to $150,000 per year for a maximum of $300,000 over two years.

Application Information: Applications are made to EPA Headquarters listed below.

Deadline: Applications must be received 45 days after the EPA's yearly solicitation in the Commerce Business Daily.

Contact: William Frietsch
Risk Reduction Engineering Laboratory
Cincinnati, OH 45268
(513) 569-7659

or

Stephen James, Chief
SITE Demonstration and Evaluation Branch
SITE Program
Office of Research and Development
Risk Reduction Engineering Laboratory
26 West Martin Luther King Street
Cincinnati, OH 45268
(513) 569-7976

Headquarters contact:
Richard Nalesnik, above address

TOXIC SUBSTANCE RESEARCH

**Environmental
Protection Agency**
Grants Administration
Division, Room 216
Washington, DC 20460
(202) 260-7473

Description: Project grants to states, universities and colleges, hospitals, laboratories, public or private institutes, and individuals who have demonstrated unusually high scientific ability.
$ Given: Range: $10,000–$700,000; average: $86,000.
Application Information: Request application from above address.
Deadline: None
Contact: Your state and/or regional EPA office

Alabama
William McBride
Grants and Contracts
Administration Section
Management Division
345 Courtland Street, NE
Atlanta, GA 30365
(404) 347-2200

Alaska
Oddvar Aurdal, Chief
Grants Administration
Section, MS 321
1200 6th Avenue
Seattle, WA 98101
(206) 442-2930

American Samoa
Mike Schulz, Chief
1235 Missouri Street
Grants and Policy Branch
San Francisco, CA 94105
(415) 744-1623

Arizona
Mike Schulz, Chief
1235 Missouri Street
Grants and Policy Branch
San Francisco, CA 94105
(415) 744-1623

Arkansas
Julie Jensen, Chief
First International Building
1445 Ross Avenue
Grants Audit Section
(6M-PG)
Management Division
Dallas, TX 75270
(214) 655-6530

California
Mike Schulz, Chief
1235 Missouri Street
Grants and Policy Branch
San Francisco, CA 94105
(415) 744-1623

Connecticut
Robert Goetzl
John F. Kennedy Federal
Building, Tenth Floor
(PAS-205)
Grants Information and
Management Section
Boston, MA 02203
(617) 565-3395

Colorado
Martha Nicodemus, Chief
Grants Administration
Branch, 8PM-GFM
999 18th Street, Suite 1300
Denver, CO 80202-2413
(303) 293-1672

Delaware
Fred Warren
Grants Management Section
Office of the Comptroller,
3PM32
841 Chestnut Building
Philadelphia, PA 19107
(215) 597-6166

District of Columbia
Fred Warren
Grants Management Section
Office of the Comptroller,
3PM32
841 Chestnut Building
Philadelphia, PA 19107
(215) 597-6166

Florida
William McBride
Grants and Contracts
Administration Section
Management Division
345 Courtland Street, NE
Atlanta, GA 30365
(404) 347-2200

Georgia
William McBride
Grants and Contracts
Administration Section
Management Division
345 Courtland Street, NE
Atlanta, GA 30365
(404) 347-2200

Environment/Conservation

Hawaii
Mike Schulz, Chief
1235 Missouri Street
Grants and Policy Branch
San Francisco, CA 94105
(415) 744-1623

Idaho
Oddvar Aurdal, Chief
Grants Administration
Section, MS 321
1200 6th Avenue
Seattle, WA 98101
(206) 442-2930

Illinois
Ivavs Anteus, Contracts
and Grants Branch
230 South Dearborn Street
Chicago, IL 60604
(312) 886-9841

Indiana
Ivavs Anteus, Contracts
and Grants Branch
230 South Dearborn Street
Chicago, IL 60604
(312) 886-9841

Iowa
Carol Rompage
726 Minnesota Avenue
Grants Administration
Branch
Kansas City, KS 66101
(913) 551-7346

Kansas
Carol Rompage
726 Minnesota Avenue
Grants Administration
Branch
Kansas City, KS 66101
(913) 551-7346

Kentucky
William McBride
Grants and Contracts
Administration Section
Management Division
345 Courtland Street, NE
Atlanta, GA 30365
(404) 347-2200

Louisiana
Julie Jensen, Chief
First International Building
1445 Ross Avenue
Grants Audit Section
(6M-PG)
Management Division
Dallas, TX 75270
(214) 655-6530

Maine
Robert Goetzl
John F. Kennedy Federal
Building, Tenth Floor
(PAS-205)
Grants Information and
Management Section
Boston, MA 02203
(617) 565-3395

Maryland
Fred Warren
Grants Management Section
Office of the Comptroller,
3PM32
841 Chestnut Building
Philadelphia, PA 19107
(215) 597-6166

Massachusetts
Robert Goetzl
John F. Kennedy Federal
Building, Tenth Floor
(PAS-205)
Grants Information and
Management Section
Boston, MA 02203
(617) 565-3395

Michigan
Ivavs Anteus, Contracts
and Grants Branch
230 South Dearborn Street
Chicago, IL 60604
(312) 886-9841

Minnesota
Ivavs Anteus, Contracts
and Grants Branch
230 South Dearborn Street
Chicago, IL 60604
(312) 886-9841

Mississippi
William McBride
Grants and Contracts
Administration Section
Management Division
345 Courtland Street, NE
Atlanta, GA 30365
(404) 347-2200

Missouri
Carol Rompage
726 Minnesota Avenue
Grants Administration
Branch
Kansas City, KS 66101
(913) 551-7346

Montana
Martha Nicodemus, Chief
Grants Administration
Branch, 8PM-GFM
999 18th Street, Suite 1300
Denver, CO 80202-2413
(303) 293-1672

Nebraska
Carol Rompage
726 Minnesota Avenue
Grants Administration
Branch
Kansas City, KS 66101
(913) 551-7346

Nevada
Mike Schulz, Chief
1235 Missouri Street
Grants and Policy Branch
San Francisco, CA 94105
(415) 744-1623

New Hampshire
Robert Goetzl
John F. Kennedy Federal
Building, Tenth Floor
(PAS-205)
Grants Information and
Management Section
Boston, MA 02203
(617) 565-3395

New Jersey
Helen Beggun, Chief
Grants Administration
Branch, 2MGT
26 Federal Plaza, Room 937A
New York, NY 10278
(212) 264-9860

New Mexico
Julie Jensen, Chief
First International Building
1445 Ross Avenue
Grants Audit Section
(6M-PG)
Management Division
Dallas, TX 75270
(214) 655-6530

New York
Helen Beggun, Chief
Grants Administration
Branch, 2MGT
26 Federal Plaza, Room 937A
New York, NY 10278
(212) 264-9860

North Carolina
William McBride
Grants and Contracts
Administration Section
Management Division
345 Courtland Street, NE
Atlanta, GA 30365
(404) 347-2200

North Dakota
Martha Nicodemus, Chief
Grants Administration
Branch, 8PM-GFM
999 18th Street, Suite 1300
Denver, CO 80202-2413
(303) 293-1672

Ohio
Ivavs Anteus, Contracts
and Grants Branch
230 South Dearborn Street
Chicago, IL 60604
(312) 886-9841

Oklahoma
Julie Jensen, Chief
First International Building
1445 Ross Avenue
Grants Audit Section
(6M-PG)
Management Division
Dallas, TX 75270
(214) 655-6530

Oregon
Oddvar Aurdal, Chief
Grants Administration
Section, MS 321
1200 6th Avenue
Seattle, WA 98101
(206) 442-2930

Pennsylvania
Fred Warren
Grants Management Section
Office of the Comptroller,
3PM32
841 Chestnut Building
Philadelphia, PA 19107
(215) 597-6166

Puerto Rico
Helen Beggun, Chief
Grants Administration
Branch, 2MGT
26 Federal Plaza, Room 937A
New York, NY 10278
(212) 264-9860

Rhode Island
Robert Goetzl
John F. Kennedy Federal
Building, Tenth Floor
(PAS-205)
Grants Information and
Management Section
Boston, MA 02203
(617) 565-3395

South Carolina
William McBride
Grants and Contracts
Administration Section
Management Division
345 Courtland Street, NE
Atlanta, GA 30365
(404) 347-2200

South Dakota
Martha Nicodemus, Chief
Grants Administration
Branch, 8PM-GFM
999 18th Street, Suite 1300
Denver, CO 80202-2413
(303) 293-1672

Tennessee
William McBride
Grants and Contracts
Administration Section
Management Division
345 Courtland Street, NE
Atlanta, GA 30365
(404) 347-2200

Environment/Conservation

Texas
Julie Jensen, Chief
First International Building
1445 Ross Avenue
Grants Audit Section
(6M-PG)
Management Division
Dallas, TX 75270
(214) 655-6530

Utah
Martha Nicodemus, Chief
Grants Administration
Branch, 8PM-GFM
999 18th Street, Suite 1300
Denver, CO 80202-2413
(303) 293-1672

Vermont
Robert Goetzl
John F. Kennedy Federal
Building, Tenth Floor
(PAS-205)
Grants Information and
Management Section
Boston, MA 02203
(617) 565-3395

Virgin Islands
Helen Beggun, Chief
Grants Administration
Branch, 2MGT
26 Federal Plaza, Room 937A
New York, NY 10278
(212) 264-9860

Virginia
Fred Warren
Grants Management Section
Office of the Comptroller,
3PM32
841 Chestnut Building
Philadelphia, PA 19107
(215) 597-6166

Washington
Oddvar Aurdal, Chief
Grants Administration
Section, MS 321
1200 6th Avenue
Seattle, WA 98101
(206) 442-2930

West Virginia
Fred Warren
Grants Management Section
Office of the Comptroller,
3PM32
841 Chestnut Building
Philadelphia, PA 19107
(215) 597-6166

Wisconsin
Ivavs Anteus, Contracts
and Grants Branch
230 South Dearborn Street
Chicago, IL 60604
(312) 886-9841

Wyoming
Martha Nicodemus, Chief
Grants Administration
Branch, 8PM-GFM
999 18th Street, Suite 1300
Denver, CO 80202-2413
(303) 293-1672

WATER POLLUTION CONTROL—RESEARCH, DEVELOPMENT, AND DEMONSTRATION

Environmental Protection Agency
Washington, DC 20460
(202) 260-7473

Description: Project grants (cooperative agreements) given on an infrequent basis to profit-making organizations to facilitate research in water pollution. Nonprofit organizations are usually recipients of grants.

$ Given: Nationwide FY 93 est. $6 million. Range: $6,300–$999,000; average: $117,000.

Application Information: Request application forms and return to EPA. Preliminary discussions are advisable.

Deadline: None

Contact: Communicate with regional EPA offices. For information concerning procedures and applications, contact Grants Administration Division, PM-216, above address; for information concerning program scope, contact Director, Research Grants Staff, RD-675, above address.

Alabama
William McBride
Grants and Contracts
Administration Section
Management Division
345 Courtland Street, NE
Atlanta, GA 30365

Alaska
Oddvar Aurdal, Chief
Grants Administration
Section, MS 321
1200 6th Avenue
Seattle, WA 98101
(206) 442-2930

American Samoa
Mike Schulz, Chief
1235 Missouri Street
Grants and Policy Branch
San Francisco, CA 94105
(415) 556-6196

Arizona
Mike Schulz, Chief
1235 Missouri Street
Grants and Policy Branch
San Francisco, CA 94105
(415) 556-6196

Arkansas
Julie Jensen, Chief
First International Building
1445 Ross Avenue
Grants Audit Section
(6M-PG)
Management Division
Dallas, TX 75270
(214) 655-6530

California
Mike Schulz, Chief
1235 Missouri Street
Grants and Policy Branch
San Francisco, CA 94105
(415) 556-6196

Colorado
Martha Nicodemus, Chief
Grants Administration
Branch, 8PM-GFM
999 18th Street, Suite 1300
Denver, CO 80202-2413
(303) 330-1672

Connecticut
Robert Goetzl
John F. Kennedy Federal
Building, Room 2300
Grants Information and
Management Section
Boston, MA 02203
(617) 835-3395

Delaware
Fred Warren
Grants Management Section
Office of the Comptroller,
3PM32
841 Chestnut Building
Philadelphia, PA 19107

District of Columbia
Fred Warren
Grants Management Section
Office of the Comptroller,
3PM32
841 Chestnut Building
Philadelphia, PA 19107

Florida
William McBride
Grants and Contracts
Administration Section
Management Division
345 Courtland Street, NE
Atlanta, GA 30365

Georgia
William McBride
Grants and Contracts
Administration Section
Management Division
345 Courtland Street, NE
Atlanta, GA 30365

Guam
Mike Schulz, Chief
1235 Missouri Street
Grants and Policy Branch
San Francisco, CA 94105
(415) 556-6196

Hawaii
Mike Schulz, Chief
1235 Missouri Street
Grants and Policy Branch
San Francisco, CA 94105
(415) 556-6196

Idaho
Oddvar Aurdal, Chief
Grants Administration
Section, MS 321
1200 6th Avenue
Seattle, WA 98101
(206) 442-2930

Illinois
Elissa Speizman, Contracts
and Grants Branch
230 South Dearborn Street
Chicago, IL 60604

Indiana
Elissa Speizman, Contracts
and Grants Branch
230 South Dearborn Street
Chicago, IL 60604

Iowa
Carol Rompage
726 Minnesota Avenue
Grants Administration
Branch
Kansas City, KS 66101
(913) 276-7346

Kansas
Carol Rompage
726 Minnesota Avenue
Grants Administration
Branch
Kansas City, KS 66101
(913) 276-7346

Kentucky
William McBride
Grants and Contracts
Administration Section
Management Division
345 Courtland Street, NE
Atlanta, GA 30365

Louisiana
Julie Jensen, Chief
First International Building
1445 Ross Avenue
Grants Audit Section
(6M-PG)
Management Division
Dallas, TX 75270
(214) 655-6530

Maine
Robert Goetzl
John F. Kennedy Federal
Building, Room 2300
Grants Information and
Management Section
Boston, MA 02203
(617) 835-3395

Maryland
Fred Warren
Grants Management Section
Office of the Comptroller,
3PM32
841 Chestnut Building
Philadelphia, PA 19107

Massachusetts
Robert Goetzl
John F. Kennedy Federal
Building, Room 2300
Grants Information and
Management Section
Boston, MA 02203
(617) 835-3395

Michigan
Elissa Speizman, Contracts
and Grants Branch
230 South Dearborn Street
Chicago, IL 60604

Minnesota
Elissa Speizman, Contracts
and Grants Branch
230 South Dearborn Street
Chicago, IL 60604

Mississippi
William McBride
Grants and Contracts
Administration Section
Management Division
345 Courtland Street, NE
Atlanta, GA 30365

Missouri
Carol Rompage
726 Minnesota Avenue
Grants Administration
Branch
Kansas City, KS 66101
(913) 276-7346

Montana
Martha Nicodemus, Chief
Grants Administration
Branch, 8PM-GFM
999 18th Street, Suite 1300
Denver, CO 80202-2413
(303) 330-1672

Nebraska
Carol Rompage
726 Minnesota Avenue
Grants Administration
Branch
Kansas City, KS 66101
(913) 276-7346

Nevada
Mike Schulz, Chief
1235 Missouri Street
Grants and Policy Branch
San Francisco, CA 94105
(415) 556-6196

New Hampshire
Robert Goetzl
John F. Kennedy Federal
Building, Room 2300
Grants Information and
Management Section
Boston, MA 02203
(617) 835-3395

New Jersey
Helen Beggun, Chief
Grants Administration
Branch, 2MGT
26 Federal Plaza, Room 973A
New York, NY 10278
(212) 264-9860

New Mexico
Julie Jensen, Chief
First International Building
1445 Ross Avenue
Grants Audit Section
(6M-PG)
Management Division
Dallas, TX 75270
(214) 655-6530

New York
Helen Beggun, Chief
Grants Administration
Branch, 2MGT
26 Federal Plaza, Room 973A
New York, NY 10278
(212) 264-9860

North Carolina
William McBride
Grants and Contracts
Administration Section
Management Division
345 Courtland Street, NE
Atlanta, GA 30365

North Dakota
Martha Nicodemus, Chief
Grants Administration
Branch, 8PM-GFM
999 18th Street, Suite 1300
Denver, CO 80202-2413
(303) 330-1672

Ohio
Elissa Speizman, Contracts
and Grants Branch
230 South Dearborn Street
Chicago, IL 60604

Oklahoma
Julie Jensen, Chief
First International Building
1445 Ross Avenue
Grants Audit Section
(6M-PG)
Management Division
Dallas, TX 75270
(214) 655-6530

Oregon
Oddvar Aurdal, Chief
Grants Administration
Section, MS 321
1200 6th Avenue
Seattle, WA 98101
(206) 442-2930

Pennsylvania
Fred Warren
Grants Management Section
Office of the Comptroller,
3PM32
841 Chestnut Building
Philadelphia, PA 19107

Puerto Rico
Helen Beggun, Chief
Grants Administration
Branch, 2MGT
26 Federal Plaza, Room 973A
New York, NY 10278
(212) 264-9860

Rhode Island
Robert Goetzl
John F. Kennedy Federal
Building, Room 2300
Grants Information and
Management Section
Boston, MS 02203
(617) 835-3395

South Carolina
William McBride
Grants and Contracts
Administration Section
Management Division
345 Courtland Street, NE
Atlanta, GA 30365

South Dakota
Martha Nicodemus, Chief
Grants Administration
Branch, 8PM-GFM
999 18th Street, Suite 1300
Denver, CO 80202-2413
(303) 330-1672

Environment/Conservation

Tennessee
William McBride
Grants and Contracts
Administration Section
Management Division
345 Courtland Street, NE
Atlanta, GA 30365

**Trust Territories of
Pacific Islands**
Mike Schulz, Chief
1235 Missouri Street
Grants and Policy Branch
San Francisco, CA 94105
(415) 556-6196

Texas
Julie Jensen, Chief
First International Building
1445 Ross Avenue
Grants Audit Section
(6M-PG)
Management Division
Dallas, TX 75270
(214) 655-6530

Utah
Martha Nicodemus, Chief
Grants Administration
Branch, 8PM-GFM
999 18th Street, Suite 1300
Denver, CO 80202-2413
(303) 330-1672

Vermont
Robert Goetzl
John F. Kennedy Federal
Building, Room 2300
Grants Information and
Management Section
Boston, MA 02203
(617) 835-3395

Virgin Islands
Helen Beggun, Chief
Grants Administration
Branch, 2MGT
26 Federal Plaza, Room 973A
New York, NY 10278
(212) 264-9860

Virginia
Fred Warren
Grants Management Section
Office of the Comptroller,
3PM32
841 Chestnut Building
Philadelphia, PA 19107

Wake Island
Mike Schulz, Chief
1235 Missouri Street
Grants and Policy Branch
San Francisco, CA 94105
(415) 556-6196

Washington
Oddvar Aurdal, Chief
Grants Administration
Section, MS 321
1200 6th Avenue
Seattle, WA 98101
(206) 442-2930

West Virginia
Fred Warren
Grants Management Section
Office of the Comptroller,
3PM32
841 Chestnut Building
Philadelphia, PA 19107

Wisconsin
Elissa Speizman, Contracts
and Grants Branch
230 South Dearborn Street
Chicago, IL 60604

Wyoming
Martha Nicodemus, Chief
Grants Administration
Branch, 8PM-GFM
999 18th Street, Suite 1300
Denver, CO 80202-2413
(303) 330-1672

General Business

Assistance is widely available from the federal government for general business and individuals operating small businesses for the following:

1. Assistance to small businesses for expansion, renovation, or development; small businesses located in rural areas; for U.S. fishermen or the fishing industry
2. Advisory services to small businesses to help them improve their management skills or labor-management relations
3. Loans to general business owners, low-income business owners, or businesses owned by handicapped individuals, disabled individuals, or veterans for working capital, construction, or equipment acquisition; loans to U.S. businesses overseas; also monies available to small business investment companies to distribute funds to small businesses

You will need to consult the list of addresses in this chapter for your nearest local or regional Small Business Administration office.

AMERICANS WITH DISABILITIES ACT TECHNICAL ASSISTANCE PROGRAM (ADA)

Department of Justice
Office of the Americans
with Disabilities Act
Civil Rights Division
P.O. Box 66738
Washington, DC
20035-6118
(202) 514-0301,
(202) 514-0381

Description: Project grants and provision of specialized services to businesses impacted by ADA.
$ Given: Nationwide FY 93 est. $2.3 million.
Application Information: Notice of solicitation for applications published in Federal Register. Submit various standard forms.
Deadline: Variable
Contact: John Wodatch, Director, above address

BUSINESS DEVELOPMENT ASSISTANCE TO SMALL BUSINESSES

**Small Business
Administration**
Loan Policy and
Procedures Branch
409 Third Street, SW
Washington, DC 20416
(202) 205-6570

Description: Advisory services, counseling, training, and dissemination of technical information to help persons improve skills to manage and operate a prospective or present small business. Limited to creditworthy individuals with income below basic needs or businesses in areas of high unemployment and/or low income, where business finances have been denied. Business must meet SBA size standards and be independently owned.
$ Given: N/A
Application Information: Application filed in field office serving territory of business location.
Deadline: None
Contact: Director

Alabama

Regional Office
1375 Peachtree Street, NE,
Fifth Floor
Atlanta, GA 30367-8102
(404) 347-2797

District Office
Birmingham District Office
2121 8th Avenue North,
Suite 200
Birmingham, AL 35203-2398
(205) 731-1344

Alaska

Regional Office
2615 4th Avenue, Room 440
Seattle, WA 98121
(206) 442-5676

District Office
Anchorage District Office
222 West 8th Avenue,
Room A36
Anchorage, AK 99513
(907) 271-4022

Arizona

Regional Office
71 Stevenson Street,
Twentieth Floor
San Francisco, CA
94105-2939
(415) 744-6402

District Office
Phoenix District Office
2828 North Central Avenue,
Suite 800
Phoenix, AZ 85004-1025
(602) 379-3732

Arkansas
Regional Office
8625 King George Drive,
Building C
Dallas, TX 75235-3391
(214) 767-7643

District Office
Little Rock District Office
Post Office and Court House
Building, Room 601
320 West Capitol Avenue
Little Rock, AR 722201
(501) 378-5871

California
Regional Office
71 Stevenson Street,
Twentieth Floor
San Francisco, CA
94105-2939
(415) 744-6402

District Offices
Santa Ana District Office
901 West Civic Center Drive,
Suite 160
Santa Ana, CA 92703-2352
(714) 836-2494

San Diego District Office
880 Front Street,
Room 4-S-29
San Diego, CA 92188-0270
(619) 557-5440

San Francisco District Office
211 Main Street,
Fourth Floor
San Francisco, CA
94105-1988
(415) 744-6804

Fresno District Office
2719 North Air Fresno Drive
Fresno, CA 93727-1547
(209) 487-5189

Los Angeles District Office
330 North Grand Boulevard,
Suite 1200
Glendale, CA 91203-2304
(213) 894-2956

Colorado
Regional Office
999 18th Street, Suite 701
Denver, CO 80202
(303) 294-7001

District Office
Denver District Office
721 19th Street, Room 407
Denver, CO 80201-0660
(303) 844-3984

Connecticut
Regional Office
155 Federal Street,
Ninth Floor
Boston, MA 02110
(617) 451-2023

District Office
Hartford District Office
Federal Building,
Second Floor
330 Main Street
Hartford, CT 06106
(203) 240-4700

Delaware
Regional Office
475 Allendale Road,
Suite 201
King of Prussia, PA 19406
(215) 962-3700

Florida
Regional Office
1375 Peachtree Street, NE,
Fifth Floor
Atlanta, GA 30367-8102
(404) 347-2797

District Offices
Jacksonville District Office
7825 Baymeadows Way,
Suite 100-B
Jacksonville, FL 32256-7504
(904) 443-1900

Miami District Office
1320 South Dixie Highway,
Suite 501
Coral Gables, FL 33146
(305) 536-5521

Georgia
Regional Office
1375 Peachtree Street, NE,
Fifth Floor
Atlanta, GA 30367-8102
(404) 347-2797

District Office
Atlanta District Office
1720 Peachtree Road, NW,
Sixth Floor
Atlanta, GA 30309
(404) 347-4749

Hawaii
Regional Office
71 Stevenson Street,
Twentieth Floor
San Francisco, CA
94105-2939
(415) 744-6402

District Office
Honolulu District Office
300 Ala Moana Boulevard,
Room 2213
Honolulu, HI 96850-4981
(808) 541-2990

Idaho
Regional Office
2615 4th Avenue, Room 440
Seattle, WA 98121
(206) 442-5676

District Office
Boise District Office
1020 Main Street, Suite 290
Boise, ID 83702
(208) 334-9635

Illinois

Regional Office
Federal Building, Room 1975
300 South Riverside Plaza
Chicago, IL 60606-6611
(312) 353-0359

District Office
Chicago District Office
500 West Madison Street,
Room 1250
Chicago, IL 60661
(312) 353-4528

Indiana

Regional Office
Federal Building, Room 1975
300 South Riverside Plaza
Chicago, IL 60606-6611
(312) 353-0359

District Office
Indianapolis District Office
429 North Pennsylvania
Street, Suite 100
Indianapolis, IN 46204-1873
(317) 226-7272

Iowa

Regional Office
911 Walnut Street,
Thirteenth Floor
Kansas City, MO 64106
(816) 426-3608

District Offices
Des Moines District Office
New Federal Building,
Room 749
210 Walnut Street
Des Moines, IA 50309
(515) 284-4762

Cedar Rapids District Office
373 Collins Road, NE,
Room 100
Cedar Rapids, IA 52402-3147
(319) 393-8630

Kansas

Regional Office
911 Walnut Street,
Thirteenth Floor
Kansas City, MO 64106
(816) 426-3608

District Office
Wichita District Office
110 East Waterman Street,
First Floor
Wichita, KS 67202
(316) 269-6273

Kentucky

Regional Office
1375 Peachtree Street, NE,
Fifth Floor
Atlanta, GA 30367-8102
(404) 347-2797

District Office
Louisville District Office
Federal Building, Room 188
600 Martin Luther King Jr.
Place
Louisville, KY 40202
(502) 582-5976

Louisiana

Regional Office
8625 King George Drive,
Building C
Dallas, TX 75235-3391
(214) 767-7643

District Office
New Orleans District Office
1661 Canal Street,
Suite 2000
New Orleans, LA 70112
(504) 589-6685

Maine

Regional Office
155 Federal Street,
Ninth Floor
Boston, MA 02110
(617) 451-2023

District Office
Augusta District Office
Federal Building, Room 512
40 Western Avenue
Augusta, ME 04330
(207) 622-8378

Massachusetts

Regional Office
155 Federal Street,
Ninth Floor
Boston, MA 02110
(617) 451-2023

District Office
Boston District Office
10 Causeway Street,
Room 265
Boston, MA 02222-1093
(617) 565-5590

Michigan

Regional Office
Federal Building, Room 1975
300 South Riverside Plaza
Chicago, IL 60606-6611
(312) 353-0359

District Office
Detroit District Office
477 Michigan Avenue,
Room 515
Detroit, MI 48226
(313) 226-6075

Minnesota

Regional Office
Federal Building, Room 1975
300 South Riverside Plaza
Chicago, IL 60606-6611
(312) 353-0359

District Office
Minneapolis District Office
100 North 6th Street,
Suite 610
Minneapolis, MN 55403-1563
(612) 370-2324

Mississippi
Regional Office
1375 Peachtree Street, NE,
Fifth Floor
Atlanta, GA 30367-8102
(404) 347-2797

District Office
Jackson District Office
100 West Capitol Street,
Suite 400
Jackson, MS 39201
(601) 965-5325

Missouri
Regional Office
911 Walnut Street,
Thirteenth Floor
Kansas City, MO 64106
(816) 426-3608

District Offices
St. Louis District Office
815 Olive Street, Room 242
St. Louis, MO 63101
(314) 539-6600

Kansas City District Office
323 West 8th Street,
Suite 501
Kansas City, MO 64105
(816) 374-6762

Montana
Regional Office
999 18th Street, Suite 701
Denver, CO 80202
(303) 294-7001

District Office
Helena District Office
301 South Park Avenue,
Room 528
Helena, MT 59626
(406) 449-5381

Nebraska
Regional Office
911 Walnut Street,
Thirteenth Floor
Kansas City, MO 64106
(816) 426-3608

District Office
Omaha District Office
11145 Mill Valley Road
Omaha, NB 64154
(402) 221-3604

Nevada
Regional Office
71 Stevenson Street,
Twentieth Floor
San Francisco, CA
94105-2939
(415) 744-6402

District Office
Las Vegas District Office
301 East Steward Street,
Room 301
Las Vegas, NV 89125-2527
(702) 388-6611

New Hampshire
Regional Office
155 Federal Street,
Ninth Floor
Boston, MA 02110
(617) 451-2023

District Office
Concord District Office
143 North Main Street,
Suite 202
Concord, NH 03302-1257
(603) 225-1400

New Jersey
Regional Office
26 Federal Plaza,
Room 31-08
New York, NY 10278
(212) 264-7772

District Office
Newark District Office
Military Park Building,
Fourth Floor
60 Park Place
Newark, NJ 07102
(201) 341-2434

New Mexico
Regional Office
8625 King George Drive,
Building C
Dallas, TX 75235-3391
(214) 767-7643

District Office
Albuquerque District Office
625 Silver Avenue, SW,
Suite 320
Albuquerque, NM 87102
(505) 766-1870

New York
Regional Office
26 Federal Plaza,
Room 31-08
New York, NY 10278
(212) 264-7772

District Offices
Buffalo District Office
Federal Building 1311
111 West Huron Street
Buffalo, NY 14202
(716) 846-4301

Syracuse District Office
100 South Clinton Street,
Room 1071
Syracuse, NY 13260
(315) 423-5383

North Carolina
Regional Office
1375 Peachtree Street, NE,
Fifth Floor
Atlanta, GA 30367-8102
(404) 347-2797

District Office
Charlotte District Office
200 North College Street
Charlotte, NC 28202
(704) 344-6563

North Dakota
Regional Office
999 18th Street, Suite 701
Denver, CO 80202
(303) 294-7001

District Office
Federal Building, Room 218
657 2nd Avenue, North
Fargo, ND 58108-3086
(701) 239-5131

Ohio
Regional Office
Federal Building, Room 1975
300 South Riverside Plaza
Chicago, IL 60606-6611
(312) 353-0359

District Office
Columbus District Office
85 Marconi Boulevard,
Room 512
Columbus, OH 43215
(614) 469-6860

Oklahoma
Regional Office
8625 King George Drive,
Building C
Dallas, TX 75235-3391
(214) 767-7643

District Office
Oklahoma City District Office
200 NW 5th Street, Suite 670
Oklahoma City, OK 73102
(405) 231-4301

Oregon
Regional Office
2615 4th Avenue, Room 440
Seattle, WA 98121
(206) 442-5676

District Office
Portland District Office
222 SW Columbia Street,
Suite 500
Portland, OR 97201-6605
(503) 326-2682

Pacific Islands
Regional Office
71 Stevenson Street,
Twentieth Floor
San Francisco, CA
94105-2939
(415) 744-6402

District Office
Agana Branch Office
Pacific Daily News Building,
Room 508
238 Archbishop F.C. Flores
Street
Agana, GM 96910
(671) 472-7277

Pennsylvania
Regional Office
475 Allendale Road,
Suite 201
King of Prussia, PA 19406
(215) 962-3700

District Office
Pittsburgh District Office
960 Penn Avenue, Fifth Floor
Pittsburgh, PA 15222
(412) 644-2780

Puerto Rico
Regional Office
26 Federal Plaza,
Room 31-08
New York, NY 10278
(212) 264-7772

District Office
Federico Degetau Federal
Building, Room 691
Carlos Chardon Avenue
Hato Rey, PR 00918
(809) 766-5002

Rhode Island
Regional Office
155 Federal Street,
Ninth Floor
Boston, MA 02110
(617) 451-2023

District Office
Providence District Office
380 Westminster Mall,
Fifth Floor
Providence, RI 02903
(401) 528-4561

South Carolina
Regional Office
1375 Peachtree Street, NE,
Fifth Floor
Atlanta, GA 30367-8102
(404) 347-2797

District Office
Columbia District Office
1835 Assembly Street,
Room 358
Columbia, SC 29202
(803) 765-5376

South Dakota
Regional Office
999 18th Street, Suite 701
Denver, CO 80202
(303) 294-7001

District Office
Sioux Falls District Office
101 South Main Avenue,
Suite 101
Sioux Falls, SD 57102-0527
(605) 336-4231

Tennessee
Regional Office
1375 Peachtree Street, NE,
Fifth Floor
Atlanta, GA 30367-8102
(404) 347-2797

District Office
Nashville District Office
50 Vantage Way, Suite 201
Nashville, TN 37338-1500
(615) 736-7176

Texas

Regional Office
8625 King George Drive,
Building C
Dallas, TX 75235-3391
(214) 767-7643

District Offices
San Antonio District Office
7400 Blanco Road, Suite 200
San Antonio, TX 78216
(512) 229-4535

Dallas District Office
1100 Commerce Street,
Room 3C36
Dallas, TX 75242
(214) 767-0608

El Paso District Office
10737 Gateway West,
Suite 320
El Paso, TX 79935
(915) 541-5586

Utah

Regional Office
999 18th Street, Suite 701
Denver, CO 80202
(303) 294-7001

District Office
Salt Lake City District Office
Federal Building, Room 2237
125 South State Street
Salt Lake City, UT
84138-1195
(801) 524-5800

Vermont

Regional Office
155 Federal Street,
Ninth Floor
Boston, MA 02110
(617) 451-2023

District Office
Montpelier District Office
Federal Building, Room 205
87 State Street
Montpelier, VT 05602
(802) 828-4474

Virgin Islands

Regional Office
26 Federal Plaza,
Room 31-08
New York, NY 10278
(212) 264-7772

District Offices
Federico Degetau Federal
Building, Room 691
Carlos Chardon Avenue
Hato Rey, PR 00918
(809) 766-5002

St. Croix Post-of-Duty
United Shopping Plaza
4C & 4D Este Sion Farm,
Room 7
Christiansted, St. Croix, VI
00820
(809) 778-5380

St. Thomas Post-of-Duty
Federal Office Building,
Room 283
Veterans Drive
St. Thomas, VI 00801
(809) 774-8530

Virginia

Regional Office
475 Allendale Road,
Suite 201
King of Prussia, PA 19406
(215) 962-3700

District Office
Richmond District Office
Federal Building, Room 3015
400 North 8th Street
Richmond, VA 23240
(804) 771-2400

Washington

Regional Office
2615 4th Avenue, Room 440
Seattle, WA 98121
(206) 442-5676

District Offices
Spokane District Office
West 601 First Avenue,
Tenth Floor East
Spokane, WA 99204
(509) 353-2807

Seattle District Office
915 Second Avenue,
Room 1792
Seattle, WA 98174-1088
(206) 553-1420

Washington, DC

Regional Office
475 Allendale Road,
Suite 201
King of Prussia, PA 19406
(215) 962-3700

District Office
Washington District Office
1111 18th Street, NW,
Sixth Floor
Washington, DC 20036
(202) 634-1500

West Virginia

Regional Office
475 Allendale Road,
Suite 201
King of Prussia, PA 19406
(215) 962-3700

District Office
Clarksburg District Office
168 West Main Street,
Fifth Floor
Clarksburg, WV 26301
(304) 623-5631

Wisconsin

Regional Office
Federal Building, Room 1975
300 South Riverside Plaza
Chicago, IL 60606-6611
(312) 353-0359

District Office
Madison District Office
212 East Washington Avenue,
Room 213
Madison, WI 53703
(608) 264-5261

Wyoming
Regional Office
999 18th Street, Suite 701
Denver, CO 80202
(303) 294-7001

District Office
Casper District Office
Federal Building, Room 4001
100 East B Street
Casper, WY 82602-2839
(307) 261-5761

BUSINESS LOANS FOR SBA PROGRAM PARTICIPANTS

**Small Business
Administration
Loan Policy and
Procedures Branch**
409 3rd Street, SW
Washington, DC 20416
(202) 205-6570

Description: Loans to small businesses for construction, development, expansion, renovation, and acquisition of equipment. Limited to small businesses owned by socially and economically disadvantaged persons.
$ Given: Nationwide FY 93 est. $5 million. Average direct loan: $113,636; guaranteed loans up to $750,000.
Application Information: Applications for direct loans are filed by the loan applicant; guaranteed loans are filed by financial institution through SBA field office.
Deadline: N/A
Contact: Regional Small Business Administration office for your state

Alabama
Small Business
Administration, Region IV
1375 Peachtree Street, NE,
Fifth Floor
Atlanta, GA 30367-8102
(404) 347-2797

Alaska
Small Business
Administration, Region X
2615 4th Avenue, Room 440
Seattle, WA 98121
(206) 442-5676

Arizona
Small Business
Administration, Region IX
71 Stevenson Street,
Twentieth Floor
San Francisco, CA
94105-2939
(415) 744-6402

Arkansas
Small Business
Administration, Region VI
8625 King George Drive,
Building C
Dallas, TX 75235-3391
(214) 767-7643

California
Small Business
Administration, Region IX
71 Stevenson Street,
Twentieth Floor
San Francisco, CA
94105-2939
(415) 744-6402

Colorado
Small Business
Administration, Region VIII
999 18th Street, Suite 701
Denver, CO 80202
(303) 294-7001

Connecticut
Small Business
Administration, Region I
155 Federal Street,
Ninth Floor
Boston, MA 02110
(617) 451-2023

Delaware
Small Business
Administration, Region III
475 Allendale Road,
Suite 201
King of Prussia, PA 19406
(215) 962-3700

District of Columbia
Small Business
Administration, Region III
475 Allendale Road,
Suite 201
King of Prussia, PA 19406
(215) 962-3700

Florida
Small Business
Administration, Region IV
1375 Peachtree Street, NE,
Fifth Floor
Atlanta, GA 30367-8102
(404) 347-2797

Georgia
Small Business
Administration, Region IV
1375 Peachtree Street, NE,
Fifth Floor
Atlanta, GA 30367-8102
(404) 347-2797

Hawaii
Small Business
Administration, Region IX
71 Stevenson Street,
Twentieth Floor
San Francisco, CA
94105-2939
(415) 744-6402

Idaho
Small Business
Administration, Region X
2615 4th Avenue, Room 440
Seattle, WA 98121
(206) 442-5676

Illinois
Small Business
Administration, Region V
Federal Building, Room 1975
300 South Riverside Plaza
Chicago, IL 60606-6611
(312) 353-0359

Indiana
Small Business
Administration, Region V
Federal Building, Room 1975
300 South Riverside Plaza
Chicago, IL 60606-6611
(312) 353-0359

Iowa
Small Business
Administration, Region VII
911 Walnut Street,
Thirteenth Floor
Kansas City, MO 64106
(816) 426-3608

Kansas
Small Business
Administration, Region VII
911 Walnut Street,
Thirteenth Floor
Kansas City, MO 64106
(816) 426-3608

Kentucky
Small Business
Administration, Region IV
1375 Peachtree Street, NE,
Fifth Floor
Atlanta, GA 30367-8102
(404) 347-2797

Louisiana
Small Business
Administration, Region VI
8625 King George Drive,
Building C
Dallas, TX 75235-3391
(214) 767-7643

Maine
Small Business
Administration, Region I
155 Federal Street,
Ninth Floor
Boston, MA 02110
(617) 451-2023

Maryland
Small Business
Administration, Region III
475 Allendale Road,
Suite 201
King of Prussia, PA 19406
(215) 962-3700

Massachusetts
Small Business
Administration, Region I
155 Federal Street,
Ninth Floor
Boston, MA 02110
(617) 451-2023

Michigan
Small Business
Administration, Region V
Federal Building, Room 1975
300 South Riverside Plaza
Chicago, IL 60606-6611
(312) 353-0359

Minnesota
Small Business
Administration, Region V
Federal Building, Room 1975
300 South Riverside Plaza
Chicago, IL 60606-6611
(312) 353-0359

Mississippi
Small Business
Administration, Region IV
1375 Peachtree Street, NE,
Fifth Floor
Atlanta, GA 30367-8102
(404) 347-2797

Missouri
Small Business
Administration, Region VII
911 Walnut Street,
Thirteenth Floor
Kansas City, MO 64106
(816) 426-3608

Montana
Small Business
Administration, Region VIII
999 18th Street, Suite 701
Denver, CO 80202
(303) 294-7001

Nebraska
Small Business
Administration, Region VII
911 Walnut Street,
Thirteenth Floor
Kansas City, MO 64106
(816) 426-3608

Nevada
Small Business
Administration, Region IX
71 Stevenson Street,
Twentieth Floor
San Francisco, CA
94105-2939
(415) 744-6402

New Hampshire
Small Business
Administration, Region I
155 Federal Street,
Ninth Floor
Boston, MA 02110
(617) 451-2023

New Jersey
Small Business
Administration, Region II
26 Federal Plaza,
Room 31-08
New York, NY 10278
(212) 264-7772

New Mexico
Small Business
Administration, Region VI
8625 King George Drive,
Building C
Dallas, TX 75235-3391
(214) 767-7643

New York
Small Business
Administration, Region II
26 Federal Plaza,
Room 31-08
New York, NY 10278
(212) 264-7772

North Carolina
Small Business
Administration, Region IV
1375 Peachtree Street, NE,
Fifth Floor
Atlanta, GA 30367-8102
(404) 347-2797

North Dakota
Small Business
Administration, Region VIII
999 18th Street, Suite 701
Denver, CO 80202
(303) 294-7001

Ohio
Small Business
Administration, Region V
Federal Building, Room 1975
300 South Riverside Plaza
Chicago, IL 60606-6611
(312) 353-0359

Oklahoma
Small Business
Administration, Region VI
8625 King George Drive,
Building C
Dallas, TX 75235-3391
(214) 767-7643

Oregon
Small Business
Administration, Region X
2615 4th Avenue, Room 440
Seattle, WA 98121
(206) 442-5676

Pennsylvania
Small Business
Administration, Region III
475 Allendale Road,
Suite 201
King of Prussia, PA 19406
(215) 962-3700

Puerto Rico
Small Business
Administration, Region II
26 Federal Plaza,
Room 31-08
New York, NY 10278
(212) 264-7772

Rhode Island
Small Business
Administration, Region I
155 Federal Street,
Ninth Floor
Boston, MA 02110
(617) 451-2023

South Carolina
Small Business
Administration, Region IV
1375 Peachtree Street, NE,
Fifth Floor
Atlanta, GA 30367-8102
(404) 347-2797

South Dakota
Small Business
Administration, Region VIII
999 18th Street, Suite 701
Denver, CO 80202
(303) 294-7001

Tennessee
Small Business
Administration, Region IV
1375 Peachtree Street, NE,
Fifth Floor
Atlanta, GA 30367-8102
(404) 347-2797

Texas
Small Business
Administration, Region VI
8625 King George Drive,
Building C
Dallas, TX 75235-3391
(214) 767-7643

Utah
Small Business
Administration, Region VIII
999 18th Street, Suite 701
Denver, CO 80202
(303) 294-7001

Vermont
Small Business
Administration, Region I
155 Federal Street,
Ninth Floor
Boston, MA 02110
(617) 451-2023

Virgin Islands
Small Business
Administration, Region II
26 Federal Plaza,
Room 31-08
New York, NY 10278
(212) 264-7772

Virginia
Small Business
Administration, Region III
475 Allendale Road,
Suite 201
King of Prussia, PA 19406
(215) 962-3700

Washington
Small Business
Administration, Region X
2615 4th Avenue, Room 440
Seattle, WA 98121
(206) 442-5676

West Virginia
Small Business
Administration, Region III
475 Allendale Road,
Suite 201
King of Prussia, PA 19406
(215) 962-3700

Wisconsin
Small Business
Administration, Region V
Federal Building, Room 1975
300 South Riverside Plaza
Chicago, IL 60606-6611
(312) 353-0359

Wyoming
Small Business
Administration, Region VIII
999 18th Street, Suite 701
Denver, CO 80202
(303) 294-7001

CAPITAL CONSTRUCTION FUND (CCF)

**Department of
Transportation**
Associate Administrator
for Maritime Aids
Maritime Administration
400 Seventh Street, SW
Washington, DC 20590
(202) 366-0364

Description: Direct payments for specified use (in the form of tax deferments) to promote trade ship construction and reconstruction. Applicant must be a U.S. citizen and own at least one vessel.
$ Given: Tax benefits to applicants not stated. Total monies deferred $5 billion.
Application Information: Contact Marine Administration, Office of Ship Financing.
Deadline: Prior to due date for filing federal tax forms.
Contact: Local Marine Administration regional office

General Business

Alabama
F. X. McNerney
Maritime Administration
365 Canal Street, Suite 2590
New Orleans, LA 70130-1137
(504) 589-6556

Alaska
Robert A. Bryan
Maritime Administration
211 Main Street, Room 1112
San Francisco, CA 94105
(415) 744-2580

Arizona
Robert A. Bryan
Maritime Administration
211 Main Street, Room 1112
San Francisco, CA 94105
(415) 744-2580

Arkansas
F. X. McNerney
Maritime Administration
365 Canal Street, Suite 2590
New Orleans, LA 70130-1137
(504) 589-6556

California
Robert A. Bryan
Maritime Administration
211 Main Street, Room 1112
San Francisco, CA 94105
(415) 744-2580

Colorado
Robert A. Bryan
Maritime Administration
211 Main Street, Room 1112
San Francisco, CA 94105
(415) 744-2580

Connecticut
Robert F. McKeon
Maritime Administration
26 Federal Plaza, Room 3737
New York, NY 10278
(212) 264-1300

Delaware
Robert F. McKeon
Maritime Administration
26 Federal Plaza, Room 3737
New York, NY 10278
(212) 264-1300

Florida
(Eastern Half)
William S. Chambers
Maritime Administration
7737 Hampton Boulevard,
Building 4D, Room 211
Norfolk, VA 23505
(804) 441-6393

(Western Half)
F. X. McNerney
Maritime Administration
365 Canal Street, Suite 2590
New Orleans, LA 70130-1137
(504) 589-6556

Georgia
William S. Chambers
Maritime Administration
7737 Hampton Boulevard,
Building 4D, Room 211
Norfolk, VA 23505
(804) 441-6393

Hawaii
Robert A. Bryan
Maritime Administration
211 Main Street, Room 1112
San Francisco, CA 94105
(415) 744-2580

Idaho
Robert A. Bryan
Maritime Administration
211 Main Street, Room 1112
San Francisco, CA 94105
(415) 744-2580

Illinois
Alpha H. Ames, Jr.
Maritime Administration
2300 East Devon Avenue,
Suite 366
Des Plaines, IL 60018-4605
(708) 298-4535

Indiana
Alpha H. Ames, Jr.
Maritime Administration
2300 East Devon Avenue,
Suite 366
Des Plaines, IL 60018-4605
(708) 298-4535

Iowa
F. X. McNerney
Maritime Administration
365 Canal Street, Suite 2590
New Orleans, LA 70130-1137
(504) 589-6556

Kansas
F. X. McNerney
Maritime Administration
365 Canal Street, Suite 2590
New Orleans, LA 70130-1137
(504) 589-6556

Kentucky
F. X. McNerney
Maritime Administration
365 Canal Street, Suite 2590
New Orleans, LA 70130-1137
(504) 589-6556

Louisiana
F. X. McNerney
Maritime Administration
365 Canal Street, Suite 2590
New Orleans, LA 70130-1137
(504) 589-6556

Maine
Robert F. McKeon
Maritime Administration
26 Federal Plaza, Room 3737
New York, NY 10278
(212) 264-1300

Maryland
Robert F. McKeon
Maritime Administration
26 Federal Plaza, Room 3737
New York, NY 10278
(212) 264-1300

Massachusetts
Robert F. McKeon
Maritime Administration
26 Federal Plaza, Room 3737
New York, NY 10278
(212) 264-1300

Michigan
Alpha H. Ames, Jr.
Maritime Administration
2300 East Devon Avenue,
Suite 366
Des Plaines, IL 60018-4605
(708) 298-4535

Minnesota
Alpha H. Ames, Jr.
Maritime Administration
2300 East Devon Avenue,
Suite 366
Des Plaines, IL 60018-4605
(708) 298-4535

Mississippi
F. X. McNerney
Maritime Administration
365 Canal Street, Suite 2590
New Orleans, LA 70130-1137
(504) 589-6556

Missouri
F. X. McNerney
Maritime Administration
365 Canal Street, Suite 2590
New Orleans, LA 70130-1137
(504) 589-6556

Montana
Robert A. Bryan
Maritime Administration
211 Main Street, Room 1112
San Francisco, CA 94105
(415) 744-2580

Nebraska
F. X. McNerney
Maritime Administration
365 Canal Street, Suite 2590
New Orleans, LA 70130-1137
(504) 589-6556

Nevada
Robert A. Bryan
Maritime Administration
211 Main Street, Room 1112
San Francisco, CA 94105
(415) 744-2580

New Hampshire
Robert F. McKeon
Maritime Administration
26 Federal Plaza, Room 3737
New York, NY 10278
(212) 264-1300

New Jersey
Robert F. McKeon
Maritime Administration
26 Federal Plaza, Room 3737
New York, NY 10278
(212) 264-1300

New Mexico
Robert A. Bryan
Maritime Administration
211 Main Street, Room 1112
San Francisco, CA 94105
(415) 744-2580

New York
(Except Lake Coastal Area)
Robert F. McKeon
Maritime Administration
26 Federal Plaza, Room 3737
New York, NY 10278
(212) 264-1300

(Lake Coastal Area)
Alpha H. Ames, Jr.
Maritime Administration
2300 East Devon Avenue,
Suite 366
Des Plaines, IL 60018-4605
(708) 298-4535

North Carolina
William S. Chambers
Maritime Administration
7737 Hampton Boulevard,
Building 4D, Room 211
Norfolk, VA 23505
(804) 441-6393

North Dakota
Robert A. Bryan
Maritime Administration
211 Main Street, Room 1112
San Francisco, CA 94105
(415) 744-2580

Ohio
Alpha H. Ames, Jr.
Maritime Administration
2300 East Devon Avenue,
Suite 366
Des Plaines, IL 60018-4605
(708) 298-4535

Oklahoma
F. X. McNerney
Maritime Administration
365 Canal Street, Suite 2590
New Orleans, LA 70130-1137
(504) 589-6556

Oregon
Robert A. Bryan
Maritime Administration
211 Main Street, Room 1112
San Francisco, CA 94105
(415) 744-2580

Pennsylvania
(Except Lake Coastal Area)
Robert F. McKeon
Maritime Administration
26 Federal Plaza, Room 3737
New York, NY 10278
(212) 264-1300

(Lake Coastal Area)
Alpha H. Ames, Jr.
Maritime Administration
2300 East Devon Avenue,
Suite 366
Des Plaines, IL 60018-4605
(708) 298-4535

Puerto Rico
William S. Chambers
Maritime Administration
7737 Hampton Boulevard,
Building 4D, Room 211
Norfolk, VA 23505
(804) 441-6393

Rhode Island
Robert F. McKeon
Maritime Administration
26 Federal Plaza, Room 3737
New York, NY 10278
(212) 264-1300

South Carolina
William S. Chambers
Maritime Administration
7737 Hampton Boulevard,
Building 4D, Room 211
Norfolk, VA 23505
(804) 441-6393

South Dakota
Robert A. Bryan
Maritime Administration
211 Main Street, Room 1112
San Francisco, CA 94105
(415) 744-2580

Tennessee
F. X. McNerney
Maritime Administration
365 Canal Street, Suite 2590
New Orleans, LA 70130-1137
(504) 589-6556

Texas
F. X. McNerney
Maritime Administration
365 Canal Street, Suite 2590
New Orleans, LA 70130-1137
(504) 589-6556

Utah
Robert A. Bryan
Maritime Administration
211 Main Street, Room 1112
San Francisco, CA 94105
(415) 744-2580

Vermont
Robert F. McKeon
Maritime Administration
26 Federal Plaza, Room 3737
New York, NY 10278
(212) 264-1300

Virginia
William S. Chambers
Maritime Administration
7737 Hampton Boulevard,
Building 4D, Room 211
Norfolk, VA 23505
(804) 441-6393

Washington
Robert A. Bryan
Maritime Administration
211 Main Street, Room 1112
San Francisco, CA 94105
(415) 744-2580

West Virginia
William S. Chambers
Maritime Administration
7737 Hampton Boulevard,
Building 4D, Room 211
Norfolk, VA 23505
(804) 441-6393

Wisconsin
Alpha H. Ames, Jr.
Maritime Administration
2300 East Devon Avenue,
Suite 366
Des Plaines, IL 60018-4605
(708) 298-4535

Wyoming
Robert A. Bryan
Maritime Administration
211 Main Street, Room 1112
San Francisco, CA 94105
(415) 744-2580

Field Office
Paul L. Krinsky
United States Merchant
Marine Academy
Kings Point, NY 11024-1699
(516) 773-5000

CERTIFIED DEVELOPMENT COMPANY LOANS

Small Business Administration
Office of Rural Affairs and Economic Development
409 3rd Street, SW
Washington, DC 20416
(202) 205-6485

Description: Guaranteed and insured loans to small businesses independently owned and operated for profit, to acquire land and buildings, as well as construction, expansion, renovation, and modernization of machinery and equipment. Loan may have either a 10- or 20-year term.
$ Given: Loans up to $1 million; average: $292,200.
Application Information: Application must be made on SBA Form 1244 and the requirements set forth thereon must be complied with.
Deadline: None
Contact: Your state and/or regional office

Alabama
1375 Peachtree Street, NE,
Fifth Floor
Atlanta, GA 30367-8102
(404) 347-2797

Alaska
2615 4th Avenue, Room 440
Seattle, WA 98121
(206) 553-5676

Arizona
71 Stevenson Street,
Twentieth Floor
San Francisco, CA
94105-2939
(415) 744-6402

Arkansas
8625 King George Drive,
Building C
Dallas, TX 75235-3391
(214) 767-7633

California
71 Stevenson Street,
Twentieth Floor
San Francisco, CA
94105-2939
(415) 744-6402

Colorado
999 18th Street, Suite 701
Denver, CO 80202
(303) 294-7186

Connecticut
155 Federal Street,
Ninth Floor
Boston, MA 02110
(617) 451-2023

Delaware
475 Allendale Road,
Suite 201
King of Prussia, PA 19406
(215) 962-3700

District of Columbia
475 Allendale Road,
Suite 201
King of Prussia, PA 19406
(215) 962-3700

Florida
1375 Peachtree Street, NE,
Fifth Floor
Atlanta, GA 30367-8102
(404) 347-2797

Georgia
1375 Peachtree Street, NE,
Fifth Floor
Atlanta, GA 30367-8102
(404) 347-2797

Hawaii
71 Stevenson Street,
Twentieth Floor
San Francisco, CA
94105-2939
(415) 744-6402

Idaho
2615 4th Avenue, Room 440
Seattle, WA 98121
(206) 553-5676

Illinois
Federal Building
300 South Riverside Plaza,
1975 South
Chicago, IL 60606-6617
(312) 353-5000

Iowa
911 Walnut Street,
Thirteenth Floor
Kansas City, MO 64106
(816) 426-3608

Indiana
Federal Building
300 South Riverside Plaza,
1975 South
Chicago, IL 60606-6617
(312) 353-5000

Kansas
911 Walnut Street,
Thirteenth Floor
Kansas City, MO 64106
(816) 426-3608

Kentucky
1375 Peachtree Street, NE,
Fifth Floor
Atlanta, GA 30367-8102
(404) 347-2797

Louisiana
8625 King George Drive,
Building C
Dallas, TX 75235-3391
(214) 767-7633

Maine
155 Federal Street,
Ninth Floor
Boston, MA 02110
(617) 451-2023

Maryland
475 Allendale Road,
Suite 201
King of Prussia, PA 19406
(215) 962-3700

Massachusetts
155 Federal Street,
Ninth Floor
Boston, MA 02110
(617) 451-2023

Michigan
Federal Building
300 South Riverside Plaza,
1975 South
Chicago, IL 60606-6617
(312) 353-5000

Minnesota
Federal Building
300 South Riverside Plaza,
1975 South
Chicago, IL 60606-6617
(312) 353-5000

Mississippi
1375 Peachtree Street, NE,
Fifth Floor
Atlanta, GA 30367-8102
(404) 347-2797

Missouri
911 Walnut Street,
Thirteenth Floor
Kansas City, MO 64106
(816) 426-3608

Montana
999 18th Street, Suite 701
Denver, CO 80202
(303) 294-7186

Nebraska
911 Walnut Street,
Thirteenth Floor
Kansas City, MO 64106
(816) 426-3608

Nevada
71 Stevenson Street,
Twentieth Floor
San Francisco, CA
94105-2939
(415) 744-6402

New Hampshire
155 Federal Street,
Ninth Floor
Boston, MA 02110
(617) 451-2023

New Jersey
26 Federal Plaza,
Room 31-08
New York, NY 10278
(212) 264-7772

New Mexico
8625 King George Drive,
Building C
Dallas, TX 75235-3391
(214) 767-7633

New York
26 Federal Plaza,
Room 31-08
New York, NY 10278
(212) 264-7772

North Carolina
1375 Peachtree Street, NE,
Fifth Floor
Atlanta, GA 30367-8102
(404) 347-2797

North Dakota
999 18th Street, Suite 701
Denver, CO 80202
(303) 294-7186

Ohio
Federal Building
300 South Riverside Plaza,
1975 South
Chicago, IL 60606-6617
(312) 353-5000

Oklahoma
8625 King George Drive,
Building C
Dallas, TX 75235-3391
(214) 767-7633

Oregon
2615 4th Avenue, Room 440
Seattle, WA 98121
(206) 553-5676

Pacific Islands
71 Stevenson Street,
Twentieth Floor
San Francisco, CA
94105-2939
(415) 744-6402

Pennsylvania
475 Allendale Road,
Suite 201
King of Prussia, PA 19406
(215) 962-3700

Puerto Rico
26 Federal Plaza,
Room 31-08
New York, NY 10278
(212) 264-7772

Rhode Island
155 Federal Street,
Ninth Floor
Boston, MA 02110
(617) 451-2023

South Carolina
1375 Peachtree Street, NE,
Fifth Floor
Atlanta, GA 30367-8102
(404) 347-2797

South Dakota
999 18th Street, Suite 701
Denver, CO 80202
(303) 294-7186

Tennessee
1375 Peachtree Street, NE,
Fifth Floor
Atlanta, GA 30367-8102
(404) 347-2797

Texas
8625 King George Drive,
Building C
Dallas, TX 75235-3391
(214) 767-7633

Utah
999 18th Street, Suite 701
Denver, CO 80202
(303) 294-7186

Vermont
155 Federal Street,
Ninth Floor
Boston, MA 02110
(617) 451-2023

Virgin Islands
26 Federal Plaza,
Room 31-08
New York, NY 10278
(212) 264-7772

Virginia
475 Allendale Road,
Suite 201
King of Prussia, PA 19406
(215) 962-3700

Washington
2615 4th Avenue, Room 440
Seattle, WA 98121
(206) 553-5676

West Virginia
475 Allendale Road,
Suite 201
King of Prussia, PA 19406
(215) 962-3700

Wisconsin
Federal Building
300 South Riverside Plaza,
1975 South
Chicago, IL 60606-6617
(312) 353-5000

Wyoming
999 18th Street, Suite 701
Denver, CO 80202
(303) 294-7186

CONSTRUCTION RESERVE FUND (CRF)

Department of Transportation
Associate Administrator for Maritime Aids
Maritime Administration
400 Seventh Street, SW
Washington, DC 20590
(202) 366-0364

Description: Direct payments for specified use (tax deferments) to promote construction of U.S. maritime trade vessels. In this case, deposited funds are those obtained from sale of vessels or indemnification for lost vessels.
$ Given: Tax benefits to depositors not stated. Total CRFs: $500,000.
Application Information: Contact Maritime Administration, Office of Ship Financing, prior to formal application.
Deadline: CRF must be established within 60 days after owner's receipt of proceeds or indemnifications.
Contact: Local Maritime Administration regional office

Alabama
F. X. McNerney
Maritime Administration
365 Canal Street, Suite 2590
New Orleans, LA 70130-1137
(504) 589-6556

Alaska
Robert A. Bryan
Maritime Administration
211 Main Street, Room 1112
San Francisco, CA 94105
(415) 744-2580

Arizona
Robert A. Bryan
Maritime Administration
211 Main Street, Room 1112
San Francisco, CA 94105
(415) 744-2580

Arkansas
F. X. McNerney
Maritime Administration
365 Canal Street, Suite 2590
New Orleans, LA 70130-1137
(504) 589-6556

California
Robert A. Bryan
Maritime Administration
211 Main Street, Room 1112
San Francisco, CA 94105
(415) 744-2580

Colorado
Robert A. Bryan
Maritime Administration
211 Main Street, Room 1112
San Francisco, CA 94105
(415) 744-2580

Connecticut
Robert F. McKeon
Maritime Administration
26 Federal Plaza, Room 3737
New York, NY 10278
(212) 264-1300

Delaware
Robert F. McKeon
Maritime Administration
26 Federal Plaza, Room 3737
New York, NY 10278
(212) 264-1300

Florida
(Eastern Half)
William S. Chambers
Maritime Administration
7737 Hampton Boulevard,
Building 4D, Room 211
Norfolk, VA 23505
(804) 441-6393

(Western Half)
F. X. McNerney
Maritime Administration
365 Canal Street, Suite 2590
New Orleans, LA 70130-1137
(504) 589-6556

Georgia
William S. Chambers
Maritime Administration
7737 Hampton Boulevard,
Building 4D, Room 211
Norfolk, VA 23505
(804) 441-6393

Hawaii
Robert A. Bryan
Maritime Administration
211 Main Street, Room 1112
San Francisco, CA 94105
(415) 744-2580

Idaho
Robert A. Bryan
Maritime Administration
211 Main Street, Room 1112
San Francisco, CA 94105
(415) 744-2580

Illinois
Alpha H. Ames, Jr.
Maritime Administration
2300 East Devon Avenue,
Suite 366
Des Plaines, IL 60018-4605
(708) 298-4535

Indiana
Alpha H. Ames, Jr.
Maritime Administration
2300 East Devon Avenue,
Suite 366
Des Plaines, IL 60018-4605
(708) 298-4535

Iowa
F. X. McNerney
Maritime Administration
365 Canal Street, Suite 2590
New Orleans, LA 70130-1137
(504) 589-6556

Kansas
F. X. McNerney
Maritime Administration
365 Canal Street, Suite 2590
New Orleans, LA 70130-1137
(504) 589-6556

Kentucky
F. X. McNerney
Maritime Administration
365 Canal Street, Suite 2590
New Orleans, LA 70130-1137
(504) 589-6556

Louisiana
F. X. McNerney
Maritime Administration
365 Canal Street, Suite 2590
New Orleans, LA 70130-1137
(504) 589-6556

Maine
Robert F. McKeon
Maritime Administration
26 Federal Plaza, Room 3737
New York, NY 10278
(212) 264-1300

Maryland
Robert F. McKeon
Maritime Administration
26 Federal Plaza, Room 3737
New York, NY 10278
(212) 264-1300

Massachusetts
Robert F. McKeon
Maritime Administration
26 Federal Plaza, Room 3737
New York, NY 10278
(212) 264-1300

Michigan
Alpha H. Ames, Jr.
Maritime Administration
2300 East Devon Avenue,
Suite 366
Des Plaines, IL 60018-4605
(708) 298-4535

Minnesota
Alpha H. Ames, Jr.
Maritime Administration
2300 East Devon Avenue,
Suite 366
Des Plaines, IL 60018-4605
(708) 298-4535

Mississippi
F. X. McNerney
Maritime Administration
365 Canal Street, Suite 2590
New Orleans, LA 70130-1137
(504) 589-6556

Missouri
F. X. McNerney
Maritime Administration
365 Canal Street, Suite 2590
New Orleans, LA 70130-1137
(504) 589-6556

Montana
Robert A. Bryan
Maritime Administration
211 Main Street, Room 1112
San Francisco, CA 94105
(415) 744-2580

Nebraska
F. X. McNerney
Maritime Administration
365 Canal Street, Suite 2590
New Orleans, LA 70130-1137
(504) 589-6556

Nevada
Robert A. Bryan
Maritime Administration
211 Main Street, Room 1112
San Francisco, CA 94105
(415) 744-2580

New Hampshire
Robert F. McKeon
Maritime Administration
26 Federal Plaza, Room 3737
New York, NY 10278
(212) 264-1300

New Jersey
Robert F. McKeon
Maritime Administration
26 Federal Plaza, Room 3737
New York, NY 10278
(212) 264-1300

New Mexico
Robert A. Bryan
Maritime Administration
211 Main Street, Room 1112
San Francisco, CA 94105
(415) 744-2580

New York
(Except Lake Coastal Area)
Robert F. McKeon
Maritime Administration
26 Federal Plaza, Room 3737
New York, NY 10278
(212) 264-1300

(Lake Coastal Area)
Alpha H. Ames, Jr.
Maritime Administration
2300 East Devon Avenue,
Suite 366
Des Plaines, IL 60018-4605
(708) 298-4535

North Carolina
William S. Chambers
Maritime Administration
7737 Hampton Boulevard,
Building 4D, Room 211
Norfolk, VA 23505
(804) 441-6393

North Dakota
Robert A. Bryan
Maritime Administration
211 Main Street, Room 1112
San Francisco, CA 94105
(415) 744-2580

Ohio
Alpha H. Ames, Jr.
Maritime Administration
2300 East Devon Avenue,
Suite 366
Des Plaines, IL 60018-4605
(708) 298-4535

Oklahoma
F. X. McNerney
Maritime Administration
365 Canal Street, Suite 2590
New Orleans, LA 70130-1137
(504) 589-6556

Oregon
Robert A. Bryan
Maritime Administration
211 Main Street, Room 1112
San Francisco, CA 94105
(415) 744-2580

Pennsylvania
(Except Lake Coastal Area)
Robert F. McKeon
Maritime Administration
26 Federal Plaza, Room 3737
New York, NY 10278
(212) 264-1300

(Lake Coastal Area)
Alpha H. Ames, Jr.
Maritime Administration
2300 East Devon Avenue,
Suite 366
Des Plaines, IL 60018-4605
(708) 298-4535

Puerto Rico
William S. Chambers
Maritime Administration
7737 Hampton Boulevard,
Building 4D, Room 211
Norfolk, VA 23505
(804) 441-6393

Rhode Island
Robert F. McKeon
Maritime Administration
26 Federal Plaza, Room 3737
New York, NY 10278
(212) 264-1300

South Carolina
William S. Chambers
Maritime Administration
7737 Hampton Boulevard,
Building 4D, Room 211
Norfolk, VA 23505
(804) 441-6393

South Dakota
Robert A. Bryan
Maritime Administration
211 Main Street, Room 1112
San Francisco, CA 94105
(415) 744-2580

Tennessee
F. X. McNerney
Maritime Administration
365 Canal Street, Suite 2590
New Orleans, LA 70130-1137
(504) 589-6556

Texas
F. X. McNerney
Maritime Administration
365 Canal Street, Suite 2590
New Orleans, LA 70130-1137
(504) 589-6556

Utah
Robert A. Bryan
Maritime Administration
211 Main Street, Room 1112
San Francisco, CA 94105
(415) 744-2580

Vermont
Robert F. McKeon
Maritime Administration
26 Federal Plaza, Room 3737
New York, NY 10278
(212) 264-1300

Virginia
William S. Chambers
Maritime Administration
7737 Hampton Boulevard,
Building 4D, Room 211
Norfolk, VA 23505
(804) 441-6393

Washington
Robert A. Bryan
Maritime Administration
211 Main Street, Room 1112
San Francisco, CA 94105
(415) 744-2580

West Virginia
William S. Chambers
Maritime Administration
7737 Hampton Boulevard,
Building 4D, Room 211
Norfolk, VA 23505
(804) 441-6393

Wisconsin
Alpha H. Ames, Jr.
Maritime Administration
2300 East Devon Avenue,
Suite 366
Des Plaines, IL 60018-4605
(708) 298-4535

Wyoming
Robert A. Bryan
Maritime Administration
211 Main Street, Room 1112
San Francisco, CA 94105
(415) 744-2580

Field Office
Paul L. Krinsky
United States Merchant
Marine Academy
Kings Point, NY 11024-1699
(516) 773-5000

DIRECT INVESTMENT LOANS

Overseas Private Investment Corporation (OPIC)
1615 M Street, NW
Washington, DC 20527
(202) 457-7033

Description: Direct loans to small businesses to promote overseas investment in developing countries. Must be small business (i.e., non-Fortune 1000 size).
$ Given: Nationwide FY 93 est. $30 million in loans. Range: $700,000–$7 million; average: $3 million.
Application Information: Request free "Investment Finance Handbook." For application, send letter with required preliminary information.
Deadline: None
Contact: Daven Oswalt, Information Officer, above address

FEDERAL SHIP FINANCING FUND LIQUIDATING ACCOUNT

Department of Commerce
National Marine Fisheries Service
1335 East West Highway
Silver Spring, MD 20910
(301) 713-2390

Description: Private loans guaranteed/insured by U.S. government to finance or upgrade U.S. fishing vessels or shoreside facilities. For guarantees of obligations up to 80 percent of cost. Must have an approved lender providing reasonable terms and an owner/operator able to operate and maintain project.
$ Given: Nationwide FY 92 est. $24 million (FY 93 est. $0). Range: $100,000–$25 million; average: $500,000.
Application Information: Submit application for "fisheries obligation guarantee" to above address.
Deadline: N/A
Contact: Chief, Financial Services Division, above address

165

FISHERMEN'S CONTINGENCY FUND

**Department of
Commerce**
National Marine Fisheries
Service
1335 East West Highway
Silver Spring, MD 20910
(301) 713-2396

Description: Direct payments with unrestricted use to
compensate U.S. commercial fishermen for damage
and loss of fishing gear and 50 percent of resulting
economic loss due to oil- and gas-related activities in
any area of the Outer Continental Shelf.
$ Given: Nationwide FY 93 est. $989,000. Range:
$500–$25,000; average: $6,000.
Application Information: Submit application to above
address.
Deadline: Within 90 days of loss. Presumption of
causation allowed if reported within 15 days of vessel's
return to port.
Contact: Chief, Financial Services Division, above
address

FISHERMEN'S GUARANTY FUND

Department of State
Office of Fisheries Affairs
Bureau of Oceans
Room 5806
Washington, DC
20520-7818
(202) 647-2009

Description: Insurance reimbursement for commercial
U.S. fishing vessels seized by foreign governments.
Vessel must have been seized under territorial claims
or on other basis not recognized by the State
Department.
$ Given: Nationwide FY 93 est. $900,000
reimbursement of losses.
Application Information: Obtain standard application
forms from above address.
Deadline: None
Contact: Stetson Tinkham, above address

FISHING VESSEL AND GEAR DAMAGE COMPENSATION FUND

Department of Commerce
National Marine Fisheries Service
1335 East West Highway
Silver Spring, MD 20910
(301) 713-2396

Description: Direct payments with unrestricted use to compensate U.S. fishermen for loss, damage, or destruction of their vessels by foreign fishing vessels and their gear by any vessel.
$ Given: Nationwide FY 93 est. $1.3 million. Range: $600–$150,000; average: $6,922.
Application Information: Submit application to above address.
Deadline: Within 90 days.
Contact: Chief, Financial Services Division, above address

FOREIGN INVESTMENT GUARANTEES

Overseas Private Investment Corporation
1615 M Street, NW
Washington, DC 20527
(202) 457-7033

Description: Guaranteed/insured loans and direct loans to eligible investors in friendly developing countries and areas. Individual must be U.S. citizen; corporation must be substantially owned by U.S. citizens; foreign subsidiary must be 95 percent owned by U.S. citizens.
$ Given: Nationwide FY 93 est. $500 million in guarantees. Range: $4 million–$50 million; average: $15.6 million.
Application Information: Letter followed by discussions with OPIC, which will provide application instructions to eligible applicants.
Deadline: None
Contact: Daven Oswalt, Information Office, above address

FOREIGN INVESTMENT INSURANCE (POLITICAL RISK INSURANCE)

Overseas Private Investment Corporation
1615 M Street, NW
Washington, DC 20527
(202) 457-7033

Description: Insurance to guarantee U.S. investors in friendly foreign countries against risk of war, revolution, etc. Investors must contribute to welfare of host country without adversely affecting U.S. jobs. Special criteria may be applied to extraction of mineral resources and other large, sensitive projects. Registration with OPIC must be made before investment. Approval of foreign government for the investment must be obtained. Individual must be U.S. citizen; corporation must be created under U.S. law and be 50 percent owned by U.S. citizens; foreign subsidiary must be 95 percent owned by U.S. citizens.
$ Given: Nationwide FY 93 est. $22.3 million in insurance.
Application Information: Registration letter followed by formal application.
Deadline: See above. Registration must precede commitment of investment.
Contact: Daven Oswalt, Information Office, above address

HANDICAPPED ASSISTANCE LOANS

Small Business Administration
Loan Policy and Procedures Branch
409 3rd Street, SW
Washington, DC 20416
(202) 205-6570

Description: Direct loans for construction, expansion, or conversion of facilities; to purchase buildings, equipment, or materials; and for working capital to independently owned and operated small businesses that are 100 percent owned by handicapped individuals. Excludes speculation, publishing media, radio, television, nonprofit entities, speculators in property lending or investment enterprises, and financing of real property held for sale or investment.
$ Given: Range: $500–$350,000; average: $93,305.
Application Information: Write for guidelines.
Deadline: None
Contact: Your state and/or regional office

Alabama
1375 Peachtree Street, NE,
Fifth Floor
Atlanta, GA 30367-8102
(404) 347-2797

Alaska
2615 4th Avenue, Room 440
Seattle, WA 98121
(206) 553-5676

Arizona
71 Stevenson Street,
Twentieth Floor
San Francisco, CA
94105-2939
(415) 744-6402

Arkansas
8625 King George Drive,
Building C
Dallas, TX 75235-3391
(214) 767-7633

California
71 Stevenson Street,
Twentieth Floor
San Francisco, CA
94105-2939
(415) 744-6402

Colorado
999 18th Street, Suite 701
Denver, CO 80202
(303) 294-7186

Connecticut
155 Federal Street,
Ninth Floor
Boston, MA 02110
(617) 451-2023

Delaware
475 Allendale Road,
Suite 201
King of Prussia, PA 19406
(215) 962-3700

District of Columbia
475 Allendale Road,
Suite 201
King of Prussia, PA 19406
(215) 962-3700

Florida
1375 Peachtree Street, NE,
Fifth Floor
Atlanta, GA 30367-8102
(404) 347-2797

Georgia
1375 Peachtree Street, NE,
Fifth Floor
Atlanta, GA 30367-8102
(404) 347-2797

Hawaii
71 Stevenson Street,
Twentieth Floor
San Francisco, CA
94105-2939
(415) 744-6402

Idaho
2615 4th Avenue, Room 440
Seattle, WA 98121
(206) 553-5676

Illinois
Federal Building
300 South Riverside Plaza,
1975 South
Chicago, IL 60606-6617
(312) 353-5000

Iowa
911 Walnut Street,
Thirteenth Floor
Kansas City, MO 64106
(816) 426-3608

Indiana
Federal Building
300 South Riverside Plaza,
1975 South
Chicago, IL 60606-6617
(312) 353-5000

Kansas
911 Walnut Street,
Thirteenth Floor
Kansas City, MO 64106
(816) 426-3608

Kentucky
1375 Peachtree Street, NE,
Fifth Floor
Atlanta, GA 30367-8102
(404) 347-2797

Louisiana
8625 King George Drive,
Building C
Dallas, TX 75235-3391
(214) 767-7633

Maine
155 Federal Street,
Ninth Floor
Boston, MA 02110
(617) 451-2023

Maryland
475 Allendale Road,
Suite 201
King of Prussia, PA 19406
(215) 962-3700

Massachusetts
155 Federal Street,
Ninth Floor
Boston, MA 02110
(617) 451-2023

Michigan
Federal Building
300 South Riverside Plaza,
1975 South
Chicago, IL 60606-6617
(312) 353-5000

Minnesota
Federal Building
300 South Riverside Plaza,
1975 South
Chicago, IL 60606-6617
(312) 353-5000

Mississippi
1375 Peachtree Street, NE,
Fifth Floor
Atlanta, GA 30367-8102
(404) 347-2797

Missouri
911 Walnut Street,
Thirteenth Floor
Kansas City, MO 64106
(816) 426-3608

Montana
999 18th Street, Suite 701
Denver, CO 80202
(303) 294-7186

Nebraska
911 Walnut Street,
Thirteenth Floor
Kansas City, MO 64106
(816) 426-3608

Nevada
71 Stevenson Street,
Twentieth Floor
San Francisco, CA
94105-2939
(415) 744-6402

New Hampshire
155 Federal Street,
Ninth Floor
Boston, MA 02110
(617) 451-2023

New Jersey
26 Federal Plaza,
Room 31-08
New York, NY 10278
(212) 264-7772

New Mexico
8625 King George Drive,
Building C
Dallas, TX 75235-3391
(214) 767-7633

New York
26 Federal Plaza,
Room 31-08
New York, NY 10278
(212) 264-7772

North Carolina
1375 Peachtree Street, NE,
Fifth Floor
Atlanta, GA 30367-8102
(404) 347-2797

North Dakota
999 18th Street, Suite 701
Denver, CO 80202
(303) 294-7186

Ohio
Federal Building
300 South Riverside Plaza,
1975 South
Chicago, IL 60606-6617
(312) 353-5000

Oklahoma
8625 King George Drive,
Building C
Dallas, TX 75235-3391
(214) 767-7633

Oregon
2615 4th Avenue, Room 440
Seattle, WA 98121
(206) 553-5676

Pacific Islands
71 Stevenson Street,
Twentieth Floor
San Francisco, CA
94105-2939
(415) 744-6402

Pennsylvania
475 Allendale Road,
Suite 201
King of Prussia, PA 19406
(215) 962-3700

Puerto Rico
26 Federal Plaza,
Room 31-08
New York, NY 10278
(212) 264-7772

Rhode Island
155 Federal Street,
Ninth Floor
Boston, MA 02110
(617) 451-2023

South Carolina
1375 Peachtree Street, NE,
Fifth Floor
Atlanta, GA 30367-8102
(404) 347-2797

South Dakota
999 18th Street, Suite 701
Denver, CO 80202
(303) 294-7186

Tennessee
1375 Peachtree Street, NE,
Fifth Floor
Atlanta, GA 30367-8102
(404) 347-2797

Texas
8625 King George Drive,
Building C
Dallas, TX 75235-3391
(214) 767-7633

Utah
999 18th Street, Suite 701
Denver, CO 80202
(303) 294-7186

Vermont
155 Federal Street,
Ninth Floor
Boston, MA 02110
(617) 451-2023

Virgin Islands
26 Federal Plaza,
Room 31-08
New York, NY 10278
(212) 264-7772

Virginia
475 Allendale Road,
Suite 201
King of Prussia, PA 19406
(215) 962-3700

Washington
2615 4th Avenue, Room 440
Seattle, WA 98121
(206) 553-5676

West Virginia
475 Allendale Road,
Suite 201
King of Prussia, PA 19406
(215) 962-3700

Wisconsin
Federal Building
300 South Riverside Plaza,
1975 South
Chicago, IL 60606-6617
(312) 353-5000

Wyoming
999 18th Street, Suite 701
Denver, CO 80202
(303) 294-7186

IMPORT RELIEF (INDUSTRY) (ESCAPE CLAUSE)

**International Trade
Commission (ITC)**
500 East Street, SW
Washington, DC 20436
(202) 252-1000

Description: Provision of specialized services (tariffs, import quotas, and adjustments) to industries and workers adversely affected by imports. Applicants must be found eligible by the ITC and the president.
$ Given: N/A
Application Information: Preliminary conference with ITC staff recommended. Submit petition to Secretary, address given.
Deadline: None
Contact: Kenneth R. Mason, Secretary, above address

LABOR-MANAGEMENT RELATIONS AND COOPERATIVE PROGRAMS

Department of Labor
Bureau of Labor-
Management Relations
and Cooperative
Programs
200 Constitution Avenue,
NW
Washington, DC 20210
(202) 523-6098

Description: Advisory services and counseling to businesses to promote better labor-management relations through establishment of voluntary cooperative programs.
$ Given: N/A
Application Information: Oral or written communication with headquarters.
Deadline: None
Contact: James L. Perlmutter or (for airlines) B. Kelley Andrews, above address

LOCAL DEVELOPMENT COMPANY LOANS

**Small Business
Administration
Office of Rural Affairs
and Economic
Development**
409 3rd Street, SW
Washington, DC 20416
(202) 205-6485

Description: Loans administered by local development companies to small businesses for purposes of construction, land purchases, machinery, and equipment. Limited to small, independently owned businesses that are not dominant in their fields. Loans are not provided for working capital or for refinancing.
$ Given: Nationwide FY 93 est. $36.5 million (guarantee). Range: $62,000–$1 million; average: $358,646.
Application Information: Applicants must contact local agent or broker of surety bonds. For program particulars, contact regional SBA office (Program #502 Loans).
Deadline: N/A
Contact: Regional Small Business Administration office for your state

LOW-INCOME HOME ENERGY ASSISTANCE (LIHEAP)

**Department of Health
and Human Services**
Division of Energy
Assistance
Office of Community
Services
Administration for
Children and Families
370 L'Enfant Promenade,
SW
Washington, DC 20447
(202) 401-9351

Description: Technical and training assistance grants
to business concerns to help low-income households
meet their home energy costs. Business concern must
apply jointly with a private nonprofit organization.
$ Given: Nationwide FY 93 est. $500,000.
Application Information: Submit request. Applicable
requirements are published in the Federal Register or
Commerce Business Daily.
Deadline: Published in Federal Register or contact
headquarters office.
Contact: Janet M. Fox, Director, above address

MARITIME WAR RISK INSURANCE

**Department of
Transportation**
Office of Trade Analysis
and Insurance
Maritime Administration
Washington, DC 20590
(202) 366-2400

Description: Provision of war risk insurance not
available on reasonable terms from insurance
companies.
$ Given: Not stated.
Application Information: File application and
supporting documents according to guidelines.
Deadline: None
Contact: Edmond J. Fitzgerald, Director, above address

OPERATING-DIFFERENTIAL SUBSIDIES (ODS)

**Department of
Transportation**
Associate Administrator
for Maritime Aids
Maritime Administration
400 Seventh Street, SW
Washington, DC 20590
(202) 366-0364

Description: Direct payments for specified use to any
U.S. citizen able to operate a maritime vessel, to
equalize cost of operating a U.S. flag ship with cost of
operating a vessel under foreign registry.
$ Given: Subsidies to individual ships $7,400–$13,500;
average: $9,700.
Application Information: Submit standard
applications.
Deadline: None
Contact: Local Maritime Administration regional office

General Business

Alabama
F. X. McNerney
Maritime Administration
365 Canal Street, Suite 2590
New Orleans, LA 70130-1137
(504) 589-6556

Alaska
Robert A. Bryan
Maritime Administration
211 Main Street, Room 1112
San Francisco, CA 94105
(415) 744-2580

Arizona
Robert A. Bryan
Maritime Administration
211 Main Street, Room 1112
San Francisco, CA 94105
(415) 744-2580

Arkansas
F. X. McNerney
Maritime Administration
365 Canal Street, Suite 2590
New Orleans, LA 70130-1137
(504) 589-6556

California
Robert A. Bryan
Maritime Administration
211 Main Street, Room 1112
San Francisco, CA 94105
(415) 744-2580

Colorado
Robert A. Bryan
Maritime Administration
211 Main Street, Room 1112
San Francisco, CA 94105
(415) 744-2580

Connecticut
Robert F. McKeon
Maritime Administration
26 Federal Plaza, Room 3737
New York, NY 10278
(212) 264-1300

Delaware
Robert F. McKeon
Maritime Administration
26 Federal Plaza, Room 3737
New York, NY 10278
(212) 264-1300

Florida
(Eastern Half)
William S. Chambers
Maritime Administration
7737 Hampton Boulevard,
Building 4D, Room 211
Norfolk, VA 23505
(804) 441-6393

(Western Half)
F. X. McNerney
Maritime Administration
365 Canal Street, Suite 2590
New Orleans, LA 70130-1137
(504) 589-6556

Georgia
William S. Chambers
Maritime Administration
7737 Hampton Boulevard,
Building 4D, Room 211
Norfolk, VA 23505
(804) 441-6393

Hawaii
Robert A. Bryan
Maritime Administration
211 Main Street, Room 1112
San Francisco, CA 94105
(415) 744-2580

Idaho
Robert A. Bryan
Maritime Administration
211 Main Street, Room 1112
San Francisco, CA 94105
(415) 744-2580

Illinois
Alpha H. Ames, Jr.
Maritime Administration
2300 East Devon Avenue,
Suite 366
Des Plaines, IL 60018-4605
(708) 298-4535

Indiana
Alpha H. Ames, Jr.
Maritime Administration
2300 East Devon Avenue,
Suite 366
Des Plaines, IL 60018-4605
(708) 298-4535

Iowa
F. X. McNerney
Maritime Administration
365 Canal Street, Suite 2590
New Orleans, LA 70130-1137
(504) 589-6556

Kansas
F. X. McNerney
Maritime Administration
365 Canal Street, Suite 2590
New Orleans, LA 70130-1137
(504) 589-6556

Kentucky
F. X. McNerney
Maritime Administration
365 Canal Street, Suite 2590
New Orleans, LA 70130-1137
(504) 589-6556

Louisiana
F. X. McNerney
Maritime Administration
365 Canal Street, Suite 2590
New Orleans, LA 70130-1137
(504) 589-6556

Maine
Robert F. McKeon
Maritime Administration
26 Federal Plaza, Room 3737
New York, NY 10278
(212) 264-1300

Maryland
Robert F. McKeon
Maritime Administration
26 Federal Plaza, Room 3737
New York, NY 10278
(212) 264-1300

Massachusetts
Robert F. McKeon
Maritime Administration
26 Federal Plaza, Room 3737
New York, NY 10278
(212) 264-1300

Michigan
Alpha H. Ames, Jr.
Maritime Administration
2300 East Devon Avenue,
Suite 366
Des Plaines, IL 60018-4605
(708) 298-4535

Minnesota
Alpha H. Ames, Jr.
Maritime Administration
2300 East Devon Avenue,
Suite 366
Des Plaines, IL 60018-4605
(708) 298-4535

Mississippi
F. X. McNerney
Maritime Administration
365 Canal Street, Suite 2590
New Orleans, LA 70130-1137
(504) 589-6556

Missouri
F. X. McNerney
Maritime Administration
365 Canal Street, Suite 2590
New Orleans, LA 70130-1137
(504) 589-6556

Montana
Robert A. Bryan
Maritime Administration
211 Main Street, Room 1112
San Francisco, CA 94105
(415) 744-2580

Nebraska
F. X. McNerney
Maritime Administration
365 Canal Street, Suite 2590
New Orleans, LA 70130-1137
(504) 589-6556

Nevada
Robert A. Bryan
Maritime Administration
211 Main Street, Room 1112
San Francisco, CA 94105
(415) 744-2580

New Hampshire
Robert F. McKeon
Maritime Administration
26 Federal Plaza, Room 3737
New York, NY 10278
(212) 264-1300

New Jersey
Robert F. McKeon
Maritime Administration
26 Federal Plaza, Room 3737
New York, NY 10278
(212) 264-1300

New Mexico
Robert A. Bryan
Maritime Administration
211 Main Street, Room 1112
San Francisco, CA 94105
(415) 744-2580

New York
(Except Lake Coastal Area)
Robert F. McKeon
Maritime Administration
26 Federal Plaza, Room 3737
New York, NY 10278
(212) 264-1300

(Lake Coastal Area)
Alpha H. Ames, Jr.
Maritime Administration
2300 East Devon Avenue,
Suite 366
Des Plaines, IL 60018-4605
(708) 298-4535

North Carolina
William S. Chambers
Maritime Administration
7737 Hampton Boulevard,
Building 4D, Room 211
Norfolk, VA 23505
(804) 441-6393

North Dakota
Robert A. Bryan
Maritime Administration
211 Main Street, Room 1112
San Francisco, CA 94105
(415) 744-2580

Ohio
Alpha H. Ames, Jr.
Maritime Administration
2300 East Devon Avenue,
Suite 366
Des Plaines, IL 60018-4605
(708) 298-4535

Oklahoma
F. X. McNerney
Maritime Administration
365 Canal Street, Suite 2590
New Orleans, LA 70130-1137
(504) 589-6556

General Business

Oregon
Robert A. Bryan
Maritime Administration
211 Main Street, Room 1112
San Francisco, CA 94105
(415) 744-2580

Pennsylvania
(Except Lake Coastal Area)
Robert F. McKeon
Maritime Administration
26 Federal Plaza, Room 3737
New York, NY 10278
(212) 264-1300

(Lake Coastal Area)
Alpha H. Ames, Jr.
Maritime Administration
2300 East Devon Avenue,
Suite 366
Des Plaines, IL 60018-4605
(708) 298-4535

Puerto Rico
William S. Chambers
Maritime Administration
7737 Hampton Boulevard,
Building 4D, Room 211
Norfolk, VA 23505
(804) 441-6393

Rhode Island
Robert F. McKeon
Maritime Administration
26 Federal Plaza, Room 3737
New York, NY 10278
(212) 264-1300

South Carolina
William S. Chambers
Maritime Administration
7737 Hampton Boulevard,
Building 4D, Room 211
Norfolk, VA 23505
(804) 441-6393

South Dakota
Robert A. Bryan
Maritime Administration
211 Main Street, Room 1112
San Francisco, CA 94105
(415) 744-2580

Tennessee
F. X. McNerney
Maritime Administration
365 Canal Street, Suite 2590
New Orleans, LA 70130-1137
(504) 589-6556

Texas
F. X. McNerney
Maritime Administration
365 Canal Street, Suite 2590
New Orleans, LA 70130-1137
(504) 589-6556

Utah
Robert A. Bryan
Maritime Administration
211 Main Street, Room 1112
San Francisco, CA 94105
(415) 744-2580

Vermont
Robert F. McKeon
Maritime Administration
26 Federal Plaza, Room 3737
New York, NY 10278
(212) 264-1300

Virginia
William S. Chambers
Maritime Administration
7737 Hampton Boulevard,
Building 4D, Room 211
Norfolk, VA 23505
(804) 441-6393

Washington
Robert A. Bryan
Maritime Administration
211 Main Street, Room 1112
San Francisco, CA 94105
(415) 744-2580

West Virginia
William S. Chambers
Maritime Administration
7737 Hampton Boulevard,
Building 4D, Room 211
Norfolk, VA 23505
(804) 441-6393

Wisconsin
Alpha H. Ames, Jr.
Maritime Administration
2300 East Devon Avenue,
Suite 366
Des Plaines, IL 60018-4605
(708) 298-4535

Wyoming
Robert A. Bryan
Maritime Administration
211 Main Street, Room 1112
San Francisco, CA 94105
(415) 744-2580

Field Office
Paul L. Krinsky
United States Merchant
Marine Academy
Kings Point, NY 11024-1699
(516) 773-5000

PENSION PLAN TERMINATION INSURANCE (ERISA)

**Pension Benefit
Guaranty Corporation**
2020 K Street, NW
Washington, DC
20006-1806
(202) 778-8800

Description: Insurance to businesses to encourage establishment and maintenance of voluntary private pension funds. Employer must prove certain distress criteria.
$ Given: Nationwide FY 93 est. $894.3 million in benefit payments to retirees; $4.3 million in financial assistance to plans.
Application Information: Submit application.
Deadline: 60 days prior to termination of distressed plan. Annual premium must be paid for coverage.
Contact: Regional Pension and Welfare Benefits Administration offices below or Premium Operation Division, (202) 778-8825, above address

David Ganz
3660 Wilshire Boulevard,
Room 718
Los Angeles, CA 90010
(213) 252-7556

Leonard Garofolo
71 Stevenson Street,
Suite 915
P.O. Box 190250
San Francisco, CA
94119-0250
(415) 744-6700

Rebecca Marshall
Riddell Building, Room 556
1730 K Street, NW
Washington, DC 20006
(202) 254-7013

Jesse Day
Washington Square Building
111 NW 183rd Street,
Suite 504
Miami, FL 33169
(305) 651-6464

Howard Marsh
1371 Peachtree Street, NE,
Room 205
Atlanta, GA 30367
(404) 347-4090

Kenneth M. Bazar
401 South State Street,
Suite 840
Chicago, IL 60605
(312) 353-0900
(312) 353-1023

Joseph Menez
Fort Wright Executive
Building, Suite 210
1885 Dixie Highway
Fort Wright, KY 41011
(606) 292-3121

James Benages
J. W. McCormack POCH
Building, Suite L-2
Boston, MA 02109
(617) 223-9837

Robert Jogan
Federal Building and U.S.
Courthouse, Room 619
231 West Lafayette Street
Detroit, MI 48226
(313) 226-7450

Gregory Egan
Federal Office Building,
Room 2200
911 Walnut
Kansas City, MO 64106
(816) 426-5131

Francis C. Clisham
815 Olive Street
St. Louis, MO 63101
(314) 425-4691

John Wehrum
1633 Broadway, Room 226
New York, NY 10019
(212) 399-5191

Gerard Gumpertz
Gateway Building,
Room M300
3535 Market Street
Philadelphia, PA 19104
(215) 596-1134

Pension Administrator
Federal Office Building,
Room 707
525 Griffin Street
Dallas, TX 75202
(214) 767-6831

John Scanlon
111 Third Avenue, Room 860
Seattle, WA 98101
(206) 553-4244

PROCUREMENT AUTOMATED SOURCE SYSTEM (PASS)

**Small Business
Administration
Associate Administrator
for Procurement
Assistance**
409 3rd Street, SW
Washington, DC 20416
(202) 205-6469

Description: PASS is a computerized database available to government agencies nationwide that lists and profiles small businesses as potential bidders on government contracts. Participation in the program is restricted to small, independently owned businesses as defined by the Small Business Administration.
$ Given: N/A
Application Information: Fill out and submit a Company Profile Form (SBA 1167) available from the SBA office in your region listed below.
Deadline: N/A
Contact: Regional SBA office listed below

Alabama
Small Business
Administration, Region IV
1375 Peachtree Street, NE,
Fifth Floor
Atlanta, GA 30367-8102
(404) 347-2797

Alaska
Small Business
Administration, Region X
2615 4th Avenue, Room 440
Seattle, WA 98121
(206) 442-5676

Arizona
Small Business
Administration, Region IX
71 Stevenson Street,
Twentieth Floor
San Francisco, CA
94105-2939
(415) 744-6402

Arkansas
Small Business
Administration, Region VI
8625 King George Drive,
Building C
Dallas, TX 75235-3391
(214) 767-7643

California
Small Business
Administration, Region IX
71 Stevenson Street,
Twentieth Floor
San Francisco, CA
94105-2939
(415) 744-6402

Colorado
Small Business
Administration, Region VIII
999 18th Street, Suite 701
Denver, CO 80202
(303) 294-7001

Connecticut
Small Business
Administration, Region I
155 Federal Street,
Ninth Floor
Boston, MA 02110
(617) 451-2023

Delaware
Small Business
Administration, Region III
475 Allendale Road,
Suite 201
King of Prussia, PA 19406
(215) 962-3700

District of Columbia
Small Business
Administration, Region III
475 Allendale Road,
Suite 201
King of Prussia, PA 19406
(215) 962-3700

Florida
Small Business
Administration, Region IV
1375 Peachtree Street, NE,
Fifth Floor
Atlanta, GA 30367-8102
(404) 347-2797

Georgia
Small Business
Administration, Region IV
1375 Peachtree Street, NE,
Fifth Floor
Atlanta, GA 30367-8102
(404) 347-2797

Hawaii
Small Business
Administration, Region IX
71 Stevenson Street,
Twentieth Floor
San Francisco, CA
94105-2939
(415) 744-6402

Idaho
Small Business
Administration, Region X
2615 4th Avenue, Room 440
Seattle, WA 98121
(206) 442-5676

Illinois
Small Business
Administration, Region V
Federal Building, Room 1975
300 South Riverside Plaza
Chicago, IL 60606-6611
(312) 353-0359

Indiana
Small Business
Administration, Region V
Federal Building, Room 1975
300 South Riverside Plaza
Chicago, IL 60606-6611
(312) 353-0359

Iowa
Small Business
Administration, Region VII
911 Walnut Street,
Thirteenth Floor
Kansas City, MO 64106
(816) 426-3608

Kansas
Small Business
Administration, Region VII
911 Walnut Street,
Thirteenth Floor
Kansas City, MO 64106
(816) 426-3608

Kentucky
Small Business
Administration, Region IV
1375 Peachtree Street, NE,
Fifth Floor
Atlanta, GA 30367-8102
(404) 347-2797

Louisiana
Small Business
Administration, Region VI
8625 King George Drive,
Building C
Dallas, TX 75235-3391
(214) 767-7643

Maine
Small Business
Administration, Region I
155 Federal Street,
Ninth Floor
Boston, MA 02110
(617) 451-2023

Maryland
Small Business
Administration, Region III
475 Allendale Road,
Suite 201
King of Prussia, PA 19406
(215) 962-3700

Massachusetts
Small Business
Administration, Region I
155 Federal Street,
Ninth Floor
Boston, MA 02110
(617) 451-2023

Michigan
Small Business
Administration, Region V
Federal Building, Room 1975
300 South Riverside Plaza
Chicago, IL 60606-6611
(312) 353-0359

Minnesota
Small Business
Administration, Region V
Federal Building, Room 1975
300 South Riverside Plaza
Chicago, IL 60606-6611
(312) 353-0359

Mississippi
Small Business
Administration, Region IV
1375 Peachtree Street, NE,
Fifth Floor
Atlanta, GA 30367-8102
(404) 347-2797

Missouri
Small Business
Administration, Region VII
911 Walnut Street,
Thirteenth Floor
Kansas City, MO 64106
(816) 426-3608

Montana
Small Business
Administration, Region VIII
999 18th Street, Suite 701
Denver, CO 80202
(303) 294-7001

Nebraska
Small Business
Administration, Region VII
911 Walnut Street,
Thirteenth Floor
Kansas City, MO 64106
(816) 426-3608

Nevada
Small Business
Administration, Region IX
71 Stevenson Street,
Twentieth Floor
San Francisco, CA
94105-2939
(415) 744-6402

New Hampshire
Small Business
Administration, Region I
155 Federal Street,
Ninth Floor
Boston, MA 02110
(617) 451-2023

New Jersey
Small Business
Administration, Region II
26 Federal Plaza,
Room 31-08
New York, NY 10278
(212) 264-7772

New Mexico
Small Business
Administration, Region VI
8625 King George Drive,
Building C
Dallas, TX 75235-3391
(214) 767-7643

New York
Small Business
Administration, Region II
26 Federal Plaza,
Room 31-08
New York, NY 10278
(212) 264-7772

North Carolina
Small Business
Administration, Region IV
1375 Peachtree Street, NE,
Fifth Floor
Atlanta, GA 30367-8102
(404) 347-2797

North Dakota
Small Business
Administration, Region VIII
999 18th Street, Suite 701
Denver, CO 80202
(303) 294-7001

Ohio
Small Business
Administration, Region V
Federal Building, Room 1975
300 South Riverside Plaza
Chicago, IL 60606-6611
(312) 353-0359

Oklahoma
Small Business
Administration, Region VI
8625 King George Drive,
Building C
Dallas, TX 75235-3391
(214) 767-7643

Oregon
Small Business
Administration, Region X
2615 4th Avenue, Room 440
Seattle, WA 98121
(206) 442-5676

Pennsylvania
Small Business
Administration, Region III
475 Allendale Road,
Suite 201
King of Prussia, PA 19406
(215) 962-3700

Puerto Rico
Small Business
Administration, Region II
26 Federal Plaza,
Room 31-08
New York, NY 10278
(212) 264-7772

Rhode Island
Small Business
Administration, Region I
155 Federal Street,
Ninth Floor
Boston, MA 02110
(617) 451-2023

South Carolina
Small Business
Administration, Region IV
1375 Peachtree Street, NE,
Fifth Floor
Atlanta, GA 30367-8102
(404) 347-2797

South Dakota
Small Business
Administration, Region VIII
999 18th Street, Suite 701
Denver, CO 80202
(303) 294-7001

Tennessee
Small Business
Administration, Region IV
1375 Peachtree Street, NE,
Fifth Floor
Atlanta, GA 30367-8102
(404) 347-2797

Texas
Small Business
Administration, Region VI
8625 King George Drive,
Building C
Dallas, TX 75235-3391
(214) 767-7643

Utah
Small Business
Administration, Region VIII
999 18th Street, Suite 701
Denver, CO 80202
(303) 294-7001

Vermont
Small Business
Administration, Region I
155 Federal Street,
Ninth Floor
Boston, MA 02110
(617) 451-2023

Virgin Islands
Small Business
Administration, Region II
26 Federal Plaza,
Room 31-08
New York, NY 10278
(212) 264-7772

Virginia
Small Business
Administration, Region III
475 Allendale Road,
Suite 201
King of Prussia, PA 19406
(215) 962-3700

Washington
Small Business
Administration, Region X
2615 4th Avenue, Room 440
Seattle, WA 98121
(206) 442-5676

West Virginia
Small Business
Administration, Region III
475 Allendale Road,
Suite 201
King of Prussia, PA 19406
(215) 962-3700

Wisconsin
Small Business
Administration, Region V
Federal Building, Room 1975
300 South Riverside Plaza
Chicago, IL 60606-6611
(312) 353-0359

Wyoming
Small Business
Administration, Region VIII
999 18th Street, Suite 701
Denver, CO 80202
(303) 294-7001

PROTECTION OF SHIPS FROM FOREIGN SEIZURE

Department of State
International Claims and
Investment Disputes
Office of the Legal
Adviser
2100 K Street, NW,
Suite 402
Washington, DC
20037-7180
(202) 632-7810

Description: Insurance reimbursement to owners of private fishing vessels seized by a foreign country. Claims must satisfy guidelines of the State Department.
$ Given: Nationwide FY 93 est. $100,000 claims paid.
Application Information: Submit sworn statement in triplicate with other forms.
Deadline: None
Contact: Ronald J. Bettauer, Assistant Legal Adviser, above address

RURAL DEVELOPMENT GRANTS

**Department of
Agriculture
Farmers Home
Administration
Community Facilities
Loan Division**
Washington, DC 20250
(202) 720-1490

Description: Grants given to aid development of small private businesses and industries in rural areas. Limited to private businesses that will employ 50 or fewer new employees, have less than $1.0 million projected gross revenue, and will emphasize technological innovation and commercialization of new products. Priority is given to businesses in communities of less than 25,000, with a large proportion of the inhabitants having low incomes.
$ Given: Total nationwide est. FY 93 $35 million. Range: $7,000–$500,000; average: $180,555.
Application Information: Inquire at county or district Farmers Home Administration, or State office listed below.
Deadline: N/A
Contact: Local office of Farmers Home Administration

Alabama
Aronov Building, Room 717
474 South Court Street
Montgomery, AL 36104
(205) 223-7077

Alaska
634 South Bailey, Suite 103
Palmer, AK 99645
(907) 745-2176

Arizona
201 East Indianola, Suite 275
Phoenix, AZ 85012
(602) 640-5086

Arkansas
700 West Capitol
For letter mail: P.O. Box 2778
Little Rock, AR 72203
(501) 324-6281

California
194 West Main Street,
Suite F
Woodland, CA 95695-2915
(916) 666-3382

Colorado
655 Parfet Street,
Room E-100
Lakewood, CO 80215
(303) 236-2801

Connecticut
451 West Street
Amherst, MA 01002
(413) 253-4300

Delaware
4611 South Dupont Highway
P.O. Box 400
Camden, DE 19934-9998
(302) 697-4300

District of Columbia
4611 South Dupont Highway
P.O. Box 400
Camden, DE 19934-9998
(302) 697-4300

Florida
Federal Building
4440 NW 25th Place
P.O. Box 147010
Gainesville, FL 32614-7010
(904) 338-3400

Georgia
355 East Hancock Avenue
Stephens Federal Building
Athens, GA 30610
(404) 546-2162

Hawaii
Federal Building, Room 311
154 Waianuenue Avenue
Hilo, HI 96720
(808) 933-3000

Idaho
3232 Elder Street
Boise, ID 83705
(208) 334-1301

Illinois
Illini Plaza, Suite 103
1817 South Neil Street
Champaign, IL 61320
(217) 398-5235

Indiana
5975 Lakeside Boulevard
Indianapolis, IN 46278
(317) 290-3100

Iowa
Federal Building, Room 873
210 Walnut Street
Des Moines, IA 50309
(515) 284-4663

Kansas
1201 SW Summit Executive
Court
P.O. Box 4653
Topeka, KS 66604
(913) 271-7300

Kentucky
333771 Corporate Plaza,
Suite 200
Lexington, KY 40503
(606) 224-7300

Louisiana
3727 Government Street
Alexandria, LA 71302
(318) 473-7920

Maine
444 Stillwater Avenue,
Suite 2
P.O. Box 405
Bangor, ME 04402-0405
(207) 990-9106

Maryland
4611 South Dupont Highway
P.O. Box 400
Camden, DE 19934-9998

Massachusetts
451 West Street
Amherst, MA 01002
(413) 253-4300

Michigan
Manly Miles Building,
Room 209
1405 South Harrison Road
East Lansing, MI 48823
(517) 337-6631

Minnesota
410 Farm Credit Building
375 Jackson Street
St. Paul, MN 55101
(612) 290-3842

Mississippi
Federal Building, Suite 831
100 West Capitol
Jackson, MS 39269
(601) 965-4316

Missouri
601 Business Loop, 70 West
Parkade Center, Suite 235
Columbia, MO 65203
(314) 876-0976

Montana
900 Technology Boulevard,
Suite B
P.O. Box 850
Bozeman, MT 59771
(406) 585-2500

Nebraska
Federal Building, Room 308
100 Centennial Mall North
Lincoln, NE 68508
(402) 437-5551

Nevada
194 West Main Street,
Suite F
Woodland, CA 95695-2915
(916) 666-3382

New Hampshire
City Center, Third Floor
89 Main Street
Montpelier, VT 05602
(802) 223-2371

New Jersey
Tarnsfield and
Woodlane Roads
Tarnsfield Plaza, Suite 22
Mount Holly, NJ 08060
(609) 265-3600

New Mexico
Federal Building, Room 3414
517 Gold Avenue, SW
Albuquerque, NM 87102
(505) 766-2462

New York
Federal Building
100 South Clinton Street,
Room 871
Syracuse, NY 13261-7318
(315) 423-5290

North Carolina
4405 South Bland Road,
Suite 260
Raleigh, NC 27609
(919) 790-2731

North Dakota
Federal Building, Room 208
For letter mail:
Third and Rosser
P.O. Box 1737
Bismark, ND 58502
(701) 250-4781

General Business

Ohio
Federal Building, Room 507
200 North High Street
Columbus, OH 43215
(614) 469-5606

Oklahoma
USDA Agricultural Center
Office Building
Stillwater, OK 74074
(405) 624-4250

Oregon
Federal Building, Room 1590
1220 SW 3rd Avenue
Portland, OR 97204
(503) 326-2731

Pennsylvania
One Credit Union Place,
Suite 330
Harrisburg, PA 17110-2996
(717) 782-4476

Puerto Rico
New San Juan Center
Building, Room 501
159 Carlos E. Chardon Street
For letter mail:
G.P.O. Box 6106G
Hato Rey, PR 00918-5481
(809) 766-5095

Rhode Island
451 West Street
Amherst, MA 01002
(413) 253-4300

South Carolina
Strom Thurmond Federal
Building, Room 1007
1835 Assembly Street
Columbia, SC 29201
(803) 765-5163

South Dakota
Huron Federal Building,
Room 308
200 Fourth Street, SW
Huron, SD 57350
(605) 353-1430

Tennessee
Small Business
Administration, Region IV
1375 Peachtree Street, NE,
Fifth Floor
Atlanta, GA 30367-8102
(404) 347-2797

Texas
Federal Building, Suite 102
101 South Main
Temple, TX 76501
(817) 774-1301

Utah
Federal Building, Room 5438
125 South State Street
Salt Lake City, UT 84138
(801) 524-4063

Vermont
City Center, Third Floor
89 Main Street
Montpelier, VT 05602
(802) 223-2371

Virgin Islands
City Center, Third Floor
89 Main Street
Montpelier, VT 05602
(802) 223-2371

Virginia
Federal Building, Room 8213
400 North 8th Street
Richmond, VA 23240
(804) 771-2451

Washington
Federal Building, Room 319
P.O. Box 2427
Wenatchee, WA 98807
(509) 662-4352

West Virginia
75 High Street
P.O. Box 678
Morgantown, WV 26505
(304) 291-4791

Wisconsin
4949 Kirschling Court
Stevens Point, WI 54481
(715) 345-7600

Wyoming
Federal Building, Room 1005
100 East B Street
For letter mail: P.O. Box 820
Casper, WY 82602
(307) 261-5271

SMALL BUSINESS INNOVATION RESEARCH

Department of Agriculture
Cooperative State Research Service
Aerospace Building, Room 323
14th and Independence Avenue, SW
Washington, DC 20250
(202) 401-6852

Description: Project grants for small businesses. Must be organized for professional independently owned and operated business that is not dominant in the proposed research field. The principal places of business must be located within the United States and must have no more than 500 employees.
$ Given: Range: $46,720–$225,000.
Application Information: Send formal proposals to the SBIR coordinator, Office Research Systems, Cooperative State Research Service.
Deadline: Announced in the Federal Register and the SBIR Program Guidelines.
Contact: SBIR coordinator at above address

SMALL BUSINESS INVESTMENT COMPANIES

Small Business Administration
Investment Division
Office of Operations
409 3rd Street, SW
Washington, DC 20416
(202) 205-6510

Description: Direct, guaranteed, and insured loans, as well as advisory services and counseling to any chartered small business investment company having a combined paid-in capital and paid-in surplus of not less than $2.5 million, having qualified management, filing evidence of sound operation, and establishing the need for SBIC financing in geographic areas where applicant proposes to operate. Investment company must be chartered as a corporation or limited partnership.
$ Given: Guaranteed loan range: $50,000–$35 million; average: $1 million.
Application Information: Request information and appropriate forms from SBA office. Complete appropriate requirements and submit with application fee payments of $5,000 to SBA headquarters office.
Deadline: None
Contact: Your state and/or regional offices

General Business

Alabama
1375 Peachtree Street, NE,
Fifth Floor
Atlanta, GA 30367-8102
(404) 347-2797

Alaska
2615 4th Avenue, Room 440
Seattle, WA 98121
(206) 553-5676

Arizona
71 Stevenson Street,
Twentieth Floor
San Francisco, CA
94105-2939
(415) 744-6402

Arkansas
8625 King George Drive,
Building C
Dallas, TX 75235-3391
(214) 767-7633

California
71 Stevenson Street,
Twentieth Floor
San Francisco, CA
94105-2939
(415) 744-6402

Colorado
999 18th Street, Suite 701
Denver, CO 80202
(303) 294-7186

Connecticut
155 Federal Street,
Ninth Floor
Boston, MA 02110
(617) 451-2023

Delaware
475 Allendale Road,
Suite 201
King of Prussia, PA 19406
(215) 962-3700

District of Columbia
475 Allendale Road,
Suite 201
King of Prussia, PA 19406
(215) 962-3700

Florida
1375 Peachtree Street, NE,
Fifth Floor
Atlanta, GA 30367-8102
(404) 347-2797

Georgia
1375 Peachtree Street, NE,
Fifth Floor
Atlanta, GA 30367-8102
(404) 347-2797

Hawaii
71 Stevenson Street,
Twentieth Floor
San Francisco, CA
94105-2939
(415) 744-6402

Idaho
2615 4th Avenue, Room 440
Seattle, WA 98121
(206) 553-5676

Illinois
Federal Building
300 South Riverside Plaza,
1975 South
Chicago, IL 60606-6617
(312) 353-5000

Iowa
911 Walnut Street,
Thirteenth Floor
Kansas City, MO 64106
(816) 426-3608

Indiana
Federal Building
300 South Riverside Plaza,
1975 South
Chicago, IL 60606-6617
(312) 353-5000

Kansas
911 Walnut Street,
Thirteenth Floor
Kansas City, MO 64106
(816) 426-3608

Kentucky
1375 Peachtree Street, NE,
Fifth Floor
Atlanta, GA 30367-8102
(404) 347-2797

Louisiana
8625 King George Drive,
Building C
Dallas, TX 75235-3391
(214) 767-7633

Maine
155 Federal Street,
Ninth Floor
Boston, MA 02110
(617) 451-2023

Maryland
475 Allendale Road,
Suite 201
King of Prussia, PA 19406
(215) 962-3700

Massachusetts
155 Federal Street,
Ninth Floor
Boston, MA 02110
(617) 451-2023

Michigan
Federal Building
300 South Riverside Plaza,
1975 South
Chicago, IL 60606-6617
(312) 353-5000

Minnesota
Federal Building
300 South Riverside Plaza,
1975 South
Chicago, IL 60606-6617
(312) 353-5000

Mississippi
1375 Peachtree Street, NE,
Fifth Floor
Atlanta, GA 30367-8102
(404) 347-2797

Missouri
911 Walnut Street,
Thirteenth Floor
Kansas City, MO 64106
(816) 426-3608

Montana
999 18th Street, Suite 701
Denver, CO 80202
(303) 294-7186

Nebraska
911 Walnut Street,
Thirteenth Floor
Kansas City, MO 64106
(816) 426-3608

Nevada
71 Stevenson Street,
Twentieth Floor
San Francisco, CA
94105-2939
(415) 744-6402

New Hampshire
155 Federal Street,
Ninth Floor
Boston, MA 02110
(617) 451-2023

New Jersey
26 Federal Plaza,
Room 31-08
New York, NY 10278
(212) 264-7772

New Mexico
8625 King George Drive,
Building C
Dallas, TX 75235-3391
(214) 767-7633

New York
26 Federal Plaza,
Room 31-08
New York, NY 10278
(212) 264-7772

North Carolina
1375 Peachtree Street, NE,
Fifth Floor
Atlanta, GA 30367-8102
(404) 347-2797

North Dakota
999 18th Street, Suite 701
Denver, CO 80202
(303) 294-7186

Ohio
Federal Building
300 South Riverside Plaza,
1975 South
Chicago, IL 60606-6617
(312) 353-5000

Oklahoma
8625 King George Drive,
Building C
Dallas, TX 75235-3391
(214) 767-7633

Oregon
2615 4th Avenue, Room 440
Seattle, WA 98121
(206) 553-5676

Pacific Islands
71 Stevenson Street,
Twentieth Floor
San Francisco, CA
94105-2939
(415) 744-6402

Pennsylvania
475 Allendale Road,
Suite 201
King of Prussia, PA 19406
(215) 962-3700

Puerto Rico
26 Federal Plaza,
Room 31-08
New York, NY 10278
(212) 264-7772

Rhode Island
155 Federal Street,
Ninth Floor
Boston, MA 02110
(617) 451-2023

South Carolina
1375 Peachtree Street, NE,
Fifth Floor
Atlanta, GA 30367-8102
(404) 347-2797

South Dakota
999 18th Street, Suite 701
Denver, CO 80202
(303) 294-7186

Tennessee
1375 Peachtree Street, NE,
Fifth Floor
Atlanta, GA 30367-8102
(404) 347-2797

Texas
8625 King George Drive,
Building C
Dallas, TX 75235-3391
(214) 767-7633

Utah
999 18th Street, Suite 701
Denver, CO 80202
(303) 294-7186

Vermont
155 Federal Street,
Ninth Floor
Boston, MA 02110
(617) 451-2023

Virgin Islands
26 Federal Plaza,
Room 31-08
New York, NY 10278
(212) 264-7772

Virginia
475 Allendale Road,
Suite 201
King of Prussia, PA 19406
(215) 962-3700

Washington
2615 4th Avenue, Room 440
Seattle, WA 98121
(206) 553-5676

West Virginia
475 Allendale Road,
Suite 201
King of Prussia, PA 19406
(215) 962-3700

Wisconsin
Federal Building
300 South Riverside Plaza,
1975 South
Chicago, IL 60606-6617
(312) 353-5000

Wyoming
999 18th Street, Suite 701
Denver, CO 80202
(303) 294-7186

SMALL BUSINESS LOANS

**Small Business
Administration**
Loan Policy and
Procedures Branch
409 3rd Street, SW
Washington, DC 20416
(202) 205-6570

Description: Guaranteed and insured loans to small,
independently owned businesses not dominant in
their field to construct, expand, or convert facilities, to
purchase building equipment, or for working capital.
Excluded are gambling establishments, publishing
media, nonprofit enterprises, property speculators,
lending or investment enterprises, and financing of
real property held for investment.
$ Given: Loans up to $750,000; average: $192,126.
Application Information: Applications should be filed
by lender in field office serving territory in which
applicant's business is located.
Deadline: None
Contact: Your state and/or regional office

Alabama
1375 Peachtree Street, NE,
Fifth Floor
Atlanta, GA 30367-8102
(404) 347-2797

Alaska
2615 4th Avenue, Room 440
Seattle, WA 98121
(206) 553-5676

Arizona
71 Stevenson Street,
Twentieth Floor
San Francisco, CA
94105-2939
(415) 744-6402

Arkansas
8625 King George Drive,
Building C
Dallas, TX 75235-3391
(214) 767-7633

California
71 Stevenson Street,
Twentieth Floor
San Francisco, CA
94105-2939
(415) 744-6402

Colorado
999 18th Street, Suite 701
Denver, CO 80202
(303) 294-7186

Connecticut
155 Federal Street,
Ninth Floor
Boston, MA 02110
(617) 451-2023

Delaware
475 Allendale Road,
Suite 201
King of Prussia, PA 19406
(215) 962-3700

District of Columbia
475 Allendale Road,
Suite 201
King of Prussia, PA 19406
(215) 962-3700

Florida
1375 Peachtree Street, NE,
Fifth Floor
Atlanta, GA 30367-8102
(404) 347-2797

Georgia
1375 Peachtree Street, NE,
Fifth Floor
Atlanta, GA 30367-8102
(404) 347-2797

Hawaii
71 Stevenson Street,
Twentieth Floor
San Francisco, CA
94105-2939
(415) 744-6402

Idaho
2615 4th Avenue, Room 440
Seattle, WA 98121
(206) 553-5676

Illinois
Federal Building
300 South Riverside Plaza,
1975 South
Chicago, IL 60606-6617
(312) 353-5000

Iowa
911 Walnut Street,
Thirteenth Floor
Kansas City, MO 64106
(816) 426-3608

Indiana
Federal Building
300 South Riverside Plaza,
1975 South
Chicago, IL 60606-6617
(312) 353-5000

Kansas
911 Walnut Street,
Thirteenth Floor
Kansas City, MO 64106
(816) 426-3608

Kentucky
1375 Peachtree Street, NE,
Fifth Floor
Atlanta, GA 30367-8102
(404) 347-2797

Louisiana
8625 King George Drive,
Building C
Dallas, TX 75235-3391
(214) 767-7633

Maine
155 Federal Street,
Ninth Floor
Boston, MA 02110
(617) 451-2023

Maryland
475 Allendale Road,
Suite 201
King of Prussia, PA 19406
(215) 962-3700

Massachusetts
155 Federal Street,
Ninth Floor
Boston, MA 02110
(617) 451-2023

Michigan
Federal Building
300 South Riverside Plaza,
1975 South
Chicago, IL 60606-6617
(312) 353-5000

Minnesota
Federal Building
300 South Riverside Plaza,
1975 South
Chicago, IL 60606-6617
(312) 353-5000

Mississippi
1375 Peachtree Street, NE,
Fifth Floor
Atlanta, GA 30367-8102
(404) 347-2797

Missouri
911 Walnut Street,
Thirteenth Floor
Kansas City, MO 64106
(816) 426-3608

Montana
999 18th Street, Suite 701
Denver, CO 80202
(303) 294-7186

Nebraska
911 Walnut Street,
Thirteenth Floor
Kansas City, MO 64106
(816) 426-3608

Nevada
71 Stevenson Street,
Twentieth Floor
San Francisco, CA
94105-2939
(415) 744-6402

New Hampshire
155 Federal Street,
Ninth Floor
Boston, MA 02110
(617) 451-2023

New Jersey
26 Federal Plaza,
Room 31-08
New York, NY 10278
(212) 264-7772

New Mexico
8625 King George Drive,
Building C
Dallas, TX 75235-3391
(214) 767-7633

New York
26 Federal Plaza,
Room 31-08
New York, NY 10278
(212) 264-7772

North Carolina
1375 Peachtree Street, NE,
Fifth Floor
Atlanta, GA 30367-8102
(404) 347-2797

North Dakota
999 18th Street, Suite 701
Denver, CO 80202
(303) 294-7186

Ohio
Federal Building
300 South Riverside Plaza,
1975 South
Chicago, IL 60606-6617
(312) 353-5000

Oklahoma
8625 King George Drive,
Building C
Dallas, TX 75235-3391
(214) 767-7633

Oregon
2615 4th Avenue, Room 440
Seattle, WA 98121
(206) 553-5676

Pacific Islands
71 Stevenson Street,
Twentieth Floor
San Francisco, CA
94105-2939
(415) 744-6402

Pennsylvania
475 Allendale Road,
Suite 201
King of Prussia, PA 19406
(215) 962-3700

Puerto Rico
26 Federal Plaza,
Room 31-08
New York, NY 10278
(212) 264-7772

Rhode Island
155 Federal Street,
Ninth Floor
Boston, MA 02110
(617) 451-2023

South Carolina
1375 Peachtree Street, NE,
Fifth Floor
Atlanta, GA 30367-8102
(404) 347-2797

South Dakota
999 18th Street, Suite 701
Denver, CO 80202
(303) 294-7186

Tennessee
1375 Peachtree Street, NE,
Fifth Floor
Atlanta, GA 30367-8102
(404) 347-2797

Texas
8625 King George Drive,
Building C
Dallas, TX 75235-3391
(214) 767-7633

Utah
999 18th Street, Suite 701
Denver, CO 80202
(303) 294-7186

Vermont
155 Federal Street,
Ninth Floor
Boston, MA 02110
(617) 451-2023

Virgin Islands
26 Federal Plaza,
Room 31-08
New York, NY 10278
(212) 264-7772

Virginia
475 Allendale Road,
Suite 201
King of Prussia, PA 19406
(215) 962-3700

Washington
2615 4th Avenue, Room 440
Seattle, WA 98121
(206) 553-5676

West Virginia
475 Allendale Road,
Suite 201
King of Prussia, PA 19406
(215) 962-3700

Wisconsin
Federal Building
300 South Riverside Plaza,
1975 South
Chicago, IL 60606-6617
(312) 353-5000

Wyoming
999 18th Street, Suite 701
Denver, CO 80202
(303) 294-7186

SUPERFUND PERMANENT RELOCATION ASSISTANCE PROGRAM

Federal Emergency Management Agency
Superfund and Relocation Assistance Branch
Individual Assistance Division
Washington, DC 20472
(202) 646-4262

Description: Direct payments for restricted and nonrestricted use as well as advisory services and counseling to assist individuals and corporations in relocating from areas impacted by a Superfund hazardous substance response action and clean-up. Funds will not be provided if available elsewhere. Funds will not necessarily cover total losses of applicant.
$ Given: Nationwide FY 92 est. $1.8 million (FY 93 $0) in grants that have averaged $80,000.
Application Information: EPA determines eligibility automatically. However, individuals and corporations may appeal EPA determination.
Deadline: N/A
Contact: Local FEMA regional office or Charles D. Robinson, Chief, above address

General Business

Alabama
Major P. May
Regional Director
1371 Peachtree Street, NE,
Suite 700
Atlanta, GA 30309-3108
(404) 853-4200

Alaska
Kim Whitman
Regional Director
Federal Regional Center
130-228th Street, SW
Bothell, WA 98021-9796
(206) 487-4604

American Samoa
William Medigovich
Regional Director
Building 105
Presidio of San Francisco
San Francisco, CA
94129-1250
(415) 923-7100

Arizona
William Medigovich
Regional Director
Building 105
Presidio of San Francisco
San Francisco, CA
94129-1250
(415) 923-7100

Arkansas
Bradley M. Harris
Regional Director
Federal Regional Center,
Room 206-800,
North Loop 288
Denton, TX 76201-3698
(817) 898-5104

California
William Medigovich
Regional Director
Building 105
Presidio of San Francisco
San Francisco, CA
94129-1250
(415) 923-7100

Colorado
Marian L. Olson
Regional Director
Denver Federal Center,
Building 710, Box 25267
Denver, CO 80225-0267
(303) 235-4812

Connecticut
Richard H. Strome
Regional Director
J. W. McCormack Post Office
and Courthouse Building,
Room 442
Boston, MA 02109-4595
(617) 223-9540

Delaware
Paul P. Giordano
Regional Director
Liberty Square Building,
Second Floor
105 South Seventh Street
Philadelphia, PA 19106-3316
(215) 931-5608

District of Columbia
Paul P. Giordano
Regional Director
Liberty Square Building,
Second Floor
105 South Seventh Street
Philadelphia, PA 19106-3316
(215) 931-5608

Florida
Major P. May
Regional Director
1371 Peachtree Street, NE,
Suite 700
Atlanta, GA 30309-3108
(404) 853-4200

Georgia
Major P. May
Regional Director
1371 Peachtree Street, NE,
Suite 700
Atlanta, GA 30309-3108
(404) 853-4200

Guam
William Medigovich
Regional Director
Building 105
Presidio of San Francisco
San Francisco, CA
94129-1250
(415) 923-7100

Hawaii
William Medigovich
Regional Director
Building 105
Presidio of San Francisco
San Francisco, CA
94129-1250
(415) 923-7100

Idaho
Kim Whitman
Regional Director
Federal Regional Center
130-228th Street, SW
Bothell, WA 98021-9796
(206) 487-4604

Illinois
Arlyn F. Brower
Regional Director
175 West Jackson Boulevard,
Fourth Floor
Chicago, IL 60604-2698
(312) 408-5501

Indiana
Arlyn F. Brower
Regional Director
175 West Jackson Boulevard,
Fourth Floor
Chicago, IL 60604-2698
(312) 408-5501

Iowa
S. Richard Mellinger
Regional Director
911 Walnut Street, Room 200
Kansas City, MO 64106-2085
(816) 283-7061

Kansas
S. Richard Mellinger
Regional Director
911 Walnut Street, Room 200
Kansas City, MO 64106-2085
(816) 283-7061

Kentucky
Major P. May
Regional Director
1371 Peachtree Street, NE,
Suite 700
Atlanta, GA 30309-3108
(404) 853-4200

Louisiana
Bradley M. Harris
Regional Director
Federal Regional Center,
Room 206-800,
North Loop 288
Denton, TX 76201-3698
(817) 898-5104

Maine
Richard H. Strome
Regional Director
J. W. McCormack Post Office
and Courthouse Building,
Room 442
Boston, MA 02109-4595
(617) 223-9540

Maryland
Paul P. Giordano
Regional Director
Liberty Square Building,
Second Floor
105 South Seventh Street
Philadelphia, PA 19106-3316
(215) 931-5608

Massachusetts
Richard H. Strome
Regional Director
J. W. McCormack Post Office
and Courthouse Building,
Room 442
Boston, MA 02109-4595
(617) 223-9540

Michigan
Arlyn F. Brower
Regional Director
175 West Jackson Boulevard,
Fourth Floor
Chicago, IL 60604-2698
(312) 408-5501

Minnesota
Arlyn F. Brower
Regional Director
175 West Jackson Boulevard,
Fourth Floor
Chicago, IL 60604-2698
(312) 408-5501

Mississippi
Major P. May
Regional Director
1371 Peachtree Street, NE,
Suite 700
Atlanta, GA 30309-3108
(404) 853-4200

Missouri
S. Richard Mellinger
Regional Director
911 Walnut Street, Room 200
Kansas City, MO 64106-2085
(816) 283-7061

Montana
Marian L. Olson
Regional Director
Denver Federal Center,
Building 710, Box 25267
Denver, CO 80225-0267
(303) 235-4812

Nebraska
S. Richard Mellinger
Regional Director
911 Walnut Street, Room 200
Kansas City, MO 64106-2085
(816) 283-7061

Nevada
William Medigovich
Regional Director
Building 105
Presidio of San Francisco
San Francisco, CA
94129-1250
(415) 923-7100

New Hampshire
Richard H. Strome
Regional Director
J. W. McCormack Post Office
and Courthouse Building,
Room 442
Boston, MA 02109-4595
(617) 223-9540

General Business

New Jersey
Stephen Kempf, Jr.
Regional Director
26 Federal Plaza, Room 1337
New York, NY 10278-0002
(212) 225-7209

New Mexico
Bradley M. Harris
Regional Director
Federal Regional Center,
Room 206-800,
North Loop 288
Denton, TX 76201-3698
(817) 898-5104

New York
Stephen Kempf, Jr.
Regional Director
26 Federal Plaza, Room 1337
New York, NY 10278-0002
(212) 225-7209

North Carolina
Major P. May
Regional Director
1371 Peachtree Street, NE,
Suite 700
Atlanta, GA 30309-3108
(404) 853-4200

North Dakota
Marian L. Olson
Regional Director
Denver Federal Center,
Building 710, Box 25267
Denver, CO 80225-0267
(303) 235-4812

Northern Mariana Islands
William Medigovich
Regional Director
Building 105
Presidio of San Francisco
San Francisco, CA
94129-1250
(415) 923-7100

Ohio
Arlyn F. Brower
Regional Director
175 West Jackson Boulevard,
Fourth Floor
Chicago, IL 60604-2698
(312) 408-5501

Oklahoma
Bradley M. Harris
Regional Director
Federal Regional Center,
Room 206-800,
North Loop 288
Denton, TX 76201-3698
(817) 898-5104

Oregon
Kim Whitman
Regional Director
Federal Regional Center
130-228th Street, SW
Bothell, WA 98021-9796
(206) 487-4604

Pennsylvania
Paul P. Giordano
Regional Director
Liberty Square Building,
Second Floor
105 South Seventh Street
Philadelphia, PA 19106-3316
(215) 931-5608

Puerto Rico
Stephen Kempf, Jr.
Regional Director
26 Federal Plaza, Room 1337
New York, NY 10278-0002
(212) 225-7209

Rhode Island
Richard H. Strome
Regional Director
J. W. McCormack Post Office
and Courthouse Building,
Room 442
Boston, MA 02109-4595
(617) 223-9540

South Carolina
Major P. May
Regional Director
1371 Peachtree Street, NE,
Suite 700
Atlanta, GA 30309-3108
(404) 853-4200

South Dakota
Marian L. Olson
Regional Director
Denver Federal Center,
Building 710, Box 25267
Denver, CO 80225-0267
(303) 235-4812

Tennessee
Major P. May
Regional Director
1371 Peachtree Street, NE,
Suite 700
Atlanta, GA 30309-3108
(404) 853-4200

Texas
Bradley M. Harris
Regional Director
Federal Regional Center,
Room 206-800,
North Loop 288
Denton, TX 76201-3698
(817) 898-5104

Trust Territories of the Pacific Islands
William Medigovich
Regional Director
Building 105
Presidio of San Francisco
San Francisco, CA
94129-1250
(415) 923-7100

Utah
Marian L. Olson
Regional Director
Denver Federal Center,
Building 710, Box 25267
Denver, CO 80225-0267
(303) 235-4812

Vermont
Richard H. Strome
Regional Director
J. W. McCormack Post Office
and Courthouse Building,
Room 442
Boston, MA 02109-4595
(617) 223-9540

Virgin Islands
Stephen Kempf, Jr.
Regional Director
26 Federal Plaza, Room 1337
New York, NY 10278-0002
(212) 225-7209

Virginia
Paul P. Giordano
Regional Director
Liberty Square Building,
Second Floor
105 South Seventh Street
Philadelphia, PA 19106-3316
(215) 931-5608

Washington
Kim Whitman
Regional Director
Federal Regional Center
130-228th Street, SW
Bothell, WA 98021-9796
(206) 487-4604

West Virginia
Paul P. Giordano
Regional Director
Liberty Square Building,
Second Floor
105 South Seventh Street
Philadelphia, PA 19106-3316
(215) 931-5608

Wisconsin
Arlyn F. Brower
Regional Director
175 West Jackson Boulevard,
Fourth Floor
Chicago, IL 60604-2698
(312) 408-5501

Wyoming
Marian L. Olson
Regional Director
Denver Federal Center,
Building 710, Box 25267
Denver, CO 80225-0267
(303) 235-4812

TRADE ADJUSTMENT ASSISTANCE

Department of Commerce
Trade Adjustment
Assistance Division
Economic Development
Administration
Attn.: Daniel F. Harrington
14th and Constitution
Avenue, NW
Washington, DC 20230
(202) 377-3373

Description: Grants (cooperative agreements) to firms and industries adversely affected by increased imports; funds will be used to render recipient technically competitive. Firms must be certified by Secretary of Commerce as eligible. Industries must demonstrate hardship and have a substantial number of certified firms or worker groups. Firms must share 25 percent of cost, industries 50 percent.
$ Given: Grants to firms ranging $5,000–$150,000; grants to industries ranging $25,000–$500,000.
Application Information: Certified firms and eligible industries must submit acceptable adjustment proposals and applications for technical assistance.
Deadline: For firms, within two years of certification. No limit for industries, but funds available on first come, first served basis
Contact: Above address for general information

VETERANS LOAN PROGRAM

**Small Business
Administration
Loan Policy and
Procedures Branch**
409 Third Street, SW
Washington, DC 20416
(202) 205-6570

Description: Direct loans given to small businesses owned by Vietnam-era and disabled veterans for construction, working capital, or equipment. Business must be 51 percent owned by eligible veteran(s) who served more than 180 days any part between 8/5/64 and 5/7/75 and was discharged other than dishonorably. Also loans for disabled vets of any era with a minimum compensable disability of 30 percent or a vet of any era discharged for disability.
$ Given: Range: $1,000–$150,000; average: $75,845.
Application Information: Application filed in field office serving territory in which business is located.
Deadline: None
Contact: Director, above addresses or Regional Offices below.

Alabama
Regional Office
1375 Peachtree Street, NE,
Fifth Floor
Atlanta, GA 30367-8102
(404) 347-2797

District Office
Birmingham District Office
2121 8th Avenue North,
Suite 200
Birmingham, AL 35203-2398
(205) 731-1344

Alaska
Regional Office
2615 4th Avenue, Room 440
Seattle, WA 98121
(206) 442-5676

District Office
Anchorage District Office
222 West 8th Avenue,
Room A36
Anchorage, AK 99513
(907) 271-4022

Arizona
Regional Office
71 Stevenson Street,
Twentieth Floor
San Francisco, CA
94105-2939
(415) 744-6402

District Office
Phoenix District Office
2828 North Central Avenue,
Suite 800
Phoenix, AZ 85004-1025
(602) 379-3732

Arkansas
Regional Office
8625 King George Drive,
Building C
Dallas, TX 75235-3391
(214) 767-7643

District Office
Little Rock District Office
Post Office and Court House
Building, Room 601
320 West Capitol Avenue
Little Rock, AR 72201
(501) 378-5871

California
Regional Office
71 Stevenson Street,
Twentieth Floor
San Francisco, CA
94105-2939
(415) 744-6402

District Offices
Santa Ana District Office
901 West Civic Center Drive,
Suite 160
Santa Ana, CA 92703-2352
(714) 836-2494

San Diego District Office
880 Front Street,
Room 4-S-29
San Diego, CA 92188-0270
(619) 557-5440

San Francisco District Office
211 Main Street,
Fourth Floor
San Francisco, CA
94105-1988
(415) 744-6804

Fresno District Office
2719 North Air Fresno Drive
Fresno, CA 93727-1547
(209) 487-5189

Los Angeles District Office
330 North Grand Boulevard,
Suite 1200
Glendale, CA 91203-2304
(213) 894-2956

Colorado
Regional Office
999 18th Street, Suite 701
Denver, CO 80202
(303) 294-7001

District Office
Denver District Office
721 19th Street, Room 407
Denver, CO 80201-0660
(303) 844-3984

Connecticut
Regional Office
155 Federal Street,
Ninth Floor
Boston, MA 02110
(617) 451-2023

District Office
Hartford District Office
Federal Building,
Second Floor
330 Main Street
Hartford, CT 06106
(203) 240-4700

Delaware
Regional Office
475 Allendale Road,
Suite 201
King of Prussia, PA 19406
(215) 962-3700

Florida
Regional Office
1375 Peachtree Street, NE,
Fifth Floor
Atlanta, GA 30367-8102
(404) 347-2797

District Offices
Jacksonville District Office
7825 Baymeadows Way,
Suite 100-B
Jacksonville, FL 32256-7504
(904) 443-1900

Miami District Office
1320 South Dixie Highway,
Suite 501
Coral Gables, FL 33146
(305) 536-5521

Georgia
Regional Office
1375 Peachtree Street, NE,
Fifth Floor
Atlanta, GA 30367-8102
(404) 347-2797

District Office
Atlanta District Office
1720 Peachtree Road, NW,
Sixth Floor
Atlanta, GA 30309
(404) 347-4749

Hawaii
Regional Office
71 Stevenson Street,
Twentieth Floor
San Francisco, CA
94105-2939
(415) 744-6402

District Office
Honolulu District Office
300 Ala Moana Boulevard,
Room 2213
Honolulu, HI 96850-4981
(808) 541-2990

Idaho
Regional Office
2615 4th Avenue, Room 440
Seattle, WA 98121
(206) 442-5676

District Office
Boise District Office
1020 Main Street, Suite 290
Boise, ID 83702
(208) 334-9635

Illinois
Regional Office
Federal Building, Room 1975
300 South Riverside Plaza
Chicago, IL 60606-6611
(312) 353-0359

District Office
Chicago District Office
500 West Madison Street,
Room 1250
Chicago, IL 60661
(312) 353-4528

Indiana
Regional Office
Federal Building, Room 1975
300 South Riverside Plaza
Chicago, IL 60606-6611
(312) 353-0359

District Office
Indianapolis District Office
429 North Pennsylvania
Street, Suite 100
Indianapolis, IN 46204-1873
(317) 226-7272

Iowa
Regional Office
911 Walnut Street,
Thirteenth Floor
Kansas City, MO 64106
(816) 426-3608

District Offices
Des Moines District Office
New Federal Building,
Room 749
210 Walnut Street
Des Moines, IA 50309
(515) 284-4762

Cedar Rapids District Office
373 Collins Road, NE,
Room 100
Cedar Rapids, IA 52402-3147
(319) 393-8630

Kansas
Regional Office
911 Walnut Street,
Thirteenth Floor
Kansas City, MO 64106
(816) 426-3608

District Office
Wichita District Office
110 East Waterman Street,
First Floor
Wichita, KS 67202
(316) 269-6273

Kentucky
Regional Office
1375 Peachtree Street, NE,
Fifth Floor
Atlanta, GA 30367-8102
(404) 347-2797

District Office
Louisville District Office
Federal Building, Room 188
600 Martin Luther King Jr.
Place
Louisville, KY 40202
(502) 582-5976

Louisiana
Regional Office
8625 King George Drive,
Building C
Dallas TX 75235-3391
(214) 767-7643

District Office
New Orleans District Office
1661 Canal Street,
Suite 2000
New Orleans, LA 70112
(504) 589-6685

Maine
Regional Office
155 Federal Street,
Ninth Floor
Boston, MA 02110
(617) 451-2023

District Office
Augusta District Office
Federal Building, Room 512
40 Western Avenue
Augusta, ME 04330
(207) 622-8378

Massachusetts
Regional Office
155 Federal Street,
Ninth Floor
Boston, MA 02110
(617) 451-2023

District Office
Boston District Office
10 Causeway Street,
Room 265
Boston, MA 02222-1093
(617) 565-5590

Michigan
Regional Office
Federal Building, Room 1975
300 South Riverside Plaza
Chicago, IL 60606-6611
(312) 353-0359

District Office
Detroit District Office
477 Michigan Avenue,
Room 515
Detroit, MI 48226
(313) 226-6075

Minnesota
Regional Office
Federal Building, Room 1975
300 South Riverside Plaza
Chicago, IL 60606-6611
(312) 353-0359

District Office
Minneapolis District Office
100 North 6th Street,
Suite 610
Minneapolis, MN 55403-1563
(612) 370-2324

Mississippi
Regional Office
1375 Peachtree Street, NE,
Fifth Floor
Atlanta, GA 30367-8102
(404) 347-2797

District Office
Jackson District Office
100 West Capitol Street,
Suite 400
Jackson, MS 39201
(601) 965-5325

Missouri
Regional Office
911 Walnut Street,
Thirteenth Floor
Kansas City, MO 64106
(816) 426-3608

District Offices
St. Louis District Office
815 Olive Street, Room 242
St. Louis, MO 63101
(314) 539-6600

Kansas City District Office
323 West 8th Street,
Suite 501
Kansas City, MO 64105
(816) 374-6762

Montana
Regional Office
999 18th Street, Suite 701
Denver, CO 80202
(303) 294-7001

District Office
Helena District Office
301 South Park Avenue,
Room 528
Helena, MT 59626
(406) 449-5381

Nebraska
Regional Office
911 Walnut Street,
Thirteenth Floor
Kansas City, MO 64106
(816) 426-3608

District Office
Omaha District Office
11145 Mill Valley Road
Omaha, NB 64154
(402) 221-3604

Nevada
Regional Office
71 Stevenson Street,
Twentieth Floor
San Francisco, CA
94105-2939
(415) 744-6402

District Office
Las Vegas District Office
301 East Steward Street,
Room 301
Las Vegas, NV 89125-2527
(702) 388-6611

New Hampshire
Regional Office
155 Federal Street,
Ninth Floor
Boston, MA 02110
(617) 451-2023

District Office
Concord District Office
143 North Main Street,
Suite 202
Concord, NH 03302-1257
(603) 225-1400

New Jersey
Regional Office
26 Federal Plaza,
Room 31-08
New York, NY 10278
(212) 264-7772

District Office
Newark District Office
Military Park Building,
Fourth Floor
60 Park Place
Newark, NJ 07102
(201) 341-2434

New Mexico
Regional Office
8625 King George Drive,
Building C
Dallas, TX 75235-3391
(214) 767-7643

District Office
Albuquerque District Office
625 Silver Avenue, SW,
Suite 320
Albuquerque, NM 87102
(505) 766-1870

New York
Regional Office
26 Federal Plaza,
Room 31-08
New York, NY 10278
(212) 264-7772

District Offices
Buffalo District Office
Federal Building 1311
111 West Huron Street
Buffalo, NY 14202
(716) 846-4301

Syracuse District Office
100 South Clinton Street,
Room 1071
Syracuse, NY 13260
(315) 423-5383

North Carolina
Regional Office
1375 Peachtree Street, NE,
Fifth Floor
Atlanta, GA 30367-8102
(404) 347-2797

District Office
Charlotte District Office
200 North College Street
Charlotte, NC 28202
(704) 344-6563

North Dakota
Regional Office
999 18th Street, Suite 701
Denver, CO 80202
(303) 294-7001

District Office
Federal Building, Room 218
657 2nd Avenue, North
Fargo, ND 58108-3086
(701) 239-5131

Ohio .
Regional Office
Federal Building, Room 1975
300 South Riverside Plaza
Chicago, IL 60606-6611
(312) 353-0359

District Office
Columbus District Office
85 Marconi Boulevard,
Room 512
Columbus, OH 43215
(614) 469-6860

Oklahoma
Regional Office
8625 King George Drive,
Building C
Dallas, TX 75235-3391
(214) 767-7643

District Office
Oklahoma City District Office
200 NW 5th Street, Suite 670
Oklahoma City, OK 73102
(405) 231-4301

Oregon
Regional Office
2615 4th Avenue, Room 440
Seattle, WA 98121
(206) 442-5676

General Business

District Office
Portland District Office
222 SW Columbia Street,
Suite 500
Portland, OR 97201-6605
(503) 326-2682

Pacific Islands
Regional Office
71 Stevenson Street,
Twentieth Floor
San Francisco, CA
94105-2939
(415) 744-6402

District Office
Agana Branch Office
Pacific Daily News Building,
Room 508
238 Archbishop F.C. Flores
Street
Agana, GM 96910
(671) 472-7277

Pennsylvania
Regional Office
475 Allendale Road,
Suite 201
King of Prussia, PA 19406
(215) 962-3700

District Office
Pittsburgh District Office
960 Penn Avenue, Fifth Floor
Pittsburgh, PA 15222
(412) 644-2780

Puerto Rico
Regional Office
26 Federal Plaza,
Room 31-08
New York, NY 10278
(212) 264-7772

District Office
Federico Degetau Federal
Building, Room 691
Carlos Chardon Avenue
Hato Rey, PR 00918
(809) 766-5002

Rhode Island
Regional Office
155 Federal Street,
Ninth Floor
Boston, MA 02110
(617) 451-2023

District Office
Providence District Office
380 Westminster Mall,
Fifth Floor
Providence, RI 02903
(401) 528-4561

South Carolina
Regional Office
1375 Peachtree Street, NE,
Fifth Floor
Atlanta, GA 30367-8102
(404) 347-2797

District Office
Columbia District Office
1835 Assembly Street,
Room 358
Columbia, SC 29202
(803) 765-5376

South Dakota
Regional Office
999 18th Street, Suite 701
Denver, CO 80202
(303) 294-7001

District Office
Sioux Falls District Office
101 South Main Avenue,
Suite 101
Sioux Falls, SD 57102-0527
(605) 336-4231

Tennessee
Regional Office
1375 Peachtree Street, NE,
Fifth Floor
Atlanta, GA 30367-8102
(404) 347-2797

District Office
Nashville District Office
50 Vantage Way, Suite 201
Nashville, TN 37338-1500
(615) 736-7176

Texas
Regional Office
8625 King George Drive,
Building C
Dallas, TX 75235-3391
(214) 767-7643

District Offices
San Antonio District Office
7400 Blanco Road, Suite 200
San Antonio, TX 78216
(512) 229-4535

Dallas District Office
1100 Commerce Street,
Room 3C36
Dallas, TX 75242
(214) 767-0608

El Paso District Office
10737 Gateway West,
Suite 320
El Paso, TX 79935
(915) 541-5586

Utah
Regional Office
999 18th Street, Suite 701
Denver, CO 80202
(303) 294-7001

District Office
Salt Lake City District Office
Federal Building, Room 2237
125 South State Street
Salt Lake City, UT
84138-1195
(801) 524-5800

Vermont
Regional Office
155 Federal Street,
Ninth Floor
Boston, MA 02110
(617) 451-2023

District Office
Montpelier District Office
Federal Building, Room 205
87 State Street
Montpelier, VT 05602
(802) 828-4474

Virgin Islands
Regional Office
26 Federal Plaza,
Room 31-08
New York, NY 10278
(212) 264-7772

District Offices
Federico Degetau Federal
Building, Room 691
Carlos Chardon Avenue
Hato Rey, PR 00918
(809) 766-5002

St. Croix Post-of-Duty
United Shopping Plaza
4C & 4D Este Sion Farm,
Room 7
Christiansted, St. Croix, VI
00820
(809) 778-5380

St. Thomas Post-of-Duty
Federal Office Building,
Room 283
Veterans Drive
St. Thomas, VI 00801
(809) 774-8530

Virginia
Regional Office
475 Allendale Road,
Suite 201
King of Prussia, PA 19406
(215) 962-3700

District Office
Richmond District Office
Federal Building, Room 3015
400 North 8th Street
Richmond, VA 23240
(804) 771-2400

Washington
Regional Office
2615 4th Avenue, Room 440
Seattle, WA 98121
(206) 442-5676

District Offices
Spokane District Office
West 601 First Avenue,
Tenth Floor East
Spokane, WA 99204
(509) 353-2807

Seattle District Office
915 Second Avenue,
Room 1792
Seattle, WA 98174-1088
(206) 553-1420

Washington, DC
Regional Office
475 Allendale Road,
Suite 201
King of Prussia, PA 19406
(215) 962-3700

District Office
Washington District Office
1111 18th Street, NW,
Sixth Floor
Washington, DC 20036
(202) 634-1500

West Virginia
Regional Office
475 Allendale Road,
Suite 201
King of Prussia, PA 19406
(215) 962-3700

District Office
Clarksburg District Office
168 West Main Street,
Fifth Floor
Clarksburg, WV 26301
(304) 623-5631

Wisconsin
Regional Office
Federal Building, Room 1975
300 South Riverside Plaza
Chicago, IL 60606-6611
(312) 353-0359

District Office
Madison District Office
212 East Washington Avenue,
Room 213
Madison, WI 53703
(608) 264-5261

Wyoming
Regional Office
999 18th Street, Suite 701
Denver, CO 80202
(303) 294-7001

District Office
Casper District Office
Federal Building, Room 4001
100 East B Street
Casper, WY 82602-2839
(307) 261-5761

Research and Development

Many funds are available from the federal government for business research and development for the following:

1. Assistance for companies to research and develop new products or to develop research centers (i.e., support for energy technology, biomedical research, or biomass technology)
2. Counseling services for export companies to facilitate trade development

You will need to consult the list of addresses in this chapter for your nearest local Department of Commerce field office.

ADVANCED TECHNOLOGY PROGRAM (ATP)

Department of Commerce
National Institute of Standards and Technology (NIST)
Gaithersburg, MD 20899
(301) 975-5187

Description: Project grants to U.S. businesses, joint research and development ventures, and independent research organizations to improve U.S. industry competitiveness by assisting in creating and applying precompetitive generic technology and research necessary to commercialize significant new discoveries and refine manufacturing technologies. Single recipients must pay indirect costs.
$ Given: Nationwide FY 93 est. $63.7 million. Range: $500,00–$13 million; average: $4.4 million.
Application Information: Submit proposals only in response to periodically published program notices.
Deadline: Variable. Contact NIST for details.
Contact: For application kits, contact Gail Killen, Advanced Technology Program, above address, (301) 975-2636

AGING RESEARCH

Department of Health and Human Services
National Institute on Aging
National Institutes of Health
Public Health Service
Bethesda, MD 20892

Description: Project grants to profit-making organizations (SBIRs included) to foster research and technological innovation related to the biomedical, social, and behavioral aspects of aging. Funds to be used for research. Usual restrictions apply for SBIRs.
$ Given: Nationwide FY 93 est. $311.4 million (SBIRs $4.2 million). Range: $5,000–$2.6 million; average: $247,241.
Application Information: Submit formal proposal.
Deadline: February 1, June 1, October 1; SBIRs: April 15, August 15, December 15.
Contact: Biology: Dr. Richard L. Sprott, (301) 496-4996
Geriatrics/Clinical: Dr. Evan Hadley, (301) 496-6761
Behavioral/Social: Dr. Matilda W. Riley, (301) 496-3136
Neuroscience: Dr. Z. Khachaturian, (301) 496-9350
SBIRs: Dr. Miriam F. Kelty, (301) 496-9373
at above address

ALLERGY, IMMUNOLOGY, AND TRANSPLANTATION RESEARCH

Department of Health and Human Services
National Institute of Allergy and Infectious Diseases
National Institutes of Health
Public Health Service
Bethesda, MD 20892
(301) 496-7291

Description: Project grants to profit-making organizations (SBIRs included) to foster research and technological innovation related to allergies and immunological pathologies. Funds to be used for research. Usual restrictions apply for SBIRs.
$ Given: Nationwide FY 93 est. $2.6 million in grants. Range: $1,000–$1.8 million; average: $189,617.
Application Information: Submit formal proposal.
Deadline: February 1, June 1, October 1; SBIRs: April 15, August 15, December 15.
Contact: Dr. John T. McGowan, above address

ANTERIOR SEGMENT DISEASES RESEARCH

Department of Health and Human Services
National Eye Institute
National Institutes of Health
Public Health Service
Bethesda, MD 20892
(301) 496-5884

Description: Project grants to profit-making organizations (SBIRs included) to foster research and technological innovation related to the cornea and external structures of the eye. Funds to be used for research. Usual restrictions apply for SBIRs.
$ Given: Nationwide FY 93 est. $77 million (SBIRs $1.4 million) in grants. Range: $5,000–$605,000; average: $155,000.
Application Information: Submit formal proposal.
Deadline: February 1, June 1, October 1; SBIRs: April 15, August 15, December 15.
Contact: Dr. Lore Anne McNicol, Chief, Anterior Segment Diseases Branch, above address

ARTHRITIS, MUSCULOSKELETAL, AND SKIN DISEASES RESEARCH

Department of Health and Human Services
National Institute of Arthritis and Musculoskeletal and Skin Diseases
National Institutes of Health
Public Health Service
Bethesda, MD 20892

Description: Project grants to profit-making organizations (SBIRs included) to foster research and technological innovation related to arthritis and musculoskeletal and skin diseases. Funds to be used for research. Usual restrictions apply for SBIRs.
$ Given: Nationwide FY 93 est. $177.7 million in grants. Range: $10,000–$1.3 million; average: $188,875.
Application Information: Submit formal applications.
Deadline: February 1, June 1, October 1; SBIRs: April 15, August 15, December 15.
Contact: Dr. M. Lockshin, Director, Extramural Program, Building 31, Room 4C32, above address. For SBIRs, contact Diane Watson, Grants Management Officer, Division of Extramural Activities, Westwood Building, Room 403, above address

BIOLOGICAL BASIS RESEARCH IN THE NEUROSCIENCES

Department of Health and Human Services
National Institute of Neurological Disorders and Stroke
National Institutes of Health
Public Health Service
Bethesda, MD 20892
(301) 496-4188

Description: Project grants to profit-making organizations (SBIRs included) to foster research and technological innovation related to biologic bases of neurological pathologies. Funds to be used for research. Usual restrictions apply for SBIRs.
$ Given: Nationwide FY 93 est. $297 million in grants. Range: $20,000–$1 million; average: $170,000.
Application Information: Submit formal proposals.
Deadline: February 1, June 1, October 1. SBIRs: April 15, August 15, December 15.
Contact: Edward M. Donohue, Division of Extramural Activities, Federal Building, Room 1016, above address

BIOLOGICAL SCIENCES

National Science Foundation
Biological Sciences
1800 G Street, NW
Washington, DC 20550
(202) 357-9854

Description: Project grants to private for-profit organizations to promote biological research. Funds must be used for research, salaries, equipment, travel, etc.
$ Given: Nationwide FY 93 est. $320.6 million. Range: $5,000–$3.5 million; average $90,000.
Application Information: Submit formal proposal.
Deadline: Published in NSF bulletin.
Contact: Assistant Director, above address

BIOPHYSICS AND PHYSIOLOGICAL SCIENCES

Department of Health and Human Services
National Institute of General Medical Sciences
National Institutes of Health
Public Health Service
Bethesda, MD 20892
(301) 496-7061

Description: Project grants to profit-making organizations (SBIRs included) to foster research in biomedical engineering and technology. Funds to be used for research. Usual restrictions apply for SBIRs.
$ Given: Nationwide FY 93 est. $177.1 million in grants including $8.8 million for SBIRs. Range: $21,000–$1 million; average $183,853.
Application Information: Submit formal proposals.
Deadline: February 1, June 1, October 1; SBIRs: April 15, August 15, December 15.
Contact: Dr. James Cassatt, Program Director, Biophysics and Physiological Sciences, above address. For SBIRs, contact Dr. W. Sue Shafer, above address, (301) 496-7061

BLOOD DISEASES AND RESOURCES RESEARCH

Department of Health and Human Services
National Heart, Lung, and Blood Institute
National Institutes of Health
Public Health Service
Bethesda, MD 20892
(301) 496-4868

Description: Project grants to profit-making organizations (SBIRs included) to foster research and technological innovation related to blood diseases and resources. Funds to be used for research. Usual restrictions apply for SBIRs.
$ Given: Nationwide FY 93 est. $174.7 million in grants including SBIRs. Range: $1,000–$2.3 million; average: $245,654.
Application Information: Submit formal proposals.
Deadline: February 1, June 1, October 1; SBIRs: April 15, August 15, December 15.
Contact: Director or Allan Czarra, Program Planning and Prevention Research, Division of Blood Diseases and Resources, above address, (301) 496-4186. For SBIRs, contact Dr. Henry G. Roscoe, Deputy Director, Division of Extramural Affairs, above address, (301) 496-7225

CELLULAR AND MOLECULAR BASIS OF DISEASE RESEARCH

Department of Health and Human Services
National Institute of General Medical Sciences
National Institutes of Health
Public Health Service
Bethesda, MD 20892
(301) 496-7021

Description: Project grants to profit-making organizations (SBIRs included) to foster research and technological innovation related to disturbed or abnormal cellular activity. Funds to be used for research. Usual restrictions apply for SBIRs.
$ Given: Nationwide FY 93 est. $237.9 million in grants. Range: $21,000–$1 million; average: $165,245.
Application Information: Submit formal proposal.
Deadline: February 1, June 1, October 1; SBIRs: April 15, August 15, December 15.
Contact: Dr. Charles Miller, Program Director, Cellular and Molecular Basis of Disease, above address. For SBIRs, contact Dr. W. Sue Shafer, (301) 496-7061

CLEAN COAL TECHNOLOGY PROGRAM

Department of Energy (DOE)
Fossil Energy Program
FE-22
Clean Coal Technology
Washington, DC 20585
(703) 235-2450

Description: Formula grants (cooperative agreements) to corporations to conduct innovative clean coal technology projects. Grants to finance not more than 50 percent of cost of any project.
$ Given: Nationwide FY 93 est. $490.6 million in grants. Range: $227,736–$6.4 million.
Application Information: Submit standard application form according to Office of Management and Budget guidelines.
Deadline: Five months after release of solicitation.
Contact: C. Lowell Miller, above address

CLINICAL RESEARCH RELATED TO NEUROLOGICAL DISORDERS

Department of Health and Human Services
National Institute of Neurological Disorders and Stroke
National Institutes of Health
Public Health Service
Bethesda, MD 20892
(301) 496-4188

Description: Project grants to profit-making organizations (SBIRs included) to foster research and technological innovation related to neurological pathologies. Funds to be used for research. Usual restrictions apply for SBIRs.
$ Given: Nationwide FY 93 est. $189.5 million in grants. Range: $20,000–$3 million; average: $470,000.
Application Information: Submit formal proposals.
Deadline: February 1, June 1, October 1; SBIRs: April 15, August 15, December 15.
Contact: Edward M. Donohue, Division of Extramural Activities, Federal Building, Room 1016, above address

COMPARATIVE MEDICINE PROGRAM (ANIMAL RESEARCH)

Department of Health and Human Services
National Center for Research Resources
National Institutes of Health
Public Health Service
Bethesda, MD 20892
(301) 496-5175

Description: Project grants to profit-making organizations (SBIRs included) to promote research and technological innovation in comparative medicine (use of animals in human medical research). Funds to be used for research. Usual restrictions for SBIRs apply.

$ Given: Nationwide FY 93 est. $73.2 million in grants. Range: $38,475–$612,570; average: $210,985.

Application Information: Submit formal applications.

Deadline: February 1, June 1, October 1; SBIRs: April 15, August 15, December 15.

Contact: Primate Research, Dr. Don C. Gibson
Laboratory Animals, Dr. Denise O. Johnson
AIDS Animal Models, Dr. Milton April
at above address, (301) 496-5175

SBIRs, Dr. Judith Vaitukaitis
at above address, (301) 496-6023

COMPUTER AND INFORMATION SCIENCE AND ENGINEERING (CISE)

National Science Foundation
Computer and Information Science and Engineering
1800 G Street, NW, Room 306
Washington, DC 20550
(202) 357-7936

Description: Project grants to small businesses and other profit-making organizations for research into computer and information processing. Funds must be used for research, salaries, equipment, travel, access to advanced computer networking, etc.

$ Given: Nationwide FY 93 est. $272.2 million. Range: $15,000–$5 million; average: $145,000.

Application Information: Preliminary discussion with relevant program officer encouraged. Submit formal proposal following guidelines.

Deadline: None in most cases

Contact: Assistant Director, above address

CONSERVATION RESEARCH AND DEVELOPMENT

Department of Energy
Office of Management
and Resources
Conservation and
Renewable Energy
Washington, DC 20585
(202) 586-8714

Description: Project grants (cost-shared contracts and cooperative agreements) to for-profit organizations to conduct research and transfer technology in the areas of buildings, industry, and transportation energy conservation.
$ Given: Nationwide FY 93 est. $2 million in grants. Range: $50,000–$500,000; average: $200,000.
Application Information: Preapplication coordination recommended for unsolicited proposals, which are to be submitted in accordance with DOE guidelines. See the department's publication "Guide for the Submission of Unsolicited Proposals."
Deadline: None
Contact: Barbara Twigg, above address

COOPERATIVE AGREEMENTS FOR RESEARCH IN PUBLIC LANDS MANAGEMENT

Department of the Interior
Bureau of Land
Management (BLM)
Washington, DC 20240
(202) 653-9200

Description: Project grants (cooperative agreements) to individuals and corporations for mutually beneficial studies on enhancing management and value of public lands. Must include mutually beneficial objectives. BLM must play substantial role in research.
$ Given: Not stated. Approximately $1 million yearly operating expenses.
Application Information: Coordinate with BLM state office.
Deadline: None
Contact: Chief, Resource Sciences Staff, above address

DIABETES, ENDOCRINOLOGY, AND METABOLISM RESEARCH

Department of Health and Human Services
National Institute of Diabetes, Digestive, and Kidney Diseases
National Institutes of Health
Public Health Service
Bethesda, MD 20892
(301) 496-7348

Description: Project grants to profit-making organizations (SBIRs included) to foster research and technological innovation related to diabetes and its underlying causes. Funds to be used for research. Usual restrictions apply for SBIRs.
$ Given: Nationwide FY 93 est. $274.2 million in grants. Range: $16,600–$2.1 million; average: $180,100.
Application Information: Submit formal proposals.
Deadline: February 1, June 1, October 1; SBIRs: April 15, August 15, December 15.
Contact: Director, Division of Diabetes, Endocrinology, and Metabolic Diseases, Room 9A16, Building 31, above address. For SBIRs, contact John Garthune, Assistant Director, Division of Extramural Activities, Westwood Building, Room 637, above address, (301) 496-7793 (same for FTS)

DIGESTIVE DISEASES AND NUTRITION RESEARCH

Department of Health and Human Services
National Institute of Diabetes, Digestive, and Kidney Diseases
National Institutes of Health
Public Health Service
Bethesda, MD 20892
(301) 496-1333

Description: Project grants to profit-making organizations (SBIRs included) to foster research and technological innovation related to digestive diseases and allied studies. Funds to be used for research. Usual restrictions apply for SBIRs.
$ Given: Nationwide FY 93 est. $128.5 million in grants. Range: $26,547–$1.4 million; average: $164,900.
Application Information: Submit formal proposals.
Deadline: February 1, June 1, October 1; SBIRs: April 15, August 15, December 15.
Contact: Dr. Jay Hoofnagle, Director, Division of Digestive Diseases and Nutrition, Room 9A23, Building 31, above address. For SBIRs, contact John Garthune, Assistant Director, Division of Extramural Activities, Westwood Building, Room 637, above address, (301) 496-7793 (same for FTS)

EARTHQUAKE HAZARDS REDUCTION PROGRAM

Department of the Interior
Office of Earthquakes, Volcanoes, and Engineering
Geologic Division
Geological Survey
National Center,
Mail Stop 905
Reston, VA 22092
(703) 648-6722
(FTS 959-6722)

Description: Project grants (cooperative agreements) to profit-making organizations to mitigate earthquake losses by research into prediction, land-use planning, engineering design, and emergency preparedness. Applicant must prove qualifications.
$ Given: Nationwide FY 93 est. $8 million. Range: $16,000–$200,000; average: $65,000.
Application Information: Submit formal proposal package.
Deadline: January/February
Contact: Deputy Chief, Grants and Contracts, above address

EDUCATION AND HUMAN RESOURCES (EHR)

National Science Foundation
Education and Human Resources
1800 G Street, NW,
Room 516
Washington, DC 20550
(202) 357-7557

Description: Project grants to private organizations to facilitate research aimed at improving the U.S. educational system. Funds must be used for research, salaries, equipment, travel, etc.
$ Given: Nationwide FY 93 est. $480 million. Range: $7,500–$2 million; average: $157,000.
Application Information: Discussion with NSF staff strongly encouraged. Submit formal proposal.
Deadline: Published in NSF bulletin.
Contact: Assistant Director, above address

ENERGY-RELATED INVENTIONS

Department of Energy
Office of Technology
Evaluation and
Assessment
National Institute of
Standards and Technology
Gaithersburg, MD 20899
(301) 975-5500
or
Department of Energy
Inventions and Innovation
Division
Energy-Related Inventions
Programs
1000 Independence
Avenue, SW
Washington, DC 20585
(202) 586-1479

Description: Project grants and advisory services especially to small businesses, individual inventors, and entrepreneurs developing non-nuclear energy technology. Funding assistance limited. Mainly evaluation of inventions and advice concerning engineering, etc.
$ Given: Nationwide FY 93 est. $6 million in grants. Average: $80,000.
Application Information: Submit new technology or invention to NIST, formerly National Bureau of Standards (NBS).
Deadline: None
Contact: George Lewett, Director, Office of Technology Evaluation and Assessment, above address

ENGINEERING GRANTS

National Science
Foundation
Directorate for
Engineering
1800 G Street, NW,
Room 1126E
Washington, DC 20550
(202) 357-9774

Description: Project grants (cooperative agreements) to small businesses to promote progress of engineering and technology. Funds must be used for research (salaries, supplies, travel, etc.). Funds must not be used to support inventions (product development, marketing, pilot plants, etc.).
$ Given: Nationwide FY 93 est. $313 million. Range: $1,000–$5 million; average: $79,000.
Application Information: Send proposals following standard guidelines. Preliminary conferences with relevant program officer encouraged.
Deadline: None for unsolicited proposals.
Contact: Glen Larsen, Program Analyst, above address

EXPORT PROMOTION SERVICES

Department of Commerce
International Trade Administration
Office of the Director General
U.S. and Foreign Commercial Service
Room 3804
Washington, DC 20230
(202) 377-5777

Description: Advisory services and counseling to encourage and assist U.S. firms in expanding their export efforts.
$ Given: N/A
Application Information: N/A
Deadline: N/A
Contact: Local Department of Commerce ITA field office

Alabama
Gayle C. Shelton, Jr., Director
Berry Building, Room 302
2015 2nd Avenue, North
Birmingham, AL 35203
(205) 731-1331

Alaska
Charles Becker, Director
World Trade Center Alaska
4201 Tudor Center Drive,
Suite 319
Anchorage, AK 99508
(907) 271-6237

Arizona
Donald W. Fry, Director
Federal Building, Room 3412
230 North 1st Avenue
Phoenix, AZ 85025
(602) 379-3285

Arkansas
Lon J. Hardin, Director
Savers Federal Building,
Suite 811
320 West Capitol Avenue
Little Rock, AR 72201
(501) 324-5794

California
Steven Arlinghaus, Director
11000 Wilshire Boulevard,
Room 9200
Los Angeles, CA 90024
(212) 575-7105

Jesse Campos,
Trade Specialist
116A West 4th Street,
Suite #1
Santa Ana, CA 92701
(714) 836-2461

Richard Powell, Director
6363 Greenwich Drive,
Suite 145
San Diego, CA 92122
(619) 557-5395

Betty D. Neuhart, Director
250 Montgomery Street,
Fourteenth Floor
San Francisco, CA 94104
(415) 705-2300

Colorado
Paul Bergman,
Acting Director
1625 Broadway, Suite 680
Denver, CO 80202
(303) 844-3246

Connecticut
Eric B. Outwater, Director
Federal Office Building,
Room 610-B
450 Main Street
Hartford, CT 06103
(203) 240-3530

Delaware
Robert E. Kistler, Director
475 Allendale Road,
Suite 202
King of Prussia, PA 19406
(215) 962-4980

Florida
Ivan A. Cosimi, Director
Federal Building, Suite 224
51 SW First Avenue
Miami, FL 33130
(305) 536-5267

George L. Martinez,
Trade Specialist
128 North Osceola Avenue
Clearwater, FL 34615
(813) 461-0011

John Marshall,
Trade Specialist
c/o College of Business
Administration
CEBA II, Room 346,
University of Central Florida
Orlando, FL 32816
(407) 648-6235

Michael E. Higgins,
Trade Specialist
Collins Building, Room 40
107 West Gains Street
Tallahassee, FL 32304
(904) 488-6469

Georgia
Barbara H. Prieto,
Trade Specialist-in-Charge
120 Barnard Street,
Room A-107
Savannah, GA 31401
(912) 652-4204

George T. Norton, Jr.,
Director
Plaza Square North,
Suite 310
4360 Chamblee-Dunwoody
Road
Atlanta, GA 30341

Hawaii
George Dolan, Director
P.O. Box 50026
400 Ala Moana Boulevard,
Room 4106
Honolulu, HI 96850
(808) 541-1782

Idaho
(Portland, Oregon District)
Steve Thompson,
Trade Specialist
Joe R. Williams Building,
Second Floor
700 West State Street
Boise, ID 83720
(208) 334-3857

Illinois
LoRee Silloway, Director
Mid-Continental Plaza
Building, Room 1406
55 East Monroe Street
Chicago, IL 60603
(312) 353-4450

Oscar L. Dube,
Trade Specialist
Illinois Institute of
Technology
201 East Loop Road
Wheaton, IL 60187
(312) 353-4332

Thomas J. DeSeve
515 North Court Street
P.O. Box 1747
Rockford, IL 61110-0247
(815) 987-8123

Indiana
Andrew Thress, Director
One North Capitol, Suite 520
Indianapolis, IN 46204
(317) 226-6214

Iowa
John H. Steuber, Jr., Director
Federal Building, Room 817
210 Walnut Street
Des Moines, IA 50309
(515) 284-4222

Kansas
(Kansas City,
Missouri District)
George D. Lavid,
Trade Specialist
151 North Volutsia
Wichita, KS 67214-4695
(316) 269-6160

Kentucky
John Autin, Director
Gene Synder Courthouse
and Customhouse Building,
Room 636 B
601 West Broadway
Louisville, KY 40202
(502) 582-5066

Louisiana
Paul Guidry, Director
432 World Trade Center
No. 2 Canal Street
New Orleans, LA 70130
(504) 589-6546

Maine
(Boston, Massachusetts
District)
Stephen N. Nyulaszi,
Trade Specialist
77 Sewell Street
Augusta, ME 04330
(207) 622-8249

Maryland
David Earle, Director
U.S. Customhouse,
Room 413
40 South Gay Street
Baltimore, MD 21202
(301) 962-3560

Steve Hall, Trade Specialist
c/o National Institute of
Standards and Technology
Building 411
Gaithersburg, MD 20899
(301) 962-3560

Massachusetts
Francis J. O'Connor, Director
World Trade Center, Suit 307
Commonwealth Pier Area
Boston, MA 02210-2071
(617) 565-8563

Michigan
1140 McNamara Building
477 Michigan Avenue
Detroit, MI 48226
(313) 226-3650

Thomas J. Maquire,
Trade Specialist
300 Monroe Avenue, NW,
Room 406A
Grand Rapids, MI 49503-2291
(616) 456-2411

Minnesota
Ronald E. Kramer, Director
Federal Building, Room 108
110 South Fourth Street
Minneapolis, MN 55401
(612) 348-1638

Research and Development

Mississippi
Mark E. Spinney, Director
Jackson Mall Office Center,
Suite 328
300 Woodrow Wilson
Boulevard
Jackson, MS 39213
(601) 965-4388

Missouri
Donald R. Loso, Director
7911 Forsyth Boulevard,
Suite 610
St. Louis, MO 63105
(314) 425-3302

John Kupfer, Director
601 East 12th Street,
Room 635
Kansas City, MO 64106
(816) 426-3141

Montana
(Portland, Oregon District)
Steve Thompson,
Trade Specialist
Joe R. Williams Building,
Second Floor
700 West State Street
Boise, ID 83720
(208) 334-3857

Nebraska
George H. Payne, Director
11133 "O" Street
Omaha, NE 68137
(402) 221-3664

Nevada
Joseph J. Jeremy, Director
1755 East Plumb Lane,
Room 152
Reno, NV 89502
(702) 784-5203

New Hampshire
Harvey Timberlake
c/o State of New Hampshire
Department of Resources
and Economic Development
172 Pennbroke Road
P.O. Box 856
Concord, NH 03302-0856

New Jersey
Thomas J. Murray, Director
3131 Princeton Pike
Building #6, Suite 100
Trenton, NJ 08648
(609) 989-2100

New Mexico
(Dallas, Texas District)
Sandy Necessary,
Trade Specialist
625 Silver, SW, Third Floor
Albuquerque, NM 87102
(505) 766-2070

New York
George Buchanan, Director
Federal Building, Room 1312
111 West Huron Street
Buffalo, NY 14202
(716) 846-4191

Joel Barkan, Director
26 Federal Plaza, Room 3718
New York, NY 10278
(212) 264-0634

William Freiert,
Trade Specialist
111 East Avenue, Room 220
Rochester, NY 14604
(716) 263-6480

North Carolina
Samuel P. Troy, Director
324 West Market Street
P.O. Box 1950, Room 203
Greensboro, NC 27402
(919) 333-5345

North Dakota
George H. Payne, Director
11133 "O" Street
Omaha, NE 68137
(402) 221-3664

Ohio
Gordon B. Thomas, Director
Federal Building, Room 9504
550 Main Street
Cincinnati, OH 45202
(513) 684-2944

Toby T. Zettler, Director
668 Euclid Avenue,
Room 600
Cleveland, OH 44114
(216) 522-4750

Oklahoma
Ronald L. Wilson, Director
6601 Broadway Extension
Oklahoma City, OK 73116
(405) 231-5302

Thomas Strauss,
Trade Specialist
440 South Houston Street
Tulsa, OK 74127
(918) 581-7650

Oregon
William Schrage, Director
One World Trade Center,
Suite 242
121 SW Salmon
Portland, OR 97204
(503) 326-3001

Pennsylvania
John McCartney, Director
Federal Building, Room 2002
1000 Liberty Avenue
Pittsburgh, PA 15222
(412) 644-2850

Robert E. Kistler, Director
475 Allendale Road,
Suite 202
King of Prussia, PA 19406
(215) 962-4980

Puerto Rico
(Hato Rey)
J. Enrique Vilella, Director
Federal Building, Room G-55
San Juan, PR 00918
(809) 766-5555

Rhode Island
(Boston, Massachusetts
District)
Raimond Meerbach,
Trade Specialist
7 Jackson Walkway
Providence, RI 02903
(401) 528-5104

South Carolina
Edgar Rojas, Director
Strom Thurmond Federal
Building, Suite 172
1835 Assembly Street
Columbia, SC 29201
(803) 765-5345

Margaret Patrick,
Trade Specialist
J. C. Long Building,
Room 128
9 Liberty Street
Charleston, SC 29424
(803) 724-4361

South Dakota
George H. Payne, Director
11133 "O" Street
Omaha, NE 68137
(402) 221-3664

Tennessee
Jeanne Marie Russell,
Trade Specialist
Falls Building, Suite 200
22 North Front Street
Memphis, TN 38103
(901) 544-4137

Jim E. Charlet, Jr., Director
Parkway Towers, Suite 1114
404 James Robertson
Parkway
Nashville, TN 37219-1504
(615) 736-5161

W. Bryan Smith,
Trade Specialist
301 East Church Avenue
Knoxville, TN 37915
(615) 549-9268

Texas
Karen C. Parker,
Trade Reference Assistant
816 Congress Avenue,
Suite 1200
P.O. Box 12728
Austin, TX 78711
(512) 482-5939

James D. Cook, Director
515 Rusk Street, Room 2625
Houston, TX 77002
(713) 229-2578

Donald Schilke, Director
1100 Commerce Street,
Room 7A5
Dallas, TX 75242-0787
(214) 767-0542

Utah
Stephen Smoot, Director
324 South State Street,
Suite 105
Salt Lake City, UT 84111
(801) 524-5116

Vermont
Francis J. O'Connor, Director
World Trade Center,
Suite 307
Commonwealth Pier Area
Boston, MA 02210-2071
(617) 565-8563

Virginia
Philip A. Ouzts, Director
Federal Building, Room 8010
400 North Eighth Street
Richmond, VA 23240
(804) 771-2246

Washington
Charles Buck, Director
3131 Elliott Avenue,
Suite 290
Seattle, WA 98121
(206) 553-5615

West Virginia
Roger L. Fortner, Director
4405 Capitol Street,
Suite 809
Charleston, WV 25301
(304) 347-5123

Wisconsin
Johnny E. Brown, Director
517 East Wisconsin Avenue,
Room 606
Milwaukee, WI 53202
(414) 297-3473

Wyoming
Paul Bergman,
Acting Director
1625 Broadway, Suite 680
Denver, CO 80202
(303) 844-3246

FISHERIES DEVELOPMENT AND UTILIZATION RESEARCH AND DEVELOPMENT GRANTS AND COOPERATIVE AGREEMENTS PROGRAM

Department of Commerce
Office of Trade and Industry Services
National Marine Fisheries Service
National Oceanic and Atmospheric Administration
1335 East West Highway
Silver Spring, MD 20910
(301) 713-2358
(FTS 713-2358)

Description: Project grants (cooperative agreements) to foster development and strengthening of U.S. fishing industry. Recent projects included development of Alaskan bottom fish resources and shellfish toxin detection. Any individual or group may apply.
$ Given: Nationwide FY 92 est. $512,000 (FY 93 est. $0). Range: $5,000–$400,000; average: $100,000.
Application Information: Submit standard application form and proposal and budget following guidelines.
Deadline: Generally 60 days after published solicitation.
Contact: National Oceanic and Atmospheric Administration regional office

Northeast Region
Richard B. Roe, Director
One Blackburn Drive
Gloucester, MA 01930
(508) 281-9300

Southeast Region
Andrew Kemmerer, Director
9450 Koger Boulevard
St. Petersburg, FL 33702
(813) 893-3141

Northwest Region
Rolland A. Schmitten, Director
7600 Sand Point Way, NE
Seattle, WA 90731-7415
(206) 526-6150

Southwest Region
E. Charles Fullerton, Director
300 South Ferry Street
Terminal Island, CA 90731-7415
(213) 514-6196

Alaska Region
Steven Pennoyer, Director
P.O. Box 21668
Juneau, AK 99802
(907) 586-7221

Field Areas
Virginia
Atlantic Marine Center
R. Adm. Freddie L. Jeffries, Director
439 West York Street
Norfolk, VA 23510-1114
(804) 441-6776

Washington
Pacific Marine Center
R. Adm. Raymond L. Spear, Director
1801 Fairview Avenue East
Seattle, WA 98102
(206) 442-7656

FOOD AND DRUG ADMINISTRATION—RESEARCH

Department of Health and Human Services
Grants and Assistance Agreements Section
Division of Contracts and Grants
Food and Drug Administration
Public Health Service
HFA-520, Room 3-20
Parklawn Building
5600 Fishers Lane
Rockville, MD 20857
(301) 443-6170

Description: Project grants to private businesses to encourage medical research (AIDS, poison control, drug hazards, medical devices, etc.). Conference grants provide partial support for medical conferences. Small Business Innovation Research (SBIR) grants included in program. Funds to be used for salaries, equipment, travel, and the like. SBIRs in two phases—Phase I to determine feasibility, Phase II to ensure competitive continuation of research.

$ Given: Nationwide FY 93 est. $15 million in grants. Range: $10,000–$425,000; average: $116,000. Only about 3 SBIR Phase I are expected to be made in FY 93.

Application Information: If wished, consult headquarters staff. Submit formal proposal.

Deadline: Conference grants: October 15, January 15, April 15 and July 15; SBIRs: December 15; unsolicited applications: February 1, June 1, October 1.

Contact: Robert L. Robins, Chief, above address

FOSSIL ENERGY RESEARCH AND DEVELOPMENT

Department of Energy
Fossil Energy Program
Germantown, MD 20545

Description: Project grants and cooperative agreements to commercial corporations to fund high-risk research and development of fossil fuel technologies with high potential payoff; goals are either to increase oil and gas production or to switch to the use of coal and oil shale. Emphasis on fundamental research and technology development.

$ Given: Nationwide FY 93 est. $36 million in grants and cooperative agreements. Range: $5,000–$15 million.

Application Information: Preapplication coordination recommended for unsolicited proposals, which must be submitted in accordance with DOE guidelines.

Deadline: None

Contact: Pittsburgh Energy Technology Center
Supervisor
Proposal Operations, OP-20
P.O. Box 10940
Pittsburgh, PA 15276

or

Dwight Mottet, headquarters address

GENETICS RESEARCH

Department of Health and Human Services
National Institute of General Medical Sciences
National Institutes of Health
Public Health Service
Bethesda, MD 20892
(301) 496-7175

Description: Project grants to profit-making organizations (SBIRs included) to foster research and technological innovation related to genetics. Funds to be used for research. Usual restrictions apply for SBIRs.
$ Given: Nationwide FY 93 est. $239.8 million in grants. Range: $21,000–$1 million; average: $192,452.
Application Information: Submit formal proposal.
Deadline: February 1, June 1, October 1; SBIRs: April 15, August 15, December 15.
Contact: Dr. Judith H. Greenberg, Program Director (Genetics), above address. For SBIRs, contact Dr. W. Sue Shafer, (301) 496-7061, above address

GEOLOGICAL SURVEY—RESEARCH AND DATA ACQUISITION

Department of the Interior
Geological Survey
Research
National Center,
Mail Stop 104
12201 Sunrise Valley Drive
Reston, VA 22092
(703) 648-4451

Description: Project grants (cooperative agreements) to profit-making organizations to support any research beneficial to the Geological Survey's mission to gathering and interpreting geological, hydrological, and topological data pertaining to water, land, and energy resources, etc. Conferences and symposia not ordinarily supported. Office furniture and equipment, foreign travel not supported.
$ Given: Nationwide FY 93 est. $6.5 million. Range: $4,000—$200,000; average: $50,000.
Application Information: Limited discussion followed by standard application.
Deadline: None
Contact: One of the following regional offices:

Alaska:
Director's Representative, Alaska
U.S. Geological Survey
4230 University Drive, Suite 201
Anchorage, AK 99508
(907) 271-4138

Pacific Coast Area:
Director's Representative, Western Region
U.S. Geological Survey
345 Middlefield Road
Menlo Park, CA 94025
(415) 323-8111 ext. 2711

Rocky Mountain Area:
Director's Representative,
Central Region
U.S. Geological Survey
Federal Center
Denver, CO 80225
(303) 236-5438

All Other States:
Assistant Director for
Intergovernmental Affairs
U.S. Geological Survey,
National Center
12201 Sunrise Valley Drive
Reston, VA 22092
(703) 648-4427

GEOSCIENCES

National Science Foundation
1800 G Street, NW
Washington, DC 20550
(202) 357-9859

Description: Project grants to private for-profit organizations to promote earth science research. Funds to be used for salaries, equipment, travel costs, etc.
$ Given: Nationwide FY 93 est. $494.4 million in grants. Range: $1,000–$3 million; average: $99,205.
Application Information: Formal submission of proposal. Preliminary conference with relevant program officer encouraged.
Deadline: Write for specifics.
Contact: Atmospheric (Dr. Eugene W. Bierly) (202) 357-9874
Earth (Dr. James F. Hayes) (202) 357-7958
Ocean (Dr. M. Grant Gross) (202) 357-9639
Polar (Dr. Peter E. Wilkniss) (202) 357-7766
all at above address

GRANTS FOR AGRICULTURAL RESEARCH—COMPETITIVE RESEARCH GRANTS (NATIONAL RESEARCH INITIATIVE COMPETITIVE GRANTS PROGRAM)

Department of Agriculture
Aerospace Building,
Room 323
14th and Independence
Avenue, SW
Washington, DC
20250-2200
(201) 401-5022

Description: Grants to individuals or corporations to promote research in food and agriculture, markets, trade and policy, and processes to add value or develop new products.
$ Given: Range: $4,000–$540,000; average: $117,295.
Application Information: Send formal proposal.
Deadline: January 13, April 13
Contact: Chief Scientist, National Research Initiative Competitive Grants Program, above address

GRANTS FOR AGRICULTURAL RESEARCH, SPECIAL RESEARCH GRANTS

Department of Agriculture
Cooperative State Research Service
Washington, DC 20250
(202) 720-4423

Description: Project grants to universities, other research institutions and organizations, federal agencies, private organizations, or corporations and individuals with demonstrable capacity to facilitate promising breakthroughs in areas of food and agricultural science.
$ Given: Range: $6,000–$352,000; average: $100,426.
Application Information: Submit formal proposals to Grants Administrative Management, CSRS USDA. Application procedures are contained in the research grant application kit.
Deadline: January 21, March 2, March 20
Contact: Administrator at above address

HEART AND VASCULAR DISEASES RESEARCH

Department of Health and Human Services
National Heart, Lung, and Blood Institute
National Institutes of Health
Public Health Service
Bethesda, MD 20892
(301) 496-2553

Description: Project grants to profit-making organizations (SBIRs included) to foster research and technological innovation related to heart and vascular diseases. Funds to be used for research. Usual restrictions apply for SBIRs.
$ Given: Nationwide FY 93 est. $562.9 million including SBIRs. Range: $8,100–$2.7 million; average: $234,796.
Application Information: Submit formal proposals.
Deadline: February 1, June 1, October 1; SBIRs: April 15, August 15, December 15.
Contact: Dr. David Robinson, Special Assistant to the Director, Division of Heart and Vascular Diseases, above address. For SBIRs, contact Dr. Henry G. Roscoe, Deputy Director, Division of Extramural Affairs, above address, (301) 496-7225

HUMAN GENOME RESEARCH

Department of Health and Human Services
National Center for Human Genome Research
National Institutes of Health
Public Health Service
Bethesda, MD 20892
(301) 496-7531

Description: Project grants to stimulate research in human genetics (obtain genetic maps, study DNA sequences, etc.). Funds to be used for salaries, equipment, travel, publication costs, etc. Usual restrictions and deadlines for SBIRs apply.
$ Given: Nationwide FY 93 est. $96.9 million in grants and $1.2 million in SBIRs. Range: $50,000–$2.4 million; average: $314,092.
Application Information: Application forms and information obtainable from Division of Research Grants, above address.
Deadline: New projects: February 1, June 1, October 1; SBIRs: April 15, August 15, December 15.
Contact: Dr. Mark Guyer, (301) 496-0844, or Dr. Bettie Graham (301) 496-7531

INJURY PREVENTION AND CONTROL RESEARCH PROJECTS

Department of Health and Human Services
Division of Injury Epidemiology and Control
National Center for Environmental Health and Injury Control
Centers for Disease Control
Public Health Service
Atlanta, GA 30333
(404) 488-4265

Description: Project grants to any for-profit organization to support injury control research and to implement aspects of all related disciplines in prevention of injuries. Funds to be spent on research only. Grantees may not subgrant, but may contract.
$ Given: Nationwide FY 93 est. $14.5 million in grants. Range: $60,000–$300,000.
Application Information: Preapplication coordination desired but not required. Submit formal application.
Deadline: Contact headquarters office.
Contact: Ted Jones, Research Grants, above address

INTERGOVERNMENTAL CLIMATE—PROGRAMS

Department of Commerce
National Weather Service
World Weather Building
5200 Auth Road
Camp Springs, MD 20746
(301) 763-8071

Description: Project grants to aid states in installation of regional climate information/data centers. Individual or institution must be qualified to conduct climate-related studies or provide climate-related services.
$ Given: Nationwide FY 93 est. $3 million. Grants of $300,000 per center.

Application Information: Submit standard application with proposal and budget estimate.
Deadline: None
Contact: Climate Analysis Center, National Meteorological Center, above address

KIDNEY DISEASES, UROLOGY, AND HEMATOLOGY RESEARCH

Department of Health and Human Services
National Institute of Diabetes, Digestive, and Kidney Diseases
National Institutes of Health
Public Health Service
Bethesda, MD 20892
(301) 496-6325

Description: Project grants to profit-making organizations (SBIRs included) to foster research and technological innovation related to kidney diseases and blood studies. Funds to be used for research. Usual restrictions apply for SBIRs.
$ Given: Nationwide FY 93 est. $143 million in grants. Range: $15,000–$1.6 million; average: $171,000.
Application Information: Submit formal proposal.
Deadline: February 1, June 1, October 1; SBIRs: April 15, August 15, December 15.
Contact: Dr. G. Striker, Director, Division of Kidney, Urologic, and Hematologic Diseases, Room 9A17, Building 31, above address. For SBIRs, contact John Garthune, Assistant Director, Division of Extramural Activities, Westwood Building, Room 637, above address, (301) 496-7793 (same for FTS)

LUNG DISEASE RESEARCH

Department of Health and Human Services
National Heart, Lung, and Blood Institute
National Institutes of Health
Public Health Service
Bethesda, MD 20892
(301) 496-7208

Description: Project grants to profit-making organizations (SBIRs included) to foster research and technological innovation related to lung diseases. Funds to be used for research. Usual restrictions apply for SBIRs.
$ Given: Nationwide FY 93 est. $184.8 million for grants. Range: $3,769–$2.1 million; average: $218,852.
Application Information: Submit formal proposals.
Deadline: February 1, June 1, October 1; SBIRs: April 15, August 15, December 15.
Contact: Director, Division of Lung Diseases, or Loretta Layton, Administrative Office, (301) 496-7984, above address. For SBIRs, contact Dr. Henry G. Roscoe, Deputy Director, Division of Extramural Affairs, above address, (301) 496-7225

MARINE FISHERIES INITIATIVE (MARFIN)

Department of Commerce
National Marine Fisheries Service
9450 Koger Boulevard
St. Petersburg, FL 33702
(813) 893-3720
(FTS 826-3720)

Description: Project grants to individual or corporation to understand and enhance fishery resources in the Gulf of Mexico. Must be used for fisheries in the Gulf of Mexico. Funds not to be used for loans. Funds may be used to develop harvest methods, analyze fishery economics and processing methods, improve stock, etc.
$ Given: Nationwide FY 93 est. $2 million. Range: $10,000–$100,000; average: $50,000.
Application Information: Submit standard application form with detailed standard proposal and line-by-line budget.
Deadline: Contact office for deadlines.
Contact: Donald R. Ekberg, above address

MATERNAL AND CHILD HEALTH FEDERAL CONSOLIDATED PROGRAMS (SPECIAL PROJECTS OF REGIONAL AND NATIONAL SIGNIFICANCE [SPRANS])

Department of Health and Human Services
Maternal and Child Health Bureau
Health Resources and Services Administration
Public Health Service
5600 Fishers Lane, Room 9-11
Rockville, MD 20857
(301) 443-2170

Description: Project grants to private entities to foster genetic disease testing and counseling; to support centers for hemophilia diagnosis and treatment; and other projects that may be shown to benefit mothers and children.
$ Given: Nationwide FY 93 est. $93 million in total grants to nonprofit and for-profit entities. Grants to for-profit entities for genetic, hemophilia, and other projects not stated.
Application Information: Informal discussion followed by standard application.
Deadline: March 1–August 1, depending on program.
Contact: Regional DHHS office or Dr. Vince L. Hutchins, above address

Alabama
Earl Forsythe
101 Marietta Tower, Suite 1515
Atlanta, GA 30323
(404) 331-2442

Alaska
Elizabeth G. Healy
2201 Sixth Avenue, RX-01
Seattle, WA 98121
(206) 553-0420

American Samoa
Emory Lee
Federal Office Building, Room 431
50 United Nations Plaza
San Francisco, CA 94102
(415) 556-1961

Research and Development

Arizona
Emory Lee
Federal Office Building,
Room 431
50 United Nations Plaza
San Francisco, CA 94102
(415) 556-1961

Arkansas
J. B. Keith
1200 Main Tower Building,
Room 1100
Dallas, TX 75202
(214) 767-3301

California
Emory Lee
Federal Office Building,
Room 431
50 United Nations Plaza
San Francisco, CA 94102
(415) 556-1961

Colorado
Paul Denham
Federal Building, Room 325
1961 Stout Street
Denver, CO 80294-3538
(303) 844-3372

Connecticut
Maureen Osolnik
John F. Kennedy Federal
Building, Room 1500
Government Center
Boston, MA 02203
(617) 565-1500

Delaware
James Mengel
Gateway Building,
Room 11480
3535 Market Street
Philadelphia, PA 19104
(215) 596-6492

Mail Address:
P.O. Box 13716,
Mail Stop No. 1
Philadelphia, PA 19101

District of Columbia
James Mengel
Gateway Building,
Room 11480
3535 Market Street
Philadelphia, PA 19104
(215) 596-6492

Mail Address:
P.O. Box 13716,
Mail Stop No. 1
Philadelphia, PA 19101

Florida
Earl Forsythe
101 Marietta Tower,
Suite 1515
Atlanta, GA 30323
(404) 331-2442

Georgia
Earl Forsythe
101 Marietta Tower,
Suite 1515
Atlanta, GA 30323
(404) 331-2442

Guam
Emory Lee
Federal Office Building,
Room 431
50 United Nations Plaza
San Francisco, CA 94102
(415) 556-1961

Hawaii
Emory Lee
Federal Office Building,
Room 431
50 United Nations Plaza
San Francisco, CA 94102
(415) 556-1961

Idaho
Elizabeth G. Healy
2201 Sixth Avenue, RX-01
Seattle, WA 98121
(206) 553-0420

Illinois
Hiroshi Kanno
105 West Adams,
Twenty-third Floor
Chicago, IL 60603
(312) 353-5132

Indiana
Hiroshi Kanno
105 West Adams,
Twenty-third Floor
Chicago, IL 60603
(312) 353-5132

Iowa
Danny K. Sakata
601 East 12th Street,
Room 210
Kansas City, MO 64106
(816) 426-2829

Kansas
Danny K. Sakata
601 East 12th Street,
Room 210
Kansas City, MO 64106
(816) 426-2829

Kentucky
Earl Forsythe
101 Marietta Tower,
Suite 1515
Atlanta, GA 30323
(404) 331-2442

Louisiana
J. B. Keith
1200 Main Tower Building,
Room 1100
Dallas, TX 75202
(214) 767-3301

Maine
Maureen Osolnik
John F. Kennedy Federal
Building, Room 1500
Government Center
Boston, MA 02203
(617) 565-1500

Maryland
James Mengel
Gateway Building, Room
11480
3535 Market Street
Philadelphia, PA 19104
(215) 596-6492

Mail Address:
P.O. Box 13716,
Mail Stop No. 1
Philadelphia, PA 19101

Massachusetts
Maureen Osolnik
John F. Kennedy Federal
Building, Room 1500
Government Center
Boston, MA 02203
(617) 565-1500

Michigan
Hiroshi Kanno
105 West Adams,
Twenty-third Floor
Chicago, IL 60603
(312) 353-5132

Minnesota
Hiroshi Kanno
105 West Adams,
Twenty-third Floor
Chicago, IL 60603
(312) 353-5132

Mississippi
Earl Forsythe
101 Marietta Tower,
Suite 1515
Atlanta, GA 30323
(404) 331-2442

Missouri
Danny K. Sakata
601 East 12th Street,
Room 210
Kansas City, MO 64106
(816) 426-2829

Montana
Paul Denham
Federal Building, Room 325
1961 Stout Street
Denver, CO 80294-3538
(303) 844-3372

Nebraska
Danny K. Sakata
601 East 12th Street,
Room 210
Kansas City, MO 64106
(816) 426-2829

Nevada
Emory Lee
Federal Office Building,
Room 431
50 United Nations Plaza
San Francisco, CA 94102
(415) 556-1961

New Hampshire
Maureen Osolnik
John F. Kennedy Federal
Building, Room 1500
Government Center
Boston, MA 02203
(617) 565-1500

New Jersey
Kathleen Harten
26 Federal Plaza, Room 3835
New York, NY 10278
(212) 264-4600

New Mexico
J. B. Keith
1200 Main Tower Building,
Room 1100
Dallas, TX 75202
(214) 767-3301

New York
Kathleen Harten
26 Federal Plaza, Room 3835
New York, NY 10278
(212) 264-4600

North Carolina
Earl Forsythe
101 Marietta Tower,
Suite 1515
Atlanta, GA 30323
(404) 331-2442

North Dakota
Paul Denham
Federal Building, Room 325
1961 Stout Street
Denver, CO 80294-3538
(303) 844-3372

North Mariana Islands
Emory Lee
Federal Office Building,
Room 431
50 United Nations Plaza
San Francisco, CA 94102
(415) 556-1961

Ohio
Hiroshi Kanno
105 West Adams,
Twenty-third Floor
Chicago, IL 60603
(312) 353-5132

Oklahoma
J. B. Keith
1200 Main Tower Building,
Room 1100
Dallas, TX 75202
(214) 767-3301

Oregon
Elizabeth G. Healy
2201 Sixth Avenue, RX-01
Seattle, WA 98121
(206) 553-0420

Pennsylvania
James Mengel
Gateway Building,
Room 11480
3535 Market Street
Philadelphia, PA 19104
(215) 596-6492

Research and Development

Mail Address:
P.O. Box 13716,
Mail Stop No. 1
Philadelphia, PA 19101

Puerto Rico
Kathleen Harten
26 Federal Plaza, Room 3835
New York, NY 10278
(212) 264-4600

Rhode Island
Maureen Osolnik
John F. Kennedy Federal
Building, Room 1500
Government Center
Boston, MA 02203
(617) 565-1500

South Carolina
Earl Forsythe
101 Marietta Tower,
Suite 1515
Atlanta, GA 30323
(404) 331-2442

South Dakota
Paul Denham
Federal Building, Room 325
1961 Stout Street
Denver, CO 80294-3538
(303) 844-3372

Tennessee
Earl Forsythe
101 Marietta Tower,
Suite 1515
Atlanta, GA 30323
(404) 331-2442

Texas
J. B. Keith
1200 Main Tower Building,
Room 1100
Dallas, TX 75202
(214) 767-3301

Trust Territories of the Pacific Islands
Emory Lee
Federal Office Building,
Room 431
50 United Nations Plaza
San Francisco, CA 94102
(415) 556-1961

Utah
Paul Denham
Federal Building, Room 325
1961 Stout Street
Denver, CO 80294-3538
(303) 844-3372

Vermont
Maureen Osolnik
John F. Kennedy Federal
Building, Room 1500
Government Center
Boston, MA 02203
(617) 565-1500

Virgin Islands
Kathleen Harten
26 Federal Plaza, Room 3835
New York, NY 10278
(212) 264-4600

Virginia
James Mengel
Gateway Building,
Room 11480
3535 Market Street
Philadelphia, PA 19104
(215) 596-6492

Mail Address:
P.O. Box 13716,
Mail Stop No. 1
Philadelphia, PA 19101

Washington
Elizabeth G. Healy
2201 Sixth Avenue, RX-01
Seattle, WA 98121
(206) 553-0420

West Virginia
James Mengel
Gateway Building,
Room 11480
3535 Market Street
Philadelphia, PA 19104
(215) 596-6492

Mail Address:
P.O. Box 13716,
Mail Stop No. 1
Philadelphia, PA 19101

Wisconsin
Hiroshi Kanno
105 West Adams,
Twenty-third Floor
Chicago, IL 60603
(312) 353-5132

Wyoming
Paul Denham
Federal Building, Room 325
1961 Stout Street
Denver, CO 80294-3538
(303) 844-3372

MATHEMATICAL AND PHYSICAL SCIENCES

National Science Foundation
Mathematical and Physical Sciences
1800 G Street, NW
Washington, DC 20550
(202) 357-9742

Description: Project grants (cooperative agreements) to small businesses to promote progress of science. Funds must be used for research (salaries, supplies, travel, etc.).
$ Given: Nationwide FY 93 est. $726 million. Range: $10,000–$4.2 million; average: $70,000.
Application Information: Send proposals following standard guidelines.
Deadline: None
Contact: Assistant Director, above address

MICROBIOLOGY AND INFECTIOUS DISEASES RESEARCH

Department of Health and Human Services
National Institute of Allergy and Infectious Diseases
National Institutes of Health
Public Health Service
Bethesda, MD 20892
(301) 496-7291

Description: Project grants to profit-making organizations (SBIRs included) to foster research and technological innovation related to the microbiology of infectious and parasitic diseases. Funds to be used for research. Usual restrictions apply for SBIRs.
$ Given: Nationwide FY 93 est. $7.5 million in grants. Range: $1,000–$2.8 million; average: $222,710.
Application Information: Submit formal proposal.
Deadline: February 1, June 1, October 1; SBIRs: April 15, August 15, December 15.
Contact: Dr. John T. McGowan, above address

NATIONAL WATER RESOURCES RESEARCH PROGRAM (WATER RESOURCES RESEARCH GRANT PROGRAM)

Department of the Interior
Geological Survey
MS 424 National Center
Reston, VA 22092
(703) 648-6811

Description: Project grants to private firms and individuals to research water resource related problems in national interest. No proposals accepted for 1993.
$ Given: Nationwide FY 93 est. $1.8 million. Range: $35,000–$175,000; average: $121,000.
Application Information: Submit application based on periodic Geological Survey announcements.
Deadline: None
Contact: Melvin Lew, Program Coordinator, Office of External Research, above address

NUCLEAR ENERGY, REACTOR SYSTEMS, DEVELOPMENT, AND TECHNOLOGY

Department of Energy
Office of Nuclear Energy
B-410
Germantown Building
Washington, DC 20545

Description: Project grants (cooperative agreements), in whole or part, to individuals and corporations to promote research in nuclear energy technology. Funds to be used for salaries, materials, travel, publication costs, etc.
$ Given: Nationwide FY 92 est. $3.5 million (FY 93 est. $0) in grants ranging up to $5 million maximum.
Application Information: Informal communication followed by formal proposal following OMB guidelines.
Deadline: None
Contact: J. Greenwood
          Policy and Analysis Division
          Chicago Operations Office
          or
          H. Rohm, headquarters address

OCCUPATIONAL SAFETY AND HEALTH RESEARCH GRANTS

Department of Health and Human Services
National Institute for Occupational Safety and Health
Centers for Disease Control
Public Health Service
1600 Clifton Road, NE
MS-D30
Atlanta, GA 30333
(404) 639-3343

Description: Project grants to profit-making organizations (SBIRs included) to research occupational health and safety questions and foster technological innovations. Funds to be used for research purposes only. Usual restrictions apply to SBIRs.
$ Given: Nationwide FY 93 est. $6.7 million in grants. Range: $10,000–$300,000; average: $160,000.
Application Information: Submit formal applications.
Deadline: February 1, June 1, October 1; SBIRs: December 15.
Contact: Dr. Roy M. Fleming, above address

ORAL DISEASE AND DISORDERS RESEARCH

Department of Health and Human Services
Extramural Program
National Institute of Dental Research
National Institutes of Health
Public Health Service
Bethesda, MD 20892

Description: Project grants to businesses (SBIRs included) to promote research on oral diseases and disorders. SBIRs in two phases, I and II (feasibility and continuation). Maximum funds $50,000 for Phase I, $500,000 for Phase II. Various other restrictions apply. Funds to be used in manner consistent with research grants.
$ Given: Nationwide FY 93 est. $118 million. Range: $5,000–$1.5 million; average $156,000.
Application Information: Request and submit application form.
Deadline: Grants: February 1, June 1, October 1; SBIRs: April 15, August 15, December 15.
Contact: Periodontal and Soft Tissue
Dr. Matthew Kinnard
(301) 496-7784

Craniofacial Anomalies, Pain Control and Behavior
Dr. John D. Townsley
(301) 496-7807

Caries, Restorative Materials, and Salivary Research
Dr. Gerassismos J. Roussos
(301) 496-7437

All care of headquarters address

POPULATION RESEARCH

Department of Health and Human Services
National Institute of Child Health and Human Development
National Institutes of Health
Public Health Service
Bethesda, MD 20892
(301) 496-1848

Description: Project grants to profit-making organizations (SBIRs included) to foster research and technological innovation related to population control and contraception. Funds to be used for research. Usual restrictions apply for SBIRs.
$ Given: Nationwide FY 93 est. $125.3 million ($1.6 million SBIRs) in grants. Range: $15,500–$1.3 million; average: $165,500.
Application Information: Submit formal proposal.
Deadline: February 1, June 1, October 1; SBIRs: April 15, August 15, December 15.
Contact: Hildegard P. Topper, Building 31, Room 2A04, above address

REGIONAL BIOMASS PROGRAMS

Department of Energy
Office of National
Programs CE-52
Washington, DC 20585
(202) 586-1480

Description: Project grants to profit-motivated organizations to develop and transfer to nonfederal sector biomass technologies relating to feedstock production, conversion technologies, and municipal solid waste. Regional needs must be addressed.
$ Given: Nationwide FY 93 est. $2 million in grants.
Application Information: Standard application forms. Unsolicited proposals should be submitted in accordance with DOE guidelines.
Deadline: None
Contact: Any of the below in your area of the country.

James Cooke
Oak Ridge Field Office
P.O. Box 2008
Oak Ridge, TN 37831-8613
(615) 576-0737

Russell O'Connell
Northeast Biomass Energy
Program
400 North Capitol Street,
NW
Washington, DC 20001
(202) 624-8450

Phillip Badger
Southeast Biomass Energy
Program
Tennessee Valley Authority
Muscle Shoals, AL 35660
(205) 386-3086

Pat Fox
Northwest Biomass Energy
Program
Bonneville Power
Administration
905 11th Avenue, NE
Portland, OR 97232
(503) 230-3449

David Swanson
Western Biomass Energy
Program
1627 Cole Boulevard, P.O.
Box 3402
Building 18, MS-0450
Golden, CO 80401
(303) 231-1615

Fred Kuzel
Great Lakes Governors
35 East Walker Drive
Chicago, IL 60601
(312) 407-0177

Mike Voorhies
Department of Energy
Office of National
Programs CE-52
Washington, DC 20585
(202) 586-1480

REGULATION OF SURFACE COAL MINING AND SURFACE EFFECTS OF UNDERGROUND COAL MINING

Department of the Interior
Office of Surface Mining Reclamation and Enforcement
1951 Constitution Avenue, NW
Washington, DC 20240
(202) 208-2651

Description: Project grants and direct payments for specified use to small coal mine operators for contracting with qualified laboratories to provide hydrologic and geologic data.
$ Given: Nationwide FY 93 est. $1.8 million.
Application Information: Consult local OSM office, submit formal application.
Deadline: None
Contact: Nearest local OSM field office

Field Offices

Office of Surface Mining
U.S. Department of the Interior
Director
1951 Constitutional Avenue, NW
Washington, DC 20240
(202) 208-4006

Office of Surface Mining
U.S. Department of the Interior
Director, Indianapolis Field Office
575 North Pennsylvania Street, Room 301
Indianapolis, IN 46204
(317) 226-6700

Office of Surface Mining
U.S. Department of the Interior
Director, Albuquerque Field Office
625 Silver Avenue, SW, Suite 310
Albuquerque, NM 87102
(505) 766-1486

Office of Surface Mining
U.S. Department of the Interior
Director, Birmingham Field Office
135 Gemini Circle, Suite 215
Homewood, AL 35209
(205) 290-7282

Office of Surface Mining
U.S. Department of the Interior
Director, Lexington Field Office
340 Legion Drive, Suite 28
Lexington, KY 40504
(606) 233-2896

Office of Surface Mining
U.S. Department of the Interior
Director, Columbus Field Office
2242 South Hamilton Road, Room 202
Columbus, OH 43232
(614) 866-0578

Office of Surface Mining
U.S. Department of the Interior
Director, Springfield Field Office
511 West Capitol Avenue
Springfield, IL 62704
(217) 492-4495

Office of Surface Mining
U.S. Department of the Interior
Director, Kansas City Field Office
934 Wyandotte Street, Room 500
Kansas City, MO 64105
(816) 374-6405

Office of Surface Mining
U.S. Department of the Interior
Director, Tulsa Field Office
5100 East Skelly Drive, Suite 550
Tulsa, OK 74135
(918) 581-6430

Office of Surface Mining
U.S. Department of the
Interior
Director, Harrisburg Field
Office
4th and Market Streets,
Suite 3C
Harrisburg, PA 17101
(717) 782-4036

Office of Surface Mining
U.S. Department of the
Interior
Director, Knoxville Field
Office
530 Gay Street, SW,
Suite 500
Knoxville, TN 37902
(615) 673-4504

Office of Surface Mining
U.S. Department of the
Interior
Director, Big Stone Gap Field
Office
P.O. Box 1216
Big Stone Gap, VA 24219
(703) 523-4303

Office of Surface Mining
U.S. Department of the
Interior
Director, Charleston Field
Office
603 Morris Street
Charleston, WV 25301
(304) 347-7158

Office of Surface Mining
U.S. Department of the
Interior
Director, Casper Field Office
Federal Building, Room 2128
100 East B Street
Casper, WY 82601-1918
(307) 261-5776

**Assistant Directors Support
Centers**
Office of Surface Mining
U.S. Department of the
Interior
Assistant Director, Western
Support Center
Brooks Towers
1020 15th Street,
Second Floor
Denver, CO 80202
(303) 844-2459

Office of Surface Mining
U.S. Department of the
Interior
Assistant Director, Eastern
Support Center
Ten Parkway Center
Pittsburgh, PA 15220
(412) 937-2828

RENEWABLE ENERGY RESEARCH
AND DEVELOPMENT

Department of Energy
Office of Management
and Resources
Washington, DC 20585
(202) 586-8714

Description: Project grants to profit organizations to
develop and transfer to the nonfederal sector the
following energy technologies: solar buildings,
photovoltaics, solar thermal, biomass, alcohol fuels,
urban waste, wind, ocean, and geothermal.
$ Given: Nationwide FY 93 est. $100,000 in grants.
Range: $10,000–$100,000.
Application Information: Preapplication coordination
recommended for unsolicited proposals, which must
be submitted in accordance with DOE guidelines.
Deadline: None
Contact: Barbara Twigg, above address

RESEARCH AND TECHNOLOGY DEVELOPMENT

Department of Defense
Defense Advanced
Research Projects Agency
3701 North Fairfax Drive
Arlington, VA 22203
(703) 696-2404

Description: Project grants (cooperative agreements) to commercial firms to support basic and applied research in state-of-the-art military technology. Individuals not eligible. Programs to encourage careers in science, particularly among underrepresented minority groups. Applicants must not appear on Department of Defense debarred or suspended list.
$ Given: Nationwide FY 93 est. $75 million. Range: $100,000–$100 million; average: $1.4 million.
Application Information: Submit proposals or white papers in response to relevant Broad Agency Announcements.
Deadline: See Broad Agency Announcements in Commerce Business Daily.
Contact: Above address

RESEARCH FOR MOTHERS AND CHILDREN

**Department of Health
and Human Services**
National Institute of Child
Health and Human
Development
National Institutes of
Health
Public Health Service
Bethesda, MD 20892
(301) 496-1848

Description: Project grants to profit-making organizations (SBIRs included) to foster research and technological innovation related to childhood development from conception to maturity. Funds to be used for research. Usual restrictions apply for SBIRs.
$ Given: Nationwide FY 93 est. $249.5 million (SBIRs $3.6 million) in grants. Range: $18,300–$2 million; average: $200,000.
Application Information: Submit formal proposal.
Deadline: February 1, June 1, October 1; SBIRs: April 15, August 15, December 15.
Contact: Hildegard P. Topper, Building 31, Room 2A04, above address

RESEARCH RELATED TO DEAFNESS AND COMMUNICATION DISORDERS

Department of Health and Human Services
National Institute on Deafness and Other Communication Disorders
National Institutes of Health
Public Health Service
Executive Plaza South, Room 400-B
Bethesda, MD 20892
(301) 496-1804

Description: Project grants to businesses (SBIRs included) to promote research into deafness and disorders of hearing, balance, smell, taste, voice, speech, language, etc. Funds to be used for salaries, equipment, travel, publication costs, etc. Usual restrictions apply to SBIRs. For-profit institutions not eligible for some grants.

$ Given: Nationwide FY 93 est. $134.7 million in grants. Range: $72,486–$458,342; average: $186,000.

Application Information: Submit standard application forms.

Deadline: New grants: February 1, June 1, October 1; SBIRs: April 15, August 15, December 15.

Contact: Dr. Ralph F. Naunton, above address, or Sharon Hunt, (301) 402-0909, for grants management

RETINAL AND CHOROIDAL DISEASE RESEARCH

Department of Health and Human Services
National Eye Institute
National Institutes of Health
Public Health Service
Bethesda, MD 20892
(301) 496-5884

Description: Project grants to profit-making organizations (SBIRs included) to foster research and technological innovation related to the retina. Funds to be used for research. Usual restrictions apply for SBIRs.

$ Given: Nationwide FY 93 est. $102.6 million (SBIRs $495,000) in grants. Range: $5,000–$2.8 million; average: $158,000.

Application Information: Submit formal proposal.

Deadline: February 1, June 1, October 1; SBIRs: April 15, August 15, December 15.

Contact: Dr. Peter A. Dudley, Chief, Retinal and Choroidal Diseases Branch, above address

SEA GRANT SUPPORT

Department of Commerce
National Oceanic and Atmospheric Administration
1335 East West Highway
Silver Spring, MD 20910
(301) 713-2448

Description: Project grants to support establishment and operation of major university centers for marine resources research, education, and training, and to support marine advisory services. "Some individual efforts receive funding." Limited to individuals or private corporations. Funds must be used for research, development, education, etc. Funds must not be used to purchase or construct ships or facilities.
$ Given: Nationwide FY 93 est. $22.5 million. Range: $45,000–$3.3 million.
Application Information: Use standard application forms. Submit proposal to headquarters.
Deadline: None
Contact: Director, National Sea Grant College Program, above address

SMALL BUSINESS INNOVATION RESEARCH (SBIR PROGRAM)

Department of Health and Human Services
Parklawn Building
5600 Fishers Lane
Rockville, MD 20857
(301) 443-3107

Description: Project grants to stimulate research by small businesses in various fields of research and development pertaining to the Alcohol, Drug Abuse, and Mental Health Administration's mission. Grants given in two phases, I and II. Only Phase I grantees eligible for Phase II. Grants of no more than $50,000 and $500,000 respectively. Businesses must be independently owned and operated and not be dominant in their field. Primary employment of principal investigator must be with firm. Minority and disadvantaged firms encouraged.

$ Given: Nationwide FY 93 est. $10 million.

Application Information: May consult official Omnibus Solicitation. Submit formal application.

Deadline: April 15, August 15, December 15

Contact: Dr. Laurie Faudin
National Institute on Alcohol Abuse and Alcoholism
Room 16C-05
(301) 443-4223

Jackie Downing
National Institute on Drug Abuse
Room 10A-55
(301) 443-1056

James Moynihan
National Institute of Mental Health
Room 11-95
(301) 443-3107

All at headquarters address

SOCIAL, BEHAVIORAL, AND ECONOMIC SCIENCES (SBE)

National Science Foundation
Social, Behavioral, and Economic Sciences
1800 G Street, NW
Washington, DC 20550
(202) 357-9859

Description: Project grants to private for-profit organizations to facilitate cooperative activities with foreign scientists, engineers, and institutions. Funds must be used for studies, research, salaries, equipment, travel (on U.S. flag vessels only), etc.
$ Given: Nationwide FY 93 est. $107.8 million. Range: $1,000–$900,000; average: $46,819.
Application Information: Proposals by the applicant and foreign peers should be submitted simultaneously to their respective agencies. Initial inquiries encouraged.
Deadline: Published in NSF bulletin.
Contact: Assistant Director, above address

SOCIOECONOMIC AND DEMOGRAPHIC RESEARCH, DATA, AND OTHER INFORMATION

Department of Energy
Forrestal Building,
Room 5B-110
Washington, DC 20585
(202) 586-1593

Description: Project grants to energy-related industry (particularly small and disadvantaged businesses) and national laboratories to research minority energy use. Funds must be used for salaries, materials and supplies, equipment, travel, publication costs, etc.
$ Given: Nationwide FY 93 est. $830,000 in grants.
Application Information: Proposals to be submitted in accordance with DOE guidelines.
Deadline: None
Contact: Georgia R. Johnson, above address

STRABISMUS, AMBLYOPIA, AND VISUAL PROCESSING

Department of Health and Human Services
National Eye Institute
National Institutes of Health
Public Health Service
Bethesda, MD 20892
(301) 496-5301

Description: Project grants to profit-making organizations (SBIRs included) to foster research and technological innovation related to various eye pathologies, with emphasis on strabismus, amblyopia, and oculomotor disorders. Funds to be used for research. Usual restrictions apply for SBIRs.
$ Given: Nationwide FY 93 est. $47.5 million (SBIRs $1 million) in grants. Range: $5,000–$363,000; average: $134,000.
Application Information: Submit formal proposal.
Deadline: February 1, June 1, October 1; SBIRs: April 15, August 15, December 15.
Contact: Dr. Constance W. Atwell, Chief, Strabismus, Amblyopia, and Visual Processing Branch, above address

TECHNOLOGY INTEGRATION (TIP)

Department of Energy
Office of Technology Development
Environmental Restoration and Waste Management
EM-52
Washington, DC 20545
(301) 903-7928
(FTS 233-7928)

Description: Project grants to all organizations to transfer technology and information from DOE to public sector and vice versa, to increase public participation in nation's energy needs, and to develop public/private partnership with companies of all sizes. Other restrictions will depend on nature of contract.
$ Given: None stated. Nationwide FY 93 est. "obligations" $11 million.
Application Information: After informal communication, formal proposal to headquarters office. Applicant must demonstrate qualifications.
Deadline: None
Contact: Local DOE field offices or C. Sink, above address

Department of Energy
San Francisco Field Office
1333 Broadway
Oakland, CA 94612
(415) 273-4237

Department of Energy
Idaho Field Office
785 Idaho Place
Idaho Falls, ID 83402
(208) 526-0111

Department of Energy
Chicago Field Office
9800 South Cass Avenue
Argonne, IL 60439
(708) 972-2001

Department of Energy
Albuquerque Field Office
P.O. Box 5400
Albuquerque, NM 87115
(505) 845-3118

Department of Energy
Nevada Field Office
P.O. Box 98518
Las Vegas, NV 89193-8518
(702) 295-1212

Pittsburgh Energy
Technology Center
P.O. Box 10940
Pittsburgh, PA 15236-0940
(412) 892-6000

Department of Energy
Savannah River Field Office
P.O. Box A
Aiken, SC 29808
(803) 725-6211

Department of Energy
Oak Ridge Field Office
P.O. Box 2001
Oak Ridge, TN 37831
(615) 576-5454

Department of Energy
Richland Field Office
825 Jadwin Avenue
P.O. Box 550
Richland, WA 99352
(509) 376-7411

Morgantown Energy
Technology Center
P.O. Box 880
3610 Collins Ferry Road
Morgantown, WV 26505
(304) 291-4764

State Energy Offices

Alabama
Terri Adams, Conservation
Section Chief
Alabama Department of
Economic and Community
Affairs
P.O. Box 250347
Montgomery, AL 36125-0347
(205) 284-8936

Alaska
Robert Braen, Director
Department of Community
and Regional Affairs
Rural Development Division
949 East 36th Avenue,
Suite 400
Anchorage, AK 99508
(907) 563-1073

American Samoa
Mat Lei, Director
Territorial Energy Office
Office of the Governor
Pago, AS 96799
(684) 633-1306, 4136, 4137,
4138 (via overseas operator)

Arizona
Arizona Energy Office
3800 North Central Avenue,
Suite 1200
Phoenix, AZ 85012
(602) 280-1402

Arkansas
Jim Blakley, Director
Arkansas Energy Office
One State Capitol Mall,
Suite 4B215
Little Rock, AR 72201
(501) 682-7315

California
Richard Sybert, Director
Governor's Office of Planning
and Research
1400 10th Street
Sacramento, CA 95814
(916) 322-2318

Charles Imbrecht, Chairman
California Energy
Commission
1516 9th Street
Sacramento, CA 95814
(916) 324-3326

Colorado
Executive Director
Colorado Office of Energy
Conservation
1675 Broadway, Suite 1300
Denver, CO 80202-4613
(303) 620-4292

Connecticut
Susan Shimelman,
Undersecretary
Policy Development and
Planning
Office of Policy and
Management
80 Washington Street
Hartford, CT 06106
(203) 566-2800

Delaware
George P. Donnelly, Director
Division of Facilities
Management
P.O. Box 1401
Dover, DE 19901
(302) 739-5644

District of Columbia
Charles Clinton, Director
District of Columbia Energy
Office
613 G Street, NW, Fifth Floor
Washington, DC 20001
(202) 727-1800

Research and Development

Florida
Jim Tait, Director
Florida Energy Office,
Department of Community
Affairs
2740 Centralview
Tallahassee, FL 32399-2100
(904) 488-6764

Georgia
Paul Burks, Director
Office of Energy Resources
254 Washington Street, SW,
Suite 401
Atlanta, GA 30334
(404) 656-5176

Guam
Jerry Rivera, Director
Guam Energy Office
P.O. Box 2950
Agana, GU 96910
(671) 472-8711 (or use
overseas operator)
9-0-11-671-734-4453 or 4530

Hawaii
Murray E. Towill, Director
Business Economic
Development and Tourism
P.O. Box 2359
Honolulu, HI 96804
(808) 548-3033

Idaho
Robert Hoppie,
Administrator
Idaho Department of Water
Resources
Energy Division
1301 North Orchard
Boise, ID 83706
(208) 327-7900

Illinois
John S. Moore, Director
Department of Energy and
Natural Resources
325 West Adams Street,
Room 300
Springfield, IL 62704-1892
(217) 785-2200

Indiana
Amy Stewart, Director
Department of Commerce,
Office of Energy Policy
Indiana Commerce Center
One North Capitol, Suite 700
Indianapolis, IN 46204-2248
(317) 232-8940

Iowa
Larry Bean, Administrator
Iowa Department of Natural
Resources
Energy and Geological
Resources Division
Wallace State Office Building
Des Moines, IA 50319
(515) 281-4368

Kansas
Kansas Corporation
Commission
1500 Southwest Arrowhead
Road
Topeka, KS 66604
(913) 271-3260

Kentucky
John M. Stapleton,
Assistant Director
Natural Resources and
Environmental Protection
Cabinet
691 Teton Trail
Frankfort, KY 40661
(502) 564-7192

Louisiana
Diane Smith, Director
Louisiana Department of
Natural Resources
P.O. Box 94156
Baton Rouge, LA 70804-4156
(504) 342-2133

Maine
Leonard A. Dow,
Development Director
Office of Community
Development
Maine Office of Community
and Economic Development
219 Capital Street
Augusta, ME 04333
(207) 289-6800

Maryland
Dr. Donald E. Milsten,
Deputy Director
Maryland Energy
Administration
45 Calvert Street,
Second Floor
Annapolis, MD 21401
(301) 974-3755

Massachusetts
Paul W. Gromer,
Commissioner
Division of Energy Resources
Leverett Saltonstall Building,
Room 1500
100 Cambridge Street
Boston, MA 02202
(617) 727-4732

Michigan
Steven M. Fetter,
Chairperson
Michigan Public Service
Commission
6546 Mercantile Way
P.O. Box 30221
Lansing, MI 48909
(517) 334-6270

Minnesota
Krista L. Sanda,
Commissioner
Department of Public Service
900 American Center
Building
150 East Kellogg Boulevard
St. Paul, MN 55101
(612) 296-6025

Mississippi
Andrew Jenkins,
Executive Director
Mississippi Department of
Economic and Community
Development
Energy and Transportation
Division
510 George Street, Suite 101
Jackson, MS 39202-3096
(601) 359-6600

Missouri
Robert Jackson, Director
Missouri Department of
Natural Resources
Division of Energy
P.O. Box 176
Jefferson City, MO 65102
(314) 751-4000

Montana
Van Jamison, Administrator
Energy Division
Department of Natural
Resources and Conservation
1520 East Sixth Avenue
Helena, MT 59620-2301
(406) 444-6697

Nebraska
Robert Harris, Director
Nebraska Energy Office
P.O. Box 95085
State Capitol Building,
Ninth Floor
Lincoln, NE 68509
(402) 471-2867

Nevada
Jane Hawke, Director
Nevada State Office of
Community Services
Capital Complex
Carson City, NV 89701
(702) 687-4990

New Hampshire
Jonathan S. Osgood, Director
Governor's Energy Office
2½ Beacon Street
Concord, NH 03301-4498
(603) 271-2711

New Jersey
Scott A. Werner,
Commissioner
Department of
Environmental Protection
and Energy
401 East State Street
Trenton, NJ 08625
(609) 292-2885

New Mexico
Jack McGowan, Director
Energy Conservation and
Management Division
Department of Energy,
Minerals, and Natural
Resources
240 South Pacheer
Santa Fe, NM 87505
(505) 827-5906

New York
William D. Cotter,
Commissioner
New York State Energy Office
2 Rockefeller Plaza
Albany, NY 12223
(518) 473-4376

North Carolina
Carson D. Culbreth, Jr.,
Director
North Carolina Department
of Economic and
Community Development
Energy Division
430 North Salisbury Street
Raleigh, NC 27611
(919) 733-2230

North Dakota
Shirley R. Dykshoorn,
Director
Office of Intergovernmental
Assistance
State Capitol Building
600 East Boulevard Avenue
Bismarck, ND 58505-0170
(701) 224-2094

Northern Mariana Islands
Jocelyn Guerrero, Energy
Administrator
Commonwealth Energy
Office
P.O. Box 340
Saipan, CM 96950
(855) 099-7174 or 7284 (via
overseas operator)

Ohio
Donald E. Jakeway, Director
Ohio Department of
Development
Community Development
Division
Office of Energy
Conservation
77 South High Street,
Twenty-ninth Floor
Columbus, OH 43266-0101
(614) 466-3465

Research and Development

Oklahoma
Sherwood Washington,
Director
Division of Community
Affairs and Development
Oklahoma Department of
Commerce
P.O. Box 26980
Oklahoma City, OK
73126-0980
(405) 843-9326

Oregon
Christine Ervin, Director
Oregon Department of
Energy
625 Marion Street, NE
Salem, OR 97310-0831
(503) 378-0063

Pennsylvania
Brian T. Castelli,
Executive Director
Pennsylvania Energy Office
116 Pine Street
Harrisburg, PA 17101
(717) 783-9981

Puerto Rico
Carmon Vanessa Davila,
Assistant Secretary
Commonwealth of Puerto
Rico
Department of Consumer
Affairs
P.O. Box 4105, Minillas
Station
Santurce, PR 00940-1059
(809) 721-2573

Rhode Island
J. Scott Wolf, Director
Governor's Office of Housing,
Energy, Intergovernmental
Relations
Statehouse, Room 111
Providence, RI 02903-5872
(401) 277-2850

South Carolina
John McMillian
Energy, Agriculture, and
Natural Resources
1205 Pendleton Street,
Third Floor
Columbia, SC 29201
(803) 734-0447

South Dakota
Ron Reed, Commissioner
Governor's Office of Energy
Policy
217 West Missouri, Suite 200
Pierre, SD 57501
(605) 773-3603

Tennessee
Cynthia Oliphant
Energy Division
Tennessee Department of
Economic and Community
Development
320 6th Avenue North,
Sixth Floor
Nashville, TN 37219-5308
(615) 741-2994

Texas
Bob Armstrong, Director
Governor's Energy Office
P.O. Box 12428,
Capitol Station
Austin, TX 78711
(512) 463-1931

Utah
Richard M. Anderson,
Director
Utah Energy Office
355 West North Temple
3 Triad Center, Suite 450
Salt Lake City, UT
84180-1204
(801) 538-5428

Vermont
Louise McCarren,
Commissioner
Department of Public
Services
State Office Building
120 State Street
Montpelier, VT 05602
(802) 828-2811

Virgin Islands
Claudette Young-Hinds,
Director
Virgin Islands Energy Office
Castle Coakley
Christiansted, St. Croix
U.S. Virgin Islands. 00823
(809) 772-2616

Virginia
Ronald J. Desroches, Director
Division of Energy
Department of Mines,
Minerals, and Energy
2201 West Broad Street
Richmond, VA 23220
(804) 367-0979

Washington
Richard Watson, Director
Washington State Energy
Office
809 Legion Way, SE
Olympia, WA 98504
(206) 506-5000

West Virginia
John F. Herholdt, Jr.,
Manager
Governor's Office of
Community and Industrial
Development
Fuel and Energy Office
Capital Complex Building
Charleston, WV 25315
(304) 348-4010

Wisconsin
John Bilotti, Administrator
Wisconsin Division of Energy
and Intergovernmental
Relations
101 South Webster Street,
Sixth Floor
P.O. Box 7868
Madison, WI 53707-7868
(608) 266-8234

Wyoming
Steven Schmitz
Division of Economic and
Community Development
Energy Division
Herschler Building,
Second Floor
Cheyenne, WY 82002
(307) 777-7284

TRADE DEVELOPMENT

**Department of
Commerce**
International Trade
Administration
14th and Constitution
Avenue, NW
Washington, DC 20230
(202) 377-3373

Description: Advisory services and counseling to any individual or corporation to foster competitiveness and growth of U.S. industries and to promote their increased participation in international markets.
$ Given: N/A
Application Information: Inquire in person, write, or call.
Deadline: N/A
Contact: Local Department of Commerce ITA field office

Alabama
Gayle C. Shelton, Jr., Director
Berry Building, Room 302
2015 2nd Avenue, North
Birmingham, AL 35203
(205) 731-1331

Alaska
Charles Becker, Director
World Trade Center Alaska
4201 Tudor Center Drive,
Suite 319
Anchorage, AK 99508
(907) 271-6237

Arizona
Donald W. Fry, Director
Federal Building, Room 3412
230 North 1st Avenue
Phoenix, AZ 85025
(602) 379-3285

Arkansas
Lon J. Hardin, Director
Savers Federal Building,
Suite 811
320 West Capitol Avenue
Little Rock, AR 72201
(501) 324-5794

California
Steven Arlinghaus, Director
11000 Wilshire Boulevard,
Room 9200
Los Angeles, CA 90024
(212) 575-7105

Jesse Campos,
Trade Specialist
116A West 4th Street,
Suite #1
Santa Ana, CA 92701
(714) 836-2461

Richard Powell, Director
6363 Greenwich Drive,
Suite 145
San Diego, CA 92122
(619) 557-5395

Betty D. Neuhart, Director
250 Montgomery Street,
Fourteenth Floor
San Francisco, CA 94104
(415) 705-2300

Colorado
Paul Bergman,
Acting Director
1625 Broadway, Suite 680
Denver, CO 80202
(303) 844-3246

Research and Development

Connecticut
Eric B. Outwater, Director
Federal Office Building,
Room 610-B
450 Main Street
Hartford, CT 06103
(203) 240-3530

Delaware
Robert E. Kistler, Director
475 Allendale Road,
Suite 202
King of Prussia, PA 19406
(215) 962-4980

Florida
Ivan A. Cosimi, Director
Federal Building, Suite 224
51 SW First Avenue
Miami, FL 33130
(305) 536-5267

George L. Martinez,
Trade Specialist
128 North Osceola Avenue
Clearwater, FL 34615
(813) 461-0011

John Marshall,
Trade Specialist
c/o College of Business
Administration
CEBA II, Room 346,
University of Central Florida
Orlando, FL 32816
(407) 648-6235

Michael E. Higgins,
Trade Specialist
Collins Building, Room 40
107 West Gains Street
Tallahassee, FL 32304
(904) 488-6469

Georgia
Barbara H. Prieto, Trade
Specialist-in-Charge
120 Barnard Street,
Room A-107
Savannah, GA 31401
(912) 652-4204

George T. Norton, Jr.,
Director
Plaza Square North,
Suite 310
4360 Chamblee-Dunwoody
Road
Atlanta, GA 30341
(404) 452-9101

Hawaii
George Dolan, Director
P.O. Box 50026
400 Ala Moana Boulevard,
Room 4106
Honolulu, HI 96850
(808) 541-1782

Idaho
(Portland, Oregon District)
Steven Thompson,
Trade Specialist
Joe R. Williams Building,
Second Floor
700 West State Street
Boise, ID 83720
(208) 334-3857

Illinois
LoRee Silloway, Director
Mid-Continental Plaza
Building, Room 1406
55 East Monroe Street
Chicago, IL 60603
(312) 353-4450

Oscar L. Dube,
Trade Specialist
Illinois Institute of
Technology
201 East Loop Road
Wheaton, IL 60187
(312) 353-4332

Thomas J. DeSeve
515 North Court Street
P.O. Box 1747
Rockford, IL 61110-0247
(815) 987-8123

Indiana
Andrew Thress, Director
One North Capitol, Suite 520
Indianapolis, IN 46204
(317) 226-6214

Iowa
John H. Steuber, Jr., Director
Federal Building, Room 817
210 Walnut Street
Des Moines, IA 50309
(515) 284-4222

Kansas
(Kansas City, Missouri
District)
George D. Lavid,
Trade Specialist
151 North Volutsia
Wichita, KS 67214-4695
(316) 269-6160

Kentucky
John Autin, Director
Gene Snyder Courthouse
and Customhouse Building,
Room 636 B
601 West Broadway
Louisville, KY 40202
(502) 582-5066

Louisiana
Paul Guidry, Director
432 World Trade Center
No. 2 Canal Street
New Orleans, LA 70130
(504) 589-6546

Maine
(Boston, Massachusetts
District)
Stephen M. Nyulaszi,
Trade Specialist
77 Sewell Street
Augusta, ME 04330
(207) 622-8249

Maryland
David Earle, Director
U.S. Customhouse,
Room 413
40 South Gay Street
Baltimore, MD 21202
(301) 962-3560

Steve Hall, Trade Specialist
c/o National Institute of
Standards and Technology
Building 411
Gaithersburg, MD 20899
(301) 962-3560

Massachusetts
Francis J. O'Connor, Director
World Trade Center,
Suite 307
Commonwealth Pier Area
Boston, MA 02210-2071
(617) 565-8563

Michigan
Vacant
1140 McNamara Building
477 Michigan Avenue
Detroit, MI 48226
(313) 226-3650

Thomas J. Maquire,
Trade Specialist
300 Monroe Avenue, NW,
Room 406A
Grand Rapids, MI 49503-2291
(616) 456-2411

Minnesota
Ronald E. Kramer, Director
Federal Building, Room 108
110 South Fourth Street
Minneapolis, MN 55401
(612) 348-1638

Mississippi
Mark E. Spinney, Director
Jackson Mall Office Center,
Suite 328
300 Woodrow Wilson
Boulevard
Jackson, MS 39213
(601) 965-4388

Missouri
Donald R. Loso, Director
7911 Forsyth Boulevard,
Suite 610
St. Louis, MO 63105
(314) 425-3302

John Kupfer, Director
601 East 12th Street,
Room 635
Kansas City, MO 64106
(816) 426-3141

Montana
(Portland, Oregon District)
Steve Thompson,
Trade Specialist
Joe R. Williams Building,
Second Floor
700 West State Street
Boise, ID 83720
(208) 334-3857

Nebraska
George H. Payne, Director
11133 "O" Street
Omaha, NE 68137
(402) 221-3664

Nevada
Joseph J. Jeremy, Director
1755 East Plumb Lane,
Room 152
Reno, NV 89502
(702) 784-5203

New Hampshire
Harvey Timberlake
c/o State of New Hampshire
Department of Resources
and Economic Development
172 Pennbroke Road
P.O. Box 856
Concord, NH 03302-0856

New Jersey
Thomas J. Murray, Director
3131 Princeton Pike
Building #6, Suite 100
Trenton, NJ 08648
(609) 989-2100

New Mexico
(Dallas, Texas District)
Sandy Necessary,
Trade Specialist
625 Silver, SW, Third Floor
Albuquerque, NM 87102
(505) 766-2070
FTS 474-2070

New York
George Buchanan, Director
Federal Building, Room 1312
111 West Huron Street
Buffalo, NY 14202
(716) 846-4191

Joel Barkan, Director
26 Federal Plaza, Room 3718
New York, NY 10278
(212) 264-0634

William Freiert,
Trade Specialist
111 East Avenue, Room 220
Rochester, NY 14604
(716) 263-6480

North Carolina
Samuel P. Troy, Director
324 West Market Street
P.O. Box 1950, Room 203
Greensboro, NC 27402
(919) 333-5345

North Dakota
George H. Payne, Director
11133 "O" Street
Omaha, NE 68137
(402) 221-3664

Ohio
Gordon B. Thomas, Director
Federal Building, Room 9504
550 Main Street
Cincinnati, OH 45202
(513) 684-2944

Toby T. Zettler, Director
668 Euclid Avenue,
Room 600
Cleveland, OH 44114
(216) 522-4750

Research and Development

Oklahoma
Ronald L. Wilson, Director
6601 Broadway Extension
Oklahoma City, OK 73116
(405) 231-5302

Thomas Strauss,
Trade Specialist
440 South Houston Street
Tulsa, OK 74127
(918) 581-7650

Oregon
William Schrage, Director
One World Trade Center,
Suite 242
121 SW Salmon
Portland, OR 97204
(503) 326-3001

Pennsylvania
John McCartney, Director
Federal Building, Room 2002
1000 Liberty Avenue
Pittsburgh, PA 15222
(412) 644-2850

Robert E. Kistler, Director
475 Allendale Road,
Suite 202
King of Prussia, PA 19406
(215) 962-4980

Puerto Rico
(Hato Rey)
J. Enrique Vilella, Director
Federal Building, Room G-55
San Juan, PR 00918
(809) 766-5555

Rhode Island
(Boston, Massachusetts
District)
Raimond Meerbach,
Trade Specialist
7 Jackson Walkway
Providence, RI 02903
(401) 528-5104

South Carolina
Edgar Rojas, Director
Strom Thurmond Federal
Building, Suite 172
1835 Assembly Street
Columbia, SC 29201
(803) 765-5345

Margaret Patrick,
Trade Specialist
J. C. Long Building, Room
128
9 Liberty Street
Charleston, SC 29424
(803) 724-4361

South Dakota
George H. Payne, Director
11133 "O" Street
Omaha, NE 68137
(402) 221-3664

Tennessee
Jeanne Marie Russell,
Trade Specialist
Falls Building, Suite 200
22 North Front Street
Memphis, TN 38103
(901) 544-4137

Jim E. Charlet, Jr., Director
Parkway Towers, Suite 1114
404 James Robertson
Parkway
Nashville, TN 37219-1504
(615) 736-5161

W. Bryan Smith,
Trade Specialist
301 East Church Avenue
Knoxville, TN 37915
(615) 549-9268

Texas
Karen C. Parker, Trade
Reference Assistant
816 Congress Avenue,
Suite 1200
P.O. Box 12728
Austin, TX 78711
(512) 482-5939

James D. Cook, Director
515 Rusk Street, Room 2625
Houston, TX 77002
(713) 229-2578

Donald Schilke, Director
1100 Commerce Street,
Room 7A5
Dallas, TX 75242-0787
(214) 767-0542

Utah
Stephen Smoot, Director
324 South State Street,
Suite 105
Salt Lake City, UT 84111
(801) 524-5116

Vermont
Francis J. O'Connor, Director
World Trade Center,
Suite 307
Commonwealth Pier Area
Boston, MA 02210-2071
(617) 565-8563

Virginia
Philip A. Ouzts, Director
Federal Building, Room 8010
400 North Eighth Street
Richmond, VA 23240
(804) 771-2246

Washington
Charles Buck, Director
3131 Elliott Avenue,
Suite 290
Seattle, WA 98121
(206) 553-5615

West Virginia
Roger L. Fortner, Director
4405 Capitol Street,
Suite 809
Charleston, WV 25301
(304) 347-5123

Wisconsin
Johnny E. Brown, Director
517 East Wisconsin Avenue,
Room 606
Milwaukee, WI 53202
(414) 297-3473

Wyoming
Paul Bergman,
Acting Director
1625 Broadway, Suite 680
Denver, CO 80202
(303) 844-3246

UNDERSEA RESEARCH

Department of Commerce
National Oceanic and Atmospheric Administration
1335 East West Highway
Silver Spring, MD 20910
(301) 713-2427

Description: Project grants to foster undersea research. Any individual, technical school, or laboratory may apply. Must have professional interest in marine science engineering.
$ Given: Nationwide FY 93 est. $50,000. Range: $10,000–$4 million.
Application Information: Submit standard application form and formal proposal.
Deadline: None
Contact: Director, Office of Undersea Research, above address

WEIGHTS AND MEASURES SERVICE

Department of Commerce
National Institute of Standards and Technology
Gaithersburg, MD 20899
(301) 975-4004

Description: Advisory services, counseling, and training to individuals and corporations to promote an accurate system of weights and measures.
$ Given: N/A
Application Information: Send letter to contact.
Deadline: N/A
Contact: Chief, Weights and Measures Program, above address

Minorities

Assistance is widely available from the federal government for minority-owned businesses or for businesses serving minorities or the disadvantaged (the word "minority" in this book refers to people who are either African American, Hispanic, Asian American, American Indian, or female) for the following:

1. Assistance to Indian-owned businesses; native American employment and training programs; and programs that promote the business and economic development of Indian reservations

2. Advisory services to promote the development of businesses owned by economically or socially disadvantaged individuals as well as counseling services for businesses owned by women

3. Assistance to minority firms and individuals for business expansion and development

You will need to consult the list of addresses in this chapter for your nearest local or regional Bureau of Indian Affairs office, tribal contact office, or Minority Business Development office.

ACQUIRED IMMUNODEFICIENCY SYNDROME (AIDS) ACTIVITY

Department of Health and Human Services
Grants Management Branch
Procurement and Grants Office
Centers for Disease Control
Public Health Service
255 East Paces Ferry Road, NE
Atlanta, GA 30305
(404) 842-6575

Description: Project grants (cooperative agreements) to businesses (with emphasis on small, minority-, and women-owned businesses) to promote HIV prevention programs of information and education.
$ Given: Nationwide FY 93 est. $224.3 million in cooperative agreement grants. Range $20,000–$2.8 million; average: $300,000.
Application Information: Submit standard application form (PHS-5161.1) to CDC.
Deadline: Varies. Contact headquarters office.
Contact: Clara Jenkins, above address

AMERICAN INDIAN PROGRAM (AIP)

Department of Commerce
Minority Business Development Agency
14th and Constitution Avenue, NW
Washington, DC 20230
(202) 377-8015

Description: Project grants to provide business development service to American Indians interested in entering, expanding, or improving their efforts in the marketplace. Limited to individuals and nonprofit organizations.
$ Given: Range: $157,500–$303,000 (based on availability of agency funds).
Application Information: Standard application form as furnished by federal agency.
Deadline: Outlined in the Federal Register and Commerce Business Daily.
Contact: Bharat Bhargava

Alabama
Carlton Eccles, Director
401 West Peachtree Street, NW, Room 1930
Atlanta, GA 30308-3516
(404) 730-3300

Alaska
Xavier Mena, Director
221 Main Street, Room 1280
San Francisco, CA 94105
(415) 744-3001

Arkansas
Melda Cabrera, Director
1100 Commerce Street, Room 7B23
Dallas, TX 75242
(214) 767-8001

Minorities

Arizona
Xavier Mena, Director
221 Main Street, Room 1280
San Francisco, CA 94105
(415) 744-3001

American Somoa
Xavier Mena, Director
221 Main Street, Room 1280
San Francisco, CA 94105
(415) 744-3001

California
Xavier Mena, Director
221 Main Street, Room 1280
San Francisco, CA 94105
(415) 744-3001

Rudy Guerra, District Officer
977 North Broadway,
Suite 201
Los Angeles, CA 90012
(213) 894-7157

Colorado
Melda Cabrera, Director
1100 Commerce Street,
Room 7B23
Dallas, TX 75242
(214) 767-8001

Connecticut
John Iglehart, Director
26 Federal Plaza, Room 3720
New York, NY 10278
(212) 264-3262

District of Columbia
Georgina Sanchez, Director
14th and Constitution
Avenue, NW, Room 6711
Washington, DC 20230
(202) 377-8275

Delaware
Georgina Sanchez, Director
14th and Constitution
Avenue, NW, Room 6711
Washington, DC 20230
(202) 377-8275

Florida
Carlton Eccles, Director
401 West Peachtree Street,
NW, Room 1930
Atlanta, GA 30308-3516
(404) 730-3300

Rudy Suarez, District Officer
Federal Building, Room 928
51 SW First Avenue
P.O. Box 25
Miami, FL 33130
(305) 536-5054

Georgia
Carlton Eccles, Director
401 West Peachtree Street,
NW, Room 1930
Atlanta, GA 30308-3516
(404) 730-3300

Guam
Xavier Mena, Director
221 Main Street, Room 1280
San Francisco, CA 94105
(415) 744-3001

Hawaii
Xavier Mena, Director
221 Main Street, Room 1280
San Francisco, CA 94105
(415) 744-3001

Idaho
Xavier Mena, Director
221 Main Street, Room 1280
San Francisco, CA 94105
(415) 744-3001

Illinois
David Vega, Director
55 East Monroe Street,
Suite 1440
Chicago, IL 60603
(312) 353-0182

Indiana
David Vega, Director
55 East Monroe Street,
Suite 1440
Chicago, IL 60603
(312) 353-0182

Iowa
David Vega, Director
55 East Monroe Street,
Suite 1440
Chicago, IL 60603
(312) 353-0182

Kansas
David Vega, Director
55 East Monroe Street,
Suite 1440
Chicago, IL 60603
(312) 353-0182

Kentucky
Carlton Eccles, Director
401 West Peachtree Street,
NW, Room 1930
Atlanta, GA 30308-3516
(404) 730-3300

Louisiana
Melda Cabrera, Director
1100 Commerce Street,
Room 7B23
Dallas, TX 75242
(214) 767-8001

Maine
John Iglehart, Director
26 Federal Plaza, Room 3720
New York, NY 10278
(212) 264-3262

Maryland
Georgina Sanchez, Director
14th and Constitution
Avenue, NW, Room 6711
Washington, DC 20230
(202) 377-8275

Massachusetts
John Iglehart, Director
26 Federal Plaza, Room 3720
New York, NY 10278
(212) 264-3262

R. K. Schwartz,
District Officer
10 Causeway Street,
Room 418
Boston, MA 02222-1041
(617) 565-6850

Michigan
David Vega, Director
55 East Monroe Street,
Suite 1440
Chicago, IL 60603
(312) 353-0182

Minnesota
David Vega, Director
55 East Monroe Street,
Suite 1440
Chicago, IL 60603
(312) 353-0182

Mississippi
Carlton Eccles, Director
401 West Peachtree Street,
NW, Room 1930
Atlanta, GA 30308-3516
(404) 730-3300

Missouri
David Vega, Director
55 East Monroe Street,
Suite 1440
Chicago, IL 60603
(312) 353-0182

Montana
Melda Cabrera, Director
1100 Commerce Street,
Room 7B23
Dallas, TX 75242
(214) 767-8001

Nebraska
David Vega, Director
55 East Monroe Street,
Suite 1440
Chicago, IL 60603
(312) 353-0182

Nevada
Xavier Mena, Director
221 Main Street, Room 1280
San Francisco, CA 94105
(415) 744-3001

New Hampshire
John Iglehart, Director
26 Federal Plaza, Room 3720
New York, NY 10278
(212) 264-3262

New Jersey
John Iglehart, Director
26 Federal Plaza, Room 3720
New York, NY 10278
(212) 264-3262

New Mexico
Melda Cabrera, Director
1100 Commerce Street,
Room 7B23'
Dallas, TX 75242
(214) 767-8001

New York
John Iglehart, Director
26 Federal Plaza, Room 3720
New York, NY 10278
(212) 264-3262

North Carolina
Carlton Eccles, Director
401 West Peachtree Street,
NW, Room 1930
Atlanta, GA 30308-3516
(404) 730-3300

North Dakota
Melda Cabrera, Director
1100 Commerce Street,
Room 7B23
Dallas, TX 75242
(214) 767-8001

Ohio
David Vega, Director
55 East Monroe Street,
Suite 1440
Chicago, IL 60603
(312) 353-0182

Oklahoma
Melda Cabrera, Director
1100 Commerce Street,
Room 7B23
Dallas, TX 75242
(214) 767-8001

Oregon
Xavier Mena, Director
221 Main Street, Room 1280
San Francisco, CA 94105
(415) 744-3001

Pennsylvania
Georgina Sanchez, Director
14th and Constitution
Avenue, NW, Room 6711
Washington, DC 20230
(202) 377-8275

Alfonso Jackson,
District Officer
Federal Office Building,
Room 10128
600 Arch Street
Philadelphia, PA 19106
(215) 597-9236

District Officer
614-16 Federal Office
Building
1000 Liberty Avenue
Pittsburgh, PA 15222
(412) 722-6659

Puerto Rico
John Iglehart, Director
26 Federal Plaza, Room 3720
New York, NY 10278
(212) 264-3262

Rhode Island
John Iglehart, Director
26 Federal Plaza, Room 3720
New York, NY 10278
(212) 264-3262

South Carolina
Carlton Eccles, Director
401 West Peachtree Street,
NW, Room 1930
Atlanta, GA 30308-3516
(404) 730-3300

South Dakota
Melda Cabrera, Director
1100 Commerce Street,
Room 7B23
Dallas, TX 75242
(214) 767-8001

Tennessee
Carlton Eccles, Director
401 West Peachtree Street,
NW, Room 1930
Atlanta, GA 30308-3516
(404) 730-3300

Texas
Melda Cabrera, Director
1100 Commerce Street,
Room 7B23
Dallas, TX 75242
(214) 767-8001

Utah
Melda Cabrera, Director
1100 Commerce Street,
Room 7B23
Dallas, TX 75242
(214) 767-8001

Vermont
John Iglehart, Director
26 Federal Plaza, Room 3720
New York, NY 10278
(212) 264-3262

Virgin Islands
John Iglehart, Director
26 Federal Plaza, Room 3720
New York, NY 10278
(212) 264-3262

Virginia
Georgina Sanchez, Director
14th and Constitution
Avenue, NW, Room 6711
Washington, DC 20230
(202) 377-8275

Washington
Xavier Mena, Director
221 Main Street, Room 1280
San Francisco, CA 94105
(415) 744-3001

West Virginia
Georgina Sanchez, Director
14th and Constitution
Avenue, NW, Room 6711
Washington, DC 20230
(202) 377-8275

Wisconsin
David Vega, Director
55 East Monroe Street,
Suite 1440
Chicago, IL 60603
(312) 353-0182

Wyoming
Melda Cabrera, Director
1100 Commerce Street,
Room 7B23
Dallas, TX 75242
(214) 767-8001

INDIAN ARTS AND CRAFTS DEVELOPMENT

**Department of the
Interior
Indian Arts and Crafts
Board**
Main Interior Building,
Room 4004
Washington, DC 20240
(202) 208-3773

Description: Use of property, facilities, and equipment along with advisory services and counseling given to encourage and promote development of American Indian arts and crafts. Assistance for development of economic concepts related to native culture. Limited to native Americans, Indians, Eskimos, and Aleut individuals and organizations.
$ Given: N/A
Application Information: N/A
Deadlines: None
Contact: Robert G. Hart

Alaska

Juneau Area Office
P.O. Box 25520
Juneau, AK 99801
(907) 586-7177

Field Agencies
Anchorage Agency
1675 C Street
Anchorage, AK 99501
(907) 271-4088

Bethel Agency
P.O. Box 347
Bethel, AK 99559
(907) 543-2726

Fairbanks Agency
101 12th Avenue
Box 16
Fairbanks, AK 99707
(907) 452-0222

Nome Agency
Box 1108
Nome, AK 99762
(907) 443-2284

Southeast Agency
P.O. Box 3-8000
Juneau, AK 99802
(907) 586-7304

Arizona

Phoenix Area Office
1 North First Street
Phoenix, AZ 85001
(602) 379-6760

Field Agencies
Chinle Agency
P.O. Box 10-H
Chinle, AZ 86503
(505) 674-5211

Colorado River Agency
Route 1, Box 9-C
Parker, AZ 85344
(602) 669-2134

Fort Apache Agency
Whiteriver, AZ 85941
(602) 338-4364

Fort Defiance Agency
P.O. Box 619
Fort Defiance, AZ 86504
(602) 729-5041

Fort Yuma Agency
P.O. Box 1591
Yuma, AZ 85364
(714) 572-0248

Hopi Agency
Keams Canyon, AZ 86034
(602) 738-2228

Papago Agency
Sells, AZ 85634
(602) 729-7284

Pima Agency
Sacaton, AZ 85247
(602) 383-7286

Salt River Agency
Route 1, Box 117
Scottsdale, AZ 85256
(602) 241-2842

San Carlos Agency
San Carlos, AZ 85550
(602) 475-2321

San Carlos Irrigation Project
Coolidge, AZ 85228
(602) 723-5439

Truxton Canon Agency
Valentine, AZ 86437
(602) 769-2241

Western Navajo Agency
P.O. Box 127
Tuba City, AZ 86045
(602) 283-6265

Navajo Area Office
P.O. Box #1060
Gallup, NM 87301
(505) 863-9501

California
(See also Arizona [Phoenix])

Sacramento Area Office
Federal Office Building,
Room W-2550
2800 Cottage Way
Sacramento, CA 95825-1884
(916) 978-4689

Field Agencies
Central California Agency
1800 Tribute Road, Suite 111
Sacramento, CA 95815
(916) 484-4357

Hoopa Agency
P.O. Box 367
Hoopa, CA 95546
(916) 625-4285

Palm Springs Area Field
Office
P.O. Box 2245
441 South Calle Encilla,
Suite 8
Palm Springs, CA 92262
(916) 325-2086

Southern California Agency
P.O. Box 2900, Suite 201
5750 Division Street
Riverside, CA 92506
(714) 351-6624

Colorado
(See New Mexico)

Field Agencies
Southern Ute Agency
P.O. Box 315
Ignacio, CO 81137
(303) 563-4511

Ute Mountain Ute Agency
Towaoc, CO 81334
(303) 565-8471

District of Columbia

Eastern Area Office
3701 North Fairfax Drive,
Suite 260-Mailroom
Arlington, VA 22203
(703) 235-2735

Deputy Assistant Secretary
Indian Affairs (Operations)
1849 C Street, NW,
MS-334A, SIB
Washington, DC 20240
(202) 208-2809

Florida
(See District of Columbia,
Eastern Area Office)

Field Agencies
Miccosukee Agency
P.O. Box 44021
Tamiami Station
Miami, FL 33144
(305) 223-8380

Minorities

Seminole Agency
6075 Stirling Road
Hollywood, FL 33024
(305) 581-7050

Idaho
(see Arizona [Phoenix] and Oregon)
Field Agencies
Fort Hall Agency
Fort Hall, ID 83203
(208) 237-0600

Northern Idaho Agency
P.O. Drawer 277
Lapwai, ID 83540
(208) 843-2267

Iowa
(See Minnesota)
Field Agency
Sac and Fox Area Field Office
Tama, IA 52339
(515) 484-4041

Kansas
(See Oklahoma [Anadarko])
Field Agencies
Haskell Indian Junior College
Lawrence, KS 66604
(913) 843-1831

Horton Agency
Horton, KS 66439
(913) 486-2161

Louisiana
(See District of Columbia, Eastern Area Office)

Michigan
(See Minnesota)

Minnesota
Minneapolis Area Office
331 South 2nd Avenue
Minneapolis, MN 55402
(612) 373-1037

Field Agencies
Minnesota Agency
P.O. Box 97
Cass Lake, MN 56633
(218) 335-6913

Red Lake Agency
Red Lake, MN 56671
(218) 679-3361

Minnesota Sioux Area Field Office
2330 Sioux Trail, NW
Prior Lake, MN 55372
(612) 445-6565

Mississippi
(See District of Columbia, Eastern Area Office)
Field Agency
Choctaw Agency
421 Powell
Philadelphia, MS 39350
(601) 656-1521

Montana
Billings Area Office
316 North 26th Street
Billings, MT 59101-1397
(406) 657-6313
Field Agencies
Blackfeet Agency
Browning, MT 59417
(406) 338-7511

Crow Agency
Crow Agency, MT 59022
(406) 638-2671

Flathead Agency
Ronan, MT 59864
(406) 676-4700

Flathead Irrigation Project
Ignatius, MT 59865
(406) 745-2661

Fort Belknap Agency
P.O. Box 80
Harlem, MT 59526
(406) 353-2205

Fort Peck Agency
P.O. Box 637
Poplar, MT 59225
(406) 768-5311

Northern Cheyenne Agency
Lame Deer, MT 59043
(406) 477-6242

Rocky Boy's Agency
Box Elder, MT 59521
(406) 395-4476

Nebraska
(See South Dakota)
Field Agency
Winnebago Agency
Winnebago, NE 68071
(402) 878-2201

Nevada
(See Arizona [Phoenix])
Field Agencies
Western Nevada Agency
1677 Hotsprings Road
Carson City, NV 89706
(702) 887-3500

Eastern Nevada Agency
Elko, NV 89801
(702) 738-5165

New Mexico
(See also Arizona [Navajo])

Albuquerque Area Office
615 1st Street
P.O. Box 26567
Albuquerque, NM 87103
(505) 766-2996
Field Agencies
Eastern Navajo Agency
P.O. Box 328
Crownpoint, NM 87313
(505) 786-5228

Institute of American Indian Arts
Santa Fe, NM 87501
(505) 982-3801

Jicarilla Agency
Dulce, NM 87528
(505) 759-3651

Mescalero Agency
Mescalero, NM 88340
(505) 671-4421

Navajo Irrigation Project
Energy Building, Room 103
3539 East 30th Street, NW
Farmington, NM 87401
(505) 325-1864

Northern Pueblos Agency
Federal P.O. Building
P.O. Box 849
Santa Fe, NM 87501
(505) 988-6431

Ramah-Navajo Agency
Ramah, NM 87321
(505) 783-5731

Shiprock Agency
P.O. Box 966
Shiprock, NM 87420
(505) 368-4427

Southern Pueblos Agency
P.O. Box 1667
Albuquerque, NM 87103
(505) 766-3021

Southwestern Indian
Polytechnic Institute
1000 Indian School Road,
NW
Albuquerque, NM 87103
(505) 843-3033

Zuni Agency
P.O. Box 338
Zuni, NM 87327
(505) 782-4481

New York
(See District of Columbia,
Eastern Area Office)
Field Agency
New York Field Office
Federal Building, No. 523
100 South Clinton Street
Syracuse, NY 13202
(315) 423-5476

North Carolina
(See District of Columbia,
Eastern Area Office)
Field Agency
Cherokee Agency
Cherokee, NC 28719
(704) 497-9131

North Dakota
(See South Dakota)
Field Agencies
Fort Berthold Agency
New Town, ND 58763
(701) 627-4707

Fort Totten Agency
Fort Totten, ND 58335
(701) 766-4545

Standing Rock Agency
Fort Yates, ND 58538
(701) 854-3431

Turtle Mountain Agency
Belcourt, ND 58316
(701) 477-3191

Oklahoma
Anadarko Area Office
P.O. Box 368
Anadarko, OK 73005-0368
(405) 247-6673

Muskogee Area Office
Federal Building,
U.S. Courthouse
Muskogee, OK 74401-4898
(918) 687-2230
Field Agencies
Anadarko Agency
P.O. Box 309
Anadarko, OK 73005
(405) 247-6673

Ardmore Agency
P.O. Box 997
Ardmore, OK 73401
(405) 223-6767

Concho Agency
Concho, OK 73022
(405) 262-4855

Okmulgee Agency
P.O. Box 370
Okulgee, OK 74447
(918) 756-3950

Osage Agency
Pawhuska, OK 74056
(918) 287-2481

Miami Agency
P.O. Box 391
Miami, OK 74354
(918) 542-3396

Pawnee Agency
P.O. Box 440
Pawness, OK 74058
(918) 762-2585

Shawnee Agency
Federal Building
Shawnee, OK 74801
(405) 273-0317

Tahlequah Agency
P.O. Box 828
Tahlequah, OK 74465
(918) 456-6164

Talihina Agency
Drawer H
Talihina, OK 74571
(918) 567-2207

Wewoka Agency
P.O. Box 1060
Wewoka, OK 74884
(918) 257-6257

Oregon
(See also Arizona [Phoenix])

Portland Area Office
911 NE 11th Avenue
Portland, OR 97232-4169
(503) 231-6757
Field Agencies
Umatilla Agency
P.O. Box 520
Pendleton, OR 97801
(503) 276-3811

Warm Springs Agency
Warm Springs, OR 97761
(503) 553-1121

South Dakota

Aberdeen Area Office
Federal Building
115th Avenue, SE
Aberdeen, SD 57401-4382
(605) 226-7426
Field Agencies
Cheyenne River Agency
P.O. Box 325
Eagle Butte, SD 57625
(605) 964-6611

Crow Creek Agency
P.O. Box 616
Fort Thompson, SD 57339
(605) 245-2311

Lower Brule Agency
Lower Brule, SD 57548
(606) 473-5512

Pine Ridge Agency
Pine Ridge, SD 57770
(605) 867-5121

Rosebud Agency
Rosebud, SD 57570
(605) 747-2224

Sisseton Agency
Sisseton, SD 57262
(605) 698-7676

Yankton Agency
Wagner, SD 57380
(605) 384-3651

Utah
(See Arizona [Navajo and
Phoenix] and Oregon)

Field Agency
Uintah and Ouray Agency
Fort Duchesne, UT 84026
(801) 722-2406

Washington
(See Oregon)

Field Agencies
Colville Agency
P.O. Box 111-0111
Nespelem, WA 99155
(509) 634-4901

Spokane Agency
P.O. Box 389
Wellpinit, WA 99040
(509) 258-4561

Wapato Irrigation Project
P.O. Box 220
Wapato, WA 98951
(509) 877-3155

Puget Sound Agency
Federal Building
3006 Colby Avenue
Everett, WA 98201
(206) 258-2651

Yakima Agency
P.O. Box 632
Toppenish, WA 98948
(509) 865-2255

Wisconsin
(See Minnesota)

Field Agency
Great Lakes Agency
Ashland, WI 54806
(715) 682-4527

Wyoming
(See Montana)

Field Agency
Wind River Agency
Fort Washakie, WY 82514
(307) 225-8301

INDIAN EMPLOYMENT ASSISTANCE

Department of the Interior
Bureau of Indian Affairs (BIA)
Office of Tribal Services
Division of Job Placement and Training
1849 C Street NW
Washington, DC 20240
(202) 208-2570

Description: Direct payments for specialized use to provide eligible American Indians with vocational training and employment opportunities. Must be a member of federally recognized tribe, band, or group of Indians who live near or on reservation under the jurisdiction of the BIA, in need of financial assistance.
$ Given: Range: $800–$6,500 per year; average: $5,000.
Application Information: BIA Form BIA-8205 available at nearest Bureau Employment Assistance Office or tribal contact office at place of residence.
Deadline: None
Contact: Dean Poleahla

Alaska

Juneau Area Office
P.O. Box 25520
Juneau, AK 99801
(907) 586-7177

Field Agencies

Anchorage Agency
1675 C Street
Anchorage, AK 99501
(907) 271-4088

Bethel Agency
P.O. Box 347
Bethel, AK 99559
(907) 543-2726

Fairbanks Agency
101 12th Avenue
Box 16
Fairbanks, AK 99707
(907) 452-0222

Nome Agency
Box 1108
Nome, AK 99762
(907) 443-2284

Southeast Agency
P.O. Box 3-8000
Juneau, AK 99802
(907) 586-7304

Arizona

Phoenix Area Office
1 North First Street
Phoenix, AZ 85001
(602) 379-6760

Field Agencies

Chinle Agency
P.O. Box 10-H
Chinle, AZ 86503
(505) 674-5211

Colorado River Agency
Route 1, Box 9-C
Parker, AZ 85344
(602) 669-2134

Fort Apache Agency
Whiteriver, AZ 85941
(602) 338-4364

Fort Defiance Agency
P.O. Box 619
Fort Defiance, AZ 86504
(602) 729-5041

Fort Yuma Agency
P.O. Box 1591
Yuma, AZ 85364
(714) 572-0248

Hopi Agency
Keams Canyon, AZ 86034
(602) 738-2228

Papago Agency
Sells, AZ 85634
(602) 729-7284

Pima Agency
Sacaton, AZ 85247
(602) 383-7286

Salt River Agency
Route 1, Box 117
Scottsdale, AZ 85256
(602) 241-2842

San Carlos Agency
San Carlos, AZ 85550
(602) 475-2321

San Carlos Irrigation Project
Coolidge, AZ 85228
(602) 723-5439

Truxton Canon Agency
Valentine, AZ 86437
(602) 769-2241

Western Navajo Agency
P.O. Box 127
Tuba City, AZ 86045
(602) 283-6265

Navajo Area Office
P.O. Box #1060
Gallup, NM 87301
(505) 863-9501

California

(See also Arizona [Phoenix])

Sacramento Area Office
Federal Office Building,
Room W-2550
2800 Cottage Way
Sacramento, CA 95825-1884
(916) 978-4689

Field Agencies

Central California Agency
1800 Tribute Road, Suite 111
Sacramento, CA 95815
(916) 484-4357

Hoopa Agency
P.O. Box 367
Hoopa, CA 95546
(916) 625-4285

Palm Springs Area Field
Office
P.O. Box 2245
441 South Calle Encilla,
Suite 8
Palm Springs, CA 92262
(916) 325-2086

Southern California Agency
P.O. Box 2900, Suite 201
5750 Division Street
Riverside, CA 92506
(714) 351-6624

Colorado

(See New Mexico)

Field Agencies

Southern Ute Agency
P.O. Box 315
Ignacio, CO 81137
(303) 563-4511

Ute Mountain Ute Agency
Towaoc, CO 81334
(303) 565-8471

District of Columbia

Eastern Area Office
3701 North Fairfax Drive,
Suite 260-Mailroom
Arlington, VA 22203
(703) 235-2735

Deputy Assistant Secretary
Indian Affairs (Operations)
1849 C Street, NW,
MS-334A, SIB
Washington, DC 20240
(202) 208-2809

Florida

(See District of Columbia,
Eastern Area Office)

Field Agencies

Miccosukee Agency
P.O. Box 44021
Tamiami Station
Miami, FL 33144
(305) 223-8380

Seminole Agency
6075 Stirling Road
Hollywood, FL 33024
(305) 581-7050

Idaho
(see Arizona [Phoenix] and
Oregon)
Field Agencies
Fort Hall Agency
Fort Hall, ID 83203
(208) 237-0600

Northern Idaho Agency
P.O. Drawer 277
Lapwai, ID 83540
(208) 843-2267

Iowa
(See Minnesota)
Field Agency
Sac and Fox Area Field
Office
Tama, IA 52339
(515) 484-4041

Kansas
(See Oklahoma [Anadarko])
Field Agencies
Haskell Indian Junior College
Lawrence, KS 66604
(913) 843-1831

Horton Agency
Horton, KS 66439
(913) 486-2161

Louisiana
(See District of Columbia,
Eastern Area Office)

Michigan
(See Minnesota)

Minnesota
Minneapolis Area Office
331 South 2nd Avenue
Minneapolis, MN 55402
(612) 373-1037

Field Agencies
Minnesota Agency
P.O. Box 97
Cass Lake, MN 56633
(218) 335-6913

Red Lake Agency
Red Lake, MN 56671
(218) 679-3361

Minnesota Sioux Area Field
Office
2330 Sioux Trail, NW
Prior Lake, MN 55372
(612) 445-6565

Mississippi
(See District of Columbia,
Eastern Area Office)
Field Agency
Choctaw Agency
421 Powell
Philadelphia, MS 39350
(601) 656-1521

Montana
Billings Area Office
316 North 26th Street
Billings, MT 59101-1397
(406) 657-6313
Field Agencies
Blackfeet Agency
Browning, MT 59417
(406) 338-7511

Crow Agency
Crow Agency, MT 59022
(406) 638-2671

Flathead Agency
Ronan, MT 59864
(406) 676-4700

Flathead Irrigation Project
Ignatius, MT 59865
(406) 745-2661

Fort Belknap Agency
P.O. Box 80
Harlem, MT 59526
(406) 353-2205

Fort Peck Agency
P.O. Box 637
Poplar, MT 59225
(406) 768-5311

Northern Cheyenne Agency
Lame Deer, MT 59043
(406) 477-6242

Rocky Boy's Agency
Box Elder, MT 59521
(406) 395-4476

Nebraska
(See South Dakota)
Field Agency
Winnebago Agency
Winnebago, NE 68071
(402) 878-2201

Nevada
(See Arizona [Phoenix])
Field Agencies
Western Nevada Agency
1677 Hotsprings Road
Carson City, NV 89706
(702) 887-3500

Eastern Nevada Agency
Elko, NV 89801
(702) 738-5165

New Mexico
(See also Arizona [Navajo])

Albuquerque Area Office
615 1st Street
P.O. Box 26567
Albuquerque, NM 87103
(505) 766-2996
Field Agencies
Eastern Navajo Agency
P.O. Box 328
Crownpoint, NM 87313
(505) 786-5228

Institute of American Indian
Arts
Santa Fe, NM 87501
(505) 982-3801

Jicarilla Agency
Dulce, NM 87528
(505) 759-3651

Mescalero Agency
Mescalero, NM 88340
(505) 671-4421

Navajo Irrigation Project
Energy Building, Room 103
3539 East 30th Street, NW
Farmington, NM 87401
(505) 325-1864

Northern Pueblos Agency
Federal P.O. Building
P.O. Box 849
Santa Fe, NM 87501
(505) 988-6431

Ramah-Navajo Agency
Ramah, NM 87321
(505) 783-5731

Shiprock Agency
P.O. Box 966
Shiprock, NM 87420
(505) 368-4427

Southern Pueblos Agency
P.O. Box 1667
Albuquerque, NM 87103
(505) 766-3021

Southwestern Indian
Polytechnic Institute
1000 Indian School Road,
NW
Albuquerque, NM 87103
(505) 843-3033

Zuni Agency
P.O. Box 338
Zuni, NM 87327
(505) 782-4481

New York
(See District of Columbia,
Eastern Area Office)
Field Agency
New York Field Office
Federal Building, No. 523
100 South Clinton Street
Syracuse, NY 13202
(315) 423-5476

North Carolina
(See District of Columbia,
Eastern Area Office)
Field Agency
Cherokee Agency
Cherokee, NC 28719
(704) 497-9131

North Dakota
(See South Dakota)
Field Agencies
Fort Berthold Agency
New Town, ND 58763
(701) 627-4707

Fort Totten Agency
Fort Totten, ND 58335
(701) 766-4545

Standing Rock Agency
Fort Yates, ND 58538
(701) 854-3431

Turtle Mountain Agency
Belcourt, ND 58316
(701) 477-3191

Oklahoma
Anadarko Area Office
P.O. Box 368
Anadarko, OK 73005-0368
(405) 247-6673

Muskogee Area Office
Federal Building,
U.S. Courthouse
Muskogee, OK 74401-4898
(918) 687-2230
Field Agencies
Anadarko Agency
P.O. Box 309
Anadarko, OK 73005
(405) 247-6673

Ardmore Agency
P.O. Box 997
Ardmore, OK 73401
(405) 223-6767

Concho Agency
Concho, OK 73022
(405) 262-4855

Okmulgee Agency
P.O. Box 370
Okulgee, OK 74447
(918) 756-3950

Osage Agency
Pawhuska, OK 74056
(918) 287-2481

Miami Agency
P.O. Box 391
Miami, OK 74354
(918) 542-3396

Pawnee Agency
P.O. Box 440
Pawness, OK 74058
(918) 762-2585

Shawnee Agency
Federal Building
Shawnee, OK 74801
(405) 273-0317

Tahlequah Agency
P.O. Box 828
Tahlequah, OK 74465
(918) 456-6164

Talihina Agency
Drawer H
Talihina, OK 74571
(918) 567-2207

Wewoka Agency
P.O. Box 1060
Wewoka, OK 74884
(918) 257-6257

Oregon
(See also Arizona [Phoenix])

Portland Area Office
911 NE 11th Avenue
Portland, OR 97232-4169
(503) 231-6757
Field Agencies
Umatilla Agency
P.O. Box 520
Pendleton, OR 97801
(503) 276-3811

Warm Springs Agency
Warm Springs, OR 97761
(503) 553-1121

South Dakota
Aberdeen Area Office
Federal Building
115th Avenue, SE
Aberdeen, SD 57401-4382
(605) 226-7426
Field Agencies
Cheyenne River Agency
P.O. Box 325
Eagle Butte, SD 57625
(605) 964-6611

Crow Creek Agency
P.O. Box 616
Fort Thompson, SD 57339
(605) 245-2311

Lower Brule Agency
Lower Brule, SD 57548
(605) 473-5512

Pine Ridge Agency
Pine Ridge, SD 57770
(605) 867-5121

Rosebud Agency
Rosebud, SD 57570
(605) 747-2224

Sisseton Agency
Sisseton, SD 57262
(605) 698-7676

Yankton Agency
Wagner, SD 57380
(605) 384-3651

Utah
(See Arizona [Navajo and
Phoenix] and Oregon)

Field Agency
Uintah and Ouray Agency
Fort Duchesne, UT 84026
(801) 722-2406

Washington
(See Oregon)
Field Agencies
Colville Agency
P.O. Box 111-0111
Nespelem, WA 99155
(509) 634-4901

Spokane Agency
P.O. Box 389
Wellpinit, WA 99040
(509) 258-4561

Wapato Irrigation Project
P.O. Box 220
Wapato, WA 98951
(509) 877-3155

Puget Sound Agency
Federal Building
3006 Colby Avenue
Everett, WA 98201
(206) 258-2651

Yakima Agency
P.O. Box 632
Toppenish, WA 98948
(509) 865-2255

Wisconsin
(See Minnesota)
Field Agency
Great Lakes Agency
Ashland, WI 54806
(715) 682-4527

Wyoming
(See Montana)
Field Agency
Wind River Agency
Fort Washakie, WY 82514
(307) 225-8301

INDIAN GRANTS—ECONOMIC DEVELOPMENT (INDIAN GRANT PROGRAM)

**Department of the
Interior
Bureau of Indian Affairs
Office of Trust and
Economic Development**
1849 and C Street, NW,
Room 4060
Washington, DC 20240
(202) 208-3662

Description: Provides seed money to attract financing from other sources for developing Indian-owned businesses; to improve reservation economics by providing employment and goods services where needed. Grants must be used for development of profit-oriented businesses that will have positive economic impact on Indian reservations. Grant no more than 25 percent of project costs.
$ Given: Limited to $100,000 for individuals; $250,000 for tribes. Range: $810–$250,000; average: $39,400.
Application Information: Application initiated at local agency and submitted on forms approved by the Office of Management and Budget.
Deadline: None
Contact: Ray Quinn

Alaska

Juneau Area Office
P.O. Box 25520
Juneau, AK 99801
(907) 586-7177

Field Agencies
Anchorage Agency
1675 C Street
Anchorage, AK 99501
(907) 271-4088

Bethel Agency
P.O. Box 347
Bethel, AK 99559
(907) 543-2726

Fairbanks Agency
101 12th Avenue
Box 16
Fairbanks, AK 99707
(907) 452-0222

Nome Agency
Box 1108
Nome, AK 99762
(907) 443-2284

Southeast Agency
P.O. Box 3-8000
Juneau, AK 99802
(907) 586-7304

Arizona

Phoenix Area Office
1 North First Street
Phoenix, AZ 85001
(602) 379-6760

Field Agencies
Chinle Agency
P.O. Box 10-H
Chinle, AZ 86503
(505) 674-5211

Colorado River Agency
Route 1, Box 9-C
Parker, AZ 85344
(602) 669-2134

Fort Apache Agency
Whiteriver, AZ 85941
(602) 338-4364

Fort Defiance Agency
P.O. Box 619
Fort Defiance, AZ 86504
(602) 729-5041

Fort Yuma Agency
P.O. Box 1591
Yuma, AZ 85364
(714) 572-0248

Hopi Agency
Keams Canyon, AZ 86034
(602) 738-2228

Papago Agency
Sells, AZ 85634
(602) 729-7284

Pima Agency
Sacaton, AZ 85247
(602) 383-7286

Salt River Agency
Route 1, Box 117
Scottsdale, AZ 85256
(602) 241-2842

San Carlos Agency
San Carlos, AZ 85550
(602) 475-2321

San Carlos Irrigation Project
Coolidge, AZ 85228
(602) 723-5439

Truxton Canon Agency
Valentine, AZ 86437
(602) 769-2241

Western Navajo Agency
P.O. Box 127
Tuba City, AZ 86045
(602) 283-6265

Navajo Area Office
P.O. Box #1060
Gallup, NM 87301
(505) 863-9501

California

(See also Arizona [Phoenix])

Sacramento Area Office
Federal Office Building,
Room W-2550
2800 Cottage Way
Sacramento, CA 95825-1884
(916) 978-4689

Field Agencies
Central California Agency
1800 Tribute Road, Suite 111
Sacramento, CA 95815
(916) 484-4357

Hoopa Agency
P.O. Box 367
Hoopa, CA 95546
(916) 625-4285

Palm Springs Area Field
Office
P.O. Box 2245
441 South Calle Encilla,
Suite 8
Palm Springs, CA 92262
(916) 325-2086

Southern California Agency
P.O. Box 2900, Suite 201
5750 Divsion Street
Riverside, CA 92506
(714) 351-6624

Colorado

(See New Mexico)
Field Agencies
Southern Ute Agency
P.O. Box 315
Ignacio, CO 81137
(303) 563-4511

Ute Mountain Ute Agency
Towaoc, CO 81334
(303) 565-8471

District of Columbia

Eastern Area Office
3701 North Fairfax Drive,
Suite 260-Mailroom
Arlington, VA 22203
(703) 235-2735

Deputy Assistant Secretary
Indian Affairs (Operations)
1849 C Street, NW,
MS-334A, SIB
Washington, DC 20240
(202) 208-2809

Florida

(See District of Columbia,
Eastern Area Office)
Field Agencies
Miccosukee Agency
P.O. Box 44021
Tamiami Station
Miami, FL 33144
(305) 223-8380

Seminole Agency
6075 Stirling Road
Hollywood, FL 33024
(305) 581-7050

Idaho
(see Arizona [Phoenix] and
Oregon)
Field Agencies
Fort Hall Agency
Fort Hall, ID 83203
(208) 237-0600

Northern Idaho Agency
P.O. Drawer 277
Lapwai, ID 83540
(208) 843-2267

Iowa
(See Minnesota)
Field Agency
Sac and Fox Area Field
Office
Tama, IA 52339
(515) 484-4041

Kansas
(See Oklahoma [Anadarko])
Field Agencies
Haskell Indian Junior College
Lawrence, KS 66604
(913) 843-1831

Horton Agency
Horton, KS 66439
(913) 486-2161

Louisiana
(See District of Columbia,
Eastern Area Office)

Michigan
(See Minnesota)

Minnesota
Minneapolis Area Office
331 South 2nd Avenue
Minneapolis, MN 55402
(612) 373-1037

Field Agencies
Minnesota Agency
P.O. Box 97
Cass Lake, MN 56633
(218) 335-6913

Red Lake Agency
Red Lake, MN 56671
(218) 679-3361

Minnesota Sioux Area Field
Office
2330 Sioux Trail, NW
Prior Lake, MN 55372
(612) 445-6565

Mississippi
(See District of Columbia,
Eastern Area Office)
Field Agency
Choctaw Agency
421 Powell
Philadelphia, MS 39350
(601) 656-1521

Montana
Billings Area Office
316 North 26th Street
Billings, MT 59101-1397
(406) 657-6313
Field Agencies
Blackfeet Agency
Browning, MT 59417
(406) 338-7511

Crow Agency
Crow Agency, MT 59022
(406) 638-2671

Flathead Agency
Ronan, MT 59864
(406) 676-4700

Flathead Irrigation Project
Ignatius, MT 59865
(406) 745-2661

Fort Belknap Agency
P.O. Box 80
Harlem, MT 59526
(406) 353-2205

Fort Peck Agency
P.O. Box 637
Poplar, MT 59225
(406) 768-5311

Northern Cheyenne Agency
Lame Deer, MT 59043
(406) 477-6242

Rocky Boy's Agency
Box Elder, MT 59521
(406) 395-4476

Nebraska
(See South Dakota)
Field Agency
Winnebago Agency
Winnebago, NE 68071
(402) 878-2201

Nevada
(See Arizona [Phoenix])
Field Agencies
Western Nevada Agency
1677 Hotsprings Road
Carson City, NV 89706
(702) 887-3500

Eastern Nevada Agency
Elko, NV 89801
(702) 738-5165

New Mexico
(See also Arizona [Navajo])

Albuquerque Area Office
615 1st Street
P.O. Box 26567
Albuquerque, NM 87103
(505) 766-2996

Field Agencies
Eastern Navajo Agency
P.O. Box 328
Crownpoint, NM 87313
(505) 786-5228

Institute of American Indian
Arts
Santa Fe, NM 87501
(505) 982-3801

Jicarilla Agency
Dulce, NM 87528
(505) 759-3651

Mescalero Agency
Mescalero, NM 88340
(505) 671-4421

Navajo Irrigation Project
Energy Building, Room 103
3539 East 30th Street, NW
Farmington, NM 87401
(505) 325-1864

Northern Pueblos Agency
Federal P.O. Building
P.O. Box 849
Santa Fe, NM 87501
(505) 988-6431

Ramah-Navajo Agency
Ramah, NM 87321
(505) 783-5731

Shiprock Agency
P.O. Box 966
Shiprock, NM 87420
(505) 368-4427

Southern Pueblos Agency
P.O. Box 1667
Albuquerque, NM 87103
(505) 766-3021

Southwestern Indian
Polytechnic Institute
1000 Indian School Road,
NW
Albuquerque, NM 87103
(505) 843-3033

Zuni Agency
P.O. Box 338
Zuni, NM 87327
(505) 782-4481

New York
(See District of Columbia,
Eastern Area Office)
Field Agency
New York Field Office
Federal Building, No. 523
100 South Clinton Street
Syracuse, NY 13202
(315) 423-5476

North Carolina
(See District of Columbia,
Eastern Area Office)
Field Agency
Cherokee Agency
Cherokee, NC 28719
(704) 497-9131

North Dakota
(See South Dakota)
Field Agencies
Fort Berthold Agency
New Town, ND 58763
(701) 627-4707

Fort Totten Agency
Fort Totten, ND 58335
(701) 766-4545

Standing Rock Agency
Fort Yates, ND 58538
(701) 854-3431

Turtle Mountain Agency
Belcourt, ND 58316
(701) 477-3191

Oklahoma
Anadarko Area Office
P.O. Box 368
Anadarko, OK 73005-0368
(405) 247-6673

Muskogee Area Office
Federal Building,
U.S. Courthouse
Muskogee, OK 74401-4898
(918) 687-2230
Field Agencies
Anadarko Agency
P.O. Box 309
Anadarko, OK 73005
(405) 247-6673

Ardmore Agency
P.O. Box 997
Ardmore, OK 73401
(405) 223-6767

Concho Agency
Concho, OK 73022
(405) 262-4855

Okmulgee Agency
P.O. Box 370
Okulgee, OK 74447
(918) 756-3950

Osage Agency
Pawhuska, OK 74056
(918) 287-2481

Miami Agency
P.O. Box 391
Miami, OK 74354
(918) 542-3396

Pawnee Agency
P.O. Box 440
Pawness, OK 74058
(918) 762-2585

Shawnee Agency
Federal Building
Shawnee, OK 74801
(405) 273-0317

Tahlequah Agency
P.O. Box 828
Tahlequah, OK 74465
(918) 456-6164

Talihina Agency
Drawer H
Talihina, OK 74571
(918) 567-2207

Wewoka Agency
P.O. Box 1060
Wewoka, OK 74884
(918) 257-6257

Oregon
(See also Arizona [Phoenix])

Portland Area Office
911 NE 11th Avenue
Portland, OR 97232-4169
(503) 231-6757
Field Agencies
Umatilla Agency
P.O. Box 520
Pendleton, OR 97801
(503) 276-3811

Warm Springs Agency
Warm Springs, OR 97761
(503) 553-1121

South Dakota

Aberdeen Area Office
Federal Building
115th Avenue, SE
Aberdeen, SD 57401-4382
(605) 226-7426
Field Agencies
Cheyenne River Agency
P.O. Box 325
Eagle Butte, SD 57625
(605) 964-6611

Crow Creek Agency
P.O. Box 616
Fort Thompson, SD 57339
(605) 245-2311

Lower Brule Agency
Lower Brule, SD 57548
(605) 473-5512

Pine Ridge Agency
Pine Ridge, SD 57770
(605) 867-5121

Rosebud Agency
Rosebud, SD 57570
(605) 747-2224

Sisseton Agency
Sisseton, SD 57262
(605) 698-7676

Yankton Agency
Wagner, SD 57380
(605) 384-3651

Utah
(See Arizona [Navajo and
Phoenix] and Oregon)

Field Agency
Uintah and Ouray Agency
Fort Duchesne, UT 84026
(801) 722-2406

Washington
(See Oregon)
Field Agencies
Colville Agency
P.O. Box 111-0111
Nespelem, WA 99155
(509) 634-4901

Spokane Agency
P.O. Box 389
Wellpinit, WA 99040
(509) 258-4561

Wapato Irrigation Project
P.O. Box 220
Wapato, WA 98951
(509) 877-3155

Puget Sound Agency
Federal Building
3006 Colby Avenue
Everett, WA 98201
(206) 258-2651

Yakima Agency
P.O. Box 632
Toppenish, WA 98948
(509) 865-2255

Wisconsin
(See Minnesota)
Field Agency
Great Lakes Agency
Ashland, WI 54806
(715) 682-4527

Wyoming
(See Montana)
Field Agency
Wind River Agency
Fort Washakie, WY 82514
(307) 225-8301

Indian Loans—Economic Development
(Indian Credit Program)

**Department of the
Interior
Bureau of Indian Affairs
Office of Trust and
Economic Development**
1849 and C Street, NW,
Room 4060
Washington, DC 20240
(202) 208-5324

Description: Assistance given to Indians, Alaska
natives, tribes, and Indian organizations to obtain
financing from private and governmental sources to
promote economic development of federal Indian
reservation. Funds must be unavailable from other
sources at reasonable terms and conditions. Funds
cannot be used for speculation.
$ Given: Range: $1,000–over $1 million; average:
$100,000.
Application Information: Application initiated at local
agency level and submitted on forms approved by the
Deputy to Assistant Secretary, Indian Affairs.
Deadline: N/A
Contact: R. K. Nephew

Alaska

Juneau Area Office
P.O. Box 25520
Juneau, AK 99801
(907) 586-7177

Field Agencies

Anchorage Agency
1675 C Street
Anchorage, AK 99501
(907) 271-4088

Bethel Agency
P.O. Box 347
Bethel, AK 99559
(907) 543-2726

Fairbanks Agency
101 12th Avenue
Box 16
Fairbanks, AK 99707
(907) 452-0222

Nome Agency
Box 1108
Nome, AK 99762
(907) 443-2284

Southeast Agency
P.O. Box 3-8000
Juneau, AK 99802
(907) 586-7304

Arizona

Phoenix Area Office
1 North First Street
Phoenix, AZ 85001
(602) 379-6760

Field Agencies

Chinle Agency
P.O. Box 10-H
Chinle, AZ 86503
(505) 674-5211

Colorado River Agency
Route 1, Box 9-C
Parker, AZ 85344
(602) 669-2134

Fort Apache Agency
Whiteriver, AZ 85941
(602) 338-4364

Fort Defiance Agency
P.O. Box 619
Fort Defiance, AZ 86504
(602) 729-5041

Fort Yuma Agency
P.O. Box 1591
Yuma, AZ 85364
(714) 572-0248

Hopi Agency
Keams Canyon, AZ 86034
(602) 738-2228

Papago Agency
Sells, AZ 85634
(602) 729-7284

Pima Agency
Sacaton, AZ 85247
(602) 383-7286

Salt River Agency
Route 1, Box 117
Scottsdale, AZ 85256
(602) 241-2842

San Carlos Agency
San Carlos, AZ 85550
(602) 475-2321

San Carlos Irrigation Project
Coolidge, AZ 85228
(602) 723-5439

Truxton Canon Agency
Valentine, AZ 86437
(602) 769-2241

Western Navajo Agency
P.O. Box 127
Tuba City, AZ 86045
(602) 283-6265

Navajo Area Office
P.O. Box #1060
Gallup, NM 87301
(505) 863-9501

California
(See also Arizona [Phoenix])

Sacramento Area Office
Federal Office Building,
Room W-2550
2800 Cottage Way
Sacramento, CA 95825-1884
(916) 978-4689

Field Agencies

Central California Agency
1800 Tribute Road, Suite 111
Sacramento, CA 95815
(916) 484-4357

Hoopa Agency
P.O. Box 367
Hoopa, CA 95546
(916) 625-4285

Palm Springs Area Field
Office
P.O. Box 2245
441 South Calle Encilla,
Suite 8
Palm Springs, CA 92262
(916) 325-2086

Southern California Agency
P.O. Box 2900, Suite 201
5750 Division Street
Riverside, CA 92506
(714) 351-6624

Colorado
(See New Mexico)

Field Agencies

Southern Ute Agency
P.O. Box 315
Ignacio, CO 81137
(303) 563-4511

Ute Mountain Ute Agency
Towaoc, CO 81334
(303) 565-8471

District of Columbia

Eastern Area Office
3701 North Fairfax Drive,
Suite 260-Mailroom
Arlington, VA 22203
(703) 235-2735

Deputy Assistant Secretary
Indian Affairs (Operations)
1849 C Street, NW,
MS-334A, SIB
Washington, DC 20240
(202) 208-2809

Florida
(See District of Columbia,
Eastern Area Office)

Field Agencies

Miccosukee Agency
P.O. Box 44021
Tamiami Station
Miami, FL 33144
(305) 223-8380

Seminole Agency
6075 Stirling Road
Hollywood, FL 33024
(305) 581-7050

Idaho
(see Arizona [Phoenix] and
Oregon)
Field Agencies
Fort Hall Agency
Fort Hall, ID 83203
(208) 237-0600

Northern Idaho Agency
P.O. Drawer 277
Lapwai, ID 83540
(208) 843-2267

Iowa
(See Minnesota)
Field Agency
Sac and Fox Area Field
Office
Tama, IA 52339
(515) 484-4041

Kansas
(See Oklahoma [Anadarko])
Field Agencies
Haskell Indian Junior College
Lawrence, KS 66604
(913) 843-1831

Horton Agency
Horton, KS 66439
(913) 486-2161

Louisiana
(See District of Columbia,
Eastern Area Office)

Michigan
(See Minnesota)

Minnesota

Minneapolis Area Office
331 South 2nd Avenue
Minneapolis, MN 55402
(612) 373-1037

Field Agencies
Minnesota Agency
P.O. Box 97
Cass Lake, MN 56633
(218) 335-6913
Red Lake Agency
Red Lake, MN 56671
(218) 679-3361
Minnesota Sioux Area Field
Office
2330 Sioux Trail, NW
Prior Lake, MN 55372
(612) 445-6565

Mississippi
(See District of Columbia,
Eastern Area Office)
Field Agency
Choctaw Agency
421 Powell
Philadelphia, MS 39350
(601) 656-1521

Montana
Billings Area Office
316 North 26th Street
Billings, MT 59101-1397
(406) 657-6313
Field Agencies
Blackfeet Agency
Browning, MT 59417
(406) 338-7511
Crow Agency
Crow Agency, MT 59022
(406) 638-2671
Flathead Agency
Ronan, MT 59864
(406) 676-4700
Flathead Irrigation Project
Ignatius, MT 59865
(406) 745-2661
Fort Belknap Agency
P.O. Box 80
Harlem, MT 59526
(406) 353-2205
Fort Peck Agency
P.O. Box 637
Poplar, MT 59225
(406) 768-5311

Northern Cheyenne Agency
Lame Deer, MT 59043
(406) 477-6242

Rocky Boy's Agency
Box Elder, MT 59521
(406) 395-4476

Nebraska
(See South Dakota)
Field Agency
Winnebago Agency
Winnebago, NE 68071
(402) 878-2201

Nevada
(See Arizona [Phoenix])
Field Agencies
Western Nevada Agency
1677 Hotsprings Road
Carson City, NV 89706
(702) 887-3500

Eastern Nevada Agency
Elko, NV 89801
(702) 738-5165

New Mexico
(See also Arizona [Navajo])
Albuquerque Area Office
615 1st Street
P.O. Box 26567
Albuquerque, NM 87103
(505) 766-2996
Field Agencies
Eastern Navajo Agency
P.O. Box 328
Crownpoint, NM 87313
(505) 786-5228

Institute of American Indian
Arts
Santa Fe, NM 87501
(505) 982-3801

Jicarilla Agency
Dulce, NM 87528
(505) 759-3651

Mescalero Agency
Mescalero, NM 88340
(505) 671-4421

Navajo Irrigation Project
Energy Building, Room 103
3539 East 30th Street, NW
Farmington, NM 87401
(505) 325-1864

Northern Pueblos Agency
Federal P.O. Building
P.O. Box 849
Santa Fe, NM 87501
(505) 988-6431

Ramah-Navajo Agency
Ramah, NM 87321
(505) 783-5731

Shiprock Agency
P.O. Box 966
Shiprock, NM 87420
(505) 368-4427

Southern Pueblos Agency
P.O. Box 1667
Albuquerque, NM 87103
(505) 766-3021

Southwestern Indian
Polytechnic Institute
1000 Indian School Road,
NW
Albuquerque, NM 87103
(505) 843-3033

Zuni Agency
P.O. Box 338
Zuni, NM 87327
(505) 782-4481

New York
(See District of Columbia,
Eastern Area Office)
Field Agency
New York Field Office
Federal Building, No. 523
100 South Clinton Street
Syracuse, NY 13202
(315) 423-5476

North Carolina
(See District of Columbia,
Eastern Area Office)
Field Agency
Cherokee Agency
Cherokee, NC 28719
(704) 497-9131

North Dakota
(See South Dakota)
Field Agencies
Fort Berthold Agency
New Town, ND 58763
(701) 627-4707

Fort Totten Agency
Fort Totten, ND 58335
(701) 766-4545

Standing Rock Agency
Fort Yates, ND 58538
(701) 854-3431

Turtle Mountain Agency
Belcourt, ND 58316
(701) 477-3191

Oklahoma
Anadarko Area Office
P.O. Box 368
Anadarko, OK 73005-0368
(405) 247-6673

Muskogee Area Office
Federal Building,
U.S. Courthouse
Muskogee, OK 74401-4898
(918) 687-2230
Field Agencies
Anadarko Agency
P.O. Box 309
Anadarko, OK 73005
(405) 247-6673

Ardmore Agency
P.O. Box 997
Ardmore, OK 73401
(405) 223-6767

Concho Agency
Concho, OK 73022
(405) 262-4855

Okmulgee Agency
P.O. Box 370
Okulgee, OK 74447
(918) 756-3950

Osage Agency
Pawhuska, OK 74056
(918) 287-2481

Miami Agency
P.O. Box 391
Miami, OK 74354
(918) 542-3396

Pawnee Agency
P.O. Box 440
Pawness, OK 74058
(918) 762-2585

Shawnee Agency
Federal Building
Shawnee, OK 74801
(405) 273-0317

Tahlequah Agency
P.O. Box 828
Tahlequah, OK 74465
(918) 456-6164

Talihina Agency
Drawer H
Talihina, OK 74571
(918) 567-2207

Wewoka Agency
P.O. Box 1060
Wewoka, OK 74884
(918) 257-6257

Oregon
(See also Arizona [Phoenix])

Portland Area Office
911 NE 11th Avenue
Portland, OR 97232-4169
(503) 231-6757
Field Agencies
Umatilla Agency
P.O. Box 520
Pendleton, OR 97801
(503) 276-3811

Warm Springs Agency
Warm Springs, OR 97761
(503) 553-1121

South Dakota

Aberdeen Area Office
Federal Building
115th Avenue SE
Aberdeen, SD 57401-4382
(605) 226-7426
Field Agencies
Cheyenne River Agency
P.O. Box 325
Eagle Butte, SD 57625
(605) 964-6611

Crow Creek Agency
P.O. Box 616
Fort Thompson, SD 57339
(605) 245-2311

Lower Brule Agency
Lower Brule, SD 57548
(605) 473-5512

Pine Ridge Agency
Pine Ridge, SD 57770
(605) 867-5121

Rosebud Agency
Rosebud, SD 57570
(605) 747-2224

Sisseton Agency
Sisseton, SD 57262
(605) 698-7676

Yankton Agency
Wagner, SD 57380
(605) 384-3651

Utah
(See Arizona |Navajo and
Phoenix| and Oregon)

Field Agency
Uintah and Ouray Agency
Fort Duchesne, UT 84026
(801) 722-2406

Washington
(See Oregon)
Field Agencies
Colville Agency
P.O. Box 111-0111
Nespelem, WA 99155
(509) 634-4901

Spokane Agency
P.O. Box 389
Wellpinit, WA 99040
(509) 258-4561

Wapato Irrigation Project
P.O. Box 220
Wapato, WA 98951
(509) 877-3155

Puget Sound Agency
Federal Building
3006 Colby Avenue
Everett, WA 98201
(206) 258-2651

Yakima Agency
P.O. Box 632
Toppenish, WA 98948
(509) 865-2255

Wisconsin
(See Minnesota)
Field Agency
Great Lakes Agency
Ashland, WI 54806
(715) 682-4527

Wyoming
(See Montana)
Field Agency
Wind River Agency
Fort Washakie, WY 82514

MENTAL HEALTH SERVICES FOR CUBAN ENTRANTS

**Department of Health
and Human Services**
Refugee Mental Health
Program
National Institute of
Mental Health
Alcohol, Drug Abuse, and
Mental Health
Administration
Public Health Service
Parklawn Building,
Room 18-49
5600 Fishers Lane
Rockville, MD 20857
(301) 443-2130

Description: Project grants (cooperative agreements) to for-profit organizations to provide complete range of treatment to mentally ill and developmentally disabled Cuban entrants currently in federal custody. Applicant must demonstrate qualifications and work closely with federal officials.
$ Given: Nationwide FY 93 est. $3.6 million in cooperative agreements. Range: $819,710–$2.8 million; average: $1.8 million.
Application Information: Submit standard application to Grants Management Branch, above address.
Deadline: None
Contact: Dr. Thomas H. Bornemann, above address

MINORITY BUSINESS DEVELOPMENT

Small Business Administration (SBA)
Office of Minority Small Business Development Administration
409 Third Street, SW
Washington, DC 20416
(202) 205-6410

Description: Provision of specialized services to foster business ownership and competitive viability to individuals who are both socially and economically disadvantaged. Limited to small business with at least 51 percent ownership by an American citizen who is disadvantaged but demonstrates potential for success.
$ Given: N/A
Application Information: Written application to SBA district offices. Assistance given in completing forms.
Deadline: None
Contact: See appropriate field office

Alabama

Regional Office
1375 Peachtree Street, NE, Fifth Floor
Atlanta, GA 30367-8102
(404) 347-2797

District Office
Birmingham District Office
2121 8th Avenue North, Suite 200
Birmingham, AL 35203-2398
(205) 731-1344

Alaska

Regional Office
2615 4th Avenue, Room 440
Seattle, WA 98121
(206) 442-5676

District Office
Anchorage District Office
222 West 8th Avenue, Room A36
Anchorage, AK 99513
(907) 271-4022

Arizona

Regional Office
71 Stevenson Street, Twentieth Floor
San Francisco, CA 94105-2939
(415) 744-6402

District Office
Phoenix District Office
2828 North Central Avenue, Suite 800
Phoenix, AZ 85004-1025
(602) 379-3732

Arkansas

Regional Office
8625 King George Drive, Building C
Dallas, TX 75235-3391
(214) 767-7643

District Office
Little Rock District Office
Post Office and Court House Building, Room 601
320 West Capitol Avenue
Little Rock, AR 722201
(501) 378-5871

California

Regional Office
71 Stevenson Street, Twentieth Floor
San Francisco, CA 94105-2939
(415) 744-6402

District Offices
Santa Ana District Office
901 West Civic Center Drive, Suite 160
Santa Ana, CA 92703-2352
(714) 836-2494

San Diego District Office
880 Front Street, Room 4-S-29
San Diego, CA 92188-0270
(619) 557-5440

San Francisco District Office
211 Main Street, Fourth Floor
San Francisco, CA 94105-1988
(415) 744-6804

Fresno District Office
2719 North Air Fresno Drive
Fresno, CA 93727-1547
(209) 487-5189

Los Angeles District Office
330 North Grand Boulevard, Suite 1200
Glendale, CA 91203-2304
(213) 894-2956

Colorado

Regional Office
999 18th Street, Suite 701
Denver, CO 80202
(303) 294-7001

Minorities

District Office
Denver District Office
721 19th Street, Room 407
Denver, CO 80201-0660
(303) 844-3984

Connecticut

Regional Office
155 Federal Street,
Ninth Floor
Boston, MA 02110
(617) 451-2023

District Office
Hartford District Office
Federal Building,
Second Floor
330 Main Street
Hartford, CT 06106
(203) 240-4700

Delaware

475 Allendale Road,
Suite 201
King of Prussia, PA 19406
(215) 962-3700

Florida

Regional Office
1375 Peachtree Street, NE,
Fifth Floor
Atlanta, GA 30367-8102
(404) 347-2797

District Offices
Jacksonville District Office
7825 Baymeadows Way,
Suite 100-B
Jacksonville, FL 32256-7504
(904) 443-1900

Miami District Office
1320 South Dixie Highway,
Suite 501
Coral Gables, FL 33146
(305) 536-5521

Georgia

Regional Office
1375 Peachtree Street, NE,
Fifth Floor
Atlanta, GA 30367-8102
(404) 347-2797

District Office
Atlanta District Office
1720 Peachtree Road, NW,
Sixth Floor
Atlanta, GA 30309
(404) 347-4749

Hawaii

Regional Office
71 Stevenson Street,
Twentieth Floor
San Francisco, CA
94105-2939
(415) 744-6402

District Office
Honolulu District Office
300 Ala Moana Boulevard,
Room 2213
Honolulu, HI 96850-4981
(808) 541-2990

Idaho

Regional Office
2615 4th Avenue, Room 440
Seattle, WA 98121
(206) 442-5676

District Office
Boise District Office
1020 Main Street, Suite 290
Boise, ID 83702
(208) 334-9635

Illinois

Regional Office
Federal Building, Room 1975
300 South Riverside Plaza
Chicago, IL 60606-6611
(312) 353-0359

District Office
Chicago District Office
500 West Madison Street,
Room 1250
Chicago, IL 60661
(312) 353-4528

Indiana

Regional Office
Federal Building, Room 1975
300 South Riverside Plaza
Chicago, IL 60606-6611
(312) 353-0359

District Office
Indianapolis District Office
429 North Pennsylvania
Street, Suite 100
Indianapolis, IN 46204-1873
(317) 226-7272

Iowa

Regional Office
911 Walnut Street,
Thirteenth Floor
Kansas City, MO 64106
(816) 426-3608

District Offices
Des Moines District Office
New Federal Building,
Room 749
210 Walnut Street
Des Moines, IA 50309
(515) 284-4762

Cedar Rapids District Office
373 Collins Road, NE,
Room 100
Cedar Rapids, IA 52402-3147
(319) 393-8630

Kansas

Regional Office
911 Walnut Street,
Thirteenth Floor
Kansas City, MO 64106
(816) 426-3608

District Office
Wichita District Office
110 East Waterman Street,
First Floor
Wichita, KS 67202
(316) 269-6273

Kentucky

Regional Office
1375 Peachtree Street, NE,
Fifth Floor
Atlanta, GA 30367-8102
(404) 347-2797

District Office
Louisville District Office
Federal Building, Room 188
600 Martin Luther King Jr.
Place
Louisville, KY 40202
(502) 582-5976

Louisiana

Regional Office
8625 King George Drive,
Building C
Dallas, TX 75235-3391
(214) 767-7643

District Office
New Orleans District Office
1661 Canal Street,
Suite 2000
New Orleans, LA 70112
(504) 589-6685

Maine

Regional Office
155 Federal Street,
Ninth Floor
Boston, MA 02110
(617) 451-2023

District Office
Augusta District Office
Federal Building, Room 512
40 Western Avenue
Augusta, ME 04330
(207) 622-8378

Massachusetts

Regional Office
155 Federal Street,
Ninth Floor
Boston, MA 02110
(617) 451-2023

District Office
Boston District Office
10 Causeway Street,
Room 265
Boston, MA 02222-1093
(617) 565-5590

Michigan

Regional Office
Federal Building, Room 1975
300 South Riverside Plaza
Chicago, IL 60606-6611
(312) 353-0359

District Office
Detroit District Office
477 Michigan Avenue,
Room 515
Detroit, MI 48226
(313) 226-6075

Minnesota

Regional Office
Federal Building, Room 1975
300 South Riverside Plaza
Chicago, IL 60606-6611
(312) 353-0359

District Office
Minneapolis District Office
100 North 6th Street,
Suite 610
Minneapolis, MN 55403-1563
(612) 370-2324

Mississippi

Regional Office
1375 Peachtree Street, NE,
Fifth Floor
Atlanta, GA 30367-8102
(404) 347-2797

District Office
Jackson District Office
100 West Capitol Street,
Suite 400
Jackson, MS 39201
(601) 965-5325

Missouri

Regional Office
911 Walnut Street,
Thirteenth Floor
Kansas City, MO 64106
(816) 426-3608

District Offices
St. Louis District Office
815 Olive Street, Room 242
St. Louis, MO 63101
(314) 539-6600

Kansas City District Office
323 West 8th Street,
Suite 501
Kansas City, MO 64105
(816) 374-6762

Montana

Regional Office
999 18th Street, Suite 701
Denver, CO 80202
(303) 294-7001

District Office
Helena District Office
301 South Park Avenue,
Room 528
Helena, MT 59626
(406) 449-5381

Nebraska

Regional Office
911 Walnut Street,
Thirteenth Floor
Kansas City, MO 64106
(816) 426-3608

District Office
Omaha District Office
11145 Mill Valley Road
Omaha, NB 64154
(402) 221-3604

Nevada

Regional Office
71 Stevenson Street,
Twentieth Floor
San Francisco, CA
94105-2939
(415) 744-6402

District Office
Las Vegas District Office
301 East Steward Street,
Room 301
Las Vegas, NV 89125-2527
(702) 388-6611

New Hampshire

Regional Office
155 Federal Street,
Ninth Floor
Boston, MA 02110
(617) 451-2023

District Office
Concord District Office
143 North Main Street,
Suite 202
Concord, NH 03302-1257
(603) 225-1400

New Jersey

Regional Office
26 Federal Plaza,
Room 31-08
New York, NY 10278
(212) 264-7772

District Office
Newark District Office
Military Park Building,
Fourth Floor
60 Park Place
Newark, NJ 07102
(201) 341-2434

New Mexico

Regional Office
8625 King George Drive,
Building C
Dallas, TX 75235-3391
(214) 767-7643

District Office
Albuquerque District Office
625 Silver Avenue, SW,
Suite 320
Albuquerque, NM 87102
(505) 766-1870

New York

Regional Office
26 Federal Plaza,
Room 31-08
New York, NY 10278
(212) 264-7772

District Offices
Buffalo District Office
Federal Building 1311
111 West Huron Street
Buffalo, NY 14202
(716) 846-4301

Syracuse District Office
100 South Clinton Street,
Room 1071
Syracuse, NY 13260
(315) 423-5383

North Carolina

Regional Office
1375 Peachtree Street, NE,
Fifth Floor
Atlanta, GA 30367-8102
(404) 347-2797

District Office
Charlotte District Office
200 North College Street
Charlotte, NC 28202
(704) 344-6563

North Dakota

Regional Office
999 18th Street, Suite 701
Denver, CO 80202
(303) 294-7001

District Office
Federal Building, Room 218
657 2nd Avenue, North
Fargo, ND 58108-3086
(701) 239-5131

Ohio

Regional Office
Federal Building, Room 1975
300 South Riverside Plaza
Chicago, IL 60606-6611
(312) 353-0359

District Office
Columbus District Office
85 Marconi Boulevard,
Room 512
Columbus, OH 43215
(614) 469-6860

Oklahoma

Regional Office
8625 King George Drive,
Building C
Dallas, TX 75235-3391
(214) 767-7643

District Office
Oklahoma City District Office
200 NW 5th Street, Suite 670
Oklahoma City, OK 73102
(405) 231-4301

Oregon

Regional Office
2615 4th Avenue, Room 440
Seattle, WA 98121
(206) 442-5676

District Office
Portland District Office
222 SW Columbia Street,
Suite 500
Portland, OR 97201-6605
(503) 326-2682

Pacific Islands

Regional Office
71 Stevenson Street,
Twentieth Floor
San Francisco, CA
94105-2939
(415) 744-6402

District Office
Agana Branch Office
Pacific Daily News Building,
Room 508
238 Archbishop F.C. Flores
Street
Agana, GM 96910
(671) 472-7277

Pennsylvania

Regional Office
475 Allendale Road,
Suite 201
King of Prussia, PA 19406
(215) 962-3700

District Office
Pittsburgh District Office
960 Penn Avenue, Fifth Floor
Pittsburgh, PA 15222
(412) 644-2780

Puerto Rico

Regional Office
26 Federal Plaza,
Room 31-08
New York, NY 10278
(212) 264-7772

District Office
Federico Degetau Federal
Building, Room 691
Carlos Chardon Avenue
Hato Rey, PR 00918
(809) 766-5002

Rhode Island

Regional Office
155 Federal Street,
Ninth Floor
Boston, MA 02110
(617) 451-2023

District Office
Providence District Office
380 Westminster Mall,
Fifth Floor
Providence, RI 02903
(401) 528-4561

South Carolina

Regional Office
1375 Peachtree Street, NE,
Fifth Floor
Atlanta, GA 30367-8102
(404) 347-2797

District Office
Columbia District Office
1835 Assembly Street,
Room 358
Columbia, SC 29202
(803) 765-5376

South Dakota

Regional Office
999 18th Street, Suite 701
Denver, CO 80202
(303) 294-7001

District Office
Sioux Falls District Office
101 South Main Avenue,
Suite 101
Sioux Falls, SD 57102-0527
(605) 336-4231

Tennessee

Regional Office
1375 Peachtree Street, NE,
Fifth Floor
Atlanta, GA 30367-8102
(404) 347-2797

District Office
Nashville District Office
50 Vantage Way, Suite 201
Nashville, TN 37338-1500
(615) 736-7176

Texas

Regional Office
8625 King George Drive,
Building C
Dallas, TX 75235-3391
(214) 767-7643

District Offices
San Antonio District Office
7400 Blanco Road, Suite 200
San Antonio, TX 78216
(512) 229-4535

Dallas District Office
1100 Commerce Street,
Room 3C36
Dallas, TX 75242
(214) 767-0608

El Paso District Office
10737 Gateway West,
Suite 320
El Paso, TX 79935
(915) 541-5586

Utah

Regional Office
999 18th Street, Suite 701
Denver, CO 80202
(303) 294-7001

District Office
Salt Lake City District Office
Federal Building, Room 2237
125 South State Street
Salt Lake City, UT
84138-1195
(801) 524-5800

Vermont

Regional Office
155 Federal Street,
Ninth Floor
Boston, MA 02110
(617) 451-2023

District Office
Montpelier District Office
Federal Building, Room 205
87 State Street
Montpelier, VT 05602
(802) 828-4474

Virgin Islands

Regional Office
26 Federal Plaza,
Room 31-08
New York, NY 10278
(212) 264-7772

District Office
Federico Degetau Federal
Building, Room 691
Carlos Chardon Avenue
Hato Rey, PR 00918
(809) 766-5002

St. Croix Post-of-Duty
United Shopping Plaza
4C & 4D Este Sion Farm,
Room 7
Christiansted, St. Croix, VI
00820
(809) 778-5380

St. Thomas Post-of-Duty
Federal Office Building,
Room 283
Veterans Drive
St. Thomas, VI 00801
(809) 774-8530

Virginia
Regional Office
475 Allendale Road,
Suite 201
King of Prussia, PA 19406
(215) 962-3700

District Office
Richmond District Office
Federal Building, Room 3015
400 North 8th Street
Richmond, VA 23240
(804) 771-2400

Washington
Regional Office
2615 4th Avenue, Room 440
Seattle, WA 98121
(206) 442-5676

District Office
Spokane District Office
West 601 First Avenue
Tenth Floor East
Spokane, WA 99204
(509) 353-2807

Seattle District Office
915 Second Avenue,
Room 1792
Seattle, WA 98174-1088
(206) 553-1420

Washington, DC
Regional Office
475 Allendale Road,
Suite 201
King of Prussia, PA 19406
(215) 962-3700

District Office
Washington District Office
1111 18th Street, NW,
Sixth Floor
Washington, DC 20036
(202) 634-1500

West Virginia
Regional Office
475 Allendale Road,
Suite 201
King of Prussia, PA 19406
(215) 962-3700

District Office
Clarksburg District Office
168 West Main Street,
Fifth Floor
Clarksburg, WV 26301
(304) 623-5631

Wisconsin
Regional Office
Federal Building, Room 1975
300 South Riverside Plaza
Chicago, IL 60606-6611
(312) 353-0359

District Office
Madison District Office
212 East Washington Avenue,
Room 213
Madison, WI 53703
(608) 264-5261

Wyoming
Regional Office
999 18th Street, Suite 701
Denver, CO 80202
(303) 294-7001

District Office
Casper District Office
Federal Building, Room 4001
100 East B Street
Casper, WY 82602-2839
(307) 261-5761

MINORITY BUSINESS DEVELOPMENT CENTERS

Department of Commerce Minority Business Agency
14th and Constitution Avenue, NW
Washington, DC 20230
(202) 377-8015

Description: Project grants to provide business development services for a minimal fee to minority firms and individuals interested in entering, expanding, or improving their efforts in the marketplace.
$ Given: Range: $165,000–$622,000; average: $212,000.
Application Information: Standard application forms as furnished by the federal agency.
Deadline: See Federal Register and Commerce Business Daily.
Contact: Bharat Bhargava
          Assistant Director
          Office of Operations
          Room 5063

Alabama
Carlton Eccles, Director
401 West Peachtree Street, NW, Room 1930
Atlanta, GA 30308-3516
(404) 730-3300

Alaska
Xavier Mena, Director
221 Main Street, Room 1280
San Francisco, CA 94105
(415) 744-3001

Arkansas
Melda Cabrera, Director
1100 Commerce Street, Room 7B23
Dallas, TX 75242
(214) 767-8001

Arizona
Xavier Mena, Director
221 Main Street, Room 1280
San Francisco, CA 94105
(415) 744-3001

American Somoa
Xavier Mena, Director
221 Main Street, Room 1280
San Francisco, CA 94105
(415) 744-3001

California
Xavier Mena, Director
221 Main Street, Room 1280
San Francisco, CA 94105
(415) 744-3001

Rudy Guerra, District Officer
977 North Broadway, Suite 201
Los Angeles, CA 90012
(213) 894-7157

Colorado
Melda Cabrera, Director
1100 Commerce Street, Room 7B23
Dallas, TX 75242
(214) 767-8001

Connecticut
John Iglehart, Director
26 Federal Plaza, Room 3720
New York, NY 10278
(212) 264-3262

District of Columbia
Georgina Sanchez, Director
14th and Constitution Avenue, NW, Room 6711
Washington, DC 20230
(202) 377-8275

Delaware
Georgina Sanchez, Director
14th and Constitution Avenue, NW, Room 6711
Washington, DC 20230
(202) 377-8275

Florida
Carlton Eccles, Director
401 West Peachtree Street, NW, Room 1930
Atlanta, GA 30308-3516
(404) 730-3300

Rudy Suarez, District Officer
Federal Building, Room 928
51 SW First Avenue
P.O. Box 25
Miami, FL 33130
(305) 536-5054

Minorities

Georgia
Carlton Eccles, Director
401 West Peachtree Street,
NW, Room 1930
Atlanta, GA 30308-3516
(404) 730-3300

Guam
Xavier Mena, Director
221 Main Street, Room 1280
San Francisco, CA 94105
(415) 744-3001

Hawaii
Xavier Mena, Director
221 Main Street, Room 1280
San Francisco, CA 94105
(415) 744-3001

Idaho
Xavier Mena, Director
221 Main Street, Room 1280
San Francisco, CA 94105
(415) 744-3001

Illinois
David Vega, Director
55 East Monroe Street,
Suite 1440
Chicago, IL 60603
(312) 353-0182

Indiana
David Vega, Director
55 East Monroe Street,
Suite 1440
Chicago, IL 60603
(312) 353-0182

Iowa
David Vega, Director
55 East Monroe Street,
Suite 1440
Chicago, IL 60603
(312) 353-0182

Kansas
David Vega, Director
55 East Monroe Street,
Suite 1440
Chicago, IL 60603
(312) 353-0182

Kentucky
Carlton Eccles, Director
401 West Peachtree Street,
NW, Room 1930
Atlanta, GA 30308-3516
(404) 730-3300

Louisiana
Melda Cabrera, Director
1100 Commerce Street,
Room 7B23
Dallas, TX 75242
(214) 767-8001

Maine
John Iglehart, Director
26 Federal Plaza, Room 3720
New York, NY 10278
(212) 264-3262

Maryland
Georgina Sanchez, Director
14th and Constitution
Avenue, NW, Room 6711
Washington, DC 20230
(202) 377-8275

Massachusetts
John Iglehart, Director
26 Federal Plaza, Room 3720
New York, NY 10278
(212) 264-3262

R. K. Schwartz,
District Officer
10 Causeway Street,
Room 418
Boston, MA 02222-1041
(617) 565-6850

Michigan
David Vega, Director
55 East Monroe Street,
Suite 1440
Chicago, IL 60603
(312) 353-0182

Minnesota
David Vega, Director
55 East Monroe Street,
Suite 1440
Chicago, IL 60603
(312) 353-0182

Mississippi
Carlton Eccles, Director
401 West Peachtree Street,
NW, Room 1930
Atlanta, GA 30308-3516
(404) 730-3300

Missouri
David Vega, Director
55 East Monroe Street,
Suite 1440
Chicago, IL 60603
(312) 353-0182

Montana
Melda Cabrera, Director
1100 Commerce Street,
Room 7B23
Dallas, TX 75242
(214) 767-8001

Nebraska
David Vega, Director
55 East Monroe Street,
Suite 1440
Chicago, IL 60603
(312) 353-0182

Nevada
Xavier Mena, Director
221 Main Street, Room 1280
San Francisco, CA 94105
(415) 744-3001

New Hampshire
John Iglehart, Director
26 Federal Plaza, Room 3720
New York, NY 10278
(212) 264-3262

New Jersey
John Iglehart, Director
26 Federal Plaza, Room 3720
New York, NY 10278
(212) 264-3262

New Mexico
Melda Cabrera, Director
1100 Commerce Street,
Room 7B23
Dallas, TX 75242
(214) 767-8001

New York
John Iglehart, Director
26 Federal Plaza, Room 3720
New York, NY 10278
(212) 264-3262

North Carolina
Carlton Eccles, Director
401 West Peachtree Street,
NW, Room 1930
Atlanta, GA 30308-3516
(404) 730-3300

North Dakota
Melda Cabrera, Director
1100 Commerce Street,
Room 7B23
Dallas, TX 75242
(214) 767-8001

Ohio
David Vega, Director
55 East Monroe Street,
Suite 1440
Chicago, IL 60603
(312) 353-0182

Oklahoma
Melda Cabrera, Director
1100 Commerce Street,
Room 7B23
Dallas, TX 75242
(214) 767-8001

Oregon
Xavier Mena, Director
221 Main Street, Room 1280
San Francisco, CA 94105
(415) 744-3001

Pennsylvania
Georgina Sanchez, Director
14th and Constitution
Avenue, NW, Room 6711
Washington, DC 20230
(202) 377-8275

Alfonso Jackson,
District Officer
Federal Office Building,
Room 10128
600 Arch Street
Philadelphia, PA 19106
(215) 597-9236

District Officer
614-16 Federal Office
Building
1000 Liberty Avenue
Pittsburgh, PA 15222
(412) 722-6659

Puerto Rico
John Iglehart, Director
26 Federal Plaza, Room 3720
New York, NY 10278
(212) 264-3262

Rhode Island
John Iglehart, Director
26 Federal Plaza, Room 3720
New York, NY 10278
(212) 264-3262

South Carolina
Carlton Eccles, Director
401 West Peachtree Street,
NW, Room 1930
Atlanta, GA 30308-3516
(404) 730-3300

South Dakota
Melda Cabrera, Director
1100 Commerce Street,
Room 7B23
Dallas, TX 75242
(214) 767-8001

Tennessee
Carlton Eccles, Director
401 West Peachtree Street,
NW, Room 1930
Atlanta, GA 30308-3516
(404) 730-3300

Texas
Melda Cabrera, Director
1100 Commerce Street,
Room 7B23
Dallas, TX 75242
(214) 767-8001

Utah
Melda Cabrera, Director
1100 Commerce Street,
Room 7B23
Dallas, TX 75242
(214) 767-8001

Vermont
John Iglehart, Director
26 Federal Plaza, Room 3720
New York, NY 10278
(212) 264-3262

Virgin Islands
John Iglehart, Director
26 Federal Plaza, Room 3720
New York, NY 10278
(212) 264-3262

Virginia
Georgina Sanchez, Director
14th and Constitution
Avenue, NW, Room 6711
Washington, DC 20230
(202) 377-8275

West Virginia
Georgina Sanchez, Director
14th and Constitution
Avenue, NW, Room 6711
Washington, DC 20230
(202) 377-8275

Wyoming
Melda Cabrera, Director
1100 Commerce Street,
Room 7B23
Dallas, TX 75242
(214) 767-8001

Washington
Xavier Mena, Director
221 Main Street, Room 1280
San Francisco, CA 94105
(415) 744-3001

Wisconsin
David Vega, Director
55 East Monroe Street,
Suite 1440
Chicago, IL 60603
(312) 353-0182

NATIVE AMERICAN EMPLOYMENT AND TRAINING PROGRAMS

**Department of Labor
Employment and
Training Administration
Division of Indian and
Native American
Programs**
200 Constitution Avenue,
NW, Room N4641
Washington, DC 20210
(202) 535-0500

Description: Funds for employment, training programs, and services given to afford job training to native Americans facing barriers to employment. Limited to Indian tribes, bands or groups, Alaska native villages/groups, and Hawaiian native communities.
$ Given: Range: $13,732–$6.6 million; average: $331,250.
Application Information: Standard application forms as furnished by Federal agency required. Grantees must prepare four-year master plan addressing administrative, planning, and operational elements.
Deadline: January 1 of every year for notices of intent to apply.
Contact: Paul Mayrand

WOMEN'S SPECIAL EMPLOYMENT ASSISTANCE

Department of Labor
Women's Bureau
Office of the Secretary
Room 53305
Washington, DC 20210
(202) 523-6606

Description: Advisory services/counseling and dissemination of technical information for expansion, training, and employment opportunities for women especially in new technology and nontraditional occupations. Available for any individual (especially women) located in the United States or its territories.
$ Given: N/A
Application Information: Requests made to appropriate Department of Labor
Deadline: None
Contact: Dora E. Carrington, Chief
        Office of Administration Management
        or Regional Administrator in respective state

Alabama
Delores L. Crockett
Regional Administrator
1371 Peachtree Street, NE,
Room 323
Atlanta, GA 30367
(404) 347-4461

Alaska
Lazelle S. Johnson
Regional Administrator
1111 Third Avenue,
Room 885
Seattle, WA 98101-3211
(206) 553-1534

Arizona
Madeline Mixer
Regional Administrator
71 Stevenson Street,
Room 927
San Francisco, CA 94105
(415) 774-6678

Arkansas
Evelyn Smith
Regional Administrator
Federal Building, Suite 731
525 Griffin Street
Dallas, TX 75202
(214) 767-6985

California
Madeline Mixer
Regional Administrator
71 Stevenson Street,
Room 927
San Francisco, CA 94105
(415) 774-6678

Colorado
Oleta Crain
Regional Administrator
Federal Office Building,
Room 1452
1801 California Street,
Suite 905
Denver, CO 80202-2614
(303) 391-6755

Connecticut
Martha Izzi
Regional Administrator
One Congress Street
Boston, MA 02214
(617) 565-1988

Delaware
Helen E. Sherwood
Regional Administrator
Gateway Building,
Room 13280
3535 Market Street
Philadelphia, PA 19104
(215) 596-1183

Florida
Delores L. Crockett
Regional Administrator
1371 Peachtree Street, NE,
Room 323
Atlanta, GA 30367
(404) 347-4461

Georgia
Delores L. Crockett
Regional Administrator
1371 Peachtree Street, NE,
Room 323
Atlanta, GA 30367
(404) 347-4461

Hawaii
Madeline Mixer
Regional Administrator
71 Stevenson Street,
Room 927
San Francisco, CA 94105
(415) 774-6678

Idaho
Lazelle S. Johnson
Regional Administrator
1111 Third Avenue,
Room 885
Seattle, WA 98101-3211
(206) 553-1534

Minorities

Illinois
Sandra K. Frank
Regional Administrator
230 South Dearborn Street,
Room 1022
Chicago, IL 60604
(312) 353-6985

Indiana
Sandra K. Frank
Regional Administrator
230 South Dearborn Street,
Room 1022
Chicago, IL 60604
(312) 353-6985

Iowa
Rose A. Kemp
Regional Administrator
Federal Building, Room 2511
911 Walnut Street
Kansas City, MO 64106
(816) 426-6108

Kansas
Rose A. Kemp
Regional Administrator
Federal Building, Room 2511
911 Walnut Street
Kansas City, MO 64106
(816) 426-6108

Kentucky
Delores L. Crockett
Regional Administrator
1371 Peachtree Street, NE,
Room 323
Atlanta, GA 30367
(404) 347-4461

Louisiana
Evelyn Smith
Regional Administrator
Federal Building, Suite 731
525 Griffin Street
Dallas, TX 75202
(214) 767-6985

Maine
Martha Izzi
Regional Administrator
One Congress Street
Boston, MA 02214
(617) 565-1988

Maryland
Helen E. Sherwood
Regional Administrator
Gateway Building,
Room 13280
3535 Market Street
Philadelphia, PA 19104
(215) 596-1183

Massachusetts
Martha Izzi
Regional Administrator
One Congress Street
Boston, MA 02214
(617) 565-1988

Michigan
Sandra K. Frank
Regional Administrator
230 South Dearborn Street,
Room 1022
Chicago, IL 60604
(312) 353-6985

Minnesota
Sandra K. Frank
Regional Administrator
230 South Dearborn Street,
Room 1022
Chicago, IL 60604
(312) 353-6985

Mississippi
Delores L. Crockett
Regional Administrator
1371 Peachtree Street, NE,
Room 323
Atlanta, GA 30367
(404) 347-4461

Missouri
Rose A. Kemp
Regional Administrator
Federal Building, Room 2511
911 Walnut Street
Kansas City, MO 64106
(816) 426-6108

Montana
Oleta Crain
Regional Administrator
Federal Office Building,
Room 1452
1801 California Street,
Suite 905
Denver, CO 80202-2614
(303) 391-6755

Nebraska
Rose A. Kemp
Regional Administrator
Federal Building, Room 2511
911 Walnut Street
Kansas City, MO 64106
(816) 426-6108

Nevada
Madeline Mixer
Regional Administrator
71 Stevenson Street,
Room 927
San Francisco, CA 94105
(415) 774-6678

New Hampshire
Martha Izzi
Regional Administrator
One Congress Street
Boston, MA 02214
(617) 565-1988

New Jersey
Mary C. Murphree
Regional Administrator
201 Varick Street, Room 601
New York, NY 10014
(212) 337-2389

New Mexico
Evelyn Smith
Regional Administrator
Federal Building, Suite 731
525 Griffin Street
Dallas, TX 75202
(214) 767-6985

New York
Mary C. Murphree
Regional Administrator
201 Varick Street, Room 601
New York, NY 10014
(212) 337-2389

North Carolina
Delores L. Crockett
Regional Administrator
1371 Peachtree Street, NE,
Room 323
Atlanta, GA 30367
(404) 347-4461

North Dakota
Oleta Crain
Regional Administrator
Federal Office Building,
Room 1452
1801 California Street,
Suite 905
Denver, CO 80202-2614
(303) 391-6755

Ohio
Sandra K. Frank
Regional Administrator
230 South Dearborn Street,
Room 1022
Chicago, IL 60604
(312) 353-6985

Oklahoma
Evelyn Smith
Regional Administrator
Federal Building, Suite 731
525 Griffin Street
Dallas, TX 75202
(214) 767-6985

Oregon
Lazelle S. Johnson
Regional Administrator
1111 Third Avenue,
Room 885
Seattle, WA 98101-3211
(206) 553-1534

Pennsylvania
Helen E. Sherwood
Regional Administrator
Gateway Building,
Room 13280
3535 Market Street
Philadelphia, PA 19104
(215) 596-1183

Puerto Rico
Mary C. Murphree
Regional Administrator
201 Varick Street, Room 601
New York, NY 10014
(212) 337-2389

Rhode Island
Martha Izzi
Regional Administrator
One Congress Street
Boston, MA 02214
(617) 565-1988

South Carolina
Delores L. Crockett
Regional Administrator
1371 Peachtree Street, NE,
Room 323
Atlanta, GA 30367
(404) 347-4461

South Dakota
Oleta Crain
Regional Administrator
Federal Office Building,
Room 1452
1801 California Street,
Suite 905
Denver, CO 80202-2614
(303) 391-6755

Tennessee
Delores L. Crockett
Regional Administrator
1371 Peachtree Street, NE,
Room 323
Atlanta, GA 30367
(404) 347-4461

Texas
Evelyn Smith
Regional Administrator
Federal Building, Suite 731
525 Griffin Street
Dallas, TX 75202
(214) 767-6985

Utah
Oleta Crain
Regional Administrator
Federal Office Building,
Room 1452
1801 California Street,
Suite 905
Denver, CO 80202-2614
(303) 391-6755

Vermont
Martha Izzi
Regional Administrator
One Congress Street
Boston, MA 02214
(617) 565-1988

Virgin Islands
Mary C. Murphree
Regional Administrator
201 Varick Street, Room 601
New York, NY 10014
(212) 337-2389

Virginia
Helen E. Sherwood
Regional Administrator
Gateway Building,
Room 13280
3535 Market Street
Philadelphia, PA 19104
(215) 596-1183

Minorities

Washington
Lazelle S. Johnson
Regional Administrator
1111 Third Avenue,
Room 885
Seattle, WA 98101-3211
(206) 553-1534

Washington, DC
Helen E. Sherwood
Regional Administrator
Gateway Building,
Room 13280
3535 Market Street
Philadelphia, PA 19104
(215) 596-1183

West Virginia
Helen E. Sherwood
Regional Administrator
Gateway Building,
Room 13280
3535 Market Street
Philadelphia, PA 19104
(215) 596-1183

Wisconsin
Sandra K. Frank
Regional Administration
230 South Dearborn Street,
Room 1022
Chicago, IL 60604
(312) 353-6985

Wyoming
Oleta Crain
Regional Administrator
Federal Office Building,
Room 1452
1801 California Street,
Suite 905
Denver, CO 80202-2614
(303) 391-6755

Housing

Assistance is widely available from the federal government for owners and builders of housing units for the following:

1. Assistance for owners and builders of multifamily housing projects, low- or moderate-income projects, and nursing homes and housing for the elderly; funds are available for restoration, maintenance, or construction

2. Guaranteed insured loans to businesses to provide mortgage insurance for rental units or single-room occupancy units, or to develop condominium projects, manufactured home parks, or rental housing in urban renewal areas

3. Loans for individuals to finance home improvements, repairs, or home purchases or to refinance building units

You will need to consult the list of addresses in this chapter for your nearest local or regional Housing and Urban Development office.

MANUFACTURED HOME LOAN INSURANCE—FINANCING PURCHASE OF MANUFACTURED HOMES AS PRINCIPAL RESIDENCES OF BORROWERS

Department of Housing and Urban Development (HUD)
Title I Insurance Division
Washington, DC 20410
(800) 733-4663
(202) 708-2880

Description: Guaranteed/insured loans to all persons to make possible reasonable financing of home purchases. Buyers must intend to use homes as principal place of residence. Maximum loan: $40,500.
$ Given: Through September 30, 1991, 403,696 loans approved for $7 billion.
Application Information: Apply through HUD-approved lender or dealer.
Deadline: None
Contact: Director, above address

MORTGAGE INSURANCE—CONSTRUCTION OR SUBSTANTIAL REHABILITATION OF CONDOMINIUM PROJECTS

Department of Housing and Urban Development
Policies and Procedures Division
Office of Insured Multifamily Housing Development
Washington, DC 20410
(202) 708-2556

Description: Guaranteed/insured loans for private, profit-motivated individuals to develop condominium projects. Restrictions vary with size of project.
$ Given: Nationwide FY 93 est. $10. 3 million insured mortgages.
Application Information: Initial conference with local HUD field office. If project feasible, formal mortgage insurance application submitted through HUD-approved mortgagee to local HUD Office.
Deadline: Established on case-by-case basis at local HUD offices.
Contact: Nearest local HUD field office

Alabama
Robert E. Lunsford, Manager
600 Beacon Parkway West, Suite 300
Birmingham, AL 35209-3144
(205) 731-1617

Alaska
Arlene Patton, Manager
222 West 8th Avenue, #64
Anchorage, AK 99513-7537
(907) 271-4170

Community Planning and Development Division
222 West 8th Avenue, #64
Anchorage, AK 99513-7537
(907) 271-3669

American Samoa
Gordon Y. Furutani, Manager
300 Ala Moana Boulevard,
Room 3318
Honolulu, HI 96850-4991
(808) 546-2136

Arizona
Dwight Peterson, Manager
400 North First Street,
Suite 1600
P.O. Box 13468
Phoenix, AZ 85004-2361
(602) 261-4434

Charles Ming, Manager
1615 West Olympic
Boulevard
Los Angeles, CA 90015-3801
(213) 251-7122

Jean Staley, Manager
Pioneer Plaza, 100 North
Stone Avenue, Suite 410
P.O. Box 2648
Tucson, AZ 86701-1467
(602) 629-6237

Arkansas
Roger Zachritz, Acting
Manager
Lafayette Building, Suite 200
523 Louisiana
Little Rock, AR 72201-3523
(501) 378-5931

California
Lilly Lee, Manager
1630 East Shaw Avenue,
Suite 138
Fresno, CA 93710-8193
(209) 487-5033

(San Francisco Regional
Office)
Robert De Monte, Regional
Housing Commissioner
Phillip Burton Federal
Building and U.S Courthouse
450 Golden Gate Avenue
P.O. Box 36003
San Francisco, CA
94102-3448
(415) 556-4752

(North California)
Office of Indian Programs
Community Planning and
Development Division
San Francisco Program
Management Team
Phillip Burton Federal
Building and U.S.
Courthouse
450 Golden Gate Avenue
P.O. Box 36003
San Francisco, CA
94102-3448
(415) 556-9200

(Northeast California)
Anthony A. Randolph,
Manager
777 12th Street, Suite 200
P.O. Box 1978
Sacramento, CA 95814-1997
(916) 551-1351

(Imperial and San Diego
Counties)
Charles J. Wilson, Manager
Federal Office Building,
Room 563
880 Front Street
San Diego, CA 92188-0100
(619) 557-5310

(Orange, Riverside and San
Bernardino Counties, for
home mortgages)
Harold A. Matzoll, Acting
Manager
34 Civic Center Plaza,
Box 12850
Santa Ana, CA 92712-2850
(714) 836-2451

(South California)
Charles Ming, Manager
1615 West Olympic
Boulevard
Los Angeles, CA 90015-3801
(213) 251-7122

Colorado
Michael Chitwood, Regional
Administrator
Regional Housing
Commissioner
HUD Denver Regional Office
Executive Tower Building
1405 Curtis Street
Denver, CO 80202-2349
(303) 844-4513

Office of Indian Programs
Housing and Community
Development Division
Executive Tower Building
1405 Curtis Street
Denver, CO 80202-2349
(303) 844-2861

Connecticut
William Hernandez, Jr.,
Manager
330 Main Street, First Floor
Hartford, CT 06106-1860
(203) 240-4523

Delaware
A. David Sharbaugh, Chief
Federal Building, Room 1304
844 King Street
Wilmington, DE 19801-3519
(302) 573-6300

District of Columbia
(Washington, D.C. Regional
Office)
Toni Thomas, Manager
Union Center Plaza, Phase II
820 First Street, NE,
Suite 300
Washington, DC 20002-4205
(202) 275-9200

Florida
James T. Chaplin, Manager
325 West Adams Street
Jacksonville, FL 32202-4303
(904) 791-2626

Housing

(Counties of Citrus, Sumter,
Hernando, Pasco, Pinellas,
Hillsborough, Polk, Manatee,
Hardee, Highlands, DeSoto,
Sarasota, Charlotte, Olaoes,
Hendry, Lake Okeechobee)
George A. Milburn, Jr.,
Manager
Timberlake Federal Building
Annex, Suite 700
501 East Polk Street
Tampa, FL 33602-3945
(813) 228-2501

(Counties of Volusia, Lake,
Seminole, Orange, Brevard,
Osceola, Indian River,
Okeechobee, St. Lucie)
M. Jeanette Porter, Manager
Langley Building, Suite 270
3751 Maguire Boulevard
Orlando, FL 32803-3032
(407) 648-6441

(South Florida)
Orlando L. Lorie, Manager
Gables 1 Tower
1320 South Dixie Highway
Coral Gables, FL 33146-2911
(305) 662-4510

Georgia
Raymond A. Harris, Regional
Housing Commissioner
Richard B. Russell Federal
Building
75 Spring Street, SW
Atlanta, GA 30303-3388
(404) 331-5136

Guam
Gordon Y. Furutani, Manager
300 Ala Moana Boulevard,
Room 3318
Honolulu, HI 96850-4991
(808) 546-2136

Hawaii
Gordon Y. Furutani, Manager
300 Ala Moana Boulevard,
Room 3318
Honolulu, HI 96850-4991
(808) 546-2136

Idaho
(North Idaho)
Keith R. Green, Manager
Farm Credit Bank Building,
Eighth Floor East
West 601 1st Avenue
Spokane, WA 99204-0317
(509) 456-2624

(West-Central Idaho)
Gary Gillespie, Manager
Federal Building and U.S.
Courthouse
P.O. Box 042
550 West Fort Street
Boise, ID 83724-0420
(208) 334-1990

(South Idaho)
Richard C. Brinck, Manager
Cascade Building
520 SW 6th Avenue
Portland, OR 97204-1596
(503) 221-2561

Illinois
Chicago Office of Indian
Programs
Housing Development
Division
626 West Jackson Boulevard
Chicago, IL 60606-5601
(312) 353-1684

(Chicago Regional Office)
Gertrude Jordan,
Regional Housing
Commissioner
626 West Jackson Boulevard
Chicago, IL 60606-5601
(312) 353-5680

(Central and South Illinois)
John Lawler, Acting
Supervisory Appraiser
Lincoln Towers Plaza,
Suite 672
524 South Second Street
Springfield, IL 62701-1774
(217) 492-4085

Indiana
J. Nicholas Shelley, Manager
151 North Delaware Street
Indianapolis, IN 46204-2526
(317) 226-6303

Iowa
Roger M. Massey, Manager
Braiker/Brandeis Building
210 South 16th Street
Omaha, NE 68102-1622
(402) 221-3703

William R. McNarney,
Manager
HUD Des Moines Office
Federal Building, Room 259
210 Walnut Street
Des Moines, IA 50309-2155
(515) 284-4512

Kansas
William H. Brown, Regional
Administrator
Regional Housing
Commissioner
HUD Kansas City, Regional
Office
Gateway Tower II
400 State Avenue
Kansas City, KS 66101-2406
(913) 236-2162

Kentucky
Verna V. Van Ness, Manager
601 West Broadway
P.O. Box 1044
Louisville, KY 40201-1044
(502) 582-5251

Louisiana
Robert Vasquez, Manager
Fisk Federal Building,
1661 Canal Street
P.O. Box 70288
New Orleans, LA 70112-2887
(504) 589-7200

(North Louisiana)
David E. Gleason, Manager
New Federal Building
500 Fannin Street
Shreveport, LA 71101-3077
(318) 226-5385

Maine
Richard Young, Supervisory
Appraiser
Casco Northern Bank
Building
23 Main Street
Bangor, ME 04401-4318
(207) 945-0467

James Barry, Manager
Norris Cotton Federal
Building
275 Chestnut Street
Manchester, NH 03101-2487
(603) 666-7681

Maryland
(Except Montgomery and
Prince Georges Counties)
Maxine Saunders, Manager
The Equitable Building,
Third Floor
10 North Calvert Street
Baltimore, MD 21202-1865
(301) 962-2121

(Montgomery and Prince
Georges Counties)
Toni Thomas, Manager
Union Center Plaza, Phase II
820 First Street, NE,
Suite 300
Washington, DC 20002-4205
(202) 275-9200

Massachusetts
John Mastropietro,
Acting Regional
Administrator
Regional Housing
Commissioner
Boston Federal Office
Building, Room 375
10 Causeway Street
Boston, MA 02222-1092
(617) 565-5234

Michigan
Harry I. Sharrott, Manager
Patrick V. McNamara Federal
Building
477 Michigan Avenue
Detroit, MI 48226-2592
(313) 226-6280

(East Michigan)
Gary T. LeVine, Manager
Gil Sabuco Building,
Room 200
352 South Saginaw Street
Flint, MI 48502-1953
(313) 766-5112

(West and North Michigan)
Ronald Weston, Manager
Northbrook Building, No. II
2922 Fuller Avenue, NE
Grand Rapids, MI 48505-3409
(616) 456-2100

Minnesota
Thomas Feeney, Manager
Bridge Place Building
220 Second Street, South
Minneapolis, MN 55401-2195
(612) 370-3000

Mississippi
Sandra Freeman, Manager
Dr. A. H. McCoy Federal
Building, Room 910
100 West Capitol Street
Jackson, MS 39269-1096
(601) 965-4702

Missouri
Kenneth G. Lange, Manager
210 North Tucker Boulevard
St. Louis, MO 63101-1997
(314) 425-4761

Montana
Christian KaFentzis, Manager
Federal Office Building,
Room 340
Drawer 10095
301 South Park
Helena, MT 59626-0095
(406) 449-5205

Nebraska
Roger M. Massey, Manager
Braiker/Brandeis Building
210 South 16th Street
Omaha, NE 68102-1622
(402) 221-3703

Nevada
Andrew D. Whitten, Jr.,
Manager
1050 Bible Way
P.O. Box 4700
Reno, NV 89505-4700
(702) 784-5356

Andrew Robertson, Manager
1500 East Tropicana Avenue,
Second Floor
Las Vegas, NV 89119-6516
(702) 388-6500

(North Nevada)
Office of Indian Programs
Community Planning and
Development Division
San Francisco Program
Management Team
Phillip Burton Federal
Building and U.S.
Courthouse
450 Golden Gate Avenue
P.O. Box 36003
San Francisco, CA
94102-3448
(415) 556-9200

New Hampshire
James Barry, Manager
Norris Cotton Federal
Building
275 Chestnut Street
Manchester, NH 03101-2487
(603) 666-7681

New Jersey
(North New Jersey)
Theodore Britton, Jr.,
Manager
Military Park Building
60 Park Place
Newark, NJ 07102-5504
(201) 887-1662

Housing

(South New Jersey)
Elmer Roy, Manager
The Parkade Building
519 Federal Street
Camden, NJ 08103-9998
(609) 757-5081

New Mexico
Michael R. Griego, Manager
625 Truman Street, NE
Albuquerque, NM
87110-6443
(505) 262-6463

C. Don Babers, Acting
Manager
555 Griffin Square Building,
Room 106
525 Griffin Street
Dallas, TX 75202-5007
(214) 767-8308

New York
Dr. Anthony Villane, Regional
Housing Commissioner
26 Federal Plaza
New York, NY 10278-0068
(212) 264-8068

(North New York)
John Petricco, Manager
Leo W. O'Brien Federal
Building
North Pearl Street and
Clinton Avenue
Albany, NY 12207-2395
(518) 472-3567

(West New York)
Joseph Lynch, Manager
465 Main Street, Fifth Floor
Lafayette Court
Buffalo, NY 14203-1780
(716) 846-5755

North Carolina
Larry J. Parker, Manager
415 North Edgeworth Street
Greensboro, NC 27401-2107
(919) 333-5363

North Dakota
Keith Elliot, Chief
Federal Building, Room 300
653 2nd Avenue, North
P.O. Box 2483
Fargo, ND 58108-2483
(701) 239-5136

Ohio
Robert W. Dolin, Manager
New Federal Building
200 North High Street
Columbus, OH 43215-2499
(614) 469-5737

(North Ohio)
George L. Engel, Manager
One Playhouse Square
1375 Euclid Avenue,
Room 420
Cleveland, OH 44115-1832
(216) 522-4065

(Southwest Ohio)
William Harris, Manager
Federal Office Building,
Room 9002
550 Main Street
Cincinnati, OH 45202-3253
(513) 684-2884

Oklahoma
Edwin I. Gardner, Manager
Murrah Federal Building
200 NW 5th Street
Oklahoma City, OK
73102-3202
(405) 231-4181

Indian Programs Division
Hugh Johnson, Director
Community Planning and
Development Branch
Murrah Federal Building
200 NW 5th Street
Oklahoma City, OK
73102-3202
(405) 231-4101

(East Oklahoma)
Robert H. Gardner, Manager
Robert S. Kerr Building,
Room 200
440 South Houston Avenue
Tulsa, OK 74127-8923
(918) 581-7435

Oregon
Richard C. Brinck, Manager
Cascade Building
520 SW 6th Avenue
Portland, OR 97204-1596
(503) 221-2561

Panama Canal Zone
Rosa Villalonga, Acting
Manager
159 Carlos Chardon Avenue
San Juan, PR 00918-1804
(809) 766-5201 or
(809) 498-5201

Pennsylvania
(Philadelphia Regional
Office)
Michael A. Smerconish,
Regional Administrator
Regional Housing
Commissioner
Liberty Square Building
105 South 7th Street
Philadelphia, PA 19106-3392
(215) 597-2560

(West Pennsylvania)
William Costello, Acting
Manager
412 Old Post Office
Courthouse Building
7th Avenue and Grant Street
Pittsburgh, PA 15219-1906
(412) 644-6428

Puerto Rico
Rosa Villalonga, Acting
Manager
159 Carlos Chardon Avenue
San Juan, PR 00918-1804
(809) 766-5201 or
(809) 498-5201

Rhode Island
Casimir J. Kolaski, Jr.,
Manager
Federal Building and U.S.
Post Office, Room 330
Kennedy Plaza
Providence, RI 02903-1745
(401) 528-5351

South Carolina
Ted B. Freeman, Manager
Strom Thurmond Federal
Building
1835-45 Assembly Street
Columbia, SC 29201-2480
(803) 765-5592

South Dakota
Don Olson, Chief
Courthouse Plaza, Suite 116
300 North Dakota Avenue
Sioux Falls, SD 57102-0311
(605) 330-4223

Tennessee
Richard B. Barnwell,
Manager
John J. Duncan Federal
Building
710 Locust Street, SW
Knoxville, TN 37902-2526
(615) 549-9384

(Central Tennessee)
John H. Fisher, Manager
251 Cumberland Bend Drive,
Suite 200
Nashville, TN 37228-1803
(615) 736-5213

(West Tennessee)
Bob Atkins, Manager
One Memphis Place,
Suite 1200
200 Jefferson Avenue
Memphis, TN 38103-2335
(901) 521-3367

Texas
(Fort Worth Regional Office)
Sam R. Moseley, Regional
Housing Commissioner
Regional Housing
Commissioner
1600 Throckmorton
P.O. Box 2905
Forth Worth, TX 76113-2905
(817) 885-5401

(Northwest Texas)
Henry E. Whitney, Manager
Federal Office Building
1205 Texas Avenue
Lubbock, TX 79401-4093
(806) 743-7265

(East, North, and West
Texas)
C. Don Babers, Acting
Manager
555 Griffin Square Building,
Room 106
525 Griffin Street
Dallas, TX 75202-5007
(214) 767-8308

(Five Counties in East Texas)
David E. Gleason, Manager
New Federal Building
500 Fannin Street
Shreveport, LA 71101-3077
(318) 226-5385

(East-Central Texas)
William Robertson, Jr.,
Manager
National Bank of Texas
Building, Suite 300
221 Norfolk
Houston, TX 77098-4096
(713) 229-3589

(Bowie County)
Roger Zachritz, Acting
Manager
Lafayette Building, Suite 200
523 Louisiana
Little Rock, AR 72201-3523
(501) 378-5931

(Southwest Texas)
Don Creed, Manager
Washington Square Building
800 Dolorosa Street
San Antonio, TX 78207-4563
(512) 229-6781

Utah
Richard Bell, Manager
324 South State Street,
Suite 220
Salt Lake City, UT
84111-2321
(801) 524-5237

Vermont
William Peters, Chief
Federal Building, Room B311
11 Elmwood Avenue
P.O. Box 879
Burlington, VT 05402-0879
(802) 951-6290

James Barry, Manager
Norris Cotton Federal
Building
275 Chestnut Street
Manchester, NH 03101-2487
(603) 666-7681

Virgin Islands
Rosa Villalonga, Acting
Manager
159 Carlos Chardon Avenue
San Juan, PR 00918-1804
(809) 766-5201 or
(809) 498-5201

Virginia
(North Virginia)
Toni Thomas, Manager
Union Center Plaza, Phase II
820 First Street, NE,
Suite 300
Washington, DC 20002-4205
(202) 275-9200

(South Virginia)
Mary Ann Wilson, Manager
Federal Building, First Floor
400 North Eighth Street
Richmond, VA 23240-0170
(804) 771-2721

Washington
Office of Indian Programs
Community Planning and
Development Division
Arcade Plaza Building
1321 Second Avenue
Seattle, WA 98101-2058
(206) 442-0760

(Seattle Regional Office)
Richard Bauer,
Regional Housing
Commissioner
Arcade Plaza Building
1321 Second Avenue
Seattle, WA 98101-2054
(206) 442-5414

(East Washington)
Keith R. Green, Manager
Farm Credit Bank Building,
Eighth Floor East
West 601 1st Avenue
Spokane, WA 99204-0317
(509) 456-2624

(Clark, Klickitat, and
Skamania Counties)
Richard C. Brinck, Manager
Cascade Building
520 SW 6th Avenue
Portland, OR 97204-1596
(503) 221-2561

West Virginia
William Costello, Acting
Manager
412 Old Post Office
Courthouse Building
7th Avenue and Grant Street
Pittsburgh, PA 15219-1906
(412) 644-6428

or:

405 Capitol Street, Suite 708
Charleston, WV 25301-1795
(304) 347-7000

Wisconsin
Delbert F. Reynolds,
Manager
Henry S. Reuss Federal Plaza
310 West Wisconsin Avenue,
Suite 1380
Milwaukee, WI 53203-2289
(414) 291-3214

Wyoming
Lawrence Gosnell, Chief
4225 Federal Office Building
100 East B Street
P.O. Box 580
Casper, WY 82602-1918
(307) 261-5252

MORTGAGE INSURANCE—EXPERIMENTAL HOMES

**Department of Housing
and Urban Development**
Policy Development and
Research
Division of Innovative
Technology
451 7th Street, SW
Washington, DC 20410
(202) 708-0640

Description: Guaranteed/insured loans to home
builders to provide mortgage insurance for homes
incorporating new or untried construction concepts
that may reduce housing costs, raise living standards,
and improve neighborhood design.
$ Given: To date, 600 units insured for $10 million.
Application Information: Submit application to local
HUD field office.
Deadline: Established on case-by-case basis at local
HUD field office.
Contact: Nearest local HUD field office

Alabama
Robert E. Lunsford, Manager
600 Beacon Parkway West,
Suite 300
Birmingham, AL 35209-3144
(205) 731-1617

Alaska
Arlene Patton, Manager
222 West 8th Avenue, #64
Anchorage, AK 99513-7537
(907) 271-4170

Community Planning and
Development Division
222 West 8th Avenue, #64
Anchorage, AK 99513-7537
(907) 271-3669

American Samoa
Gordon Y. Furutani, Manager
300 Ala Moana Boulevard,
Room 3318
Honolulu, HI 96850-4991
(808) 546-2136

Arizona
Dwight Peterson, Manager
P.O. Box 13468
Phoenix, AZ 85004-2361
(602) 261-4434

Charles Ming, Manager
1615 West Olympic
Boulevard
Los Angeles, CA 90015-3801
(213) 251-7122

Jean Staley, Manager
Pioneer Plaza, 100 North
Stone Avenue, Suite 410
P.O. Box 2648
Tucson, AZ 86701-1467
(602) 629-6237

Arkansas
Roger Zachritz, Acting
Manager
Lafayette Building, Suite 200
523 Louisiana
Little Rock, AR 72201-3523
(501) 378-5931

California
Lilly Lee, Manager
1630 East Shaw Avenue,
Suite 138
Fresno, CA 93710-8193
(209) 487-5033

(San Francisco Regional
Office)
John Wilson, Regional
Housing Commissioner
Phillip Burton Federal
Building and U.S Courthouse
450 Golden Gate Avenue
P.O. Box 36003
San Francisco, CA
94102-3448
(415) 556-4752

(North California)
Office of Indian Programs
Community Planning and
Development Division
San Francisco Program
Management Team
Phillip Burton Federal
Building and U.S.
Courthouse
450 Golden Gate Avenue
P.O. Box 36003
San Francisco, CA
94102-3448
(415) 556-9200

(Northeast California)
Anthony A. Randolph,
Manager
777 12th Street, Suite 200
P.O. Box 1978
Sacramento, CA 95814-1997
(916) 551-1351

(Imperial and San Diego
Counties)
Charles J. Wilson, Manager
Federal Office Building,
Room 563
880 Front Street
San Diego, CA 92188-0100
(619) 557-5310

(Orange, Riverside and San
Bernardino Counties, for
home mortgages)
Earl Fields, Manager
34 Civic Center Plaza,
Box 12850
Santa Ana, CA 92712-2850
(714) 836-2451

(South California)
Charles Ming, Manager
1615 West Olympic
Boulevard
Los Angeles, CA 90015-3801
(213) 251-7122

Colorado
Michael Chitwood, Regional
Administrator
Regional Housing
Commissioner
HUD Denver Regional Office
Executive Tower Building
1405 Curtis Street
Denver, CO 80202-2349
(303) 844-4513

Office of Indian Programs
Housing and Community
Development Division
Executive Tower Building
1405 Curtis Street
Denver, CO 80202-2349
(303) 844-2861

Connecticut
William Hernandez, Jr.,
Manager
330 Main Street, First Floor
Hartford, CT 06106-1860
(203) 240-4523

Delaware
A. David Sharbaugh, Chief
Federal Building, Room 1304
844 King Street
Wilmington, DE 19801-3519
(302) 573-6300

District of Columbia
(Washington, D.C. Regional
Office)
Toni Thomas, Manager
Union Center Plaza, Phase II
820 First Street, NE,
Suite 300
Washington, DC 20002-4205
(202) 275-9200

Florida
James T. Chaplin, Manager
325 West Adams Street
Jacksonville, FL 32202-4303
(904) 791-2626

Housing

(Counties of Citrus, Sumter, Hernando, Pasco, Pinellas, Hillsborough, Polk, Manatee, Hardee, Highlands, DeSoto, Sarasota, Charlotte, Olaoes, Hendry, Lake Okeechobee)
George A. Milburn, Jr., Manager
Timberlake Federal Building Annex, Suite 700
501 East Polk Street
Tampa, FL 33602-3945
(813) 228-2501

(Counties of Volusia, Lake, Seminole, Orange, Brevard, Osceola, Indian River, Okeechobee, St. Lucie)
M. Jeanette Porter, Manager
Langley Building, Suite 270
3751 Maguire Boulevard
Orlando, FL 32803-3032
(407) 648-6441

(South Florida)
Orlando L. Lorie, Manager
Gables I Tower
1320 South Dixie Highway
Coral Gables, FL 33146-2911
(305) 662-4510

Georgia
Raymond A. Harris, Regional Housing Commissioner
Richard B. Russell Federal Building
75 Spring Street, SW
Atlanta, GA 30303-3388
(404) 331-5136

Guam
Gordon Y. Furutani, Manager
300 Ala Moana Boulevard, Room 3318
Honolulu, HI 96850-4991
(808) 546-2136

Hawaii
Gordon Y. Furutani, Manager
300 Ala Moana Boulevard, Room 3318
Honolulu, HI 96850-4991
(808) 546-2136

Idaho
(North Idaho)
Keith R. Green, Manager
Farm Credit Bank Building, Eighth Floor East
West 601 1st Avenue
Spokane, WA 99204-0317
(509) 456-2624

(West-Central Idaho)
Gary Gillespie, Manager
Federal Building and U.S. Courthouse
P.O. Box 042
550 West Fort Street
Boise, ID 83724-0420
(208) 334-1990

(South Idaho)
Richard C. Brinck, Manager
Cascade Building
520 SW 6th Avenue
Portland, OR 97204-1596
(503) 221-2561

Illinois
Chicago Office of Indian Programs
Housing Development Division
626 West Jackson Boulevard
Chicago, IL 60606-5601
(312) 353-1684

(Chicago Regional Office)
Gertrude Jordan,
Regional Housing Commissioner
626 West Jackson Boulevard
Chicago, IL 60606-5601
(312) 353-5680

(Central and South Illinois)
William Fattic, Manager
Lincoln Towers Plaza, Suite 672
524 South Second Street
Springfield, IL 62701-1774
(217) 492-4085

Indiana
J. Nicholas Shelley, Manager
151 North Delaware Street
Indianapolis, IN 46204-2526
(317) 226-6303

Iowa
Roger M. Massey, Manager
Braiker/Brandeis Building
210 South 16th Street
Omaha, NE 68102-1622
(402) 221-3703

William R. McNarney, Manager
HUD Des Moines Office
Federal Building, Room 259
210 Walnut Street
Des Moines, IA 50309-2155
(515) 284-4512

Kansas
William H. Brown, Regional Administrator
Regional Housing Commissioner
HUD Kansas City, Regional Office
Gateway Tower II
400 State Avenue
Kansas City, KS 66101-2406
(913) 236-2162

Kentucky
Verna V. Van Ness, Manager
601 West Broadway
P.O. Box 1044
Louisville, KY 40201-1044
(502) 582-5251

Louisiana
Robert Vasquez, Manager
Fisk Federal Building,
1661 Canal Street
P.O. Box 70288
New Orleans, LA 70112-2887
(504) 589-7200

(North Louisiana)
David E. Gleason, Manager
New Federal Building
500 Fannin Street
Shreveport, LA 71101-3077
(318) 226-5385

Housing

Maine
Richard Young, Supervisory
Appraiser
Casco Northern Bank
Building
23 Main Street
Bangor, ME 04401-4318
(207) 945-0467

James Barry, Manager
Norris Cotton Federal
Building
275 Chestnut Street
Manchester, NH 03101-2487
(603) 666-7681

Maryland
(Except Montgomery and
Prince Georges Counties)
Maxine Saunders, Manager
The Equitable Building,
Third Floor
10 North Calvert Street
Baltimore, MD 21202-1865
(301) 962-2121

(Montgomery and Prince
Georges Counties)
Toni Thomas, Manager
Union Center Plaza, Phase II
820 First Street, NE,
Suite 300
Washington, DC 20002-4205
(202) 275-9200

Massachusetts
John Mastropietro,
Acting Regional
Administrator
Regional Housing
Commissioner
Boston Federal Office
Building, Room 375
10 Causeway Street
Boston, MA 02222-1092
(617) 565-5234

Michigan
Harry I. Sharrott, Manager
Patrick V. McNamara Federal
Building
477 Michigan Avenue
Detroit, MI 48226-2592
(313) 226-6280

(East Michigan)
Gary T. LeVine, Manager
Gil Sabuco Building, Room
200
352 South Saginaw Street
Flint, MI 48502-1953
(313) 766-5112

(West and North Michigan)
Ronald Weston, Manager
Northbrook Building, No. II
2922 Fuller Avenue, NE
Grand Rapids, MI 48505-3409
(616) 456-2100

Minnesota
Thomas Feeney, Manager
Bridge Place Building
220 Second Street, South
Minneapolis, MN 55401-2195
(612) 370-3000

Mississippi
Sandra Freeman, Manager
Dr. A. H. McCoy Federal
Building, Room 910
100 West Capitol Street
Jackson, MS 39269-1096
(601) 965-4702

Missouri
Kenneth G. Lange, Manager
210 North Tucker Boulevard
St. Louis, MO 63101-1997
(314) 425-4761

Montana
Christian KaFentzis, Manager
Federal Office Building,
Room 340
Drawer 10095
301 South Park
Helena, MT 59626-0095
(406) 449-5205

Nebraska
Roger M. Massey, Manager
Braiker/Brandeis Building
210 South 16th Street
Omaha, NE 68102-1622
(402) 221-3703

Nevada
Andrew D. Whitten, Jr.,
Manager
1050 Bible Way
P.O. Box 4700
Reno, NV 89505-4700
(702) 784-5356

Andrew Robertson, Manager
1500 East Tropicana Avenue,
Second Floor
Las Vegas, NV 89119-6516
(702) 388-6500

(North Nevada)
Office of Indian Programs
Community Planning and
Development Division
San Francisco Program
Management Team
Phillip Burton Federal
Building and U.S.
Courthouse
450 Golden Gate Avenue
P.O. Box 36003
San Francisco, CA
94102-3448
(415) 556-9200

New Hampshire
David B. Harrity, Manager
Norris Cotton Federal
Building
275 Chestnut Street
Manchester, NH 03101-2487
(603) 666-7681

New Jersey
(North New Jersey)
Diane J. Johnson, Deputy
Manager
Military Park Building
60 Park Place
Newark, NJ 07102-5504
(201) 877-1662

Housing

(South New Jersey)
Elmer Roy, Manager
The Parkade Building
519 Federal Street
Camden, NJ 08103-9998
(609) 757-5081

New Mexico
Michael R. Griego, Manager
625 Truman Street, NE
Albuquerque, NM
87110-6443
(505) 262-6463

C. Don Babers, Acting
Manager
555 Griffin Square Building,
Room 106
525 Griffin Street
Dallas, TX 75202-5007
(214) 767-8308

New York
Dr. Anthony Villane, Regional
Housing Commissioner
26 Federal Plaza
New York, NY 10278-0068
(212) 264-8068

(North New York)
John Petricco, Manager
Leo W. O'Brien Federal
Building
North Pearl Street and
Clinton Avenue
Albany, NY 12207-2395
(518) 472-3567

(West New York)
Joseph Lynch, Manager
465 Main Street, Fifth Floor
Lafayette Court
Buffalo, NY 14203-1780
(716) 846-5755

North Carolina
Larry J. Parker, Manager
415 North Edgeworth Street
Greensboro, NC 27401-2107
(919) 333-5363

North Dakota
Keith Elliot, Chief
Federal Building, Room 300
653 2nd Avenue, North
P.O. Box 2483
Fargo, ND 58108-2483
(701) 239-5136

Ohio
Robert W. Dolin, Manager
New Federal Building
200 North High Street
Columbus, OH 43215-2499
(614) 469-5737

(North Ohio)
George L. Engel, Manager
One Playhouse Square
1375 Euclid Avenue, Room
420
Cleveland, OH 44115-1832
(216) 522-4065

(Southwest Ohio)
William Harris, Manager
Federal Office Building,
Room 9002
550 Main Street
Cincinnati, OH 45202-3253
(513) 684-2884

Oklahoma
Edwin I. Gardner, Manager
Murrah Federal Building
200 NW 5th Street
Oklahoma City, OK
73102-3202
(405) 231-4181

Indian Programs Division
Hugh Johnson, Director
Community Planning and
Development Branch
Murrah Federal Building
200 NW 5th Street
Oklahoma City, OK
73102-3202
(405) 231-4101

(East Oklahoma)
James Colgan, Manager
Robert S. Kerr Building,
Room 200
440 South Houston Avenue
Tulsa, OK 74127-8923
(918) 581-7435

Oregon
Richard C. Brinck, Manager
Cascade Building
520 SW 6th Avenue
Portland, OR 97204-1596
(503) 221-2561

Panama Canal Zone
Rosa Villalonga, Acting
Manager
159 Carlos Chardon Avenue
San Juan, PR 00918-1804
(809) 766-5201 or
(809) 498-5201

Pennsylvania
(Philadelphia Regional
Office)
Michael A. Smerconish,
Regional Administrator
Regional Housing
Commissioner
Liberty Square Building
105 South 7th Street
Philadelphia, PA 19106-3392
(215) 597-2560

(West Pennsylvania)
Choice Edwards, Manager
412 Old Post Office
Courthouse Building
7th Avenue and Grant Street
Pittsburgh, PA 15219-1906
(412) 644-6428

Puerto Rico
Rosa Villalonga, Acting
Manager
159 Carlos Chardon Avenue
San Juan, PR 00918-1804
(809) 766-5201 or
(809) 498-5201

Rhode Island
Casimir J. Kolaski, Jr.,
Manager
Federal Building and U.S.
Post Office, Room 330
Kennedy Plaza
Providence, RI 02903-1745
(401) 528-5351

South Carolina
Ted B. Freeman, Manager
Strom Thurmond Federal
Building
1835-45 Assembly Street
Columbia, SC 29201-2480
(803) 765-5592

South Dakota
Don Olson, Chief
Courthouse Plaza, Suite 116
300 North Dakota Avenue
Sioux Falls, SD 57102-0311
(605) 330-4223

Tennessee
Richard B. Barnwell,
Manager
John J. Duncan Federal
Building
710 Locust Street, SW
Knoxville, TN 37902-2526
(615) 549-9384

(Central Tennessee)
John H. Fisher, Manager
251 Cumberland Bend Drive,
Suite 200
Nashville, TN 37228-1803
(615) 736-5213

(West Tennessee)
Bob Atkins, Manager
One Memphis Place,
Suite 1200
200 Jefferson Avenue
Memphis, TN 38103-2335
(901) 521-3367

Texas
(Fort Worth Regional Office)
Sam R. Moseley, Regional
Housing Commissioner
1600 Throckmorton
P.O. Box 2905
Forth Worth, TX 76113-2905
(817) 885-5401

(Northwest Texas)
Henry E. Whitney, Manager
Federal Office Building
1205 Texas Avenue
Lubbock, TX 79401-4093
(806) 743-7265

(East, North, and West
Texas)
C. Don Babers, Acting
Manager
555 Griffin Square Building,
Room 106
525 Griffin Street
Dallas, TX 75202-5007
(214) 767-8308

(Five Counties in East Texas)
David E. Gleason, Manager
New Federal Building
500 Fannin Street
Shreveport, LA 71101-3077
(318) 226-5385

(East-Central Texas)
William Robertson, Jr.,
Manager
National Bank of Texas
Building, Suite 300
221 Norfolk
Houston, TX 77098-4096
(713) 229-3589

(Bowie County)
John T. Suskie, Manager
Lafayette Building, Suite 200
523 Louisiana
Little Rock, AR 72201-3523
(501) 378-5931

(Southwest Texas)
Cynthia Leon, Manager
Washington Square Building
800 Dolorosa Street
San Antonio, TX 78207-4563
(512) 229-6781

Utah
Richard Bell, Manager
324 South State Street,
Suite 220
Salt Lake City, UT
84111-2321
(801) 524-5237

Vermont
William Peters, Chief
Federal Building, Room B311
11 Elmwood Avenue
P.O. Box 879
Burlington, VT 05402-0879
(802) 951-6290

James Barry, Manager
Norris Cotton Federal
Building
275 Chestnut Street
Manchester, NH 03101-2487
(603) 666-7681

Virgin Islands
Rosa Villalonga, Acting
Manager
159 Carlos Chardon Avenue
San Juan, PR 00918-1804
(809) 766-5201 or
(809) 498-5201

Virginia
(North Virginia)
Toni Thomas, Manager
Union Center Plaza, Phase II
820 First Street, NE,
Suite 300
Washington, DC 20002-4205
(202) 275-9200

(South Virginia)
Mary Ann Wilson, Manager
Federal Building, First Floor
400 North Eighth Street
Richmond, VA 23240-0170
(804) 771-2721

Washington
Office of Indian Programs
Community Planning and
Development Division
Arcade Plaza Building
1321 Second Avenue
Seattle, WA 98101-2058
(206) 442-0760

(Seattle Regional Office)
Richard Bauer,
Regional Housing
Commissioner
Arcade Plaza Building
1321 Second Avenue
Seattle, WA 98101-2054
(206) 442-5414

(East Washington)
Keith R. Green, Manager
Farm Credit Bank Building,
Eighth Floor East
West 601 1st Avenue
Spokane, WA 99204-0317
(509) 456-2624

(Clark, Klickitat, and
Skamania Counties)
Richard C. Brinck, Manager
Cascade Building
520 SW 6th Avenue
Portland, OR 97204-1596
(503) 221-2561

West Virginia
William Costello, Acting
Manager
412 Old Post Office
Courthouse Building
7th Avenue and Grant Street
Pittsburgh, PA 15219-1906
(412) 644-6428

Fred Roncaglione, Acting
Manager
405 Capitol Street, Suite 708
Charleston, WV 25301-1795
(304) 347-7000

Wisconsin
Delbert F. Reynolds,
Manager
Henry S. Reuss Federal Plaza
310 West Wisconsin Avenue,
Suite 1380
Milwaukee, WI 53203-2289
(414) 291-3214

Wyoming
Lawrence Gosnell, Chief
4225 Federal Office Building
100 East B Street
P.O. Box 580
Casper, WY 82602-1918
(307) 261-5252

MORTGAGE INSURANCE—EXPERIMENTAL PROJECTS OTHER THAN HOUSING

**Department of Housing
and Urban Development**
Policy Development and
Research
Division of Innovative
Technology
451 7th Street, SW
Washington, DC 20410
(202) 708-0640

Description: Guaranteed/insured loans to
builders/owners of group medical facilities
incorporating experimental building methods.
Applicants must prove that new technology represents
an acceptable risk to HUD.
$ Given: To date, 5,000 units insured for $100 million.
Average $2.3 million per project.
Application Information: Initial conference with local
HUD field office followed by formal application.
Deadline: Established on case-by-case basis by local
HUD field office.
Contact: Local HUD field office

Alabama
Robert E. Lunsford, Manager
600 Beacon Parkway West,
Suite 300
Birmingham, AL 35209-3144
(205) 731-1617

Alaska
Arlene Patton, Manager
222 West 8th Avenue, #64
Anchorage, AK 99513-7537
(907) 271-4170

Community Planning and
Development Division
222 West 8th Avenue, #64
Anchorage, AK 99513-7537
(907) 271-3669

American Samoa
Gordon Y. Furutani, Manager
300 Ala Moana Boulevard,
Room 3318
Honolulu, HI 96850-4991
(808) 546-2136

Arizona
Dwight Peterson, Manager
400 North First Street,
Suite 1600
P.O. Box 13468
Phoenix, AZ 85004-2361
(602) 261-4434

Charles Ming, Manager
1615 West Olympic
Boulevard
Los Angeles, CA 90015-3801
(213) 251-7122

Jean Staley, Manager
Pioneer Plaza, 100 North
Stone Avenue, Suite 410
P.O. Box 2648
Tucson, AZ 86701-1467
(602) 629-6237

Arkansas
Roger Zachritz, Acting
Manager
Lafayette Building, Suite 200
523 Louisiana
Little Rock, AR 72201-3523
(501) 378-5931

California
Lilly Lee, Manager
1630 East Shaw Avenue,
Suite 138
Fresno, CA 93710-8193
(209) 487-5033

(San Francisco Regional
Office)
Robert De Monte, Regional
Housing Commissioner
Phillip Burton Federal
Building and U.S Courthouse
450 Golden Gate Avenue
P.O. Box 36003
San Francisco, CA
94102-3448
(415) 556-4752

(North California)
Office of Indian Programs
Community Planning and
Development Division
San Francisco Program
Management Team
Phillip Burton Federal
Building and U.S.
Courthouse
450 Golden Gate Avenue
P.O. Box 36003
San Francisco, CA
94102-3448
(415) 556-9200

(Northeast California)
Anthony A. Randolph,
Manager
777 12th Street, Suite 200
P.O. Box 1978
Sacramento, CA 95814-1997
(916) 551-1351

(Imperial and San Diego
Counties)
Charles J. Wilson, Manager
Federal Office Building,
Room 563
880 Front Street
San Diego, CA 92188-0100
(619) 557-5310

(Orange, Riverside and San
Bernardino Counties, for
home mortgages)
Harold A. Matzoll, Acting
Manager
34 Civic Center Plaza,
Box 12850
Santa Ana, CA 92712-2850
(714) 836-2451

(South California)
Charles Ming, Manager
1615 West Olympic
Boulevard
Los Angeles, CA 90015-3801
(213) 251-7122

Colorado
Michael Chitwood, Regional
Administrator
Regional Housing
Commissioner
HUD Denver Regional Office
Executive Tower Building
1405 Curtis Street
Denver, CO 80202-2349
(303) 844-4513

Office of Indian Programs
Housing and Community
Development Division
Executive Tower Building
1405 Curtis Street
Denver, CO 80202-2349
(303) 844-2861

Connecticut
William Hernandez, Jr.,
Manager
330 Main Street, First Floor
Hartford, CT 06106-1860
(203) 240-4523

Delaware
A. David Sharbaugh, Chief
Federal Building, Room 1304
844 King Street
Wilmington, DE 19801-3519
(302) 573-6300

District of Columbia
(Washington, D.C. Regional
Office)
Toni Thomas, Manager
Union Center Plaza, Phase II
820 First Street, NE,
Suite 300
Washington, DC 20002-4205
(202) 275-9200

Florida
James T. Chaplin, Manager
325 West Adams Street
Jacksonville, FL 32202-4303
(904) 791-2626

Housing

(Counties of Citrus, Sumter, Hernando, Pasco, Pinellas, Hillsborough, Polk, Manatee, Hardee, Highlands, DeSoto, Sarasota, Charlotte, Olaoes, Hendry, Lake Okeechobee)
George A. Milburn, Jr., Manager
Timberlake Federal Building Annex, Suite 700
501 East Polk Street
Tampa, FL 33602-3945
(813) 228-2501

(Counties of Volusia, Lake, Seminole, Orange, Brevard, Osceola, Indian River, Okeechobee, St. Lucie)
M. Jeanette Porter, Manager
Langley Building, Suite 270
3751 Maguire Boulevard
Orlando, FL 32803-3032
(407) 648-6441

(South Florida)
Orlando L. Lorie, Manager
Gables 1 Tower
1320 South Dixie Highway
Coral Gables, FL 33146-2911
(305) 662-4510

Georgia
Raymond A. Harris, Regional Housing Commissioner
Richard B. Russell Federal Building
75 Spring Street, SW
Atlanta, GA 30303-3388
(404) 331-5136

Guam
Gordon Y. Furutani, Manager
300 Ala Moana Boulevard, Room 3318
Honolulu, HI 96850-4991
(808) 546-2136

Hawaii
Gordon Y. Furutani, Manager
300 Ala Moana Boulevard, Room 3318
Honolulu, HI 96850-4991
(808) 546-2136

Idaho
(North Idaho)
Keith R. Green, Manager
Farm Credit Bank Building, Eighth Floor East
West 601 1st Avenue
Spokane, WA 99204-0317
(509) 456-2624

(West-Central Idaho)
Gary Gillespie, Manager
Federal Building and U.S. Courthouse
P.O. Box 042
550 West Fort Street
Boise, ID 83724-0420
(208) 334-1990

(South Idaho)
Richard C. Brinck, Manager
Cascade Building
520 SW 6th Avenue
Portland, OR 97204-1596
(503) 221-2561

Illinois
Chicago Office of Indian Programs
Housing Development Division
626 West Jackson Boulevard
Chicago, IL 60606-5601
(312) 353-1684

(Chicago Regional Office)
Gertrude Jordan, Regional Housing Commissioner
626 West Jackson Boulevard
Chicago, IL 60606-5601
(312) 353-5680

(Central and South Illinois)
John Lawler, Acting Supervisory Appraiser
Lincoln Towers Plaza, Suite 672
524 South Second Street
Springfield, IL 62701-1774
(217) 492-4085

Indiana
J. Nicholas Shelley, Manager
151 North Delaware Street
Indianapolis, IN 46204-2526
(317) 226-6303

Iowa
Roger M. Massey, Manager
Braiker/Brandeis Building
210 South 16th Street
Omaha, NE 68102-1622
(402) 221-3703

William R. McNarney, Manager
HUD Des Moines Office
Federal Building, Room 259
210 Walnut Street
Des Moines, IA 50309-2155
(515) 284-4512

Kansas
William H. Brown, Regional Administrator
Regional Housing Commissioner
HUD Kansas City, Regional Office
Gateway Tower II
400 State Avenue
Kansas City, KS 66101-2406
(913) 236-2162

Kentucky
Verna V. Van Ness, Manager
601 West Broadway
P.O. Box 1044
Louisville, KY 40201-1044
(502) 582-5251

Louisiana
Robert Vasquez, Manager
Fisk Federal Building,
1661 Canal Street
P.O. Box 70288
New Orleans, LA 70112-2887
(504) 589-7200

(North Louisiana)
David E. Gleason, Manager
New Federal Building
500 Fannin Street
Shreveport, LA 71101-3077
(318) 226-5385

Maine
Richard Young, Supervisory
Appraiser
Casco Northern Bank
Building
23 Main Street
Bangor, ME 04401-4318
(207) 945-0467

James Barry, Manager
Norris Cotton Federal
Building
275 Chestnut Street
Manchester, NH 03101-2487
(603) 666-7681

Maryland
(Except Montgomery and
Prince Georges Counties)
Maxine Saunders, Manager
The Equitable Building,
Third Floor
10 North Calvert Street
Baltimore, MD 21202-1865
(301) 962-2121

(Montgomery and Prince
Georges Counties)
Toni Thomas, Manager
Union Center Plaza, Phase II
820 First Street, NE,
Suite 300
Washington, DC 20002-4205
(202) 275-9200

Massachusetts
John Mastropietro,
Acting Regional
Administrator
Regional Housing
Commissioner
Boston Federal Office
Building, Room 375
10 Causeway Street
Boston, MA 02222-1092
(617) 565-5234

Michigan
Harry I. Sharrott, Manager
Patrick V. McNamara Federal
Building
477 Michigan Avenue
Detroit, MI 48226-2592
(313) 226-6280

(East Michigan)
Gary T. LeVine, Manager
Gil Sabuco Building,
Room 200
352 South Saginaw Street
Flint, MI 48502-1953
(313) 766-5112

(West and North Michigan)
Ronald Weston, Manager
Northbrook Building, No. II
2922 Fuller Avenue, NE
Grand Rapids, MI 48505-3409
(616) 456-2100

Minnesota
Thomas Feeney, Manager
Bridge Place Building
220 Second Street, South
Minneapolis, MN 55401-2195
(612) 370-3000

Mississippi
Sandra Freeman, Manager
Dr. A. H. McCoy Federal
Building, Room 910
100 West Capitol Street
Jackson, MS 39269-1096
(601) 965-4702

Missouri
Kenneth G. Lange, Manager
210 North Tucker Boulevard
St. Louis, MO 63101-1997
(314) 425-4761

Montana
Christian KaFentzis, Manager
Federal Office Building,
Room 340
Drawer 10095
301 South Park
Helena, MT 59626-0095
(406) 449-5205

Nebraska
Roger M. Massey, Manager
Braiker/Brandeis Building
210 South 16th Street
Omaha, NE 68102-1622
(402) 221-3703

Nevada
Andrew D. Whitten, Jr.,
Manager
1050 Bible Way
P.O. Box 4700
Reno, NV 89505-4700
(702) 784-5356

Andrew Robertson, Manager
1500 East Tropicana Avenue,
Second Floor
Las Vegas, NV 89119-6516
(702) 388-6500

(North Nevada)
Office of Indian Programs
Community Planning and
Development Division
San Francisco Program
Management Team
Phillip Burton Federal
Building and U.S.
Courthouse
450 Golden Gate Avenue
P.O. Box 36003
San Francisco, CA
94102-3448
(415) 556-9200

New Hampshire
James Barry, Manager
Norris Cotton Federal
Building
275 Chestnut Street
Manchester, NH 03101-2487
(603) 666-7681

New Jersey
(North New Jersey)
Theodore Britton, Jr.,
Manager
Military Park Building
60 Park Place
Newark, NJ 07102-5504
(201) 887-1662

Housing

(South New Jersey)
Elmer Roy, Manager
The Parkade Building
519 Federal Street
Camden, NJ 08103-9998
(609) 757-5081

New Mexico
Michael R. Griego, Manager
625 Truman Street, NE
Albuquerque, NM
87110-6443
(505) 262-6463

C. Don Babers, Acting
Manager
555 Griffin Square Building,
Room 106
525 Griffin Street
Dallas, TX 75202-5007
(214) 767-8308

New York
Dr. Anthony Villane, Regional
Housing Commissioner
26 Federal Plaza
New York, NY 10278-0068
(212) 264-8068

(North New York)
John Petricco, Manager
Leo W. O'Brien Federal
Building
North Pearl Street and
Clinton Avenue
Albany, NY 12207-2395
(518) 472-3567

(West New York)
Joseph Lynch, Manager
465 Main Street, Fifth Floor
Lafayette Court
Buffalo, NY 14203-1780
(716) 846-5755

North Carolina
Larry J. Parker, Manager
415 North Edgeworth Street
Greensboro, NC 27401-2107
(919) 333-5363

North Dakota
Keith Elliot, Chief
Federal Building, Room 300
653 2nd Avenue, North
P.O. Box 2483
Fargo, ND 58108-2483
(701) 239-5136

Ohio
Robert W. Dolin, Manager
New Federal Building
200 North High Street
Columbus, OH 43215-2499
(614) 469-5737

(North Ohio)
George L. Engel, Manager
One Playhouse Square
1375 Euclid Avenue,
Room 420
Cleveland, OH 44115-1832
(216) 522-4065

(Southwest Ohio)
William Harris, Manager
Federal Office Building,
Room 9002
550 Main Street
Cincinnati, OH 45202-3253
(513) 684-2884

Oklahoma
Edwin I. Gardner, Manager
Murrah Federal Building
200 NW 5th Street
Oklahoma City, OK
73102-3202
(405) 231-4181

Indian Programs Division
Hugh Johnson, Director
Community Planning and
Development Branch
Murrah Federal Building
200 NW 5th Street
Oklahoma City, OK
73102-3202
(405) 231-4101

(East Oklahoma)
Robert H. Gardner, Manager
Robert S. Kerr Building,
Room 200
440 South Houston Avenue
Tulsa, OK 74127-8923
(918) 581-7435

Oregon
Richard C. Brinck, Manager
Cascade Building
520 SW 6th Avenue
Portland, OR 97204-1596
(503) 221-2561

Panama Canal Zone
Rosa Villalonga, Acting
Manager
159 Carlos Chardon Avenue
San Juan, PR 00918-1804
(809) 766-5201 or
(809) 498-5201

Pennsylvania
(Philadelphia Regional
Office)
Michael A. Smerconish,
Regional Administrator
Regional Housing
Commissioner
Liberty Square Building
105 South 7th Street
Philadelphia, PA 19106-3392
(215) 597-2560

(West Pennsylvania)
William Costello, Acting
Manager
412 Old Post Office
Courthouse Building
7th Avenue and Grant Street
Pittsburgh, PA 15219-1906
(412) 644-6428

Puerto Rico
Rosa Villalonga, Acting
Manager
159 Carlos Chardon Avenue
San Juan, PR 00918-1804
(809) 766-5201 or
(809) 498-5201

Rhode Island
Casimir J. Kolaski, Jr.,
Manager
Federal Building and U.S.
Post Office, Room 330
Kennedy Plaza
Providence, RI 02903-1745
(401) 528-5351

South Carolina
Ted B. Freeman, Manager
Strom Thurmond Federal
Building
1835-45 Assembly Street
Columbia, SC 29201-2480
(803) 765-5592

South Dakota
Don Olson, Chief
Courthouse Plaza, Suite 116
300 North Dakota Avenue
Sioux Falls, SD 57102-0311
(605) 330-4223

Tennessee
Richard B. Barnwell,
Manager
John J. Duncan Federal
Building
710 Locust Street, SW
Knoxville, TN 37902-2526
(615) 549-9384

(Central Tennessee)
John H. Fisher, Manager
251 Cumberland Bend Drive,
Suite 200
Nashville, TN 37228-1803
(615) 736-5213

(West Tennessee)
Bob Atkins, Manager
One Memphis Place,
Suite 1200
200 Jefferson Avenue
Memphis, TN 38103-2335
(901) 521-3367

Texas
(Fort Worth Regional Office)
Sam R. Moseley, Regional
Housing Commissioner
1600 Throckmorton
P.O. Box 2905
Forth Worth, TX 76113-2905
(817) 885-5401

(Northwest Texas)
Henry E. Whitney, Manager
Federal Office Building
1205 Texas Avenue
Lubbock, TX 79401-4093
(806) 743-7265

(East, North, and West
Texas)
C. Don Babers, Acting
Manager
555 Griffin Square Building,
Room 106
525 Griffin Street
Dallas, TX 75202-5007
(214) 767-8308

(Five Counties in East Texas)
David E. Gleason, Manager
New Federal Building
500 Fannin Street
Shreveport, LA 71101-3077
(318) 226-5385

(East-Central Texas)
William Robertson, Jr.,
Manager
National Bank of Texas
Building, Suite 300
221 Norfolk
Houston, TX 77098-4096
(713) 229-3589

(Bowie County)
Roger Zachritz, Acting
Manager
Lafayette Building, Suite 200
523 Louisiana
Little Rock, AR 72201-3523
(501) 378-5931

(Southwest Texas)
Don Creed, Manager
Washington Square Building
800 Dolorosa Street
San Antonio, TX 78207-4563
(512) 229-6781

Utah
Richard Bell, Manager
324 South State Street,
Suite 220
Salt Lake City, UT
84111-2321
(801) 524-5237

Vermont
William Peters, Chief
Federal Building, Room B311
11 Elmwood Avenue
P.O. Box 879
Burlington, VT 05402-0879
(802) 951-6290

James Barry, Manager
Norris Cotton Federal
Building
275 Chestnut Street
Manchester, NH 03101-2487
(603) 666-7681

Virgin Islands
Rosa Villalonga, Acting
Manager
159 Carlos Chardon Avenue
San Juan, PR 00918-1804
(809) 766-5201 or
(809) 498-5201

Virginia
(North Virginia)
Toni Thomas, Manager
Union Center Plaza, Phase II
820 First Street, NE,
Suite 300
Washington, DC 20002-4205
(202) 275-9200

(South Virginia)
Mary Ann Wilson, Manager
Federal Building, First Floor
400 North Eighth Street
Richmond, VA 23240-0170
(804) 771-2721

Washington
Office of Indian Programs
Community Planning and
Development Division
Arcade Plaza Building
1321 Second Avenue
Seattle, WA 98101-2058
(206) 442-0760

(Seattle Regional Office)
Richard Bauer,
Regional Housing
Commissioner
Arcade Plaza Building
1321 Second Avenue
Seattle, WA 98101-2054
(206) 442-5414

(East Washington)
Keith R. Green, Manager
Farm Credit Bank Building,
Eighth Floor East
West 601 1st Avenue
Spokane, WA 99204-0317
(509) 456-2624

(Clark, Klickitat, and
Skamania Counties)
Richard C. Brinck, Manager
Cascade Building
520 SW 6th Avenue
Portland, OR 97204-1596
(503) 221-2561

West Virginia
William Costello, Acting
Manager
412 Old Post Office
Courthouse Building
7th Avenue and Grant Street
Pittsburgh, PA 15219-1906
(412) 644-6428

or:

405 Capitol Street, Suite 708
Charleston, WV 25301-1795
(304) 347-7000

Wisconsin
Delbert F. Reynolds,
Manager
Henry S. Reuss Federal Plaza
310 West Wisconsin Avenue,
Suite 1380
Milwaukee, WI 53203-2289
(414) 291-3214

Wyoming
Lawrence Gosnell, Chief
4225 Federal Office Building
100 East B Street
P.O. Box 580
Casper, WY 82602-1918
(307) 261-5252

MORTGAGE INSURANCE—EXPERIMENTAL RENTAL HOUSING

Department of Housing and Urban Development
Policy Development and
Research
Division of Innovative
Technology
451 7th Street, SW
Washington, DC 20410
(202) 708-0640

Description: Guaranteed/insured loans to builders/owners of multifamily housing facilities incorporating experimental building methods. Applicants must prove that new technology represents an acceptable risk to HUD.
$ Given: To date, 5,000 units insured for $100 million. Average $2.3 million per project.
Application Information: Initial conference with local HUD field office followed by formal application.
Deadline: Established on case-by-case basis by local HUD field office.
Contact: Local HUD field office

Alabama
Robert E. Lunsford, Manager
600 Beacon Parkway West,
Suite 300
Birmingham, AL 35209-3144
(205) 731-1617

Alaska
Arlene Patton, Manager
222 West 8th Avenue, #64
Anchorage, AK 99513-7537
(907) 271-4170

Community Planning and
Development Division
222 West 8th Avenue, #64
Anchorage, AK 99513-7537
(907) 271-3669

American Samoa
Gordon Y. Furutani, Manager
300 Ala Moana Boulevard,
Room 3318
Honolulu, HI 96850-4991
(808) 546-2136

Arizona
Dwight Peterson, Manager
400 North First Street,
Suite 1600
P.O. Box 13468
Phoenix, AZ 85004-2361
(602) 261-4434

Charles Ming, Manager
1615 West Olympic
Boulevard
Los Angeles, CA 90015-3801
(213) 251-7122

Jean Staley, Manager
Pioneer Plaza, 100 North
Stone Avenue, Suite 410
P.O. Box 2648
Tucson, AZ 86701-1467
(602) 629-6237

Arkansas
Roger Zachritz, Acting
Manager
Lafayette Building, Suite 200
523 Louisiana
Little Rock, AR 72201-3523
(501) 378-5931

California
Lilly Lee, Manager
1630 East Shaw Avenue,
Suite 138
Fresno, CA 93710-8193
(209) 487-5033

(San Francisco Regional
Office)
Robert De Monte, Regional
Housing Commissioner
Phillip Burton Federal
Building and U.S Courthouse
450 Golden Gate Avenue
P.O. Box 36003
San Francisco, CA
94102-3448
(415) 556-4752

(North California)
Office of Indian Programs
Community Planning and
Development Division
San Francisco Program
Management Team
Phillip Burton Federal
Building and U.S.
Courthouse
450 Golden Gate Avenue
P.O. Box 36003
San Francisco, CA
94102-3448
(415) 556-9200

(Northeast California)
Anthony A. Randolph,
Manager
777 12th Street, Suite 200
P.O. Box 1978
Sacramento, CA 95814-1997
(916) 551-1351

(Imperial and San Diego
Counties)
Charles J. Wilson, Manager
Federal Office Building,
Room 563
880 Front Street
San Diego, CA 92188-0100
(619) 557-5310

(Orange, Riverside and San
Bernardino Counties, for
home mortgages)
Harold A. Matzoll, Acting
Manager
34 Civic Center Plaza,
Box 12850
Santa Ana, CA 92712-2850
(714) 836-2451

(South California)
Charles Ming, Manager
1615 West Olympic
Boulevard
Los Angeles, CA 90015-3801
(213) 251-7122

Colorado
Michael Chitwood, Regional
Administrator
Regional Housing
Commissioner
HUD Denver Regional Office
Executive Tower Building
1405 Curtis Street
Denver, CO 80202-2349
(303) 844-4513

Office of Indian Programs
Housing and Community
Development Division
Executive Tower Building
1405 Curtis Street
Denver, CO 80202-2349
(303) 844-2861

Connecticut
William Hernandez, Jr.,
Manager
330 Main Street, First Floor
Hartford, CT 06106-1860
(203) 240-4523

Delaware
A. David Sharbaugh, Chief
Federal Building, Room 1304
844 King Street
Wilmington, DE 19801-3519
(302) 573-6300

District of Columbia
(Washington, D.C. Regional
Office)
Toni Thomas, Manager
Union Center Plaza, Phase II
820 First Street, NE,
Suite 300
Washington, DC 20002-4205
(202) 275-9200

Florida
James T. Chaplin, Manager
325 West Adams Street
Jacksonville, FL 32202-4303
(904) 791-2626

Housing

(Counties of Citrus, Sumter, Hernando, Pasco, Pinellas, Hillsborough, Polk, Manatee, Hardee, Highlands, DeSoto, Sarasota, Charlotte, Olaoes, Hendry, Lake Okeechobee)
George A. Milburn, Jr., Manager
Timberlake Federal Building Annex, Suite 700
501 East Polk Street
Tampa, FL 33602-3945
(813) 228-2501

(Counties of Volusia, Lake, Seminole, Orange, Brevard, Osceola, Indian River, Okeechobee, St. Lucie)
M. Jeanette Porter, Manager
Langley Building, Suite 270
3751 Maguire Boulevard
Orlando, FL 32803-3032
(407) 648-6441

(South Florida)
Orlando L. Lorie, Manager
Gables 1 Tower
1320 South Dixie Highway
Coral Gables, FL 33146-2911
(305) 662-4510

Georgia
Raymond A. Harris, Regional Housing Commissioner
Richard B. Russell Federal Building
75 Spring Street, SW
Atlanta, GA 30303-3388
(404) 331-5136

Guam
Gordon Y. Furutani, Manager
300 Ala Moana Boulevard, Room 3318
Honolulu, HI 96850-4991
(808) 546-2136

Hawaii
Gordon Y. Furutani, Manager
300 Ala Moana Boulevard, Room 3318
Honolulu, HI 96850-4991
(808) 546-2136

Idaho
(North Idaho)
Keith R. Green, Manager
Farm Credit Bank Building, Eighth Floor East
West 601 1st Avenue
Spokane, WA 99204-0317
(509) 456-2624

(West-Central Idaho)
Gary Gillespie, Manager
Federal Building and U.S. Courthouse
P.O. Box 042
550 West Fort Street
Boise, ID 83724-0420
(208) 334-1990

(South Idaho)
Richard C. Brinck, Manager
Cascade Building
520 SW 6th Avenue
Portland, OR 97204-1596
(503) 221-2561

Illinois
Chicago Office of Indian Programs
Housing Development Division
626 West Jackson Boulevard
Chicago, IL 60606-5601
(312) 353-1684

(Chicago Regional Office)
Gertrude Jordan, Regional Housing Commissioner
626 West Jackson Boulevard
Chicago, IL 60606-5601
(312) 353-5680

(Central and South Illinois)
John Lawler, Acting Supervisory Appraiser
Lincoln Towers Plaza, Suite 672
524 South Second Street
Springfield, IL 62701-1774
(217) 492-4085

Indiana
J. Nicholas Shelley, Manager
151 North Delaware Street
Indianapolis, IN 46204-2526
(317) 226-6303

Iowa
Roger M. Massey, Manager
Braiker/Brandeis Building
210 South 16th Street
Omaha, NE 68102-1622
(402) 221-3703

William R. McNarney, Manager
HUD Des Moines Office
Federal Building, Room 259
210 Walnut Street
Des Moines, IA 50309-2155
(515) 284-4512

Kansas
William H. Brown, Regional Administrator
Regional Housing Commissioner
HUD Kansas City, Regional Office
Gateway Tower II
400 State Avenue
Kansas City, KS 66101-2406
(913) 236-2162

Kentucky
Verna V. Van Ness, Manager
601 West Broadway
P.O. Box 1044
Louisville, KY 40201-1044
(502) 582-5251

Louisiana
Robert Vasquez, Manager
Fisk Federal Building,
1661 Canal Street
P.O. Box 70288
New Orleans, LA 70112-2887
(504) 589-7200

(North Louisiana)
David E. Gleason, Manager
New Federal Building
500 Fannin Street
Shreveport, LA 71101-3077
(318) 226-5385

Maine
Richard Young, Supervisory
Appraiser
Casco Northern Bank
Building
23 Main Street
Bangor, ME 04401-4318
(207) 945-0467

James Barry, Manager
Norris Cotton Federal
Building
275 Chestnut Street
Manchester, NH 03101-2487
(603) 666-7681

Maryland
(Except Montgomery and
Prince Georges Counties)
Maxine Saunders, Manager
The Equitable Building,
Third Floor
10 North Calvert Street
Baltimore, MD 21202-1865
(301) 962-2121

(Montgomery and Prince
Georges Counties)
Toni Thomas, Manager
Union Center Plaza, Phase II
820 First Street, NE,
Suite 300
Washington, DC 20002-4205
(202) 275-9200

Massachusetts
John Mastropietro,
Acting Regional
Administrator
Regional Housing
Commissioner
Boston Federal Office
Building, Room 375
10 Causeway Street
Boston, MA 02222-1092
(617) 565-5234

Michigan
Harry I. Sharrott, Manager
Patrick V. McNamara Federal
Building
477 Michigan Avenue
Detroit, MI 48226-2592
(313) 226-6280

(East Michigan)
Gary T. LeVine, Manager
Gil Sabuco Building,
Room 200
352 South Saginaw Street
Flint, MI 48502-1953
(313) 766-5112

(West and North Michigan)
Ronald Weston, Manager
Northbrook Building, No. II
2922 Fuller Avenue, NE
Grand Rapids, MI 48505-3409
(616) 456-2100

Minnesota
Thomas Feeney, Manager
Bridge Place Building
220 Second Street, South
Minneapolis, MN 55401-2195
(612) 370-3000

Mississippi
Sandra Freeman, Manager
Dr. A. H. McCoy Federal
Building, Room 910
100 West Capitol Street
Jackson, MS 39269-1096
(601) 965-4702

Missouri
Kenneth G. Lange, Manager
210 North Tucker Boulevard
St. Louis, MO 63101-1997
(314) 425-4761

Montana
Christian KaFentzis, Manager
Federal Office Building,
Room 340
Drawer 10095
301 South Park
Helena, MT 59626-0095
(406) 449-5205

Nebraska
Roger M. Massey, Manager
Braiker/Brandeis Building
210 South 16th Street
Omaha, NE 68102-1622
(402) 221-3703

Nevada
Andrew D. Whitten, Jr.,
Manager
1050 Bible Way
P.O. Box 4700
Reno, NV 89505-4700
(702) 784-5356

Andrew Robertson, Manager
1500 East Tropicana Avenue,
Second Floor
Las Vegas, NV 89119-6516
(702) 388-6500

(North Nevada)
Office of Indian Programs
Community Planning and
Development Division
San Francisco Program
Management Team
Phillip Burton Federal
Building and U.S.
Courthouse
450 Golden Gate Avenue
P.O. Box 36003
San Francisco, CA
94102-3448
(415) 556-9200

New Hampshire
James Barry, Manager
Norris Cotton Federal
Building
275 Chestnut Street
Manchester, NH 03101-2487
(603) 666-7681

New Jersey
(North New Jersey)
Theodore Britton, Jr.,
Manager
Military Park Building
60 Park Place
Newark, NJ 07102-5504
(201) 887-1662

Housing

(South New Jersey)
Elmer Roy, Manager
The Parkade Building
519 Federal Street
Camden, NJ 08103-9998
(609) 757-5081

New Mexico
Michael R. Griego, Manager
625 Truman Street, NE
Albuquerque, NM
87110-6443
(505) 262-6463

C. Don Babers, Acting
Manager
555 Griffin Square Building,
Room 106
525 Griffin Street
Dallas, TX 75202-5007
(214) 767-8308

New York
Dr. Anthony Villane, Regional
Housing Commissioner
26 Federal Plaza
New York, NY 10278-0068
(212) 264-8068

(North New York)
John Petricco, Manager
Leo W. O'Brien Federal
Building
North Pearl Street and
Clinton Avenue
Albany, NY 12207-2395
(518) 472-3567

(West New York)
Joseph Lynch, Manager
465 Main Street, Fifth Floor
Lafayette Court
Buffalo, NY 14203-1780
(716) 846-5755

North Carolina
Larry J. Parker, Manager
415 North Edgeworth Street
Greensboro, NC 27401-2107
(919) 333-5363

North Dakota
Keith Elliot, Chief
Federal Building, Room 300
653 2nd Avenue, North
P.O. Box 2483
Fargo, ND 58108-2483
(701) 239-5136

Ohio
Robert W. Dolin, Manager
New Federal Building
200 North High Street
Columbus, OH 43215-2499
(614) 469-5737

(North Ohio)
George L. Engel, Manager
One Playhouse Square
1375 Euclid Avenue,
Room 420
Cleveland, OH 44115-1832
(216) 522-4065

(Southwest Ohio)
William Harris, Manager
Federal Office Building,
Room 9002
550 Main Street
Cincinnati, OH 45202-3253
(513) 684-2884

Oklahoma
Edwin I. Gardner, Manager
Murrah Federal Building
200 NW 5th Street
Oklahoma City, OK
73102-3202
(405) 231-4181

Indian Programs Division
Hugh Johnson, Director
Community Planning and
Development Branch
Murrah Federal Building
200 NW 5th Street
Oklahoma City, OK
73102-3202
(405) 231-4101

(East Oklahoma)
Robert H. Gardner, Manager
Robert S. Kerr Building,
Room 200
440 South Houston Avenue
Tulsa, OK 74127-8923
(918) 581-7435

Oregon
Richard C. Brinck, Manager
Cascade Building
520 SW 6th Avenue
Portland, OR 97204-1596
(503) 221-2561

Panama Canal Zone
Rosa Villalonga, Acting
Manager
159 Carlos Chardon Avenue
San Juan, PR 00918-1804
(809) 766-5201 or
(809) 498-5201

Pennsylvania
(Philadelphia Regional
Office)
Michael A. Smerconish,
Regional Administrator
Regional Housing
Commissioner
Liberty Square Building
105 South 7th Street
Philadelphia, PA 19106-3392
(215) 597-2560

(West Pennsylvania)
William Costello, Acting
Manager
412 Old Post Office
Courthouse Building
7th Avenue and Grant Street
Pittsburgh, PA 15219-1906
(412) 644-6428

Puerto Rico
Rosa Villalonga, Acting
Manager
159 Carlos Chardon Avenue
San Juan, PR 00918-1804
(809) 766-5201 or
(809) 498-5201

Rhode Island
Casimir J. Kolaski, Jr.,
Manager
Federal Building and U.S.
Post Office, Room 330
Kennedy Plaza
Providence, RI 02903-1745
(401) 528-5351

South Carolina
Ted B. Freeman, Manager
Strom Thurmond Federal
Building
1835-45 Assembly Street
Columbia, SC 29201-2480
(803) 765-5592

South Dakota
Don Olson, Chief
Courthouse Plaza, Suite 116
300 North Dakota Avenue
Sioux Falls, SD 57102-0311
(605) 330-4223

Tennessee
Richard B. Barnwell,
Manager
John J. Duncan Federal
Building
710 Locust Street, SW
Knoxville, TN 37902-2526
(615) 549-9384

(Central Tennessee)
John H. Fisher, Manager
251 Cumberland Bend Drive,
Suite 200
Nashville, TN 37228-1803
(615) 736-5213

(West Tennessee)
Bob Atkins, Manager
One Memphis Place,
Suite 1200
200 Jefferson Avenue
Memphis, TN 38103-2335
(901) 521-3367

Texas
(Fort Worth Regional Office)
Sam R. Moseley, Regional
Housing Commissioner
1600 Throckmorton
P.O. Box 2905
Forth Worth, TX 76113-2905
(817) 885-5401

(Northwest Texas)
Henry E. Whitney, Manager
Federal Office Building
1205 Texas Avenue
Lubbock, TX 79401-4093
(806) 743-7265

(East, North, and West
Texas)
C. Don Babers, Acting
Manager
555 Griffin Square Building,
Room 106
525 Griffin Street
Dallas, TX 75202-5007
(214) 767-8308

(Five Counties in East Texas)
David E. Gleason, Manager
New Federal Building
500 Fannin Street
Shreveport, LA 71101-3077
(318) 226-5385

(East-Central Texas)
William Robertson, Jr.,
Manager
National Bank of Texas
Building, Suite 300
221 Norfolk
Houston, TX 77098-4096
(713) 229-3589

(Bowie County)
Roger Zachritz, Acting
Manager
Lafayette Building, Suite 200
523 Louisiana
Little Rock, AR 72201-3523
(501) 378-5931

(Southwest Texas)
Don Creed, Manager
Washington Square Building
800 Dolorosa Street
San Antonio, TX 78207-4563
(512) 229-6781

Utah
Richard Bell, Manager
324 South State Street,
Suite 220
Salt Lake City, UT
84111-2321
(801) 524-5237

Vermont
William Peters, Chief
Federal Building, Room B311
11 Elmwood Avenue
P.O. Box 879
Burlington, VT 05402-0879
(802) 951-6290

James Barry, Manager
Norris Cotton Federal
Building
275 Chestnut Street
Manchester, NH 03101-2487
(603) 666-7681

Virgin Islands
Rosa Villalonga, Acting
Manager
159 Carlos Chardon Avenue
San Juan, PR 00918-1804
(809) 766-5201 or
(809) 498-5201

Virginia
(North Virginia)
Toni Thomas, Manager
Union Center Plaza, Phase II
820 First Street, NE,
Suite 300
Washington, DC 20002-4205
(202) 275-9200

(South Virginia)
Mary Ann Wilson, Manager
Federal Building, First Floor
400 North Eighth Street
Richmond, VA 23240-0170
(804) 771-2721

Washington
Office of Indian Programs
Community Planning and
Development Division
Arcade Plaza Building
1321 Second Avenue
Seattle, WA 98101-2058
(206) 442-0760

(Seattle Regional Office)
Richard Bauer,
Regional Housing
Commissioner
Arcade Plaza Building
1321 Second Avenue
Seattle, WA 98101-2054
(206) 442-5414

(East Washington)
Keith R. Green, Manager
Farm Credit Bank Building,
Eighth Floor East
West 601 1st Avenue
Spokane, WA 99204-0317
(509) 456-2624

(Clark, Klickitat, and
Skamania Counties)
Richard C. Brinck, Manager
Cascade Building
520 SW 6th Avenue
Portland, OR 97204-1596
(503) 221-2561

West Virginia
William Costello, Acting
Manager
412 Old Post Office
Courthouse Building
7th Avenue and Grant Street
Pittsburgh, PA 15219-1906
(412) 644-6428

or:

405 Capitol Street, Suite 708
Charleston, WV 25301-1795
(304) 347-7000

Wisconsin
Delbert F. Reynolds,
Manager
Henry S. Reuss Federal Plaza
310 West Wisconsin Avenue,
Suite 1380
Milwaukee, WI 53203-2289
(414) 291-3214

Wyoming
Lawrence Gosnell, Chief
4225 Federal Office Building
100 East B Street
P.O. Box 580
Casper, WY 82602-1918
(307) 261-5252

MORTGAGE INSURANCE—MANUFACTURED HOME PARKS

**Department of Housing
and Urban Development**
Policies and Procedures
Division
Office of Insured
Multifamily Housing
Development
Washington, DC 20410
(202) 708-2556

Description: Guaranteed/insured loans to investors, builders, and developers to make possible construction or rehabilitation of manufactured home parks. Must meet HUD requirements. Documentation required.
$ Given: Through September 30, 1991, 390 projects with 66,872 spaces insured at $212.7 million.
Application Information: Initial conference at local HUD office followed by formal application.
Deadline: Established on case-by-case basis at local HUD offices.
Contact: Local HUD field office

Alabama
Robert E. Lunsford, Manager
600 Beacon Parkway West,
Suite 300
Birmingham, AL 35209-3144
(205) 731-1617

Alaska
Arlene Patton, Manager
222 West 8th Avenue, #64
Anchorage, AK 99513-7537
(907) 271-4170

Community Planning and
Development Division
222 West 8th Avenue, #64
Anchorage, AK 99513-7537
(907) 271-3669

American Samoa
Gordon Y. Furutani, Manager
300 Ala Moana Boulevard,
Room 3318
Honolulu, HI 96850-4991
(808) 546-2136

Arizona
Dwight Peterson, Manager
400 North First Street,
Suite 1600
P.O. Box 13468
Phoenix, AZ 85004-2361
(602) 261-4434

Charles Ming, Manager
1615 West Olympic
Boulevard
Los Angeles, CA 90015-3801
(213) 251-7122

Jean Staley, Manager
Pioneer Plaza, 100 North
Stone Avenue, Suite 410
P.O. Box 2648
Tucson, AZ 86701-1467
(602) 629-6237

Arkansas
Roger Zachritz, Acting
Manager
Lafayette Building, Suite 200
523 Louisiana
Little Rock, AR 72201-3523
(501) 378-5931

California
Lilly Lee, Manager
1630 East Shaw Avenue,
Suite 138
Fresno, CA 93710-8193
(209) 487-5033

(San Francisco Regional
Office)
Robert De Monte, Regional
Housing Commissioner
Phillip Burton Federal
Building and U.S Courthouse
450 Golden Gate Avenue
P.O. Box 36003
San Francisco, CA
94102-3448
(415) 556-4752

(North California)
Office of Indian Programs
Community Planning and
Development Division
San Francisco Program
Management Team
Phillip Burton Federal
Building and U.S.
Courthouse
450 Golden Gate Avenue
P.O. Box 36003
San Francisco, CA
94102-3448
(415) 556-9200

(Northeast California)
Anthony A. Randolph,
Manager
777 12th Street, Suite 200
P.O. Box 1978
Sacramento, CA 95814-1997
(916) 551-1351

(Imperial and San Diego
Counties)
Charles J. Wilson, Manager
Federal Office Building,
Room 563
880 Front Street
San Diego, CA 92188-0100
(619) 557-5310

(Orange, Riverside and San
Bernardino Counties, for
home mortgages)
Harold A. Matzoll, Acting
Manager
34 Civic Center Plaza,
Box 12850
Santa Ana, CA 92712-2850
(714) 836-2451

(South California)
Charles Ming, Manager
1615 West Olympic
Boulevard
Los Angeles, CA 90015-3801
(213) 251-7122

Colorado
Michael Chitwood, Regional
Administrator
Regional Housing
Commissioner
HUD Denver Regional Office
Executive Tower Building
1405 Curtis Street
Denver, CO 80202-2349
(303) 844-4513

Office of Indian Programs
Housing and Community
Development Division
Executive Tower Building
1405 Curtis Street
Denver, CO 80202-2349
(303) 844-2861

Connecticut
William Hernandez, Jr.,
Manager
330 Main Street, First Floor
Hartford, CT 06106-1860
(203) 240-4523

Delaware
A. David Sharbaugh, Chief
Federal Building, Room 1304
844 King Street
Wilmington, DE 19801-3519
(302) 573-6300

District of Columbia
(Washington, D.C. Regional
Office)
Toni Thomas, Manager
Union Center Plaza, Phase II
820 First Street, NE,
Suite 300
Washington, DC 20002-4205
(202) 275-9200

Florida
James T. Chaplin, Manager
325 West Adams Street
Jacksonville, FL 32202-4303
(904) 791-2626

Housing

(Counties of Citrus, Sumter, Hernando, Pasco, Pinellas, Hillsborough, Polk, Manatee, Hardee, Highlands, DeSoto, Sarasota, Charlotte, Olaoes, Hendry, Lake Okeechobee)
George A. Milburn, Jr., Manager
Timberlake Federal Building Annex, Suite 700
501 East Polk Street
Tampa, FL 33602-3945
(813) 228-2501

(Counties of Volusia, Lake, Seminole, Orange, Brevard, Osceola, Indian River, Okeechobee, St. Lucie)
M. Jeanette Porter, Manager
Langley Building, Suite 270
3751 Maguire Boulevard
Orlando, FL 32803-3032
(407) 648-6441

(South Florida)
Orlando L. Lorie, Manager
Gables 1 Tower
1320 South Dixie Highway
Coral Gables, FL 33146-2911
(305) 662-4510

Georgia
Raymond A. Harris, Regional Housing Commissioner
Richard B. Russell Federal Building
75 Spring Street, SW
Atlanta, GA 30303-3388
(404) 331-5136

Guam
Gordon Y. Furutani, Manager
300 Ala Moana Boulevard, Room 3318
Honolulu, HI 96850-4991
(808) 546-2136

Hawaii
Gordon Y. Furutani, Manager
300 Ala Moana Boulevard, Room 3318
Honolulu, HI 96850-4991
(808) 546-2136

Idaho
(North Idaho)
Keith R. Green, Manager
Farm Credit Bank Building, Eighth Floor East
West 601 1st Avenue
Spokane, WA 99204-0317
(509) 456-2624

(West-Central Idaho)
Gary Gillespie, Manager
Federal Building and U.S. Courthouse
P.O. Box 042
550 West Fort Street
Boise, ID 83724-0420
(208) 334-1990

(South Idaho)
Richard C. Brinck, Manager
Cascade Building
520 SW 6th Avenue
Portland, OR 97204-1596
(503) 221-2561

Illinois
Chicago Office of Indian Programs
Housing Development Division
626 West Jackson Boulevard
Chicago, IL 60606-5601
(312) 353-1684

(Chicago Regional Office)
Gertrude Jordan,
Regional Housing Commissioner
626 West Jackson Boulevard
Chicago, IL 60606-5601
(312) 353-5680

(Central and South Illinois)
John Lawler, Acting Supervisory Appraiser
Lincoln Towers Plaza, Suite 672
524 South Second Street
Springfield, IL 62701-1774
(217) 492-4085

Indiana
J. Nicholas Shelley, Manager
151 North Delaware Street
Indianapolis, IN 46204-2526
(317) 226-6303

Iowa
Roger M. Massey, Manager
Braiker/Brandeis Building
210 South 16th Street
Omaha, NE 68102-1622
(402) 221-3703

William R. McNarney, Manager
HUD Des Moines Office
Federal Building, Room 259
210 Walnut Street
Des Moines, IA 50309-2155
(515) 284-4512

Kansas
William H. Brown, Regional Administrator
Regional Housing Commissioner
HUD Kansas City, Regional Office
Gateway Tower II
400 State Avenue
Kansas City, KS 66101-2406
(913) 236-2162

Kentucky
Verna V. Van Ness, Manager
601 West Broadway
P.O. Box 1044
Louisville, KY 40201-1044
(502) 582-5251

Louisiana
Robert Vasquez, Manager
Fisk Federal Building,
1661 Canal Street
P.O. Box 70288
New Orleans, LA 70112-2887
(504) 589-7200

(North Louisiana)
David E. Gleason, Manager
New Federal Building
500 Fannin Street
Shreveport, LA 71101-3077
(318) 226-5385

Maine
Richard Young, Supervisory
Appraiser
Casco Northern Bank
Building
23 Main Street
Bangor, ME 04401-4318
(207) 945-0467

James Barry, Manager
Norris Cotton Federal
Building
275 Chestnut Street
Manchester, NH 03101-2487
(603) 666-7681

Maryland
(Except Montgomery and
Prince Georges Counties)
Maxine Saunders, Manager
The Equitable Building,
Third Floor
10 North Calvert Street
Baltimore, MD 21202-1865
(301) 962-2121

(Montgomery and Prince
Georges Counties)
Toni Thomas, Manager
Union Center Plaza, Phase II
820 First Street, NE,
Suite 300
Washington, DC 20002-4205
(202) 275-9200

Massachusetts
John Mastropietro,
Acting Regional
Administrator
Regional Housing
Commissioner
Boston Federal Office
Building, Room 375
10 Causeway Street
Boston, MA 02222-1092
(617) 565-5234

Michigan
Harry I. Sharrott, Manager
Patrick V. McNamara Federal
Building
477 Michigan Avenue
Detroit, MI 48226-2592
(313) 226-6280

(East Michigan)
Gary T. LeVine, Manager
Gil Sabuco Building,
Room 200
352 South Saginaw Street
Flint, MI 48502-1953
(313) 766-5112

(West and North Michigan)
Ronald Weston, Manager
Northbrook Building, No. II
2922 Fuller Avenue, NE
Grand Rapids, MI 48505-3409
(616) 456-2100

Minnesota
Thomas Feeney, Manager
Bridge Place Building
220 Second Street, South
Minneapolis, MN 55401-2195
(612) 370-3000

Mississippi
Sandra Freeman, Manager
Dr. A. H. McCoy Federal
Building, Room 910
100 West Capitol Street
Jackson, MS 39269-1096
(601) 965-4702

Missouri
Kenneth G. Lange, Manager
210 North Tucker Boulevard
St. Louis, MO 63101-1997
(314) 425-4761

Montana
Christian KaFentzis, Manager
Federal Office Building,
Room 340
Drawer 10095
301 South Park
Helena, MT 59626-0095
(406) 449-5205

Nebraska
Roger M. Massey, Manager
Braiker/Brandeis Building
210 South 16th Street
Omaha, NE 68102-1622
(402) 221-3703

Nevada
Andrew D. Whitten, Jr.,
Manager
1050 Bible Way
P.O. Box 4700
Reno, NV 89505-4700
(702) 784-5356

Andrew Robertson, Manager
1500 East Tropicana Avenue,
Second Floor
Las Vegas, NV 89119-6516
(702) 388-6500

(North Nevada)
Office of Indian Programs
Community Planning and
Development Division
San Francisco Program
Management Team
Phillip Burton Federal
Building and U.S.
Courthouse
450 Golden Gate Avenue
P.O. Box 36003
San Francisco, CA
94102-3448
(415) 556-9200

New Hampshire
James Barry, Manager
Norris Cotton Federal
Building
275 Chestnut Street
Manchester, NH 03101-2487
(603) 666-7681

New Jersey
(North New Jersey)
Theodore Britton, Jr.,
Manager
Military Park Building
60 Park Place
Newark, NJ 07102-5504
(201) 887-1662

Housing

(South New Jersey)
Elmer Roy, Manager
The Parkade Building
519 Federal Street
Camden, NJ 08103-9998
(609) 757-5081

New Mexico
Michael R. Griego, Manager
625 Truman Street, NE
Albuquerque, NM
87110-6443
(505) 262-6463

C. Don Babers, Acting
Manager
555 Griffin Square Building,
Room 106
525 Griffin Street
Dallas, TX 75202-5007
(214) 767-8308

New York
Dr. Anthony Villane, Regional
Housing Commissioner
26 Federal Plaza
New York, NY 10278-0068
(212) 264-8068

(North New York)
John Petricco, Manager
Leo W. O'Brien Federal
Building
North Pearl Street and
Clinton Avenue
Albany, NY 12207-2395
(518) 472-3567

(West New York)
Joseph Lynch, Manager
465 Main Street, Fifth Floor
Lafayette Court
Buffalo, NY 14203-1780
(716) 846-5755

North Carolina
Larry J. Parker, Manager
415 North Edgeworth Street
Greensboro, NC 27401-2107
(919) 333-5363

North Dakota
Keith Elliot, Chief
Federal Building, Room 300
653 2nd Avenue, North
P.O. Box 2483
Fargo, ND 58108-2483
(701) 239-5136

Ohio
Robert W. Dolin, Manager
New Federal Building
200 North High Street
Columbus, OH 43215-2499
(614) 469-5737

(North Ohio)
George L. Engel, Manager
One Playhouse Square
1375 Euclid Avenue,
Room 420
Cleveland, OH 44115-1832
(216) 522-4065

(Southwest Ohio)
William Harris, Manager
Federal Office Building,
Room 9002
550 Main Street
Cincinnati, OH 45202-3253
(513) 684-2884

Oklahoma
Edwin I. Gardner, Manager
Murrah Federal Building
200 NW 5th Street
Oklahoma City, OK
73102-3202
(405) 231-4181

Indian Programs Division
Hugh Johnson, Director
Community Planning and
Development Branch
Murrah Federal Building
200 NW 5th Street
Oklahoma City, OK
73102-3202
(405) 231-4101

(East Oklahoma)
Robert H. Gardner, Manager
Robert S. Kerr Building,
Room 200
440 South Houston Avenue
Tulsa, OK 74127-8923
(918) 581-7435

Oregon
Richard C. Brinck, Manager
Cascade Building
520 SW 6th Avenue
Portland, OR 97204-1596
(503) 221-2561

Panama Canal Zone
Rosa Villalonga, Acting
Manager
159 Carlos Chardon Avenue
San Juan, PR 00918-1804
(809) 766-5201 or
(809) 498-5201

Pennsylvania
(Philadelphia Regional
Office)
Michael A. Smerconish,
Regional Administrator
Regional Housing
Commissioner
Liberty Square Building
105 South 7th Street
Philadelphia, PA 19106-3392
(215) 597-2560

(West Pennsylvania)
William Costello, Acting
Manager
412 Old Post Office
Courthouse Building
7th Avenue and Grant Street
Pittsburgh, PA 15219-1906
(412) 644-6428

Puerto Rico
Rosa Villalonga, Acting
Manager
159 Carlos Chardon Avenue
San Juan, PR 00918-1804
(809) 766-5201 or
(809) 498-5201

Rhode Island
Casimir J. Kolaski, Jr.,
Manager
Federal Building and U.S.
Post Office, Room 330
Kennedy Plaza
Providence, RI 02903-1745
(401) 528-5351

South Carolina
Ted B. Freeman, Manager
Strom Thurmond Federal
Building
1835-45 Assembly Street
Columbia, SC 29201-2480
(803) 765-5592

South Dakota
Don Olson, Chief
Courthouse Plaza, Suite 116
300 North Dakota Avenue
Sioux Falls, SD 57102-0311
(605) 330-4223

Tennessee
Richard B. Barnwell,
Manager
John J. Duncan Federal
Building
710 Locust Street, SW
Knoxville, TN 37902-2526
(615) 549-9384

(Central Tennessee)
John H. Fisher, Manager
251 Cumberland Bend Drive,
Suite 200
Nashville, TN 37228-1803
(615) 736-5213

(West Tennessee)
Bob Atkins, Manager
One Memphis Place,
Suite 1200
200 Jefferson Avenue
Memphis, TN 38103-2335
(901) 521-3367

Texas
(Fort Worth Regional Office)
Sam R. Moseley, Regional
Housing Commissioner
1600 Throckmorton
P.O. Box 2905
Forth Worth, TX 76113-2905
(817) 885-5401

(Northwest Texas)
Henry E. Whitney, Manager
Federal Office Building
1205 Texas Avenue
Lubbock, TX 79401-4093
(806) 743-7265

(East, North, and West
Texas)
C. Don Babers, Acting
Manager
555 Griffin Square Building,
Room 106
525 Griffin Street
Dallas, TX 75202-5007
(214) 767-8308

(Five Counties in East Texas)
David E. Gleason, Manager
New Federal Building
500 Fannin Street
Shreveport, LA 71101-3077
(318) 226-5385

(East-Central Texas)
William Robertson, Jr.,
Manager
National Bank of Texas
Building, Suite 300
221 Norfolk
Houston, TX 77098-4096
(713) 229-3589

(Bowie County)
Roger Zachritz, Acting
Manager
Lafayette Building, Suite 200
523 Louisiana
Little Rock, AR 72201-3523
(501) 378-5931

(Southwest Texas)
Don Creed, Manager
Washington Square Building
800 Dolorosa Street
San Antonio, TX 78207-4563
(512) 229-6781

Utah
Richard Bell, Manager
324 South State Street,
Suite 220
Salt Lake City, UT
84111-2321
(801) 524-5237

Vermont
William Peters, Chief
Federal Building, Room B311
11 Elmwood Avenue
P.O. Box 879
Burlington, VT 05402-0879
(802) 951-6290

James Barry, Manager
Norris Cotton Federal
Building
275 Chestnut Street
Manchester, NH 03101-2487
(603) 666-7681

Virgin Islands
Rosa Villalonga, Acting
Manager
159 Carlos Chardon Avenue
San Juan, PR 00918-1804
(809) 766-5201 or
(809) 498-5201

Virginia
(North Virginia)
Toni Thomas, Manager
Union Center Plaza, Phase II
820 First Street, NE,
Suite 300
Washington, DC 20002-4205
(202) 275-9200

(South Virginia)
Mary Ann Wilson, Manager
Federal Building, First Floor
400 North Eighth Street
Richmond, VA 23240-0170
(804) 771-2721

Housing

Washington
Office of Indian Programs
Community Planning and
Development Division
Arcade Plaza Building
1321 Second Avenue
Seattle, WA 98101-2058
(206) 442-0760

(Seattle Regional Office)
Richard Bauer,
Regional Housing
Commissioner
Arcade Plaza Building
1321 Second Avenue
Seattle, WA 98101-2054
(206) 442-5414

(East Washington)
Keith R. Green, Manager
Farm Credit Bank Building,
Eighth Floor East
West 601 1st Avenue
Spokane, WA 99204-0317
(509) 456-2624

(Clark, Klickitat, and
Skamania Counties)
Richard C. Brinck, Manager
Cascade Building
520 SW 6th Avenue
Portland, OR 97204-1596
(503) 221-2561

West Virginia
William Costello, Acting
Manager
412 Old Post Office
Courthouse Building
7th Avenue and Grant Street
Pittsburgh, PA 15219-1906
(412) 644-6428

or:

405 Capitol Street, Suite 708
Charleston, WV 25301-1795
(304) 347-7000

Wisconsin
Delbert F. Reynolds,
Manager
Henry S. Reuss Federal Plaza
310 West Wisconsin Avenue,
Suite 1380
Milwaukee, WI 53203-2289
(414) 291-3214

Wyoming
Lawrence Gosnell, Chief
4225 Federal Office Building
100 East B Street
P.O. Box 580
Casper, WY 82602-1918
(307) 261-5252

MORTGAGE INSURANCE—NURSING HOMES, INTERMEDIATE CARE FACILITIES, AND BOARD AND CARE HOMES

**Department of Housing
and Urban Development**
Policies and Procedures
Division
Office of Insured
Multifamily Housing
Development
Washington, DC 20412
(202) 708-2556

Description: Guaranteed/insured loans to investors, builders, developers, and corporations to make possible construction and rehabilitation of nursing homes and the like. Applicants must be licensed or regulated by the state.
$ Given: Nationwide FY 93 est. $913.5 million in insured mortgages.
Application Information: Initial conference at local HUD office followed by formal application.
Deadline: Established on case-by-case basis, mutually agreed to conference.
Contact: Local HUD field office

Alabama
Robert E. Lunsford, Manager
600 Beacon Parkway West,
Suite 300
Birmingham, AL 35209-3144
(205) 731-1617

Alaska
Arlene Patton, Manager
222 West 8th Avenue, #64
Anchorage, AK 99513-7537
(907) 271-4170

Community Planning and
Development Division
222 West 8th Avenue, #64
Anchorage, AK 99513-7537
(907) 271-3669

American Samoa
Gordon Y. Furutani, Manager
300 Ala Moana Boulevard,
Room 3318
Honolulu, HI 96850-4991
(808) 546-2136

Arizona
Dwight Peterson, Manager
400 North First Street,
Suite 1600
P.O. Box 13468
Phoenix, AZ 85004-2361
(602) 261-4434

Charles Ming, Manager
1615 West Olympic
Boulevard
Los Angeles, CA 90015-3801
(213) 251-7122

Jean Staley, Manager
Pioneer Plaza, 100 North
Stone Avenue, Suite 410
P.O. Box 2648
Tucson, AZ 86701-1467
(602) 629-6237

Arkansas
Roger Zachritz, Acting
Manager
Lafayette Building, Suite 200
523 Louisiana
Little Rock, AR 72201-3523
(501) 378-5931

California
Lilly Lee, Manager
1630 East Shaw Avenue,
Suite 138
Fresno, CA 93710-8193
(209) 487-5033

(San Francisco Regional
Office)
Robert De Monte, Regional
Housing Commissioner
Phillip Burton Federal
Building and U.S Courthouse
450 Golden Gate Avenue
P.O. Box 36003
San Francisco, CA
94102-3448
(415) 556-4752

(North California)
Office of Indian Programs
Community Planning and
Development Division
San Francisco Program
Management Team
Phillip Burton Federal
Building and U.S.
Courthouse
450 Golden Gate Avenue
P.O. Box 36003
San Francisco, CA
94102-3448
(415) 556-9200

(Northeast California)
Anthony A. Randolph,
Manager
777 12th Street, Suite 200
P.O. Box 1978
Sacramento, CA 95814-1997
(916) 551-1351

(Imperial and San Diego
Counties)
Charles J. Wilson, Manager
Federal Office Building,
Room 563
880 Front Street
San Diego, CA 92188-0100
(619) 557-5310

(Orange, Riverside and San
Bernardino Counties, for
home mortgages)
Harold A. Matzoll, Acting
Manager
34 Civic Center Plaza,
Box 12850
Santa Ana, CA 92712-2850
(714) 836-2451

(South California)
Charles Ming, Manager
1615 West Olympic
Boulevard
Los Angeles, CA 90015-3801
(213) 251-7122

Colorado
Michael Chitwood, Regional
Administrator
Regional Housing
Commissioner
HUD Denver Regional Office
Executive Tower Building
1405 Curtis Street
Denver, CO 80202-2349
(303) 844-4513

Office of Indian Programs
Housing and Community
Development Division
Executive Tower Building
1405 Curtis Street
Denver, CO 80202-2349
(303) 844-2861

Connecticut
William Hernandez, Jr.,
Manager
330 Main Street, First Floor
Hartford, CT 06106-1860
(203) 240-4523

Delaware
A. David Sharbaugh, Chief
Federal Building, Room 1304
844 King Street
Wilmington, DE 19801-3519
(302) 573-6300

District of Columbia
(Washington, D.C. Regional
Office)
Toni Thomas, Manager
Union Center Plaza, Phase II
820 First Street, NE,
Suite 300
Washington, DC 20002-4205
(202) 275-9200

Florida
James T. Chaplin, Manager
325 West Adams Street
Jacksonville, FL 32202-4303
(904) 791-2626

(Counties of Citrus, Sumter, Hernando, Pasco, Pinellas, Hillsborough, Polk, Manatee, Hardee, Highlands, DeSoto, Sarasota, Charlotte, Olaoes, Hendry, Lake Okeechobee)
George A. Milburn, Jr., Manager
Timberlake Federal Building Annex, Suite 700
501 East Polk Street
Tampa, FL 33602-3945
(813) 228-2501

(Counties of Volusia, Lake, Seminole, Orange, Brevard, Osceola, Indian River, Okeechobee, St. Lucie)
M. Jeanette Porter, Manager
Langley Building, Suite 270
3751 Maguire Boulevard
Orlando, FL 32803-3032
(407) 648-6441

(South Florida)
Orlando L. Lorie, Manager
Gables 1 Tower
1320 South Dixie Highway
Coral Gables, FL 33146-2911
(305) 662-4510

Georgia
Raymond A. Harris, Regional Housing Commissioner
Richard B. Russell Federal Building
75 Spring Street, SW
Atlanta, GA 30303-3388
(404) 331-5136

Guam
Gordon Y. Furutani, Manager
300 Ala Moana Boulevard, Room 3318
Honolulu, HI 96850-4991
(808) 546-2136

Hawaii
Gordon Y. Furutani, Manager
300 Ala Moana Boulevard, Room 3318
Honolulu, HI 96850-4991
(808) 546-2136

Idaho
(North Idaho)
Keith R. Green, Manager
Farm Credit Bank Building, Eighth Floor East
West 601 1st Avenue
Spokane, WA 99204-0317
(509) 456-2624

(West-Central Idaho)
Gary Gillespie, Manager
Federal Building and U.S. Courthouse
P.O. Box 042
550 West Fort Street
Boise, ID 83724-0420
(208) 334-1990

(South Idaho)
Richard C. Brinck, Manager
Cascade Building
520 SW 6th Avenue
Portland, OR 97204-1596
(503) 221-2561

Illinois
Chicago Office of Indian Programs
Housing Development Division
626 West Jackson Boulevard
Chicago, IL 60606-5601
(312) 353-1684

(Chicago Regional Office)
Gertrude Jordan, Regional Housing Commissioner
626 West Jackson Boulevard
Chicago, IL 60606-5601
(312) 353-5680

(Central and South Illinois)
John Lawler, Acting Supervisory Appraiser
Lincoln Towers Plaza, Suite 672
524 South Second Street
Springfield, IL 62701-1774
(217) 492-4085

Indiana
J. Nicholas Shelley, Manager
151 North Delaware Street
Indianapolis, IN 46204-2526
(317) 226-6303

Iowa
Roger M. Massey, Manager
Braiker/Brandeis Building
210 South 16th Street
Omaha, NE 68102-1622
(402) 221-3703

William R. McNarney, Manager
HUD Des Moines Office
Federal Building, Room 259
210 Walnut Street
Des Moines, IA 50309-2155
(515) 284-4512

Kansas
William H. Brown, Regional Administrator
Regional Housing Commissioner
HUD Kansas City, Regional Office
Gateway Tower II
400 State Avenue
Kansas City, KS 66101-2406
(913) 236-2162

Kentucky
Verna V. Van Ness, Manager
601 West Broadway
P.O. Box 1044
Louisville, KY 40201-1044
(502) 582-5251

Louisiana
Robert Vasquez, Manager
Fisk Federal Building,
1661 Canal Street
P.O. Box 70288
New Orleans, LA 70112-2887
(504) 589-7200

(North Louisiana)
David E. Gleason, Manager
New Federal Building
500 Fannin Street
Shreveport, LA 71101-3077
(318) 226-5385

Maine
Richard Young, Supervisory
Appraiser
Casco Northern Bank
Building
23 Main Street
Bangor, ME 04401-4318
(207) 945-0467

James Barry, Manager
Norris Cotton Federal
Building
275 Chestnut Street
Manchester, NH 03101-2487
(603) 666-7681

Maryland
(Except Montgomery and
Prince Georges Counties)
Maxine Saunders, Manager
The Equitable Building,
Third Floor
10 North Calvert Street
Baltimore, MD 21202-1865
(301) 962-2121

(Montgomery and Prince
Georges Counties)
Toni Thomas, Manager
Union Center Plaza, Phase II
820 First Street, NE,
Suite 300
Washington, DC 20002-4205
(202) 275-9200

Massachusetts
John Mastropietro,
Acting Regional
Administrator
Regional Housing
Commissioner
Boston Federal Office
Building, Room 375
10 Causeway Street
Boston, MA 02222-1092
(617) 565-5234

Michigan
Harry I. Sharrott, Manager
Patrick V. McNamara Federal
Building
477 Michigan Avenue
Detroit, MI 48226-2592
(313) 226-6280

(East Michigan)
Gary T. LeVine, Manager
Gil Sabuco Building,
Room 200
352 South Saginaw Street
Flint, MI 48502-1953
(313) 766-5112

(West and North Michigan)
Ronald Weston, Manager
Northbrook Building, No. II
2922 Fuller Avenue, NE
Grand Rapids, MI 48505-3409
(616) 456-2100

Minnesota
Thomas Feeney, Manager
Bridge Place Building
220 Second Street, South
Minneapolis, MN 55401-2195
(612) 370-3000

Mississippi
Sandra Freeman, Manager
Dr. A. H. McCoy Federal
Building, Room 910
100 West Capitol Street
Jackson, MS 39269-1096
(601) 965-4702

Missouri
Kenneth G. Lange, Manager
210 North Tucker Boulevard
St. Louis, MO 63101-1997
(314) 425-4761

Montana
Christian KaFentzis, Manager
Federal Office Building,
Room 340
Drawer 10095
301 South Park
Helena, MT 59626-0095
(406) 449-5205

Nebraska
Roger M. Massey, Manager
Braiker/Brandeis Building
210 South 16th Street
Omaha, NE 68102-1622
(402) 221-3703

Nevada
Andrew D. Whitten, Jr.,
Manager
1050 Bible Way
P.O. Box 4700
Reno, NV 89505-4700
(702) 784-5356

Andrew Robertson, Manager
1500 East Tropicana Avenue,
Second Floor
Las Vegas, NV 89119-6516
(702) 388-6500

(North Nevada)
Office of Indian Programs
Community Planning and
Development Division
San Francisco Program
Management Team
Phillip Burton Federal
Building and U.S.
Courthouse
450 Golden Gate Avenue
P.O. Box 36003
San Francisco, CA
94102-3448
(415) 556-9200

New Hampshire
James Barry, Manager
Norris Cotton Federal
Building
275 Chestnut Street
Manchester, NH 03101-2487
(603) 666-7681

New Jersey
(North New Jersey)
Theodore Britton, Jr.,
Manager
Military Park Building
60 Park Place
Newark, NJ 07102-5504
(201) 887-1662

Housing

(South New Jersey)
Elmer Roy, Manager
The Parkade Building
519 Federal Street
Camden, NJ 08103-9998
(609) 757-5081

New Mexico
Michael R. Griego, Manager
625 Truman Street, NE
Albuquerque, NM
87110-6443
(505) 262-6463

C. Don Babers, Acting
Manager
555 Griffin Square Building,
Room 106
525 Griffin Street
Dallas, TX 75202-5007
(214) 767-8308

New York
Dr. Anthony Villane, Regional
Housing Commissioner
26 Federal Plaza
New York, NY 10278-0068
(212) 264-8068

(North New York)
John Petricco, Manager
Leo W. O'Brien Federal
Building
North Pearl Street and
Clinton Avenue
Albany, NY 12207-2395
(518) 472-3567

(West New York)
Joseph Lynch, Manager
465 Main Street, Fifth Floor
Lafayette Court
Buffalo, NY 14203-1780
(716) 846-5755

North Carolina
Larry J. Parker, Manager
415 North Edgeworth Street
Greensboro, NC 27401-2107
(919) 333-5363

North Dakota
Keith Elliot, Chief
Federal Building, Room 300
653 2nd Avenue, North
P.O. Box 2483
Fargo, ND 58108-2483
(701) 239-5136

Ohio
Robert W. Dolin, Manager
New Federal Building
200 North High Street
Columbus, OH 43215-2499
(614) 469-5737

(North Ohio)
George L. Engel, Manager
One Playhouse Square
1375 Euclid Avenue,
Room 420
Cleveland, OH 44115-1832
(216) 522-4065

(Southwest Ohio)
William Harris, Manager
Federal Office Building,
Room 9002
550 Main Street
Cincinnati, OH 45202-3253
(513) 684-2884

Oklahoma
Edwin I. Gardner, Manager
Murrah Federal Building
200 NW 5th Street
Oklahoma City, OK
73102-3202
(405) 231-4181

Indian Programs Division
Hugh Johnson, Director
Community Planning and
Development Branch
Murrah Federal Building
200 NW 5th Street
Oklahoma City, OK
73102-3202
(405) 231-4101

(East Oklahoma)
Robert H. Gardner, Manager
Robert S. Kerr Building,
Room 200
440 South Houston Avenue
Tulsa, OK 74127-8923
(918) 581-7435

Oregon
Richard C. Brinck, Manager
Cascade Building
520 SW 6th Avenue
Portland, OR 97204-1596
(503) 221-2561

Panama Canal Zone
Rosa Villalonga, Acting
Manager
159 Carlos Chardon Avenue
San Juan, PR 00918-1804
(809) 766-5201 or
(809) 498-5201

Pennsylvania
(Philadelphia Regional
Office)
Michael A. Smerconish,
Regional Administrator
Regional Housing
Commissioner
Liberty Square Building
105 South 7th Street
Philadelphia, PA 19106-3392
(215) 597-2560

(West Pennsylvania)
William Costello, Acting
Manager
412 Old Post Office
Courthouse Building
7th Avenue and Grant Street
Pittsburgh, PA 15219-1906
(412) 644-6428

Puerto Rico
Rosa Villalonga, Acting
Manager
159 Carlos Chardon Avenue
San Juan, PR 00918-1804
(809) 766-5201 or
(809) 498-5201

Rhode Island
Casimir J. Kolaski, Jr.,
Manager
Federal Building and U.S.
Post Office, Room 330
Kennedy Plaza
Providence, RI 02903-1745
(401) 528-5351

South Carolina
Ted B. Freeman, Manager
Strom Thurmond Federal
Building
1835-45 Assembly Street
Columbia, SC 29201-2480
(803) 765-5592

South Dakota
Don Olson, Chief
Courthouse Plaza, Suite 116
300 North Dakota Avenue
Sioux Falls, SD 57102-0311
(605) 330-4223

Tennessee
Richard B. Barnwell,
Manager
John J. Duncan Federal
Building
710 Locust Street, SW
Knoxville, TN 37902-2526
(615) 549-9384

(Central Tennessee)
John H. Fisher, Manager
251 Cumberland Bend Drive,
Suite 200
Nashville, TN 37228-1803
(615) 736-5213

(West Tennessee)
Bob Atkins, Manager
One Memphis Place,
Suite 1200
200 Jefferson Avenue
Memphis, TN 38103-2335
(901) 521-3367

Texas
(Fort Worth Regional Office)
Sam R. Moseley, Regional
Housing Commissioner
1600 Throckmorton
P.O. Box 2905
Forth Worth, TX 76113-2905
(817) 885-5401

(Northwest Texas)
Henry E. Whitney, Manager
Federal Office Building
1205 Texas Avenue
Lubbock, TX 79401-4093
(806) 743-7265

(East, North, and West
Texas)
C. Don Babers, Acting
Manager
555 Griffin Square Building,
Room 106
525 Griffin Street
Dallas, TX 75202-5007
(214) 767-8308

(Five Counties in East Texas)
David E. Gleason, Manager
New Federal Building
500 Fannin Street
Shreveport, LA 71101-3077
(318) 226-5385

(East-Central Texas)
William Robertson, Jr.,
Manager
National Bank of Texas
Building, Suite 300
221 Norfolk
Houston, TX 77098-4096
(713) 229-3589

(Bowie County)
Roger Zachritz, Acting
Manager
Lafayette Building, Suite 200
523 Louisiana
Little Rock, AR 72201-3523
(501) 378-5931

(Southwest Texas)
Don Creed, Manager
Washington Square Building
800 Dolorosa Street
San Antonio, TX 78207-4563
(512) 229-6781

Utah
Richard Bell, Manager
324 South State Street,
Suite 220
Salt Lake City, UT
84111-2321
(801) 524-5237

Vermont
William Peters, Chief
Federal Building, Room B311
11 Elmwood Avenue
P.O. Box 879
Burlington, VT 05402-0879
(802) 951-6290

James Barry, Manager
Norris Cotton Federal
Building
275 Chestnut Street
Manchester, NH 03101-2487
(603) 666-7681

Virgin Islands
Rosa Villalonga, Acting
Manager
159 Carlos Chardon Avenue
San Juan, PR 00918-1804
(809) 766-5201 or
(809) 498-5201

Virginia
(North Virginia)
Toni Thomas, Manager
Union Center Plaza, Phase II
820 First Street, NE,
Suite 300
Washington, DC 20002-4205
(202) 275-9200

(South Virginia)
Mary Ann Wilson, Manager
Federal Building, First Floor
400 North Eighth Street
Richmond, VA 23240-0170
(804) 771-2721

Washington
Office of Indian Programs
Community Planning and
Development Division
Arcade Plaza Building
1321 Second Avenue
Seattle, WA 98101-2058
(206) 442-0760

(Seattle Regional Office)
Richard Bauer,
Regional Housing
Commissioner
Arcade Plaza Building
1321 Second Avenue
Seattle, WA 98101-2054
(206) 442-5414

(East Washington)
Keith R. Green, Manager
Farm Credit Bank Building,
Eighth Floor East
West 601 1st Avenue
Spokane, WA 99204-0317
(509) 456-2624

(Clark, Klickitat, and
Skamania Counties)
Richard C. Brinck, Manager
Cascade Building
520 SW 6th Avenue
Portland, OR 97204-1596
(503) 221-2561

West Virginia
William Costello, Acting
Manager
412 Old Post Office
Courthouse Building
7th Avenue and Grant Street
Pittsburgh, PA 15219-1906
(412) 644-6428

or:

405 Capitol Street, Suite 708
Charleston, WV 25301-1795
(304) 347-7000

Wisconsin
Delbert F. Reynolds,
Manager
Henry S. Reuss Federal Plaza
310 West Wisconsin Avenue,
Suite 1380
Milwaukee, WI 53203-2289
(414) 291-3214

Wyoming
Lawrence Gosnell, Chief
4225 Federal Office Building
100 East B Street
P.O. Box 580
Casper, WY 82602-1918
(307) 261-5252

MORTGAGE INSURANCE—RENTAL AND COOPERATIVE HOUSING FOR MODERATE-INCOME FAMILIES AND ELDERLY, MARKET INTEREST RATE

**Department of Housing
and Urban Development**
Policies and Procedures
Division
Office of Insured
Multifamily Housing
Development
Washington, DC 20412
(202) 708-2556

Description: Guaranteed/insured loans to profit-motivated sponsors, builders-sellers, and others to provide good quality rental or cooperative housing for moderate-income families and the elderly and handicapped. Housing must consist of five or more units. Various other restrictions.
$ Given: Through September 30, 1991, 11,075 projects with 1.2 million units valued at $29.3 billion.
Application Information: Initial conference with local HUD field office before submission of formal proposal.
Deadline: Established on case-by-case basis.
Contact: Nearest local HUD field office

Alabama
Robert E. Lunsford, Manager
600 Beacon Parkway West,
Suite 300
Birmingham, AL 35209-3144
(205) 731-1617

Alaska
Arlene Patton, Manager
222 West 8th Avenue, #64
Anchorage, AK 99513-7537
(907) 271-4170

Community Planning and
Development Division
222 West 8th Avenue, #64
Anchorage, AK 99513-7537
(907) 271-3669

American Samoa
Gordon Y. Furutani, Manager
300 Ala Moana Boulevard,
Room 3318
Honolulu, HI 96850-4991
(808) 546-2136

Arizona
Dwight Peterson, Manager
400 North First Street,
Suite 1600
P.O. Box 13468
Phoenix, AZ 85004-2361
(602) 261-4434

Charles Ming, Manager
1615 West Olympic
Boulevard
Los Angeles, CA 90015-3801
(213) 251-7122

Jean Staley, Manager
Pioneer Plaza, 100 North
Stone Avenue, Suite 410
P.O. Box 2648
Tucson, AZ 86701-1467
(602) 629-6237

Arkansas
Roger Zachritz, Acting
Manager
Lafayette Building, Suite 200
523 Louisiana
Little Rock, AR 72201-3523
(501) 378-5931

California
Lilly Lee, Manager
1630 East Shaw Avenue,
Suite 138
Fresno, CA 93710-8193
(209) 487-5033

(San Francisco Regional
Office)
Robert De Monte, Regional
Housing Commissioner
Phillip Burton Federal
Building and U.S Courthouse
450 Golden Gate Avenue
P.O. Box 36003
San Francisco, CA
94102-3448
(415) 556-4752

(North California)
Office of Indian Programs
Community Planning and
Development Division
San Francisco Program
Management Team
Phillip Burton Federal
Building and U.S.
Courthouse
450 Golden Gate Avenue
P.O. Box 36003
San Francisco, CA
94102-3448
(415) 556-9200

(Northeast California)
Anthony A. Randolph,
Manager
777 12th Street, Suite 200
P.O. Box 1978
Sacramento, CA 95814-1997
(916) 551-1351

(Imperial and San Diego
Counties)
Charles J. Wilson, Manager
Federal Office Building,
Room 563
880 Front Street
San Diego, CA 92188-0100
(619) 557-5310

(Orange, Riverside and San
Bernardino Counties, for
home mortgages)
Harold A. Matzoll, Acting
Manager
34 Civic Center Plaza,
Box 12850
Santa Ana, CA 92712-2850
(714) 836-2451

(South California)
Charles Ming, Manager
1615 West Olympic
Boulevard
Los Angeles, CA 90015-3801
(213) 251-7122

Colorado
Michael Chitwood, Regional
Administrator
Regional Housing
Commissioner
HUD Denver Regional Office
Executive Tower Building
1405 Curtis Street
Denver, CO 80202-2349
(303) 844-4513

Office of Indian Programs
Housing and Community
Development Division
Executive Tower Building
1405 Curtis Street
Denver, CO 80202-2349
(303) 844-2861

Connecticut
William Hernandez, jr.,
Manager
330 Main Street, First Floor
Hartford, CT 06106-1860
(203) 240-4523

Delaware
A. David Sharbaugh, Chief
Federal Building, Room 1304
844 King Street
Wilmington, DE 19801-3519
(302) 573-6300

District of Columbia
(Washington, D.C. Regional
Office)
Toni Thomas, Manager
Union Center Plaza, Phase II
820 First Street, NE,
Suite 300
Washington, DC 20002-4205
(202) 275-9200

Florida
James T. Chaplin, Manager
325 West Adams Street
Jacksonville, FL 32202-4303
(904) 791-2626

Housing

(Counties of Citrus, Sumter, Hernando, Pasco, Pinellas, Hillsborough, Polk, Manatee, Hardee, Highlands, DeSoto, Sarasota, Charlotte, Olaoes, Hendry, Lake Okeechobee)
George A. Milburn, Jr., Manager
Timberlake Federal Building Annex, Suite 700
501 East Polk Street
Tampa, FL 33602-3945
(813) 228-2501

(Counties of Volusia, Lake, Seminole, Orange, Brevard, Osceola, Indian River, Okeechobee, St. Lucie)
M. Jeanette Porter, Manager
Langley Building, Suite 270
3751 Maguire Boulevard
Orlando, FL 32803-3032
(407) 648-6441

(South Florida)
Orlando L. Lorie, Manager
Gables 1 Tower
1320 South Dixie Highway
Coral Gables, FL 33146-2911
(305) 662-4510

Georgia
Raymond A. Harris, Regional Housing Commissioner
Richard B. Russell Federal Building
75 Spring Street, SW
Atlanta, GA 30303-3388
(404) 331-5136

Guam
Gordon Y. Furutani, Manager
300 Ala Moana Boulevard, Room 3318
Honolulu, HI 96850-4991
(808) 546-2136

Hawaii
Gordon Y. Furutani, Manager
300 Ala Moana Boulevard, Room 3318
Honolulu, HI 96850-4991
(808) 546-2136

Idaho
(North Idaho)
Keith R. Green, Manager
Farm Credit Bank Building, Eighth Floor East
West 601 1st Avenue
Spokane, WA 99204-0317
(509) 456-2624

(West-Central Idaho)
Gary Gillespie, Manager
Federal Building and U.S. Courthouse
P.O. Box 042
550 West Fort Street
Boise, ID 83724-0420
(208) 334-1990

(South Idaho)
Richard C. Brinck, Manager
Cascade Building
520 SW 6th Avenue
Portland, OR 97204-1596
(503) 221-2561

Illinois
Chicago Office of Indian Programs
Housing Development Division
626 West Jackson Boulevard
Chicago, IL 60606-5601
(312) 353-1684

(Chicago Regional Office)
Gertrude Jordan, Regional Housing Commissioner
626 West Jackson Boulevard
Chicago, IL 60606-5601
(312) 353-5680

(Central and South Illinois)
John Lawler, Acting Supervisory Appraiser
Lincoln Towers Plaza, Suite 672
524 South Second Street
Springfield, IL 62701-1774
(217) 492-4085

Indiana
J. Nicholas Shelley, Manager
151 North Delaware Street
Indianapolis, IN 46204-2526
(317) 226-6303

Iowa
Roger M. Massey, Manager
Braiker/Brandeis Building
210 South 16th Street
Omaha, NE 68102-1622
(402) 221-3703

William R. McNarney, Manager
HUD Des Moines Office
Federal Building, Room 259
210 Walnut Street
Des Moines, IA 50309-2155
(515) 284-4512

Kansas
William H. Brown, Regional Administrator
Regional Housing Commissioner
HUD Kansas City, Regional Office
Gateway Tower II
400 State Avenue
Kansas City, KS 66101-2406
(913) 236-2162

Kentucky
Verna V. Van Ness, Manager
601 West Broadway
P.O. Box 1044
Louisville, KY 40201-1044
(502) 582-5251

Louisiana
Robert Vasquez, Manager
Fisk Federal Building,
1661 Canal Street
P.O. Box 70288
New Orleans, LA 70112-2887
(504) 589-7200

(North Louisiana)
David E. Gleason, Manager
New Federal Building
500 Fannin Street
Shreveport, LA 71101-3077
(318) 226-5385

Maine
Richard Young, Supervisory
Appraiser
Casco Northern Bank
Building
23 Main Street
Bangor, ME 04401-4318
(207) 945-0467

James Barry, Manager
Norris Cotton Federal
Building
275 Chestnut Street
Manchester, NH 03101-2487
(603) 666-7681

Maryland
(Except Montgomery and
Prince Georges Counties)
Maxine Saunders, Manager
The Equitable Building,
Third Floor
10 North Calvert Street
Baltimore, MD 21202-1865
(301) 962-2121

(Montgomery and Prince
Georges Counties)
Toni Thomas, Manager
Union Center Plaza, Phase II
820 First Street, NE,
Suite 300
Washington, DC 20002-4205
(202) 275-9200

Massachusetts
John Mastropietro,
Acting Regional
Administrator
Regional Housing
Commissioner
Boston Federal Office
Building, Room 375
10 Causeway Street
Boston, MA 02222-1092
(617) 565-5234

Michigan
Harry I. Sharrott, Manager
Patrick V. McNamara Federal
Building
477 Michigan Avenue
Detroit, MI 48226-2592
(313) 226-6280

(East Michigan)
Gary T. LeVine, Manager
Gil Sabuco Building,
Room 200
352 South Saginaw Street
Flint, MI 48502-1953
(313) 766-5112

(West and North Michigan)
Ronald Weston, Manager
Northbrook Building, No. II
2922 Fuller Avenue, NE
Grand Rapids, MI 48505-3409
(616) 456-2100

Minnesota
Thomas Feeney, Manager
Bridge Place Building
220 Second Street, South
Minneapolis, MN 55401-2195
(612) 370-3000

Mississippi
Sandra Freeman, Manager
Dr. A. H. McCoy Federal
Building, Room 910
100 West Capitol Street
Jackson, MS 39269-1096
(601) 965-4702

Missouri
Kenneth G. Lange, Manager
210 North Tucker Boulevard
St. Louis, MO 63101-1997
(314) 425-4761

Montana
Christian KaFentzis, Manager
Federal Office Building,
Room 340
Drawer 10095
301 South Park
Helena, MT 59626-0095
(406) 449-5205

Nebraska
Roger M. Massey, Manager
Braiker/Brandeis Building
210 South 16th Street
Omaha, NE 68102-1622
(402) 221-3703

Nevada
Andrew D. Whitten, Jr.,
Manager
1050 Bible Way
P.O. Box 4700
Reno, NV 89505-4700
(702) 784-5356

Andrew Robertson, Manager
1500 East Tropicana Avenue,
Second Floor
Las Vegas, NV 89119-6516
(702) 388-6500

(North Nevada)
Office of Indian Programs
Community Planning and
Development Division
San Francisco Program
Management Team
Phillip Burton Federal
Building and U.S.
Courthouse
450 Golden Gate Avenue
P.O. Box 36003
San Francisco, CA
94102-3448
(415) 556-9200

New Hampshire
James Barry, Manager
Norris Cotton Federal
Building
275 Chestnut Street
Manchester, NH 03101-2487
(603) 666-7681

New Jersey
(North New Jersey)
Theodore Britton, Jr.,
Manager
Military Park Building
60 Park Place
Newark, NJ 07102-5504
(201) 887-1662

Housing

(South New Jersey)
Elmer Roy, Manager
The Parkade Building
519 Federal Street
Camden, NJ 08103-9998
(609) 757-5081

New Mexico
Michael R. Griego, Manager
625 Truman Street, NE
Albuquerque, NM
87110-6443
(505) 262-6463

C. Don Babers, Acting
Manager
555 Griffin Square Building,
Room 106
525 Griffin Street
Dallas, TX 75202-5007
(214) 767-8308

New York
Dr. Anthony Villane, Regional
Housing Commissioner
26 Federal Plaza
New York, NY 10278-0068
(212) 264-8068

(North New York)
John Petricco, Manager
Leo W. O'Brien Federal
Building
North Pearl Street and
Clinton Avenue
Albany, NY 12207-2395
(518) 472-3567

(West New York)
Joseph Lynch, Manager
465 Main Street, Fifth Floor
Lafayette Court
Buffalo, NY 14203-1780
(716) 846-5755

North Carolina
Larry J. Parker, Manager
415 North Edgeworth Street
Greensboro, NC 27401-2107
(919) 333-5363

North Dakota
Keith Elliot, Chief
Federal Building, Room 300
653 2nd Avenue, North
P.O. Box 2483
Fargo, ND 58108-2483
(701) 239-5136

Ohio
Robert W. Dolin, Manager
New Federal Building
200 North High Street
Columbus, OH 43215-2499
(614) 469-5737

(North Ohio)
George L. Engel, Manager
One Playhouse Square
1375 Euclid Avenue,
Room 420
Cleveland, OH 44115-1832
(216) 522-4065

(Southwest Ohio)
William Harris, Manager
Federal Office Building,
Room 9002
550 Main Street
Cincinnati, OH 45202-3253
(513) 684-2884

Oklahoma
Edwin I. Gardner, Manager
Murrah Federal Building
200 NW 5th Street
Oklahoma City, OK
73102-3202
(405) 231-4181

Indian Programs Division
Hugh Johnson, Director
Community Planning and
Development Branch
Murrah Federal Building
200 NW 5th Street
Oklahoma City, OK
73102-3202
(405) 231-4101

(East Oklahoma)
Robert H. Gardner, Manager
Robert S. Kerr Building,
Room 200
440 South Houston Avenue
Tulsa, OK 74127-8923
(918) 581-7435

Oregon
Richard C. Brinck, Manager
Cascade Building
520 SW 6th Avenue
Portland, OR 97204-1596
(503) 221-2561

Panama Canal Zone
Rosa Villalonga, Acting
Manager
159 Carlos Chardon Avenue
San Juan, PR 00918-1804
(809) 766-5201 or
(809) 498-5201

Pennsylvania
(Philadelphia Regional
Office)
Michael A. Smerconish,
Regional Administrator
Regional Housing
Commissioner
Liberty Square Building
105 South 7th Street
Philadelphia, PA 19106-3392
(215) 597-2560

(West Pennsylvania)
William Costello, Acting
Manager
412 Old Post Office
Courthouse Building
7th Avenue and Grant Street
Pittsburgh, PA 15219-1906
(412) 644-6428

Puerto Rico
Rosa Villalonga, Acting
Manager
159 Carlos Chardon Avenue
San Juan, PR 00918-1804
(809) 766-5201 or
(809) 498-5201

Rhode Island
Casimir J. Kolaski, Jr.,
Manager
Federal Building and U.S.
Post Office, Room 330
Kennedy Plaza
Providence, RI 02903-1745
(401) 528-5351

South Carolina
Ted B. Freeman, Manager
Strom Thurmond Federal
Building
1835-45 Assembly Street
Columbia, SC 29201-2480
(803) 765-5592

South Dakota
Don Olson, Chief
Courthouse Plaza, Suite 116
300 North Dakota Avenue
Sioux Falls, SD 57102-0311
(605) 330-4223

Tennessee
Richard B. Barnwell,
Manager
John J. Duncan Federal
Building
710 Locust Street, SW
Knoxville, TN 37902-2526
(615) 549-9384

(Central Tennessee)
John H. Fisher, Manager
251 Cumberland Bend Drive,
Suite 200
Nashville, TN 37228-1803
(615) 736-5213

(West Tennessee)
Bob Atkins, Manager
One Memphis Place,
Suite 1200
200 Jefferson Avenue
Memphis, TN 38103-2335
(901) 521-3367

Texas
(Fort Worth Regional Office)
Sam R. Moseley, Regional
Housing Commissioner
1600 Throckmorton
P.O. Box 2905
Forth Worth, TX 76113-2905
(817) 885-5401

(Northwest Texas)
Henry E. Whitney, Manager
Federal Office Building
1205 Texas Avenue
Lubbock, TX 79401-4093
(806) 743-7265

(East, North, and West
Texas)
C. Don D. Babers, Acting
Manager
555 Griffin Square Building,
Room 106
525 Griffin Street
Dallas, TX 75202-5007
(214) 767-8308

(Five Counties in East Texas)
David E. Gleason, Manager
New Federal Building
500 Fannin Street
Shreveport, LA 71101-3077
(318) 226-5385

(East-Central Texas)
William Robertson, Jr.,
Manager
National Bank of Texas
Building, Suite 300
221 Norfolk
Houston, TX 77098-4096
(713) 229-3589

(Bowie County)
Roger Zachritz, Acting
Manager
Lafayette Building, Suite 200
523 Louisiana
Little Rock, AR 72201-3523
(501) 378-5931

(Southwest Texas)
Don Creed, Manager
Washington Square Building
800 Dolorosa Street
San Antonio, TX 78207-4563
(512) 229-6781

Utah
Richard Bell, Manager
324 South State Street,
Suite 220
Salt Lake City, UT
84111-2321
(801) 524-5237

Vermont
William Peters, Chief
Federal Building, Room B311
11 Elmwood Avenue
P.O. Box 879
Burlington, VT 05402-0879
(802) 951-6290

James Barry, Manager
Norris Cotton Federal
Building
275 Chestnut Street
Manchester, NH 03101-2487
(603) 666-7681

Virgin Islands
Rosa Villalonga, Acting
Manager
159 Carlos Chardon Avenue
San Juan, PR 00918-1804
(809) 766-5201 or
(809) 498-5201

Virginia
(North Virginia)
Toni Thomas, Manager
Union Center Plaza, Phase II
820 First Street, NE,
Suite 300
Washington, DC 20002-4205
(202) 275-9200

(South Virginia)
Mary Ann Wilson, Manager
Federal Building, First Floor
400 North Eighth Street
Richmond, VA 23240-0170
(804) 771-2721

Housing

Washington

Office of Indian Programs
Community Planning and
Development Division
Arcade Plaza Building
1321 Second Avenue
Seattle, WA 98101-2058
(206) 442-0760

(Seattle Regional Office)
Richard Bauer,
Regional Housing
Commissioner
Arcade Plaza Building
1321 Second Avenue
Seattle, WA 98101-2054
(206) 442-5414

(East Washington)
Keith R. Green, Manager
Farm Credit Bank Building,
Eighth Floor East
West 601 1st Avenue
Spokane, WA 99204-0317
(509) 456-2624

(Clark, Klickitat, and
Skamania Counties)
Richard C. Brinck, Manager
Cascade Building
520 SW 6th Avenue
Portland, OR 97204-1596
(503) 221-2561

West Virginia

William Costello, Acting
Manager
412 Old Post Office
Courthouse Building
7th Avenue and Grant Street
Pittsburgh, PA 15219-1906
(412) 644-6428

or:

405 Capitol Street, Suite 708
Charleston, WV 25301-1795
(304) 347-7000

Wisconsin

Delbert F. Reynolds,
Manager
Henry S. Reuss Federal Plaza
310 West Wisconsin Avenue,
Suite 1380
Milwaukee, WI 53203-2289
(414) 291-3214

Wyoming

Lawrence Gosnell, Chief
4225 Federal Office Building
100 East B Street
P.O. Box 580
Casper, WY 82602-1918
(307) 261-5252

MORTGAGE INSURANCE—RENTAL HOUSING

**Department of Housing
and Urban Development**
Office of Insured
Multifamily Housing
Development
Policies and Procedures
Division
Washington, DC 20410
(202) 708-2556

Description: Guaranteed and insured loans to
investors, builders, developers, and others meeting
HUD requirements to finance, construct, or
rehabilitate rental detached, semidetached, row, walk-
up, or elevator type structures with five or more units.
$ Given: N/A
Application Information: Initial conference with local
HUD field office to determine preliminary feasibility of
project is required.
Deadline: Established on a case-by-case basis.
Contact: Your local, state, and/or regional HUD office

Alabama

Robert E. Lunsford, Manager
600 Beacon Parkway West,
Suite 300
Birmingham, AL 35209-3144
(205) 731-1617

Alaska

Arlene Patton, Manager
222 West 8th Avenue, #64
Anchorage, AK 99513-7537
(907) 271-4170

Arizona

Dwight Peterson, Manager
P.O. Box 13468
Phoenix, AZ 85004-2361
(602) 261-4434

Jean Staley, Manager
Pioneer Plaza, 100 North
Stone Avenue, Suite 410
P.O. Box 2648
Tucson, AZ 86701-1467
(602) 629-6237

Charles Ming, Manager
1615 West Olympic
Boulevard
Los Angeles, CA 90015-3801
(213) 251-7122

(HUD Indian Programs)
C. Raphael Macham, Director
One North First Street,
Suite 400
Phoenix, AZ 85004-2360
(602) 261-4156

Arkansas
John T. Suskie, Manager
Lafayette Building, Suite 200
523 Louisiana
Little Rock, AR 72201-3523
(501) 378-5931

(Indian Programs)
Hugh Johnson, Director
Community Planning and
Development Branch
Murrah Federal Building
200 NW 5th Street
Oklahoma City, OK
73102-3202
(405) 231-4101

California
(Southern Region)
Charles Ming, Manager
1615 West Olympic
Boulevard
Los Angeles, CA 90015-3801
(213) 251-7122

(San Francisco Area)
John Wilson, Regional
Housing Commissioner
Phillip Burton Federal
Building and U.S.
Courthouse
450 Golden Gate Avenue P.O.
Box 36003
San Francisco, CA
94102-3448
(415) 556-4752

(Fresno)
Lilly Lee, Manager
1630 East Shaw Avenue,
Suite 138
Fresno, CA 93710-8193
(209) 487-5033

(Northeastern Region)
Paul Pradia, Acting
777 12th Street, Suite 200
P.O. Box 1978
Sacramento, CA 95814-1997
(916) 551-1351

(Imperial and San Diego
Counties)
Charles J. Wilson, Manager
Federal Office Building,
Room 563
880 Front Street
San Diego, CA 92188-0100
(619) 557-5310

(Orange, Riverside, and San
Bernardino Counties)
Earl Fields, Manager
34 Civic Center Plaza,
Box 12850
Santa Ana, CA 92712-2850
(714) 836-2451

Colorado
Michael Chitwood, Regional
Administrator
Regional Housing
Commissioner
HUD-Denver Regional Office
Executive Tower Building
1405 Curtis Street
Denver, CO 80202-2349
(303) 844-4513

(Indian Programs)
Housing and Community
Development Division
Executive Tower Building
1405 Curtis Street
Denver, CO 80202-2349
(303) 844-2861

Connecticut
William Hernandez, Jr.,
Manager
330 Main Street, First Floor
Hartford, CT 06106-1860
(203) 565-5234

Delaware
A. David Sharbaugh, Chief
Federal Building, Room 1304
844 King Street
Wilmington, DE 19801-3519
(302) 573-6300

District of Columbia
Toni Thomas, Manager
Union Center Plaza, Phase II
820 First Street, NE,
Suite 300
Washington, DC 20002-4205
(202) 275-9200

Florida
(Northern Region)
James T. Chaplin, Manager
325 West Adams Street
Jacksonville, FL 32202-4303
(904) 791-2626

(Southern Region)
Orlando L. Lorie, Manager
Gables 1 Tower
1320 South Dixie Highway
Coral Gables, FL 33146-2911
(305) 662-4510

(Central Western Counties)
George A. Milburn, Jr.,
Manager
Timberlake Federal Building
Annex, Suite 700
501 East Polk Street
Tampa, FL 33602-3945
(813) 228-2501

Housing

(Central Eastern Counties)
M. Jeanette Porter, Manager
Langley Building, Suite 270
3751 Maguire Boulevard
Orlando, FL 32803-3032
(407) 648-6441

Georgia
Raymond A. Harris, Regional
Housing Commissioner
Richard B. Russell Federal
Building
75 Spring Street, SW
Atlanta, GA 30303-3388
(404) 331-5136

Guam
Gordon Y. Furutani, Manager
300 Ala Moana Boulevard,
Room 3318
Honolulu, HI 96850-4991
(808) 546-2136

Hawaii
Gordon Y. Furutani, Manager
300 Ala Moana Boulevard,
Room 3318
Honolulu, HI 96850-4991
(808) 546-2136

Idaho
(West-Central Region)
Gary Gillespie, Manager
Federal Building and U.S.
Courthouse
P.O. Box 042
550 West Fort Street
Boise, ID 83724-0420
(208) 334-1990

(Southern Region)
Richard C. Brinck, Manager
Cascade Building
520 SW 6th Avenue
Portland, OR 97204-1596
(503) 221-2561

(Northern Region)
Keith R. Green, Manager
Farm Credit Bank Building
8th Floor East
West 601 1st Avenue
Spokane, WA 99204-0317
(509) 456-2624

Illinois
Gertrude Jordan, Regional
Housing Commissioner
626 West Jackson Boulevard
Chicago, IL 60606-5601
(312) 353-5680

(Central and Southern
Region)
William Fattic, Manager
Lincoln Towers Plaza,
Suite 672
524 South Second Street
Springfield, IL 62701-1774
(217) 492-4085

(Indian Programs)
Housing Development
Division
626 West Jackson Boulevard
Chicago, IL 60606-5601
(312) 353-1684

Indiana
J. Nicholas Shelley, Manager
151 North Delaware Street
Indianapolis, IN 46204-2526
(317) 226-6303

Iowa
William R. McNarney,
Manager
HUD Des Moines Office
Federal Building, Room 259
210 Walnut Street
Des Moines, IA 50309-2155
(515) 284-4512

Gertrude Jordan, Regional
Housing Commissioner
626 West Jackson Boulevard
Chicago, IL 60606-5601
(312) 353-5680

Roger M. Massey, Manager
Braiker/Brandeis Building
210 South 16th Street
Omaha, NE 68102-1622
(402) 221-3703

Kansas
William H. Brown, Regional
Administrator
Regional Housing
Commissioner
HUD Kansas City, Regional
Office
Gateway Tower II
400 State Avenue
Kansas City, KS 66101-2406
(913) 236-2162

(Indian Programs)
Hugh Johnson, Director
Community Planning and
Development Branch
Murrah Federal Building
200 NW 5th Street
Oklahoma City, OK
73102-3202
(405) 231-4101

Kentucky
Verna V. Van Ness, Manager
601 West Broadway
P.O. Box 1044
Louisville, KY 40201-1044
(502) 582-5251

Gertrude Jordan, Regional
Housing Commissioner
626 West Jackson Boulevard
Chicago, IL 60606-5601
(312) 353-5680

Louisiana
Robert Vasquez, Manager
Fisk Federal Building,
1661 Canal Street
P.O. Box 70288
New Orleans, LA 70112-2887
(504) 589-7200

(Northern Region)
David E. Gleason, Manager
New Federal Building
500 Fannin Street
Shreveport, LA 71101-3077
(318) 226-5385

(Indian Programs)
Hugh Johnson, Director
Community Planning and
Development Branch
Murrah Federal Building
200 NW 5th Street
Oklahoma City, OK
73102-3202
(405) 231-4101

Maine
Richard Young, Supervisory
Appraiser
Casco Northern Bank
Building
23 Main Street
Bangor, ME 04401-4318
(207) 945-0467

Maryland
Maxine Saunders, Manager
The Equitable Building,
Third Floor
10 North Calvert Street
Baltimore, MD 21202-1865
(301) 962-2121

(Montgomery and Prince
Georges Counties)
Toni Thomas, Manager
Union Center Plaza, Phase II
820 First Street, NE,
Suite 300
Washington, DC 20002-4205
(202) 275-9200

Massachusetts
John Mastropietro,
Acting Regional
Administrator
Regional Housing
Commissioner
Boston Federal Office
Building, Room 375
10 Causeway Street
Boston, MA 02222-1092
(617) 565-5234

Michigan
Harry I. Sharrott, Manager
Patrick V. McNamara Federal
Building
477 Michigan Avenue
Detroit, MI 48226-2592
(313) 226-6280

(Eastern Region)
Gary T. LeVine, Manager
Gil Sabuco Building,
Room 200
352 South Saginaw Street
Flint, MI 48502-1953
(313) 766-5112

(Western and Northern
Region)
Ronald Weston, Manager
Northbrook Building, No. II
2922 Fuller Avenue, NE
Grand Rapids, MI 48505-3409
(616) 456-2100

Minnesota
Thomas Feeney, Manager
Bridge Place Building
220 Second Street, South
Minneapolis, MN 55401-2195
(612) 370-3000

Mississippi
Sandra Freeman, Manager
Dr. A. H. McCoy Federal
Building, Room 910
100 West Capitol Street
Jackson, MS 39269-1096
(601) 965-4702

Missouri
Kenneth G. Lange, Manager
210 North Tucker Boulevard
St. Louis, MO 63101-1997
(314) 425-4761

(Indian Programs)
Hugh Johnson, Director
Community Planning and
Development Branch
Murrah Federal Building
200 NW 5th Street
Oklahoma City, OK
73102-3202
(405) 231-4101

Montana
Christian KaFentzis, Manager
Federal Office Building,
Room 340
Drawer 10095
301 South Park
Helena, MT 59626-0095
(406) 449-5205

Nebraska
Roger M. Massey, Manager
Braiker/Brandeis Building
210 South 16th Street
Omaha, NE 68102-1622
(402) 221-3703

Nevada
Andrew D. Whitten, Jr.,
Manager
1050 Bible Way
P.O. Box 4700
Reno, NV 89505-4700
(702) 784-5356

Andrew Robertson, Manager
1500 East Tropicana Avenue,
Second Floor
Las Vegas, NV 89119-6516
(702) 388-6500

New Hampshire
David B. Harrity, Manager
Norris Cotton Federal
Building
275 Chestnut Street
Manchester, NH 03101-2487
(603) 666-7681

New Jersey
(Northern Region)
Diane J. Johnson, Deputy
Manager
Military Park Building
60 Park Place
Newark, NJ 07102-5504
(201) 877-1662

(Southern Region)
Elmer Roy, Manager
The Parkade Building
519 Federal Street
Camden, NJ 08103-9998
(609) 757-5081

Housing

New Mexico
Michael R. Griego, Manager
625 Truman Street, NE
Albuquerque, NM
87110-6443
(505) 262-6463

Clarence D. Babers, Manager
555 Griffin Square Building,
Room 106
525 Griffin Street
Dallas, TX 75202-5007
(214) 767-8308

New York
Dr. Anthony Villane, Regional
Housing Commissioner
26 Federal Plaza
New York, NY 10278-0068
(212) 264-8068

(Western Region)
Joseph Lynch, Manager
465 Main Street, Fifth Floor
Lafayette Court
Buffalo, NY 14203-1780
(716) 846-5755

(Northern Region)
John Petricco, Manager
Leo W. O'Brien Federal
Building
North Pearl Street and
Clinton Avenue
Albany, NY 12207-2395
(518) 472-3567

North Carolina
Larry J. Parker, Manager
415 North Edgeworth Street
Greensboro, NC 27401-2107
(919) 333-5363

North Dakota
Keith Elliot, Chief
Federal Building, Room 300
653 2nd Avenue, North
P.O. Box 2483
Fargo, ND 58108-2483
(701) 239-5136

Ohio
Robert W. Dolin, Manager
New Federal Building
200 North High Street
Columbus, OH 43215-2499
(614) 469-5737

(Northern Region)
George L. Engel, Manager
One Playhouse Square
1375 Euclid Avenue,
Room 420
Cleveland, OH 44115-1832
(216) 522-4065

(Southwestern Region)
William Harris, Manager
Federal Office Building,
Room 9002
550 Main Street
Cincinnati, OH 45202-3253
(513) 684-2884

Oklahoma
Edwin I. Gardner, Manager
Murrah Federal Building
200 NW 5th Street
Oklahoma City, OK
73102-3202
(405) 231-4181

(Eastern Region)
James Colgan, Manager
Robert S. Kerr Building,
Room 200
440 South Houston Avenue
Tulsa, OK 74127-8923
(918) 581-7435

(Indian Programs)
Hugh Johnson, Director
Community Planning and
Development Branch
Murrah Federal Building
200 NW 5th Street
Oklahoma City, OK
73102-3202
(405) 231-4101

Oregon
Richard C. Brinck, Manager
Cascade Building
520 SW 6th Avenue
Portland, OR 97204-1596
(503) 221-2561

Pennsylvania
Michael A. Smerconish,
Regional Administrator
Regional Housing
Commissioner
Liberty Square Building
105 South 7th Street
Philadelphia, PA 19106-3392
(215) 597-2560

(Western Region)
Choice Edwards, Manager
412 Old Post Office
Courthouse Building
7th Avenue and Grant Street
Pittsburgh, PA 15219-1906
(412) 644-6428

Puerto Rico
Rosa Villalonga, Acting
Manager
159 Carlos Chardon Avenue
San Juan, PR 00918-1804
(809) 766-5201

Rhode Island
Casimir J. Kolaski, Jr.,
Manager
Federal Building and U.S.
Post Office, Room 330
Kennedy Plaza
Providence, RI 02903-1745
(401) 528-5351

South Carolina
Ted B. Freeman, Manager
Strom Thurmond Federal
Building
1835-45 Assembly Street
Columbia, SC 29201-2480
(803) 765-5592

South Dakota
Don Olson, Chief
Courthouse Plaza, Suite 116
300 North Dakota Avenue
Sioux Falls, SD 57102-0311
(605) 330-4223

Housing

Tennessee
Richard B. Barnwell,
Manager
John J. Duncan Federal
Building
710 Locust Street, SW
Knoxville, TN 37902-2526
(615) 549-9384

(Western Region)
Bob Atkins, Manager
One Memphis Place,
Suite 1200
200 Jefferson Avenue
Memphis, TN 38103-2335
(901) 521-3367

(Central Region)
John H. Fisher, Manager
251 Cumberland Bend Drive,
Suite 200
Nashville, TN 37228-1803
(615) 736-5213

Texas
Sam R. Moseley, Regional
Housing Commissioner
1600 Throckmorton
P.O. Box 2905
Forth Worth, TX 76113-2905
(817) 885-5401

(Southwest Region)
A. Cynthia Leon, Manager
Washington Square Building
800 Dolorosa Street
San Antonio, TX 78207-4563
(512) 229-6781

(East Central Region)
William Robertson, Jr.,
Manager
National Bank of Texas
Building, Suite 300
221 Norfolk
Houston, TX 77098-4096
(713) 229-3589

(Northwest Region)
Henry E. Whitney, Manager
Federal Office Building
1205 Texas Avenue
Lubbock, TX 79401-4093
(806) 743-7265

(Five Easternmost Counties)
David E. Gleason, Manager
New Federal Building
500 Fannin Street
Shreveport, LA 71101-3077
(318) 226-5385

(Eastern, Northern, and
Western Region)
Clarence D. Babers, Manager
555 Griffin Square Building,
Room 106
525 Griffin Street
Dallas, TX 75202-5007
(214) 767-8308

(Bowie County)
John T. Suskie, Manager
Lafayette Building, Suite 200
523 Louisiana
Little Rock, AR 72201-3523
(501) 378-5931

(Indian Programs)
Hugh Johnson, Director
Community Planning and
Development Branch
Murrah Federal Building
200 NW 5th Street
Oklahoma City, OK
73102-3202
(405) 231-4101

Utah
Richard Bell, Manager
324 South State Street,
Suite 220
Salt Lake City, UT
84111-2321
(801) 524-5237

Vermont
William Peters, Chief
Federal Building, Room B311
11 Elmwood Avenue
P.O. Box 879
Burlington, VT 05402-0879
(802) 951-6290

Virgin Islands
Rosa Villalonga, Acting
Manager
159 Carlos Chardon Avenue
San Juan, PR 00918-1804
(809) 766-5201

Virginia
(Northern Region)
Toni Thomas, Manager
Union Center Plaza, Phase II
820 First Street, NE,
Suite 300
Washington, DC 20002-4205
(202) 275-9200

(Southern Region)
Mary Ann Wilson, Manager
Federal Building, First Floor
400 North Eighth Street
Richmond, VA 23240-0170
(804) 771-2721

Washington
Richard Bauer,
Regional Housing
Commissioner
Arcade Plaza Building
1321 Second Avenue
Seattle, WA 98101-2054
(206) 442-5414

(Eastern Region)
Keith R. Green, Manager
Farm Credit Bank Building,
Eighth Floor East
West 601 1st Avenue
Spokane, WA 99204-0317
(509) 456-2624

(Clark, Klickitat, and
Skamania Counties)
Richard C. Brinck, Manager
Cascade Building
520 SW 6th Avenue
Portland, OR 97204-1596
(503) 221-2561

(Indian Programs)
Community Planning and
Development Division
Arcade Plaza Building
1321 Second Avenue
Seattle, WA 98101-2058
(206) 442-0760

West Virginia
Fred Roncaglione, Acting
Manager
405 Capitol Street, Suite 708
Charleston, WV 25301-1795
(304) 347-7000

Choice Edwards, Manager
412 Old Post Office
Courthouse Building
7th Avenue and Grant Street
Pittsburgh, PA 15219-1906
(412) 644-6428

Wisconsin
Delbert F. Reynolds,
Manager
Henry S. Reuss Federal Plaza
310 West Wisconsin Avenue,
Suite 1380
Milwaukee, WI 53203-2289
(414) 291-3214

Wyoming
William Garrett, Chief
4225 Federal Office Building
100 East B Street
P.O. Box 580
Casper, WY 82602-1918
(307) 261-5252

MORTGAGE INSURANCE—RENTAL HOUSING FOR THE ELDERLY

**Department of Housing
and Urban Development**
Office of Insured
Multifamily Housing
Development
Policies and Procedures
Division
Washington, DC 20410
(202) 708-2556

Description: Guaranteed and insured loans to private, profit-motivated developers, public bodies, and nonprofit sponsors to finance, construct, or rehabilitate rental detached, semidetached, row, walk-up, or elevator type structures for the occupancy of elderly or handicapped individuals with five or more units.
$ Given: N/A
Application Information: Initial conference with local HUD field office to determine preliminary feasibility of project is required.
Deadline: Established on a case-by-case basis.
Contact: Your local, state, and/or regional HUD office

Alabama
Robert E. Lunsford, Manager
600 Beacon Parkway West,
Suite 300
Birmingham, AL 35209-3144
(205) 731-1617

Alaska
Arlene Patton, Manager
222 West 8th Avenue, #64
Anchorage, AK 99513-7537
(907) 271-4170

Arizona
Dwight Peterson, Manager
P.O. Box 13468
Phoenix, AZ 85004-2361
(602) 261-4434

Jean Staley, Manager
Pioneer Plaza, 100 North
Stone Avenue, Suite 410
P.O. Box 2648
Tucson, AZ 86701-1467
(602) 629-6237

Charles Ming, Manager
1615 West Olympic
Boulevard
Los Angeles, CA 90015-3801
(213) 251-7122

(HUD Indian Programs)
C. Raphael Macham, Director
One North First Street,
Suite 400
Phoenix, AZ 85004-2360
(602) 261-4156

Arkansas
John T. Suskie, Manager
Lafayette Building, Suite 200
523 Louisiana
Little Rock, AR 72201-3523
(501) 378-5931

(Indian Programs)
Hugh Johnson, Director
Community Planning and
Development Branch
Murrah Federal Building
200 NW 5th Street
Oklahoma City, OK
73102-3202
(405) 231-4101

California
(Southern Region)
Charles Ming, Manager
1615 West Olympic
Boulevard
Los Angeles, CA 90015-3801
(213) 251-7122

(San Francisco Area)
John Wilson, Regional
Housing Commissioner
Phillip Burton Federal
Building and U.S.
Courthouse
450 Golden Gate Avenue P.O.
Box 36003
San Francisco, CA
94102-3448
(415) 556-4752

(Fresno)
Lilly Lee, Manager
1630 East Shaw Avenue,
Suite 138
Fresno, CA 93710-8193
(209) 487-5033

(Northeastern Region)
Paul Pradia, Acting
777 12th Street, Suite 200
P.O. Box 1978
Sacramento, CA 95814-1997
(916) 551-1351

(Imperial and San Diego
Counties)
Charles J. Wilson, Manager
Federal Office Building,
Room 563
880 Front Street
San Diego, CA 92188-0100
(619) 557-5310

(Orange, Riverside, and San
Bernardino Counties)
Earl Fields, Manager
34 Civic Center Plaza,
Box 12850
Santa Ana, CA 92712-2850
(714) 836-2451

Colorado
Michael Chitwood, Regional
Administrator
Regional Housing
Commissioner
HUD-Denver Regional Office
Executive Tower Building
1405 Curtis Street
Denver, CO 80202-2349
(303) 844-4513

(Indian Programs)
Housing and Community
Development Division
Executive Tower Building
1405 Curtis Street
Denver, CO 80202-2349
(303) 844-2861

Connecticut
William Hernandez, Jr.,
Manager
330 Main Street, First Floor
Hartford, CT 06106-1860
(203) 565-5234

Delaware
A. David Sharbaugh, Chief
Federal Building, Room 1304
844 King Street
Wilmington, DE 19801-3519
(302) 573-6300

District of Columbia
Toni Thomas, Manager
Union Center Plaza, Phase II
820 First Street, NE,
Suite 300
Washington, DC 20002-4205
(202) 275-9200

Florida
(Northern Region)
James T. Chaplin, Manager
325 West Adams Street
Jacksonville, FL 32202-4303
(904) 791-2626

(Southern Region)
Orlando L. Lorie, Manager
Gables 1 Tower
1320 South Dixie Highway
Coral Gables, FL 33146-2911
(305) 662-4510

(Central Western Counties)
George A. Milburn, Jr.,
Manager
Timberlake Federal Building
Annex, Suite 700
501 East Polk Street
Tampa, FL 33602-3945
(813) 228-2501

(Central Eastern Counties)
M. Jeanette Porter, Manager
Langley Building, Suite 270
3751 Maguire Boulevard
Orlando, FL 32803-3032
(407) 648-6441

Georgia
Raymond A. Harris, Regional
Housing Commissioner
Richard B. Russell Federal
Building
75 Spring Street, SW
Atlanta, GA 30303-3388
(404) 331-5136

Guam
Gordon Y. Furutani, Manager
300 Ala Moana Boulevard,
Room 3318
Honolulu, HI 96850-4991
(808) 546-2136

Hawaii
Gordon Y. Furutani, Manager
300 Ala Moana Boulevard,
Room 3318
Honolulu, HI 96850-4991
(808) 546-2136

Housing

Idaho
(West-Central Region)
Gary Gillespie, Manager
Federal Building and U.S.
Courthouse
P.O. Box 042
550 West Fort Street
Boise, ID 83724-0420
(208) 334-1990

(Southern Region)
Richard C. Brinck, Manager
Cascade Building
520 SW 6th Avenue
Portland, OR 97204-1596
(503) 221-2561

(Northern Region)
Keith R. Green, Manager
Farm Credit Bank Building
8th Floor East
West 601 1st Avenue
Spokane, WA 99204-0317
(509) 456-2624

Illinois
Gertrude Jordan, Regional
Housing Commissioner
626 West Jackson Boulevard
Chicago, IL 60606-5601
(312) 353-5680

(Central and Southern
Region)
William Fattic, Manager
Lincoln Towers Plaza,
Suite 672
524 South Second Street
Springfield, IL 62701-1774
(217) 492-4085

(Indian Programs)
Housing Development
Division
626 West Jackson Boulevard
Chicago, IL 60606-5601
(312) 353-1684

Indiana
J. Nicholas Shelley, Manager
151 North Delaware Street
Indianapolis, IN 46204-2526
(317) 226-6303

Iowa
William R. McNarney,
Manager
HUD Des Moines Office
Federal Building, Room 259
210 Walnut Street
Des Moines, IA 50309-2155
(515) 284-4512

Gertrude Jordan, Regional
Housing Commissioner
626 West Jackson Boulevard
Chicago, IL 60606-5601
(312) 353-5680

Roger M. Massey, Manager
Braiker/Brandeis Building
210 South 16th Street
Omaha, NE 68102-1622
(402) 221-3703

Kansas
William H. Brown, Regional
Administrator
Regional Housing
Commissioner
HUD Kansas City, Regional
Office
Gateway Tower II
400 State Avenue
Kansas City, KS 66101-2406
(913) 236-2162

(Indian Programs)
Hugh Johnson, Director
Community Planning and
Development Branch
Murrah Federal Building
200 NW 5th Street
Oklahoma City, OK
73102-3202
(405) 231-4101

Kentucky
Verna V. Van Ness, Manager
601 West Broadway
P.O. Box 1044
Louisville, KY 40201-1044
(502) 582-5251

Gertrude Jordan, Regional
Housing Commissioner
626 West Jackson Boulevard
Chicago, IL 60606-5601
(312) 353-5680

Louisiana
Robert Vasquez, Manager
Fisk Federal Building,
1661 Canal Street
P.O. Box 70288
New Orleans, LA 70112-2887
(504) 589-7200

(Northern Region)
David E. Gleason, Manager
New Federal Building
500 Fannin Street
Shreveport, LA 71101-3077
(318) 226-5385

(Indian Programs)
Hugh Johnson, Director
Community Planning and
Development Branch
Murrah Federal Building
200 NW 5th Street
Oklahoma City, OK
73102-3202
(405) 231-4101

Maine
Richard Young, Supervisory
Appraiser
Casco Northern Bank
Building
23 Main Street
Bangor, ME 04401-4318
(207) 945-0467

Maryland
Maxine Saunders, Manager
The Equitable Building,
Third Floor
10 North Calvert Street
Baltimore, MD 21202-1865
(301) 962-2121

(Montgomery and Prince
Georges Counties)
Toni Thomas, Manager
Union Center Plaza, Phase II
820 First Street, NE,
Suite 300
Washington, DC 20002-4205
(202) 275-9200

Massachusetts
John Mastropietro,
Acting Regional
Administrator
Regional Housing
Commissioner
Boston Federal Office
Building, Room 375
10 Causeway Street
Boston, MA 02222-1092
(617) 565-5234

Michigan
Harry I. Sharrott, Manager
Patrick V. McNamara Federal
Building
477 Michigan Avenue
Detroit, MI 48226-2592
(313) 226-6280

(Eastern Region)
Gary T. LeVine, Manager
Gil Sabuco Building,
Room 200
352 South Saginaw Street
Flint, MI 48502-1953
(313) 766-5112

(Western and Northern
Region)
Ronald Weston, Manager
Northbrook Building, No. II
2922 Fuller Avenue, NE
Grand Rapids, MI 48505-3409
(616) 456-2100

Minnesota
Thomas Feeney, Manager
Bridge Place Building
220 Second Street, South
Minneapolis, MN 55401-2195
(612) 370-3000

Mississippi
Sandra Freeman, Manager
Dr. A. H. McCoy Federal
Building, Room 910
100 West Capitol Street
Jackson, MS 39269-1096
(601) 965-4702

Missouri
Kenneth G. Lange, Manager
210 North Tucker Boulevard
St. Louis, MO 63101-1997
(314) 425-4761

(Indian Programs)
Hugh Johnson, Director
Community Planning and
Development Branch
Murrah Federal Building
200 NW 5th Street
Oklahoma City, OK
73102-3202
(405) 231-4101

Montana
Christian KaFentzis, Manager
Federal Office Building,
Room 340
Drawer 10095
301 South Park
Helena, MT 59626-0095
(406) 449-5205

Nebraska
Roger M. Massey, Manager
Braiker/Brandeis Building
210 South 16th Street
Omaha, NE 68102-1622
(402) 221-3703

Nevada
Andrew D. Whitten, Jr.,
Manager
1050 Bible Way
P.O. Box 4700
Reno, NV 89505-4700
(702) 784-5356

Andrew Robertson, Manager
1500 East Tropicana Avenue,
Second Floor
Las Vegas, NV 89119-6516
(702) 388-6500

New Hampshire
David Harrity, Manager
Norris Cotton Federal
Building
275 Chestnut Street
Manchester, NH 03101-2487
(603) 666-7681

New Jersey
(Northern Region)
Diane J. Johnson, Deputy
Manager
Military Park Building
60 Park Place
Newark, NJ 07102-5504
(201) 877-1662

(Southern Region)
Elmer Roy, Manager
The Parkade Building
519 Federal Street
Camden, NJ 08103-9998
(609) 757-5081

New Mexico
Michael R. Griego, Manager
625 Truman Street, NE
Albuquerque, NM
87110-6443
(505) 262-6463

Clarence D. Babers, Manager
555 Griffin Square Building,
Room 106
525 Griffin Street
Dallas, TX 75202-5007
(214) 767-8308

New York
Dr. Anthony Villane, Regional
Housing Commissioner
26 Federal Plaza
New York, NY 10278-0068
(212) 264-8068

(Western Region)
Joseph Lynch, Manager
465 Main Street, Fifth Floor
Lafayette Court
Buffalo, NY 14203-1780
(716) 846-5755

(Northern Region)
John Petricco, Manager
Leo W. O'Brien Federal
Building
North Pearl Street and
Clinton Avenue
Albany, NY 12207-2395
(518) 472-3567

Housing

North Carolina
Larry J. Parker, Manager
415 North Edgeworth Street
Greensboro, NC 27401-2107
(919) 333-5363

North Dakota
Keith Elliot, Chief
Federal Building, Room 300
653 2nd Avenue, North
P.O. Box 2483
Fargo, ND 58108-2483
(701) 239-5136

Ohio
Robert W. Dolin, Manager
New Federal Building
200 North High Street
Columbus, OH 43215-2499
(614) 469-5737

(Northern Region)
George L. Engel, Manager
One Playhouse Square
1375 Euclid Avenue,
Room 420
Cleveland, OH 44115-1832
(216) 522-4065

(Southwestern Region)
William Harris, Manager
Federal Office Building,
Room 9002
550 Main Street
Cincinnati, OH 45202-3253
(513) 684-2884

Oklahoma
Edwin I. Gardner, Manager
Murrah Federal Building
200 NW 5th Street
Oklahoma City, OK
73102-3202
(405) 231-4181

(Eastern Region)
James Colgan, Manager
Robert S. Kerr Building,
Room 200
440 South Houston Avenue
Tulsa, OK 74127-8923
(918) 581-7435

(Indian Programs)
Hugh Johnson, Director
Community Planning and
Development Branch
Murrah Federal Building
200 NW 5th Street
Oklahoma City, OK
73102-3202
(405) 231-4101

Oregon
Richard C. Brinck, Manager
Cascade Building
520 SW 6th Avenue
Portland, OR 97204-1596
(503) 221-2561

Pennsylvania
Michael A. Smerconish,
Regional Administrator
Regional Housing
Commissioner
Liberty Square Building
105 South 7th Street
Philadelphia, PA 19106-3392
(215) 597-2560

(Western Region)
Choice Edwards, Manager
412 Old Post Office
Courthouse Building
7th Avenue and Grant Street
Pittsburgh, PA 15219-1906
(412) 644-6428

Puerto Rico
Rosa Villalonga, Acting
Manager
159 Carlos Chardon Avenue
San Juan, PR 00918-1804
(809) 766-5201

Rhode Island
Casimir J. Kolaski, Jr.,
Manager
Federal Building and U.S.
Post Office, Room 330
Kennedy Plaza
Providence, RI 02903-1745
(401) 528-5351

South Carolina
Ted B. Freeman, Manager
Strom Thurmond Federal
Building
1835-45 Assembly Street
Columbia, SC 29201-2480
(803) 765-5592

South Dakota
Don Olson, Chief
Courthouse Plaza, Suite 116
300 North Dakota Avenue
Sioux Falls, SD 57102-0311
(605) 330-4223

Tennessee
Richard B. Barnwell,
Manager
John J. Duncan Federal
Building
710 Locust Street, SW
Knoxville, TN 37902-2526
(615) 549-9384

(Western Region)
Bob Atkins, Manager
One Memphis Place,
Suite 1200
200 Jefferson Avenue
Memphis, TN 38103-2335
(901) 521-3367

(Central Region)
John H. Fisher, Manager
251 Cumberland Bend Drive,
Suite 200
Nashville, TN 37228-1803
(615) 736-5213

Texas
Sam R. Moseley, Regional
Housing Commissioner
1600 Throckmorton
P.O. Box 2905
Forth Worth, TX 76113-2905
(817) 885-5401

(Southwest Region)
A. Cynthia Leon, Manager
Washington Square Building
800 Dolorosa Street
San Antonio, TX 78207-4563
(512) 229-6781

(East Central Region)
William Robertson, Jr.,
Manager
National Bank of Texas
Building, Suite 300
221 Norfolk
Houston, TX 77098-4096
(713) 229-3589

(Northwest Region)
Henry E. Whitney, Manager
Federal Office Building
1205 Texas Avenue
Lubbock, TX 79401-4093
(806) 743-7265

(Five Easternmost Counties)
David E. Gleason, Manager
New Federal Building
500 Fannin Street
Shreveport, LA 71101-3077
(318) 226-5385

(Eastern, Northern, and
Western Region)
Clarence D. Babers, Manager
555 Griffin Square Building,
Room 106
525 Griffin Street
Dallas, TX 75202-5007
(214) 767-8308

(Bowie County)
John T. Suskie, Manager
Lafayette Building, Suite 200
523 Louisiana
Little Rock, AR 72201-3523
(501) 378-5931

(Indian Programs)
Hugh Johnson, Director
Community Planning and
Development Branch
Murrah Federal Building
200 NW 5th Street
Oklahoma City, OK
73102-3202
(405) 231-4101

Utah
Richard Bell, Manager
324 South State Street,
Suite 220
Salt Lake City, UT
84111-2321
(801) 524-5237

Vermont
William Peters, Chief
Federal Building, Room B311
11 Elmwood Avenue
P.O. Box 879
Burlington, VT 05402-0879
(802) 951-6290

Virgin Islands
Rosa Villalonga, Acting
Manager
159 Carlos Chardon Avenue
San Juan, PR 00918-1804
(809) 766-5201

Virginia
(Northern Region)
Toni Thomas, Manager
Union Center Plaza, Phase II
820 First Street, NE,
Suite 300
Washington, DC 20002-4205
(202) 275-9200

(Southern Region)
Mary Ann Wilson, Manager
Federal Building, First Floor
400 North Eighth Street
Richmond, VA 23240-0170
(804) 771-2721

Washington
Richard Bauer,
Regional Housing
Commissioner
Arcade Plaza Building
1321 Second Avenue
Seattle, WA 98101-2054
(206) 442-5414

(Eastern Region)
Keith R. Green, Manager
Farm Credit Bank Building,
Eighth Floor East
West 601 1st Avenue
Spokane, WA 99204-0317
(509) 456-2624

(Clark, Klickitat, and
Skamania Counties)
Richard C. Brinck, Manager
Cascade Building
520 SW 6th Avenue
Portland, OR 97204-1596
(503) 221-2561

(Indian Programs)
Community Planning and
Development Division
Arcade Plaza Building
1321 Second Avenue
Seattle, WA 98101-2058
(206) 442-0760

West Virginia
Fred Roncaglione, Acting
Manager
405 Capitol Street, Suite 708
Charleston, WV 25301-1795
(304) 347-7000

Choice Edwards, Manager
412 Old Post Office
Courthouse Building
7th Avenue and Grant Street
Pittsburgh, PA 15219-1906
(412) 644-6428

Wisconsin
Delbert F. Reynolds,
Manager
Henry S. Reuss Federal Plaza
310 West Wisconsin Avenue,
Suite 1380
Milwaukee, WI 53203-2289
(414) 291-3214

Wyoming
William Garrett, Chief
4225 Federal Office Building
100 East B Street
P.O. Box 580
Casper, WY 82602-1918
(307) 261-5252

MORTGAGE INSURANCE—RENTAL HOUSING IN URBAN RENEWAL AREAS

Department of Housing and Urban Development
Policies and Procedures Division
Office of Insured Multifamily Housing Development
Washington, DC 20412
(202) 708-2556

Description: Guaranteed/insured loans to eligible profit-motivated mortgagers to provide housing in urban renewal areas, code enforcement areas, and other areas designated for revitalization. Applicants must meet HUD requirements. At least two units per structure. Program falling into disuse due to termination of urban renewal and code enforcement programs.
$ Given: Nationwide FY 93 est $7.6 million mortgages insured.
Application Information: Initial conference followed by formal application.
Deadline: Established on case-by-case basis.
Contact: Nearest local HUD field office

Alabama
Robert E. Lunsford, Manager
600 Beacon Parkway West, Suite 300
Birmingham, AL 35209-3144
(205) 731-1617

Alaska
Arlene Patton, Manager
222 West 8th Avenue, #64
Anchorage, AK 99513-7537
(907) 271-4170

Community Planning and Development Division
222 West 8th Avenue, #64
Anchorage, AK 99513-7537
(907) 271-3669

American Samoa
Gordon Y. Furutani, Manager
300 Ala Moana Boulevard, Room 3318
Honolulu, HI 96850-4991
(808) 546-2136

Arizona
Dwight Peterson, Manager
400 North First Street, Suite 1600
P.O. Box 13468
Phoenix, AZ 85004-2361
(602) 261-4434

Charles Ming, Manager
1615 West Olympic Boulevard
Los Angeles, CA 90015-3801
(213) 251-7122

Jean Staley, Manager
Pioneer Plaza, 100 North Stone Avenue, Suite 410
P.O. Box 2648
Tucson, AZ 86701-1467
(602) 629-6237

Arkansas
Roger Zachritz, Acting Manager
Lafayette Building, Suite 200
523 Louisiana
Little Rock, AR 72201-3523
(501) 378-5931

California
Lilly Lee, Manager
1630 East Shaw Avenue, Suite 138
Fresno, CA 93710-8193
(209) 487-5033

(San Francisco Regional Office)
Robert De Monte, Regional Housing Commissioner
Phillip Burton Federal Building and U.S Courthouse
450 Golden Gate Avenue
P.O. Box 36003
San Francisco, CA 94102-3448
(415) 556-4752

(North California)
Office of Indian Programs
Community Planning and Development Division
San Francisco Program Management Team
Phillip Burton Federal Building and U.S. Courthouse
450 Golden Gate Avenue
P.O. Box 36003
San Francisco, CA 94102-3448
(415) 556-9200

(Northeast California)
Anthony A. Randolph,
Manager
777 12th Street, Suite 200
P.O. Box 1978
Sacramento, CA 95814-1997
(916) 551-1351

(Imperial and San Diego
Counties)
Charles J. Wilson, Manager
Federal Office Building,
Room 563
880 Front Street
San Diego, CA 92188-0100
(619) 557-5310

(Orange, Riverside and San
Bernardino Counties, for
home mortgages)
Harold A. Matzoll, Acting
Manager
34 Civic Center Plaza,
Box 12850
Santa Ana, CA 92712-2850
(714) 836-2451

(South California)
Charles Ming, Manager
1615 West Olympic
Boulevard
Los Angeles, CA 90015-3801
(213) 251-7122

Colorado
Michael Chitwood, Regional
Administrator
Regional Housing
Commissioner
HUD Denver Regional Office
Executive Tower Building
1405 Curtis Street
Denver, CO 80202-2349
(303) 844-4513

Office of Indian Programs
Housing and Community
Development Division
Executive Tower Building
1405 Curtis Street
Denver, CO 80202-2349
(303) 844-2861

Connecticut
William Hernandez, Jr.,
Manager
330 Main Street, First Floor
Hartford, CT 06106-1860
(203) 240-4523

Delaware
A. David Sharbaugh, Chief
Federal Building, Room 1304
844 King Street
Wilmington, DE 19801-3519
(302) 573-6300

District of Columbia
(Washington, D.C. Regional
Office)
Toni Thomas, Manager
Union Center Plaza, Phase II
820 First Street, NE,
Suite 300
Washington, DC 20002-4205
(202) 275-9200

Florida
James T. Chaplin, Manager
325 West Adams Street
Jacksonville, FL 32202-4303
(904) 791-2626

(Counties of Citrus, Sumter,
Hernando, Pasco, Pinellas,
Hillsborough, Polk, Manatee,
Hardee, Highlands, DeSoto,
Sarasota, Charlotte, Olaoes,
Hendry, Lake Okeechobee)
George A. Milburn, Jr.,
Manager
Timberlake Federal Building
Annex, Suite 700
501 East Polk Street
Tampa, FL 33602-3945
(813) 228-2501

(Counties of Volusia, Lake,
Seminole, Orange, Brevard,
Osceola, Indian River,
Okeechobee, St. Lucie)
M. Jeanette Porter, Manager
Langley Building, Suite 270
3751 Maguire Boulevard
Orlando, FL 32803-3032
(407) 648-6441

(South Florida)
Orlando L. Lorie, Manager
Gables 1 Tower
1320 South Dixie Highway
Coral Gables, FL 33146-2911
(305) 662-4510

Georgia
Raymond A. Harris, Regional
Housing Commissioner
Richard B. Russell Federal
Building
75 Spring Street, SW
Atlanta, GA 30303-3388
(404) 331-5136

Guam
Gordon Y. Furutani, Manager
300 Ala Moana Boulevard,
Room 3318
Honolulu, HI 96850-4991
(808) 546-2136

Hawaii
Gordon Y. Furutani, Manager
300 Ala Moana Boulevard,
Room 3318
Honolulu, HI 96850-4991
(808) 546-2136

Idaho
(North Idaho)
Keith R. Green, Manager
Farm Credit Bank Building,
Eighth Floor East
West 601 1st Avenue
Spokane, WA 99204-0317
(509) 456-2624

(West-Central Idaho)
Gary Gillespie, Manager
Federal Building and U.S.
Courthouse
P.O. Box 042
550 West Fort Street
Boise, ID 83724-0420
(208) 334-1990

(South Idaho)
Richard C. Brinck, Manager
Cascade Building
520 SW 6th Avenue
Portland, OR 97204-1596
(503) 221-2561

Housing

Illinois

Chicago Office of Indian Programs
Housing Development Division
626 West Jackson Boulevard
Chicago, IL 60606-5601
(312) 353-1684

(Chicago Regional Office)
Gertrude Jordan,
Regional Housing Commissioner
626 West Jackson Boulevard
Chicago, IL 60606-5601
(312) 353-5680

(Central and South Illinois)
John Lawler, Acting Supervisory Appraiser
Lincoln Towers Plaza,
Suite 672
524 South Second Street
Springfield, IL 62701-1774
(217) 492-4085

Indiana

J. Nicholas Shelley, Manager
151 North Delaware Street
Indianapolis, IN 46204-2526
(317) 226-6303

Iowa

Roger M. Massey, Manager
Braiker/Brandeis Building
210 South 16th Street
Omaha, NE 68102-1622
(402) 221-3703

William R. McNarney,
Manager
HUD Des Moines Office
Federal Building, Room 259
210 Walnut Street
Des Moines, IA 50309-2155
(515) 284-4512

Kansas

William H. Brown, Regional Administrator
Regional Housing Commissioner
HUD Kansas City, Regional Office
Gateway Tower II
400 State Avenue
Kansas City, KS 66101-2406
(913) 236-2162

Kentucky

Verna V. Van Ness, Manager
601 West Broadway
P.O. Box 1044
Louisville, KY 40201-1044
(502) 582-5251

Louisiana

Robert Vasquez, Manager
Fisk Federal Building,
1661 Canal Street
P.O. Box 70288
New Orleans, LA 70112-2887
(504) 589-7200

(North Louisiana)
David E. Gleason, Manager
New Federal Building
500 Fannin Street
Shreveport, LA 71101-3077
(318) 226-5385

Maine

Richard Young, Supervisory Appraiser
Casco Northern Bank Building
23 Main Street
Bangor, ME 04401-4318
(207) 945-0467

James Barry, Manager
Norris Cotton Federal Building
275 Chestnut Street
Manchester, NH 03101-2487
(603) 666-7681

Maryland

(Except Montgomery and Prince Georges Counties)
Maxine Saunders, Manager
The Equitable Building,
Third Floor
10 North Calvert Street
Baltimore, MD 21202-1865
(301) 962-2121

(Montgomery and Prince Georges Counties)
Toni Thomas, Manager
Union Center Plaza, Phase II
820 First Street, NE,
Suite 300
Washington, DC 20002-4205
(202) 275-9200

Massachusetts

John Mastropietro,
Acting Regional Administrator
Regional Housing Commissioner
Boston Federal Office Building, Room 375
10 Causeway Street
Boston, MA 02222-1092
(617) 565-5234

Michigan

Harry I. Sharrott, Manager
Patrick V. McNamara Federal Building
477 Michigan Avenue
Detroit, MI 48226-2592
(313) 226-6280

(East Michigan)
Gary T. LeVine, Manager
Gil Sabuco Building,
Room 200
352 South Saginaw Street
Flint, MI 48502-1953
(313) 766-5112

(West and North Michigan)
Ronald Weston, Manager
Northbrook Building, No. II
2922 Fuller Avenue, NE
Grand Rapids, MI 48505-3409
(616) 456-2100

Minnesota
Thomas Feeney, Manager
Bridge Place Building
220 Second Street, South
Minneapolis, MN 55401-2195
(612) 370-3000

Mississippi
Sandra Freeman, Manager
Dr. A. H. McCoy Federal
Building, Room 910
100 West Capitol Street
Jackson, MS 39269-1096
(601) 965-4702

Missouri
Kenneth G. Lange, Manager
210 North Tucker Boulevard
St. Louis, MO 63101-1997
(314) 425-4761

Montana
Christian KaFentzis, Manager
Federal Office Building,
Room 340
Drawer 10095
301 South Park
Helena, MT 59626-0095
(406) 449-5205

Nebraska
Roger M. Massey, Manager
Braiker/Brandeis Building
210 South 16th Street
Omaha, NE 68102-1622
(402) 221-3703

Nevada
Andrew D. Whitten, Jr.,
Manager
1050 Bible Way
P.O. Box 4700
Reno, NV 89505-4700
(702) 784-5356

Andrew Robertson, Manager
1500 East Tropicana Avenue,
Second Floor
Las Vegas, NV 89119-6516
(702) 388-6500

(North Nevada)
Office of Indian Programs
Community Planning and
Development Division
San Francisco Program
Management Team
Phillip Burton Federal
Building and U.S.
Courthouse
450 Golden Gate Avenue
P.O. Box 36003
San Francisco, CA
94102-3448
(415) 556-9200

New Hampshire
James Barry, Manager
Norris Cotton Federal
Building
275 Chestnut Street
Manchester, NH 03101-2487
(603) 666-7681

New Jersey
(North New Jersey)
Theodore Britton, Jr.,
Manager
Military Park Building
60 Park Place
Newark, NJ 07102-5504
(201) 887-1662

(South New Jersey)
Elmer Roy, Manager
The Parkade Building
519 Federal Street
Camden, NJ 08103-9998
(609) 757-5081

New Mexico
Michael R. Griego, Manager
625 Truman Street, NE
Albuquerque, NM
87110-6443
(505) 262-6463

C. Don Babers, Acting
Manager
555 Griffin Square Building,
Room 106
525 Griffin Street
Dallas, TX 75202-5007
(214) 767-8308

New York
Dr. Anthony Villane, Regional
Housing Commissioner
26 Federal Plaza
New York, NY 10278-0068
(212) 264-8068

(North New York)
John Petricco, Manager
Leo W. O'Brien Federal
Building
North Pearl Street and
Clinton Avenue
Albany, NY 12207-2395
(518) 472-3567

(West New York)
Joseph Lynch, Manager
465 Main Street, Fifth Floor
Lafayette Court
Buffalo, NY 14203-1780
(716) 846-5755

North Carolina
Larry J. Parker, Manager
415 North Edgeworth Street
Greensboro, NC 27401-2107
(919) 333-5363

North Dakota
Keith Elliot, Chief
Federal Building, Room 300
653 2nd Avenue, North
P.O. Box 2483
Fargo, ND 58108-2483
(701) 239-5136

Ohio
Robert W. Dolin, Manager
New Federal Building
200 North High Street
Columbus, OH 43215-2499
(614) 469-5737

(North Ohio)
George L. Engel, Manager
One Playhouse Square
1375 Euclid Avenue,
Room 420
Cleveland, OH 44115-1832
(216) 522-4065

Housing

(Southwest Ohio)
William Harris, Manager
Federal Office Building,
Room 9002
550 Main Street
Cincinnati, OH 45202-3253
(513) 684-2884

Oklahoma
Edwin I. Gardner, Manager
Murrah Federal Building
200 NW 5th Street
Oklahoma City, OK
73102-3202
(405) 231-4181

Indian Programs Division
Hugh Johnson, Director
Community Planning and
Development Branch
Murrah Federal Building
200 NW 5th Street
Oklahoma City, OK
73102-3202
(405) 231-4101

(East Oklahoma)
Robert H. Gardner, Manager
Robert S. Kerr Building,
Room 200
440 South Houston Avenue
Tulsa, OK 74127-8923
(918) 581-7435

Oregon
Richard C. Brinck, Manager
Cascade Building
520 SW 6th Avenue
Portland, OR 97204-1596
(503) 221-2561

Panama Canal Zone
Rosa Villalonga, Acting
Manager
159 Carlos Chardon Avenue
San Juan, PR 00918-1804
(809) 766-5201 or
(809) 498-5201

Pennsylvania
(Philadelphia Regional
Office)
Michael A. Smerconish,
Regional Administrator
Regional Housing
Commissioner
Liberty Square Building
105 South 7th Street
Philadelphia, PA 19106-3392
(215) 597-2560

(West Pennsylvania)
William Costello, Acting
Manager
412 Old Post Office
Courthouse Building
7th Avenue and Grant Street
Pittsburgh, PA 15219-1906
(412) 644-6428

Puerto Rico
Rosa Villalonga, Acting
Manager
159 Carlos Chardon Avenue
San Juan, PR 00918-1804
(809) 766-5201 or
(809) 498-5201

Rhode Island
Casimir J. Kolaski, Jr.,
Manager
Federal Building and U.S.
Post Office, Room 330
Kennedy Plaza
Providence, RI 02903-1745
(401) 528-5351

South Carolina
Ted B. Freeman, Manager
Strom Thurmond Federal
Building
1835-45 Assembly Street
Columbia, SC 29201-2480
(803) 765-5592

South Dakota
Don Olson, Chief
Courthouse Plaza, Suite 116
300 North Dakota Avenue
Sioux Falls, SD 57102-0311
(605) 330-4223

Tennessee
Richard B. Barnwell,
Manager
John J. Duncan Federal
Building
710 Locust Street, SW
Knoxville, TN 37902-2526
(615) 549-9384

(Central Tennessee)
John H. Fisher, Manager
251 Cumberland Bend Drive,
Suite 200
Nashville, TN 37228-1803
(615) 736-5213

(West Tennessee)
Bob Atkins, Manager
One Memphis Place,
Suite 1200
200 Jefferson Avenue
Memphis, TN 38103-2335
(901) 521-3367

Texas
(Fort Worth Regional Office)
Sam R. Moseley, Regional
Housing Commissioner
1600 Throckmorton
P.O. Box 2905
Forth Worth, TX 76113-2905
(817) 885-5401

(Northwest Texas)
Henry E. Whitney, Manager
Federal Office Building
1205 Texas Avenue
Lubbock, TX 79401-4093
(806) 743-7265

(East, North, and West
Texas)
C. Don Babers, Acting
Manager
555 Griffin Square Building,
Room 106
525 Griffin Street
Dallas, TX 75202-5007
(214) 767-8308

(Five Counties in East Texas)
David E. Gleason, Manager
New Federal Building
500 Fannin Street
Shreveport, LA 71101-3077
(318) 226-5385

(East-Central Texas)
William Robertson, Jr.,
Manager
National Bank of Texas
Building, Suite 300
221 Norfolk
Houston, TX 77098-4096
(713) 229-3589

(Bowie County)
Roger Zachritz, Acting
Manager
Lafayette Building, Suite 200
523 Louisiana
Little Rock, AR 72201-3523
(501) 378-5931

(Southwest Texas)
Don Creed, Manager
Washington Square Building
800 Dolorosa Street
San Antonio, TX 78207-4563
(512) 229-6781

Utah
Richard Bell, Manager
324 South State Street,
Suite 220
Salt Lake City, UT
84111-2321
(801) 524-5237

Vermont
William Peters, Chief
Federal Building, Room B311
11 Elmwood Avenue
P.O. Box 879
Burlington, VT 05402-0879
(802) 951-6290

James Barry, Manager
Norris Cotton Federal
Building
275 Chestnut Street
Manchester, NH 03101-2487
(603) 666-7681

Virgin Islands
Rosa Villalonga, Acting
Manager
159 Carlos Chardon Avenue
San Juan, PR 00918-1804
(809) 766-5201 or
(809) 498-5201

Virginia
(North Virginia)
Toni Thomas, Manager
Union Center Plaza, Phase II
820 First Street, NE,
Suite 300
Washington, DC 20002-4205
(202) 275-9200

(South Virginia)
Mary Ann Wilson, Manager
Federal Building, First Floor
400 North Eighth Street
Richmond, VA 23240-0170
(804) 771-2721

Washington
Office of Indian Programs
Community Planning and
Development Division
Arcade Plaza Building
1321 Second Avenue
Seattle, WA 98101-2058
(206) 442-0760

(Seattle Regional Office)
Richard Bauer,
Regional Housing
Commissioner
Arcade Plaza Building
1321 Second Avenue
Seattle, WA 98101-2054
(206) 442-5414

(East Washington)
Keith R. Green, Manager
Farm Credit Bank Building,
Eighth Floor East
West 601 1st Avenue
Spokane, WA 99204-0317
(509) 456-2624

(Clark, Klickitat, and
Skamania Counties)
Richard C. Brinck, Manager
Cascade Building
520 SW 6th Avenue
Portland, OR 97204-1596
(503) 221-2561

West Virginia
William Costello, Acting
Manager
412 Old Post Office
Courthouse Building
7th Avenue and Grant Street
Pittsburgh, PA 15219-1906
(412) 644-6428

405 Capitol Street, Suite 708
Charleston, WV 25301-1795
(304) 347-7000

Wisconsin
Delbert F. Reynolds,
Manager
Henry S. Reuss Federal Plaza
310 West Wisconsin Avenue,
Suite 1380
Milwaukee, WI 53203-2289
(414) 291-3214

Wyoming
Lawrence Gosnell, Chief
4225 Federal Office Building
100 East B Street
P.O. Box 580
Casper, WY 82602-1918
(307) 261-5252

MORTGAGE INSURANCE—SINGLE-ROOM OCCUPANCY (SRO) PROJECTS

Department of Housing and Urban Developmpent
Policies and Procedures Division
Office of Insured Multifamily Housing Development
Washington, DC 20410
(202) 708-2556

Description: Guaranteed/insured loans to profit-motivated entities and builders/sellers to provide mortgage insurance for SROs. Dwellings must consist of at least five SRO units, with no more than 10 percent gross floor space devoted to commercial use (20 percent for substantial rehabilitation projects).
$ Given: Nationwide FY 93 est. $40 million mortgages insured.
Application Information: Initial conference followed by formal application submission.
Deadline: Established on case-by-case basis at local HUD field office.
Contact: Local HUD field office

Alabama
Robert E. Lunsford, Manager
600 Beacon Parkway West, Suite 300
Birmingham, AL 35209-3144
(205) 731-1617

Alaska
Arlene Patton, Manager
222 West 8th Avenue, #64
Anchorage, AK 99513-7537
(907) 271-4170

Community Planning and Development Division
222 West 8th Avenue, #64
Anchorage, AK 99513-7537
(907) 271-3669

American Samoa
Gordon Y. Furutani, Manager
300 Ala Moana Boulevard, Room 3318
Honolulu, HI 96850-4991
(808) 546-2136

Arizona
Dwight Peterson, Manager
400 North First Street, Suite 1600
P.O. Box 13468
Phoenix, AZ 85004-2361
(602) 261-4434

Charles Ming, Manager
1615 West Olympic Boulevard
Los Angeles, CA 90015-3801
(213) 251-7122

Jean Staley, Manager
Pioneer Plaza, 100 North Stone Avenue, Suite 410
P.O. Box 2648
Tucson, AZ 86701-1467
(602) 629-6237

Arkansas
Roger Zachritz, Acting Manager
Lafayette Building, Suite 200
523 Louisiana
Little Rock, AR 72201-3523
(501) 378-5931

California
Lilly Lee, Manager
1630 East Shaw Avenue, Suite 138
Fresno, CA 93710-8193
(209) 487-5033

(San Francisco Regional Office)
Robert De Monte, Regional Housing Commissioner
Phillip Burton Federal Building and U.S Courthouse
450 Golden Gate Avenue
P.O. Box 36003
San Francisco, CA 94102-3448
(415) 556-4752

(North California)
Office of Indian Programs
Community Planning and Development Division
San Francisco Program Management Team
Phillip Burton Federal Building and U.S. Courthouse
450 Golden Gate Avenue
P.O. Box 36003
San Francisco, CA 94102-3448
(415) 556-9200

(Northeast California)
Anthony A. Randolph,
Manager
777 12th Street, Suite 200
P.O. Box 1978
Sacramento, CA 95814-1997
(916) 551-1351

(Imperial and San Diego
Counties)
Charles J. Wilson, Manager
Federal Office Building,
Room 563
880 Front Street
San Diego, CA 92188-0100
(619) 557-5310

(Orange, Riverside and San
Bernardino Counties, for
home mortgages)
Harold A. Matzoll, Acting
Manager
34 Civic Center Plaza,
Box 12850
Santa Ana, CA 92712-2850
(714) 836-2451

(South California)
Charles Ming, Manager
1615 West Olympic
Boulevard
Los Angeles, CA 90015-3801
(213) 251-7122

Colorado
Michael Chitwood, Regional
Administrator
Regional Housing
Commissioner
HUD Denver Regional Office
Executive Tower Building
1405 Curtis Street
Denver, CO 80202-2349
(303) 844-4513

Office of Indian Programs
Housing and Community
Development Division
Executive Tower Building
1405 Curtis Street
Denver, CO 80202-2349
(303) 844-2861

Connecticut
William Hernandez, Jr.,
Manager
330 Main Street, First Floor
Hartford, CT 06106-1860
(203) 240-4523

Delaware
A. David Sharbaugh, Chief
Federal Building, Room 1304
844 King Street
Wilmington, DE 19801-3519
(302) 573-6300

District of Columbia
(Washington, D.C. Regional
Office)
Toni Thomas, Manager
Union Center Plaza, Phase II
820 First Street, NE,
Suite 300
Washington, DC 20002-4205
(202) 275-9200

Florida
James T. Chaplin, Manager
325 West Adams Street
Jacksonville, FL 32202-4303
(904) 791-2626

(Counties of Citrus, Sumter,
Hernando, Pasco, Pinellas,
Hillsborough, Polk, Manatee,
Hardee, Highlands, DeSoto,
Sarasota, Charlotte, Olaoes,
Hendry, Lake Okeechobee)
George A. Milburn, Jr.,
Manager
Timberlake Federal Building
Annex, Suite 700
501 East Polk Street
Tampa, FL 33602-3945
(813) 228-2501

(Counties of Volusia, Lake,
Seminole, Orange, Brevard,
Osceola, Indian River,
Okeechobee, St. Lucie)
M. Jeanette Porter, Manager
Langley Building, Suite 270
3751 Maguire Boulevard
Orlando, FL 32803-3032
(407) 648-6441

(South Florida)
Orlando L. Lorie, Manager
Gables 1 Tower
1320 South Dixie Highway
Coral Gables, FL 33146-2911
(305) 662-4510

Georgia
Raymond A. Harris, Regional
Housing Commissioner
Richard B. Russell Federal
Building
75 Spring Street, SW
Atlanta, GA 30303-3388
(404) 331-5136

Guam
Gordon Y. Furutani, Manager
300 Ala Moana Boulevard,
Room 3318
Honolulu, HI 96850-4991
(808) 546-2136

Hawaii
Gordon Y. Furutani, Manager
300 Ala Moana Boulevard,
Room 3318
Honolulu, HI 96850-4991
(808) 546-2136

Idaho
(North Idaho)
Keith R. Green, Manager
Farm Credit Bank Building,
Eighth Floor East
West 601 1st Avenue
Spokane, WA 99204-0317
(509) 456-2624

(West-Central Idaho)
Gary Gillespie, Manager
Federal Building and U.S.
Courthouse
P.O. Box 042
550 West Fort Street
Boise, ID 83724-0420
(208) 334-1990

(South Idaho)
Richard C. Brinck, Manager
Cascade Building
520 SW 6th Avenue
Portland, OR 97204-1596
(503) 221-2561

Housing

Illinois
Chicago Office of Indian Programs
Housing Development Division
626 West Jackson Boulevard
Chicago, IL 60606-5601
(312) 353-1684

(Chicago Regional Office)
Gertrude Jordan,
Regional Housing Commissioner
626 West Jackson Boulevard
Chicago, IL 60606-5601
(312) 353-5680

(Central and South Illinois)
John Lawler, Acting Supervisory Appraiser
Lincoln Towers Plaza,
Suite 672
524 South Second Street
Springfield, IL 62701-1774
(217) 492-4085

Indiana
J. Nicholas Shelley, Manager
151 North Delaware Street
Indianapolis, IN 46204-2526
(317) 226-6303

Iowa
Roger M. Massey, Manager
Braiker/Brandeis Building
210 South 16th Street
Omaha, NE 68102-1622
(402) 221-3703

William R. McNarney,
Manager
HUD Des Moines Office
Federal Building, Room 259
210 Walnut Street
Des Moines, IA 50309-2155
(515) 284-4512

Kansas
William H. Brown, Regional Administrator
Regional Housing Commissioner
HUD Kansas City, Regional Office
Gateway Tower II
400 State Avenue
Kansas City, KS 66101-2406
(913) 236-2162

Kentucky
Verna V. Van Ness, Manager
601 West Broadway
P.O. Box 1044
Louisville, KY 40201-1044
(502) 582-5251

Louisiana
Robert Vasquez, Manager
Fisk Federal Building,
1661 Canal Street
P.O. Box 70288
New Orleans, LA 70112-2887
(504) 589-7200

(North Louisiana)
David E. Gleason, Manager
New Federal Building
500 Fannin Street
Shreveport, LA 71101-3077
(318) 226-5385

Maine
Richard Young, Supervisory Appraiser
Casco Northern Bank Building
23 Main Street
Bangor, ME 04401-4318
(207) 945-0467

James Barry, Manager
Norris Cotton Federal Building
275 Chestnut Street
Manchester, NH 03101-2487
(603) 666-7681

Maryland
(Except Montgomery and Prince Georges Counties)
Maxine Saunders, Manager
The Equitable Building,
Third Floor
10 North Calvert Street
Baltimore, MD 21202-1865
(301) 962-2121

(Montgomery and Prince Georges Counties)
Toni Thomas, Manager
Union Center Plaza, Phase II
820 First Street, NE,
Suite 300
Washington, DC 20002-4205
(202) 275-9200

Massachusetts
John Mastropietro,
Acting Regional Administrator
Regional Housing Commissioner
Boston Federal Office Building, Room 375
10 Causeway Street
Boston, MA 02222-1092
(617) 565-5234

Michigan
Harry I. Sharrott, Manager
Patrick V. McNamara Federal Building
477 Michigan Avenue
Detroit, MI 48226-2592
(313) 226-6280

(East Michigan)
Gary T. LeVine, Manager
Gil Sabuco Building,
Room 200
352 South Saginaw Street
Flint, MI 48502-1953
(313) 766-5112

(West and North Michigan)
Ronald Weston, Manager
Northbrook Building, No. II
2922 Fuller Avenue, NE
Grand Rapids, MI 48505-3409
(616) 456-2100

Minnesota
Thomas Feeney, Manager
Bridge Place Building
220 Second Street, South
Minneapolis, MN 55401-2195
(612) 370-3000

Mississippi
Sandra Freeman, Manager
Dr. A. H. McCoy Federal
Building, Room 910
100 West Capitol Street
Jackson, MS 39269-1096
(601) 965-4702

Missouri
Kenneth G. Lange, Manager
210 North Tucker Boulevard
St. Louis, MO 63101-1997
(314) 425-4761

Montana
Christian KaFentzis, Manager
Federal Office Building,
Room 340
Drawer 10095
301 South Park
Helena, MT 59626-0095
(406) 449-5205

Nebraska
Roger M. Massey, Manager
Braiker/Brandeis Building
210 South 16th Street
Omaha, NE 68102-1622
(402) 221-3703

Nevada
Andrew D. Whitten, Jr.,
Manager
1050 Bible Way
P.O. Box 4700
Reno, NV 89505-4700
(702) 784-5356

Andrew Robertson, Manager
1500 East Tropicana Avenue,
Second Floor
Las Vegas, NV 89119-6516
(702) 388-6500

(North Nevada)
Office of Indian Programs
Community Planning and
Development Division
San Francisco Program
Management Team
Phillip Burton Federal
Building and U.S.
Courthouse
450 Golden Gate Avenue
P.O. Box 36003
San Francisco, CA
94102-3448
(415) 556-9200

New Hampshire
James Barry, Manager
Norris Cotton Federal
Building
275 Chestnut Street
Manchester, NH 03101-2487
(603) 666-7681

New Jersey
(North New Jersey)
Theodore Britton, Jr.,
Manager
Military Park Building
60 Park Place
Newark, NJ 07102-5504
(201) 887-1662

(South New Jersey)
Elmer Roy, Manager
The Parkade Building
519 Federal Street
Camden, NJ 08103-9998
(609) 757-5081

New Mexico
Michael R. Griego, Manager
625 Truman Street, NE
Albuquerque, NM
87110-6443
(505) 262-6463

C. Don Babers, Acting
Manager
555 Griffin Square Building,
Room 106
525 Griffin Street
Dallas, TX 75202-5007
(214) 767-8308

New York
Dr. Anthony Villane, Regional
Housing Commissioner
26 Federal Plaza
New York, NY 10278-0068
(212) 264-8068

(North New York)
John Petricco, Manager
Leo W. O'Brien Federal
Building
North Pearl Street and
Clinton Avenue
Albany, NY 12207-2395
(518) 472-3567

(West New York)
Joseph Lynch, Manager
465 Main Street, Fifth Floor
Lafayette Court
Buffalo, NY 14203-1780
(716) 846-5755

North Carolina
Larry J. Parker, Manager
415 North Edgeworth Street
Greensboro, NC 27401-2107
(919) 333-5363

North Dakota
Keith Elliot, Chief
Federal Building, Room 300
653 2nd Avenue, North
P.O. Box 2483
Fargo, ND 58108-2483
(701) 239-5136

Ohio
Robert W. Dolin, Manager
New Federal Building
200 North High Street
Columbus, OH 43215-2499
(614) 469-5737

(North Ohio)
George L. Engel, Manager
One Playhouse Square
1375 Euclid Avenue,
Room 420
Cleveland, OH 44115-1832
(216) 522-4065

Housing

(Southwest Ohio)
William Harris, Manager
Federal Office Building,
Room 9002
550 Main Street
Cincinnati, OH 45202-3253
(513) 684-2884

Oklahoma
Edwin I. Gardner, Manager
Murrah Federal Building
200 NW 5th Street
Oklahoma City, OK
73102-3202
(405) 231-4181

Indian Programs Division
Hugh Johnson, Director
Community Planning and
Development Branch
Murrah Federal Building
200 NW 5th Street
Oklahoma City, OK
73102-3202
(405) 231-4101

(East Oklahoma)
Robert H. Gardner, Manager
Robert S. Kerr Building,
Room 200
440 South Houston Avenue
Tulsa, OK 74127-8923
(918) 581-7435

Oregon
Richard C. Brinck, Manager
Cascade Building
520 SW 6th Avenue
Portland, OR 97204-1596
(503) 221-2561

Panama Canal Zone
Rosa Villalonga, Acting
Manager
159 Carlos Chardon Avenue
San Juan, PR 00918-1804
(809) 766-5201 or
(809) 498-5201

Pennsylvania
(Philadelphia Regional
Office)
Michael A. Smerconish,
Regional Administrator
Regional Housing
Commissioner
Liberty Square Building
105 South 7th Street
Philadelphia, PA 19106-3392
(215) 597-2560

(West Pennsylvania)
William Costello, Acting
Manager
412 Old Post Office
Courthouse Building
7th Avenue and Grant Street
Pittsburgh, PA 15219-1906
(412) 644-6428

Puerto Rico
Rosa Villalonga, Acting
Manager
159 Carlos Chardon Avenue
San Juan, PR 00918-1804
(809) 766-5201 or
(809) 498-5201

Rhode Island
Casimir J. Kolaski, Jr.,
Manager
Federal Building and U.S.
Post Office, Room 330
Kennedy Plaza
Providence, RI 02903-1745
(401) 528-5351

South Carolina
Ted B. Freeman, Manager
Strom Thurmond Federal
Building
1835-45 Assembly Street
Columbia, SC 29201-2480
(803) 765-5592

South Dakota
Don Olson, Chief
Courthouse Plaza, Suite 116
300 North Dakota Avenue
Sioux Falls, SD 57102-0311
(605) 330-4223

Tennessee
Richard B. Barnwell,
Manager
John J. Duncan Federal
Building
710 Locust Street, SW
Knoxville, TN 37902-2526
(615) 549-9384

(Central Tennessee)
John H. Fisher, Manager
251 Cumberland Bend Drive,
Suite 200
Nashville, TN 37228-1803
(615) 736-5213

(West Tennessee)
Bob Atkins, Manager
One Memphis Place,
Suite 1200
200 Jefferson Avenue
Memphis, TN 38103-2335
(901) 521-3367

Texas
(Fort Worth Regional Office)
Sam R. Moseley, Regional
Housing Commissioner
1600 Throckmorton
P.O. Box 2905
Forth Worth, TX 76113-2905
(817) 885-5401

(Northwest Texas)
Henry E. Whitney, Manager
Federal Office Building
1205 Texas Avenue
Lubbock, TX 79401-4093
(806) 743-7265

(East, North, and West
Texas)
C. Don D. Babers, Acting
Manager
555 Griffin Square Building,
Room 106
525 Griffin Street
Dallas, TX 75202-5007
(214) 767-8308

(Five Counties in East Texas)
David E. Gleason, Manager
New Federal Building
500 Fannin Street
Shreveport, LA 71101-3077
(318) 226-5385

(East-Central Texas)
William Robertson, Jr.,
Manager
National Bank of Texas
Building, Suite 300
221 Norfolk
Houston, TX 77098-4096
(713) 229-3589

(Bowie County)
Roger Zachritz, Acting
Manager
Lafayette Building, Suite 200
523 Louisiana
Little Rock, AR 72201-3523
(501) 378-5931

(Southwest Texas)
Don Creed, Manager
Washington Square Building
800 Dolorosa Street
San Antonio, TX 78207-4563
(512) 229-6781

Utah
Richard Bell, Manager
324 South State Street,
Suite 220
Salt Lake City, UT
84111-2321
(801) 524-5237

Vermont
William Peters, Chief
Federal Building, Room B311
11 Elmwood Avenue
P.O. Box 879
Burlington, VT 05402-0879
(802) 951-6290

James Barry, Manager
Norris Cotton Federal
Building
275 Chestnut Street
Manchester, NH 03101-2487
(603) 666-7681

Virgin Islands
Rosa Villalonga, Acting
Manager
159 Carlos Chardon Avenue
San Juan, PR 00918-1804
(809) 766-5201 or
(809) 498-5201

Virginia
(North Virginia)
Toni Thomas, Manager
Union Center Plaza, Phase II
820 First Street, NE,
Suite 300
Washington, DC 20002-4205
(202) 275-9200

(South Virginia)
Mary Ann Wilson, Manager
Federal Building, First Floor
400 North Eighth Street
Richmond, VA 23240-0170
(804) 771-2721

Washington
Office of Indian Programs
Community Planning and
Development Division
Arcade Plaza Building
1321 Second Avenue
Seattle, WA 98101-2058
(206) 442-0760

(Seattle Regional Office)
Richard Bauer,
Regional Housing
Commissioner
Arcade Plaza Building
1321 Second Avenue
Seattle, WA 98101-2054
(206) 442-5414

(East Washington)
Keith R. Green, Manager
Farm Credit Bank Building,
Eighth Floor East
West 601 1st Avenue
Spokane, WA 99204-0317
(509) 456-2624

(Clark, Klickitat, and
Skamania Counties)
Richard C. Brinck, Manager
Cascade Building
520 SW 6th Avenue
Portland, OR 97204-1596
(503) 221-2561

West Virginia
William Costello, Acting
Manager
412 Old Post Office
Courthouse Building
7th Avenue and Grant Street
Pittsburgh, PA 15219-1906
(412) 644-6428

405 Capitol Street, Suite 708
Charleston, WV 25301-1795
(304) 347-7000

Wisconsin
Delbert F. Reynolds,
Manager
Henry S. Reuss Federal Plaza
310 West Wisconsin Avenue,
Suite 1380
Milwaukee, WI 53203-2289
(414) 291-3214

Wyoming
Lawrence Gosnell, Chief
4225 Federal Office Building
100 East B Street
P.O. Box 580
Casper, WY 82602-1918
(307) 261-5252

MORTGAGE INSURANCE—TWO-YEAR OPERATING LOSS LOANS (TWO-YEAR OPERATING LOSS LOANS)

Department of Housing and Urban Development
Policies and Procedures Division
Office of Insured Multifamily Housing Development
Washington, DC 20410
(202) 708-3730

Description: Guaranteed/insured loans to owners of multifamily projects or facilities subject to a mortgage insured or held by HUD to insure a separate loan covering operating losses during first two years after a first HUD mortgage. Limited to currently insured HUD projects, and to term of mortgage.

$ Given: Nationwide FY 93 est. $10.9 million.

Application Information: Initial conference at local HUD field office followed by formal application accompanied by financial statement prepared by an independent CPA.

Deadline: Three years after end of two-year operating loss period.

Contact: Local HUD field office

Alabama
Robert E. Lunsford, Manager
600 Beacon Parkway West,
Suite 300
Birmingham, AL 35209-3144
(205) 731-1617

Alaska
Arlene Patton, Manager
222 West 8th Avenue, #64
Anchorage, AK 99513-7537
(907) 271-4170

Community Planning and Development Division
222 West 8th Avenue, #64
Anchorage, AK 99513-7537
(907) 271-3669

American Samoa
Gordon Y. Furutani, Manager
300 Ala Moana Boulevard,
Room 3318
Honolulu, HI 96850-4991
(808) 546-2136

Arizona
Dwight Peterson, Manager
400 North First Street,
Suite 1600
P.O. Box 13468
Phoenix, AZ 85004-2361
(602) 261-4434

Charles Ming, Manager
1615 West Olympic Boulevard
Los Angeles, CA 90015-3801
(213) 251-7122

Jean Staley, Manager
Pioneer Plaza, 100 North Stone Avenue, Suite 410
P.O. Box 2648
Tucson, AZ 86701-1467
(602) 629-6237

Arkansas
Roger Zachritz, Acting Manager
Lafayette Building, Suite 200
523 Louisiana
Little Rock, AR 72201-3523
(501) 378-5931

California
Lilly Lee, Manager
1630 East Shaw Avenue,
Suite 138
Fresno, CA 93710-8193
(209) 487-5033

(San Francisco Regional Office)
Robert De Monte, Regional Housing Commissioner
Phillip Burton Federal Building and U.S Courthouse
450 Golden Gate Avenue
P.O. Box 36003
San Francisco, CA 94102-3448
(415) 556-4752

(North California)
Office of Indian Programs
Community Planning and Development Division
San Francisco Program Management Team
Phillip Burton Federal Building and U.S. Courthouse
450 Golden Gate Avenue
P.O. Box 36003
San Francisco, CA 94102-3448
(415) 556-9200

(Northeast California)
Anthony A. Randolph,
Manager
777 12th Street, Suite 200
P.O. Box 1978
Sacramento, CA 95814-1997
(916) 551-1351

(Imperial and San Diego
Counties)
Charles J. Wilson, Manager
Federal Office Building,
Room 563
880 Front Street
San Diego, CA 92188-0100
(619) 557-5310

(Orange, Riverside and San
Bernardino Counties, for
home mortgages)
Harold A. Matzoll, Acting
Manager
34 Civic Center Plaza,
Box 12850
Santa Ana, CA 92712-2850
(714) 836-2451

(South California)
Charles Ming, Manager
1615 West Olympic
Boulevard
Los Angeles, CA 90015-3801
(213) 251-7122

Colorado
Michael Chitwood, Regional
Administrator
Regional Housing
Commissioner
HUD Denver Regional Office
Executive Tower Building
1405 Curtis Street
Denver, CO 80202-2349
(303) 844-4513

Office of Indian Programs
Housing and Community
Development Division
Executive Tower Building
1405 Curtis Street
Denver, CO 80202-2349
(303) 844-2861

Connecticut
William Hernandez, Jr.,
Manager
330 Main Street, First Floor
Hartford, CT 06106-1860
(203) 240-4523

Delaware
A. David Sharbaugh, Chief
Federal Building, Room 1304
844 King Street
Wilmington, DE 19801-3519
(302) 573-6300

District of Columbia
(Washington, D.C. Regional
Office)
Toni Thomas, Manager
Union Center Plaza, Phase II
820 First Street, NE,
Suite 300
Washington, DC 20002-4205
(202) 275-9200

Florida
James T. Chaplin, Manager
325 West Adams Street
Jacksonville, FL 32202-4303
(904) 791-2626

(Counties of Citrus, Sumter,
Hernando, Pasco, Pinellas,
Hillsborough, Polk, Manatee,
Hardee, Highlands, DeSoto,
Sarasota, Charlotte, Olaoes,
Hendry, Lake Okeechobee)
George A. Milburn, Jr.,
Manager
Timberlake Federal Building
Annex, Suite 700
501 East Polk Street
Tampa, FL 33602-3945
(813) 228-2501

(Counties of Volusia, Lake,
Seminole, Orange, Brevard,
Osceola, Indian River,
Okeechobee, St. Lucie)
M. Jeanette Porter, Manager
Langley Building, Suite 270
3751 Maguire Boulevard
Orlando, FL 32803-3032
(407) 648-6441

(South Florida)
Orlando L. Lorie, Manager
Gables 1 Tower
1320 South Dixie Highway
Coral Gables, FL 33146-2911
(305) 662-4510

Georgia
Raymond A. Harris, Regional
Housing Commissioner
Richard B. Russell Federal
Building
75 Spring Street, SW
Atlanta, GA 30303-3388
(404) 331-5136

Guam
Gordon Y. Furutani, Manager
300 Ala Moana Boulevard,
Room 3318
Honolulu, HI 96850-4991
(808) 546-2136

Hawaii
Gordon Y. Furutani, Manager
300 Ala Moana Boulevard,
Room 3318
Honolulu, HI 96850-4991
(808) 546-2136

Idaho
(North Idaho)
Keith R. Green, Manager
Farm Credit Bank Building,
Eighth Floor East
West 601 1st Avenue
Spokane, WA 99204-0317
(509) 456-2624

(West-Central Idaho)
Gary Gillespie, Manager
Federal Building and U.S.
Courthouse
P.O. Box 042
550 West Fort Street
Boise, ID 83724-0420
(208) 334-1990

(South Idaho)
Richard C. Brinck, Manager
Cascade Building
520 SW 6th Avenue
Portland, OR 97204-1596
(503) 221-2561

Housing

Illinois
Chicago Office of Indian Programs
Housing Development Division
626 West Jackson Boulevard
Chicago, IL 60606-5601
(312) 353-1684

(Chicago Regional Office)
Gertrude Jordan,
Regional Housing Commissioner
626 West Jackson Boulevard
Chicago, IL 60606-5601
(312) 353-5680

(Central and South Illinois)
John Lawler, Acting
Supervisory Appraiser
Lincoln Towers Plaza,
Suite 672
524 South Second Street
Springfield, IL 62701-1774
(217) 492-4085

Indiana
J. Nicholas Shelley, Manager
151 North Delaware Street
Indianapolis, IN 46204-2526
(317) 226-6303

Iowa
Roger M. Massey, Manager
Braiker/Brandeis Building
210 South 16th Street
Omaha, NE 68102-1622
(402) 221-3703

William R. McNarney,
Manager
HUD Des Moines Office
Federal Building, Room 259
210 Walnut Street
Des Moines, IA 50309-2155
(515) 284-4512

Kansas
William H. Brown, Regional
Administrator
Regional Housing
Commissioner
HUD Kansas City, Regional
Office
Gateway Tower II
400 State Avenue
Kansas City, KS 66101-2406
(913) 236-2162

Kentucky
Verna V. Van Ness, Manager
601 West Broadway
P.O. Box 1044
Louisville, KY 40201-1044
(502) 582-5251

Louisiana
Robert Vasquez, Manager
Fisk Federal Building,
1661 Canal Street
P.O. Box 70288
New Orleans, LA 70112-2887
(504) 589-7200

(North Louisiana)
David E. Gleason, Manager
New Federal Building
500 Fannin Street
Shreveport, LA 71101-3077
(318) 226-5385

Maine
Richard Young, Supervisory
Appraiser
Casco Northern Bank
Building
23 Main Street
Bangor, ME 04401-4318
(207) 945-0467

James Barry, Manager
Norris Cotton Federal
Building
275 Chestnut Street
Manchester, NH 03101-2487
(603) 666-7681

Maryland
(Except Montgomery and
Prince Georges Counties)
Maxine Saunders, Manager
The Equitable Building,
Third Floor
10 North Calvert Street
Baltimore, MD 21202-1865
(301) 962-2121

(Montgomery and Prince
Georges Counties)
Toni Thomas, Manager
Union Center Plaza, Phase II
820 First Street, NE,
Suite 300
Washington, DC 20002-4205
(202) 275-9200

Massachusetts
John Mastropietro,
Acting Regional
Administrator
Regional Housing
Commissioner
Boston Federal Office
Building, Room 375
10 Causeway Street
Boston, MA 02222-1092
(617) 565-5234

Michigan
Harry I. Sharrott, Manager
Patrick V. McNamara Federal
Building
477 Michigan Avenue
Detroit, MI 48226-2592
(313) 226-6280

(East Michigan)
Gary T. LeVine, Manager
Gil Sabuco Building,
Room 200
352 South Saginaw Street
Flint, MI 48502-1953
(313) 766-5112

(West and North Michigan)
Ronald Weston, Manager
Northbrook Building, No. II
2922 Fuller Avenue, NE
Grand Rapids, MI 48505-3409
(616) 456-2100

Minnesota
Thomas Feeney, Manager
Bridge Place Building
220 Second Street, South
Minneapolis, MN 55401-2195
(612) 370-3000

Mississippi
Sandra Freeman, Manager
Dr. A. H. McCoy Federal
Building, Room 910
100 West Capitol Street
Jackson, MS 39269-1096
(601) 965-4702

Missouri
Kenneth G. Lange, Manager
210 North Tucker Boulevard
St. Louis, MO 63101-1997
(314) 425-4761

Montana
Christian KaFentzis, Manager
Federal Office Building,
Room 340
Drawer 10095
301 South Park
Helena, MT 59626-0095
(406) 449-5205

Nebraska
Roger M. Massey, Manager
Braiker/Brandeis Building
210 South 16th Street
Omaha, NE 68102-1622
(402) 221-3703

Nevada
Andrew D. Whitten, Jr.,
Manager
1050 Bible Way
P.O. Box 4700
Reno, NV 89505-4700
(702) 784-5356

Andrew Robertson, Manager
1500 East Tropicana Avenue,
Second Floor
Las Vegas, NV 89119-6516
(702) 388-6500

(North Nevada)
Office of Indian Programs
Community Planning and
Development Division
San Francisco Program
Management Team
Phillip Burton Federal
Building and U.S.
Courthouse
450 Golden Gate Avenue
P.O. Box 36003
San Francisco, CA
94102-3448
(415) 556-9200

New Hampshire
James Barry, Manager
Norris Cotton Federal
Building
275 Chestnut Street
Manchester, NH 03101-2487
(603) 666-7681

New Jersey
(North New Jersey)
Theodore Britton, Jr.,
Manager
Military Park Building
60 Park Place
Newark, NJ 07102-5504
(201) 887-1662

(South New Jersey)
Elmer Roy, Manager
The Parkade Building
519 Federal Street
Camden, NJ 08103-9998
(609) 757-5081

New Mexico
Michael R. Griego, Manager
625 Truman Street, NE
Albuquerque, NM
87110-6443
(505) 262-6463

C. Don Babers, Acting
Manager
555 Griffin Square Building,
Room 106
525 Griffin Street
Dallas, TX 75202-5007
(214) 767-8308

New York
Dr. Anthony Villane, Regional
Housing Commissioner
26 Federal Plaza
New York, NY 10278-0068
(212) 264-8068

(North New York)
John Petricco, Manager
Leo W. O'Brien Federal
Building
North Pearl Street and
Clinton Avenue
Albany, NY 12207-2395
(518) 472-3567

(West New York)
Joseph Lynch, Manager
465 Main Street, Fifth Floor
Lafayette Court
Buffalo, NY 14203-1780
(716) 846-5755

North Carolina
Larry J. Parker, Manager
415 North Edgeworth Street
Greensboro, NC 27401-2107
(919) 333-5363

North Dakota
Keith Elliot, Chief
Federal Building, Room 300
653 2nd Avenue, North
P.O. Box 2483
Fargo, ND 58108-2483
(701) 239-5136

Ohio
Robert W. Dolin, Manager
New Federal Building
200 North High Street
Columbus, OH 43215-2499
(614) 469-5737

(North Ohio)
George L. Engel, Manager
One Playhouse Square
1375 Euclid Avenue,
Room 420
Cleveland, OH 44115-1832
(216) 522-4065

Housing

(Southwest Ohio)
William Harris, Manager
Federal Office Building,
Room 9002
550 Main Street
Cincinnati, OH 45202-3253
(513) 684-2884

Oklahoma
Edwin I. Gardner, Manager
Murrah Federal Building
200 NW 5th Street
Oklahoma City, OK
73102-3202
(405) 231-4181

Indian Programs Division
Hugh Johnson, Director
Community Planning and
Development Branch
Murrah Federal Building
200 NW 5th Street
Oklahoma City, OK
73102-3202
(405) 231-4101

(East Oklahoma)
Robert H. Gardner, Manager
Robert S. Kerr Building,
Room 200
440 South Houston Avenue
Tulsa, OK 74127-8923
(918) 581-7435

Oregon
Richard C. Brinck, Manager
Cascade Building
520 SW 6th Avenue
Portland, OR 97204-1596
(503) 221-2561

Panama Canal Zone
Rosa Villalonga, Acting
Manager
159 Carlos Chardon Avenue
San Juan, PR 00918-1804
(809) 766-5201 or
(809) 498-5201

Pennsylvania
(Philadelphia Regional
Office)
Michael A. Smerconish,
Regional Administrator
Regional Housing
Commissioner
Liberty Square Building
105 South 7th Street
Philadelphia, PA 19106-3392
(215) 597-2560

(West Pennsylvania)
William Costello, Acting
Manager
412 Old Post Office
Courthouse Building
7th Avenue and Grant Street
Pittsburgh, PA 15219-1906
(412) 644-6428

Puerto Rico
Rosa Villalonga, Acting
Manager
159 Carlos Chardon Avenue
San Juan, PR 00918-1804
(809) 766-5201 or
(809) 498-5201

Rhode Island
Casimir J. Kolaski, Jr.,
Manager
Federal Building and U.S.
Post Office, Room 330
Kennedy Plaza
Providence, RI 02903-1745
(401) 528-5351

South Carolina
Ted B. Freeman, Manager
Strom Thurmond Federal
Building
1835-45 Assembly Street
Columbia, SC 29201-2480
(803) 765-5592

South Dakota
Don Olson, Chief
Courthouse Plaza, Suite 116
300 North Dakota Avenue
Sioux Falls, SD 57102-0311
(605) 330-4223

Tennessee
Richard B. Barnwell,
Manager
John J. Duncan Federal
Building
710 Locust Street, SW
Knoxville, TN 37902-2526
(615) 549-9384

(Central Tennessee)
John H. Fisher, Manager
251 Cumberland Bend Drive,
Suite 200
Nashville, TN 37228-1803
(615) 736-5213

(West Tennessee)
Bob Atkins, Manager
One Memphis Place,
Suite 1200
200 Jefferson Avenue
Memphis, TN 38103-2335
(901) 521-3367

Texas
(Fort Worth Regional Office)
Sam R. Moseley, Regional
Housing Commissioner
1600 Throckmorton
P.O. Box 2905
Forth Worth, TX 76113-2905
(817) 885-5401

(Northwest Texas)
Henry E. Whitney, Manager
Federal Office Building
1205 Texas Avenue
Lubbock, TX 79401-4093
(806) 743-7265

(East, North, and West
Texas)
C. Don Babers, Acting
Manager
555 Griffin Square Building,
Room 106
525 Griffin Street
Dallas, TX 75202-5007
(214) 767-8308

(Five Counties in East Texas)
David E. Gleason, Manager
New Federal Building
500 Fannin Street
Shreveport, LA 71101-3077
(318) 226-5385

(East-Central Texas)
William Robertson, Jr.,
Manager
National Bank of Texas
Building, Suite 300
221 Norfolk
Houston, TX 77098-4096
(713) 229-3589

(Bowie County)
Roger Zachritz, Acting
Manager
Lafayette Building, Suite 200
523 Louisiana
Little Rock, AR 72201-3523
(501) 378-5931

(Southwest Texas)
Don Creed, Manager
Washington Square Building
800 Dolorosa Street
San Antonio, TX 78207-4563
(512) 229-6781

Utah
Richard Bell, Manager
324 South State Street,
Suite 220
Salt Lake City, UT
84111-2321
(801) 524-5237

Vermont
William Peters, Chief
Federal Building, Room B311
11 Elmwood Avenue
P.O. Box 879
Burlington, VT 05402-0879
(802) 951-6290

James Barry, Manager
Norris Cotton Federal
Building
275 Chestnut Street
Manchester, NH 03101-2487
(603) 666-7681

Virgin Islands
Rosa Villalonga, Acting
Manager
159 Carlos Chardon Avenue
San Juan, PR 00918-1804
(809) 766-5201 or
(809) 498-5201

Virginia
(North Virginia)
Toni Thomas, Manager
Union Center Plaza, Phase II
820 First Street, NE,
Suite 300
Washington, DC 20002-4205
(202) 275-9200

(South Virginia)
Mary Ann Wilson, Manager
Federal Building, First Floor
400 North Eighth Street
Richmond, VA 23240-0170
(804) 771-2721

Washington
Office of Indian Programs
Community Planning and
Development Division
Arcade Plaza Building
1321 Second Avenue
Seattle, WA 98101-2058
(206) 442-0760

(Seattle Regional Office)
Richard Bauer,
Regional Housing
Commissioner
Arcade Plaza Building
1321 Second Avenue
Seattle, WA 98101-2054
(206) 442-5414

(East Washington)
Keith R. Green, Manager
Farm Credit Bank Building,
Eighth Floor East
West 601 1st Avenue
Spokane, WA 99204-0317
(509) 456-2624

(Clark, Klickitat, and
Skamania Counties)
Richard C. Brinck, Manager
Cascade Building
520 SW 6th Avenue
Portland, OR 97204-1596
(503) 221-2561

West Virginia
William Costello, Acting
Manager
412 Old Post Office
Courthouse Building
7th Avenue and Grant Street
Pittsburgh, PA 15219-1906
(412) 644-6428

405 Capitol Street, Suite 708
Charleston, WV 25301-1795
(304) 347-7000

Wisconsin
Delbert F. Reynolds,
Manager
Henry S. Reuss Federal Plaza
310 West Wisconsin Avenue,
Suite 1380
Milwaukee, WI 53203-2289
(414) 291-3214

Wyoming
Lawrence Gosnell, Chief
4225 Federal Office Building
100 East B Street
P.O. Box 580
Casper, WY 82602-1918
(307) 261-5252

OPERATING ASSISTANCE FOR TROUBLED MULTIFAMILY HOUSING PROJECTS (FLEXIBLE SUBSIDY FUND/TROUBLED PROJECTS)

Department of Housing and Urban Development
Office of Multifamily Housing Management
Washington, DC 20420
(202) 708-3730

Description: Direct payments for specified use to profit-motivated, limited dividend, and cooperative owners to restore or maintain physical and financial upkeep of certain approved low- to moderate-income projects. Restricted to certain projects approved by HUD. Assurance must be gained from local government that essential services will be maintained, that real estate taxes will be assessed in a normal manner, and that assistance is not inconsistent with local plans and priorities.
$ Given: Nationwide FY 92 est. $1.7 million per project. In 1991, 121 projects received $98.2 million.
Application Information: Projects identified by HUD as needing aid are asked to submit appropriate documentation.
Deadline: None
Contact: Chief, loan management branch of local HUD field office

Alabama
Robert E. Lunsford, Manager
600 Beacon Parkway West, Suite 300
Birmingham, AL 35209-3144
(205) 731-1617

Alaska
Arlene Patton, Manager
222 West 8th Avenue, #64
Anchorage, AK 99513-7537
(907) 271-4170

Community Planning and Development Division
222 West 8th Avenue, #64
Anchorage, AK 99513-7537
(907) 271-3669

American Samoa
Gordon Y. Furutani, Manager
300 Ala Moana Boulevard, Room 3318
Honolulu, HI 96850-4991
(808) 546-2136

Arizona
Dwight Peterson, Manager
400 North First Street, Suite 1600
P.O. Box 13468
Phoenix, AZ 85004-2361
(602) 261-4434

Charles Ming, Manager
1615 West Olympic Boulevard
Los Angeles, CA 90015-3801
(213) 251-7122

Jean Staley, Manager
Pioneer Plaza, 100 North Stone Avenue, Suite 410
P.O. Box 2648
Tucson, AZ 86701-1467
(602) 629-6237

Arkansas
Roger Zachritz, Acting Manager
Lafayette Building, Suite 200
523 Louisiana
Little Rock, AR 72201-3523
(501) 378-5931

California
Lilly Lee, Manager
1630 East Shaw Avenue, Suite 138
Fresno, CA 93710-8193
(209) 487-5033

(San Francisco Regional Office)
Robert De Monte, Regional Housing Commissioner
Phillip Burton Federal Building and U.S Courthouse
450 Golden Gate Avenue
P.O. Box 36003
San Francisco, CA 94102-3448
(415) 556-4752

(North California)
Office of Indian Programs
Community Planning and
Development Division
San Francisco Program
Management Team
Phillip Burton Federal
Building and U.S.
Courthouse
450 Golden Gate Avenue
P.O. Box 36003
San Francisco, CA
94102-3448
(415) 556-9200

(Northeast California)
Anthony A. Randolph,
Manager
777 12th Street, Suite 200
P.O. Box 1978
Sacramento, CA 95814-1997
(916) 551-1351

(Imperial and San Diego
Counties)
Charles J. Wilson, Manager
Federal Office Building,
Room 563
880 Front Street
San Diego, CA 92188-0100
(619) 557-5310

(Orange, Riverside and San
Bernardino Counties, for
home mortgages)
Harold A. Matzoll, Acting
Manager
34 Civic Center Plaza,
Box 12850
Santa Ana, CA 92712-2850
(714) 836-2451

(South California)
Charles Ming, Manager
1615 West Olympic
Boulevard
Los Angeles, CA 90015-3801
(213) 251-7122

Colorado
Michael Chitwood, Regional
Administrator
Regional Housing
Commissioner
HUD Denver Regional Office
Executive Tower Building
1405 Curtis Street
Denver, CO 80202-2349
(303) 844-4513

Office of Indian Programs
Housing and Community
Development Division
Executive Tower Building
1405 Curtis Street
Denver, CO 80202-2349
(303) 844-2861

Connecticut
William Hernandez, Jr.,
Manager
330 Main Street, First Floor
Hartford, CT 06106-1860
(203) 240-4523

Delaware
A. David Sharbaugh, Chief
Federal Building, Room 1304
844 King Street
Wilmington, DE 19801-3519
(302) 573-6300

District of Columbia
(Washington, D.C. Regional
Office)
Toni Thomas, Manager
Union Center Plaza, Phase II
820 First Street, NE,
Suite 300
Washington, DC 20002-4205
(202) 275-9200

Florida
James T. Chaplin, Manager
325 West Adams Street
Jacksonville, FL 32202-4303
(904) 791-2626

(Counties of Citrus, Sumter,
Hernando, Pasco, Pinellas,
Hillsborough, Polk, Manatee,
Hardee, Highlands, DeSoto,
Sarasota, Charlotte, Olaoes,
Hendry, Lake Okeechobee)
George A. Milburn, Jr.,
Manager
Timberlake Federal Building
Annex, Suite 700
501 East Polk Street
Tampa, FL 33602-3945
(813) 228-2501

(Counties of Volusia, Lake,
Seminole, Orange, Brevard,
Osceola, Indian River,
Okeechobee, St. Lucie)
M. Jeanette Porter, Manager
Langley Building, Suite 270
3751 Maguire Boulevard
Orlando, FL 32803-3032
(407) 648-6441

(South Florida)
Orlando L. Lorie, Manager
Gables 1 Tower
1320 South Dixie Highway
Coral Gables, FL 33146-2911
(305) 662-4510

Georgia
Raymond A. Harris, Regional
Housing Commissioner
Richard B. Russell Federal
Building
75 Spring Street, SW
Atlanta, GA 30303-3388
(404) 331-5136

Guam
Gordon Y. Furutani, Manager
300 Ala Moana Boulevard,
Room 3318
Honolulu, HI 96850-4991
(808) 546-2136

Hawaii
Gordon Y. Furutani, Manager
300 Ala Moana Boulevard,
Room 3318
Honolulu, HI 96850-4991
(808) 546-2136

Housing

Idaho
(North Idaho)
Keith R. Green, Manager
Farm Credit Bank Building,
Eighth Floor East
West 601 1st Avenue
Spokane, WA 99204-0317
(509) 456-2624

(West-Central Idaho)
Gary Gillespie, Manager
Federal Building and U.S.
Courthouse
P.O. Box 042
550 West Fort Street
Boise, ID 83724-0420
(208) 334-1990

(South Idaho)
Richard C. Brinck, Manager
Cascade Building
520 SW 6th Avenue
Portland, OR 97204-1596
(503) 221-2561

Illinois
Chicago Office of Indian
Programs
Housing Development
Division
626 West Jackson Boulevard
Chicago, IL 60606-5601
(312) 353-1684

(Chicago Regional Office)
Gertrude Jordan,
Regional Housing
Commissioner
626 West Jackson Boulevard
Chicago, IL 60606-5601
(312) 353-5680

(Central and South Illinois)
John Lawler, Acting
Supervisory Appraiser
Lincoln Towers Plaza,
Suite 672
524 South Second Street
Springfield, IL 62701-1774
(217) 492-4085

Indiana
J. Nicholas Shelley, Manager
151 North Delaware Street
Indianapolis, IN 46204-2526
(317) 226-6303

Iowa
Roger M. Massey, Manager
Braiker/Brandeis Building
210 South 16th Street
Omaha, NE 68102-1622
(402) 221-3703

William R. McNarney,
Manager
HUD Des Moines Office
Federal Building, Room 259
210 Walnut Street
Des Moines, IA 50309-2155
(515) 284-4512

Kansas
William H. Brown, Regional
Administrator
Regional Housing
Commissioner
HUD Kansas City, Regional
Office
Gateway Tower II
400 State Avenue
Kansas City, KS 66101-2406
(913) 236-2162

Kentucky
Verna V. Van Ness, Manager
601 West Broadway
P.O. Box 1044
Louisville, KY 40201-1044
(502) 582-5251

Louisiana
Robert Vasquez, Manager
Fisk Federal Building,
1661 Canal Street
P.O. Box 70288
New Orleans, LA 70112-2887
(504) 589-7200

(North Louisiana)
David E. Gleason, Manager
New Federal Building
500 Fannin Street
Shreveport, LA 71101-3077
(318) 226-5385

Maine
Richard Young, Supervisory
Appraiser
Casco Northern Bank
Building
23 Main Street
Bangor, ME 04401-4318
(207) 945-0467

James Barry, Manager
Norris Cotton Federal
Building
275 Chestnut Street
Manchester, NH 03101-2487
(603) 666-7681

Maryland
(Except Montgomery and
Prince Georges Counties)
Maxine Saunders, Manager
The Equitable Building,
Third Floor
10 North Calvert Street
Baltimore, MD 21202-1865
(301) 962-2121

(Montgomery and Prince
Georges Counties)
Toni Thomas, Manager
Union Center Plaza, Phase II
820 First Street, NE,
Suite 300
Washington, DC 20002-4205
(202) 275-9200

Massachusetts
John Mastropietro,
Acting Regional
Administrator
Regional Housing
Commissioner
Boston Federal Office
Building, Room 375
10 Causeway Street
Boston, MA 02222-1092
(617) 565-5234

Michigan
Harry I. Sharrott, Manager
Patrick V. McNamara Federal
Building
477 Michigan Avenue
Detroit, MI 48226-2592
(313) 226-6280

(East Michigan)
Gary T. LeVine, Manager
Gil Sabuco Building,
Room 200
352 South Saginaw Street
Flint, MI 48502-1953
(313) 766-5112

(West and North Michigan)
Ronald Weston, Manager
Northbrook Building, No. II
2922 Fuller Avenue, NE
Grand Rapids, MI 48505-3409
(616) 456-2100

Minnesota
Thomas Feeney, Manager
Bridge Place Building
220 Second Street, South
Minneapolis, MN 55401-2195
(612) 370-3000

Mississippi
Sandra Freeman, Manager
Dr. A. H. McCoy Federal
Building, Room 910
100 West Capitol Street
Jackson, MS 39269-1096
(601) 965-4702

Missouri
Kenneth G. Lange, Manager
210 North Tucker Boulevard
St. Louis, MO 63101-1997
(314) 425-4761

Montana
Christian KaFentzis, Manager
Federal Office Building,
Room 340
Drawer 10095
301 South Park
Helena, MT 59626-0095
(406) 449-5205

Nebraska
Roger M. Massey, Manager
Braiker/Brandeis Building
210 South 16th Street
Omaha, NE 68102-1622
(402) 221-3703

Nevada
Andrew D. Whitten, Jr.,
Manager
1050 Bible Way
P.O. Box 4700
Reno, NV 89505-4700
(702) 784-5356

Andrew Robertson, Manager
1500 East Tropicana Avenue,
Second Floor
Las Vegas, NV 89119-6516
(702) 388-6500

(North Nevada)
Office of Indian Programs
Community Planning and
Development Division
San Francisco Program
Management Team
Phillip Burton Federal
Building and U.S.
Courthouse
450 Golden Gate Avenue
P.O. Box 36003
San Francisco, CA
94102-3448
(415) 556-9200

New Hampshire
James Barry, Manager
Norris Cotton Federal
Building
275 Chestnut Street
Manchester, NH 03101-2487
(603) 666-7681

New Jersey
(North New Jersey)
Theodore Britton, Jr.,
Manager
Military Park Building
60 Park Place
Newark, NJ 07102-5504
(201) 887-1662

(South New Jersey)
Elmer Roy, Manager
The Parkade Building
519 Federal Street
Camden, NJ 08103-9998
(609) 757-5081

New Mexico
Michael R. Griego, Manager
625 Truman Street, NE
Albuquerque, NM
87110-6443
(505) 262-6463

C. Don Babers, Acting
Manager
555 Griffin Square Building,
Room 106
525 Griffin Street
Dallas, TX 75202-5007
(214) 767-8308

New York
Dr. Anthony Villane, Regional
Housing Commissioner
26 Federal Plaza
New York, NY 10278-0068
(212) 264-8068

(North New York)
John Petricco, Manager
Leo W. O'Brien Federal
Building
North Pearl Street and
Clinton Avenue
Albany, NY 12207-2395
(518) 472-3567

(West New York)
Joseph Lynch, Manager
465 Main Street, Fifth Floor
Lafayette Court
Buffalo, NY 14203-1780
(716) 846-5755

North Carolina
Larry J. Parker, Manager
415 North Edgeworth Street
Greensboro, NC 27401-2107
(919) 333-5363

Housing

North Dakota
Keith Elliot, Chief
Federal Building, Room 300
653 2nd Avenue, North
P.O. Box 2483
Fargo, ND 58108-2483
(701) 239-5136

Ohio
Robert W. Dolin, Manager
New Federal Building
200 North High Street
Columbus, OH 43215-2499
(614) 469-5737

(North Ohio)
George L. Engel, Manager
One Playhouse Square
1375 Euclid Avenue,
Room 420
Cleveland, OH 44115-1832
(216) 522-4065

(Southwest Ohio)
William Harris, Manager
Federal Office Building,
Room 9002
550 Main Street
Cincinnati, OH 45202-3253
(513) 684-2884

Oklahoma
Edwin I. Gardner, Manager
Murrah Federal Building
200 NW 5th Street
Oklahoma City, OK
73102-3202
(405) 231-4181

Indian Programs Division
Hugh Johnson, Director
Community Planning and
Development Branch
Murrah Federal Building
200 NW 5th Street
Oklahoma City, OK
73102-3202
(405) 231-4101

(East Oklahoma)
Robert H. Gardner, Manager
Robert S. Kerr Building,
Room 200
440 South Houston Avenue
Tulsa, OK 74127-8923
(918) 581-7435

Oregon
Richard C. Brinck, Manager
Cascade Building
520 SW 6th Avenue
Portland, OR 97204-1596
(503) 221-2561

Panama Canal Zone
Rosa Villalonga, Acting
Manager
159 Carlos Chardon Avenue
San Juan, PR 00918-1804
(809) 766-5201 or
(809) 498-5201

Pennsylvania
(Philadelphia Regional
Office)
Michael A. Smerconish,
Regional Administrator
Regional Housing
Commissioner
Liberty Square Building
105 South 7th Street
Philadelphia, PA 19106-3392
(215) 597-2560

(West Pennsylvania)
William Costello, Acting
Manager
412 Old Post Office
Courthouse Building
7th Avenue and Grant Street
Pittsburgh, PA 15219-1906
(412) 644-6428

Puerto Rico
Rosa Villalonga, Acting
Manager
159 Carlos Chardon Avenue
San Juan, PR 00918-1804
(809) 766-5201 or
(809) 498-5201

Rhode Island
Casimir J. Kolaski, Jr.,
Manager
Federal Building and U.S.
Post Office, Room 330
Kennedy Plaza
Providence, RI 02903-1745
(401) 528-5351

South Carolina
Ted B. Freeman, Manager
Strom Thurmond Federal
Building
1835-45 Assembly Street
Columbia, SC 29201-2480
(803) 765-5592

South Dakota
Don Olson, Chief
Courthouse Plaza, Suite 116
300 North Dakota Avenue
Sioux Falls, SD 57102-0311
(605) 330-4223

Tennessee
Richard B. Barnwell,
Manager
John J. Duncan Federal
Building
710 Locust Street, SW
Knoxville, TN 37902-2526
(615) 549-9384

(Central Tennessee)
John H. Fisher, Manager
251 Cumberland Bend Drive,
Suite 200
Nashville, TN 37228-1803
(615) 736-5213

(West Tennessee)
Bob Atkins, Manager
One Memphis Place,
Suite 1200
200 Jefferson Avenue
Memphis, TN 38103-2335
(901) 521-3367

Texas
(Fort Worth Regional Office)
Sam R. Moseley, Regional
Housing Commissioner
1600 Throckmorton
P.O. Box 2905
Forth Worth, TX 76113-2905
(817) 885-5401

(Northwest Texas)
Henry E. Whitney, Manager
Federal Office Building
1205 Texas Avenue
Lubbock, TX 79401-4093
(806) 743-7265

(East, North, and West
Texas)
C. Don D. Babers, Acting
Manager
555 Griffin Square Building,
Room 106
525 Griffin Street
Dallas, TX 75202-5007
(214) 767-8308

(Five Counties in East Texas)
David E. Gleason, Manager
New Federal Building
500 Fannin Street
Shreveport, LA 71101-3077
(318) 226-5385

(East-Central Texas)
William Robertson, Jr.,
Manager
National Bank of Texas
Building, Suite 300
221 Norfolk
Houston, TX 77098-4096
(713) 229-3589

(Bowie County)
Roger Zachritz, Acting
Manager
Lafayette Building, Suite 200
523 Louisiana
Little Rock, AR 72201-3523
(501) 378-5931

(Southwest Texas)
Don Creed, Manager
Washington Square Building
800 Dolorosa Street
San Antonio, TX 78207-4563
(512) 229-6781

Utah
Richard Bell, Manager
324 South State Street,
Suite 220
Salt Lake City, UT
84111-2321
(801) 524-5237

Vermont
William Peters, Chief
Federal Building, Room B311
11 Elmwood Avenue
P.O. Box 879
Burlington, VT 05402-0879
(802) 951-6290

James Barry, Manager
Norris Cotton Federal
Building
275 Chestnut Street
Manchester, NH 03101-2487
(603) 666-7681

Virgin Islands
Rosa Villalonga, Acting
Manager
159 Carlos Chardon Avenue
San Juan, PR 00918-1804
(809) 766-5201 or
(809) 498-5201

Virginia
(North Virginia)
Toni Thomas, Manager
Union Center Plaza, Phase II
820 First Street, NE,
Suite 300
Washington, DC 20002-4205
(202) 275-9200

(South Virginia)
Mary Ann Wilson, Manager
Federal Building, First Floor
400 North Eighth Street
Richmond, VA 23240-0170
(804) 771-2721

Washington
Office of Indian Programs
Community Planning and
Development Division
Arcade Plaza Building
1321 Second Avenue
Seattle, WA 98101-2058
(206) 442-0760

(Seattle Regional Office)
Richard Bauer,
Regional Housing
Commissioner
Arcade Plaza Building
1321 Second Avenue
Seattle, WA 98101-2054
(206) 442-5414

(East Washington)
Keith R. Green, Manager
Farm Credit Bank Building,
Eighth Floor East
West 601 1st Avenue
Spokane, WA 99204-0317
(509) 456-2624

(Clark, Klickitat, and
Skamania Counties)
Richard C. Brinck, Manager
Cascade Building
520 SW 6th Avenue
Portland, OR 97204-1596
(503) 221-2561

West Virginia
William Costello, Acting
Manager
412 Old Post Office
Courthouse Building
7th Avenue and Grant Street
Pittsburgh, PA 15219-1906
(412) 644-6428

405 Capitol Street, Suite 708
Charleston, WV 25301-1795
(304) 347-7000

Wisconsin
Delbert F. Reynolds,
Manager
Henry S. Reuss Federal Plaza
310 West Wisconsin Avenue,
Suite 1380
Milwaukee, WI 53203-2289
(414) 291-3214

Wyoming
Lawrence Gosnell, Chief
4225 Federal Office Building
100 East B Street
P.O. Box 580
Casper, WY 82602-1918
(307) 261-5252

PROPERTY IMPROVEMENT LOAN INSURANCE FOR IMPROVING ALL EXISTING STRUCTURES AND BUILDING OF NEW NONRESIDENTIAL STRUCTURES

Department of Housing and Urban Development
Title I Insurance Division
Washington, DC 20410
(800) 733-4663
(202) 708-2880

Description: Guaranteed/insured loans to eligible borrowers to facilitate financing home improvements and construction of nonresidential structures. Maximum loan for one-family dwelling $17,500. Maximum for multifamily dwelling $8,750 per unit, not to exceed $43,750.
$ Given: Nationwide FY 93 est. $1.4 billion.
Application Information: Borrower applies directly through insured lender or lender's approved dealer.
Deadline: None
Contact: Director, above address, for program information

REHABILITATION MORTGAGE INSURANCE

Department of Housing and Urban Development
Single Family Development Division
Office of Insured Single Family Housing
Washington, DC 20410
(202) 708-2720

Description: Guaranteed/insured loans to individual purchasers and investors to purchase, repair, improve, and refinance existing structures more than one year old. Rehabilitation costs must be at least $5,000. Condominiums not acceptable.
$ Given: Through September 30, 1991, 9,654 home units insured for $293.4 million.
Application Information: Submit application through HUD-approved lending institution.
Deadline: None
Contact: Director. Persons are encouraged to communicate with local HUD field office.

Housing

Alabama
Robert E. Lunsford, Manager
600 Beacon Parkway West,
Suite 300
Birmingham, AL 35209-3144
(205) 731-1617

Alaska
Arlene Patton, Manager
222 West 8th Avenue, #64
Anchorage, AK 99513-7537
(907) 271-4170

Community Planning and
Development Division
222 West 8th Avenue, #64
Anchorage, AK 99513-7537
(907) 271-3669

American Samoa
Gordon Y. Furutani, Manager
300 Ala Moana Boulevard,
Room 3318
Honolulu, HI 96850-4991
(808) 546-2136

Arizona
Dwight Peterson, Manager
400 North First Street,
Suite 1600
P.O. Box 13468
Phoenix, AZ 85004-2361
(602) 261-4434

Charles Ming, Manager
1615 West Olympic
Boulevard
Los Angeles, CA 90015-3801
(213) 251-7122

Jean Staley, Manager
Pioneer Plaza, 100 North
Stone Avenue, Suite 410
P.O. Box 2648
Tucson, AZ 86701-1467
(602) 629-6237

Arkansas
Roger Zachritz, Acting
Manager
Lafayette Building, Suite 200
523 Louisiana
Little Rock, AR 72201-3523
(501) 378-5931

California
Lilly Lee, Manager
1630 East Shaw Avenue,
Suite 138
Fresno, CA 93710-8193
(209) 487-5033

(San Francisco Regional
Office)
Robert De Monte, Regional
Housing Commissioner
Phillip Burton Federal
Building and U.S Courthouse
450 Golden Gate Avenue
P.O. Box 36003
San Francisco, CA
94102-3448
(415) 556-4752

(North California)
Office of Indian Programs
Community Planning and
Development Division
San Francisco Program
Management Team
Phillip Burton Federal
Building and U.S.
Courthouse
450 Golden Gate Avenue
P.O. Box 36003
San Francisco, CA
94102-3448
(415) 556-9200

(Northeast California)
Anthony A. Randolph,
Manager
777 12th Street, Suite 200
P.O. Box 1978
Sacramento, CA 95814-1997
(916) 551-1351

(Imperial and San Diego
Counties)
Charles J. Wilson, Manager
Federal Office Building,
Room 563
880 Front Street
San Diego, CA 92188-0100
(619) 557-5310

(Orange, Riverside and San
Bernardino Counties, for
home mortgages)
Harold A. Matzoll, Acting
Manager
34 Civic Center Plaza,
Box 12850
Santa Ana, CA 92712-2850
(714) 836-2451

(South California)
Charles Ming, Manager
1615 West Olympic
Boulevard
Los Angeles, CA 90015-3801
(213) 251-7122

Colorado
Michael Chitwood, Regional
Administrator
Regional Housing
Commissioner
HUD Denver Regional Office
Executive Tower Building
1405 Curtis Street
Denver, CO 80202-2349
(303) 844-4513

Office of Indian Programs
Housing and Community
Development Division
Executive Tower Building
1405 Curtis Street
Denver, CO 80202-2349
(303) 844-2861

Connecticut
William Hernandez, Jr.,
Manager
330 Main Street, First Floor
Hartford, CT 06106-1860
(203) 240-4523

Delaware
A. David Sharbaugh, Chief
Federal Building, Room 1304
844 King Street
Wilmington, DE 19801-3519
(302) 573-6300

Housing

District of Columbia
(Washington, D.C. Regional Office)
Toni Thomas, Manager
Union Center Plaza, Phase II
820 First Street, NE,
Suite 300
Washington, DC 20002-4205
(202) 275-9200

Florida
James T. Chaplin, Manager
325 West Adams Street
Jacksonville, FL 32202-4303
(904) 791-2626

(Counties of Citrus, Sumter,
Hernando, Pasco, Pinellas,
Hillsborough, Polk, Manatee,
Hardee, Highlands, DeSoto,
Sarasota, Charlotte, Olaoes,
Hendry, Lake Okeechobee)
George A. Milburn, Jr.,
Manager
Timberlake Federal Building
Annex, Suite 700
501 East Polk Street
Tampa, FL 33602-3945
(813) 228-2501

(Counties of Volusia, Lake,
Seminole, Orange, Brevard,
Osceola, Indian River,
Okeechobee, St. Lucie)
M. Jeanette Porter, Manager
Langley Building, Suite 270
3751 Maguire Boulevard
Orlando, FL 32803-3032
(407) 648-6441

(South Florida)
Orlando L. Lorie, Manager
Gables 1 Tower
1320 South Dixie Highway
Coral Gables, FL 33146-2911
(305) 662-4510

Georgia
Raymond A. Harris, Regional
Housing Commissioner
Richard B. Russell Federal
Building
75 Spring Street, SW
Atlanta, GA 30303-3388
(404) 331-5136

Guam
Gordon Y. Furutani, Manager
300 Ala Moana Boulevard,
Room 3318
Honolulu, HI 96850-4991
(808) 546-2136

Hawaii
Gordon Y. Furutani, Manager
300 Ala Moana Boulevard,
Room 3318
Honolulu, HI 96850-4991
(808) 546-2136

Idaho
(North Idaho)
Keith R. Green, Manager
Farm Credit Bank Building,
Eighth Floor East
West 601 1st Avenue
Spokane, WA 99204-0317
(509) 456-2624

(West-Central Idaho)
Gary Gillespie, Manager
Federal Building and U.S.
Courthouse
P.O. Box 042
550 West Fort Street
Boise, ID 83724-0420
(208) 334-1990

(South Idaho)
Richard C. Brinck, Manager
Cascade Building
520 SW 6th Avenue
Portland, OR 97204-1596
(503) 221-2561

Illinois
Chicago Office of Indian
Programs
Housing Development
Division
626 West Jackson Boulevard
Chicago, IL 60606-5601
(312) 353-1684

(Chicago Regional Office)
Gertrude Jordan,
Regional Housing
Commissioner
626 West Jackson Boulevard
Chicago, IL 60606-5601
(312) 353-5680

(Central and South Illinois)
John Lawler, Acting
Supervisory Appraiser
Lincoln Towers Plaza,
Suite 672
524 South Second Street
Springfield, IL 62701-1774
(217) 492-4085

Indiana
J. Nicholas Shelley, Manager
151 North Delaware Street
Indianapolis, IN 46204-2526
(317) 226-6303

Iowa
Roger M. Massey, Manager
Braiker/Brandeis Building
210 South 16th Street
Omaha, NE 68102-1622
(402) 221-3703

William R. McNarney,
Manager
HUD Des Moines Office
Federal Building, Room 259
210 Walnut Street
Des Moines, IA 50309-2155
(515) 284-4512

Kansas
William H. Brown, Regional
Administrator
Regional Housing
Commissioner
HUD Kansas City, Regional
Office
Gateway Tower II
400 State Avenue
Kansas City, KS 66101-2406
(913) 236-2162

Kentucky
Verna V. Van Ness, Manager
601 West Broadway
P.O. Box 1044
Louisville, KY 40201-1044
(502) 582-5251

Louisiana
Robert Vasquez, Manager
Fisk Federal Building,
1661 Canal Street
P.O. Box 70288
New Orleans, LA 70112-2887
(504) 589-7200

(North Louisiana)
David E. Gleason, Manager
New Federal Building
500 Fannin Street
Shreveport, LA 71101-3077
(318) 226-5385

Maine
Richard Young, Supervisory
Appraiser
Casco Northern Bank
Building
23 Main Street
Bangor, ME 04401-4318
(207) 945-0467

James Barry, Manager
Norris Cotton Federal
Building
275 Chestnut Street
Manchester, NH 03101-2487
(603) 666-7681

Maryland
(Except Montgomery and
Prince Georges Counties)
Maxine Saunders, Manager
The Equitable Building,
Third Floor
10 North Calvert Street
Baltimore, MD 21202-1865
(301) 962-2121

(Montgomery and Prince
Georges Counties)
Toni Thomas, Manager
Union Center Plaza, Phase II
820 First Street, NE,
Suite 300
Washington, DC 20002-4205
(202) 275-9200

Massachusetts
John Mastropietro,
Acting Regional
Administrator
Regional Housing
Commissioner
Boston Federal Office
Building, Room 375
10 Causeway Street
Boston, MA 02222-1092
(617) 565-5234

Michigan
Harry I. Sharrott, Manager
Patrick V. McNamara Federal
Building
477 Michigan Avenue
Detroit, MI 48226-2592
(313) 226-6280

(East Michigan)
Gary T. LeVine, Manager
Gil Sabuco Building,
Room 200
352 South Saginaw Street
Flint, MI 48502-1953
(313) 766-5112

(West and North Michigan)
Ronald Weston, Manager
Northbrook Building, No. II
2922 Fuller Avenue, NE
Grand Rapids, MI 48505-3409
(616) 456-2100

Minnesota
Thomas Feeney, Manager
Bridge Place Building
220 Second Street, South
Minneapolis, MN 55401-2195
(612) 370-3000

Mississippi
Sandra Freeman, Manager
Dr. A. H. McCoy Federal
Building, Room 910
100 West Capitol Street
Jackson, MS 39269-1096
(601) 965-4702

Missouri
Kenneth G. Lange, Manager
210 North Tucker Boulevard
St. Louis, MO 63101-1997
(314) 425-4761

Montana
Christian KaFentzis, Manager
Federal Office Building,
Room 340
Drawer 10095
301 South Park
Helena, MT 59626-0095
(406) 449-5205

Nebraska
Roger M. Massey, Manager
Braiker/Brandeis Building
210 South 16th Street
Omaha, NE 68102-1622
(402) 221-3703

Nevada
Andrew D. Whitten, Jr.,
Manager
1050 Bible Way
P.O. Box 4700
Reno, NV 89505-4700
(702) 784-5356

Andrew Robertson, Manager
1500 East Tropicana Avenue,
Second Floor
Las Vegas, NV 89119-6516
(702) 388-6500

Housing

(North Nevada)
Office of Indian Programs
Community Planning and
Development Division
San Francisco Program
Management Team
Phillip Burton Federal
Building and U.S.
Courthouse
450 Golden Gate Avenue
P.O. Box 36003
San Francisco, CA
94102-3448
(415) 556-9200

New Hampshire
James Barry, Manager
Norris Cotton Federal
Building
275 Chestnut Street
Manchester, NH 03101-2487
(603) 666-7681

New Jersey
(North New Jersey)
Theodore Britton, Jr.,
Manager
Military Park Building
60 Park Place
Newark, NJ 07102-5504
(201) 887-1662

(South New Jersey)
Elmer Roy, Manager
The Parkade Building
519 Federal Street
Camden, NJ 08103-9998
(609) 757-5081

New Mexico
Michael R. Griego, Manager
625 Truman Street, NE
Albuquerque, NM
87110-6443
(505) 262-6463

C. Don Babers, Acting
Manager
555 Griffin Square Building,
Room 106
525 Griffin Street
Dallas, TX 75202-5007
(214) 767-8308

New York
Dr. Anthony Villane, Regional
Housing Commissioner
26 Federal Plaza
New York, NY 10278-0068
(212) 264-8068

(North New York)
John Petricco, Manager
Leo W. O'Brien Federal
Building
North Pearl Street and
Clinton Avenue
Albany, NY 12207-2395
(518) 472-3567

(West New York)
Joseph Lynch, Manager
465 Main Street, Fifth Floor
Lafayette Court
Buffalo, NY 14203-1780
(716) 846-5755

North Carolina
Larry J. Parker, Manager
415 North Edgeworth Street
Greensboro, NC 27401-2107
(919) 333-5363

North Dakota
Keith Elliot, Chief
Federal Building, Room 300
653 2nd Avenue, North
P.O. Box 2483
Fargo, ND 58108-2483
(701) 239-5136

Ohio
Robert W. Dolin, Manager
New Federal Building
200 North High Street
Columbus, OH 43215-2499
(614) 469-5737

(North Ohio)
George L. Engel, Manager
One Playhouse Square
1375 Euclid Avenue,
Room 420
Cleveland, OH 44115-1832
(216) 522-4065

(Southwest Ohio)
William Harris, Manager
Federal Office Building,
Room 9002
550 Main Street
Cincinnati, OH 45202-3253
(513) 684-2884

Oklahoma
Edwin I. Gardner, Manager
Murrah Federal Building
200 NW 5th Street
Oklahoma City, OK
73102-3202
(405) 231-4181

Indian Programs Division
Hugh Johnson, Director
Community Planning and
Development Branch
Murrah Federal Building
200 NW 5th Street
Oklahoma City, OK
73102-3202
(405) 231-4101

(East Oklahoma)
Robert H. Gardner, Manager
Robert S. Kerr Building,
Room 200
440 South Houston Avenue
Tulsa, OK 74127-8923
(918) 581-7435

Oregon
Richard C. Brinck, Manager
Cascade Building
520 SW 6th Avenue
Portland, OR 97204-1596
(503) 221-2561

Panama Canal Zone
Rosa Villalonga, Acting
Manager
159 Carlos Chardon Avenue
San Juan, PR 00918-1804
(809) 766-5201 or
(809) 498-5201

Pennsylvania
(Philadelphia Regional
Office)
Michael A. Smerconish,
Regional Administrator
Regional Housing
Commissioner
Liberty Square Building
105 South 7th Street
Philadelphia, PA 19106-3392
(215) 597-2560

(West Pennsylvania)
William Costello, Acting
Manager
412 Old Post Office
Courthouse Building
7th Avenue and Grant Street
Pittsburgh, PA 15219-1906
(412) 644-6428

Puerto Rico
Rosa Villalonga, Acting
Manager
159 Carlos Chardon Avenue
San Juan, PR 00918-1804
(809) 766-5201 or
(809) 498-5201

Rhode Island
Casimir J. Kolaski, Jr.,
Manager
Federal Building and U.S.
Post Office, Room 330
Kennedy Plaza
Providence, RI 02903-1745
(401) 528-5351

South Carolina
Ted B. Freeman, Manager
Strom Thurmond Federal
Building
1835-45 Assembly Street
Columbia, SC 29201-2480
(803) 765-5592

South Dakota
Don Olson, Chief
Courthouse Plaza, Suite 116
300 North Dakota Avenue
Sioux Falls, SD 57102-0311
(605) 330-4223

Tennessee
Richard B. Barnwell,
Manager
John J. Duncan Federal
Building
710 Locust Street, SW
Knoxville, TN 37902-2526
(615) 549-9384

(Central Tennessee)
John H. Fisher, Manager
251 Cumberland Bend Drive,
Suite 200
Nashville, TN 37228-1803
(615) 736-5213

(West Tennessee)
Bob Atkins, Manager
One Memphis Place,
Suite 1200
200 Jefferson Avenue
Memphis, TN 38103-2335
(901) 521-3367

Texas
(Fort Worth Regional Office)
Sam R. Moseley, Regional
Housing Commissioner
1600 Throckmorton
P.O. Box 2905
Forth Worth, TX 76113-2905
(817) 885-5401

(Northwest Texas)
Henry E. Whitney, Manager
Federal Office Building
1205 Texas Avenue
Lubbock, TX 79401-4093
(806) 743-7265

(East, North, and West
Texas)
C. Don Babers, Acting
Manager
555 Griffin Square Building,
Room 106
525 Griffin Street
Dallas, TX 75202-5007
(214) 767-8308

(Five Counties in East Texas)
David E. Gleason, Manager
New Federal Building
500 Fannin Street
Shreveport, LA 71101-3077
(318) 226-5385

(East-Central Texas)
William Robertson, Jr.,
Manager
National Bank of Texas
Building, Suite 300
221 Norfolk
Houston, TX 77098-4096
(713) 229-3589

(Bowie County)
Roger Zachritz, Acting
Manager
Lafayette Building, Suite 200
523 Louisiana
Little Rock, AR 72201-3523
(501) 378-5931

(Southwest Texas)
Don Creed, Manager
Washington Square Building
800 Dolorosa Street
San Antonio, TX 78207-4563
(512) 229-6781

Utah
Richard Bell, Manager
324 South State Street,
Suite 220
Salt Lake City, UT
84111-2321
(801) 524-5237

Vermont
William Peters, Chief
Federal Building, Room B311
11 Elmwood Avenue
P.O. Box 879
Burlington, VT 05402-0879
(802) 951-6290

James Barry, Manager
Norris Cotton Federal
Building
275 Chestnut Street
Manchester, NH 03101-2487
(603) 666-7681

Virgin Islands
Rosa Villalonga, Acting
Manager
159 Carlos Chardon Avenue
San Juan, PR 00918-1804
(809) 766-5201 or
(809) 498-5201

Virginia

(North Virginia)
Toni Thomas, Manager
Union Center Plaza, Phase II
820 First Street, NE,
Suite 300
Washington, DC 20002-4205
(202) 275-9200

(South Virginia)
Mary Ann Wilson, Manager
Federal Building, First Floor
400 North Eighth Street
Richmond, VA 23240-0170
(804) 771-2721

Washington

Office of Indian Programs
Community Planning and
Development Division
Arcade Plaza Building
1321 Second Avenue
Seattle, WA 98101-2058
(206) 442-0760

(Seattle Regional Office)
Richard Bauer,
Regional Housing
Commissioner
Arcade Plaza Building
1321 Second Avenue
Seattle, WA 98101-2054
(206) 442-5414

(East Washington)
Keith R. Green, Manager
Farm Credit Bank Building,
Eighth Floor East
West 601 1st Avenue
Spokane, WA 99204-0317
(509) 456-2624

(Clark, Klickitat, and
Skamania Counties)
Richard C. Brinck, Manager
Cascade Building
520 SW 6th Avenue
Portland, OR 97204-1596
(503) 221-2561

West Virginia

William Costello, Acting
Manager
412 Old Post Office
Courthouse Building
7th Avenue and Grant Street
Pittsburgh, PA 15219-1906
(412) 644-6428

405 Capitol Street, Suite 708
Charleston, WV 25301-1795
(304) 347-7000

Wisconsin

Delbert F. Reynolds,
Manager
Henry S. Reuss Federal Plaza
310 West Wisconsin Avenue,
Suite 1380
Milwaukee, WI 53203-2289
(414) 291-3214

Wyoming

Lawrence Gosnell, Chief
4225 Federal Office Building
100 East B Street
P.O. Box 580
Casper, WY 82602-1918
(307) 261-5252

SUPPLEMENTAL LOAN INSURANCE—MULTIFAMILY RENTAL HOUSING

**Department of Housing
and Urban Development**
Policies and Procedures
Division
Office of Insured
Multifamily Housing
Development
Washington, DC 20412
(202) 708-2556

Description: Guaranteed/insured loans to repair and improve multifamily projects, hospitals, nursing homes, and group practice facilities already insured by HUD.
$ Given: Nationwide FY 93 est. $246.2 million in loans.
Application Information: Initial conference followed by formal application.
Deadline: Established on case-by-case basis at local HUD office.
Contact: Nearest local HUD office

Alabama
Robert E. Lunsford, Manager
600 Beacon Parkway West,
Suite 300
Birmingham, AL 35209-3144
(205) 731-1617

Alaska
Arlene Patton, Manager
222 West 8th Avenue, #64
Anchorage, AK 99513-7537
(907) 271-4170

Community Planning and
Development Division
222 West 8th Avenue, #64
Anchorage, AK 99513-7537
(907) 271-3669

American Samoa
Gordon Y. Furutani, Manager
300 Ala Moana Boulevard,
Room 3318
Honolulu, HI 96850-4991
(808) 546-2136

Arizona
Dwight Peterson, Manager
400 North First Street,
Suite 1600
P.O. Box 13468
Phoenix, AZ 85004-2361
(602) 261-4434

Charles Ming, Manager
1615 West Olympic
Boulevard
Los Angeles, CA 90015-3801
(213) 251-7122

Jean Staley, Manager
Pioneer Plaza, 100 North
Stone Avenue, Suite 410
P.O. Box 2648
Tucson, AZ 86701-1467
(602) 629-6237

Arkansas
Roger Zachritz, Acting
Manager
Lafayette Building, Suite 200
523 Louisiana
Little Rock, AR 72201-3523
(501) 378-5931

California
Lilly Lee, Manager
1630 East Shaw Avenue,
Suite 138
Fresno, CA 93710-8193
(209) 487-5033

(San Francisco Regional
Office)
Robert De Monte, Regional
Housing Commissioner
Phillip Burton Federal
Building and U.S Courthouse
450 Golden Gate Avenue
P.O. Box 36003
San Francisco, CA
94102-3448
(415) 556-4752

(North California)
Office of Indian Programs
Community Planning and
Development Division
San Francisco Program
Management Team
Phillip Burton Federal
Building and U.S.
Courthouse
450 Golden Gate Avenue
P.O. Box 36003
San Francisco, CA
94102-3448
(415) 556-9200

(Northeast California)
Anthony A. Randolph,
Manager
777 12th Street, Suite 200
P.O. Box 1978
Sacramento, CA 95814-1997
(916) 551-1351

(Imperial and San Diego
Counties)
Charles J. Wilson, Manager
Federal Office Building,
Room 563
880 Front Street
San Diego, CA 92188-0100
(619) 557-5310

(Orange, Riverside and San
Bernardino Counties, for
home mortgages)
Harold A. Matzoll, Acting
Manager
34 Civic Center Plaza,
Box 12850
Santa Ana, CA 92712-2850
(714) 836-2451

(South California)
Charles Ming, Manager
1615 West Olympic
Boulevard
Los Angeles, CA 90015-3801
(213) 251-7122

Colorado
Michael Chitwood, Regional
Administrator
Regional Housing
Commissioner
HUD Denver Regional Office
Executive Tower Building
1405 Curtis Street
Denver, CO 80202-2349
(303) 844-4513

Office of Indian Programs
Housing and Community
Development Division
Executive Tower Building
1405 Curtis Street
Denver, CO 80202-2349
(303) 844-2861

Connecticut
William Hernandez, Jr.,
Manager
330 Main Street, First Floor
Hartford, CT 06106-1860
(203) 240-4523

Delaware
A. David Sharbaugh, Chief
Federal Building, Room 1304
844 King Street
Wilmington, DE 19801-3519
(302) 573-6300

Housing

District of Columbia
(Washington, D.C. Regional Office)
Toni Thomas, Manager
Union Center Plaza, Phase II
820 First Street, NE,
Suite 300
Washington, DC 20002-4205
(202) 275-9200

Florida
James T. Chaplin, Manager
325 West Adams Street
Jacksonville, FL 32202-4303
(904) 791-2626

(Counties of Citrus, Sumter, Hernando, Pasco, Pinellas, Hillsborough, Polk, Manatee, Hardee, Highlands, DeSoto, Sarasota, Charlotte, Olaoes, Hendry, Lake Okeechobee)
George A. Milburn, Jr.,
Manager
Timberlake Federal Building Annex, Suite 700
501 East Polk Street
Tampa, FL 33602-3945
(813) 228-2501

(Counties of Volusia, Lake, Seminole, Orange, Brevard, Osceola, Indian River, Okeechobee, St. Lucie)
M. Jeanette Porter, Manager
Langley Building, Suite 270
3751 Maguire Boulevard
Orlando, FL 32803-3032
(407) 648-6441

(South Florida)
Orlando L. Lorie, Manager
Gables 1 Tower
1320 South Dixie Highway
Coral Gables, FL 33146-2911
(305) 662-4510

Georgia
Raymond A. Harris, Regional Housing Commissioner
Richard B. Russell Federal Building
75 Spring Street, SW
Atlanta, GA 30303-3388
(404) 331-5136

Guam
Gordon Y. Furutani, Manager
300 Ala Moana Boulevard,
Room 3318
Honolulu, HI 96850-4991
(808) 546-2136

Hawaii
Gordon Y. Furutani, Manager
300 Ala Moana Boulevard,
Room 3318
Honolulu, HI 96850-4991
(808) 546-2136

Idaho
(North Idaho)
Keith R. Green, Manager
Farm Credit Bank Building,
Eighth Floor East
West 601 1st Avenue
Spokane, WA 99204-0317
(509) 456-2624

(West-Central Idaho)
Gary Gillespie, Manager
Federal Building and U.S. Courthouse
P.O. Box 042
550 West Fort Street
Boise, ID 83724-0420
(208) 334-1990

(South Idaho)
Richard C. Brinck, Manager
Cascade Building
520 SW 6th Avenue
Portland, OR 97204-1596
(503) 221-2561

Illinois
Chicago Office of Indian Programs
Housing Development Division
626 West Jackson Boulevard
Chicago, IL 60606-5601
(312) 353-1684

(Chicago Regional Office)
Gertrude Jordan,
Regional Housing Commissioner
626 West Jackson Boulevard
Chicago, IL 60606-5601
(312) 353-5680

(Central and South Illinois)
John Lawler, Acting
Supervisory Appraiser
Lincoln Towers Plaza,
Suite 672
524 South Second Street
Springfield, IL 62701-1774
(217) 492-4085

Indiana
J. Nicholas Shelley, Manager
151 North Delaware Street
Indianapolis, IN 46204-2526
(317) 226-6303

Iowa
Roger M. Massey, Manager
Braiker/Brandeis Building
210 South 16th Street
Omaha, NE 68102-1622
(402) 221-3703

William R. McNarney,
Manager
HUD Des Moines Office
Federal Building, Room 259
210 Walnut Street
Des Moines, IA 50309-2155
(515) 284-4512

Kansas
William H. Brown, Regional Administrator
Regional Housing Commissioner
HUD Kansas City, Regional Office
Gateway Tower II
400 State Avenue
Kansas City, KS 66101-2406
(913) 236-2162

Kentucky
Verna V. Van Ness, Manager
601 West Broadway
P.O. Box 1044
Louisville, KY 40201-1044
(502) 582-5251

Louisiana
Robert Vasquez, Manager
Fisk Federal Building,
1661 Canal Street
P.O. Box 70288
New Orleans, LA 70112-2887
(504) 589-7200

(North Louisiana)
David E. Gleason, Manager
New Federal Building
500 Fannin Street
Shreveport, LA 71101-3077
(318) 226-5385

Maine
Richard Young, Supervisory Appraiser
Casco Northern Bank Building
23 Main Street
Bangor, ME 04401-4318
(207) 945-0467

James Barry, Manager
Norris Cotton Federal Building
275 Chestnut Street
Manchester, NH 03101-2487
(603) 666-7681

Maryland
(Except Montgomery and Prince Georges Counties)
Maxine Saunders, Manager
The Equitable Building,
Third Floor
10 North Calvert Street
Baltimore, MD 21202-1865
(301) 962-2121

(Montgomery and Prince Georges Counties)
Toni Thomas, Manager
Union Center Plaza, Phase II
820 First Street, NE,
Suite 300
Washington, DC 20002-4205
(202) 275-9200

Massachusetts
John Mastropietro,
Acting Regional Administrator
Regional Housing Commissioner
Boston Federal Office Building, Room 375
10 Causeway Street
Boston, MA 02222-1092
(617) 565-5234

Michigan
Harry I. Sharrott, Manager
Patrick V. McNamara Federal Building
477 Michigan Avenue
Detroit, MI 48226-2592
(313) 226-6280

(East Michigan)
Gary T. LeVine, Manager
Gil Sabuco Building,
Room 200
352 South Saginaw Street
Flint, MI 48502-1953
(313) 766-5112

(West and North Michigan)
Ronald Weston, Manager
Northbrook Building, No. II
2922 Fuller Avenue, NE
Grand Rapids, MI 48505-3409
(616) 456-2100

Minnesota
Thomas Feeney, Manager
Bridge Place Building
220 Second Street, South
Minneapolis, MN 55401-2195
(612) 370-3000

Mississippi
Sandra Freeman, Manager
Dr. A. H. McCoy Federal Building, Room 910
100 West Capitol Street
Jackson, MS 39269-1096
(601) 965-4702

Missouri
Kenneth G. Lange, Manager
210 North Tucker Boulevard
St. Louis, MO 63101-1997
(314) 425-4761

Montana
Christian KaFentzis, Manager
Federal Office Building,
Room 340
Drawer 10095
301 South Park
Helena, MT 59626-0095
(406) 449-5205

Nebraska
Roger M. Massey, Manager
Braiker/Brandeis Building
210 South 16th Street
Omaha, NE 68102-1622
(402) 221-3703

Nevada
Andrew D. Whitten, Jr.,
Manager
1050 Bible Way
P.O. Box 4700
Reno, NV 89505-4700
(702) 784-5356

Andrew Robertson, Manager
1500 East Tropicana Avenue,
Second Floor
Las Vegas, NV 89119-6516
(702) 388-6500

(North Nevada)
Office of Indian Programs
Community Planning and
Development Division
San Francisco Program
Management Team
Phillip Burton Federal
Building and U.S.
Courthouse
450 Golden Gate Avenue
P.O. Box 36003
San Francisco, CA
94102-3448
(415) 556-9200

New Hampshire
James Barry, Manager
Norris Cotton Federal
Building
275 Chestnut Street
Manchester, NH 03101-2487
(603) 666-7681

New Jersey
(North New Jersey)
Theodore Britton, Jr.,
Manager
Military Park Building
60 Park Place
Newark, NJ 07102-5504
(201) 887-1662

(South New Jersey)
Elmer Roy, Manager
The Parkade Building
519 Federal Street
Camden, NJ 08103-9998
(609) 757-5081

New Mexico
Michael R. Griego, Manager
625 Truman Street, NE
Albuquerque, NM
87110-6443
(505) 262-6463

C. Don Babers, Acting
Manager
555 Griffin Square Building,
Room 106
525 Griffin Street
Dallas, TX 75202-5007
(214) 767-8308

New York
Dr. Anthony Villane, Regional
Housing Commissioner
26 Federal Plaza
New York, NY 10278-0068
(212) 264-8068

(North New York)
John Petricco, Manager
Leo W. O'Brien Federal
Building
North Pearl Street and
Clinton Avenue
Albany, NY 12207-2395
(518) 472-3567

(West New York)
Joseph Lynch, Manager
465 Main Street, Fifth Floor
Lafayette Court
Buffalo, NY 14203-1780
(716) 846-5755

North Carolina
Larry J. Parker, Manager
415 North Edgeworth Street
Greensboro, NC 27401-2107
(919) 333-5363

North Dakota
Keith Elliot, Chief
Federal Building, Room 300
653 2nd Avenue, North
P.O. Box 2483
Fargo, ND 58108-2483
(701) 239-5136

Ohio
Robert W. Dolin, Manager
New Federal Building
200 North High Street
Columbus, OH 43215-2499
(614) 469-5737

(North Ohio)
George L. Engel, Manager
One Playhouse Square
1375 Euclid Avenue,
Room 420
Cleveland, OH 44115-1832
(216) 522-4065

(Southwest Ohio)
William Harris, Manager
Federal Office Building,
Room 9002
550 Main Street
Cincinnati, OH 45202-3253
(513) 684-2884

Oklahoma
Edwin I. Gardner, Manager
Murrah Federal Building
200 NW 5th Street
Oklahoma City, OK
73102-3202
(405) 231-4181

Indian Programs Division
Hugh Johnson, Director
Community Planning and
Development Branch
Murrah Federal Building
200 NW 5th Street
Oklahoma City, OK
73102-3202
(405) 231-4101

(East Oklahoma)
Robert H. Gardner, Manager
Robert S. Kerr Building,
Room 200
440 South Houston Avenue
Tulsa, OK 74127-8923
(918) 581-7435

Oregon
Richard C. Brinck, Manager
Cascade Building
520 SW 6th Avenue
Portland, OR 97204-1596
(503) 221-2561

Panama Canal Zone
Rosa Villalonga, Acting
Manager
159 Carlos Chardon Avenue
San Juan, PR 00918-1804
(809) 766-5201 or
(809) 498-5201

Pennsylvania
(Philadelphia Regional
Office)
Michael A. Smerconish,
Regional Administrator
Regional Housing
Commissioner
Liberty Square Building
105 South 7th Street
Philadelphia, PA 19106-3392
(215) 597-2560

(West Pennsylvania)
William Costello, Acting
Manager
412 Old Post Office
Courthouse Building
7th Avenue and Grant Street
Pittsburgh, PA 15219-1906
(412) 644-6428

Puerto Rico
Rosa Villalonga, Acting
Manager
159 Carlos Chardon Avenue
San Juan, PR 00918-1804
(809) 766-5201 or
(809) 498-5201

Rhode Island
Casimir J. Kolaski, Jr.,
Manager
Federal Building and U.S.
Post Office, Room 330
Kennedy Plaza
Providence, RI 02903-1745
(401) 528-5351

South Carolina
Ted B. Freeman, Manager
Strom Thurmond Federal
Building
1835-45 Assembly Street
Columbia, SC 29201-2480
(803) 765-5592

South Dakota
Don Olson, Chief
Courthouse Plaza, Suite 116
300 North Dakota Avenue
Sioux Falls, SD 57102-0311
(605) 330-4223

Tennessee
Richard B. Barnwell,
Manager
John J. Duncan Federal
Building
710 Locust Street, SW
Knoxville, TN 37902-2526
(615) 549-9384

(Central Tennessee)
John H. Fisher, Manager
251 Cumberland Bend Drive,
Suite 200
Nashville, TN 37228-1803
(615) 736-5213

(West Tennessee)
Bob Atkins, Manager
One Memphis Place,
Suite 1200
200 Jefferson Avenue
Memphis, TN 38103-2335
(901) 521-3367

Texas
(Fort Worth Regional Office)
Sam R. Moseley, Regional
Housing Commissioner
1600 Throckmorton
P.O. Box 2905
Forth Worth, TX 76113-2905
(817) 885-5401

(Northwest Texas)
Henry E. Whitney, Manager
Federal Office Building
1205 Texas Avenue
Lubbock, TX 79401-4093
(806) 743-7265

(East, North, and West
Texas)
C. Don Babers, Acting
Manager
555 Griffin Square Building,
Room 106
525 Griffin Street
Dallas, TX 75202-5007
(214) 767-8308

(Five Counties in East Texas)
David E. Gleason, Manager
New Federal Building
500 Fannin Street
Shreveport, LA 71101-3077
(318) 226-5385

(East-Central Texas)
William Robertson, Jr.,
Manager
National Bank of Texas
Building, Suite 300
221 Norfolk
Houston, TX 77098-4096
(713) 229-3589

(Bowie County)
Roger Zachritz, Acting
Manager
Lafayette Building, Suite 200
523 Louisiana
Little Rock, AR 72201-3523
(501) 378-5931

(Southwest Texas)
Don Creed, Manager
Washington Square Building
800 Dolorosa Street
San Antonio, TX 78207-4563
(512) 229-6781

Utah
Richard Bell, Manager
324 South State Street,
Suite 220
Salt Lake City, UT
84111-2321
(801) 524-5237

Vermont
William Peters, Chief
Federal Building, Room B311
11 Elmwood Avenue
P.O. Box 879
Burlington, VT 05402-0879
(802) 951-6290

James Barry, Manager
Norris Cotton Federal
Building
275 Chestnut Street
Manchester, NH 03101-2487
(603) 666-7681

Virgin Islands
Rosa Villalonga, Acting
Manager
159 Carlos Chardon Avenue
San Juan, PR 00918-1804
(809) 766-5201 or
(809) 498-5201

Housing

Virginia
(North Virginia)
Toni Thomas, Manager
Union Center Plaza, Phase II
820 First Street, NE,
Suite 300
Washington, DC 20002-4205
(202) 275-9200

(South Virginia)
Mary Ann Wilson, Manager
Federal Building, First Floor
400 North Eighth Street
Richmond, VA 23240-0170
(804) 771-2721

Washington
Office of Indian Programs
Community Planning and
Development Division
Arcade Plaza Building
1321 Second Avenue
Seattle, WA 98101-2058
(206) 442-0760

(Seattle Regional Office)
Richard Bauer,
Regional Housing
Commissioner
Arcade Plaza Building
1321 Second Avenue
Seattle, WA 98101-2054
(206) 442-5414

(East Washington)
Keith R. Green, Manager
Farm Credit Bank Building,
Eighth Floor East
West 601 1st Avenue
Spokane, WA 99204-0317
(509) 456-2624

(Clark, Klickitat, and
Skamania Counties)
Richard C. Brinck, Manager
Cascade Building
520 SW 6th Avenue
Portland, OR 97204-1596
(503) 221-2561

West Virginia
William Costello, Acting
Manager
412 Old Post Office
Courthouse Building
7th Avenue and Grant Street
Pittsburgh, PA 15219-1906
(412) 644-6428

405 Capitol Street, Suite 708
Charleston, WV 25301-1795
(304) 347-7000

Wisconsin
Delbert F. Reynolds,
Manager
Henry S. Reuss Federal Plaza
310 West Wisconsin Avenue,
Suite 1380
Milwaukee, WI 53203-2289
(414) 291-3214

Wyoming
Lawrence Gosnell, Chief
4225 Federal Office Building
100 East B Street
P.O. Box 580
Casper, WY 82602-1918
(307) 261-5252

Bibliography

Catalog of Federal Domestic Assistance. Washington, DC: U.S. Government Printing Office, 1992, published annually.

Free Dollars from the Federal Government, by Laurie Blum. New York: ARCO Publishing, Inc., 1991.

The United States Government Manual. The Office of the Federal Register. This describes the broad responsibilities of all the major federal government departments and agencies. It does not list grant programs specifically but does list various publications that are offered by each agency. If you know that an agency does give grants—and many do—you can find useful information about them in some of these publications. You can contact the relevant agencies to have your name put on their mailing lists for program information.

Government Assistance Almanac 1992–93, by J. Robert Dumouchel. Detroit: Omnigraphics, Inc.; and Washington, DC: Foggy Bottom Publications, 1992, 6th edition.

Guide to Federal Grants & Financial Aid: For Individuals and Nonprofit Organizations, edited by Calvin Fenton and Charles Edwards. Dubuque, Iowa: Kendall/Hunt Publishing Co., 1985, 2nd edition.

1992 *Guide to Federal Funding for Governments and Nonprofits*, edited by Charles Edwards. 2 vols. Arlington, Va.: Government Information Services, 1992.

The Complete Guide to Getting a Grant, by Laurie Blum. New York: Possedion Press, 1993.

To find your local U.S. Government Bookstore, call:
(202) 512-0132.

To order U.S. government publications by mail write:
U.S. Government Printing Office
Superintendent of Documents
Washington, DC 20402

Bibliography

For general information about U.S. government programs, contact the Federal Information Center nearest you. The main office is:

Federal Information Center
P.O. Box 600
Cumberland, MD 21501-600
(301) 722-9098

Federal Assistance Programs Retrieval System (FAPRS). There are designated access points in each state where you can ask for a computer search of the database. You can also access the database through some commercial computer-network companies.

For more information, contact:

Federal Domestic Assistance Catalog Staff
General Services Administration
Reporters Building, Ground Floor
300 7th Street, SW
Washington, DC 20407
(800) 669-8331
(202) 708-5126

For literature on federal business loans, write or call:

The Director
Loan Policy and Procedures Branch
Small Business Administration
409 Third Street, SW
Washington, DC 20416
(202) 205-6570

Index

Index